Lavoisier and the Chemistry of Life

An Exploration of Scientific Creativity

Antoine Lavoisier, the author of the "chemical revolution," also did much to establish the foundations for the fields of organic chemistry and biochemistry. Here, Frederic Lawrence Holmes gives us an intimate portrait of Lavoisier's investigations, ranging over twenty years, from 1773 to 1792, on respiration, fermentation, and plant and animal matter. These studies, Holmes finds, were not simply belated applications of Lavoisier's established chemical theories, but intimately bound from the beginning to his more widely known research on combustion and calcination.

Drawing on Lavoisier's daily laboratory records, unpublished notes, and successive drafts of articles, Holmes explores the interaction between this creative scientist's theories and practice, the experimental problems he encountered and his response to them, the apparently intuitive understanding that guided his choice of experiments, and the gradual refinement of his hypotheses. This thorough and comprehensive exposition of Lavoisier's scientific style forms the basis for general reflections on the nature of creative scientific imagination that will interest historians of science and biology, philosophers of science, cognitive psychologists, and all who are intrigued by the drama of pioneering scientific discovery.

1 **Death Is a Social Disease**
Public Health and Political Economy in Early Industrial France
William Coleman

2 **Ignaz Semmelweis**
The Etiology, Concept, and Prophylaxis of Childbed Fever
Translated and Edited, with an Introduction, by
K. Codell Carter

3 **The Philosophical Naturalists**
Themes in Early Nineteenth-Century British Biology
Philip F. Rehbock

Wisconsin Publications in the
History of Science and Medicine
Number 4

Detail of the painting of Antoine Laurent Lavoisier and His Wife, 1788, by Jacques Louis David. The Metropolitan Museum of Art, Purchase, Mr. and Mrs. Charles Wrightsman Gift, 1977. (1977.10)

Frederic Lawrence Holmes

Lavoisier and the Chemistry of Life

An Exploration of Scientific Creativity

The University of Wisconsin Press

Published 1985

The University of Wisconsin Press
114 North Murray Street
Madison, Wisconsin 53715

The University of Wisconsin Press, Ltd.
1 Gower Street
London WC1E 6HA, England

First printing

Printed in the United States of America

For LC CIP information see the colophon

ISBN 0-299-09980-6

To Sir Hans Krebs

1900–1981

Contents

Illustrations xi

Acknowledgments xiii

Introduction xv

1

The Grand System

1773–1780 1

1 An Ambitious Agenda 3

2 Lavoisier in Midstream 41

3 The Emergence of a Theory of Respiration 63

4 Respiration and a General Theory of Combustion 91

5 Collaboration and a Move toward Plant Chemistry 129

2

Heat, Water, and Respiration

1781–1785 149

6 The Importance of Melting Ice 151

7 Water Divided 199
8 Fixing the Composition of Fixed Air 224
9 Water and Respiration 237

3

Lavoisier in the Plant Kingdom
1785–1789 261

10 The Composition of Inflammable Plant Substances 263
11 Nature's Operations 291
12 Language, Organic Composition, and Fermentation 316
13 The Trouble with Sugar 353
14 Plant and Animal Chemistry in the New Chemical System 385

4

The Animal Economy
1790–1792 411

15 Responses to Lavoisier's Theory of Respiration 413
16 Lavoisier's Return to Respiration 440
17 Dissonant Echoes 469
18 Reflections on the Creativity of One Scientist 486

Notes 505
Index 553

Illustrations

1 Page from manuscript of "Expériences sur la décomposition de l'air dans le poulmon des animaux." 83

2 Drawings of ice calorimeter, and of apparatus for measuring effects on atmosphere of respiration and combustion. 163

3–6 Lavoisier's laboratory notebook record of respiration experiment on guinea pig carried out on May 12, 1783. 172–79

7 Apparatus used by Lavoisier and Meusnier for "gun barrel" experiments to decompose water. 212

8 Apparatus used by Claude-Joseph Geoffroy for experiments on spirit of wine. 266

9 Apparatus designed by Meusnier for Lavoisier's large-scale experiments on combustion of spirit of wine. 268

10 Lavoisier's apparatus for burning spirit of wine in a closed system. 271

11 Lavoisier's sketch of apparatus for analysis begun June 5, 1787, of products of fermentation. 330

12 Lavoisier's sketch of apparatus for distillation analysis of sugar. 338

13 Table of "calculated" and "experimental" results for composition of substances involved in fermentation of spirit of wine, as shown in Lavoisier's manuscript memoir "Sur le fermentation spiritueuse." 346

14 Fermentation apparatus described by Lavoisier in his *Elementary Treatise of Chemistry.* 381

15 Tables containing Lavoisier's balance sheets for fermentation as published in his *Elementary Treatise of Chemistry.* 394

16 Surviving apparatus intended by Lavoisier for large-scale combustion experiments on oil. 405

17 Surviving fermentation apparatus. This is a later modification of the apparatus described in the *Elementary Treatise.* 406

18 Surviving fermentation apparatus. The apparatus is identical to that described in the *Elementary Treatise*, but is viewed from the other side. 407

19 Apparatus of Adair Crawford for experiments on combustion and respiration. 419

20 Lavoisier and Seguin carrying out an experiment on respiration with subject in repose, as drawn by Madame Lavoisier. 444

21 Lavoisier and Seguin carrying out an experiment on respiration with subject performing work. 445

Acknowledgments

This study began as a small part of my effort to trace the origins of the field of metabolism in order to establish the background for a larger study of the discovery of the Krebs cycle, and the career of Sir Hans Krebs. When my work on Lavoisier quickly outgrew my original intention, Krebs gracefully and patiently welcomed my digression from the project on which he was collaborating with me. He did not live to see the completion either of this story, or of the one to which I shall now return, in which he will play the central role; but the inspiration of his example, and his spirit of commitment, remain to guide me.

Going back to Lavoisier has also meant for me recalling happy memories of a seminar on eighteenth-century chemistry that I took long ago under Henry Guerlac. At every turn in the present study I have been helped by what he taught us then.

I have received much help and encouragement from discussions with Joseph S. Fruton, who has also read the manuscript in its various versions with his customary meticulous care, and caught many inadequacies in time to rectify them. Owen Hannaway read the first draft and suggested important improvements. Charles C. Gillispie read the present Chapter 16, and helped me to understand the relation between Lavoisier's later work on respiration and contemporary ideas about work.

Pierre Berthon, the archivist of the Académie des Sciences, has assisted me warmly during my visits to the Archives to examine Lavoisier documents, and has provided me with microfilms of large amounts of them. I wish to thank the Archives de l'Académie des Sciences de Paris for permission to publish extracts and illustrations from the manuscripts of Lavoisier. The Count Guy de Chabrol has kindly granted permission to publish portions of a letter from Laplace to Lavoisier contained in his archival collection. David Corson and Elisabeth Lacaque were very gracious in helping me to use the Lavoisier manuscripts in the History of Science Collections of the Cornell University Library. The richness of the Historical Library of the Yale University Medical School has placed most of the published literature relevant to this study within a moment's reach of my desk, and immeasurably lightened the task of finding the sources I needed.

Gail Sacco typed most of the various versions of this manuscript with matchless speed and accuracy and kept the project from falling into disarray by maintaining my research materials in near-perfect order. Linda Barnett, Ann Sticco, and Selda Lippa typed the final chapters skillfully and cheerfully.

The completion of this project was made possible through a research grant from the Hannah Institute for the History of Medicine. I am particularly appreciative of the understanding of its executive director, Dr. G. R. Paterson, who allowed me to utilize for this purpose funds originally made available for a different project.

It was a pleasure to work with the very helpful and effective editors of the University of Wisconsin Press, especially with Erin Foley and Richard Jannaccio. The meticulous, perceptive copyediting of Susan Tarcov saved me from numerous subtle inconsistencies and other small errors that might otherwise have slipped into print.

My wife, Harriet, and my daughters, Catherine, Susan, and Rebecca, have not been waiting patiently for me to finish this book, because they have had equally important work to do. They have, however, created the warm, supportive environment in which scholarly preoccupations can most easily flourish.

Introduction

Few scientists have stood at the confluence of developments germinal to so many areas of modern science as did Antoine Lavoisier. His well-known studies of combustion laid the groundwork for understanding the oxidation and reduction reactions underlying a vast range of chemical phenomena. His persistent use of weight measurements, supported by his conviction that the weights of the reactants and products of any chemical change must be equal, opened the era of thoroughgoing quantitative chemistry. His pragmatic definition of an element was fundamental to the modern development of chemistry. His collaborative investigations with the mathematician Laplace were equally formative for the later science of physical chemistry.

If he had not become so firmly identified as the leader of the general "Chemical Revolution," Lavoisier would probably be as well known as a founder of physiological chemistry, the parent field for the huge domain now encompassed by biochemistry. His achievements here also were astonishingly pervasive. He devised the basic method for the elementary analysis of plant and animal matter around which the field of organic chemistry afterward coalesced. His famous study of the alcoholic fermentation of sugar was the starting point for investigations of that process which have occupied physiologists and chemists ever since. His theory that respiration is a slow combustion of carbon and hydrogen has been central to the whole of modern biology.

Historians have devoted far less attention to Lavoisier's work in the area of plant and animal chemistry and physiology than to that in general chemistry. Those who have discussed one or another aspect of it have tended to treat it as a kind of annex to the great research on combustion around which he built his celebrated revolution. Only in the last period of his life, it is suggested, did he devote his central concern to physiological problems. I hope to show instead that Lavoisier's studies of fermentation, respiration, and the composition of plant and animal matter were intimately connected with the development of his investigations of combustion in general chemistry; that they were all embedded in a common research program which Lavoisier pursued through most of his scientific career.

My aim is to portray, in as intimate detail as the record permits, the course of Lavoisier's *investigations* in the areas of respiration, plant and animal analysis, and fermentation. I have deliberately centered attention on the investigations, which incorporate ideas, rather than on the ideas themselves. Within the tradition in which the history of science is viewed as intellectual history, scientific ideas are sometimes treated as though they have lives of their own, and their connections with the evidence upon which they rest are given only subordinate attention. Within the newer movement toward a social history of science, investigations are usually treated only at the surfaces where the social dimension is assumed to impinge upon their direction and character. Yet it is the investigations themselves which are at the heart of the life of an active experimental scientist. For him ideas go into and come out of investigations, but by themselves are mere literary exercises. For him the social context is peripheral unless it becomes an impediment to his ongoing work. If we are to understand scientific activity at its core, we must immerse ourselves as fully as possible into those investigative operations, whether they be in the laboratory, the museum, the field, or the lecture hall, where scientists themselves spend the working days of their lives.

Lavoisier left behind an extraordinarily rich documentary record of his private research pathway. There are twelve volumes of laboratory notebooks, from which we can reconstruct a large part of his immediate experimental activity. Numerous informal notes and memoranda allow us to glimpse formative and transition stages in his thought about the theoretical problems he faced. Especially revealing are the drafts for his scientific papers—or memoirs, as they were customarily called in the French literature. In some cases two or three drafts, representing successive stages in the composition of the final version, have survived. Here we find that new ideas and points of view frequently emerged, changed, grew stronger or faded away, as he shaped his investigations into organized form. From these manuscript materials, together with the published writings themselves, we are able to trace a dense trail of interacting thought and experimental activity. For many of the episodes in his long research program we can recapture nearly full cycles of events, from the formation of a problem to the presentation of its solution in public form. We can observe his efforts to define the problem, can see in the design of a succession of experiments the manner in which he intended to explore it, the obstacles he encountered on the way, and modifications he made in his experimental plan to obviate the difficulties. We can watch him interpreting the immediate results of each experiment, grouping experimental results in a series that comes to represent the solution of the problem, and struggling to compose an account of the investigation. We can observe new insights come to light in the very process of writing, as he modifies his original drafts and reaches toward his final version. We see that his creativity does not reside in any one of these phases alone, but is spread through all of them.

I agree with Howard Gruber, Gerald Holton, and others that it is from finely detailed case studies of the investigations of highly creative scientists that we are most likely to reach eventually a clearer understanding of the general nature of creative imagination in science.[1] I am also encouraged that some philosophers of science are coming to believe that the processes of discovery can be made "intelligible to reason," and that to do so they must join forces with historians to follow the "routes" to important discoveries of the past.[2] The account given in the following chapters ought to provide nourishing materials for such objectives. I have myself paused here and there in the narrative to offer reflections on Lavoisier's experiences that may contribute toward such broader purposes, and have collected in a final chapter some thoughts concerning general patterns of creativity illustrated in his career. These comments are suggestive rather than systematic. My main purpose is to reconstruct the story itself, so that readers may be able to elicit from these events other insights that have not occurred to me.

There is another, especially urgent reason for following in painstaking detail the investigations of scientists of the stature of Lavoisier. Historians of science have reached a general consensus that we should judge the scientists of the past, no longer by the standards of present knowledge, but in the context of their own times. We should not award credits to scientists for contributing ideas still judged correct, and convict them of "errors" for holding ideas now viewed as incorrect. This approach has liberated us from some of the straitjackets of the older style of presentist, or Whig, history. We have, however, scarcely begun to grasp how much more difficult a task we have thereby set for ourselves. The older standard of judgment, whether meaningful or not, was at least clear. The new standards risk being no standards at all. From evaluating earlier scientific thought within its own context we can slip, almost without noticing it, to accepting at face value whatever earlier scientists wrote. We can all too readily abandon critical judgment. Then our descriptions will appear to lend themselves to the claim that scientific knowledge is whatever scientists of a given time say it is; that it is not about anything "out there" beyond the consensus of the contemporary scientific community, that it is merely the outcome of contingent social processes.

Having freed ourselves from what we declared to be the illegitimate judgments of the older presentist historians, we have taken on the responsibility to maintain tighter, rather than looser, critical standards of assessment. Doing away with the older decisions of "correct" and "incorrect" does not relieve us of the need to recognize qualitatively better and worse science. For experimental sciences the problem is even more difficult than for theoretical ones, because we cannot witness what our subjects observed, only their accounts of what they observed. What does seem clear is that cogent criteria can be identified only through deep and thorough studies of the work of the scientists of the past. Even if we are forced to fall back on the dictum that we cannot define good science but that we can recognize it when we see it, we should try to refine our powers of recognition. I cannot claim entirely to have solved the problem of evaluating the quality of the science of Lavoisier or his contemporaries without recourse to retrospective information; but I have tried to carry the description and interpretation down to the level of fine discrimination that will be required to reach such judgments.

From a more intimate reconstruction of Lavoisier's investigations we obtain a picture of his scientific character that differs in significant respects from the image that has been passed along in general historical accounts of him. Historians have repeatedly stated that Lavoisier made no novel experimental discoveries, that his originality consisted primarily in the interpretation that he gave to the discoveries of others.[3] Experiment itself, it is sometimes said, held little appeal for him. A. R. Hall has written that the element of novelty in his experiments "was limited to Lavoisier's insistence upon paying heed to the teachings of the balance."[4] That "element," however, amounted to discovering a whole new mode of chemical experimentation. Much of his scientific creativity went into the arduous, sustained effort to make this highly original form of investigation work.

It has also been said that he used the balance faithfully and persistently in his analytical work, but "not always with rigorous accuracy";[5] or that he "aimed at accurate results, but seldom achieved them."[6] Such judgments are based largely on comparisons of the values he reached for combining proportions, densities, heats of combustion, and other such constants, with the equivalent modern values. These assessments, however, miss the real problems Lavoisier faced. I think there are no grounds for doubting that he performed his weighings and other measurements with as much precision as the best balances and other instruments available in his time permitted. The difficulties he encountered were those not of weighing accurately, but of judging what was significant to weigh; of knowing how to estimate the quantities of substances he could not directly weigh; of determining what adjustments he could legitimately make when his balance sheets did not work out perfectly, as they almost never did; of deciding what degree of error was reasonable in a given type of experiment, when he lacked formal methods for computing expected errors. In staking his career on what has since become known as the principle of the conservation of mass, Lavoisier was embracing a myriad of complexities that he could never fully control. The most impressive aspect of his achievements is not that he sometimes came out with figures close to our own for the composition of this or that substance, but that he so consistently reached results that were meaningful. With them he was able to define substances and their relations to one another in ways that proved over and over to be sound starting points for the fields of chemical endeavor that flourished in his wake. Lavoisier did not achieve these remarkable results by routinely applying global methodological principles to every situation, but by analyzing each individual problem, and making complex judgments about the assumptions necessary to interpret each set of experimental measurements. Only by following Lavoisier through his individual investigations with a thoroughness approaching his own can we really comprehend both the springs of his scientific creativity and the foundations of his historical eminence.

The reduction of the data gathered in quantitative experimental investigations is generally regarded as a routine matter, necessary in practice, but a tedious subject for historical discussion. For Lavoisier, however, that task was never routine. He had, in effect, to invent the procedures he used. Just as he encountered difficulties in almost every measurement itself, so he had to contend with unprecedented problems whenever he utilized the results he had obtained to derive the conclusions for which his experiments served. Lavoisier's ability to manage his data through the calculations he imposed on them was as crucial to the success of his enterprise as were the design and execution of the experiments themselves, or the theoretical structure he built upon them. His scientific creativity is embedded as deeply in the data sheets on which he made these calculations as it is in the records of his laboratory operations or the texts of the drafts of his memoirs. I have tried to describe this phase of his activity fully enough to elucidate his approaches, the obstacles he encountered, his response to such difficulties, the assumptions and compromises he was forced to make along the way, and the manner in which he maintained through such maneuvers the integrity of investigations menaced at almost every turn by experimental pitfalls. Although Lavoisier or his collaborators sometimes made explicit what approaches they followed in these affairs, I have in many cases had to elicit his strategies and his assumptions from the numbers themselves.

Close examination of his scientific life suggests also that there are aspects of Lavoisier's personality left out of the typical characterizations of him by historians. He has been categorized as severely logical, rigidly disciplined, reserved, a man who controlled every aspect of his life and career as strictly as he controlled his experiments. In broad terms he probably fit those descriptions; but just as he was never able to control the real experiments in his laboratory as easily as he appeared to in his published reports of them, so we find in the private record of his thoughts and actions hints of a less austere person than his public representation. When we can visualize him suddenly having to break off an experiment to patch up a lute that had failed, or to replace a flask that had melted because he had allowed the heat to become too intense; when we see him making errors in his computations and later finding them; when we find him writing down words, phrases, or paragraphs, crossing them out and starting in again; when we witness him thinking out complex theoretical problems, realizing at the end of a long chain of reasoning that he had reached a conclusion quite inconsistent with one he had drawn at an earlier stage in the same chain, we may begin to appreciate that here was a human being feeling his way along as everyone else must do. The control he achieved over the larger features of his life and his scientific enterprise was neither so absolute nor so effortlessly attained as it appears from the outward surface of his activity. When we begin to look for them, we find evidences of diverse feelings, from eagerness to hesitation, from overconfidence to skeptical self-questioning, from ambition to vulnerability, in his published as well as his unpublished writings. Even this supposedly cold man needed the support of those around him, and the quality of his work was in part influenced by the quality of his various collaborators. For a person depicted as largely self-contained, he worked surprisingly well with others, particularly with others who were themselves strong. Charles Gillispie, who has called him "the most inaccessible of the great scientists," has also said that "in the laboratory Lavoisier might, perhaps, be known."[7] We could know him best if we could look through the keyhole of his laboratory and *see* how he went about his "cherished occupation"—whether he whistled while he worked, what his conversations with the friends and collaborators who gathered there with him were like.[8] We can do the next best thing. Through the records he saved, we can come to know a Lavoisier in the laboratory whom we have not previously known through his polished public performances.

The investigative trail along which we shall trace Lavoisier's footsteps spanned twenty years of his life. To reconstruct his progress at the intimate level which the documentary record makes possible, for so long a time, results inevitably in a very long book. Some would prefer that I had simplified the situation by restricting the finely detailed treatment to a few choice examples of his research, and had summarized the rest more succinctly. To do so, however, would be to lose the integrity of the investigative process. Historians of science too often attempt to fix on the nodal stage, the crucial insight, the formative experience, or some other hidden key that might seem to unlock the central core of a great scientist's creative achievement, and spare us the complexity of his overall investigative pathway. This approach condemns us to partial understanding. A great scientific investigation is not captured in a small set of great moments. It is an organic, growing, slowly changing movement, a network of intertwined problems which themselves develop, change their relationships with one another and their relative importance within the complex. If we wish to grasp its contours, we cannot shrink from telling the whole story. Few historic investigations merit exhaustive treatment more than does the subject of the present volume. Lavoisier's researches within the domain of what we now call the chemistry of life constitute one of the greatest investigations ever carried out by one man in the history of the life sciences. It was a prolonged scientific odyssey, which shaped entire fields of modern biology, and it is rich in the subtle nuances of creative scientific activity. Lavoisier left us so much information about what he did, privately as well as publicly, that we ought to describe his endeavor as completely, probe it as deeply, and reflect on it as thoughtfully, as our own capacities permit us to do.

By extending the logic of the above position one might infer that Lavoisier's investigations of respiration, fermentation, the composition of plant and animal matter, and closely related topics cannot be understood without telling the entire story of his investigations in general chemistry. It is true that this book follows only several currents within a broader stream. It has, in fact, been necessary to describe extensively some aspects of his theoretical and experimental work on the general problem of combustion; in doing so I hope to have contributed some new perspectives to that familiar story. I have done so selectively, however, giving more or less detail according to the degree of relevance to the central themes of the book. There is no pretense of a full or balanced account of his work in chemistry at large. A reviewer of an earlier draft of this book expressed disappointment that it does not integrate Lavoisier's investigations in its areas of special concern more fully into his general chemistry. Such an integration would, in principle, be highly desirable. The task is, however, much larger than one might at first suppose. It will not do to attach the finely detailed account of the selected areas of his research, presented here, to an account of the rest of his chemical research treated at the more general level available in the current historical literature. The laboratory notebooks contain the materials for detailed reconstruction of much of these other investigations as well. To comprehend Lavoisier's approach to general chemistry at this more intimate level will require, in addition, extensive analyses of the large body of traditional chemical literature with which Lavoisier was very familiar. When such a study is completed, it will occupy several volumes. I can only hope that someone among the "Lavoisier scholars" will embark on that long historical enterprise.

The present account assumes a familiarity with the broad outlines of Lavoisier's career. Those who wish to refresh their memories would do well to read Guerlac's authoritative overview in the *Dictionary of Scientific Biography,*[9] with its extensive bibliographical guide to the more specialized literature. My narrative begins just after the formative events described in Guerlac's *Lavoisier—The Crucial Year;*[10] that classic study provides a very useful background that I have not attempted to recapitulate.

Each of the problems Lavoisier took up in the domain of the chemistry of life has, of course, a prior history of its own. My concentration on Lavoisier's own investigative pathway leaves insufficient space to deal with these events in detail, and I have done no more than to indicate their points of intersection with his work. For the history of respiration the writings of Leonard Wilson, Robert Frank, Diana Hall, Everett Mendelsohn, and June Goodfield provide much of the earlier and contemporary events missing or treated in passing here.[11] An excellent summary of the history of fermentation in the eighteenth century, as well as after Lavoisier, is available in Joseph Fruton's *Molecules and Life.*[12] There is no comprehensive study of the history of plant and animal analysis prior to Lavoisier, but that topic is too complicated to deal with here. Many years ago I wrote most of a planned full-length treatment of the subject. I still hope to finish it.

Since much of my interpretation of Lavoisier's work rests on the relevant portions of the twelve volumes of his laboratory registers which have been preserved, it is necessary to ask how full and reliable a record of his actual investigations they provide. Generally they are regarded as far from complete. No one can tell, of course, how much is missing from them. It is obvious that there are time periods and blocks of research not covered. The most significant question is what kind of record they provide for those segments of his work which do appear in them. My strong impression from working with them is that they constitute the primary record of his laboratory work, that they are not selections out of some other record. It has been possible to reconstruct coherently the investigations Lavoisier carried out in the areas of respiration, fermentation, and plant and animal chemistry up until 1788 on the assumption that most of the important experiments are recorded in the notebooks. I have come to that conclusion in spite of the fact that Lavoisier often stated in his published papers that he had repeated experiments "many times," where the notebooks contain only one or a few such experiments. In most cases in which Lavoisier described an experiment in published form with sufficient detail to identify it clearly, it can be identified with a corresponding experiment in the notebooks. Gradually I have come to believe that his more general statements exaggerated the extent of his investigations. I therefore adopted the policy of not assuming that any experiments are missing except when there is a particular reason to suppose so. Clearly this choice entails the risk that in certain places knowledge of experiments which did not survive in the records would cast a different light on the interpretations I have made. That is the ordinary risk inherent in any historical interpretation.

Nomenclature

Any historical account of chemistry during the eighteenth century must contend with the contemporary state of the nomenclature. The situation was especially confusing for the period of this narrative. Lavoisier began by using the traditional terminology of his time and of the phlogiston theory. By the end of our period he and his colleagues had adopted the new nomenclature which has been ever since at the foundation of chemical discussion. For most of the years with which we are concerned, he remained in a shifting transition state, in which he coined one term after another, but did not stick consistently even with his own choices. Some historians would cut the knot by simply translating everything into modern terms; but that policy makes it almost impossible to perceive the problems with which Lavoisier and his contemporaries were contending. I have generally used whatever words they used, with the exception of a few synonyms which they seemed to interchange without making conceptual distinctions. Readers who are unfamiliar with the chemical literature of the period may, however, find this welter of terms more bewildering than it was at the time. The following brief discussion of some of the most frequently used terms and their synonyms may alleviate some of this difficulty. For fuller treatments one should read Jon Eklund's *The Incompleat Chymist*, or Maurice Crosland's *Historical Studies in the Language of Chemistry*.[13]

FIXED AIR was the term originated by Stephen Hales to mean ordinary air combined in other bodies, or in a "fixed" state. Joseph Black used the same term for the air, with specific properties distinct from ordinary air, that he could obtain from *magnesia alba* and other mild alkalis. At various times Lavoisier used the following terms for this air:

Aerial acid
Chalky acid (*acide crayeux*)
Acid of *charbon* (see below)
Acide charbonneux.

In the new nomenclature the substance became carbonic acid when in solution, and carbonic acid gas in the free state.

CHARBON traditionally meant charcoal. Gradually it took on a second meaning as a pure principle contained in charcoal and other substances. Lavoisier distinguished the pure principle by calling it *matière charbonneuse* and *substance charbonneuse*, but he did not always use these terms consistently. In the new nomenclature *charbon* became again charcoal, while the pure principle became carbon. Because the ambiguity inherent in Lavoisier's use of the older terms is lost in the nearest English equivalent, charcoal, I have retained the French words in the text.

PHLOGISTON was the hypothetical principle of inflammability. It was thought to be a constituent of all combustible bodies, and to be given off during the combustion. When defined by Georg Ernst Stahl it was applied principally to explain the relation between combustible bodies such as sulfur and the acids they formed, and between a metal and its calx. By Lavoisier's time Joseph Priestley and others were defining the newly discovered "airs" in terms of the varying amounts of phlogiston they were considered to contain. In the new nomenclature a metallic calx became an oxide.

DEPHLOGISTICATED AIR was the name given by Priestley to the new air he discovered by reducing a mercury calx without charcoal. Because he regarded air in which a combustion had taken place to be "phlogisticated," and the new air burned more readily than common air, he thought it contained less phlogiston than common air. Lavoisier also called the new air dephlogisticated air at first, and even after he invented new terms for it he often reverted to Priestley's name. Before he was certain that the air was a distinct species Lavoisier sometimes called it "the purest part of air," "air better than common air," or "pure air." Afterward he named it "eminently respirable air," a term he soon replaced with VITAL AIR. The principle which could be obtained from vital air by separating from it the "matter of fire," or caloric, which was responsible for its gaseous state, he called "acidifying," or "acidiform principle," or OXYGEN PRINCIPLE. In the new nomenclature vital air became oxygen gas.

MOPHETTE was irrespirable air, or "mephitic" air. After he had distinguished two portions of the atmosphere Lavoisier regarded mophette as a species of air, or gas. The principle which, together with caloric, formed this gas became in the new nomenclature AZOTE. English chemists adopted instead the word nitrogen.

NITROUS AIR, discovered by Priestley, formed nitrous acid when reacted with ordinary air. In the new nomenclature it became an oxide of azote (nitric oxide).

Of the three common mineral acids, NITROUS ACID became in the new nomenclature nitric aid; VITRIOLIC ACID became sulfuric acid; and MARINE ACID became muriatic acid (hydrochloric acid).

SPIRIT OF WINE was the most common name for what became in the new nomenclature alcohol. "Spirituous" or "vinous" fermentation became alcoholic fermentation.

Lavoisier utilized the most common French premetric system of weights, in which

1 pound = 16 ounces
1 ounce = 8 gros
1 gros = 72 grains

Part 1

The Grand System 1773–1780

In 1772 Antoine Lavoisier began to investigate processes that fix or release "airs." He found that burning phosphorus and sulfur absorb something from the atmosphere and gain weight. Shortly afterward he established that minium, a lead ore, gives off an air when heated. By pursuing the consequences of these historic discoveries, Lavoisier developed over the next eight years the experimental and conceptual core for a new system of chemistry. The burden of the following chapters is not to repeat that well-known story in detail, but to show how, from the earliest stages, the physiological process of respiration was an integral component of his investigative program. Lavoisier's experiments directly involving respiration are described completely, and the development of his thought on that subject is traced in as intimate detail as surviving records permit. The classical experiments on combustion, calcination, and reduction, on which most historical treatments of Lavoisier focus, remain here in the background. They are mentioned only as necessary to indicate the many points of attachment between the problem of respiration and the rest of Lavoisier's research enterprise. Certain phases of his investigations in general chemistry, however, such as the calcination and reduction of mercury, the analysis and synthesis of the atmosphere, and the relation between the composition of fixed air and ordinary air, are so intimately related to his investigation of respiration that they are treated more fully. In describing this work I hope that I have also brought some new perspective to the larger question of how Lavoisier came to replace the phlogiston theory with a new theory of combustion.

Because his experiments on respiration itself, although crucial, occupied only a small portion of Lavoisier's laboratory time during these years, Part 1 appears to place less emphasis on his experimental activities than Part 2 will do. With respect to respiration, the more complex development within this period was the gradual unfolding of his conceptual understanding of the process, in conjunction with his understanding of the other processes that absorb or disengage airs. The balance in these chapters therefore falls more on the side of thought than of operations. We should keep in mind, however, that in these years Lavoisier was spending the major part of his scientific working time carrying out those experiments on combustion and calcination that are already familiar to students of the history of chemistry.

1

An Ambitious Agenda

Between 1660 and 1674 English physicians and natural philosophers carried out a brilliant series of investigations concerning the function of the lungs in animals. In 1660 Robert Boyle found that a flame is extinguished and an animal dies in an evacuated chamber of an air pump. Four years later Robert Hooke demonstrated, by blowing air continuously through the perforated lungs of a dog, that it is a supply of fresh air, rather than the movement of the lungs, which is essential to the life of the animal. Richard Lower extended Hooke's experimental method in 1669 to show that the venous blood becomes arterial in passing through the lungs, and that the color change takes place only so long as the lungs are supplied with fresh air. The red coloring, he concluded, is "entirely due to the penetration of particles of air into the blood."[1] In 1674 John Mayow placed a small animal under a glass inverted over water, and observed that its breathing caused the water level to rise in the jar up to $1/14$ of the total volume of air enclosed. On the basis of this experiment he elaborated a theory of respiration. Animals, he asserted, consume something from the air, which he identified as "nitro-aerial particles." Because an animal could live only half as long in a jar in which a lamp had gone out as it otherwise could, Mayow assumed that respiration and combustion consume the same substance.[2]

For three-fourths of a century, despite a great deal of attention to the subject, those who concerned themselves with respiration were unable to make decisive progress beyond the state of the problem in 1674, and even the positions taken by Mayow and his colleagues fell into doubt. The difficulty in understanding how air could penetrate through the membrane separating the air passages of the lungs from the blood in the capillaries; evidence that air in the blood can be fatal; and a conception of air as a physical element which does not enter chemical combination, were among the obstacles to the view that respiration absorbs a portion of the air.[3] Mechanical theories which ascribed the source of animal heat to such processes as friction, created by the particles of blood passing thorugh the circulation, competed with the tacit comparison between respiration and combustion.[4]

During this prolonged period, the most influential experiments on respiration were those which Stephen Hales reported in his book *Vegetable Staticks,* in 1727. Hales "repeated Dr. Mayow's experiment, to find out how much air is absorbed by the breath of animals inclosed in glasses." Hales too placed the animal, a rat, in a glass vessel inverted over water, but he improved the arrangement by including a pedestal to support the animal above the water. Hales found 1/27 part of the "elastic air" absorbed in the process, the same amount as a burning candle would absorb in the vessel. By breathing into a bladder through a system of tubes and valves, he showed that the "respiration of human lungs" also absorbs a portion of the air. While thus confirming Mayow's experimental result, Hales rejected the conclusion that respiration consumes the "vivifying spirit of the air." Instead he inferred that the process causes "the loss of a considerable part of the air's elasticity," by loading it with "gross" and "dense" vapors. The sudden death of animals placed in air containing these "noxious vapors" he attributed to the collapse of the lungs, which could not be dilated by air that had lost its elasticity. He regarded his difficulty in expanding his own lungs, after he had rebreathed the same air for about a minute, as strong support for this contention.[5]

Between 1750 and 1770 the emergence of a chemistry of airs provided the foundations for a fresh approach to the problem of respiration, as to so many other chemical processes. After Joseph Black had identified what he named "fixed air" as a distinct aeriform substance which, unlike ordinary air, could combine with lime and with alkalis, he tested the effects of this air on animals. He found, in 1756, that birds died in fixed air within ten seconds, but that if their nostrils were blocked they could last three or four minutes. "I convinced myself," Black related much later, "that the change produced on wholesome air by breathing it, consisted chiefly, if not solely, in the conversion of part of it into fixed air. For I found, that by blowing through a pipe into lime-water, or a solution of caustic alkali, the lime was precipitated, and the alkali was rendered mild." Black acknowledged that he was "partly led" to do this last experiment by an observation by Stephen Hales that he could make the air he breathed "last longer for the purpose of life," if he breathed through cloth dipped in alkali. It was not until Black identified fixed air that Hales's result could suggest the conclusion Black drew from it and confirmed with his own test for fixed air. Black discovered also, by means of this same limewater test, that both fermentation and burning charcoal produce fixed air. Somewhat later he recorded in his notebook that, since animals with more highly developed respiration are also warmer, and "infect the air" more strongly, animal heat and this alteration of the air may arise from the same cause. Black therefore appears to have conceived of respiration as a process which both converted ordinary air to fixed air and released heat. He did not, however, publish these ideas. Through his course lectures his students in Glasgow learned of them, but it was not until the early 1770s that any of them alluded to his views in print.[6]

When Henry Cavendish described the properties of the inflammable air produced by certain metals in dilute acids and showed that it was distinct from either common or fixed air, the era of what he called "factitious" airs was well under way.[7] By 1772 Joseph Priestley had become the most indefatigable investigator of new "species" of airs. Priestley, like Black, brought this growing new dimension of chemistry quickly to bear on the phenomenon of respiration. Habitually he used, as one of his tests of the properties of each air, the effects it exerted upon a mouse placed in it. Inflammable air, he reported, "causes violent convulsive movements," always accompanied by the death of the animal. Fixed air also generally caused animals to "die on the spot." He thought that it did so by coagulating the blood in their lungs. Besides using respiration to test different airs, Priestley became interested in the effects of respiration on ordinary air. In 1772 he called the process a "corruption or infection" of the air: "There is no one who does not know that a candle can burn only a certain time, and that animals can only live for a limited time, in a given quantity of air; one is no more familiar with the cause of the death of the latter than with that of the extinction of the flame under the same circumstances, when a quantity of air has been corrupted by the respiration of animals placed within it." Like Hales, Priestley rejected the idea that the animals die because they have consumed something from the air. The cause could not be the lack of a "vital nourishment (*pabulum vitae*)," because they quickly die in convulsions after a single breath in noxious airs. The air must therefore be "charged with harmful emanations by respiration." The air in which an animal has respired "does not differ in any way," he thought, from that in which animal or plant matter has putrified. Both airs were equally harmful to animals, both smelled equally, both diminished in volume when put in contact with water, and both precipitated limewater. He believed, therefore, that he could adduce evidence for the effects of respiration from experiments he had performed on the effects of the dead body of a mouse on the air. Following the example of Mayow and Hales, Priestley carried these experiments out in vessels inverted over water, and he too observed that the air diminished in volume. The air, he wrote, was "disposed to deposit one of the parts which compose it." The technical innovation of inverting a vessel over mercury instead of over water, which he introduced into pneumatic chemistry, enabled him to show that under these circumstances the air was not diminished by the putrefaction. When he afterward introduced limewater into the vessel, "it was condensed and made turbid in the usual way"; that is, the limewater absorbed fixed air from the air left by the putrefaction.[8]

The experimental evidence would appear in retrospect to be leading to the same conclusion Black had reached, that respiration changes ordinary air to fixed air; but Priestley did not reason in such tidy categories. Fixed air was only one of the products he attributed to putrefaction, and by association to respiration as well. "Animal and plant substances which are corrupted furnish putrid emanations, and fixed air or inflammable air, according to the time and circumstances." One's choice of comparisons can be crucial. Although Priestley noted the similar effects of respired air on a burning candle and on an animal, he did not develop the analogy between combustion and respiration, but that between respiration and putrefaction. Consequently he did not focus his attention on the formation of fixed air as the central characteristic of respiration, as Black did, but viewed respiration as a "corruption," producing "noxious emanations." He suspected that "one of the uses of the lungs is to evacuate the putrid emanations which would perhaps corrupt a living body as promptly as a dead body."[9] Priestley's main concern was not so much to define the effects of respiration on the air as to discover how the atmosphere is restored to its fresh condition. It was obvious to him that "nature must have some means" to accomplish the reverse process; otherwise the mass of the atmosphere would after a certain time become useless for the conservation of animals. After trying various processes which proved to have no such action, Priestley tested the effects of plants on air made noxious by respiration, and made one of his most important discoveries. Green plants can restore such air, making it once again as respirable as ordinary air.[10]

II

By early in 1773 Antoine Lavoisier had performed the famous initial experiments on the combustion of phosphorus and sulfur which confirmed his suspicion that something from the air combines with these substances, increasing their weight. He had then discovered that the lead ore known as minium, heated with charcoal in a pneumatic chamber, gives off large quantities of air. Henry Guerlac, who has given a closely argued account of the origin of Lavoisier's interest in these subjects, has shown that he probably knew very little of the work of Black or Priestley when he began these studies, but was familiar with the earlier works of Hales. Sometime near the end of 1772, however, Lavoisier began to read carefully the writings of the many authors who had dealt with problems related to combustion.[11] The papers Priestley had recently published he then came to regard "as the most laborious and most interesting which have appeared since M. Hales on the fixation and disengagement of the air. No modern work appears to me more suitable to make one realize how many new pathways to follow physics and chemistry still offer." He prepared systematic reviews of Priestley's articles and others, which he later published. Since Priestley's writings constituted, in Lavoisier's view, "in some sense a tissue of experiments almost uninterrupted by reasoning, an assemblage of facts, of which the majority are new," his commentary was essentially an abstract of the individual articles making up Priestley's publications from the previous year.[12] This included the section on "air corrupted or infected by the respiration of animals."

Lavoisier's own style pervaded even his summary of Priestley's work, for he presented the observations and conclusions more systematically and succinctly than Priestley himself had done. He also called attention to contradictions typical of Priestley's writings. Priestley, for example, had written that putrefactive emanations mixed with fixed air diminish the volume of common air, but the experiments he described did not confirm that view. Moreover, the experiments were themselves sometimes contradictory. In one case putrefying animal matter diminished the volume of air, in another it increased the volume. On the positive side, Lavoisier emphasized that Priestley had repeated the experiments on putrefaction and respiration "employing mercury in place of water" for the pneumatic vessel. He summarized more clearly than Priestley had the effects of respiration on the air that Priestley had observed:

> Air which has thus served for the respiration of animals is no longer ordinary air: it approaches the state of fixed air, in that it can combine with lime and precipitate it in the form of calcareous earth; but it differs from fixed air (1) in that when mixed with common air it diminishes the volume, whereas fixed air increases it; (2) in that it can come into contact with water without being absorbed; (3) in that insects and plants can live in it, whereas they perish in fixed air.[13]

As he studied the writings of previous authors concerning phenomena relevant to his discovery of the fixation of air in calcination and combustion, Lavoisier began to perceive more clearly the great extent of the program of research on which he was embarking. On February 20, 1773, he wrote down in his laboratory notebook some ideas intended to guide him along the way. He began:

> Before commencing the long series of experiments that I propose to make on the elastic fluid which is released from bodies, whether by fermentation, or distillation, or finally by every type of combination, as well as [on] the air absorbed in the combustion of a great number of substances, I believe that I ought to put some reflections here in writing, in order to shape for myself the plan which I must follow.[14]

Lavoisier's private memorandum is celebrated for the fact that in it he seemed to foresee that his work on "the air which one disengages from and fixes in bodies" would "occasion a revolution in physics and chemistry." It is evident, however, that he was as interested in phenomena involving plants and animals as he was in purely chemical or physical processes. In the above paragraph, for example, the first process releasing an elastic fluid that he mentioned was fermentation, defined at the time as a spontaneous "intestine motion" which "plant and animal substances" undergo under appropriate conditions. In the next paragraphs he mentioned prominently other plant and animal processes. Raising the issue of whether "it was the air of the atmosphere itself," or some other elastic fluid, which combines with bodies, he included "the operations of the plant and animal economy," together with the "operations of art," as the processes which disengage or fix the substance in question. When discussing fixed air as defined by Black, he listed as the first property distinguishing it from ordinary air that "it kills the animals which respire it." Further on he commented, "An important point which the majority of authors have neglected," concerning fixed air, "is to pay attention to the origin of this air, which is found in a great number of bodies. They would have learned from M. Hales that one of the principal operations of the animal and plant economy consists in fixing the air, in combining it with water, fire, and earth in order to form all of the composed [bodies] with which we are acquainted." He concluded,

> The operations by which one can succeed in fixing air are: vegetation, the respiration of animals, combustion, under some circumstances calcination, and finally certain chemical combinations. It is with these experiments that I have concluded that I should begin.[15]

The repeated stress which Lavoisier placed on plant and animal processes does not appear accidental. Nor can it be maintained, I believe, that he saw them solely as convenient means toward his end of examining the fixation and release of air. At one point in his reflections, he wrote, "The works of the different authors I have cited, considered from this point of view [that is, of the fixation and release of air], have presented me with separate portions of a great chain; they have joined together several links. But there remains an immense series of experiments to carry out in order to forge a continuity."[16] Thus, Lavoisier envisioned the processes of the animal and plant economy, together with other chemical processes, as connected, through their participation in the absorption and release of air, in a network of phenomena which he hoped eventually to view as a coherent whole. Within an investigative program aimed at such a comprehensive picture, one might easily at one time view the physiological processes simply as means to examine fixation or release of the airs, and at another time view the latter as means to examine the nature of the physiological processes themselves. Means and ends could readily, sometimes almost imperceptibly, exchange places.

The phenomena involving the "plant and animal economy" which Lavoisier enumerated in his plan for future work included fermentation, vegetation, respiration, and the composition of bodies formed by plants and animals. There is reason to believe that from this time onward Lavoisier retained these four aspects of plant and animal chemistry among the enduring objectives of his research enterprise.

Lavoisier could not, of course, begin with his whole agenda at once. What he actually concentrated on during the next six weeks was the phenomenon which had already brought him to his new threshold—that is, the calcination of lead and the reduction of minium, the calx of lead. At the end of February he was thinking that minium was "a combination of lead and air." The air could not be "fixed air," because he had found that volatile alkali prepared with minium and sal ammoniac dissipated into the air, whereas if fixed air, which has "a prodigious affinity" for volatile alkali, were present, the two substances ought to have combined. The air combined in minium was therefore probably "the air of the atmosphere"; perhaps it did not contain enough phlogiston to enter into combination with alkalis.[17]

During March Lavoisier extended his experiments on other phenomena he had previously taken up, including the combustion of phosphorus and the calcination of other metals. In addition he began systematically to study for himself the properties of the fixed air of Joseph Black, obtained by reacting chalk with acids. Among the tests he planned to make with fixed air were "to wash it with different matters in order to observe afterward its action on animals."[18] This idea was undoubtedly inspired by Priestley who, Lavoisier noted, had asserted that every "air" harmful to respiration could be "rendered salubrious by agitating it for a long time with water."[19] Perhaps Lavoisier could not immediately carry out this intention because he was waiting for the construction of the apparatus with which to do so. During March he entered in his laboratory register that "the machines for testing the effects of the air on animals are ordered and almost completed. It is unnecessary to describe them here at the moment. One will speak of them when they are ready." His further reminder to himself—"In the experiments upon animals do not leave out frogs"—suggests that he had in mind to do a comprehensive investigation.[20] At the end of March, however, the apparatus was still not finished, owing to "the slowness of the workers." Meanwhile he carried on with his calcination experiments on lead. On March 29 he observed "with surprise" that in a closed chamber lead could be calcined only to a limited degree. "I began at that time," he put down in his notebook, "to suspect . . . that perhaps the totality of the air which we respire does not enter into the metals which one calcines, but only a portion, which is not abundant in a given quantity of air."[21]

The prominent place that Lavoisier accorded fermentation in his research plan among the operations that release air was a reflection of his keen interest in the process. One obvious attraction for him was that Priestley had discovered that fermentation produced a great quantity of fixed air. In the space above the fermenting beer vats in a brewery, Priestley found fixed air "in a state of almost perfect purity." As Robert Kohler has pointed out, however, Lavoisier probably also learned something else of great importance to him from fermentation. By connecting a bottle half full of wine to a pneumatic flask, the Abbé Rozier had shown that when wine begins to turn acidic, as it often does in the late stages of fermentation, it absorbs air. Kohler has suggested that if, as is probable, Rozier told Lavoisier about this phenomenon late in the summer of 1772, it may have been for Lavoisier the germinal source of the idea that acids contain air; and might even have stimulated Lavoisier to carry out his initial experiments on burning phosphorus to see if phosphoric acid too contained air. Lavoisier was, however, evidently also excited over the prospect that Rozier's finding raised for a new understanding of fermentation itself. In the draft of a memoir on the calcination of metals which, according to René Fric, Lavoisier probably read at the public meeting of the Academy on April 21, 1773, Lavoisier referred to Rozier's observation and generalized that if one ferments sugar, must of beer, or any other analogous plant matters, "one observes that as soon as the spirituous fermentation takes place there is a release of air in great abundance, but when through the course of the fermentation the liquor begins to turn acidic, all of the released air is soon absorbed again to enter into the composition of the acid." After noting that he had observed this absorption in every liquor that soured, he added, "These experiments throw a new light on the phenomena of fermentation; they will, I hope, soon place me in a position to give a nearly complete theory." Judging from the lack of details concerning "these experiments," Lavoisier had probably not carried out a special investigation of fermentation when he wrote this discussion.[22] Shortly afterward he did.

On May 16 Lavoisier put one ounce of flour and five ounces of water into a medicinal flask. He placed the flask under a glass jar "with an apparatus appropriate to measure the air" which might be formed or absorbed. The "apparatus" was presumably a pneumatic trough over which he inverted the jar, so that he could measure the change in the volume of air by the rise or fall of the water within the jar. He placed an identical mixture of flour and water in a second flask, but left it open so that he could test for changes that might take place in the fluid. If "spirituous" fermentation were to take place, he ought to be able to identify spirit of wine in the flask. If the "acetous" fermentation, regarded as the "second stage," were to ensue, he should be able to detect the formation of acid by means of an indicator, "blue paper." During the first day no air was released under the bell jar; but it began to form on the second day. By May 20 the water in the jar had lowered by "six lines." The next day it had gone down further, to 9½ lines, and he marked this level so that he could tell whether any more air would form afterward. Meanwhile the open flask had acquired a disagreeable odor, but Lavoisier could not tell whether any spirit of wine was present, and he could see no sign of acidity. Eight days later the volume of the air under the jar had diminished slowly, and the second flask was still not acidic. He continued the experiment until July 28, by which time the volume of air produced had diminished to little more than one-third of the maximum it had earlier reached.[23] Indecisive though it was, this experiment must have appeared to Lavoisier to support the view that he had already drawn from Rozier's observation. Despite his feeling that he was close to an important new theory of fermentation, he did not follow up this promising experimental start.

The most likely reason that he discontinued his fermentation investigation was that Lavoisier soon realized that he could not elucidate this complex process until he had established more fully the character of the simpler processes that composed it. In the preface to his *Opuscules* he remarked a few months later that he would defer the publication "of my experiments on fermentation in general, and on acidic fermentation in particular," until he had studied more deeply the nature of acids[24] themselves. He did not reach a position to give a "nearly complete theory" of fermentation for many years, but he never forgot his deep interest in the problem.

During the rest of 1773 Lavoisier concentrated his attention on calcination and reduction, combustion, and the properties of fixed air. His experiments on the calcination of lead and the combustion of phosphorus in pneumatic chambers showed that, no matter how much of either substance was present, it could not consume more than one-sixth to one-fifth of the total volume of the air enclosed. These results strengthened his belief that "not all of the air which we respire is suitable to be fixed in combination with metallic calces [or with phosphorus]; but that there exists in the atmosphere a particular elastic fluid mingled with the air, and that it is at the moment when the quantity of this fluid contained in the chamber is exhausted that the calcination [or combustion] no longer can take place." He could see no way, however, "to decide whether the fixable part is a substance essentially different from air, or whether it is the air itself to which something has been added or taken away." Considering it prudent to "suspend judgment," he usually referred to the substance, whatever it might be, by the neutral term "elastic fluid."[25]

His belief that there is in the air some kind of elastic fluid which is not identical with the atmosphere as a whole provided Lavoisier with a strong inducement to test the properties of the "air" released by reducing metal calces, as well as the remaining air in a closed space in which a metal had been calcined or phosphorus had been burnt; and to compare these properties with those of the air most distinct from common air, that is, the fixed air obtained especially from the "effervescence" of chalk with an acid. Lavoisier used the same basic tests for an air which Black and Priestley had developed—whether it forms a precipitate with limewater, whether it dissolves in water and is absorbed in caustic alkali, whether a candle can burn in it, and the effects upon an animal placed in it. Reflecting his own quantitative approach, he also calculated for each air its density relative to that of common air.

Lavoisier did not record when, or if, the "machines" he had ordered for testing the effects of airs on animals were finally delivered to him, nor did he give the promised description of them. He did begin soon after, however, either with these or some other apparatus, to carry out such tests for the various types of airs produced in his ongoing investigations. When he placed a sparrow into the elastic fluid evolved from chalk, the bird immediately "fell on its side in convulsions." Although removed within a quarter of a minute, it was already dead. A sparrow, a mouse, and a rat introduced into the elastic fluid released by the reduction of minium were likewise each "dead on the spot." Into each of these elastic fluids he also placed a burning candle, which was in both cases extinguished immediately.[26] Lavoisier bubbled the fixed air obtained from chalk through three successive bottles containing limewater. "Curious to test the effect that [the portion of the elastic fluid which had passed through all three bottles without being absorbed] would produce on animals," he introduced a small sparrow into it. "It did not appear to suffer noticeably during the first instant; but at the end of half a minute its respiration became difficult; it opened its beak, and at the end of a minute it had fallen on its side almost motionless." Removed after a half minute more, it recovered. A candle, however, was "instantly extinguished" in the same elastic fluid.[27] On July 1 he tested the "effects of air in which one has burned phosphorus on animals." "A bird plunged into a jar" of this air, he noted, "remained there for several seconds without appearing to suffer . . . it did not appear to have difficult respiration, or incipient convulsions. If it had remained in the same way in fixed air it would have died at once." A candle, however, went out in this residual air just as in fixed air.[28]

Lavoisier presented the results of his investigations at four successive meetings of the Academy of Sciences during July and August. He must have been making his conclusions public almost as quickly as he reached them. By early August he had tied these papers together into a single treatise and asked the Academy to appoint a commission to approve its publication.[29] The book, entitled *Opuscules physiques et chymiques*, came off the press in January 1774. The central purpose of his investigation, as he had organized it for publication, was "to prove the existence of an elastic fluid which is fixed in various substances."[30] Incorporated within this framework, the above experiments using animals appeared merely as one of the several types of tests which, following Priestley's example, Lavoisier utilized in order to characterize this elastic fluid, or to distinguish it from other elastic fluids. For instance, he used the fact that the elastic fluid derived from the reduction of minium and that from the effervescence of chalk produced "the same phenomena on limewater, on calcareous earth, on burning bodies [candles], and on animals" as the basis for concluding that there was "an almost perfect resemblance" between the two fluids. The fact that, of the elastic fluid obtained from chalk, that part which was not absorbed in limewater was "able, up to a point, to sustain the life of an animal" was evidence that there is another "portion of common air," distinguishable by its properties from the "fixable part."[31]

During September 1773, Lavoisier carried out additional experiments on the fixation and release of elastic fluids, in the presence of a committee appointed by the Academy to verify the results he had reported over the summer.[32] The members included Lavoisier's close friend J.-C.-P. Trudaine de Montigny, the pharmacist Louis-Claude Cadet de Gassicourt, and the chemist Pierre-Joseph Macquer, who recorded the procedures and results in Lavoisier's laboratory notebook. In one of these experiments Lavoisier examined the "effects" of the elastic fluid formed when he reduced minium with charcoal. He passed the air through two bottles of limewater, where it caused a precipitation. The elastic fluid afterward

> did not extinguish a candle nearly as quickly [as it did before passing through the limewater], but in proportion as the limewater precipitated and became less able to absorb the elastic fluid, that which passed through the jar became more effective in extinguishing the flame.
>
> A sparrow introduced into the jar full of that elastic fluid which had not passed through the limewater at all was instantly immobilized and remained as though dead; but having been placed in the open air at a window, it recovered in a relatively short time and flew away.
>
> A second sparrow placed under a small jar filled with elastic fluid which had passed through the two bottles of limewater [when the limewater had become] almost completely precipitated and saturated by this fluid took longer to become immobilized; nevertheless it was immobilized, and would have died if it had been left there longer.
>
> A third sparrow, stronger and larger than the first two, introduced into a larger jar filled with the same elastic fluid which had not passed through the limewater, was immobilized in 15 seconds and was completely dead in 20 seconds.[33]

It is particularly difficult to disentangle ends from means so as to identify the primary purpose that Lavoisier and his associates may have had in mind in carrying out these tests. From the attention they paid to the severity of the effects on the birds of samples of the elastic fluid subjected in varying degrees to the action of limewater we might surmise that they were interested in the physiological action of the elastic fluid. Yet we might equally well infer that they were simply utilizing the variable physiological effects as graded tests for the intensity of a property of an elastic fluid which could be modified in different degrees according to the strength of the action of the limewater upon it. Their motives need not have been unambiguous. In the *Opuscules* Lavoisier described an analogous, though more elaborate, experiment in which he had tested the effects on rats and mice of the residue left after the air disengaged from reductions of metallic calces had been pumped through limewater. The conclusion he then drew from the varying effects was "that it appeared confirmed that it is in the fixable part that the noxious property of this fluid [common air] resides, since it is less deadly to animals in proportion as it is more deprived of that part."[34]

On September 27, 1733, Lavoisier performed for the committee from the Academy a quite different experiment involving respiration:

> The air of respiration, introduced through a glass tube into limewater, precipitates it very promptly.
>
> Atmospheric air introduced into limewater through a bellows does not make it turbid or precipitate it.[35]

This description is too sketchy to permit a detailed reconstruction of the experiment. Although Lavoisier later added the title "air which has served for the respiration of animals," the "air of respiration" may have been simply air he had breathed out. There was nothing surprising or new in his comparison between the two airs. Black and Priestley had already shown that respired air precipitates limewater; and Lavoisier had noted in the summary of Priestley's experiments which he published in the *Opuscules* that air respired by animals is no longer like ordinary air, but "approaches the state of fixed air."[36] This entry is, therefore, little more than an indication that in the fall of 1773 Lavoisier made a start toward studying the effects of respiration upon the air, rather than merely using respiration as a means to characterize elastic fluids whose chemistry he was investigating. In other words, he was beginning to examine for himself the "operation" of respiration.

It is unlikely that Lavoisier held any developed chemical theory of respiration at this time, for in the *Opuscules* his one attempt to explain the physiological effects of the elastic fluid obtained from effervescences and from metallic reductions only underlines how slight were the foundations he had available for dealing with such problems. The sudden death of the animals in these experiments he accounted for by a theory that these elastic fluids, being soluble in water, are absorbed in the humors of the lungs, "and suddenly lose their elasticity," so that the lungs collapse.[37] The explanation was obviously an elaboration of the one Hales had given fifty years before, bolstered perhaps by the more recent knowledge of the solubility of fixed air in water.

In keeping with the tradition stretching back to Robert Boyle's experiments in an evacuated chamber, Lavoisier carried out conspicuously parallel experiments with a burning candle and with an animal. In the *Opuscules,* for example, an experiment on the "effect of the elastic fluid disengaged from effervescences on . . . enflamed bodies" was followed by a test of the effects of the same elastic fluid on animals. Tests of the effects of the air in which phosphorus was burned on animals and on lighted candles were also grouped in sequence.[38] He drew, however, no verbal comparisons between combustion and respiration. That he envisioned them in some sense as similar processes is evident from their association in his list of the operations which fix air that he intended to study. If he said nothing further about their similarities now, it may have been either because his attention was on other aspects of his investigation, or because while seeking a further definition of the resemblance he had not yet found anything suggestive enough to write about. If he had entertained comparisons, he might have been thrown off the track by the fact that in these early experiments the effects exerted upon the animals and on the candles by the various elastic fluids he tested were contrasting almost as often as they were similar. In all this, he shared the situation of his predecessors, who had also tacitly compared the two processes in the design of their experiments without explicitly describing them as analogous phenomena.

It was Priestley who gradually made explicit the implicit comparison between respiration and combustion as he continued his investigations of both processes. In 1774 he wrote, "That candles will burn only a certain time, in a given quantity of air is a fact not better known, than it is that animals can live only a certain time in it; but the cause of the death of the animal is not better known than that of the extinction of flame in the same circumstances."[39] His identification of the two processes with one another was weakened by cases similar to those Lavoisier experienced, in which burning candles and animals behaved differently. "An animal will live nearly, if not quite as long," Priestley reported, "in air in which candles have burned out, as in common air. This fact surprized me very greatly, having imagined that what is called the *consumption* of air by flame, or respiration, to have been of the same nature, and in the same degree; but I have since found, that this fact has been observed by many persons."[40]

The factor which enabled Priestley in 1774 to identify respiration and combustion in spite of such empirical discrepancies was the phlogiston theory. What he had thought of in 1772 as "putrid emanations" from the lungs he now perceived as a discharge of phlogiston. "Diminished, and noxious air," he wrote, "might have been called *phlogisticated air.*" Respiration and combustion were therefore alike because both discharged phlogiston into the air. "The death of animals in confined air" he no longer attributed to noxious effects of the emanations, but "to the want of a discharge of the phlogistic matter, with which the system was loaded; the air, when once saturated with it, being no sufficient *menstruum* to take it up."[41]

Priestley also modified his view of the source of the fixed air produced in respiration. The animal, he thought, did not actually discharge fixed air at all.

> It being now pretty clearly determined, that common air is made to deposit the fixed air which entered into the constitution of it, by means of phlogiston, in all the cases of diminished air, it will follow, that in the precipitation of lime, by breathing into lime-water, the fixed air, which incorporates with the lime, comes not from the lungs, but from the common air, decomposed by the phlogiston exhaled from them, and discharged, after having been taken in with the aliment, and having performed its function in the animal system.[42]

Priestley's identification of respiration with combustion was loosened by the fact that he attributed to a great variety of other phenomena as well—ranging from the effervescence of iron filings and the calcination of metals to the effluvia of paint—the same defining characteristic. "All these processes, I observed, agree in this one circumstance, and I believe in no other, that the principle which chymists call *phlogiston* is set loose."[43]

Priestley shaped the investigation of both repiration and combustion in these years also through the invention of his famous "nitrous air" test. Here, as in so much of the new chemistry of airs, he owed his inspiration to one of the many suggestive experiments of Stephen Hales. Hales found that the metallic ore Walton pyrites, when acted upon by the strong acid "compound *aqua fortis*," "expanded with great violence, heat and fume into a space equal to 200 cubick inches, and in a little time it condensed into its former space, and then absorbed 85 cubick inches of air."[44] In his second volume of "statical essays," Hales described the initial expansion as a "red fume." He treated the expansion and subsequent contraction as a case supporting his contention that "effervescent mixtures both generate and absorb air at the same time."[45] Priestley followed up Hales's observations in 1772, and found that solutions of various metals in spirit of nitre also generated the "red fume." By this time, however, he was, unlike Hales, looking for new "species" of airs, and he accordingly named the product of these reactions "nitrous air." Priestley found it amazing and surprising that "a quantity of air . . . devours another kind of air . . . yet is so far from gaining any addition to its bulk, that it is considerably diminished by it." He tried varying the proportions of nitrous air and common air. If, for example, he mixed one measure of nitrous air with two measures of common air, the volume diminished to "only one fifth of the original quantity of common air." Moreover, he found that this diminution "is peculiar to common air, or air *fit for respiration.*" It is remarkable, he wrote, in 1774,

> that on whatever account air is unfit for respiration, this same test is equally applicable. Thus there is not the least effervescence between nitrous and fixed air, or inflammable air, or any species of diminished air. Also the degree of diminution being from nothing at all to more than one third of the whole of any quantity of air, we are, by this means, in possession of a prodigiously large *scale*, by which we may distinguish very small degrees of difference in the goodness of air.[46]

It was Priestley, more than anyone else, who set the terms for discussion of processes involving the air which constantly reminded one of the relation with respiration. It was he who made "common air" nearly synonymous with "respirable air." In his earlier experiments he had defined the "goodness" of the air, its most significant variable property, by the length of time a mouse could live in it. After he devised the nitrous air test he still regarded this purely chemical operation as just a more convenient and accurate substitute for the mouse, one which still measured basically the "fitness" of the air for respiration.

At the time Priestley's volume *Experiments and Observations on Different Kinds of Air* appeared, containing the preceding discussions on respiration, combustion, and the nitrous air test, along with much else, Lavoisier was following Priestley's latest work with intense interest. The association Priestley made between respiration and combustion must have drawn Lavoisier's attention also to their similarities. When Lavoisier adopted the nitrous air test, along with so many other empirical procedures and discoveries he owed to Priestley, he inevitably imbibed as well some of the conceptual implications with which Priestley had imbued that operation.

III

During the year 1774 Lavoisier's most visible scientific activities were to follow up his calcination experiments in order to strengthen his conclusion that metals absorb an elastic fluid in the process, to set out on a program of repeating the experiments through which Priestley had discovered new "kinds of air," and to search for additional airs.[47] His private records show that he was, in fact, concerned with a broader range of problems. Many of the experiments he carried out involved traditional qualitative eighteenth-century mineral analysis, the characterization of the salts formed by combining various acids and bases. Lavoisier had been engaged in such work before he focused his attention on processes involving air in 1772. In retrospect that "crucial year" appears as a decisive turn to the set of problems which led him eventually to reform chemistry. In 1774, however, his success was not yet so dramatic as to preempt all of his experimental effort, and he went on with the examination of such conventional objects as the purification of epsom salts, the characterization of the salts formed by phosphoric acid, and the preparation of the acid of lemons. Concerned with the nature of the "matter of fire," Lavoisier considered a project to determine whether that substance has a measurable weight. He continued to make comparative tests on animals and candle flames of the effects of the airs disengaged in reductions and the residues left after calcinations.[48]

As he pursued several experimental lines, Lavoisier also kept trying to clarify the conceptual structure within which he was studying airs, and to extend the application of his ideas. The conclusion that there is a "fixable part" of common air invited him to view the atmosphere itself as a divisible entity. How to identify its portions and their relationships to one another, however, posed a puzzle that he could not readily solve. The unsettled state of his thought about the problem during the year 1774 is well expressed in the closing passage of a memoir on the calcination of lead in sealed vessels, which he completed in April and read, apparently unchanged, to the Academy on November 12. Air in which a metal has been calcined, he wrote, has

> in this way been deprived of its fixable part (I would almost say of the acid part which it contains); this air, I say, is in some manner decomposed, and it appeared to me that these experiments provide a means to analyze the fluid which comprises our atmosphere, and to examine the principles which constitute it. Although I have not reached entirely satisfying results in this regard, I believe that I am nevertheless in a position to affirm that the air, even when it is as pure as one may imagine it, freed of all moisture and of every substance foreign to its nature and its composition, far from being a simple entity, an element, as one ordinarily thinks, must on the contrary be included at least in the class of mixts, and perhaps even in that of compounds.[49]

Lavoisier was not merely uncertain of the rank of the atmosphere within the eighteenth-century chemist's hierarchy of degrees of composition; he could not even name the constituents he believed make up common air. The cause of his embarrassment is evident from a passage in the introduction of his memoir. In all the operations he had investigated which *disengaged* an elastic fluid—"metallic calces by reduction, plants by fermentation, or saline and earthy alkalis by dissolution in acids"—the product was the same "species of air," that which "one has improperly named *fixed air.*" One would expect, and Lavoisier had at various times attempted to infer, that in calcination, the operation which was assumed to be the reverse of a metallic reduction, this same species of air was absorbed. The evidence, however, could not be made to support such a view. He could say only, as he had said before, that "a portion of the air, or some matter contained in the air, combines with the metals."[50]

During the period when his ideas on the atmosphere had reached this stage, Lavoisier thought of an approach to respiration which fitted that process into his conceptions about the atmosphere and the matter of fire. At a time which cannot be closely specified, but which I believe was very probably between the fall of 1773 and the fall of 1774, he wrote on the front of a folded sheet of paper the following:

> Ideas
>
> One has [thought ?] up until now that animals and plants absorb air through the lungs and through the trachea only to cause it to circulate in the animal or plant economy. It is certain that it is fixed there.
>
> When an animal [is kept ?] under a pneumatic apparatus there is an absorption of air. One sees it by means of the barometer placed under the receiver.
>
> Some scientists have said that the air merely loses its elasticity, that is to say that it ceases to be in the vapor state and that it enters a combination.
>
> Couldn't one surmise *that there is only a certain portion* [Lavoisier then crossed out the words shown here in italics, and went on] that the heat of animals is sustained by nothing else than the matter of fire which is disengaged by the fixation of the air in the lungs. It would be necessary to prove that whenever there is an absorption of air there is heat.

On the second page of the folded sheet he went on: "but isn't the air itself composed of two substances, of which the lungs bring about the separation *and only absorb* [he then crossed out the preceding three words and substituted] of one of the two."[51]

There his idea ended for the time being. Although it cannot be definitely proven, I believe that Lavoisier may have written down here for the first time the germ of what grew eventually into his theory of respiration. The document has characteristics one would expect of an incipient stage in the emergence of a new insight, close to that initial flash historians strive to capture as the event at the heart of creative scientific activity. The tentative form of the final two paragraphs expressing his own views, cast as queries rather than statements, suggests that the ideas were new to him. Their simplicity, the lack of elaboration or qualification, suggest that he may not yet have pondered their implications or had time to run into counterarguments. The fact that the paragraph just preceding these two paragraphs refers to a theory similar to that of Hales, and to the one he had himself recently mentioned in the *Opuscules*, tempts us to see here traces of his own mental transition. The manner in which Lavoisier made the two alterations in the text also supports this interpretation. They were not revisions he made in these two passages after having written them out once, but changes he made as he went along. Thus he started to introduce in the first of the paragraphs the idea of two portions of air, then postponed it to the second paragraph in order to begin with the idea of the release of matter of fire. This is what we might expect of a person sorting out ideas, which can exist in no particular sequence in one's head, into the one-dimensional order required to transform them into sentences. The very heading of the note, "Ideas," also suggests a person about to put down something which has recently occurred to him.

We must be cautious, however, about inferring that this note is a direct expression of Lavoisier's flash of insight, even if it is the earliest written manifestation. Gruber has cogently argued that what appears in retrospect as a sudden insight, during which a novel view appears all at once, is most often only a nodal or threshold point in a gradual development of ideas.[52] There are many possible relationships between the first written form of an idea and the first awareness by the thinker that he has had one, ranging from an idea one tries to put down immediately, so that portions of the written statement nearly merge with the ongoing mental formulation itself, to ideas one carries around for days or weeks, subtly reshaping and amplifying them until one realizes that they are significant enough to write out.

More elusive even than the primordial state of a new insight is the occasion which triggers it. Even if the note were dated, we would probably not be able, in the absence of an account by Lavoisier himself, to define the exact circumstances under which he became aware of the conjunction of ideas expressed in it. As it is, we can only identify in broad terms the sources available to him for the component ideas associated in these paragraphs.

Since these ideas comprise the rudiments of a theory of *respiration*, we might anticipate that they arose somehow from the experiments he had performed which involved respiration. It is quickly apparent, however, that whatever underlying connections there may be, these are not on the surface. The observation that animals absorb air within a pneumatic apparatus does not seem to refer to Lavoisier's experiments, but to older work which had led others to the conclusions he summarized before coming to his own conjectures. There is no direct reference to the specific airs he had found to be noxious or respirable, or to his observation that respired air precipitates limewater. Neither is there an explicit comparison between respiration and combustion.

Lavoisier's new view of respiration incorporated two novel ideas. The first was that "the heat of animals is sustained by . . . the matter of fire which is disengaged by the fixation of the air in the lungs." Believing, along with many eighteenth-century physicists and chemists, that heat was a substance, Lavoisier had been concerned since very early in his career with the nature of what he called here the "matter of fire." By the time he wrote the *Opuscules*, he had formed the hypothesis that the matter of fire imparts the elasticity to elastic fluids, which it forms by combining with various solid or fluid bodies. When deprived of the matter of fire, the other component becomes "fixed."[53] His ideas on this subject were, however, still so loose and general in 1773 and 1774 that Guerlac has described them as a mere "covering theory."[54] The above statement about the disengagement of fire in the lungs constitutes a particular manifestation of that general hypothesis, and is correspondingly unspecific concerning the nature of the matter of fire or the elastic fluid from which it is disengaged. It may well be that little more had occurred to Lavoisier than the bare recognition that a release of that matter of fire, about which he had been speculating in other contexts, could also explain the warmth of animals. His assertion that "the fixation of the air" releases the matter of fire is no more specific. Possibly Lavoisier had in mind the formation of fixed air itself, implicitly drawing on the observation that respired air "approaches the state of fixed air," as he had put it when summarizing Priestley's experiments. Since he did not mention the air breathed back out, however, it is more likely that he was referring only to the older, more general view mentioned in the first paragraph of the present note, that the air breathed in "is fixed" in the animal economy; or, to his very definition of the matter of fire as a substance whose removal from an elastic fluid leaves behind the "fixed part." We cannot even tell if Lavoisier sorted out these various possible meanings as he wrote down his "ideas" about respiration.

Lavoisier's second basic insight was that the lungs absorb only one portion of the air, so that they separate the "two substances" of which he suspected the air was composed. Neither of the two "portions"is identified. This is just what we would expect if these ideas came to Lavoisier during that period in which he was seeking to conceive of the atmosphere as composed of separable portions, but had not yet reached a coherent view of what the portions were. As we have seen, it was from experiments on calcination and combustion that he was coming to see that only a "portion" of the air could be fixed in such operations. Although he had, since he laid out his agenda in early 1773, regarded respiration also as an operation which fixed air, he had not actually carried out any experiments to see if this operation too could fix only a portion of the air. Nevertheless, through his use of animals as tests for the properties of airs, he had become very aware that only certain of the airs he put them into were "respirable." It required hardly more than to focus his attention on respiration as such an operation, in the light of his emerging conception of the atmosphere, to conceive of it as separating respirable air from the unrespirable portions, even if he had no basis for identifying chemically the two portions of the air thus separated.

We may note finally the simplicity of Lavoisier's assumption that the matter of fire is disengaged, and the portions of the air separated, by the *lungs*. That feature of his theory of respiration was thus present from its earliest traces, and appears so self-evident there that he probably did not even need to reason about it.

I have analyzed Lavoisier's note as though what he wrote on that double sheet of paper fully expressed the degree of development his thoughts had reached at the time. It is, of course, possible that he had reasoned out more than that, and had written only an outline sketch of a more complex set of ideas. That is possible of *any* written statement, but there is little we can do to peer beyond it into the state of the author's consciousness at the time. If my own personal introspective experience is typical, the relationship between written statement and unwritten ideas is most often the other way around. The complexity of the ideas we can hold in association at one time in our heads is severely limited, and we are more likely to elaborate them as we write them out than we are to omit elements we have clearly reasoned out. The written statement may embody many unexpressed implications of which the author is not yet aware, but that is another matter.

Cyril Smith has likened the formation of a novel scientific idea to the formation of crystals in a supersaturated solution.[55] The nature and concentration of the dissolved substances, the temperature and pressure, correspond to a state of knowledge relevant to a given problem. The seed crystal or other nucleus dropped into the solution corresponds to the event which stimulates the crystallization of the idea in the mind of the scientist. Both the triggering agent and the supersaturated solution are required for the change of state to occur. In the preceding situation, as in most historical cases, we have been able to describe the conditions, but not to identify the immediate seeding agent. While we thus miss the germinal historical instant, that may be less significant than to understand the nature of the local surrounding conditions. The former may be almost accidental, determining only the timing, whereas the latter determine the form of the crystals, or ideas, which appear.

A new idea about respiration is far from a testable theory. Beyond the very general suggestion that "it would be necessary to prove that whenever there is an absorption of air there is heat," Lavoisier left no indication that he perceived at this point how to proceed either theoretically or experimentally toward a more fully developed point of view. It is not surprising, therefore, that he was not ready to discuss respiration publicly.

Lavoisier's note has not been included in previous historical accounts of his theory of respiration, most of which begin with his first publication on the subject, in 1777. The conclusion to be drawn from the note is not merely that he applied his theories of combustion and the composition of the atmosphere to the problem of respiration at an earlier stage than has hitherto been assumed;

for the ideas about a matter of fire and the separable portions of the atmosphere were not yet mature concepts ready to serve as stable foundations for further application. It is as plausible to view his ideas about respiration as a contribution toward the solidification of his conceptions of matter of fire and the atmosphere. From at least the time in early 1773 when he formulated his research agenda he had regarded respiration as one of the processes whose study would elucidate what is involved in the fixation of air. The fact that animals both fix air and emit heat may have reinforced his hypothesis that matter of fire is a component of elastic fluids, even as that hypothesis helped explain animal heat. The distinction between "respirable" and "unrespirable" air may have helped to stabilize Lavoisier's conception of an atmosphere separable into two portions, at a time when he was still unable to define these portions consistently in chemical terms. The nitrous air test, which distinguished respirable from all forms of unrespirable air, while lumping the latter together through the common property that nitrous air did not diminish their volume, could support this distinction while he was struggling without full success to fit the airs absorbed or released in combustions, calcinations, and reductions into a coherent scheme. Thus Lavoisier's "ideas" about respiration emerged in a complex, intimate, reciprocal interplay with his investigations of these chemical processes.

IV

During this same period, sometime between November 1774 and the end of February 1775, Lavoisier wrote a page and a half of "reflections on plant analysis" in his laboratory notebook. His interest in this topic probably came from several sources. Strictly speaking the subject was not an integral part of his program to investigate operations that absorb or release air, but it was associated in at least two ways with those processes. As we have seen, he had included in his discussion of his research plans early in 1773 that Stephen Hales had shown that one of the "principal operations of the animal and plant economy" was the fixation of air, combining it with other elements "to form all the composed bodies." It would therefore be relevant to Lavoisier's interest in the physiological operations that fix air to examine the composition of those bodies into which the air is fixed. Conversely, Hales had shown that the distillation of plant substances "generates" great quantities of "air," so that the decomposition procedures one applied to the analysis of plant matter led back to the very questions Lavoisier was asking about the nature of the airs which such operations release. Guerlac has shown that it was the *Vegetable Staticks*, in which Hales reported these results, which had first led Lavoisier "to appreciate the important role that air might play in chemical processes."[56] It was probably also partly the influence of this book which stimulated him to turn his interest to the subject of plant analysis itself; but he undoubtedly retained in addition a more general interest in the analysis of plant and animal matter going back to his early education as a chemist.

Ever since chemistry had coalesced as a coherent science during the seventeenth century, one of the central concerns of its practitioners had been to analyze plant and animal matters into their constituent parts. For generations they attempted to achieve this objective by improving traditional distillation methods, but by the early eighteenth century this approach was widely perceived as sterile. Toward the middle of the century a number of chemists, including the very popular teacher Guillaume-François Rouelle, began substituting for the old methods a systematic procedure of solvent extractions, whereby they could separate various substances from gross plant and animal matter without chemical alteration. They were, however, still unable to advance significantly on the problem of reducing the extracted substances to more elementary constituents.[57]

Lavoisier had followed Rouelle's "brilliant and flamboyant" lectures closely at a formative stage in his scientific education, probably during the years 1762–63. Although he was probably at that time primarily interested in Rouelle's lectures on the mineralogical problems which touched on Lavoisier's geological occupations under the tutelage of Jean-Étienne Guettard,[58] Rouelle devoted so much of his course to plant chemistry that the young student could hardly have failed to be impressed with the importance of the subject, as well as with its formidable problems. At the least, he must have been struck by Rouelle's devastating criticism of the customary distillation analyses of plants which "caused everything to be confounded together."[59]

During the years 1765–68 Lavoisier steeped himself in the older literature of chemistry. His fertile mind perceived opportunities to take up questions left unsolved by authors ranging from the first-generation member of the Academy, Samuel Cottereau Duclos, to the contemporary mineral analyst Johann Heinrich Pott. To judge from the notes he made, he continued to focus mainly on mineral chemistry;[60] but at least one note, written probably in 1765, revealed that the range of problems with which he concerned himself extended to plant and animal chemistry.

> Animal distillation
>
> When one distills an animal material, one obtains volatile alkali. Would it not be the calcareous material which comprises the skeleton of animals which disengages the volatile alkali, which was in the form of an ammoniacal salt in the [animal ?].[61]

There is no evidence that Lavoisier followed up this conjecture; but the note indicates at least that he was curious about one of the central questions in traditional animal chemistry, the source of the distillation product long regarded as the hallmark of animal matter.

These background experiences suggest that Lavoisier must have been familiar in a general way with the problems of plant and animal chemistry, and that he perceived the composition of plant and animal substances as relevant to his research on airs. There is no indication that he had at any time prior to writing his reflections on plant analysis undertaken on his own a systematic investigation of the subject, but he did sometimes utilize substances derived from plants in his investigations of airs. For example, in December 1773 he mixed spirit of nitre [nitrous acid] with spirit of wine in order to generate the air "nitrous ether," whose properties he then studied. He found during the course of the operation that inflammable air and fixed air were also generated.[62] It may have been from such occasional observations that he first came to suspect that these two airs were general components of plant matter. By 1774, therefore, Lavoisier had both some ideas on the subject of plant analysis, and reasons to connect the subject with his own investigation. Nevertheless we cannot isolate precisely what it was that immediately stimulated him to consider taking it up as a direct object of experimentation, as he clearly intended to do according to the aforementioned passage in his laboratory notebook:

> Reflections on plant analysis
>
> plant analysis is much less advanced than one believes. Ordinarily we completely destroy the composition of the plants, but the whole art consists in separating the mixts which compose it from one another (moreover we are uncertain whether or not we get as far as the mixts). We say that the wood of an oak is a compound of water, of acid, of oil and of a residue which is charcoal [*charbon*]. We go so far as to decompose the same *charbon* and to reduce it to earth and fixed alkali, but we do not know (1) What is the nature of that immense volume of air which is disengaged during the distillation. There is probably fixed air and inflammable air. (2) What the oil is. It would appear that through combustion one can reduce the oil to air and water, but we know nothing beyond that. Concerning the matter of the oil, one could ascertain its nature and determine the quantity of air and of water which it yields by means of a procedure that I have devised, and which I intend to carry out. It consists of causing a lamp to burn in a hermetically sealed vessel, weighing the vessel which contains the oil and that in which the combustion has taken place before and afterward. (3) What the *charbon* is. We know that in burning it converts the surrounding air into fixed air, but we do not know if it itself contributes fixed air, what is disengaged during the combustion, and the proportion of the air which remains to the original weight of the *charbon*. It would be still very interesting to do

> two experiments on the subject, to burn the *charbon* under a glass jar immersed in mercury and to examine the products. The difficulty is to obtain a large enough jar and enough mercury, and especially to maintain the combustion of the *charbon*. One could attain the latter by setting up a bellows under the jar which does not draw in external air and which only makes that of the interior circulate.
>
> It would be, furthermore, very interesting to burn *charbon* in a closed vessel. If a sensible quantity of the weight of this *charbon* is phlogiston, [the phlogiston] ought to pass through and escape from the vessel, and there ought to be a diminution of weight after the combustion. That experiment could be carried out in a hermetically sealed matras. [A matras was a standard distillation vessel.][63]

This assessment of the state of the problem of plant analysis was remarkably astute. From the succinct, tightly organized character of his discussion and his reference to experimental procedures he had already planned, we can surmise that Lavoisier had probably thought extensively about the subject before he wrote out this summary. The view that ordinary analytical methods destroy the composition of plants instead of separating the "mixts" composing it followed the line of criticisms that other chemists, including Rouelle, had been making since the beginning of the century. Lavoisier passed quickly over these well-rehearsed questions, however, to the aspects of the problem that impinged most directly on his own viewpoint. He had already available a preliminary answer to the problem raised by Hales's experiments, the identification of the "immense volume of air" disengaged. Concerning the oil, commonly regarded as the most characteristic constituent of plant matter, he had no new information at hand, but a clear plan for investigating the situation. Finally, the problem of the nature of the charcoal-like residue, called the *caput mortuum*, left in the retort after distillation, led him right back to one of the crucial unsolved problems he faced already in his investigations involving charcoal. When charcoal was utilized in reductions of metallic calces, fixed air was evolved; but Lavoisier had never been able to resolve the question of whether the fixed air derived from the metal or the charcoal. In the *Opuscules* he had reported an experiment in which he calcined *charbon* in a closed retort connected to a receiver over water and collected "almost no" air. This result led him to infer that the charcoal itself could not yield the fixed air produced in metallic reductions, and that that air must derive from "the union" of *charbon* with the calx of the metal. The contribution of the *charbon*, he conjectured, was "to render to the elastic fluid fixed [in the calx] the phlogiston, or matter of fire, and to restore the elasticity."[64] Later on he had subjected charcoal to distillation, and heated it with a burning glass, and had produced some air which precipitated lime-water. The results were equivocal enough, however, to leave the general issue in doubt.[65] It appears, then, that his appraisal of the problem of plant analysis pressed upon Lavoisier the need to seek a more definitive answer to this interrelated set of problems. As the passage suggests, only through a quantitatively rigorous combustion experiment on charcoal could he hope to settle the issue of what *charbon* contributes to the composition of fixed air, and by implication, what the "surrounding air" contributes. The final paragraph reminds us that he was still open to the possibility, already expressed in the *Opuscules*, that what the *charbon* contributes is phlogiston. He had not rejected the concept of phlogiston, but only modified the original theory of Stahl by suggesting that in metallic reductions the phlogiston is transferred, not to the metal, but to a substance released from the metal which forms with the phlogiston the resulting fixed air. The fact that he continued to discuss the situation in this manner in his own notebooks shows that he was not merely delaying a public attack on a concept he had privately discarded, but rather still thinking about phlogiston as though it might exist.

V

By the end of 1774 Lavoisier had consolidated the discoveries concerning calcination, combustion, and reduction which had started him off two years before on his general research program. He had confirmed with more decisive measurement that the bodies calcined and burned gain weight by absorbing a portion of the air. Metallic reductions, as well as fermentation and the solution of mild alkalis or earths in acids, release an air. The released air he had firmly identified as Black's fixed air. He had, however, reached an impasse in his efforts to identify the air fixed in those processes which absorb it, to identify the portion of common air left over in such processes, and to establish the relationship between either of these portions and the fixed air produced in the processes which release it. With his predilection for quantitative measurement of physical properties, he had tried to resolve these questions by determining the specific gravities of the airs involved, but they had not turned out to be different enough to establish unequivocably whether the air absorbed was common air itself or some distinctive component. Similarly, he was also unable clearly to differentiate fixed air from, or to identify it with, the residue of ordinary air left over after respiration, calcination, or combustion. With his "matter of fire" too he faced unresolvable ambiguities. He could not fully decide whether that substance is released from the elastic fluid or the combustible body during processes which fix air, so he allowed that some of it might come from each. Since the second of these alternatives fit the role customarily assigned to phlogiston, he did not dispense with that concept in spite of his skepticism about the traditional phlogiston theory of the followers of Stahl. Publicly and privately he continued to utilize phlogiston terminology. Clearly committed to a new point of view, and confident of the general outlines of his interpretation of these processes, Lavoisier could not bring the details into a sharply focused, logically consistent structure.

To judge from a group of reflections he wrote into his laboratory notebook, and on separate sheets of paper, Lavoisier was trying especially hard in the early part of 1775 to break through the conceptual barriers that seemed to stand between him and a theory capable of linking all of the phenomena he was investigating. In one of the most interesting of these documents, another folded sheet, dated "end of February 1775," he attempted to utilize his concept of a matter of fire to connect the composition of fixed air with that of common air. On the front page he wrote:

> On common air and fixed air
>
> If it is true that the inflammable matter of combustion comes for the most part from the air, it would follow that air in which one has burned any kind of body is in part phlogisticated and in part deprived of its elasticity, and for the most part disposed to combine in a solid or fluid form, and that is what in fact happens. But if through some means, whether it be, for example by [agitating ?] in water, one succeeds in depriving it of all of the fixable or phlogisticated part, then it returns to the state of natural air and becomes respirable and suitable once again for combustion. *In order to convert fixed air into natural air,* [*it is necessary* ?] [Lavoisier then crossed out "it is necessary," and began a new sentence.] One can thus convert an entire mass of common air into a mass of fixed air. It appears that in the same way a mass of fixed air could be converted into natural air by providing it with inflammable matter.

Turning to the back side of the first page of the folded sheet, Lavoisier wrote:

> It would appear that in every case in which there is an absorption of common air the operation begins by the disengagement of the matter of fire contained in the air. Then a portion of phlogisticated air is reduced to fixed air and is cast upon whatever is within its reach on the spot, if the operation is done upon a metal, if there is one there exposed to calcination, and other bodies in the same way.[66]

With the illumination provided by subsequent clarifications we can more easily spot the gaps in his logic than we can inhabit Lavoisier's mental world at the moment he formulated these statements. Compared with the explanatory power and consistency of his later versions, this conceptual sketch strikes us mainly by its shortcomings. The idea that fixed air is common air deprived of matter of fire seems flatly irreconcilable with his definition of the matter of fire as the source of the elasticity of all elastic fluids. If this discrepancy was not immediately apparent to him, one explanation might be that the use of the same term, "fixed air," for Stephen Hales's obsolete definition of air deprived of its elasticity and combined in solids or fluids, and for Joseph Black's distinct species of elastic fluid, papered over and obscured for Lavoisier the logical hole into which he had fallen. We may wonder also what processes he thought could convert "an entire mass of common air" into fixed air, since all of the processes which absorb air that he had investigated ceased when they had consumed only a portion of the common air in which they were enclosed. In a single paragraph Lavoisier gave two contradictory explanations for the reconversion of fixed air to "natural" air: first, that it occurs by the removal of the "fixable or phlogisticated part," and second that it occurs by the provision of inflammable matter.

To identify such incommensurable elements is not to reveal Lavoisier as a loose thinker. Creative scientists must accept temporary incoherence, for they are often in what can be seen afterward as transition states, juxtaposing residues of theories on the way to being discarded, with inchoate emerging theories on the way to maturity. Discrepancies which can be seen, after the transition is complete, as inadequacies in an interim theory may appear at the time either as evident anomalies which the scientist hopes to resolve later, or merely as blurred edges which he has not noticed or not had time to explore. In this case the anomalies were glaring enough and the structure itself weak enough, so that it is safe to assume the theory was ephemeral. We cannot be certain that he believed for any measurable period of time that it had solved the problems which evoked it. The fact that the final sentence trails off indeterminately might suggest that by the time he had written out this chain of reasoning he was already beginning to see that it was leading him astray. Nevertheless it appears that he did entertain this aggregate of ideas at least long enough to transfer them to the problem of respiration. On the third side of the folded sheet he wrote:

> Of the respiration of animals
>
> The respiration of animals is likewise only a removal of the matter of fire from common air, and thus the air which leaves the lungs is in part in the state of fixed air, that is to say in the state of phlogisticated air.
>
> This way of viewing the air in respiration explains why only the animals which respire are warm, why the heat of the blood is always increased in proportion as the respiration is more rapid. Fi-

> nally, perhaps it would be able to lead us to glimpse the cause of the movement of animals.[67]

In this fascinating passage we can see Lavoisier striving to build upon the basic conception of respiration adumbrated in his "ideas" note. What he had posed there only as a conjecture, that the release of matter of fire in the lungs sustains animal heat, he was now confident enough about to assert as an unqualified statement. Instead of looking to the future for evidence linking the fixation of air with heat, he now supported the assertion with the claim that respiration is always associated with animal heat, and in proportion to the degree of heat. He invoked no specific observations, however, apparently assuming as common knowledge that "the heat of the blood is always increased in proportion as the respiration is more rapid." He added a fundamental new dimension to his concept in the suggestion that it might lead to an understanding of "the cause of the movement of animals," although he seems to have caught only a faint glimpse of such a connection. He gave no clue about the source of this idea, or about how he might proceed to elucidate it.

With respect to the air respired, Lavoisier made a crucial modification of his earlier idea. No longer viewing the air absorbed as simply fixed in the animal, he now included within his purview the expiration of air "in the state of fixed air." He was thus finding room within his conception of respiration for the observation that Black, Priestley, and he himself had made, that the air one breathes out precipitates limewater; by referring to the expired air alternatively as phlogisticated air, he may have been allowing Priestley's interpretation of respiration also to enter his picture. At first glance it would appear that Lavoisier's new formulation supplemented and strengthened his initial ideas. Closer inspection shows, however, that the new idea was not fully compatible with the earlier one. A central idea in his first view was that the lungs separate the air into two portions, fixing only one of them; but, if we take into account that he was applying to respiration the hypothesis about the conversion of common air to fixed air that he had formulated on the same sheet of paper, his present view provided for no separation of common air into a respirable and an unrespirable portion. The lungs ought to be able to convert all of the respired air into fixed air. Thus Lavoisier had not arrived at a single conception of respiration capable of accounting for the absorption of a limited portion of the atmosphere, the exhalation of fixed air, and the release of heat. He had, at different times, formulated two separate but overlapping explanations, each of which encompassed only two of these three critical phenomena. His first idea left out the release of fixed air; the second left out the separation of the atmosphere into two components. The record of his thoughts does not reveal whether Lavoisier held both of these ideas in mind long enough to compare them and notice their discrepancy, or whether he entertained each so briefly that the details of the first had faded from his attention by the time he thought out the second. In any case, from our perspective Lavoisier appears to have been in the same predicament concerning respiration as in his thinking about calcination and combustion. He had partial explanations for each process, but none broad enough to encompass all of the observations associated with these three similar processes.

In another manuscript, also dated "end of February 1775," Lavoisier showed that he was himself aware of gaps and inconsistencies that he had not yet overcome. He began this document, which he entitled "Of elasticity and the formation of elastic fluids," as a systematic formulation, from first principles, of his theory that all substances can exist as solids, fluids, and in "the state of vaporization." He stated as an "axiom," that "a vaporous fluid is the result of the combination of the molecules of any fluid whatever, and in general of all bodies," with the matter of fire. Utilizing "the chemists's" concept of affinities, he explained the difference between condensable vapors such as water, acidic vapors soluble in water, and permanent elastic fluids, by means of differences in the relative affinities of matter of fire for these substances and for the substances with which they come into contact. In five pages of clear, tight reasoning, Lavoisier worked out the principles with which he would eventually redefine in the most fundamental way the three physical states of matter.[68] At this level his ideas were lucid and closely organized. The character of the manuscript suggests that he was dealing with arguments he had rehearsed often enough so that he was ready to lay them out in a systematic, definitive fashion. As he wrote on, however, his views acquired a more extemporaneous character. Reflecting on the way in which these principles could be applied to specific chemical substances and processes with which he had been particularly concerned, he seemed to be thinking out his explanations as he wrote, not knowing in advance quite where he was heading. "It appears very likely," he wrote,

> that fixed air is nothing but common air to which one has joined the same principle that gives nitrous air its permanence, and it appears established, in fact, that whenever [common] air is combined with the emanations from metals in calcination, it is converted to fixed air, and that it then combines with the metals and increases their weight, but it appears, at the same time, that the principle which it [the air] withdraws from metals is not pure matter of fire, since matter of fire is required to reduce it to the vaporous state.[69]

The difficulty Lavoisier sensed as he ended this paragraph relates to an earlier paragraph in which he had ascribed the permanence of nitrous air to its matter of fire. The first portion of his manuscript he had built around his premise that not only nitrous air but all elastic fluids are maintained in that state by the matter of fire. Here, on the other hand, he was again invoking the same matter of fire as the cause of the conversion of one elastic fluid to another. Perceiving, at least vaguely, that he could not attribute to precisely the same substance both the property common to all elastic fluids and the distinction between one elastic fluid and another, he could at this point evade that illogical position only by means of the weak qualification that the substance which forms fixed air from common air is not "pure" matter of fire.

The above paragraph also contradicts the interpretation of the composition of common and fixed air Lavoisier gave in the note on that subject which we have previously examined. There he described fixed air as common air *deprived* of matter of fire; here he described fixed air as formed by *adding* matter of fire to common air. Although he must have written both notes within a few days of each other, he left no indication of whether he saw at the time that the interpretation he gave in the one was the exact opposite of what he said in the other.

Lavoisier moved on to think about another prominent chemical phenomenon. "One will now ask why nitrous air diminishes common air." In effect he was challenging himself to use his conception of the role of the matter of fire in maintaining the elastic state to explain the striking alteration in the elasticity of the airs involved in Priestley's nitrous air test. Immediately he attempted to answer his question:

> The reason is that the phlogiston of the metals removed by the nitrous air and combined with it has a greater affinity for common air than for nitrous air. It happens that a portion of the nitrous and the common air is converted to fixed air, while the nitrous air, which does not retain the matter of fire except with the aid of [illegible word] . . . , reverts immediately to nitrous acid and returns to the fluid state. A portion of the fixed air . . . which has just formed combines with the nitrous acid and increases its strength.[70]

In this cumbersome interpretation we can virtually observe Lavoisier feeling his way along, following a line of reasoning without foreknowledge of how he would come out. Having just previously attributed the composition of fixed air to a union of matter of fire with common air, he has here incorporated the same conception into an assumed conversion of common to fixed air. He has also drawn in another idea he had expressed in the previous paragraph, that the matter of fire contained in the nitrous air is an "emanation from metals in calcination." What had been implicit in the earlier paragraph becomes explicit here—that Lavoisier's conception of "matter of fire" was merging with phlogiston, the substance traditionally supposed to emanate from metals when they are calcined. Lavoisier was evidently wandering through a conceptual borderland, in which he crossed almost insensibly out of and back into the theoretical territory mapped out by his distinguished contemporary in England. Perhaps with a slight start of recognition at what he was doing, he commented on what he had just written, "All of this agrees very much with the system of Priestley, but there is nevertheless a very notable difference."[71]

He did not pause to spell out the differences between his explanatory system and that of Priestley, but went on to take up another puzzling problem made prominent by Priestley's investigations. "There remains a very puzzling [*embarrassant*] fact to explain; that is the reason why agitation with water renders air respirable."[72] Priestley had discovered that he could make inflammable air respirable "by continued *agitation in a trough of water*, deprived of its air." He then tested whether "other kinds of noxious airs might be restored by the same means," and found

> that this process has never failed to restore any kinds of noxious air on which I have tried it, viz. air injured by respiration or putrefaction, air infected with the fumes of burning charcoal, and of calcined metals, air in which a mixture of iron filings and brimstone, that in which paint made of white lead and oil has stood, or air which has been diminished by a mixture of nitrous air.[73]

The prolific, inventive Priestley was seldom bothered by the lack of an explanation for how the products of such heterogeneous processes could then be subjected to one action with so uniform an outcome. The more systematic mind of Lavoisier was less easily satisfied. In this case Lavoisier was nevertheless not too daunted by the "puzzling fact" to plunge on with an attempt to explain the phenomena. First he separated the observed effects into two categories. In those cases involving "acid airs" he thought that the water absorbs these airs, leaving only the portions of common air that are normally mixed with them. "It is not the same," however, he went on,

> for the air diminished by the calcination of metals, by the burning of candles, by the burning of sulfur, etc. These airs are basically nothing but respirable air altered by phlogiston. It appears that this principle passes into the water and leaves the air pure.[74]

This passage contains several significant features. First, we see Lavoisier not only taking up a problem posed by Priestley's experiments, but thinking about it wholly within Priestley's conceptual framework of combustion, calcination, and respiration as processes that release phlogiston into the air. Second, we find a further manifestation of the ubiquity of respiration in Lavoisier's mental landscape. Almost any broad question that he explored was likely to lead him to a problem involving the relation of airs to respiration. Finally, we would note that Lavoisier was trying to explain processes that render air unrespirable by reasoning from observed inverse processes which restore air to a respirable state. Clearly the inspiration for this approach was Priestley's extensive concern with the processes which restore vitiated air. As we shall see, this way of thinking about such problems may have provided Lavoisier with an approach which he afterward applied to the investigation of respiration itself.

Lavoisier's explanation did not ease his perplexity for long, because it immediately raised for him another unsolved problem:

> But why do the [combustible] bodies burn only to a certain degree in the air? One will answer that it is because the combustible bodies cannot burn in fixed air. Now in proportion as a body burns, a part of the air is changed into fixed air, [and] then the ignited body is extinguished.[75]

Here we see that, just as easily as Lavoisier had drifted into Priestley's conceptual domain, so he slipped quickly back out of it into theoretical territory he was seeking to map out on his own. Priestley's well-known explanation for the fact that combustibles burned only to a limited degree in a given volume of air was that the air became saturated with phlogiston. Lavoisier, on the other hand, was here pursuing again the view that during combustions ordinary air is converted to fixed air.

The explanation Lavoisier posed in response to this question rather surprisingly omitted his earlier explanation for the same phenomenon; namely, that the air is divisible into two portions, of which one supports the combustion until it is consumed. The difference between these two explanations parallels the change from his first to his second note on respiration. It is improbable that he had abandoned his view that the atmosphere contains two or more kinds of elastic fluid, though he may have become more frustrated in his continued inability to specify them. Rather, I believe this passage manifests once more that he could not integrate his various conceptions of airs and the processes in which they take part so as to bring them fully into play within the confines of each separate attempt to solve a particular problem.

Lavoisier could not leave the question of why combustible bodies cease to burn, at the level represented by the above paragraph, since his aim in the manuscript as a whole was to reduce such processes to explanations based on his general theory of the role of the matter of fire. He pressed ahead:

> One could push the question further, and ask why combustible bodies do not burn in fixed air. I would answer that it is because the air must furnish its quota of the matter of fire to the flame. Now the matter of fire being joined very intimately in fixed air, the latter does not let go of it. This matter [of fire], on the contrary, adheres much less to ordinary air.[76]

At this point Lavoisier noticed that he had reasoned himself into a trap. He broke off his manuscript in disarray:

> But this answer no longer fits with the preceding ones, in which one has assumed that the phlogiston arises from combustible bodies. That becomes very puzzling.[77]

As we have seen, Lavoisier had asserted earlier in the manuscript that fixed air results from the combination of ordinary air with the "emanation of metals in calcination." In a subsequent paragraph, to which this final remark refers, he had explicitly identified that emanation with phlogiston. The misfit which appears to have struck him at the end was that in the first case he had assumed that in calcinations this principle was given off *into* the air, whereas in the latter case he included calcinations among the combustion processes which absorb this same principle *from* the air. The confusion he now discerned in his own reasoning appears from our perspective to derive from his having in one situation reasoned according to the phlogiston theory, and in the other by means of another theory with which he replaced the phlogiston theory. At the time, however, Lavoisier undoubtedly could not have viewed the situation in such terms. Whether his matter of fire represented a modification of the phlogiston concept or an alternative theory was not an immediate problem for him; rather he needed, with great urgency, to be able to explain the various phenomena that involved this principle, whatever its name, within an internally consistent theoretical framework.

The document through which we have traced Lavoisier's mental steps is remarkable for the reflection it conveys of an author beginning confidently to set forth fundamental principles that were obvious to him, moving on to tackle questions whose answers were not yet familiar to him, and finally groping his way to a point from which he looked back and saw some of the pitfalls into which he had stumbled. His mood by the time he finished the last page he wrote must have been a good bit more subdued than it had been when he took up his pen. We have no such direct record of the way in which he must have recognized the equally egregious discrepancy between the conception of fixed air embedded in the present manuscript and the conception incorporated into his independent note, written at almost the same time, on the composition of common and fixed air.

Lavoisier faced these same general issues in a more specialized context when, during this same period of intensive reflection in late February, he attempted to work out an explanation for "the detonation of nitre." That process, he began writing on another folded sheet of paper, "is nothing but the conversion of nitrous acid into fixed air and common air." Now he sallied forth boldly, with the avowed aim of discarding the conventional phlogiston interpretation of the process.

> The disciples of Stahl will not fail to say that this effect is due to the combination of phlogiston with nitrous acid; but the objective of this article is precisely to examine whether detonation cannot take place without phlogiston, and with no other matter of fire than that of the surrounding air.[78]

We may note, however, that Lavoisier did not appear here to be contesting the general validity of the phlogiston theory; but only to be questioning whether phlogiston takes part in this particular process. He opened his case by observing that all of the substances which detonate nitre share the property of absorbing air, separating from the air its matter of fire, so that the detonation which they produce may be likened to a combustion without air. We need not follow the details of his argument, since the detonation of nitre is, in itself, not pertinent to our story. In the course of it he showed that he still retained the "compromise" views expressed in the *Opuscules*, whereby the matter of fire released during combustions may derive in part from the combustible body and in part from the air. For the special case of the detonation of nitre with charcoal, he wrote that, although according to his general theory the charcoal may set the matter of fire free from the air, "I would nevertheless be rather inclined to believe that the *charbon* contains matter of fire fixed, and that it provides something during its combustion. That is a question to examine." The reason he preferred this interpretation was that in the case of metallic reductions "it appears that the *charbon* contributes the matter of fire necessary to constitute fixed air in the elastic state." He went on to consider other combustions, including that of inflammable air, and took the position that not all of such combustibles necessarily contributed matter of fire as *charbon* did. Sometime after writing this note, Lavoisier came back to it and added some afterthoughts. "It is impossible not to acknowledge that there is matter of fire in *charbon*," he had decided. His reason was that the detonation can take place in the absence of air, the only other possible source of the matter of fire. But other substances, like sulfur, which also detonate nitre, he thought probably do not furnish matter of fire.[79]

By now it should be abundantly evident how far away Lavoisier was in the spring of 1775 from a coherent theoretical structure to cover calcination, reduction, respiration, and the various forms of combustion on which he had fixed his attention for two full years. His conceptual field was filled instead with a patchwork of partial explanations that provided as often as not conflicting accounts of the same process when the latter entered into different problem situations. He called on his matter of fire to perform so many different roles—now as the principle which maintains all bodies in the elastic state; now as the substance which distinguishes fixed air from common air; now as that which distinguishes common air from fixed air; now as a substance fixed in certain nonelastic bodies, such as *charbon* and metals, but missing from other combustible bodies—that this elusive matter, so simply defined in the abstract, became in practice as malleable as ever its predecessor, phlogiston, has been reputed to be.

Accustomed to praise Lavoisier for the rigorous character of his thinking in public forums, we may at first be startled to find him in private so enmeshed in this web of ad hoc theories and contradictions. We have not caught him in some sort of lapse from his usual standard, however; rather, he has by preserving these ephemeral notes to himself allowed us the privilege of sharing the personal travail of a great theoretician struggling to extricate himself from the logical tangles that inevitably ensnare one in the process of trying to solve a deep scientific problem.

The fact that Lavoisier was particularly prone to fall into logical inconsistencies in applying his concept of the matter of fire derives from the circumstance that he had to get along without the experimental criterion that he had come to rely upon so heavily to guide him in interpreting ordinary chemical changes. That is, he could not apply his usual balance sheet checks, because he had accepted that his matter of fire must be weightless.

Even though Lavoisier did not leave written comments on all of the contradictions he encountered in these theoretical forays, there can be little doubt that he felt his discomfiture. He must have been acutely aware that no matter in what direction he turned, he was hobbled by his inability to define consistently the relationships between common air, fixed air, and the matter of fire. Since all three of these entities were central to his new ideas about respiration, he must also have sensed that, until he could straighten out these relationships, he was in a very poor position to advance his understanding of the respiratory process.

Two or three weeks after writing the manuscripts we have just considered, that is, on March 17, Lavoisier composed another, "The vaporous acids, called acid airs by M. Priestley." Pointing out that all acids seem to have the property of forming elastic fluids which are permanent, except when they are in contact with water, and the even more remarkable property of giving rise to other acids which are not absorbable in water, Lavoisier gave as the explanation for the latter phenomenon, "It is by combining with phlogiston." In the next paragraph he applied this explanation to acid of vinegar and to nitrous acid. Then he turned once again to the nature of fixed air:

> One can scarcely fail to recognize fixed air for an acid. It would therefore be very interesting to investigate its combination with *charbon* [charcoal]. Undoubtedly there would result an air which

> would no longer be absorbed by water; perhaps it would be common air. Then one could define the permanent elastic fluids in general as the combination of an acid in the vapor state with phlogiston.[80]

It was astute of Lavoisier to recognize the acidic nature of fixed air at a time when it was not yet generally regarded as an acid. Beyond that, however, we note him posing yet another explanation for the relationship between fixed air and common air. The latest version would account nicely for the phenomenon at the forefront of his attention at the moment, the conversion of soluble elastic fluids to insoluble ones; for fixed air was highly soluble in water and common air relatively insoluble. The new explanation could no more be reconciled with the several interpretations of the relationship between common and fixed air he had recently composed when trying to account for other phenomena, however, than they could be with one another. The passage thus only reinforces our image of Lavoisier grasping at ad hoc solutions for particular problems, still unable to combine these partial explanations into a theory comprehensive enough to extend throughout the network of interrelated problems with which he was contending. He concluded the present note with this reflection:

> The diminution which nitrous air undergoes would not be puzzling on this supposition, and one would return, in that respect, to the hypothesis of M. Priestley. This effect would be caused only by the passage of nitrous air from the inabsorbable state to the absorbable state.[81]

In his long manuscript on elastic fluids, Lavoisier had outlined an explanation for the diminution of nitrous air which corresponded to this one, except that he had deduced it then from his general axiom concerning the matter of fire and his assumptions about the strengths of the chemical affinities involved. Now phlogiston usurped the role of his own matter of fire in that explanation. Lavoisier seemed not only to be returning "to the hypothesis of Priestley" to deal with this particular effect, but to be acquiescing to the use of Priestley's phlogiston theory in general. In the notes of late February we observed an ambiguous relation between phlogiston and Lavoisier's matter of fire. Lavoisier had defined the latter on his own terms, but when treating particular situations he had seemed unable to keep steadily in mind the distinction between these two concepts. In the present note he did not even mention his matter of fire; there is only phlogiston. It is as though, in his weariness at the frustrated attempts to surmount obstacles to a full articulation of his own point of view, he was ready, for the moment at least, to fall back in line behind the theoretical leadership of the person whose empirical discoveries already inspired so many of his experimental moves. This is a far different picture from the conventional view of Lavoisier at this time progressing steadily away from the phlogiston theory, strengthening his case, and biding his time for an appropriate occasion to overwhelm the defenders of phlogiston.

* * *

The traces of Lavoisier's theoretical efforts during February and March 1775, recoverable in the notes described in the preceding pages, remind us of characteristics of mental life that are sometimes overlooked in intellectual histories. Often the ideas of a scientist, or other thinker, are described as though the individual can be expected to have held in mind continuously the entire conceptual landscape of a field of thought over which he has traveled during an extended period of time. Just as we can bring only a small portion of our visual field into sharp focus at any given instant, so can we consider only a small segment of our mental field in close detail at any one time. The remainder forms a background whose conceptual features we perceive only in broad outline. We can explore this mental landscape piece by piece, so that over a finite stretch of time we can come to know all of its pertinent details, but even afterward we can direct our immediate attention only to selected portions, or aspects of the overall field, and must review our knowledge of it by inspecting its parts in some kind of sequence. If one is entertaining a set of related theoretical concepts, linked to diverse observable phenomena, as Lavoisier was, it is impossible to conjure up all of their conceptual connections together, to verify in a single mental act that the whole and all of its parts are thoroughly coherent. What we have seen Lavoisier doing was what any creative thinker is constrained to do; he was exploring bit by bit the conceptual regions which together comprised his research enterprise, attempting to clarify the structural details in one region without being able at the same time to relate the portion on which he had fixed his attention to all of the other portions. If he had been capable of holding all of the portions, in their full complexity, in the center of his mental field at one sitting, it would be hard to imagine how he could have incurred the number of conspicuous internal contradictions that we can identify when we inspect and compare the several notes he produced over an interval of three or four weeks. At one point we have witnessed Lavoisier himself making such a comparison between a region of the intellectual landscape he had just reached and one he had recently traversed, and identifying an inconsistency. Undoubtedly he must in time have located the other contradictions that we so easily notice.

Even after exploring the details of such a conceptual structure portion by portion, one may not be able to adjust the parts in such a way that they fit together without leaving major fault lines. That was the disconcerting situation in which Lavoisier found himself in the spring of 1775. In such cases either the trouble may be due to some crucial theoretical or experimental clue that lies still beyond one's reach, or it could be that the foundations of the conceptual structure itself are flawed in some fundamental way. During these weeks Lavoisier probably could not have been certain which of these conditions he faced.

2

Lavoisier in Midstream

When we describe scientific puzzles we habitually resort to metaphorical language likening them to the prototypical jigsaw puzzle. We fall easily into phrases like "fitting the pieces together" to form an overall picture, or "searching for the key piece" which will join partial assemblies into larger ensembles. We imagine rearranging individual conceptual components, like physical pieces, until we ascertain the spatial relations between them which can enable us to link them tightly together into the completed framework. Almost involuntarily we envision Lavoisier, at the beginning of 1775, sitting before a set of partially assembled explanations for calcination, reduction, combustion, and respiration, searching for that observational or conceptual key which would permit him to arrange them all within an overarching theoretical picture, without gaps or overlapping edges. The metaphor is useful, but only to a point. In a conceptual puzzle one may find a key piece joining previously assembled partial solutions, but one may also have to reshape the partial assemblages; one may have included pieces which do not belong in this particular puzzle at all; and in the end one will have to settle for a fit which is not perfect in the sense that the jigsaw puzzle is when it is completed. Approaching the solution may not resemble placing the pieces in proper order and filling in the gaps, so much as it does bringing into sharper focus a picture previously present in full but with blurred outlines.[1] In one important sense, however, the jigsaw puzzle does aptly represent its conceptual metaphor. There is no single order of assembly, no particular piece predestined to be the key which ties everything together; for the puzzle can be assembled in many different sequences. Just so, Lavoisier might have found, in almost any of the various phenomena involving absorption or disengagement of airs which he had been studying, crucial clues to help him resolve the inconsistencies he was now facing within each one of them. Had he, for example, followed up immediately the plan sketched out in his reflections on plant analysis, to examine more rigorously the combustion of charcoal, he might have obtained a key there. As it happened, he found one in a special example of calcination and reduction which was at the time attracting the attention of his colleagues. Because these processes had to do with metals and minerals, we would not expect them to be directly tied to the development of Lavoisier's views on biological problems; but as we shall see when we have followed Lavoisier's investigations of the peculiar calx of mercury in detail, these events turned out to have a surprisingly close connection with the early phases of his experimental investigation of respiration.

Pierre Bayen, apothecary major to the camps and armies of the king, commented in 1774 that to explain "the augmentation of the weight of metallic calces" had been "for several years the goal of almost all of the chemists in Europe."[2] Bayen was undoubtedly exaggerating, but as Guerlac has shown, the investigations of Guyton de Morveau, summarized in 1772 in his book *Digressions academiques*, had elevated the phenomenon of the weight gain in calcinations to one of the central problems in chemistry.[3] Since then Lavoisier had taken the lead in further defining the problem, by demonstrating conclusively that metals not only absorb an elastic fluid when calcined, but release one when reduced. When Bayen wrote on the subject he defined the task ahead as the identification of Lavoisier's "elastic fluid."[4] Several of the chemists who took up the problem, including Lavoisier himself, converged upon the same metal, whose special properties they thought might offer a privileged path to the solution.

As Carl Perrin has recently elucidated, it had been known since alchemical times that by heating liquid mercury one could convert it to a red powder, from which, by further heating, one could recover the mercury. For a long time chemists debated whether the red powder was merely a modified form of mercury, or a true calx with the exceptional property that it could be reduced to the metal without charcoal. For the phlogiston theory the latter alternative posed the anomaly that the metal would arise without benefit of the normal source of the phlogiston essential to the composition of all metals.[5] Soon after Guyton's *Digressions* appeared, Bayen embarked on a systematic investigation of the formation and reduction of precipitates of mercury. Besides the red powder produced by heating mercury by itself—the *mercurius calcinatus per se*—these included various precipitates which formed when one dissolved mercury in an acid and then added an alkali. Between 1772 and early 1774, when he published his first two memoirs on the subject, Bayen focused on the second type. Following the precedent of Guyton and Lavoisier, Bayen oriented his analysis of the processes around the gains and losses of weight which accompanied them; following the example of Lavoisier alone, he utilized a pneumatic chamber over water to collect the elastic fluids given off when he reduced the various precipitates to metallic mercury. A critical feature of Bayen's experiment was that, for each precipitate he used, he compared the products of reducing the substance with charcoal with the products from heating the substance alone. The reduction was always easier and more complete with the charcoal, and from some of the precipitates he obtained little or no mercury in the absence of charcoal. Two precipitates which he had purified by heating to remove the acid yielded by themselves, however, an elastic fluid as well as liquid mercury. Calculating the specific weight of the former by dividing the weight lost from the calx by the volume change in the collecting vessel, he estimated the elastic fluid to be heavier than common air. It was so readily soluble in water that he had to spread a layer of oil over the water in the vessel in order to collect it. The elastic fluid so obtained Bayen thought to be indistinguishable from what he collected when he reduced the calx with charcoal, an identification he apparently based on nothing more than the fact that water impregnated with either fluid had the same odor. Nevertheless Bayen did not assert that the fluid was fixed air. He made various casual suggestions for what it might be, including a "saline mixt" resembling the *acidum pinque*, postulated by Johann Friedrich Meyer; but prudently he left the question open, acknowledging that "the task which I have set for myself relative to the elastic fluid has not been completed."[6]

The principal conclusion Bayen drew in April 1774 from his investigation was that charcoal is "useless" in the reduction of mercury and that, so far as this case went, the doctrine of the school of Stahl, that phlogiston is essential to the revivication of a metal, was false. The lesson to be learned was that it was "dangerous to commit oneself to systems, no matter how authoritative they may be."[7] Bayen was reflecting not only the outcome of this particular investigation, but an emerging general skepticism toward the phlogiston system among French chemists. At almost the same time there appeared in *Observations sur la physique* an anonymous "Discourse on phlogiston" which called the whole theory into question. The author made no reference to new experimental results or standards, but argued solely on the grounds of the circular reasoning and contradictions inherent in the fundamental theoretical structure, together with the fact that phlogiston itself was a purely theoretical substance.[8]

Not all of the French chemists believed that the reduction of mercury without charcoal deprived phlogiston of a role in the process. Some insisted that phlogiston entered the calx from other sources. Guyton decided that phlogiston was elementary fire, and could enter the glass vessel during the reduction. Following a suggestion by Buffon, Guyton supported this view by reducing a calx of mercury by concentrating sunlight on it through a burning glass.[9] The comte de Milly claimed to have reduced the calx by means of a "simple electric fluid," and concluded that an electric fluid too can act "exactly like" phlogiston. To evaluate Milly's result the Academy appointed a committee which included Louis-Claude Cadet de Gassicourt, Mathurin-Jacques Brisson, Antoine Baumé, and Lavoisier. The committee met, on July 28, 1774, at the home of Brisson, to investigate the reduction of mercury precipitate *per se*, with Cadet apparently carrying out the experiments. He reduced the precipitate by heating it in a retort exposed over an open flame until the retort was red hot. The committee then became embroiled in controversy, because Baumé argued that the mercury calx had only sublimed, and that it could not be reduced to metallic mercury without phlogiston. Repeating the reduction on a preparation of red precipitate of mercury supplied by Baumé himself, Cadet defended his conclusions in a report of the committee to the Academy on September 3.[10] Baumé remained unconvinced, so that it became necessary to appoint a second committee to adjudicate the issue. This committee also included Lavoisier, along with Brisson. The chemist Balthazar Sage replaced the two disputing members of the original committee. The new committee tested two preparations of the red precipitate, one provided by Cadet and one by Baumé, and verified that "both have the property of being reduced without addition." Lavoisier, Brisson, and Sage reported this conclusion at the meeting of the Academy of November 19.[11]

According to a famous story, Priestley visited Paris in October 1774, and revealed, during a dinner conversation at which Lavoisier was present, that he had obtained a "new air" from the red calx of mercury. Priestley was later convinced that it was this clue, afterward unacknowledged by Lavoisier, that led Lavoisier to take up the investigation of the air released when that calx is reduced without charcoal. Many historians have accepted that claim, but as Perrin points out, Lavoisier could have acquired the insights which moved him in this direction equally well from Bayen's investigation or from his participation in the two committees described above.[12] Whatever external stimuli Lavoisier may have received, they could only have reinforced the internal dynamic of his own reasoning, which must sooner or later have induced him to investigate the reduction of the mercury calx. As we have already noted, in reducing other metals with charcoal he had been unable to separate the contributions of the metal and of the charcoal to the composition of the fixed air which was disengaged. He need not, therefore, have anticipated that the air released when a calx is reduced "without addition" would be any different from the air released in ordinary reductions in order to perceive the advantage of experimenting with the former type. By eliminating one of the two sources to whose "union" he had vaguely attributed the fixed air, he might be able to distinguish their contributions. According to his own later account, he first attempted reduction without addition during April 1774 or earlier, using the calx of iron. In this way he obtained an air, but only with difficulty, and with an admixture of ordinary air which prevented him from examining the properties of the evolved air in a pure form.[13] The influence of the memoirs of Bayen which appeared about that time, of his participation in the two commissions, and of Priestley's hint was therefore probably not to suggest the general strategy of reducing the calx of a metal without charcoal, but to drive home to him the unique advantage of the red calx of mercury for that purpose.

Ambiguity surrounds the beginning of Lavoisier's own experiments on the mercury calx. In his memoir on the subject he stated that he first attempted to reduce the calx "during the month of November 1774." No such experiments are recorded in his laboratory notebooks. Since the second Academy committee reported on November 19, it is possible that Lavoisier may have had in mind successful reduction experiments he witnessed or participated in as a member of that committee. Yet he described his as "attempted with a burning glass," whereas the committee distilled the calx in a furnace. The subsequent set of experiments, which he carried out "with all precautions and necessary care in the laboratory of Montigny with M. de Trudaine, between February 28 and March 2, 1775," apparently does survive in his notebook.[14]

Having long believed that "mercury precipitate is mercury combined with fixed air," Lavoisier was persuaded before beginning these experiments that the air which he collected from the reduction of the mercury calx would be fixed air.[15] As Max Speter pointed out in 1918, his expectation reveals the persistence with which he clung to an idea that fixed air is the "calcifying principle,"[16] in spite of the logical disjunctions entailed and the lack of confirmation over the preceding years. Perhaps, if he had read Bayen's investigations of the previous year, his expectation was reinforced by the fact that Bayen had seen no difference between the airs released in reductions with and without charcoal. When Lavoisier, unlike Bayen, utilized the standard limewater test for fixed air, however, the air collected from mercury calx "without addition" only rendered the solution "slightly opaline," without forming a precipitate. More dramatically, he introduced a candle into the air and found that, far from being extinguished as it would be in fixed air, it was augmented in the way it would be if one placed it into nitrous air previously in contact with iron. Then, applying Priestley's nitrous air test, he learned that a mixture of this air with nitrous air contracted in volume about as common air does. These results convinced Lavoisier that the air was "in the state of common air," except that "it retains a little of the nature of inflammable air."[17]

If the mercury calx reduced without charcoal produced an air differing from that produced with charcoal, a logical next step would be to test whether charcoal added to the first air can convert it to the second. That is just what Lavoisier tried. By heating charcoal with the air derived from the calx alone, he obtained "pure fixed air." He attributed the result to the fact that charcoal has the general property of changing common air to fixed air, and inferred that the air fixed in other metallic calces, as well as in the mercury calx, is common air.[18]

On March 31, Lavoisier repeated some of these experiments in the company of the duc de La Rochefoucauld, Trudaine, Macquer, and Cadet.[19] He utilized what had now become for him an "ordinary" apparatus, a retort with a neck curved so as to fit under a jar inverted over water. Placing 6 gros of mercury precipitate in the retort, he heated it in a reverberatory furnace and collected the evolved air in the jar. Subtracting from the total air collected 1.40 cubic inches which he allowed for the dilatation of the common air already present in the retort, he estimated the volume of the disengaged air at 58 cubic inches. He collected some of the liquid mercury produced in a capsule, and found another portion of it in the neck of the retort. Together they weighed 5 gros 12½ grains, but he added 3 grains for "a few globules of mercury lost or left in the neck of the retort," and 1½ grains for mercury he thought to have been recalcined in the neck of the retort, making 5 gros 17 grains in all. Similarly, he had to make a correction in the original weight of the mercury precipitate, because he found at the end of the operation that he had "undoubtedly pushed the fire a little too much," and that a little bit of sand mixed in with the precipitate "has probably served to melt the glass and it has made there a little hole, through which several grains of sand could have been lost." Weighing the remaining sand, he found it to be 5½ grains, which he changed to 6 grains, probably to take into account the amount which might have been lost through the hole. The actual amount of precipitate operated on he therefore evaluated at only 5 gros 66 grains. The difference between this quantity and the corrected figure for the liquid mercury produced left a "loss" of 49 grains, which he could regard as the weight of the air evolved.[20] From this weight, divided by the estimated volume, he could calculate the density of the air. Although he did not do such a calculation from these specific figures, it must have been from such a calculation that he inferred in his published account that "each cubic inch" of the released air "weighs a little less than two-thirds of a grain, which does not deviate much from the density of common air."[21]

I have summarized this experiment in detail in part because, as we shall see, it illustrates the little things that typically went wrong for Lavoisier in his experiments even when he exerted "every precaution and necessary care," as well as the manner in which he attempted to improve his data by guessing at the quantities of the errors caused by factors he could not measure. Perhaps in this case he did not regard the results as reliable, because a weight of 49 grains for 58 cubic inches of air amounts to more than ⅘ of a grain per cubic inch, rather than the ⅔ of a grain per cubic inch he reported. A second reason for focusing on this experiment is that the tests he performed on the resulting air lead us back to our main themes. "One was first of all curious," Lavoisier entered in his notebook,

> to test the effect of this air on animals. For this purpose one passed it into a jar into which one introduced a bird. One left the bird inside it for a good half minute, without its appearing to suffer there in the least. Removed from the air, it flew away without having suffered in any way.[22]

He next performed Priestley's nitrous air test on the air:

> One introduced [one part of] nitrous air into two parts of this air. It appeared that the red color of the vapors was more marked, and the effect more rapid than with common air.
>
> There was a diminution of

Lavoisier here left a space in which to insert later the amount of the diminution, and below it wrote, "so that, according to this operation, one could judge that this air is more perfect than common air." When he had actually calculated the contraction of the volume, however, he changed his mind about this conclusion. Into the space he had left he crammed the following:

One employed two measures of this air, each 2.7 cubic inches, making together	5.4
One added _ _ _ nitrous air _ _ _	2.7
	8.1 cubic inches

> The 8.1 cubic inches was reduced almost immediately to 4.42.

Crossing out the first conclusion quoted above, he wrote below it, "That is to say, regarding the portion of nitrous air as probably entirely absorbed, there was one cubic inch, that is to say one-fifth, of the air absorbed. That is about the proportion of common air."[23] Filling in Lavoisier's elliptical summary of the calculation, we can see that if one assumes that the 2.7 cubic inches of nitrous air was entirely absorbed, then, subtracting from the observed diminution in volume ($3.68 = 8.1 - 4.42$) the quantity accounted for by the nitrous air, one obtains $3.68 - 2.7 = 0.98$ cubic inches, or a little less than one-fifth of the original 5.4 cubic inches of the air utilized.

After finding that the air caused no precipitate with limewater, Lavoisier tested a burning candle in it.

> One repeated the experiment of the candle two times, and in large jars. It is charming. The flame is much larger and much clearer and much more beautiful than in common air, but in color no different from an ordinary flame.[24]

The equivocal outcome of these tests should be obvious. Although they clearly ruled out fixed air, they did not decisively rule common air in or out. The test on the bird suggested that the air was very respirable, but Lavoisier did not press it far enough to discriminate between the effects of common air and something that might be better than common air. The candle flame suggested qualitatively that the air supported combustion better than common air did, and Lavoisier may have been swayed by one or both of these tests to see at first in the qualitative intensity of the reaction with nitrous air further support for an impression that the air was "more perfect" than common air. That impression faded, however, when he had examined quantitatively the result of the nitrous air test. If, as appears likely in the light of his subsequent statements, he gave priority to the nitrous air test in characterizing the air, that may not be only because he preferred conclusions resting on quantitative data; he may have been influenced also by a recent communication concerning the ongoing discoveries of Joseph Priestley.

Among the newsworthy items that Priestley's friend, the assiduous correspondent Jean Magellan, had transmitted in a letter to the Academy in January 1774 was that Priestley had tested "phlogisticated nitrous air," produced by placing liver of sulfur into a vessel containing nitrous air.[25] Even though this air was "very harmful to animal life," it did not extinguish a candle flame. The practical lesson Priestley drew from this situation, paradoxical as it was within his conceptual system, was: "Thus one will no longer decide about the noxious quality of an air in the future by the test of an illuminated candle. It would appear that the most infallible test for this injurious quality is that which M. Priestley proposed in his memoir in the Philosophical Transactions (ann. 1772) which consists of mixing the air with nitrous air" and observing whether there is a real diminution in volume. Magellan described a test Priestley had demonstrated for him on common air, and specified that Priestley had taken two phials of the air, to which he had added a "third" phial of nitrous air. The mixture took on a reddish color, then diminished to a fifth less than the two measures the original common air had occupied.[26] As we have seen, Lavoisier used these same proportions in his test of the air derived from the mercury precipitate, and it was his estimate that a fifth of the air had been absorbed that caused him to conclude that the proportion was the same as for common air. Besides being guided by Priestley's directions for the design and interpretation of the test, Lavoisier may well have been swayed by Priestley's assessment of the relative values of the nitrous air and the burning candle test. Later in the year the fuller description of the nitrous air test in Priestley's *Experiments and Observations*, described in Chapter 1, also became available to him.

Lavoisier presented the results of his investigation of the mercury precipitate at the public meeting of the Academy of April 26, 1775. The heart of his discussion was a description of comparative reductions carried out with and without charcoal. With an unusually candid acknowledgment of the extent to which a public scientific paper can become an imaginative reconstruction rather than a literal record of experimental activity, he gave no detailed results of any single real experiment, but "merged into a single account circumstances which derive from several repetitions of the same experiment." The air obtained with charcoal displayed, as expected, all of the properties of fixed air. That obtained without charcoal reacted negatively to each of the standard tests for fixed air, an outcome which he claimed to have "recognized with great surprise." It did not dissolve in water or precipitate limewater. It did not form a union with alkalies or reduce their causticity. It could serve again to calcine metals. It was diminished in nitrous air, "as common air" is. "Far from causing animals to perish as [fixed air] does, it seemed on the contrary more suitable to support their respiration. Not only were candles and burning bodies not extinguished in it, but the flame was enlarged in it in a very remarkable way; it emitted much more light, was more lucid, than in common air." He concluded with the statement which has been taken in retrospect to represent a wavering, indecisive position: "All of these circumstances have fully convinced me that this air is not only common air, but that it is, moreover, more respirable, more combustible, and consequently that it is even purer than the air in which we live." In related passages he referred to this air as "the purest portion of the air in which we live, which we respire," and "the air itself entire, without alteration, without decomposition," only rendered "more pure, more respirable, if it is permitted to use that expression, than the air of the atmosphere, and more suitable to support inflammation and the combustion of bodies."[27]

It is possible to see in these statements Lavoisier's incipient recognition that he was dealing with a special portion of atmospheric air—a recognition still inchoate, struggling to emerge more distinctly, yet already a further evolutionary development of the view he had previously expressed, that the atmosphere is a divisible entity. By the retrospective light of the subsequent development of his thought in the same direction, these ambiguous phrases appear as a classic "transition stage." In his well-known historical case study *The Overthrow of the Phlogiston Theory*, James Conant commented on these passages that they were "almost self-contradictory," for the air "is 'common air' yet also 'purer than common air.' For the moment Lavoisier wanted to have it both ways!"[28] We can even reinforce this general interpretation with evidence from Lavoisier's first "Ideas" on respiration. If respiration does indeed separate a "portion" from the atmosphere, then the description of an air as even "more respirable" than ordinary air must certainly represent an anticipatory identification of the respirable portion. Remembering, however, that in his second note on respiration Lavoisier had lost the concept that respiration separates the air into portions, we should be wary of imposing a uniform direction on the progression of his ideas. If we dissociate the present statements from earlier and later stages in his thought, the weight of his description falls clearly on the identification of the air with common air, "entire and undecomposed." By "purest portion" he seems to mean air freed of the adventitious matters traditionally assumed to contaminate the atmosphere, including moisture and fixed air. To fit Lavoisier's statements back into a conceptual evolution, we must then regard him as temporarily diverted from his earlier movement toward identifying a specific portion of the air as the entity absorbed in calcinations, combustions, and respiration. This digression can be seen as an essential detour around an "epistemological obstacle," to use Gaston Bachelard's term.[29] So long as Lavoisier had been seeking to identify for this role a specific constituent different from ordinary air, his predilection to choose fixed air had mired him in contradictions. How could he ever reach a common interpretation for calcination, combustion, and respiration, so long as the air he believed to be absorbed in the first of these processes was the same as that which extinguished candles and killed animals? We may argue that by relinquishing for a time the belief that a substance clearly distinguishable from common air as a whole was what he sought, he freed himself to identify that entity eventually as something other than fixed air.

The above provides a plausible refinement to the conventional view that Lavoisier gradually but steadily clarified his conception of an atmosphere composed of separable distinct species of airs; but it shares with that, and many other historical interpretations of analogous situations, the weaknesses of a history of science conceived of mainly as a history of ideas. Unless historians delve, as intimately as the record permits, into the connections between each step in an intellectual development and its nearest investigative counterpart, they depict scientific concepts as evolving according to some internal dynamic, reflecting only the general features of an underlying experimental or observational substratum; and they risk attributing to the intellectual pathway a misleading image of autonomous movement. From the detailed record we have just followed, of one of the experiments on the calx of mercury Lavoisier had recently completed at the time he composed his description of the air obtained from that substance, we can see that the ambivalence in his verbal identification exactly parallels the ambivalence in the test results on which he based it. If the qualitative tests of the candle and the bird created the visual impression of an air which supported combustion and respiration even better than common air did, the nitrous air test indicated more strongly to him that it was, after all, not measurably different from common air.

At first sight it would appear that during the course of these experiments on the mercury calx Lavoisier must have been able at least to clear up his difficulty relating the composition of common air to that of fixed air. If pure common air combined with *charbon* to yield fixed air, then fixed air must be a combination of *charbon* and common air. The matter was, however, not so simple. Lavoisier ended his memoir with the following remark:

> From the fact that common air is changed into fixed air when one combines it with *charbon*, it would seem natural to conclude that fixed air is nothing but a combination of common air and phlogiston. That is the opinion of M. Priestley, and one must admit that it is not without likelihood; nevertheless, when one descends to the factual details, that view is found to be so frequently contradicted that I believe I must ask physicians [Lavoisier used this word in the eighteenth-century sense roughly equivalent to

> "physical scientist"] and chemists for now to suspend judgment. I hope to be soon in a position to set forth for them the causes of my doubts.[30]

If, as historians generally assume, Lavoisier had privately rejected the phlogiston theory by this time, then he was merely being coy in this passage. What we have learned in the last chapter about his multiple, mutually contradictory attempts to straighten out the relation between common and fixed air within the preceding weeks reveals the statement to be, on the contrary, an understated public acknowledgment of his continuing private perplexity. The interpretation he gave as "not without likelihood" was not that of Priestley alone, for we have seen that he had entertained similar ideas himself, earlier in the *Opuscules* as well as in some of his most recent efforts to break through his conceptual barriers.[31] Only a few months before writing the above statement he had been contemplating an experiment on the combustion of charcoal to test whether it gave off phlogiston during the process.[32] What he had verified by reacting *charbon* with the air from mercury calx was only that the *charbon* contributes *something* to the composition of the fixed air. If that something was not the phlogiston, of which *charbon* was the richest known source, then it was hard to imagine what else it could be.

Finally, we should note the prominence of respiration in Lavoisier's definition of the air he had obtained. In the experiment described in detail we have seen that he was especially "curious" about the effects of the air on the respiration of an animal. Taken in the limited context of this experiment, the test he carried out appears only as the standard use of an animal to characterize the properties of a new air. Knowing of Lavoisier's prior musings about the process of respiration itself, however, we can be confident that he was also on the alert for any effect which might lead to an insight into the nature of that "operation." In the sense that the conclusion Lavoisier drew from this and his other tests was that the air was only very pure common air, the result offered no immediate new footholds for a theoretical interpretation of respiration; but his characterization of the new air as "the most respirable portion" of common air illustrates once again how this physiological criterion held Lavoisier's conception of the atmosphere together in the absence of a more discriminating chemical definition.

II

It is often said that to ask fruitful questions in science is as difficult and crucial as to provide conclusive answers. If, from our perspective, Lavoisier had not yet fully solved the problem of "the nature of the principle which combines with metals during their calcination"—the title of his paper based on the mercury calx—he displayed in his introduction to that paper his astute capacity to identify the fundamental questions of the area within which he was working:

> Do different species of air exist? Does it suffice that a body be in a state of permanent expansibility in order to comprise a species of air? Finally, are the different airs which nature presents us, or which we succeed in producing, separate substances or modifications of atmospheric air? [33]

Whether or not we accept Conant's opinion that for the moment Lavoisier was trying to answer some of these questions both ways, he was unlikely to rest satisfied until he could reach definitive decisions on the questions he had so lucidly posed. Joseph Priestley, less disciplined in his thought, was more comfortable having it both ways. Experimentally, however, Priestley had once more leaped ahead of Lavoisier.

On March 15 Priestley wrote John Pringle that from *mercurius calcinatus per se* he had produced a new species of air. Priestley's well-known candid narrative of the surprises he encountered and the "mistakes" he made along the way to this discovery shows that it was his nitrous air test that revealed decisively that what he had collected in his bell jar differed from common air. When he applied his standard nitrous air test, the air derived from the calx was diminished about as much as ordinary air; but when he decided, on a whim, to add a second measure of nitrous air, he found that, in striking contrast to ordinary air, the volume of the new air decreased further. [34]

As we have previously seen, notwithstanding the fact that the nitrous air test was a purely chemical one, Priestley regarded the procedure as a more accurate substitute for the use of a mouse to test the fitness of an air for respiration. In keeping with this viewpoint, he defined the new air principally with reference to the respiratory process, and in a way that affirmed the close association he had maintained between respiration and combustion. The new kind of air, he wrote, is "five or six times better than common air, for the purpose of respiration, inflammation, and, I believe, every other use of common atmospherical air. As I think I have sufficiently proved, that the fitness of air for respiration depends upon its capacity to receive the *phlogiston* exhaled from the lungs, this species may not improperly be called *dephlogisticated air.*" He had observed that "a candle burned in this air with amazing strength of flame," and that red-hot wood burned very rapidly. "But to complete the proof of the superior quality of this air, I introduced a mouse into it; and in a quantity in which, had it been in common air, it would have died in about a quarter of an hour, it lived, at two different times, a whole hour, and was taken out quite vigorous; and the remaining air appeared to be still, by the test of nitrous air, as good as common air." [35]

Thus, alerted by the contrasting behavior of the air from mercury calx and of common air subjected to the supplementary nitrous air test, Priestley could now see in the same standard tests—the reaction of an animal and of a burning candle—that in Lavoisier's eyes had suggested only that the air was very "pure" common air, additional evidence to distinguish the air from common air. While Lavoisier was still perceiving the air as the "most respirable portion of the air" and "the air itself entire and undecomposed," Priestley was calling it a new "species of air"; but Priestley was subject to a different form of ambivalence. His theory that the new air was "dephlogisticated air" implied that it was only an altered form of common air; and his continuous scale for the "goodness" of air, reinforced by the character of his nitrous air test, was leading him, despite his assertions that the air is composed of various constituents, to view it instead as one substance capable of graded qualitative modifications due to the multiform actions of phlogiston.

Historians agree that it took the stimulus of Priestley's new discovery to prod Lavoisier beyond the stage of thinking about the mercury calx and the atmosphere in general that he had reached in his memoir of April 1775. Apparently he did not learn of Priestley's progress until December, when advance copies of portions of the second volume of Priestley's *Experiments and Observations on Different Kinds of Air* reached Paris.[36] In the meantime, according to his laboratory register, Lavoisier was pursuing other facets of his general research program, and did no further work on the calx of mercury.[37]

With two pounds of red precipitate of mercury purchased from Baumé, Lavoisier began his new investigation of the air derived from that calx on February 13, 1776. Placing three ounces of it into his usual type of glass retort with its neck curved to convey the released air into an inverted jar over water, he began heating the substance in a small charcoal furnace. The first portion to come off was reddish. When he noticed that the vapors were no longer red, he changed receivers and "pushed the fire" to drive off more air. He collected a cylinder full of this air, then changed receivers again, having to "push the fire vigorously" in order to obtain more air. After he had collected another cylinder of air, "since it was late, and the experiment had lasted for seven or eight hours, I stopped." He found liquid mercury in the neck of the vessel, and the remaining red precipitate still in the retort.[38]

Probably inferring correctly that the reddish air evolved first was contaminated by nitrous air owing to impurities in the red calx, Lavoisier fixed his attention on the second, colorless portion. "The air of the second product," he recorded, "was found to be the dephlogisticated air of M. Prisley." It is not certain by what test Lavoisier made this identification, since he did not record a nitrous air test on this portion of the air. He did insert a burning candle in it, and observed that "it gave at first an extremely brilliant flame which diminished gradually until it returned to the state of an ordinary lamp in common air." The burning candle reduced the volume of the air from 2 cubic inches 8½ lines to 2 cubic inches 5 lines. A flame placed in an equal quantity of ordinary air burned only one-fourth as long, but to his surprise "it did not appear that the diminution with the dephlogisticated air was greater than with common air." The difference between the flame burning in the air from mercury calx and that burning in common air was thus scarcely more striking than the similar difference he had noticed a year before. If, as it seems, he now saw the greater brilliance of the first as the evidence that the air was dephlogisticated air, the most likely reason was that Priestley had taught him to see the same basic observations in a way he had not seen them previously. The next morning he realized that the observation that there was no greater diminution in the volume of the dephlogisticated air than in that of the common air "is false"; for the air from the mercury calx in which a candle had burned continued to be absorbed during the night, until the volume was reduced to about 1 cubic inch.[39]

Lavoisier next produced a large quantity of nitrous air by dissolving mercury in nitrous acid. Although his laboratory record does not explicitly say so, it seems evident that his objective was both to provide a supply of nitrous air for applying the nitrous air test to the air obtained from the mercury calx, and to explore the more discriminating use of the nitrous air test required to distinguish dephlogisticated air from common air. As soon as he had placed the mercury and acid in the curved-neck retort a reaction took place, and nitrous air began to evolve rapidly. Heating the retort cautiously, he carefully observed the changes in the reaction and in the character of the air coming off, and separated the latter into ten different fractions. After collecting the first six of these, he noticed that the vapor was beginning to be reddish, and there appeared to be an absorption of some of the air, even as further air was disengaged. He "judged that common air or dephlogisticated air was beginning to be disengaged," and that it "was mixing with the nitrous air, which was producing the phenomenon of absorption." He then halted the operation, and "since it was late, I wanted to stop, but having removed the distillation vessel, some water fell on it and caused it to break." He therefore had to remove the saline residue and put it into another retort. He did not say whether or not these extra operations caused him to miss his supper, but either then or on another day he continued heating the salt, until finally, on February 25, it was completely reduced to mercury, and he had collected ten fractions of the air.[40]

The fractions which he judged to be "good" nitrous air Lavoisier tested by mixing portions of them with common air, presumably in the ratio of one to two recommended by Priestley. Fraction number 5 diminished common air "between a sixth and a fifth," very nearly as it should. Fraction number 6, obviously somewhat less good, diminished common air only by "about one-seventh." Having established the essential property of his nitrous air, he now utilized it to test the portions of air which had come off in the later stages of the operation, as the mercury salt formed in the earlier stage was reduced to mercury. Of fraction number 7, he observed,

> This air was much better than that of the atmosphere. Having placed two parts of it in a vessel inverted in water, and having introduced nitrous air into it, I succeeded in obtaining a diminution of nearly one-half, around 5/12 [Lavoisier then crossed out "5/12" and wrote "7/16" instead]. The quantity of nitrous air introduced had been 1 5/8 parts [presumably to 2 parts of the air tested]. Then there was no further absorption. This air, thus diminished, still did not extinguish flames; they appeared even to be augmented rather than diminished. That proves that there was probably still room to introduce more nitrous air and that this air was still not completely vitiated at all!

Lavoisier's exclamation point tempts us to think that he was perhaps seeing this remarkable phenomenon for himself for the first time. On fractions 8 and 9 he varied the procedure, adding the nitrous air in stages.

> These two airs, especially number 9, are the best possible. I caused 4 parts of each of them to pass into a glass tube and I added nitrous air, part by part. Four parts diminished it by half. Five parts by two-thirds. Six parts by three-fourths. 7 parts by 7/8. On adding further nitrous air there was no diminution beyond that.[41]

Returning to the first fraction of the air he had collected from Baumé's red precipitate of mercury on February 13, he tested it too with nitrous air. "This air," he wrote between the lines of his original record, "was diminished by about seven-sixteenths [he afterward inserted "or by half"]. It was, consequently, much better than common air. The quantity of nitrous air added to 2 parts of this air, in order to reach the greatest possible diminution, was 1 1/2 to 1 3/4 or about 2 parts." Mixing the third fraction of this air to an equal portion of nitrous air, he found the combined volume diminished by about half.[42]

In these operations Lavoisier was simultaneously learning how to perform the nitrous air test to best advantage, and utilizing it to characterize the air derived from the reduction of mercury calces. He was assimilating into his own repertoire of concepts and practices Priestley's discovery of the new air. In the bargain he was acquiring also some of the conceptual crosscurrents which muddled Priestley's view of the nature of airs. Adopting Priestley's test, along with his term "dephlogisticated air," Lavoisier too evaluated the results as measures of the "goodness" of the samples in question, and he too described the result of burning a candle in dephlogisticated air by whether, or to what extent, it "vitiated" that air. Thus the very procedures by which he recognized the new air made it difficult to give, with respect to it, a clear answer to the question he had so clearly posed a year earlier: "Are the different airs which nature presents us, or which we succeed in producing, separate substances or modifications of atmospheric air?" More constructively, the conceptual milieu within which Priestley had defined the meaning of the nitrous air test served as a constant reminder of the potential significance of his new discovery for respiration.

So far Lavoisier had merely been catching up with Priestley. On April 7 he began to move beyond his English counterpart. In the evening of that day he put four gros of liquid mercury into a distillation flask with the usual curved neck extending under an inverted jar. The jar was filled initially with common air. The distillation flask soon broke, and he had to start over, using this time two ounces of mercury in place of the four gros. He heated the flask gently by suspending it in a furnace five or six inches above the charcoal. Although he maintained the mercury at the point of boiling throughout the evening, "not the least particle of calx formed." By the next morning a small pellicle had appeared on one side only of the globule of mercury. Carrying on through the day, he noticed a few more reddish fragments, and persisted through a part of the next night; but by the following morning he thought that the operation was producing air, rather than absorbing it as it should. He continued nevertheless, in the same manner, on into April 9, without noticing "anything remarkable." The quantity of red fragments did not seem even to be growing any more. Undaunted, Lavoisier endured for several more days, and was rewarded by seeing eventually the air in the inverted jar decrease in volume by about one-sixth. A little more than twenty grains of red calx of mercury had formed. He tested the air remaining in the jar and found that it did not precipitate limewater.[43]

Up until now Lavoisier had simply performed on mercury an experiment similar to those he had been carrying out on other metals for several years, demonstrating that their calcination absorbs a portion of atmospheric air. The details of his laboratory record reveal how arduous such an experiment could be. It was not merely a matter of waiting patiently for nearly a week for the result. To maintain a degree of heat which would just keep the mercury at its boiling point throughout this period, by means of charcoals in a traditional chemical furnace, required constant vigilance. Whether Lavoisier did all this by himself, or had assistants, the experimental effort involved merits respect.

At this point Lavoisier had to suspend his operations and move his apparatus to the Paris Arsenal, where he was taking up his new role as its effective scientific director, and equipping a new laboratory for his personal research.[44] His first experimental move there was one of the most brilliant of his career. It would be natural to infer that the air the mercury had absorbed in becoming a calx was identical to the air the red calx of mercury released when reduced without charcoal. The inference was, however, hardly infallible. By making a similar inference earlier regarding calcinations and reductions with charcoal, Lavoisier had only run into trouble. This time, however, not only was he more fortunate, but he devised a maneuver to verify the inference by the classical chemical method of analysis and synthesis. To five parts of the air remaining after the calcined mercury had absorbed one-sixth of it, he added one part of dephlogisticated air. In the resulting air a candle burned as in ordinary air.[45] Lavoisier had attained what he could later claim to be "the most complete proof one could reach in chemistry, the decomposition of the air and its recomposition."[46]

At almost the same time as he concluded these experiments with the air derived from mercury, Lavoisier presented at the Academy one of his outstanding experimental and theoretical achievements, the demonstration that nitrous acid is composed of nitrous air combined with this same air. The two investigations were obviously closely connected, for the same operations through which he acquired the nitrous air to test the properties of the new air constituted part of the proof for the composition of nitrous acid. The other part was the completion of another analysis and synthesis, in which he combined the air obtained from the calx of mercury with nitrous air to reconstitute nitrous acid. The "purest portion" of common air now began to take on a new role in Lavoisier's theoretical framework, as the characteristic "principle" contained in acids in general.[47]

These two scientific landmarks, the analysis and synthesis of the atmosphere and of nitrous acid, became the centerpieces for the new chemical system Lavoisier was in the process of constructing. It would be natural to assume, therefore, that by the time he had completed these experiments, in April 1776, he had answered decisively his own questions about whether there are distinct species of airs in the atmosphere; that he now understood the atmosphere as a combination of about one-sixth "respirable air," the same air that is absorbed in calcination and the formation of acids, with an unrespirable air incapable of entering into combustions and calcinations; and that from this vantage point he was in a position finally to discard the residues of older views based on various versions of the phlogiston theory. Certainly he had advanced on all these fronts. In his memoir on the existence of air in nitrous acid he wrote, "It appeared proven . . . that the air we respire contains only a quarter of true air; that this true air is mixed, in our atmosphere, with three or four parts of an injurious air, a species of mophette, which causes most animals to perish, if the quantity of it is a little greater."[48] Assuming that this statement appeared in the original version of his memoir, and was not a clarification added before its later publication, we might well conclude that he had resolved the ambiguity inherent until very recently in his thought, and that all that remained for him to do was to find an appropriate nomenclature to express the relation between "true air" and what had commonly been understood as true air. Yet we find him in the same article still calling the respirable air "the purest portion of the air," "air better than common air," and "a purer air (if it is permitted to utilize this expression) and more air than common air."[49] Clearly he was still struggling to reach a coherent conception of this air and its place in the atmosphere. His movement from a view of the atmosphere as a substance subject to modification, toward a view that it is composed of specific portions, was clearly not the holistic "switch" we would expect a person to make between two alternatives which in retrospect seem not to admit a logical intermediate position. It was a long passage, during which Lavoisier had to tolerate the incoherence of thinking within the conceptual frameworks of both alternatives. To us he seems still to have been living simultaneously in two conceptual worlds.

As the previous chapter has already shown, Lavoisier's conceptual world harbored a place for phlogiston for longer than is often appreciated. Max Speter pointed out eighty years ago that Lavoisier had been steeped in phlogiston chemistry during his early training as a chemist, becoming only gradually more skeptical of it over a period of twelve years before he was ready to do without it.[50] He did not, however, undergo simply a slow shift in attitude from acceptance, to guarded detachment, to eventual rejection. Unlike Bayen, who was ready to declare phlogiston chemistry a "dangerous system" as soon as he found one phenomenon for which phlogiston's previously accepted role could be dispensed with, Lavoisier responded to results incompatible with the phlogiston system by modifying the Stahlian orthodoxy. If phlogiston did not enter the metals in reductions, perhaps it entered the evolved air instead. If the phlogiston contained in *charbon* was unnecessary in the reduction of mercury calx, it might still explain the difference between the airs evolved in reductions with and without charcoal. At one time he was willing to drop phlogiston from his explanation of the combustion of some combustibles while retaining it for other cases. We have seen him in 1775 thinking about "returning" to Priestley's opinion that acidic airs are formed by adding phlogiston to acids.

By early 1776 the incisions he was making into conventional phlogiston theory were certainly cutting deeply. In his investigation of nitrous acid he had dissolved mercury in that acid, reducing the precipitate without addition. In his memoir he asked rhetorically whether the phlogiston contained in the mercury had played any part, and replied to his own question,

> Since the mercury came out of that operation in precisely the state in which it entered it, it appears that it had neither lost nor regained phlogiston, unless one thought that the phlogiston which served to reduce the metal had passed through the vessel; but that would be to acknowledge a particular kind of phlogiston; . . . it is to return to a principle of fire . . . much more ancient than that of Stahl, and very different.[51]

Here Lavoisier appeared almost to be burying phlogiston indirectly by substituting something like his own matter of fire for the concept of the "school of Stahl"; but getting rid of phlogiston was no single, discrete intellectual step attainable through a few flashes of insight. If the orthodox phlogiston of Stahl was already receding into the past, the protean variations Priestley was devising to accommodate the concept to the chemistry of airs surrounded Lavoisier at every step. In this same memoir he acknowledged that there was not a single experiment contained in it for which "M. Priestley cannot, rigorously speaking, claim the first idea." He asserted that he had drawn from these experiments diametrically opposite consequences from the conclusions Priestley had reached.[52] On the specific points in contention he had; but it was not so simple as he supposed, to isolate the consequences one draws from the operations out of which one draws them. Phlogiston was so deeply embedded in the very meaning of some of these operations that if one were to eliminate it and all its implications, one would have to reconstruct the field piece by piece in other terms. For example, when Lavoisier referred to the results of a nitrous air test as the measure of the "goodness" of the air, Priestley's definition of that property as a continuous scale of degrees of phlogistication or dephlogistication hovered in the background. To escape the theoretical context within which Priestley had embedded this indispensable test, Lavoisier would have to find some new meaning for the continuous scale of diminutions. Similarly, if he were to find a new way to understand the contribution of charcoal to those chemical changes in which it played a part, he would have to find some way to characterize that substance independent of its traditional role as a source of phlogiston.

It is too easy to picture Lavoisier in 1776, with the major blocks of his theoretical structure already in place, proceeding surely and inevitably toward the completion of his "revolution." That may not have been how he viewed himself then. By this time he had certainly traveled too far on his intellectual voyage to turn back, but he did not necessarily see just how he would reach the far shore. Gruber has pointed out some of the ways in which a system of scientific ideas undergoing change may tend to inhibit further change. As the individual departs from accepted patterns of thought, he becomes less capable of communicating with others who have not, losing the potent advantages of scientific communication for further change. Far from a solitary thinker, Lavoisier carried on his investigations in close contact with other chemists, and would have felt the disadvantages of intellectual isolation. Moreover, as one clarifies the remaining problems facing a new system, some of them may appear to be insoluble. Lavoisier still confronted many such problems. "Normally," Gruber writes, "one works within a context that defines soluble problems, and provides methods for solving them and criteria for recognizing solutions. The further one moves from this complex norm, the less likely one is to arrive at an effective solution."[53] Only individuals whose self-assurance matches their other scientific capacities can surmount such obstacles. Lavoisier was well endowed on both counts, but even he could falter. In a letter to Thomas Henry, drafted sometime during this period, he wrote, "I have been forced to disagree sometimes with the opinions of M. Priestley, but I could be deceiving myself, and in spite of the self-esteem natural to every individual, I will confess to you that I often have more confidence in the ideas of M. Priestley than in my own."[54] Addressing Priestley's countryman, Lavoisier undoubtedly found this admission a diplomatic one to make, but there is little reason to doubt his sincerity. We have seen him following Priestley's experimental leads, absorbing his procedures and his language; and we have detected him in private thinking often in Priestley's terms, ready at times to readopt the theoretical views of Priestley that he had previously tried to do without. It would not be surprising if he wondered frequently whether Priestley might be right about the crucial issues over which they differed.

III

I have repeatedly urged that the operations with which, and the language in which, Priestley and Lavoisier explored the airs involved in calcination, combustion, and the constitution of the atmosphere not only reinforced the association of these entities and processes with respiration, but even characterized the chemical processes by reference to respiratory ones. What Lavoisier did after completing the analysis and synthesis of the atmosphere by means of mercury and its calx confirms the reality of this association in his mind. On the page immediately following that experiment he recorded:

> Air vitiated by respiration
>
> I vitiated the air under a jar by my respiration, after which it extinguished flames. I then added 1⁄16 of dephlogisticated air to it, but it still extinguished flames. On mixing 5 parts of vitiated air with 1 part of dephlogisticated air, there resulted an air nearly [Lavoisier then crossed out "nearly" and went on] in which a flame burned nearly as in common air.
>
> I tested air vitiated by the respiration of animals with nitrous air. One part of the latter against 4 parts of vitiated air did not redden, but there was some absorption, and the 5 measures made about 4⅓. I added a second measure and I had 5 measures.
>
> I took 5 measures of vitiated air and I combined 1 measure of dephlogisticated air with it. I introduced 2 measures of nitrous air into these 6 measures. There were a few red vapors and much smoke, like that of a flame which has gone out. These eight measures were reduced to 5¼ or 5⅓, from which it results that this air is a little less good than common air. [We may wonder why Lavoisier added less than the standard proportion of nitrous air here, but he gave no explanation].
>
> It appears that *flames, in absorbing air, render it vitiated*

> [Lavoisier crossed out the italicized phrase, which obviously mixed up what he intended to say, and corrected it to] respiration, in absorbing air, renders a portion vitiated.[55]

The close parallels between this experiment on respiration and the one he had just carried out with mercury is a striking demonstration of the intimate way in which respiration was woven into Lavoisier's conceptual framework. Exactly as he had decomposed the atmosphere by calcining the metal, and recomposed it with air derived from the metallic calx, so now he decomposed the atmosphere by respiration and recomposed it with the same air derived from the metallic calx. His actions show that he must have expected respiration to have the same effect upon common air as did the calcination of mercury.

Lavoisier's notebook leaves unanswered whether he had, either in planning the experiment or as a consequence of it, an organized theory of respiration in mind supplanting his earlier fragmentary thoughts on the subject. The statement previously quoted from his memoir on nitrous acid—"that the air we respire contains only a quarter of true air; that this true air is mixed, in our atmosphere, with three or four parts of an injurious air, a species of mophette, which causes most animals to perish"—would suggest not only that by this time he had retrieved the notion in his first idea about respiration, that it separates the air into two portions, but that he was now in a position to specify what those portions were. The same conceptual duality which we have seen pervading his thought about these airs in general, however, seems to have impregnated also his views about respiration. In the above notebook description he did not write that respiration absorbs a *portion* of the atmosphere. He stated that "in absorbing the air it *vitiates* a portion." Having examined the ambivalence of his statements about airs and the atmosphere in other contexts, we are able to appreciate the significance of the duality lurking behind that brief phrase. In common usage "vitiated" meant "depraved, infected, spoiled," as with a vice, a poison, or a pestilence.[56] Lavoisier probably borrowed the term from Priestley, who had described air into which phlogiston had been discharged, so that animals died when placed in it, as "vitiated" air.[57] For Priestley vitiated was synonymous with "corrupted," "tainted," "spoiled," "injured," "infected," or made "noxious."[58] Lavoisier's statement therefore implied not a separation of unalterable constituents, but a more general modification of a single entity, or an imparting to it of some noxious quality which rendered a portion of it irrespirable. Undoubtedly Lavoisier was not consciously echoing Priestley's theory that respiration phlogisticates the air; but his dependence on this term, together with his use of the term "dephlogisticated air" to label the air which he identified through Priestley's methods, indicate to us that, whether Lavoisier was aware of it or not, the shadow of Priestley fell across his approach even to respiration.

* * *

I have described Lavoisier in 1775 and early 1776 as living in "two conceptual worlds." That is, however, a perspective available to us only through the mediation of later events. Lavoisier came eventually to regard phlogiston and its supporting concepts as an outmoded theoretical framework which he replaced with his own, and that perception has prevailed ever since. In April 1776 he would not yet have been able to tell which of the elements juxtaposed in his purview of his field would persist within his own system of thought, and which would ultimately be left behind in what would come to appear a discarded system. How then can we tell whether he himself perceived that his "hybrid" intellectual world of 1776 was not entirely coherent? His own contemporary statements of doubt, uncertainty, and recognition of inconsistency are rare, but pointed enough to establish that he did sense that he had not been able to put everything together. We must still be careful, however, not to identify the "puzzling" inconsistencies he noticed with those aspects of his thought that appear inconsistent to us. Despite the clarity of the alternatives he posed in his questions concerning species of air, there is no direct evidence that he was aware that in his descriptions of particular airs he blurred the very choices he had posed in general. Should we say, then, that on such points Lavoisier was simply confused? Historians of science often apply the term "confused" inappropriately to scientists of the past who have not yet stabilized certain distinctions that later become obvious.[59] There are few individuals in the history of science whose thinking was, in general, less confused than that of Lavoisier. We must instead be content to acknowledge the limits on our own ability to comprehend the mental state of a great creative thinker at such a stage in his conceptual odyssey.

3

The Emergence of a Theory of Respiration

Ever a jump ahead of Lavoisier, Joseph Priestley had concentrated his attention on respiration several months before Lavoisier performed the experiment described at the end of the previous chapter. In the second volume of *Experiments and Observations on Different Kinds of Air,* published in November 1775, Priestley had made the rather loose "conjecture" that phlogiston is the "proper nourishment of the animal body," and the "source of muscular motion." After performing these functions, and probably being altered in some unspecified way during the process, the phlogiston "is discharged as *effete* into the great common *menstruum,* the atmosphere."[1] Quickly following up his idea, he carried out a series of experiments on the interactions between blood and various airs, which he reported to the Royal Society in January 1776, under the heading "Observations on respiration, and the use of the blood." The "*use* of *respiration*" that he had already suggested, he wrote, "I have now, I think, proved to be effected by means of the *blood,* in consequence of its coming so nearly into contact with the air in the lungs; the blood appearing to be a fluid wonderfully formed to imbibe, and part with, that principle which the chemists call phlogiston, and changing its colour in consequence of being charged with it, or being freed from it."[2] Ever since Lower had proven that the blood acquires its arterial color in the lungs, and only if the lungs are aerated, physiologists had been searching with little success for an explanation of how respiration and the color change are connected.[3] Priestley now thought that he had solved that old and vexing problem. Coagulated sheep blood, he showed, became alternately "black" and "red" when he transferred it back and forth from phlogisticated to dephlogisticated air. A dark blood clot placed into five ounce measures of dephlogisticated air, and replaced ten to twelve times by successive pieces of the same clot, so altered the air that at the end of the time, when subjected to the nitrous air test, its volume decreased much less than it would have at the beginning. He concluded that "it is evident that this black blood must have communicated phlogiston to the air." In the process the blood itself became "florid red." Priestley was able to obtain a similar result even when the blood was enclosed within a bladder which separated it from the air, demonstrating, in his view, that in the lungs the blood can communicate the phlogiston to the air through the membranes which prevent them from coming into direct contact.[4]

Priestley's promising attack on the mysterious internal processes associated with respiration attracted widespread attention, including that of Lavoisier. Through Magellan Priestley sent Lavoisier a reprint of his article on April 2, 1776,[5] so that Lavoisier must have received it near the time that he carried out his own first experiment clearly designed to elucidate the effects of respiration on the air. Priestley's memoir greatly impressed him. Undoubtedly it also stimulated Lavoisier to intensify his own interest in respiration. This time, however, he did not adopt Priestley's experimental plan, as he had sometimes done in the past, but continued to develop the line of investigation he had opened up himself when he examined the vitiation of air by respiration following the similar examination of the calcination of mercury. The next step he took was to place a bird under a bell jar, as he had done many times before to test the effects of an air on respiration. This time, however, his purpose was unequivocably to test the effects of the respiration on the air, interpreted in terms of his emerging views about the constitution of the atmosphere.

The laboratory notebooks unfortunately contain no record of the first conclusive experiment of this type that he carried out, sometime between mid April and early October 1776. The account closest to the event which has survived is contained in an early draft of Lavoisier's first memoir on respiration, written in October or November and differing only slightly from the later published version. Although Lavoisier sometimes smoothed out the course of an actual investigation when he incorporated it into a manuscript, or inserted interpretations that only afterward became obvious, there is in this case no overt sign that he did not faithfully represent the actual experiment. As described, it forms a natural extension to the experiment of April on his own respiration.

> I introduced a sparrow under a glass jar filled with common air and immersed in a bowl full of mercury. The empty portion of the jar was thirty-one cubic inches [in volume]. The animal did not appear affected in any way during the first moments. It was only a little drowsy. At the end of a quarter of an hour it began to be agitated. Its respiration became labored and precipitous, and the irregularities increased more and more. Finally, after fifty-five minutes it died with a kind of convulsive movement.[6]

In spite of the heat produced by the sparrow, the volume of the air in the jar decreased slightly, being one-sixtieth less at the end than at the beginning. Lavoisier subjected the remaining air to the usual tests. It precipitated limewater, extinguished candles, was not further diminished in nitrous air, and another bird placed in it lived only a few moments. With his mind fixed on the similarity between respiration and the calcination of mercury, he saw these results as proof that the air "had become completely mephitic, and in that respect it was sufficiently similar to that which had served for calcination."[7]

To say that air had become "mephitic" was another way to say it had become unrespirable, or been vitiated, so that Lavoisier seemed in this statement only to be verifying what he had already inferred from the experiment on his own respired air in April. There was, however, a telltale further discrimination latent in the fact that this particular mephitic air precipitated limewater, whereas air which had served for calcination did not. Lavoisier was forced to carry his analysis of the situation further.

> Nevertheless a more profound examination caused me to perceive two very remarkable differences between the two airs, I mean between that of the calcination and that of the respiration. First, the diminution of the volume of the air had been much less in the latter than in the former. Second, the air of the respiration precipitated limewater, whereas the air of calcination caused no change in it.
>
> This difference, on the one hand, between the two airs, and the great analogy that they presented, on the other hand, in many respects, led me to suppose that there are two causes entangled in respiration, of which I was still acquainted with only one.[8]

By the "one cause" that he had already known about, Lavoisier obviously meant the absorption of a portion of the air. At first sight this account of how he came to recognize that there is a second effect appears incredible. Not only had he and others known for a long time that respired air precipitates limewater, but in his *Opuscules* in 1774 he had interpreted this effect to mean that "air which has . . . served for . . . respiration . . . approaches the state of fixed air";[9] and in February 1775, he had written down the idea that respiration converts common air to fixed air![10] How is it possible that he *discovered* this phenomenon only in the course of an experiment he performed between April and October 1776? I myself once regarded such a situation as so implausible that in an earlier draft of the present book I suggested that Lavoisier was imposing an ideal reconstruction, sacrificing historical veracity to the desire to develop a logical argument. Further examination, however, has led me to suppose that he was probably describing his mental development exactly as it appeared to him. His respiration experiment of April is consistent with the assumption that respiration only absorbs something from the air; for in order to reconstitute the original common air he had merely added to the residual air the air derived from mercury calx. His apparent neglect of his own prior knowledge that respiration also produces fixed air is another manifestation of a mental characteristic we have repeatedly observed. When he concentrated his attention closely on a particular set of phenomena or relationships, he was apt to lose sight of other phenomena which, from a greater distance, appear obviously essential aspects of the problem he was attacking. His preoccupation with the "grand analogy" between respiration and calcination had displaced a phenomenon which had no place in that comparison, so that it required a direct confrontation with the experimental manifestations of that phenomenon to force him to expand his purview to include it.

Once having retrieved his awareness of the evidence that fixed air formed in respiration, Lavoisier exploited that evidence brilliantly to complete his demonstration of the simultaneous occurrence of the "two causes."

> I passed twelve cubic inches of the air vitiated by respiration under a glass jar filled with mercury, and I introduced into it a thin layer of caustic fixed alkali. I would have used limewater for the same purpose, but the volume which it would have been necessary to employ would have been too large, and would have detracted from the success of the experiment.
>
> The effect of the caustic alkali was to cause a diminution of this air by one-sixth. At the same time the alkali partly lost its causticity, and it acquired the property of effervescing with acids and of crystallizing, properties that one knows can be communicated to it only insofar as one combines it with the species of air or of gas known by the name of fixed air; from which it results that air vitiated by respiration contains nearly one-sixth [part] of true fixed air.[11]

These changes in the properties of a caustic alkali when exposed to an air had been known, since the celebrated experiments of Joseph Black, as the standard indications that the alkali had absorbed fixed air and become transformed into what was traditionally designated a "mild alkali," such as soda or potash.

The air remaining after this operation was still not in the state of common air. It caused animals to perish and extinguished candles. In Lavoisier's view it was now in "exactly the same condition as the air which had served for the calcination of mercury." If so, one could now truly reconstitute common air, in the same way that he had already done from the residue left after the calcination of mercury:

> But the air which has served for the calcination of mercury is nothing else but . . . the mephitic residue of atmospheric air, of which the respirable part has combined with the mercury during the calcination. Therefore, the air which has served for respiration, since it is entirely the same, is equally nothing but the resi-

> due of common air deprived of its respirable part; and, in fact, having combined with this air about one-sixth [part] of eminently respirable air taken from the calx of mercury, I reestablished it in its original state.[12]

Thus, by taking into account the "second" effect he had overlooked in April, and compensating for it by removing the product of that effect, Lavoisier had now succeeded at what he had only partially accomplished then, duplicating fully the analysis and synthesis of air, with respiration substituted for the calcination of mercury.

By the time he completed these operations Lavoisier knew that he had achieved a major advance in the knowledge of respiration. The importance of the results demanded further confirmation of the experimental evidence. Taking advantage of the October Academy vacation to work in the laboratory maintained by his friend Trudaine at his château in Montigny, Lavoisier, Trudaine, and Etienne Mignot de Montigny, an industrial scientist, academician, and neighbor of Trudaine, together repeated the basic demonstrations and extended them by varying the conditions.[13]

At Montigny they used a robin in place of a sparrow, immersed the inverted jar in water instead of mercury, and provided the doomed bird with a pedestal so that it could perch above the liquid. Otherwise the experiment proceeded much as its prototype had gone:

> We placed a lively robin in a glass jar of about 48-cubic-inch capacity filled with common air. One had to pass the animal through the water in order to introduce it into the jar, and one introduced into the same jar a wooden pedestal, so that the animal would not be wet. The animal was introduced at nine minutes past noon. Whether it was stunned by passing through the water, or for other reasons, it immediately appeared dull and downcast, and remained motionless. From the first moment we noticed that its respiration was short and hurried; at 21 minutes past noon the animal stood up with an air of anxiety and suffering. At half past the hour its respiration was visibly painful, and the bird opened its beak during every inspiration. A few minutes later the animal made large movements. At 46 minutes after noon it was breathing with more and more difficulty. The bird opened its beak much more, and it had momentary convulsions. Finally it died, at one minute and 25 seconds after one o'clock with its wings beating and convulsions in its feet.[14]

Just as before, the "air in which the animal died was submitted to various tests. It extinguished candles, precipitated limewater, and gave no visible red vapors with nitrous air." This time, unlike in the first experiment, they were able to use limewater to remove the fixed air without disrupting the proceedings. Perhaps the use of water instead of mercury under the jar facilitated that operation. After depriving "the air of all that part absorbable by limewater," and finding as before that the remainder still extinguished candles and gave no reaction with nitrous air, they mixed this air "deprived of its fixable part" with "4 parts of dephlogisticated air reduceable to ⅑ [by the nitrous air test] against 22 parts [of the residual air], that is to say ⅙. From that mixture there resulted an air in which a candle burned and which appeared similar to common air."[15]

Lavoisier and his associates had again successfully completed an analysis of common air by respiration and synthesis by chemical operations. Now they moved beyond the simple confirmation of Lavoisier's original result.

The interpretation that respiration leaves a residue of fixed air and another unrespirable portion, or mophette, would invite a further experimental analysis in which the effects of the mophette are eliminated by placing the animal in dephlogisticated air. That is, in fact, just what the three investigators did next, carrying out a second set of experiments closely paralleling those they had already performed.

> At 25 minutes after noon we introduced, with the same precautions as in experiment 5, and maintaining very precisely the same conditions, a robin into a jar inverted in water in the apparatus of M. Priestley [apparently a pneumatic trough]. The jar was filled with dephlogisticated air reducible to ⅓.
>
> The animal appeared dull and downcast, just as the one in experiment 5 did; it soon had a rapid respiration. Nevertheless it remained quite tranquil until 1:45. By then its respiration was becoming visibly inconvenienced; it became agitated and fell several times on its side; moreover all of the phenomena were the same as in the fifth experiment. The animal experienced the same symptoms. It died at 3:21. The air at the end of the experiment was diminished by about one-quarter of its volume, that is to say by about 12 cubic inches, or perhaps more.[16]

The remainder of the experiments they carried out were tests corresponding to those they had performed on the air remaining after the experiment with ordinary air. A candle burned in it "with an enlarged flame and crackling." When they "combined dephlogisticated air vitiated by the respiration of the robin with nitrous air," copious red fumes appeared and the volume decreased considerably. By the standard of this test the air was, therefore, still quite "pure," or "dephlogisticated." Nevertheless, when they passed the air successively through six bottles filled with limewater, they observed a precipitation, principally in the first bottle, and the volume of the air was reduced by almost a fifth. When the air thus deprived of its "fixable part" was again tested with nitrous air the result was identical to the result obtained prior to that operation.[17]

These tests were all consistent with the interpretation that the bird had consumed some of the dephlogisticated air and had produced fixed air, so that after they had removed the latter the remaining residue was still dephlogisticated air. Lavoisier was evidently puzzled, however, about why the bird had died when four-fifths of the most respirable part of the air should still have been available to it. To explain that result he devised an ad hoc hypothesis which shows that he probably tacitly assumed that the death of animals is due to the absence of respirable air rather than to the effect on them of the fixed air they produce:

> We noticed that, fixed air being heavier than common air, and the latter heavier than dephlogisticated air, it was possible that the bird had suffocated in a small layer of fixed air above which there was an atmosphere of air purer than common air. It is also possible that it had died of cold.[18]

Although it is possible that he had in mind that the bird died because it was *in* the fixed air, I believe the thrust of his reasoning must have been that the layer of fixed air served to isolate the bird from the respirable air. It was an ill-considered argument, not because of the hindsight judgment that Lavoisier knew nothing of the laws of the mixture of gases, but because he had already observed in 1773 that a bird placed in pure fixed air dies instantly.[19]

To test the first of the two possibilities he had posed, the next morning Lavoisier, Trudaine, and Montigny put another bird in the dephlogisticated air in which the previous one had died, but placed it so that its head was higher in the jar. The bird nevertheless died after about an hour. In the residual air this second bird had died in, a lighted candle still burned with a large, brilliant flame. A third bird placed in the residue died quickly, but even after that a candle burned brightly. Lavoisier noted, in contrast, that a candle placed in the residue of "common air vitiated by the residue of the first bird was instantly extinguished."[20]

The last two experiments of the day consisted of tests of the effects of burning charcoal and candles in "pure dephlogisticated air." The former "gave a brilliant white light and lost much of its volume as it fell from the top to the bottom of the jar." The candle burned brightly and reduced the volume of the air by about a third before it went out. The residue, passed through water, diminished by another third, after which a candle burned in it and nitrous air reacted with it "almost as with common air." The residue therefore consisted, Lavoisier concluded, "of two-thirds fixed air, and one-third common air."[21]

II

In spite of secondary difficulties over the interpretation of the experiments in dephlogisticated air, Lavoisier must have returned from Montigny confident that the main points in his demonstration were secure. While Trudaine and Montigny planned to pursue further supporting experiments on their own,[22] Lavoisier began to prepare a paper on respiration for presentation at the Academy. As he worked on it he found that, although the results he had to report were clear enough, it was not easy to state how his own experiments and conclusions related to the existing state of the subject. He began his first draft boldly:

> Of all the phenomena of the animal economy, none is more striking than respiration. If, on the one hand, we know little about the purpose of that function, we know on the other hand that it is so essential to life that it cannot *cease for a few* [Lavoisier then crossed out "cease for a few," wrote "be interrupted for a few moments," crossed that out also, and wrote finally] be suspended for a few moments without causing the death of the animal.[23]

After adding a paragraph on the fact that there are many airs in which animals cannot respire, Lavoisier summed up the current situation in a way that reveals how central to his thinking Priestley's experiments and views on respiration had become.

> Modern experiments on the air, and especially those of M. Priestley, have begun to spread great light on this subject. M. Priestley has even believed that he is in a position to adopt an opinion on the use of respiration, and he has published a very interesting booklet on that subject. [Lavoisier had in mind the reprint of Priestley's article "Observations on respiration, and the use of the blood," discussed at the beginning of the present chapter.] I acknowledge that, notwithstanding the respect I have for the opinions of M. Priestley, it is impossible for me to share his opinions on the subject.[24]

After declaring that he could not at the moment discuss the reasons for his divergence, and that he would limit himself to a succinct description of the principal experiments he had made and the results to which they had led him, Lavoisier began abruptly to describe an experiment on the calcination of mercury. There either the manuscript ended, or the remainder has been lost.

It is evident from the foregoing that Lavoisier was straining to state diplomatically the delicate position he felt himself to be in with regard to Priestley. He was at once heavily indebted and eager to establish his intellectual independence. In his effort to express an appropriate balance between his appreciation of Priestley and his disagreement with him, Lavoisier corrected and recorrected the preceding paragraph. Perhaps to dilute the impression that Priestley was the only person with whom he had to reckon, he expanded the first sentence to read: "The experiments of Hales and those of Cigna and especially those of M. Priestley have begun to spread a great light on that important subject." As he read that revision over, however, it must have seemed to Lavoisier that the change relegated Priestley's latest investigations unfairly to a status similar to the much older efforts of Hales and of Cigna; so he eliminated "and especially those of Priestley," and elaborated instead on what he had said in the second sentence of his original paragraph:

> M. Priestley has gone much further, and he believes himself to be able, *on the basis of very delicate and very ingenious experiments* [Lavoisier afterward crossed out the phrase I have italicized] [to conclude] that the respiration of animals has the property of phlogisticating the air, as the calcination of metals and many other chemical procedures do, and that it [the air] does not cease to be respirable until the moment at which it is surcharged, or to put it a better way, is saturated with phlogiston.[25]

Lavoisier had even more trouble expressing precisely his own position regarding the views of Priestley summarized here. To enhance the impression of his admiration for Priestley he changed the original phrase "notwithstanding the respect I have for the opinions of M. Priestley" to "notwithstanding the respect for the opinions of M. Priestley with which I am imbued," and then tried, one after another, different ways of explaining why he could not agree with him. After writing, "The experiments of which I am about to give an account have not permitted me to share his view," he discarded this justification, reverting to the simple "It has not been possible for me to share his view." After trying three more ways to say he would not discuss his reasons for disagreeing, he finished this tortuous exercise by beginning the final sentence of his introduction, "Thus, without pausing to discuss the exp[eriments]," deleting the unfinished word "experiments," starting to substitute "results" but crossing out that word too before he had completed it, then crossing out "to discuss" and substituting "to refute the views of M. Priestley." Reaching for safe ground, he completed the sentence with "I shall restrict myself to making a succinct exposition of the principal experiments with which I have been occupied, and the results to which they have led me."[26] We may note that, even as Lavoisier was declining to go into his disagreement with Priestley, he was eliminating his initial impulse to include the experimental basis for Priestley's theory of respiration, restricting even the issue he would not now discuss to Priestley's "opinion."

I have described these superficially minor editorial revisions in detail because they reveal a great deal about Lavoisier's state of mind as he sought to enter the public arena in the study of respiration. They suggest that he was either reluctant or unprepared to deal with the broader significance of whatever experimental results he was ready to impart. Moreover, they betray the ambivalence he felt toward Priestley. He was searching anxiously for words which would simultaneously pay the respect due to the acknowledged leader in the field of respiration and challenge his leadership; yet he appeared unwilling to elucidate his reasons for taking up such a position.

Perhaps unsatisfied with his cursory summation, Lavoisier took a different tack, and tried to bypass the whole question of the relation of his work to that of others by asserting that previous views were not worth discussing. "Of all the subjects which have exercised physiologists," he began, but rejected that false start and began again:

> Of all the phenomena of the animal economy respiration seems to have been up until now one of the most difficult to explain, and although a great number of physiologists have written on that subject, one must agree that there exists nothing on that subject which is completely satisfying.[27]

In the next paragraph Lavoisier maintained that the new methods for investigating salubrious and injurious airs provided the means to push back the limits of knowledge about the subject. "It is incredible," he went on,

> how many systems have been imagined in order to explain the purpose of respiration. Everything that could be said has been said, but since the true, the false, and the probable were not supported, the majority of physicians afterward believed they should suspend judgment.
>
> I have nothing absolutely new to say concerning the purpose of respiration, and that acknowledgment excuses me here from giving a history of what has been done in that subject and from giving credit to those who have preceded me in the same path.[28]

Undoubtedly realizing that he could not get away with so cavalier a dismissal of what had gone before, Lavoisier returned to his first draft and reworked the paragraphs dealing with his predecessors until he had achieved a graceful acknowledgment of Priestley's preeminence in the field, balanced by a tactful, if still unilluminating, explanation for his inability to accept Priestley's conclusions:

> The experiments of several physicians, and especially of M. Hales and of M. Cigna, had begun to spread some light on this important subject; *but none of them* [Lavoisier then deleted the

> phrase I have italicized] since then M. Priestley, in a booklet he published last year in London, has pushed back the limits of our knowledge much further, and he has sought to prove, through very ingenious, very delicate experiments, of a very original type, that the respiration of animals has the property of phlogisticating the air, as the calcination of metals and many other chemical procedures do, and that it does not cease to be respirable until the moment that it is surcharged, and in some fashion saturated with phlogiston.
>
> As attractive as the theory of this celebrated physician appears to be at first glance, however numerous and well performed the experiments with which he has sought to support them, I acknowledge that I have found them deficient for explaining so many phenomena, that I believe myself justified to place them in doubt. Consequently I have worked according to another plan, and I find myself inevitably led by the succession of my experiments to conclusions entirely opposed to his. I shall not stop at this time to discuss each of the experiments of M. Priestley in detail, or to show how they all prove to support the view which I shall develop in this memoir. I shall limit myself to discussing those which are my own, and to report their result.[29]

Lavoisier's struggles with the introduction to his first memoir on respiration involve more than questions of style and good taste, for they touch on a problem deeply embedded within the scientific enterprise. One of the most serious questions a scientist must face in presenting his own conclusions is how to connect them with the collective stream of investigations to which he wishes to add his contribution. He must show both that the previous development of the subject has left important problems unsolved and that his work either achieves what his colleagues will recognize as solutions, or at least brings such solutions nearer. Only in that way can his work become part of the ongoing stream, and its reception may depend as much on how he defines its relation to the work of his colleagues as on its intrinsic merit. The task requires the writer simultaneously to credit his colleagues with what is due them, representing his contribution as building in some sense on what they have done; and to point out their shortcomings, so that they will accept his work as an advance on their own. To err on the side of generosity and modesty is to risk appearing unoriginal. To err on the other side is to risk alienating those whom one needs to convince. Lavoisier approached this aspect of his scientific writing with the same care that he devoted to the formulation of his own views, and applied to it the same consummate skill.

In the experimental section of his memoir Lavoisier described the calcination and reduction of mercury, followed by the respiration experiment already discussed above, organizing the two accounts so as to emphasize the similarity between the two sets of operations.[30] It is difficult to be certain whether or not the first of these was the same experiment that he had recorded, beginning April 9, in his notebook, and that was described in the preceding chapter. The initial weights of mercury used are different, but Lavoisier may have adjusted his figures for some reason. If he had performed another experiment, the second one did not differ in any essential way from the first.

From the results he had obtained, Lavoisier concluded,

> It therefore appeared to be proven that respiration acts only on a portion of the air that is respirable, and that this portion does not exceed a quarter of the air of the atmosphere, that the remainder enters the lungs and leaves them again as it had entered, without change or alteration.[31]

This passage, which Lavoisier left out of the subsequent drafts of the memoir, reveals, I believe, what he initially considered to be the main point he had established in these experiments. The idea he had tentatively expressed in his earliest surviving note about respiration, in 1774, that ordinary air is "composed of two substances, of which the lungs bring about the separation of one of the two,"[32] he had now triumphantly confirmed. Moreover, he could now identify, in terms of other chemical operations, what that portion separated in the lungs was; it was the same highly respirable air that one could procure by reducing a mercury calx without charcoal.

The analogy Lavoisier perceived between calcination and respiration was more than a suggestive starting point for carrying out the experiments which proved the action of respiration on the atmosphere, more even than a means to organize his understanding of respiration afterward; for the proof of the action itself depended upon the validity of that analogy. Although his demonstration was a form of analysis and synthesis, Lavoisier was not in a position to carry out the synthesis in a direct way by recombining the products of the analysis, because he had no practical access to the portion of the air he supposed to be absorbed in the lungs. Instead he supplied the air for the synthetic operation from the calx of mercury. His assumption that these airs were identical, although supported by the fact that the air obtained from mercury calx is highly respirable, rested mainly on the fact that in the reconstituted air a candle would burn and a bird could respire in the same manner as in the common air with which he had begun. Those simple qualitative tests were far from a rigorous chemical identification. Lavoisier had also reconstituted what appeared to him to be common air from respired air in the same general way during the previous spring, as we have seen, even though we can tell that since he had overlooked the presence of fixed air and therefore not removed it, the recomposed air was not really pure common air. Thus the explicit proof by analysis and synthesis was less decisive than he took it to be, and the reasoning through which he "proved" that respiration acts on a certain portion of the air was rooted in his implicit reliance on the analogy itself.

Following the paragraph in his draft that we have just analyzed, on "what appeared to be proven," Lavoisier again extended his conclusion to incorporate both of the "two causes" with which he was now familiar:

> One has just seen that in order to reestablish air vitiated by respiration, and to restore it to the state of respirable air, it was necessary to bring about two effects: (1) to remove from that air the portion of fixed air which it contained, by means of limewater or a caustic alkali; (2) to add to it a quantity of air which is better than common air, equal to that which it has lost. It is a necessary consequence that respiration produces the inverse of these two effects. It absorbs the truly respirable portion contained in the air, and it yields to it in the place [of that portion] a portion of air susceptible of being absorbed by lime and by alkalies, which is almost in the state of fixed air.[33]

Afterward Lavoisier strengthened the last statement by changing the final phrase to read "and which appears to be precisely in the state of fixed gas or air."

It will be immediately evident that here Lavoisier had reached one of the most fundamental conclusions in the history of respiration. Whatever interpretation one might place upon the phenomena, now or later, this identification of a specific portion of the air—an air not yet even given a stable name—which animals absorb from the atmosphere, and of another air, still referred to by Black's anachronistic term fixed air, which animals emit in approximately equal volumes into the air, laid the foundation for all subsequent development of the subject. Less striking from the perspective of our distant time, but no less interesting from the standpoint of Lavoisier's immediate situation, is the indirect form of the inference by which he came to the conclusion. Lavoisier treated his results as determinations not of the changes that respiration itself produces on the air, but of the changes necessary to restore respired air to ordinary air, from which one could deduce that the respiratory effects must be the inverse of these changes. The distinction is not merely semantic, but reflective of the procedures he used. There are two likely sources for this approach. It was, in the first place, an adaptation of the strategy of analysis and synthesis so central to eighteenth-century chemistry, and which Lavoisier had already applied in the case of the demonstration of the composition of the air through the calcination and reduction of mercury. The "demonstration," however, was no longer of the composition of the air itself. Instead Lavoisier utilized his prior knowledge of the composition of the air, and of the processes necessary to compose it, in order to infer the processes he needed to reverse to restore the air. A second source for this approach, as suggested in the previous chapter, was Priestley's preoccupation with processes, such as agitation in water, which restore respired air. Lavoisier had already been reasoning from the restorative operation to the inverse natural process while he was still thinking about these processes in terms of phlogiston.

A further explanation for Lavoisier's indirect approach is that at just that time there was probably no more direct way open to him. It is true that when he removed fixed air from the respired air in caustic alkali, he might have viewed his procedure as a direct determination of fixed air formed in respiration rather than as the first step in his restoration of ordinary air. (The reasons for his peculiar outlook in this case will become clearer below.) The absorption of a portion of the air in respiration—the process which most interested him—however, he could not demonstrate directly, because he had no means to identify that portion in some other form or combination afterward; nor could he decisively prove by an analysis of the residual air itself that its altered properties resulted from the loss of a particular portion of it, for the tests used to characterize such airs (the nitrous air test, the fact that candles went out and animals died in it) merely reaffirmed that it was unrespirable air. The only means open to him to establish *what* had disappeared was to argue indirectly from the fact that when he replaced it with an air from another source, the combination appeared qualitatively like the original air. Almost any other approach to the question assumes techniques for analyzing airs which he had not yet developed, or a conception of the respiratory process which at this particular time he did not have in mind. There is no written indication that Lavoisier had thought his way through alternative ways to go about the investigation until he selected this as the only one available to him; but whether he picked it through such a conscious process of sifting, or only by intuition, his choice is an admirable example of his ability to find a circuitous route where a straighter one did not yet exist, and to follow it to a conclusion of great consequence.

In this same paragraph, and in other places in the manuscript as well, Lavoisier referred to "air vitiated by respiration." I have maintained that when he used that phrase in April he may still have been living partly in the conceptual world in which respiration was perceived as qualitatively altering the air. The fact that he continued to use the word "vitiate" here, when he had become quite clear that respiration removes a portion of the air and replaces it with another air, while the remaining portion of the inspired air leaves the lungs unchanged, may seem to refute my argument. That is possible, but it is more plausible that Lavoisier's clarification of the process was altering the meaning of the word "vitiate." He might have chosen to abandon the word as connoting a conception from which he was freeing himself. Instead he imported it into his new framework, allowing a residue of the older conception to linger on in the language of the new.

When Lavoisier wrote that the difference between the air remaining after a bird had respired in common air and that left when mercury is calcined "led me to suppose that there are two causes entangled in respiration" (m'a fait présumer qu'il se compliquoit dans la respiration deux causes),[34] it was, I think, no accident that he used the verb "se compliquer." From his subsequent responses there is good reason to infer that he regarded this recognition as a complication of the problem, rather than a solution. It was, in fact, an unwelcome intrusion into the analogy between the calcination of mercury and respiration around which he had been organizing the whole investigation. As he turned to interpret his results, Lavoisier treated the formation of fixed air in respiration not as one of the objects of his research, but as an almost extraneous effect, for which he had to compensate by removing the fixed air from the respired air in order to restore the otherwise complete resemblance between respiration and the calcination. Moreover, he very nearly removed fixed air conceptually from his discussion of the significance of the results. This tendency is especially apparent in a paragraph (appearing in the third draft of his memoir, but which was perhaps included in the lost portions of one of the preceding drafts) that he used to make his transition from the experiments with mercury to those with the sparrow:

> These preliminary truths are about to lead us to some simple conclusions concerning the use of respiration in animals; like the calcination of metals, this animal function has the property of rendering the air insalubrious and of reducing it to the state of mophette. In this state candles can no longer burn, animals can no longer live; it can no longer be diminished by nitrous air, or give red vapors when one combines it with it [nitrous air]. Another conformity which is encountered between air which has served for the calcination of metals and that which has served for the respiration of animals is that in the one and in the other there is a diminution of volume; finally, that in the one and in the other the state of salubrity can be restored by an addition of the air extracted from the calx of mercury.[35]

Thus his preoccupation with the correspondence between these two processes was so intense that in the very aftermath of recognizing the significant difference between the airs resulting from respiration and calcination, Lavoisier totally ignored this difference in summing up the properties of respired air.

After reading over the fair copy of this draft, Lavoisier must have perceived the one-sidedness of his description: for he eliminated the whole paragraph, replacing it with the vague statement that, since air which has been respired "has much in common with that in which metals have been calcined, knowledge regarding the one will naturally apply to the other."[36]

In the final portion of his manuscript, a discussion of the physiological consequences of his results, Lavoisier focused exclusively upon the absorption of the respirable portion of the air. "But what becomes of that portion of the air? In what way does it contribute to the life and health of the animal? It is here that the combined aid of experiment and analogy can, up to a certain point, clarify matters."[37] (The remainder of the paragraph consists of Lavoisier's description of the *two* effects, in the passage already quoted above. It is evident, however, that this sequence resulted from his not yet having arranged his presentation into a fully logical order in this draft, for the answer to the question posed here actually began two paragraphs later):

> One cannot doubt, therefore, that the respirable portion of the air becomes fixed in the lungs, and it is very probable that it combines there with the blood. That probability is transformed to a kind of certitude if one considers that it is a recognized property of the air that is better than common air to impart a red color to the bodies with which it combines. Mercury, lead, and iron provide examples. These metals, combined with the respirable portion of atmospheric air, each form a beautiful red calx. . . . It is the same with the blood of animals, it is not bright red except to the extent that it is nearly continuously in contact with the air, it becomes dark in fixed air, in every air which is not respirable, in the vacuum of a pneumatic machine. It recovers its red color, on the other hand, when it is exposed to common air, and especially to the air that is better than common air: and it is no doubt for this reason that, according to the observations of many anatomists, the blood is much brighter upon leaving the lungs than when entering it, when taken from the pulmonary vein than from the pulmonary artery.
>
> In view of such striking analogies, does it not seem that one is justified in concluding that the red color of the blood is due to its combination with the air, or rather the respirable part of the air, and that this is one of the principal objects of the fixation of the air in the animal economy[?][38]

In his concluding paragraph Lavoisier wrote, "I believe that the Theory of respiration has been established."[39] What is most obvious to us is, first, that this theory is not what is historically meant by Lavoisier's theory of respiration; and second, that it cannot withstand critical scrutiny, even if we restrict our consideration to information he had available at that moment. On the one hand, the theory ignored one of the two respiratory actions he had just demonstrated experimentally. On the other, it rested heavily on a thin analogy between the color of arterial blood and three metallic calces. Moreover, Lavoisier apparently failed to perceive a fatal logical flaw. Mercury absorbs only the quantity of respirable air necessary to convert it to the calx. Under the experimental conditions, respiration too absorbed only a limited quantity of respirable air, but that was because that portion was diminished until the bird died. Normally it would absorb respirable air continuously; but Lavoisier's theory included no provision for the removal of that air from the blood, so that it could not account for an unlimited absorption. It appears evident that he had not thought the situation through. Finally, to explain the red color of arterial blood is hardly to establish the "principal object" of respiration, if one has no idea what the functional significance of the red color might be. Meanwhile, the theory was silent concerning his original idea that respiration provides animal heat, as well as about the attempt, in his note of February 1775, to incorporate into respiration a theory of the conversion of common to fixed air.

In this attempt at a theory of respiration we once more see Lavoisier, as we observed him in 1775, fixing his attention on a specific problem but unable to bring his solution into contact with all the relevant factors in his own conceptual field. He had still not managed to link the localized areas of that field tightly into his overarching theoretical framework. In this case he was building on only one of the two overlapping ideas about respiration that he had written down earlier on separate occasions. As we have already seen, the experimental demonstration that a portion of the air is absorbed verified the query to that effect that he had put down in his first note on respiration. In his theoretical discussion he was adorning the bare notion of "the fixation of the air in the lungs" contained in that note with a more elaborate idea that the air is fixed in a combination with the blood analogous to a metallic calx.

Lavoisier may have been attracted to his theory in part because, like Priestley, he thought that he had at last an explanation for the color change of the blood in the lungs that had puzzled "anatomists" for more than a century. Beyond that, his appeal to analogy to support the theory conformed to a mode of reasoning customary within chemistry itself. Eighteenth-century chemists commonly inferred the composition of a substance they could not analyze directly by drawing analogies with the composition of similar substances which underwent corresponding changes.[40] To view arterial blood as containing a substance analogous to a calx, because it seemed to have undergone an analogous combination with the same portion of the air, and acquired the same color in the process, was in keeping with these general practices.

The driving force behind Lavoisier's theory, however, must have been the momentum that the analogy between calcination and respiration had acquired in his thinking, through its success in stimulating and shaping his experimental investigation of respiration. Analogies are now widely acknowledged to be important to scientific creativity, because they can suggest relationships within the less well known side of the comparison before these relationships are accessible to direct inspection. In this sense Lavoisier's analogy had already proven its value, and it was therefore natural for him to press it further. The productive features of analogies are, however, often quickly exhausted, and they then limit and divert thought. From our vantage point we can see that Lavoisier had already entered such a phase in his commitment to the analogy. Because the analogy left no room for the observed formation of fixed air, Lavoisier could not find room for that process in his theory.

The restrictive influence of his analogy may also explain why Lavoisier omitted animal heat from his theory. Unlike combustion, most calcinations did not emit conspicuous quantities of heat; in fact one had to heat mercury continuously in order to calcine it. Therefore, although compatible with the idea that respiration releases heat, the analogy was not conducive to the further development of that view. Moreover it may well be that after his rather unsatisfactory efforts to introduce his conception of a matter of fire into explanations of various specific phenomena in 1775, he had become more guarded about incorporating that elusive substance into his reasoning about respiration. Related difficulties may have deterred him from extending his theory to encompass the formation of fixed air. Notwithstanding that he had already considered the possibility that respiration converts common air to fixed air—an idea readily modifiable to accommodate the subsequent solidification of his understanding that only a specific portion of the atmosphere takes part—he still had not solved the problem of how the composition of respirable air and of fixed air are related. He therefore lacked the means to envision the way in which the one may be changed to the other. He had observed "two effects" in respiration, but he had not linked them into a causal relationship with one another.

Unlike some of the ideas contained in his earlier notes, Lavoisier's theory of respiration was no casual thought tentatively entertained, or put down as a starting point for further meditation. This idea he had worked into an advanced draft of a formal scientific paper. Clearly something about the theory appealed to him strongly enough to suppress critical judgment. We might even say that, for a time, this normally cool, cautious thinker had allowed himself to be swept along by a wave of enthusiasm.

Lavoisier revised his manuscript for the fourth time as he prepared it for presentation at the public meeting of the Academy which marked its reopening after the October vacation. Aside from a final refinement of his statements about Priestley, he made only minor stylistic changes in the introduction and experimental sections. As previously described, he dropped the summary of the properties of respired air that had made it appear identical to the air in which mercury had been calcined. His statement of the immediate result that there are two effects of respiration stood unchanged. His answer to the question "What becomes of that respirable portion of the air absorbed in the lungs" also remained substantially intact; but by dropping several statements and adding others in their place, he modified significantly the tone and emphasis of his theoretical conclusions. Eliminating his reference to the "observations of many anatomists" that blood becomes red when it passes through the lungs, he inserted instead "the experiments of M. Cigna, of M._____, and of M. Priestley leave no doubt that [the respirable portion of the air] combines with the blood." He supported the assertion he had already made that the blood is red only when it is in continuous contact with the air by introducing the phrase "all of the modern experiments teach us" that this is so.[41] Thus he shifted the burden of the evidence behind this aspect of his theory from the old physiological observations to recent investigations. In view of the metamorphoses of his introductory statements discussed earlier, I believe that here too it was the latest publication of Priestley on this subject that loomed in the forefront, and that these additions reveal, as the earlier version did not, that Priestley's experiments exposing blood to dephlogisticated and phlogisticated airs had served as one of the main inspirations for Lavoisier's theory. One might infer from the fact that he put these passages only into this late draft that he had first reached his opinion on the basis of the older observations and later found more convincing support in Priestley's experiments. His preoccupation with Priestley in the introductory section from the first draft on, however, argues for a germinal influence whose specific nature he was only making clearer in this revision.

If, on the one hand, Lavoisier tried to strengthen the argument for his theory of respiration by alluding to the most recent experimental evidence, he had, on the other, already grown more circumspect about the status and significance of the theory. The most visible indication is that, in his summary of the theory, he struck out (in addition to the clause referring to the observations of the anatomists) the entire concluding paragraph asserting to have elucidated one of the "principal objects of the fixation of the air in the animal economy," and the claim in the next paragraph that "the Theory of respiration has been established." In the place of these sweeping conclusions he put a restrained resumé of the direct experimental results.[42] There is no indication that Lavoisier had detected the fallacies in his theory that appear so obvious from our distance, but he was recovering his more customary prudence concerning the theoretical inferences one can draw out of an experimental investigation. The evolution of his mood is clearly reflected in the successive titles he gave to his memoir. The original title of the third draft (the first two were untitled) was "Experiments on the decomposition of the air in the lungs and on the use of respiration in animals." Afterward he changed the second half of his title to read ". . . and on one of the principal uses of respiration in the animal economy."[43] He repeated that version in the fourth draft, but he altered it again, first changing "uses" to "effects," then deleting nearly all of the second half and ending up with "Experiments on the decomposition of the air in the lungs of animals."[44] One could not wish for a more graphic chart of Lavoisier's step-by-step retreat toward a modest appraisal of his achievement.

The public meeting of the Academy of November 13 at which Lavoisier proposed to read his memoir was too crowded to allow him time to do so.[45] Convinced that his results were important enough to warrant establishing his priority, he had the secretary of the Academy, Condorcet, date and sign the contents of his paper on November 15.[46] The postponement of his presentation thus forced on him was fortunate, for in the meantime he had some very significant second thoughts about his theory of respiration. Somehow he came to see that he must consider an alternative to his theory. On the blank pages in the sheaf of folded papers containing the manuscript Condorcet had signed, Lavoisier began to work out the consequences of this new realization (see Figure 1).

> Of two things, one, either a portion of pure air, dephlogisticated air contained in the air of the atmosphere, is absorbed during respiration and replaced by an almost equal quantity of fixed air or mephitic gas which the lungs restore to its place, or else the effect of the respiration is to change that same portion of dephlogisticated air into fixed air in the lungs.[47]

The character of this paragraph—Lavoisier made several changes in the wording as he went along, of which I have indicated only the resulting version, and he rewrote the ideas in a different order in the left-hand margin—suggests that he was here expressing for the first time the view that dephlogisticated air, or pure air, is converted in the lungs into fixed air. This alternative appears to have the major advantage that it incorporates both of the observed "effects" into a single theory.

If this is in fact the first version of his new idea, then we can almost watch the germ of Lavoisier's second, most significant theory of respiration becoming visible on this page. Lavoisier himself, however, did not at the time perceive the alternative as clearly superior, or even as preferable, to his earlier one. As he developed the two alternatives, he appeared to be debating with himself over what attitude to take to the new situation.

> One knows that, with an addition of powdered charcoal, dephlogisticated air can be completely converted into fixed air or mephitic gas, and this circumstance seems to give some weight to the second of these opinions, but on the other hand, strong analogies seem to lead one to believe that the portion of dephlogisti-

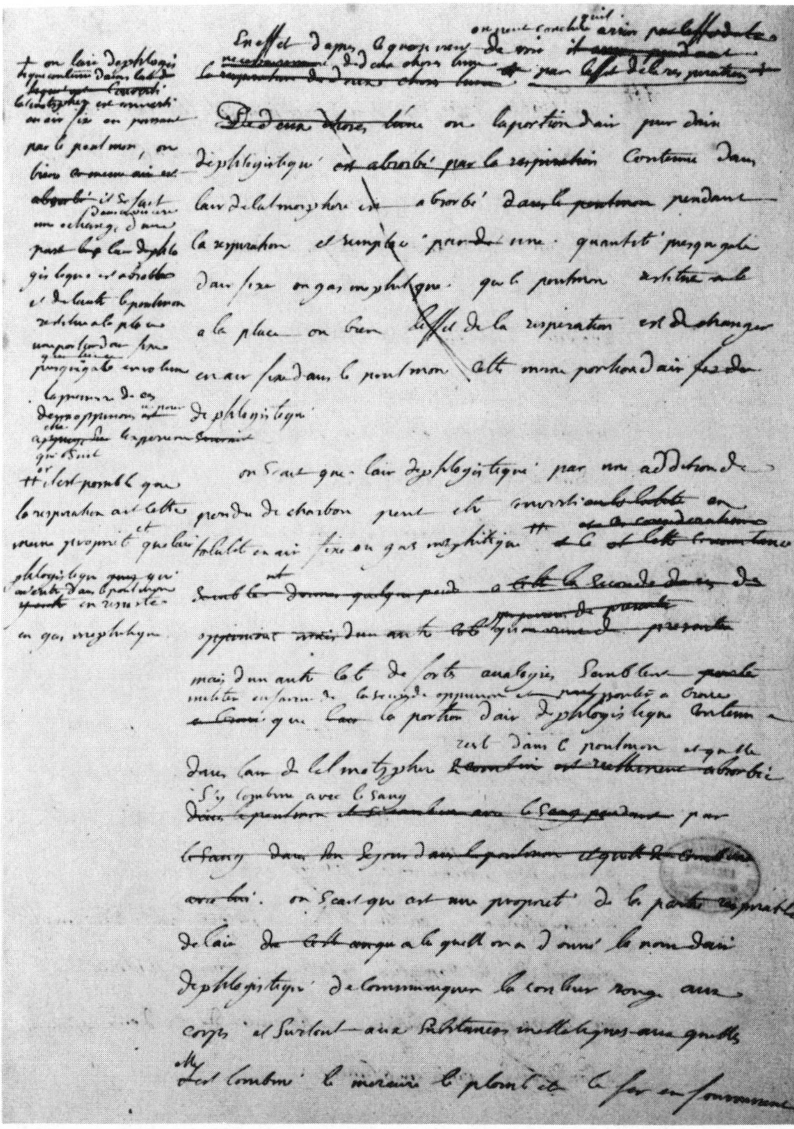

Figure 1. Page from manuscript of "Expériences sur la décomposition de l'air dans le poulmon des animaux." The main text on right includes the two paragraphs quoted on pp. 82–84. The passage beginning "Now it is possible that respiration has this same property . . ." is added in the left-hand margin. Lavoisier, Fiche 1349, Archives of the Académie des Sciences de Paris.

> cated air contained in the atmospheric air remains in the lungs and that it combines with the blood.[48]

Repeating next the argument he had already formulated in the main manuscript that dephlogisticated air imparts a red color to substances with which it combines, he again enumerated the same three metallic calces, and ended with the assertion "If one finds, as we have just seen, that in both the calcination of metals and the respiration of animals all the circumstances are the same, down to the color of the residues, *how, therefore, could one doubt* [he crossed out the italicized words and wrote instead] why, therefore, would one refuse to conclude that the red color of the blood is due to the combination of dephlogisticated air with an animal fluid." Modern experiments, especially those of Cigna and Priestley, he added, "all seem to concur in that conclusion." Recognizing after he had written this, however, that the authors of these experiments had not expressed such an opinion, Lavoisier later replaced that statement with a comment in the margin: "Although M. Cigna and M. Priestley and the other modern authors who have occupied themselves with this subject have not drawn that conclusion, I daresay that there is hardly one of their experiments that does not tend to establish it." After summarizing their results, he wrote, with unusual fervor, "So many analogies, so many probabilities approach certitude, but without taking sides between the two opinions . . . and resting only on what is purely factual, I believe I can regard as proven . . ."—Lavoisier listed as proven the direct experimental conclusions, that respiration and calcination absorb only a certain portion of the atmosphere. Not satisfied that the phrase supporting the second opinion was strong enough, he rewrote it to say "So many analogies, so many probabilities scarcely permit one to doubt that the blood results from the combination of some animal fluid with dephlogisticated air." Returning to the beginning of the same paragraph, he shifted the balance of his opinion still more in favor of his original theory, by using even stronger language to introduce it, while reducing the alternative to a mere possibility. In place of the sentence beginning "this circumstance seems to give some weight to the second of these opinions . . . ," he wrote, "Now it is possible that respiration has this same property and that the [de]phlogisticated air which has entered the lungs comes out as mephitic gas; but, on the other hand, strong analogies seem to militate in favor of the second opinion. . . ." (Mephitic gas appears in this context to have been a loose synonym for fixed air.)[49]

What all these verbal maneuvers suggest is that when it occurred to Lavoisier that the dephlogisticated air absorbed in respiration might be converted to fixed air, he was not attracted to this theory; on the contrary, it appeared to him as a threat to the theory he preferred. The weak form of his statement, "it is possible" that the inspired air is converted to fixed air, contrasts with the force of words such as "militate" in favor of the other view. Yet even if he favored so visibly his original theory, Lavoisier's critical judgment forced him in the end to attempt to detach himself from either one, subordinating them both to the conclusions he regarded as proven. Even the most disciplined of scientific thinkers must sometimes struggle to avoid becoming captive to cherished ideas.

In another effort to formulate these alternatives, contained on a different page within the same folder, Lavoisier managed to assume a more neutral attitude. "I find myself in this respect," he wrote, "led to two consequences, between which the experiments have not yet put me in a position to decide." After stating the two theories very much as in the paragraph quoted above, he ended, "Each of these two opinions has its degree of probability."[50]

On April 9, 1977, Lavoisier was finally able to read a paper on respiration to the Academy. According to the minutes of the meeting its title was "Memoir on the changes which the blood undergoes in the lungs, and on the mechanism of respiration." This paper was not published in its original form; historians disagree over which, if any, of his subsequent publications may have incorporated its contents;[51] and titles given in minutes of the Academy proceedings are not always accurate. It is therefore not possible to ascertain precisely its relation to the memoir whose development we have been following. Perhaps it was the paper he had planned to give in November, the different title reflecting the impression of the recording secretary that Lavoisier's central interest was his "first" theory of respiration with its explanation of the color change of blood.

Shortly afterward, at the public session of the Academy held during Easter, Lavoisier presented a new version of his memoir. The introductory and experimental portions were nearly identical to those in the manuscript Condorcet had signed; the paragraphs describing his conclusions were based on the pages he had added afterward to that manuscript.[52]

Lavoisier revised his memoir yet again, adding the changes in the wide left-hand margin of the fair copy, and reread it during the meeting of May 3. Once more he changed its title, from "Experiments on the decomposition of the air in the lungs and on one of the principal effects of respiration in the animal economy," to "Experiments on the respiration of animals and on the changes which the air undergoes while passing through the lungs."[53] The new title signifies that he had finally been able to subordinate his enthusiasm for his interpretation of the color change of the blood sufficiently to present the changes the *air* undergoes in the lungs as the subject of the investigation; and that he had detached himself sufficiently from his earlier preoccupation with the absorption of respirable air to encompass in that subject both of the "effects" of respiration.

In his conclusion Lavoisier now introduced the two theoretical interpretations of the experimental results as "equally probable." He gave increased attention, however, to the alternative he had reluctantly admitted at first, that "the respirable portion of the air . . . is converted to fixed air in passing through the lungs." For the sentence "One knows that . . . dephlogisticated air can be completely converted into fixed air," he substituted:

> I showed, in a memoir read at the public Easter meeting of 1775, and printed in the journal of Abbé Rozier, that dephlogisticated air can be converted entirely to fixed air by an addition of powdered charcoal, and I shall show in other memoirs that there are several other methods to carry out the same conversion.[54]

He thus reinforced the statement which came next in the memoir, "It is possible that respiration would have this same property, and that the dephlogisticated air which enters the lungs comes back out again as mephitic gas [fixed air]," with a claim to have demonstrated himself what he had earlier merely noted as "known." That interpolation did not necessarily make the inference that the same process occurs in respiration stronger—it was still only "possible"—but it indicated a growing personal interest in the possibility. The demonstration contained in the memoir of 1775 to which he referred was, in fact, less direct than he now depicted it. It had been mainly from a comparison of the airs released in the reduction of mercury calx with and without charcoal that he had then inferred that "common air is changed into fixed air when it combines with charcoal."[55] The fact that he now represented that conclusion as a direct experimental demonstration of the conversion of dephlogisticated air to fixed air suggests that he now felt a certain pressure to provide better evidence in support of this theory of respiration than he had currently available. He put the best light that he could on his older indirect evidence, pending the opportunity to obtain stronger evidence in the future.

Concomitant with the increased emphasis he gave, in making these revisions, to the theory that respiration converts respirable air to fixed air, Lavoisier subtly diluted his support for the theory that respirable air combines with the blood, by making small verbal changes. He modified the enthusiastic "So many analogies, so many probabilities combined scarcely permit one to doubt that the blood results from the combination of some animal fluid with dephlogisticated air" to "In the light of so many analogies, so many probabilities, it would seem that one is authorized to think that the blood is . . ." Then he crossed out the whole passage. Where he had written that, in view of the analogy between red blood and the red metallic calces, "why . . . would one refuse to conclude" that the color of the blood is due to respirable air, he now substituted "can one not infer" it. A residual special fondness for this theory remained, however, in his retention of the phrase "strong analogies seem to militate in favor" of it.[56]

Through the modifications in successive drafts of his memoir Lavoisier had moved from the unreserved claim "I believe that the theory of respiration has been established" to a guarded assessment of two "equally probable" alternative theories. I have treated this progression as a gradual liberation from the beguiling effect of an analogy that had guided him through a successful investigation. The repeated alterations in his attitude illustrate more, however, than the difficulty with which a scientist contends with biases introduced by his local experiences; for it is no easy matter to state accurately the degree of probability one can attribute to a theory in its formative stages. Scientific ideas are seldom proven or disproven in a single move. Scientists typically speak of results that "strengthen" or "weaken," "support" or fail to support a given view. There is a continuous range, from improbability to near certitude, through which a proposition may ascend or descend. Recently Latour and Woolgar have attempted to classify "statement types" according to their place on a scale of modalities from conjecture to that which is generally accepted as fact.[57] There are, however, neither strictly objective procedures for placing a given statement at its appropriate level, nor uniformly graded verbal forms with which to express these levels unambiguously; yet scientists must regularly make such judgments, and find language to convey the degree of certitude they wish to attach to their conclusions. Highly sensitive to these problems, Lavoisier took care to distinguish levels of probability among the various inferences he drew, and to express them accurately in ordinary language. By examining the stages in the construction of his scientific memoirs we can watch a master craftsman honing his evaluations of the scientific status of his conclusions.

In the end, Lavoisier did not confine himself to a strictly suspended decision between two alternatives, but introduced a third possibility. To the simple phrase in his conclusion "Moreover, whichever of the two opinions one embraces . . . ," he added in the margin:

> be it that the respirable portion of the air combines with the blood, be it that it is changed into fixed air, or mephitic gas; be it, finally, as I am inclined to believe, that both of these effects take place during the act of respiration . . .[58]

What did Lavoisier mean by this third choice he now favored? Looking back from the perspective of later views of respiration, we almost involuntarily see him tantalizingly close to combining the two alternatives into a unified conception: that is, that respiratory air first combines with the blood in the lungs, converting it to arterial blood, and that subsequently the respirable air is converted (by implication during the course of the circulation) into fixed air. There is, however, no evidence in his writings to support the inference that Lavoisier perceived the situation that way. His views, in fact, left no room for such an interpretation, because his unquestioned assumption that respirable air is directly converted to fixed air in the lungs precluded thinking of the absorption of respirable air into the blood as a stage within that process. Nothing in this statement indicates that he connected the two processes, and he nowhere afterward elaborated on this brief suggestion. The most probable interpretation of his position is that, unable to choose between the two alternative theories, both of which now appealed to him, he straddled the issue by allowing that both processes may occur.

Was Lavoisier's realization, midway in the development of his memoir, that respirable air might be converted to fixed air in the lungs a new idea, or a revival of the idea he had put down in his note of February 1775? There is no way to know whether he remembered the idea and consciously retrieved it, or whether the idea occurred to him anew. The ideas were not, in fact, identical. In the earlier one he had suspected that common air itself is changed to fixed air, whereas he now ascribed that change only to the respirable portion of air. That difference, however, was rooted so deeply in his clarification of the composition of the atmosphere itself that he might well not have noticed the distinction. Even if we judge the new idea to be the same in essence as the old one, it had still acquired a new force, because it now explained two specific, well-documented effects, and because it no longer ignored the evidence that respiration separates the atmosphere into two portions. Whether to regard Lavoisier's present theory as a new one bearing a family resemblance to the former one, or as a modification of the old idea, is, in the end, an arbitrary choice, because there is no sharp demarcation between fitting an existing idea into a new context and replacing the idea with another one. Idea and context are not strictly separable entities.

It requires of us a special effort not to read into Lavoisier's idea that respirable air may be converted to fixed air in the lungs more than he himself perceived in it at this time. From the comparison he made to the conversion of respirable air to fixed air in the presence of charcoal, the implication fairly leaps at us that respiration is like the combustion of charcoal. That, however, is not what Lavoisier wrote. He was describing the addition of charcoal as the laboratory condition under which one can convert respirable air to fixed air, and his attention did not necessarily extend to the role of the charcoal as a possible source of the product itself. There is little to indicate that, even at this point, he had reached a clear understanding of the relation between the composition of respirable air and of fixed air. As recently as the preceding October, when Lavoisier found during the experiments at Montigny that some air derived from heating mercury alone produced a slight precipitate with limewater, he had explained the anomaly by suspecting that a leak had permitted "a little bit of phlogiston from the charcoal to pass in and alter the air."[59] At that time, therefore, he still had nothing better than the conceptual framework of phlogiston to explain the conversion of respirable air to fixed air. In the present memoir, on the other hand, he rejected Priestley's theory that respiration phlogisticates the air. With regard to any processes which change respirable air to fixed air he was probably now caught in a conceptual limbo, unable either to accept an explanation based on phlogiston or to replace it with an explanation derived from his own theoretical structure.

As he himself insisted in his conclusion, Lavoisier's continued uncertainty over his theories of respiration did not detract from the validity or the importance of what he had proven experimentally: that respiration acts only on a portion of the atmosphere; that the calcination of a metal absorbs the same portion; that an animal in a confined atmosphere perishes when it has absorbed this portion (or converted it to fixed air); and that the "mophette" which remains afterward can be restored to atmospheric air by removing the fixed air and adding a quantity of air equal to that lost.[60] For these demonstrations Lavoisier's first paper on respiration remains a landmark event in the history of that subject. The fact that this same paper came to be regarded as a landmark demonstration of the composition of the atmosphere exemplifies the impossibility of disentangling Lavoisier's investigation of respiration from his general quest to understand the processes which fix or release airs.

* * *

In this chapter we have witnessed Lavoisier tenaciously working his way toward a theory of respiration. His progress involved the interplay between investigations carried out in the laboratory and efforts at his writing table to organize his laboratory experience. It appears that he developed much of the theoretical interpretation after the experiments were over, as he strove to place his immediate results into a framework composed of his own broader experience and the state of knowledge about respiration into which he was injecting his contribution. Through the drafts of the paper that he wrote, corrected, reconsidered, and rewrote over and over, we have been able to trace the germination and growth of certain critical ideas, as well as his changing evaluation of ideas after he had thought of them. The events which we can infer from these documents enable us, I believe, to appreciate an aspect of scientific creativity that is overlooked in the descriptions that focus on flashes of insight. The emphasis so often placed on those sudden mental inspirations that occur when a scientist is not directly immersed in his investigation—when entering a bathtub, trying to fall asleep at night, dozing before a fireplace, starting to board a bus, or riding in a carriage—has promoted a one-sided paradigm of the creative scientific act. To judge from the evidence utilized above, Lavoisier acquired some of his crucial insights through the process of writing out his ideas in the preparation of a scientific paper. We cannot always tell whether a thought that led him to modify a passage, recast an argument, or develop an alternative interpretation occurred while he was still engaged in writing what he subsequently altered, or immediately afterward, or after some interval in which he occupied himself with something else; but the timing may be less significant than the fact that the new developments were the consequence of the effort to express ideas and supporting information in writing. Hans Krebs has emphasized to me that he habitually began to write his scientific papers while the investigations they were intended to report were still in progress, because it was only in that way that he could detect the gaps in his own reasoning or evidence. I suspect that Lavoisier too had to write out his ideas in order fully to grasp them, to clarify them, to find flaws in them, or to see alternatives to what had previously preoccupied his mind. The reason for this necessity is probably similar to the reason for the inconsistencies we have found between his earlier, less fully formulated notes: that the mind cannot readily encompass at one time the entire structure of a complex argument. Only by putting it on paper, concentrating on one segment of it at a time, can one construct the conceptual edifice which has not at any single instant existed in complete detail in the center of one's mental field.

4

Respiration and a General Theory of Combustion

Lavoisier ended the first full draft of his memoir on respiration with the statement that the experiments his friends Trudaine and Montigny were continuing would "throw new light, not only on the respiration of animals, but furthermore on combustion, operations which have more in common than one would think at first sight, and we can only wait with impatience until they present them [the results of their experiments] to the public."[1]

Trudaine and Montigny never did present such results, if they ever, in fact, completed the experiments; so that we are left in the dark concerning their nature, as well as concerning what Lavoisier may have had in mind behind his hint about the relationship they might establish between respiration and combustion. To draw a general comparison between them was hardly novel, since, as we have seen, others had done so in the past, and Priestley had recently stressed their common characteristics. We cannot tell whether Lavoisier was thinking only of combustion in general, or whether he had picked out a particular form of combustion—whether that of phosphorus or sulphur, oils and waxes, or charcoal—as more especially resembling respiration.

A clue to what Lavoisier meant appears at first to lie in the fact that the last two of the experiments he had carried out with his friends in Montigny involved candles. In one of these they simply tested whether a candle would burn in the residual air left after a bird had died in the closed bell jar. In the final experiment, however, they had placed an illuminated candle into dephlogisticated air, and afterward tested the properties of the air. It extinguished a second flame. When agitated in water it was reduced to one-third of its volume, and the remainder reacted to a flame and to nitrous air as common air does. Lavoisier concluded that after a candle has gone out in dephlogisticated air, "that air is composed of two-thirds fixed air and one-third common air."[2] It would seem that Lavoisier must have been struck by the similarity of the effects of the candle on dephlogisticated air and the effects of respiration he had just examined; both converted dephlogisticated air to fixed air (although the fact that in the former case the residue remaining after the fixed air was removed appeared to be common air rather than dephlogisticated air might have introduced a further complication). Nevertheless he gave no indication that he paid special attention to this parallel.

In April 1777, Lavoisier resumed the investigation of the combustion of candles. In his notebook he wrote:

> Does the combustion of candles diminish the air? That appears to be a childish question, and there is no one who would not quickly answer in the affirmative.
>
> Nevertheless, if one considers that a part [of the air] is changed into fixed air by combustion, one might suspect that the observed diminution derives only from the combination of the fixed air with the water. I wished to verify this important point, and I saw no other way than to operate over mercury. But I encountered great difficulties.[3]

In other words, Lavoisier wanted to use his view that common air is converted to fixed air in combustions in order to subject the older assumption that combustion somehow decreases the volume of the air to a new critique. Stephen Hales had been among those who assumed that decrease; his explanation was that combustion processes "destroy the air's elasticity";[4] but as Lavoisier implied, almost everyone accepted the empirical fact of the diminution, based on experiments carried out in jars inverted over water from the time of John Mayow onward. Lavoisier now saw that that experimental circumstance may have been the cause of misleading results.

The "great difficulties" Lavoisier ran into revolved mainly around the problem of inserting a burning candle through the mercury into the inverted jar. In order to do so he had to tilt the jar momentarily, but he found that variations in the degree to which he tipped it changed the height of the mercury within the jar by different amounts, obscuring any change in the volume of air that might result from the burning of the candle. He solved this problem by floating the candle on the mercury in a capsule, then lighting it by means of a piece of phosphorus which he had in turn ignited by passing a piece of red-hot iron through the mercury. In the experiment the volume of air diminished by a small amount, which he convinced himself was due to the combustion of the phosphorus. When he added caustic alkali, the volume decreased much more, by a tenth of the initial volume. He inferred that "the combustion of candles does not really diminish the volume of the air in which it burns. In common air it consumes, or rather converts into fixed air, only the portion of pure air contained in the air of the atmosphere." Consequently, the volume should decrease much more if a candle burned "in dephlogisticated air, or pure air." To test that deduction he repeated the experiment in dephlogisticated air, and found that the caustic alkali did, in fact, reduce the residual air to one-half its previous volume.[5]

These experiments with candles, and Lavoisier's interpretation of them, correspond so closely with the experiments with birds from which he had concluded that respiration exerts "two effects," that it would almost appear that Lavoisier must have been pursuing the features common to the "operations" of combustion and respiration to which he had alluded in November when he wrote the draft of his memoir on respiration. Yet there is no supporting evidence that at the time he carried out these experiments he had such a connection in mind. In spite of the fact that he revised his memoir on respiration extensively, probably during this same period, he did nothing with his brief statement relating respiration and combustion.[6] To judge from his memoir on respiration, therefore, as late as the first week in May he was still orienting his view so strongly toward the analogy between respiration and calcination that he had not developed in any way his bare suggestion that respiration and combustion are closely related. Only one week after he had presented that memoir to the Academy for the second time, however, he read another paper in which he summarized his view of respiration with the sentence "The respiration of humans and of animals, . . . and the combustion of bodies, as I have shown in other memoirs, have the property of changing the salubrious part of the air continuously into fixed air."[7]

The disparity between this statement and the prior course of Lavoisier's thought, as we have been able to trace it through the stages of his memoir on respiration, is astonishing. Notwithstanding that he had come only gradually to treat as a possibility, and only as a possibility, that respiration converts all, or a part, of the respirable air to fixed air, he now posited that "property" as the single, unqualified conclusion of his previous work on the subject. It was as though he had never entertained the alternative that the respirable air may be absorbed in the blood as it is absorbed into calcined metals; yet a week ago he had in the same public forum expounded that alternative in detail. How could his perception of the situation shift so rapidly, and, as it seems, so inadvertently? (The possibility that he might have suppressed his alternative theory deliberately appears to be ruled out by the fact that he subsequently published the memoir on respiration with that discussion intact.) There is not sufficient evidence to establish a certain explanation, but one can offer a plausible conjecture. The special similarity between respiration and certain combustions was emerging so forcefully from Lavoisier's own investigations, especially by the time he had carried out the experiments on candles described above, that only a conceptual artifact could obscure it from him. That obstacle was, as we have seen, the research pathway that had fastened him to the analogy between respiration and the calcination of mercury. His enthusiasm for the first theory of respiration he had extracted out of that analogy had waned after he was forced to consider the alternative that the respired air may be changed to fixed air; yet, so long as he continued to develop his views by refining the manuscript that he had first drafted under the influence of that analogy, his initial orientation continued to shape his approach to the problem. If that was so, then it might well have happened that, as soon as he put that finished memoir away and began to formulate the problem anew in a fresh paper, the constraints imposed by his earlier direction fell away. The conceptual obstacle faded, and it may then have been so obvious to him that the natural analogy was between combustion and respiration, rather than calcination and respiration, that that seemed to him to have been what he had all along had in mind.

II

The meeting of May 10 at which Lavoisier delivered the paper containing his definition of respiration as a process like combustion was an auspicious occasion; for the Emperor Joseph II of Austria-Hungary, on a visit to his sister Marie-Antoinette, was present at the Academy.[8] It may have been in part that circumstance that induced Lavoisier to entertain his audience with showy demonstrations of the relation between respiration and the composition of the atmosphere. Adapting a dramatic experiment originated by the duc de Chaulnes, an academician and amateur scientist who had shown that one could pour fixed air from one flask to another because it is denser than the atmosphere, Lavoisier placed a bird in an open flask, poured fixed air from another jar into the flask, and "in less than a minute it perished, with convulsive movements and all the symptoms of animals that are drowning." He demonstrated the properties of common air, the respirable portion of the air, and the unrespirable portion, or mophette, by comparing the effects on a candle flame of samples of each type he had brought with him. Then he showed how, by mixing portions of the latter two he could compose an air with the same properties as the atmosphere. These visual displays of results Lavoisier had reached through years of investigation must have been very impressive to the august guest of the Academy. For all his virtuosity, however, he found himself upstaged in front of the whole assembly by Balthazar Sage, who revived the bird Lavoisier had left for dead by placing a few drops of volatile alkali in its beak.[9]

The special occasion of this royal visit may also have prompted Lavoisier to emphasize most of all the relevance of his new knowledge of the effects of respiration on the atmosphere to practical public problems. He addressed himself particularly to current concerns over the "salubrity" of the air in hospitals and other crowded places. The title he gave his talk was, in fact, "Observations on the alterations which take place in the air and on the means to restore vitiated air to the state of respirable air." Convinced by the experiments of the duc de Chaulnes that the airs present in the atmosphere tend to settle into layers, in the order of their relative densities, Lavoisier claimed that in buildings in which many people have breathed, the fixed air they produce sinks to the bottom, while the unrespirable mophette rises to the top. He asserted that he had verified this phenomenon by applying Priestley's nitrous air test to samples of air taken from hospitals and from various levels within public halls. Lavoisier proposed that hospitals be designed with high windows and low, unimpeded doorways, so that the mophette and fixed air could easily escape from the rooms. He even believed that the air in crowded rooms could be "disinfected" by removing the fixed air with caustic alkali and supplying additional pure respirable air produced from metallic calces. Always alert to promote the status of his science in public affairs, he complained that the Academy had not been consulted about the design of rooms presently being reconstructed in the Hôtel-Dieu. "It would undoubtedly be humiliating for the nation," he intoned, "if after [having available] a theory of the air based on precise and certain experiments, one fell, in the eighteenth century, into errors of construction that have been foreseen and avoided since the sixteenth century."[10]

During his talk Lavoisier paid generous homage to Priestley, "the celebrated English physician to whom physics and chemistry owe so much," for providing in the nitrous air test the means to estimate the salubrity of different airs. Lavoisier still retained Priestley's procedures, but he now interpreted the diminutions which result from mixing nitrous air with a sample air in terms quite different from those the inventor of the test had used:

> Of all the species of airs known by physicians, respirable air is the only one which produces this effect. This property therefore becomes a touchstone for recognizing it wherever it is found in appreciable quantities, and to determine the proportion in which it is contained in atmospheric air, or in any other air. In fact, since pure air and nitrous air mixed together mutually and almost completely absorb one another, whenever, on mixing nitrous air with any other air, one observes a decrease in volume of a third, a fourth, or an eighth, one can conclude that the air on which one is operating contains only a corresponding proportion of the true air, and that the remainder is in an unrespirable state.[11]

Priestley had interpreted the degree of diminution not in this way at all, but as a scale of quality, of the "goodness" of the air. When Lavoisier had adopted the test, he too had noted the results in terms of an air tested being "equal to," "better," or "less good" than common air. I have suggested, in fact, that his reliance on a test defined that way was one of the obstacles to viewing the atmosphere as composed of discrete species of air. By now, however, this view had become secure enough in Lavoisier's mind so that he perceived the results of the nitrous air test in a new way—as a measure not of the goodness of air, but of the proportion of "pure air" contained in a sample of any elastic fluid. This metamorphosis is typical of the way in which a major theoretical change transforms the meaning of experimental operations originally defined within the superseded conceptual framework.[12] The nitrous air test survived the demise of the conceptual system within which it had been invented, and functioned as an equally powerful tool within Lavoisier's new framework.

III

There is no reason to assume that when Lavoisier described respiration and combustion, in May 1777, as processes that change respirable air into fixed air, he had come even yet to understand the relation between the composition of respirable air and fixed air. Few aspects of the conceptual edifice he was striving to complete gave him more trouble than this vexing question. We have already seen that, two years before, he had at one time regarded fixed air as common air plus matter of fire, and at another time treated common air as fixed air plus matter of fire. He needed not merely to find a consistent theoretical interpretation for all the observed phenomena involving fixed air, but to contend with the problem of what observations to accept as valid. Some of his dilemmas derived from the importance to him of Priestley's multifarious investigations. Since Priestley was the source of many of the procedures and observations that stimulated Lavoisier's own experiments, Lavoisier was predisposed to take whatever Priestley reported quite seriously. In doing so, however, he was always in danger of being thrown off the track by certain purported phenomena which were difficult to reconcile with others.

An interesting example of the kind of impasse into which he worked himself while attempting to make sense for himself of Priestley's work is contained in a long memorandum entitled simply, "Notes extracted from M. Priestley." The document is undated, and from internal evidence was probably written before the discovery of dephlogisticated air. The difficulties Lavoisier encountered would not have been entirely resolved by that new factor, however, and may well have lingered on as late as the first part of 1777:

> M. Priestley demonstrates sufficiently well that the fixed air disengaged in the combustion of candles, and in the [other] cases in which the [volume of] the air is diminished, comes from the air itself. It appears that the same thing is true for the [matter of] fire: it comes in large part from the air, although it is not certain that all of it comes from there.
>
> Phlogisticated air is, therefore, according to me, the air deprived of matter of fire, and from which the fixed air has been precipitated. Two things are necessary to recompose the air; to restore its fixed air and its matter of fire.[13]

That is, if he accepted the correctness of Priestley's demonstration that in such combustions fixed air derives from the air consumed, then the residual air must be air minus fixed air. Adding to that his own theory that the matter of fire released in combustions derives from the air rather than the combustible, he arrived at still another divergent theory of the relation between fixed and ordinary air—that the latter consisted of the residual air (mophette) together with matter of fire and fixed air.

Immediately, however, his train of thought was derailed by another of Priestley's observations that he accepted as valid:

> But, on the other hand, how can we then conceive of the way in which agitation with water produces that phenomenon [that is, the restoration of respirable air from the residual air]?
>
> Therefore the water seems to be able to act only by removing something from the air, but then one is returning to the system of M. Priestley.[14]

Water cannot be the source of the fixed air and matter of fire which would be required to recompose the air according to his own conjecture. Since it cannot act by *adding* something essential, it must do so by removing something; but that conclusion, Lavoisier saw, leads right back to Priestley's view that the residual air is phlogisticated, and that what the water removes is phlogiston.

Leaving open this time the issue of whether one should return to the system of Priestley, Lavoisier pushed his line of reasoning a step further:

> But the air thus recomposed can still furnish more fixed air; therefore either all of the air is composed of fixed air combined with something else that constitutes it in the state of [ordinary] air, or it is composed of something which could become fixed air when required, by an addition of phlogiston or something else.[15]

Arriving at two possibilities between which he apparently saw at the moment no way to decide, he examined more critically Priestley's position on the question:

> M. Priestley considers it probable that atmospheric air is composed of an acid air combined with phlogiston. But fixed air is acid air, therefore atmospheric air must in strictness be composed of fixed air and phlogiston; but fixed air itself is an elastic fluid; it is therefore composed of matter of fire. Therefore, the air is composed of matter of fire, of phlogiston, and of aerial acid.[16]

We have seen in previous instances that Lavoisier sometimes, in thinking privately about these problems, merged his concept of a matter of fire with the conventional concept of phlogiston, or a modified version of it. In this curious mélange he seemed to entertain an explanation which included phlogiston and his matter of fire side by side in the composition of air. It is most likely, however, that he was following this line of argument largely to show himself that Priestley's conception of the composition of air was implausible. In the next paragraph he clearly appeared to be drawing Priestley into a theoretical trap:

> M. P. thinks that the diminution of the volume of the air comes only from the phlogiston, independent of any matter precipitated; but that is false, since the diminished air [that is, the air remaining after fixed air is precipitated from the residual air left by combustion] does not have a greater specific gravity.[17]

As these notes make evident, Lavoisier could more easily seize on the fatal flaws in Priestley's loosely woven explanatory network than weave together a coherent tapestry of his own. There seemed to be no consistent set of theoretical connections for all of the reputed empirical interactions between fixed air and common air. Although the subsequent identification of a portion of the latter as respirable air or dephlogisticated air modified the problems that Lavoisier saw when he wrote this note, that advance did not in itself resolve them.

Lavoisier is conventionally supposed to have all but established his general theory of combustion by early 1777, and to have been readying his positions for a broad attack on the prevailing theories. If, as I contend, he had still not "hit upon" the composition of fixed air and was therefore still unable to interpret fully those critically important combustions which produce it, it would seem, from a purely conceptual standpoint, to have been a curious blind spot in his otherwise expansive field of vision. The difficulty was not a mere failure of imagination, however, for he had, in fact, as early as the spring of 1775 "seen" what we would now take to be the germ of the solution. Sometime between February and April of that year, during the experiments on mercury calx which led to the identification of "pure air," he had formed fixed air in the usual way by combining mercury precipitate *per se* with charcoal, and had commented:

> It therefore appeared that there is charcoal employed in this operation, which also enters into the composition of the fixed air. It appeared, moreover, certain that there is more fixed air obtained in this operation than one obtains of common air in the preceding; from which it would follow that this fixed air is not common air diminished by charcoal vapor.
>
> All of this should be looked at again.[18]

This passage itself is far from clear, especially the consequence drawn in the second half. We are, however, probably not stretching Lavoisier's insight too far in taking it to mean that from the observation that the quantity of fixed air formed in reduction with charcoal is greater than the quantity of what he then took to be common air formed by reduction without, it may be concluded that fixed air may be a combination of charcoal with common air. If we then interpolate that what he considered common air here he later distinguished as "pure" or "respirable" air, then we can say that here he had had a glimpse of the way out of the labyrinth. There can be, however, a vast gap between having an idea which can be seen later on as a solution, and recognizing it at the time as the answer sought for. Nothing that Lavoisier wrote that can be dated earlier than September 1777 indicates that he knew that he had solved this problem. The reason that the answer remained for so long just beyond his grasp was that he did not have compelling experimental evidence in favor of any of the various interpretations he had entertained at one time or another.

Lavoisier's quandary is at first hard for us to appreciate, because the interpretation of the most prominent combustion involving fixed air, that of charcoal, turned out to be a direct extension of his interpretation of the combustions of phosphorus and sulfur; so that we readily presuppose that he must all along have been seeking to apply the same approach that had worked so well for his paradigm cases. The straightforward procedures by which he had been able to demonstrate that the gain in weight of the combustible bodies phosphorus and sulfur corresponded to the weight of the air consumed were of no avail to him, however, when he confronted the combustions whose product was fixed air. In his most recent experiments with candles, as in his various earlier combustions with charcoal, the volume of fixed air formed was approximately equal to that of the pure air consumed. He did regard fixed air as denser than ordinary air—that is why he postulated that it would settle to the bottom layer of an enclosed space—and might therefore have suspected that something is added to pure air when it is changed to fixed air. His efforts to distinguish airs by measuring their specific gravities had, however, proven indecisive. Merely weighing bottles filled with the respective airs, he had in his early attempts found fixed air to have the same apparent density as ordinary air.[19] In 1774 he had been able to detect only "very inconsiderable differences" between the specific gravities of the portion of air consumed in calcinations, the residue, and ordinary air.[20] His methods were, apparently, too insensitive to utilize the air densities as the basis for calculating weight gains or losses when the volume changes were slight. From the results of his combustion experiments with candles, for example, it would have been as plausible to infer that no ponderable body is combined with pure air in the conversion to fixed air as to equate the loss in weight of the candle with a weight gain in the air. It may, in fact, have been the near identity between the apparent weights of the air consumed and that produced in these conversions that had encouraged Lavoisier to entertain the various hypotheses in which he tried to distinguish them as containing or not containing a substance, such as matter of fire, or phlogiston, that he regarded as essentially weightless.

The other factor in these combustions, the nature of the combustible body, was equally problematic. Charcoal had little in common with wax candles, except that both were derived from plant matter and were assumed in orthodox theory to be rich in phlogiston. There was therefore a particular impediment to dispensing with the phlogiston theory for these cases, which may explain why Lavoisier continued to invoke it long after he had dispensed with phlogiston in his explanations of the combustion of phosphorus and sulfur. When, in the spring of 1777, he added respiration to the group of processes that convert pure air to fixed air, he increased the urgency of explaining this change, but acquired no new clues concerning the possible nature of the combustible body. There was, in short, no obvious opening for a frontal assault, utilizing his standard quantitative measures, by which Lavoisier could overcome these obstacles in his path.

I believe it unlikely that any single observation, foreseen or unforeseen, any special flash of insight, or any deliberately planned investigation revealed to Lavoisier the solution to his recalcitrant puzzle. Instead, three of the areas of research that he pursued actively during the spring and summer of 1777 indirectly helped to guide him out of his difficulties, by dissolving some of the alternatives he had previously considered, and by partially clarifying the only one which then remained viable.

IV

Lavoisier worked with such intensity, on so many of his research fronts, during the first eight months of 1777 that it is nearly impossible to sort out the temporal order of the individual investigations with respect to one another. Although we can glean a sequence for most of the key experiments from his laboratory notebook, we cannot do so for the organization of the various topics into memoirs; for he gave his first notice of them all at once, at the last meeting of the Academy of the summer. On three very neatly folded sheets, tied with a ribbon, he presented to the secretary of the Academy for his signature a "summary announcement"

> of several memoirs that M. Lavoisier proposes to read to the Academy immediately after the Saint Martin's reopening [November 12], but for which he requests a [submission] date before the holiday.
>
> The experiments relating to these memoirs are all complete, and the major portion of the memoirs themselves have been drafted and are ready to be read as soon as the Academy judges it appropriate.
>
> presented September 5, 1777.[21]

There followed summaries of ten memoirs, four of which are relevant to our theme. Because of these circumstances we should keep in mind, while examining each topic in turn, that Lavoisier was probably thinking about them concurrently, and that his ideas in the several areas developed mutually interdependently.

We have previously seen that his efforts in 1775 to incorporate his matter of fire into the explanations of specific chemical phenomena reveal mainly that Lavoisier's conception of this principle was loose enough to serve almost any purpose. During the winter or early spring of 1777, as Henry Guerlac has elucidated, Lavoisier enlisted the brilliant young mathematician Pierre-Simon Laplace to carry out with him experiments intended to substantiate the role of the matter of fire in the formation of "aeriform fluids." They approached the problem by measuring the changes of temperature that occur when volatile liquids, such as spirit of wine and ether, evaporate in a chamber as it is evacuated. From the observation that the temperature always fell, they could infer that the fluid absorbed matter of fire as it became aeriform. This was the first strong evidence Lavoisier was able to adduce for his conception that an air is a solid or liquid combined with matter of fire. Guerlac has suggested that it was these results that emboldened Lavoisier to set forth publicly his views concerning the matter of fire. He included in the notice deposited at the Academy on September 5 the abstract of a paper, "On the combination of the matter of fire with evaporable fluids, and on the formation of aeriform elastic fluids." An opportunity to read the full paper did not arise until July 1778, but we may assume that he had already worked out in the fall of 1778 the main ideas expressed in that memoir.[22]

Lavoisier now distinguished two forms of matter of fire. The free form flows from one body to another until it reaches equilibrium, its density in any given body being measured as the temperature of that body. The combined form of matter of fire is that which, joined with a fluid or solid, constitutes an air. He drew an analogy with two forms of water, the water of crystallization of a solid being combined with the solid and distinguishable from the "free" water in which a solid may be dissolved. Each specific body can combine only with a certain proportion of matter of fire, for there is a "point of saturation," just as in any other chemical combination. When a chemical decomposition or a new combination is produced, some matter of fire may be absorbed or released, depending upon whether the new combination can contain a greater or lesser quantity of that fluid than the original substances. For our present story the latter case is most relevant: when "less matter of fire enters into the new combination than existed in the former, then a portion of the igneous fluid which had been combined before the decomposition will become free "fire" after the recomposition; it will reassume its rights, it will produce the effect we call *heat*." At this time Lavoisier saw no way to measure quantitatively the heat released in such a reaction. "One can well measure under a bell jar the air which is disengaged in a reaction; but, since there is no vessel which could contain the free matter of fire without loss . . . all that one can do is to judge whether, at any given moment, there is or is not a flow of matter of fire." He suggested vaguely that he had not given up the attempt to devise a method for approximating the quantities involved. In the meantime he began to emphasize in his discussions the *idea* that matter of fire is absorbed or released in all chemical changes. The formation of heat, in particular, became a more prominent consideration in his ongoing study of combustions.[23]

It is difficult to distinguish the extent to which Lavoisier's conceptions of the nature of matter of fire were strengthened by the particular experiments on evaporation he performed with Laplace, from the effect that Laplace's disciplined thought might have had in forcing him to subject his earlier ideas to a more rigorous critique. Whatever the causes may have been, he began about this time to treat the phenomena involving matter of fire more systematically and more carefully. A significant manifestation of this care is that in his memoirs he began to introduce a terminological distinction between an air as a physical entity, a measurable isolable elastic fluid, and the component of that air which can be separated from the matter of fire by combining it with another body to form a solid or liquid. Thus he talked no longer of "pure air" in combination with a metal in a calx or a combustible body in an acid, but of the "base" of pure air in such forms. Fixed air too must contain some specific base in combination with matter of fire, even if its identity still eluded him. No longer could he speculate loosely that pure air and fixed air might be changed to one another merely by the addition or loss of matter of fire (even though he *did* assume that some matter of fire is released in the conversion of pure air to fixed air). Matter of fire imparted to all airs only their common state of elasticity. What differentiated them must now be attributed to the specific natures of their respective bases. This solidification of Lavoisier's conception of his matter of fire and of elastic fluids must have forced him to devote more thought to the unsolved problem of what the base of fixed air might be.

The experiments on candles of April 1777, which we have already discussed, appear to have been the start of a renewed experimental assault on combustion, in which Lavoisier paid particular attention to those processes that change pure air to fixed air. In May he carried out a similar set of experiments on a curious substance known as "the pyrophor of Homberg." Wilhelm Homberg, the most eminent chemist in the Academy of Sciences at the beginning of the eighteenth century, had discovered, in the residue remaining after he had distilled fecal matter, a substance which would catch fire spontaneously in the retort. In 1712 he reported several methods for producing this substance, which he believed was a "new phosphorus," from a mixture of fecal matter with the mineral alum.[24] A substance which burned by itself was always fascinating to eighteenth-century chemists, and many of them obtained it by repeating Homberg's procedures.

When it was clear that it was not phosphorus, it became known as *pyrophor.* Macquer commented in his *Dictionary of Chemistry,* in 1766, "This preparation has, up until now, no other use than to provide for the curious the truly surprising spectacle of a substance which carries within itself a principle of fire capable of igniting itself, and which is more inflammable than the most combustible body known."[25] In 1760 the Academy of Sciences published a memoir by Lejay de Suvigny, a medical doctor who was obviously also a skilled chemist, which subjected Homberg's substance to a searching reexamination. By this time the rapid development of the chemistry of salts permitted a far more systematic analysis of the process than had been possible in Homberg's era. Suvigny found that neither alum nor fecal matter was essential to produce pyrophor. He could obtain the same substance using a variety of salts that contained vitriolic acid, although alum (itself a combination of virtiolic acid with "earth of alum") still provided the best results. For the fecal matter he could substitute other plant substances. Suvigny preferred to use flour, but he could also obtain pyrophor using sugar or powdered charcoal instead. On the basis of these results he proposed that pyrophor is composed of earth of alum, sulfur, and *charbon* (charcoal), the latter two being the essential ingredients. In order to explain the formation of this substance from the starting materials, he invoked a classical phlogiston interpretation. Each of the vegetable matters which could be employed contained *charbon,* which he sometimes referred to as *matière charbonneuse* (charcoal-like matter). Some of this *charbon* gave off its phlogiston to convert the vitriolic acid to sulfur, while the remaining *charbon* formed with the sulfur a "*charbon sulfureux.*" The combustion of pyrophor then was a combined combustion of two of the best-known combustible bodies, sulfur and *charbon.*[26]

Although Suvigny did not make a clear distinction between his use of the terms *charbon* and *matière charbonneuse,* the two terms seem to touch on a significant modification that the conception of the substance to which they referred was undergoing. Like its English counterpart, "charcoal," *charbon* originally meant the black, porous matter left when one partly burned, or charred, wood or bones. Gradually, however, the term was expanded to include the very similar matter that could be obtained in this way from a variety of plant and animal substances. Macquer's dictionary defined *charbon* as

> that which remains from any compound body into the composition of which an oil enters, when this compound has been exposed to the action of fire in a closed vessel, so that all of its volatile principles are removed. . . . *Charbon* is a solid body, very dry, black, brittle, and with very little hardness.[27]

Comparing this definition with Suvigny's use of the term, we can identify an incipient division of meaning. According to Macquer, *charbon* was literally the porous black substance one could see and touch after partially burning certain substances. "*Charbon* is," he wrote, "visibly the result of the decomposition of the mixts from which it derives."[28] For Suvigny, however, *charbon* could be a substance hypothetically contained within those substances that yield it when charred, but which was capable also of entering directly into new combinations such as pyrophor, that were not necessarily black or porous. Perhaps Suvigny's alternative use of *charbon* and *matière charbonneuse* reflected some sense of this implicit difference; but if so, the distinction did not clearly emerge. It was only another of the many cases in eighteenth-century chemistry in which a word originally designating a specific, tangible substance was being applied to new situations which were almost imperceptibly transforming it from a descriptive to a theoretical term.

It is not surprising that Lavoisier was attracted to the study of pyrophor, this most combustible of bodies. In 1775 he listed among the projects he hoped to carry out during one of his sojourns at Montigny "to make the pyrophor of M. Homberg."[29] In his "Notes extracted from M. Priestley," he repeated the same direction to himself, adding the expectation "Undoubtedly there will be a rapid disengagement of air, and very rapid absorption in the combustion." He also gave an interpretation of the process in phlogiston terms which may have been his own or may have been the standard one.[30]

If Lavoisier actually made pyrophor in those years, he probably drew no significant conclusions from its properties. During the period in which he was still trying to construct a coherent theory of combustion around the processes which the simplest combustible bodies—phosphorus, sulfur, charcoal—undergo, he would have had little to gain by interjecting the complications of a body known to be a combination of combustibles. By early 1777, however, he was in a strong position to apply his previously established explanations to this substance, and to take advantage of its extraordinary combustibility. By May 31 he had prepared the substance from a mixture of alum and sugar, and was ready for the critical experiments—to burn it in ordinary air and in pure air.[31]

Simply by placing his pyrophor on a balance and allowing it to ignite, Lavoisier was able to verify that, like sulfur, it gained weight in the process. Next he prepared to burn it in atmospheric air under a bell jar to observe the change in volume of the air. Here his technical problem was the opposite of the one he faced in igniting the candle under the jar. He had to prevent the pyrophor from burning before he was ready for it. This he accomplished by inserting the substance into the jar enclosed in a capsule, then reaching through the water in which the jar was immersed and removing the capsule. The diminution when the pyrophor burned, he later wrote, "was the strongest of any I had experienced up until then." The decrease amounted to a fourth of the original volume, from which he concluded that the pyrophor consumed all of the pure air contained in the atmosphere. When he repeated the experiment with the jar immersed in limewater instead of water, the diminution was the same. Then he carried out the experiment in pure air. In view of the properties of pyrophor, he prudently used a seamless steel bell jar in place of a glass one. The pyrophor burned with great rapidity, emitting much noise, light, and heat. It did not stop burning "until the air contained in the jar had been reduced to $1/7$ of its volume." By adding further quantities of pyrophor he could "render $143/144$ of the volume of the original air absorbable by water." The immediate interpretation of these dramatic experiments was straightforward. Lavoisier needed only to apply his previous interpretations of the combustion of sulfur and of charcoal to a situation in which, as he agreed with Suvigny, both combustible bodies were present in the burning substance. The sulfur absorbed a great deal of pure air, accounting for the weight gain, whereas the *charbon* changed the rest of the pure air consumed into fixed air.[32]

On September 5, when Lavoisier deposited at the Academy the abstracts of the memoirs he hoped to read at future meetings, he had with him the full drafts of at least two of the papers, one based on his experiments with candles, the other on the experiments with pyrophor. Since both papers refer to the results of the latter, he must have composed them between June and September, but there is no way to tell in what order he wrote the two.

The memoir on candles Lavoisier organized around the same problem that he had posed for himself in his notebook when he had begun the experiments in April: to demonstrate that burning candles do not diminish the volume of the air except by changing pure air to fixed air. He described in minute detail the procedures and results with which he had verified his interpretation. In his introduction he reviewed what he believed he had already established about the airs composing the atmosphere, and noted that he would "henceforth give to fixed air the name mephitic gas, or mephitic acid vapor, or even simply mephitic acid."[33] He gave no rationale for this attempt to replace the generally accepted name that its discoverer had given to this air, but he had, in fact, begun privately to refer to fixed air by these names early in 1776, when he had carried out a series of experiments designed to show that "almost all volatile acids can exist in the form of [permanent] airs."[34] His decision to introduce these terms now probably reflects the fact that, as we shall see, he was during these same months attempting to generalize his theory of acidity.

In the conclusion of his paper Lavoisier compared the effects on the air of candles, of phosphorus, and of pyrophor. All three acted only on pure air, but whereas candles converted only two-fifths of that portion of the atmosphere into fixed air (Lavoisier had already forgotten his intention to refer to fixed air "henceforth" as mephitic acid), phosphorus consumed four-fifths of the pure air, and pyrophor "carries its action further and appears to convert in totality the pure air which the atmosphere contains into fixed air."[35]

When he composed this memoir, Lavoisier had far broader objectives in mind than these immediate conclusions, or than the limited question around which he had framed his experiments on burning candles; for he had decided to use these results as a platform from which to announce his rejection of the entire framework of phlogiston theory. In his first draft he wrote that "according to M. Priestley and many other physicians, the air in which one has burned candles is partly phlogisticated. I think, on the contrary, and I believe I have proven, that this air is only atmospheric air partially deprived of its pure, respirable portion." If Priestley were correct, then it should be necessary to remove something from the residue in order to reconstitute the air, whereas in fact it was necessary only to add a portion of pure air equivalent to that consumed. (His argument was not literally correct, since he had previously removed the fixed air formed in the process.) Then Lavoisier crossed his Rubicon:

> Besides, since I am at the point of attacking the entire doctrine of Stahl concerning phlogiston, and of undertaking to prove that it is erroneous in every respect, if my opinions are well founded M. Priestley's phlogisticated air will find itself entangled in the ruins of the edifice.[36]

Later in the manuscript Lavoisier adduced specific aspects of his experimental results that were inconsistent with a phlogiston interpretation. The details are probably less important than the fact that he had resolved to "attack" the phlogiston theory across the board, and to bury Priestley's theories in the rubble of Stahl's legacy.

These statements locate, as nearly as the written record can reveal, the time period and the context within which Lavoisier decided upon his momentous rupture with the prevailing theory of combustion of his age. Historians have given divergent interpretations of when Lavoisier opened his general "attack" on the phlogiston theory,[37] and have repeatedly questioned why he supposedly "delayed" this step until long after he had sufficient evidence to overthrow the theory. Guerlac has recently suggested that the new support he had obtained for his theory of heat in the experiments with Laplace led him to make his challenge late in 1777.[38] That development was undoubtedly a contributing factor. I do not believe, however, that it was any single decisive step toward the confirmation of his own theories, or toward the refutation of the phlogiston theory, that led him to his decision; rather, a combination of circumstances, of which the simple conditioning effect of the passage of time may have been as important as anything more specific, concurred to bring him to a stage in which he was psychologically ready to make the break. Most interpretations imply an emotionless man calculating with detachment the most opportune time to make public what he had already privately concluded. I think the situation may have been quite different. We have seen that, for longer than is often supposed, Lavoisier had continued to think privately in terms that lay both within and outside the boundaries of the phlogiston framework. The trend, from 1773 to

1777, was certainly to modify, question, and restrict the range of orthodox phlogiston explanations, but he had never indicated that he wished to dispense with them altogether. By the time he began to draft his memoir on candles, in the summer of 1777, his drift had carried him finally to a point at which he could see that he was approaching the radical denouement—that he should abandon the entire edifice within which phlogiston was housed. This was not an easy decision, I would suggest, for it did not mean that he had settled all the difficulties within his own conceptual structure. He could still easily have persuaded himself that he should wait for stronger evidence, that he ought to close the last loopholes, before issuing his challenge. At some point, however, a scientist must make the decision to commit himself personally to what he has come to believe, even though he has not resolved all of his own doubts, and can never be certain he is right. Polanyi has eloquently described the necessity for such commitment, and the risks involved, in his book *Personal Knowledge.*[39] Lavoisier had come to the watershed, and had to prepare himself to take his stand.

One of the indications that Lavoisier was preparing not simply to overthrow an "edifice" from which he had long since distanced himself was that in the very same manuscript in which he formulated the above rejection of the theory of phlogistication, he referred to "pure air" several times as "dephlogisticated air." In two places he caught himself and deleted the offending term, and in one place he substituted the phrase "the portion of pure air which M. Priestley has called dephlogisticated air"; but elsewhere he failed to dissociate himself from this residue of a mental framework he was striving to put behind him.[40] One cannot so easily erase the marks of a conceptual world one has long inhabited.

Lavoisier's decision to attack the phlogiston theory was, I believe, difficult for him also in another personal way, for it forced him to separate himself from close colleagues for whom phlogiston was one of the set pieces of chemistry. The chemists with whom he had personal contact had already begun to suspect him of secret designs against the principles they ardently maintained. Guyton de Morveau, a stalwart advocate of the phlogiston theory, had written Lavoisier to find out what he was thinking, and became convinced from the reply that Lavoisier was "getting ready to attack our phlogiston." Macquer, the senior chemist of the Academy, with whom Lavoisier associated regularly, had by this time long feared that Lavoisier was concealing some "great discovery" that would totally upset the phlogiston theory, and so destroy "our old chemistry." Lavoisier's "air of confidence," Macquer wrote later, "made me afraid to death."[41] Although Lavoisier is sometimes portrayed as an aloof personality, I do not believe that anyone who collaborated as habitually as he did with the scientists around him could be indifferent to the effects his move was bound to have on them.

Possibly the most painful aspect of his position for Lavoisier was that it forced him to attack Priestley. The conventional portrait of these two scientists as rivals obscures his predicament. Almost everything Lavoisier had written about Priestley up until this time suggests not only that he fully appreciated how much he had benefited from the English chemist's discoveries, but that in spite of his specific criticisms of some of Priestley's interpretations, he warmly admired him. We have already witnessed the labors he went through to express differences of opinion with Priestley without belittling his contributions. I think that it was not at all easy for Lavoisier to face the necessity to discredit publicly Priestley's entire theoretical structure. The passage quoted above suggests, in fact, that Lavoisier was attempting to portray Priestley not as the perpetrator of erroneous views, but as a victim trapped within the ruins of the system of Stahl. Another possible indication of his hesitancy to open a broad attack on Priestley is that, in spite of the fact that he had this paper ready at the last meeting before the closing of the Academy on September 5, he chose not to read it. He merely had Condorcet initial the pages of his fair copy,[42] and presented instead an uncontroversial memoir that he had prepared on pyrophor.

In the abstract of the memoir on candles he submitted to the Academy on that same day as part of the list of papers he wished to read in the future, Lavoisier summarized his experimental results, calling the portion of the air consumed dephlogisticated air. He included nothing to indicate he intended explicitly to refute the phlogiston explanation of the phenomenon. On the other hand, he wrote as a final one-sentence paragraph, "One can in the same manner reduce dephlogisticated air to fixed air by means of animal respiration."[43] That statement suggests he may have had in mind to develop the comparison between combustion and respiration that had been implicit in his respective investigations of these phenomena, and that he had already briefly mentioned in his talk at the Academy on May 10. In the full manuscript, however, he made no mention of that subject. One explanation for the omission would be that he still had no underlying interpretation of the process, and therefore nothing to add to the bare statement. Another explanation would be that when he decided to use the memoir to confront the phlogiston theory, he deferred a discussion of respiration for another occasion. Scientific investigations are in themselves open-ended, affording multiple attachments between the cluster of problems relevant to the overall research endeavor. Individual scientific papers would be distractingly diffuse, however, if they attempted to encompass all of the connections that could be made with the particular phase of the investigation being reported. To achieve focus the scientist must artificially limit the dimensions of his discussion, and thereby transform regions of the continuous web of his activities into a series of parcels that appear to be bounded.

The memoir on pyrophor, entitled "Experiments on the combination of alum with *matières charbonneuses*, and on the alterations which take place in the air in which one allows pyrophor to burn," was mostly a description of the experiments described above, the methods Lavoisier used to prepare pyrophor, and his interpretation of the changes of composition involved in the formation and combustion of the substance. Near the end of the paper he gave an explanation for the fact that, when he produced pyrophor by calcining alum with sugar, some fixed air formed:

> The pure air is converted to fixed air by its combination with the *matières charbonneuses*, or, what comes to the same thing, the fixed air is nothing else but a combination of *matières charbonneuses* with pure air, or rather with the base of that air. One has proof in the reduction of mercury calces; if one revivifies them alone, without addition, they give only pure air; if one adds powdered *charbon*, or any other *substance charbonneuse*, they give only fixed air. The same thing happens in the calcination of the alum with the *charbon* of sugar. The pure air, or more precisely the base of this air, contained in the vitriolic acid of the alum, combines with the *substance charbonneuse* and forms fixed air.[44]

If we assume the passage to have been part of the text Lavoisier read in September 1777, not a later addition, then in this inconspicuous form of a comment about a side effect observed during a particular process necessary to make the peculiar substance whose combustion he was studying, Lavoisier expressed for the first time the solution of his long-standing problem. He now had a very clear view of the relation between the composition of pure air and fixed air. The base of fixed air—he did not actually include the phrase "the base of fixed air," but undoubtedly meant it—was unambiguously a combination of the base of pure air and a *matière charbonneuse*.

Further on we shall consider in general how he may have found his way to this conclusion. Here we should note particularly how the differentiation of *matières charbonneuses* from *charbon* may have helped clarify the situation for him. Most likely he borrowed the term *matières charbonneuses* from the paper of Suvigny, which provided the starting point for his own investigation. Lavoisier seemed, however, to be employing it, along with *charbon*, to make a somewhat more definite distinction than Suvigny had made between tangible charcoal and a substance, or group of substances, closely related to charcoal but combined in other substances. Language alone cannot provide a viable conceptual advance, and Lavoisier's use of the terms does not signify that he had any distinct notion of how *matières charbonneuses* are related to their most concrete manifestation in charcoal. By assisting him to imagine a hypothetical substance transferable from that actual one, however, the denotation may have given him a critical insight. *Matières charbonneuses* could enter not only a substance such as pyrophor, but even one as unlike charcoal as an elastic fluid. Thus that chemical curiosity, the self-igniting pyrophor of Homberg, seems to have helped Lavoisier to clear the last great conceptual hurdle across the route he was pursuing toward his grand synthesis.

V

Lavoisier made a major effort in 1777 to develop further his theory of acids. Although his work in this direction was connected less closely to his problems with the processes common to combustion and respiration than the previously described investigations, it did contribute in a general way that will become clear further on. Moreover, a part of this investigation later became transformed into the starting point for another important field of Lavoisier's research that will be a central theme in the following chapter. We shall therefore examine the situation in some detail, even though it will divert us temporarily from the main points of the present chapter.

As is well known, and was touched on in Chapter 2, Lavoisier had reached the conclusion by early in 1776 that "the pure portion of the air enters into the composition of all acids without exception, and that it is this substance which constitutes their acidity."[45] The experimental evidence on which he based his generalization, however, was limited to nitrous acid, vitriolic acid, and phosphoric acid. During the next year he renewed his investigations of phosphoric and vitriolic acid in order to establish more accurately the proportions of pure air combined with their bases.[46] Although his case rested on three of the commonly used mineral acids, which were also the strongest known acids, his theory would obviously be more secure if he could apply his proofs to other acids. An especially promising field for such an enterprise would be the numerous partially characterized acids derivable from plant substances. These acids were, in fact, at the analytical forefront of the chemistry of the time, in an area just beginning to open up under the leadership of two outstanding chemists of the far north.

In Stockholm the extraordinarily talented apothecary Carl Wilhelm Scheele, working in collaboration with Anders Retzius, isolated the long-known acid of tartar for the first time, and fully characterized its chemical properties.[47] Scheele then turned his attention to acidic plant substances such as sorrel, from which he hoped to be able to isolate other acids. While he was engaged in that prolonged task, a student working at the University of Uppsala under the direction of the eminent chemist Torbern Bergman mixed nitrous acid with powdered sugar, placed the mixture in a retort, and distilled off a liquid containing an acid with properties distinct from any previously known acids. Bergman regarded this "acid of sugar" as contained in the sugar, and separated out during the process by the decomposition of the latter.[48] Following closely on the isolation of tartaric acid, this discovery made a great impression on chemists, raising the prospect that a whole domain of new acids might be found.

Bergman frequently exchanged news of chemical events with French chemists through a correspondence with Macquer, and Lavoisier probably heard about the discovery of acid of sugar before it appeared in the formal scientific literature accessible to him.[49] Sometime after July 22, 1777, he undertook to form acid of sugar himself, using Bergman's general method, with the important modification that he designed his apparatus to capture the airs given off.

To a retort placed in a small reverberatory furnace Lavoisier attached a double-necked receiver, the second opening of which he adapted to an inverted jar. The first vessel was intended to retain the liquids that distilled over, while the airs would collect in the jar. In the retort he mixed six gros of "royal sugar" with two ounces of nitrous acid and two ounces of water. Very gently he heated the retort over the open fire. At first the sugar dissolved quietly, but "all at once the boiling began with extreme rapidity, at the same time very abundant reddish vapors were disengaged, and all of the vessels became extremely hot." The air passed so rapidly into the jar that he had to exchange it very quickly and had soon filled three of them. The nitrous air strongly attacked the lutes connecting the parts of the apparatus, so that even though he worked as fast as possible to repair them, he suspected that he had lost a little air through leaks. By the time he had six jars full of air he noticed that there were no more red vapors. Assuming that no more nitrous acid was coming over, he disconnected the apparatus, removed the intermediate receiver, and collected the whitish vapor that was now arising directly into the inverted jars. The whitish vapors ceased while the ninth jar was filling, so he began to increase the fire, and they reappeared when the tenth was half full. The greater heat, however, caused the retort to melt, ending the operation. When he examined the retort he found nothing in it but a little bit of very porous *charbon*. The receiver contained two and a half ounces of weak nitrous acid.[50]

Lavoisier now faced the tedious task of measuring the quantities of the various airs contained in each of the ten collecting jars. Before beginning, he simply left them for thirty-six hours, during which much of the fixed air was absorbed by the water in which the jars remained immersed. To complete that process, he then agitated each jar in water, added caustic alkali, and took the total contraction in the volume of the air as a measure of the fixed air. To determine the quantities of nitrous air, he utilized Priestley's nitrous air test in reverse, adding successive portions of dephlogisticated air until he reached the saturation point, or minimum volume. From the volume of dephlogisticated air used and the combining proportions of the two airs he could calculate the volume of nitrous air. The small residue remaining after the nitrous air and fixed air had been removed he considered to be inflammable air, although he did not record that he had used specific tests to identify it as such. He did not carry out these procedures fully for each portion. By the time he reached the fifth jar, he had no more dephlogisticated air "on hand," so that for the remaining five he simply assumed that the proportions of nitrous air and inflammable air were the same as in the third and fourth jars.[51]

During the distillation, Lavoisier assumed, the nitrous acid decomposed, disengaging nitrous air and leaving dephlogisticated air to join with the sugar "to constitute [the sugar] in the acid state." The quantity of nitrous air collected in the jars ought therefore to equal the quantity that could be released by the quantity of nitrous acid decomposed. To ascertain the latter, Lavoisier first measured the amount of nitrous acid that had passed undecomposed into the intermediate receiver, by neutralizing a portion of the acidic liquor with an alkaline liquid whose acid equivalent was known. In this way he calculated that the fluid contained 6 gros 28.19 grains of nitrous acid. Therefore of the original 16 gros (or 2 ounces), 10 gros 28.19 grains had been decomposed. (Lavoisier apparently made this calculation incorrectly. The difference should have been 9 gros 43.8 grains.) Because of the loss through the lutes, he guessed that the actual amount decomposed was probably somewhat less, "but one can suppose boldly 1 ounce 2 gros" (that is, the 10 gros calculated, assuming no loss). Lavoisier's motive for estimating the maximum possible quantity decomposed was that he could see as he went through his calculations that the quantity of nitrous air expected from the nitrous acid decomposed would fall well short of the quantity estimated from his analyses of the airs in the ten collection jars. The first figure turned out to be 83.8 cubic inches, whereas for the total in the bottles he had come out with "much more"—180.36 cubic inches. He recalculated the theoretical yield in another way, using the proportion of nitrous air in nitrous acid he had published in his memoir of 1776 on the composition of nitrous acid, but still came out with only 122½ cubic inches—only two-thirds of the amount obtained. "Therefore," he was forced to conclude, "there is an error in my first memoir, or else the nitrous acid has been completely destroyed by its combination with the sugar, and what I supposed to have been nitrous acid was not really so." To eliminate the latter possibility he evaporated a portion of the remaining liquor from the receiver with alkali and obtained "pure nitre."[52] He was therefore faced with the unhappy prospect of having to question the validity of a composition he had regarded as well established. In the meantime he was left simply with an unsatisfactory experiment.

The experiment had other shortcomings besides Lavoisier's failure to make this balance come out right. Clearly in following Bergman's procedure he had expected to produce acid of sugar. In keeping with his general conception of the composition of acids, and with the analogy to the reaction of mercury with nitrous acid, he would have interpreted the reaction as a combination of the sugar with the dephlogisticated air released by the nitrous air. At the end, however, there was no acid of sugar. The retort contained only *charbon*, and in the receiver there was only nitrous acid and water.

Despite this disappointing outcome of what must have been a difficult, time-consuming experiment, Lavoisier was confident enough that he would eventually succeed to include among the abstracts of the papers he submitted on September 5 a "memoir in which one proves that a great number of bodies are capable of playing the role of an acid when one combines them with dephlogisticated air." In the first portion of his abstract he summarized evidence, based mainly on experiments by Macquer, that the calx of arsenic can be converted to an acid by combining it with dephlogisticated air. Then he continued, "The acid of sugar discovered by M. Bergman provides another example." Lavoisier asserted that by combining eight parts of nitrous acid with one part of sugar one could decompose the nitrous acid, obtaining a great quantity of nitrous air, and "dephlogisticated air, which combines with the sugar to form a particular acid."[53] Since his only attempt to achieve this result had failed,[54] Lavoisier was probably not describing an actual completed experiment, but a "chimeric" one, made up from a combination of Bergman's results, his own effort, and the interpretation he would have made of the complete result if he had been able to attain it.

Lavoisier went on to claim that one could in this same way produce a particular acid from "most gums, mucilages, etc." Finally, he concluded, it is

> a nearly universal principle, which suffers no exceptions other than that of certain metallic substances, that every time that one can succeed in combining a great quantity of dephlogisticated air with a body, one converts it into a particular acid which differs essentially from every other acid, and which has specific properties that distinguish it. Consequently I shall show that the class of acids [here Lavoisier afterward inserted "and especially of plant acids"] is capable of an infinite extension, from which it follows that there is an immense field for chemistry, which can provide work for several successive generations.[55]

Swept up in this expansive vision of future successes, Lavoisier was promising so much more than he was in a position to deliver that it is not surprising that he had no completed manuscript to back up this particular abstract.[56] In general, however, the pieces in the grand research program over which he had persevered for the past five years were now beginning to fall together so well for him that his great optimism is understandable.

VI

Soon after the Academy closed for vacation, Lavoisier made a strategic shift. The series of memoirs on specific investigations that he had planned to read at successive meetings when the Academy reopened were suddenly no longer his first priority; for he decided to formulate and present to his colleagues an overall synthesis of the theoretical structure that was now taking ever clearer form in his mind. He headed the paper in which he started to write out his views simply "On combustion." At the very beginning he tried to explain the motives for his new course:

> As dangerous as the systematic spirit is in the physical sciences, it is just as much to be feared that in accumulating too great a multiplicity of experiments without order, one may obscure the science instead of clarifying it; that one may render access difficult to those who present themselves to cross its entryway; finally that one may obtain only disorder and confusion as the reward for long and painstaking work. The facts, the observations, and the experiments are the materials for a great edifice, but if one assimilates them, one must in collecting them avoid obstructions in the science; one must, on the contrary, endeavor to classify them, to distinguish that which belongs to each category, to each part of the edifice; finally, to arrange them *to fit one day into the great whole to which they belong*. [He lined out the phrase italicized here and wrote in its place] in advance to form a part of the whole to which they belong.[57]

Dissatisfied with this awkward paragraph, Lavoisier started over and reduced it to a concise, elegant statement. The original version is, however, in some senses more revealing of what may have prompted him at this point to undertake the arrangement of the parts he had assembled into a whole. Lavoisier himself could never be justly accused of accumulating experiments without order. His searching mind invariably imposed order on every phenomenon or problem that he examined. In his own opinion, however, the series of papers he had presented over the past three years on specific aspects of his broader investigation must have begun to appear as an unorganized accumulation, in some sense as an obstruction. He felt the need of a higher order, "a grand whole" within which to fit the areas of limited order he had established. This was not, of course, his first attempt to devise a systematic structure. As he wrote a little further on, "I have already laid the first foundations of this system, pages 279 and 280 of my *Opuscules phisiques et chemiques*, but I confess *that, frightened at that time by the contradictions which a new doctrine must naturally endure* [he then replaced the phrase here italicized, toning it down a little to read] that stopped by apprehension about the contradictions, lacking confidence in my own insight, I did not dare to put forth an opinion directly opposed to the theory of Stahl and to that of many celebrated men who have adopted it."[58]

Lavoisier's recollection of his earlier feelings was probably accurate, but the passage can be misleading. Taken by itself it may appear to assert that in 1773 he had privately already rejected the phlogiston theory altogether, and merely lacked sufficient confidence in his own opposed theory to make it public. We have seen, however, that both publicly and privately he had for long afterward not reached an "opinion" consistently and generally opposed to the phlogiston theory. He had modified Stahl's original theory, dispensed with the application of phlogiston in some contexts, departed from and returned to Priestley's interpretations of phlogiston theory, and generally moved within a position somewhere between acceptance and full rejection of the theory. As for his own system, even now, he realized, he had not escaped all difficulties.

> *If, on the one hand, the reasons that have arrested me up until now are always present,* on the other hand, the facts which have multiplied and which appear to me favorable to my ideas have reinforced me in my principles, and I believe that I have enough proofs, or at least probabilities, so that even those who will not share my views cannot blame me for having written.[59]

Afterward he softened the impression conveyed in this passage by replacing the italicized part with "Although a part of the reasons . . . perhaps still remain today." Those who doubt Lavoisier's character may regard these lines as examples of his false humility, but there is no reason not to accept them as valid expressions of self-doubt. Our analysis of his pathway up until this point suggests that his experiences had long conditioned him to cycles of confidence and doubt. He had made great strides, yet when he had tried to assemble his very successful investigations and partial explanations into a "grand whole," he had repeatedly been defeated. Why was he now ready to try again? As we shall see below, perhaps the most compelling reason was that he had finally thought his way around the major obstacles that had for so long blocked him. A further motivation is, I think, suggested by the language of his first introductory statement, quoted above. Twice in that paragraph he mentioned materials for "a great edifice." It is no coincidence, I think, that only a short time before, in the first draft of his memoir on candles, he had written that Priestley's phlogisticated air was caught in the "ruins of the edifice" of Stahl. He had then been poised, as he wrote, to "attack" the entire system of Stahl. Although the evidence is only circumstantial, it is not unlikely that, having reached the point at which he was prepared to commit himself to so fundamental a break with prevailing views, he reassessed his plan for a series of "attacks" on Stahlian chemistry and found it too negative. Rather than fix his attention on the destruction of the old chemical edifice, he should make as clear as possible what he had to offer in its place.

Lavoisier began the exposition of his "new theory of combustion" by formulating three "laws," already "implicitly announced" in his earlier memoirs, concerning the phenomena that appear in every combustion. These were (1) there is always a disengagement of matter of fire; (2) combustions can take place only in pure air; and (3) in all combustions the body burned becomes an acid. Afterward he added another "third law," that "in every combustion pure air is destroyed," and made the former third law his fourth law. The same laws, except for the fact that the body becomes a metallic calx instead of an acid, apply to calcination; only the process is so much slower that the phenomena are less immediately evident. He credited Macquer with having recognized that calcination can be "considered as a slow combustion."[60]

Turning to "the hypothesis of Stahl," Lavoisier acknowledged that one could explain the same phenomena in its terms, but one must assume that "matter of fire, or fixed phlogiston, exists in metals, sulfur, and a great number of bodies." In a passage which he rephrased several times, he expressed essentially the view that to say that combustible bodies burn becuse they contain a matter of fire is to "fall into a vicious circle. . . . It is to explain combustion by combustion." If, he asserted, "I show that these same phenomena can be explained in as natural a manner" without the hypothesis that matter of fire or phlogiston exists in combustible bodies, "the system of Stahl will be undermined at its foundation, and thereby considerably shaken."[61]

Lavoisier began his own explanation by summarizing the views on matter of fire that he had developed more fully in the memoir presently "deposited with the secretary of the Academy." He emphasized particularly that each air is a combination of matter of fire with "another substance which enters as a base," and that, like a chemical solvent, the matter of fire constituted it in its physical state. It imparted to the air something of its own properties, its "elasticity, its specific lightness, its rarity." Then he applied the general principles he had outlined to particular examples. For the calcination of metals and the combustion of phosphorus and sulfur he was merely assembling in concise form the interpretations he had repeatedly given before.[62] The fourth example he included in his discussion, however, was not a mere recapitulation:

> *Charbon* and all *matières charbonneuses* have the same action on the base of the air. They appropriate it and form with it an acid *sui generis*, known by the name of fixed air or mephitic acid. The solvent of the base of the [pure] air, the matter of fire, is still disengaged in this operation, but in smaller quantity than in the combustion of sulfur and phosphorus, because a portion combines with the mephitic acid to constitute it in the elastic state of a vapor.[63]

After returning to elaborate further his conception of the role of matter of fire in maintaining the elastic state, Lavoisier concluded that "in attacking the doctrine of Stahl, I claim to substitute for it not a rigorously demonstrated theory, but only a more probable hypothesis which presents fewer contradictions . . . " Bursting the bounds of his self-imposed caution for a moment, he completed the sentence ". . . and which explains with marvelous ease almost all of the phenomena of physics and chemistry." Recovering his more customary restraint, however, he quickly replaced that visionary claim with the more modest assertion ". . . and in which a part of the phenomena of nature come to be classified almost of themselves."[64]

The shift from the hesitant, almost apprehensive tone in which Lavoisier wrote the introductory passages of his essay on combustion, to the barely repressed exuberance with which he finished it, suggests that in the process of writing out his argument he found that he had succeeded, even more felicitously than he had expected, in developing a strongly coherent overall structure. The new edifice looked very good indeed. The contrast with his similar attempt in 1775 to compose a general system beginning with his concept of the matter of fire and the elastic state is striking. There he had begun with confidence and ended in embarrassment. Here he began with caution and ended in triumph. As usual, he made numerous revisions in his draft, both as he wrote and afterward; but the changes were quite different in character from those we have analyzed in his memoir on respiration. The latter revealed him struggling with ideas and opinions he had not yet fully mastered. The changes he made here merely improved the style and tone, or stated in clearer form ideas he evidently had under firm control by the time he sat down to write.

From the vantage point of the story we have been following, the event that appears most obviously to have permitted Lavoisier to complete his theoretical structure was his recognition of the elegant way in which he could fit the combustion of charcoal, or rather of *matières charbonneuses*, into the framework. As combustible bodies, *matières charbonneuses* now conformed to the four "laws" of combustion as fully as did his paradigm cases of phosphorus and sulfur. They consumed pure air, released heat, and formed a particular acid. The only special aspect of the situation was that the acid, being itself an elastic fluid, retained a portion of the matter of fire released in the other combustions as heat and light. With that solution of the problem of the combustion of charcoal, the more general problem of the relation between the composition of pure and fixed air and the conversion of one to the other was resolved at the same time, the role of the matter of fire in the two airs was applied consistently with its definition as the cause of the state of elasticity, and mephitic acid enlarged the list to which his theory of acids applied. Two and a half years earlier Lavoisier had searched in vain for ways to force his partial solutions into the outlines of his general theory. Now his explanations of individual combustions and calcinations, his theories of matter of fire and of acids, appeared effortlessly integrated into a seamless structure. Despite his disclaimer that contradictions remained, he must at this moment have found no conspicuous flaws in his handiwork.

How had the last major piece of the puzzle been assembled? In the first place, it was probably not due to new experimental evidence obtained from the combustion of charcoal itself. Lavoisier still had no balance sheets, comparable to those for phosphorus, sulfur, or nitrous air and nitrous acid, to show that the weight of the fixed air formed equaled that of the *matières charbonneuses* and pure air consumed. Most likely it was not the solution of the immediate problem of the combustion of charcoal that enabled him to complete his theory of combustion, but the growing force of the considerations favorable to the latter that pressed the case of charcoal into line. As he strengthened his definition of the matter of fire, as he deliberately sought areas into which he could expand his theory of acids, as he dealt with situations which made it easier to view *matières charbonneuses* as substances that could be abstracted from their manifestation in charcoal, this framework of ideas relevant to the combustion of charcoal became compelling enough to shape the solution of the problem even without more direct evidence. Lavoisier may have reasoned to the solution by analogy to the cases he had characterized more fully, or by deduction from his general theory of combustion; or he may not have reasoned it out deliberately at all. One day it might simply have appeared so obvious to him as to require no further argument. In 1775 the outlines of his general theoretical structure were still too weak to show Lavoisier how to join his partial hypotheses for limited problems together. By now the architecture of that structure had become solid enough, enough of its components fit properly, so that the structure as a whole could now hold together the parts remaining unconnected by more direct evidence.

Lavoisier might have felt some satisfaction in the symmetry that attended his solution to the combustion of charcoal; for just as that step completed the system he now opposed to the system of Stahl, so had the role of charcoal stimulated the first tentative step he had taken to modify the system of Stahl, the step which he identified in the passage above as the two pages in his *Opuscules* where he had "laid the first foundations" of his system. Because he had already conceived of the matter of fire then as the source of the elasticity of elastic fluids, he had raised the possibility that in the reduction of metallic calces, "*charbon* . . . , like all *substances charbonneuses* employed in reductions, . . . renders to the elastic fluid fixed [in the calx], the phlogiston, or matter of fire, which restores its elasticity." Contrary to his later recollection, he had not presented his view then as "opposed" to Stahl: it was "remote from the view of Stahl, but perhaps not incompatible with it."[65] After three years of uncertainty and vacillation, Lavoisier was finally in a position to explain the role of charcoal in a manner fully consistent with his own early conception of the matter of fire, and fully incompatible with the system of Stahl.

In that investigative voyage on which Lavoisier had embarked even before the modest departure from Stahlian orthodoxy expressed in his *Opuscules*, he had, by the time he completed his essay on combustion, reached the far shore.

To switch to his own metaphor, he now depicted himself correctly as having constructed a new edifice to replace one which he could now view from the outside as a "ruin." For him personally, if not yet for the chemical community at large, the revolution he had predicted in 1773 had come to pass. The change he had wrought has become one of the classic examples of scientific revolutions—events in which, as Thomas Kuhn has argued persuasively, the new structure must inevitably be incompatible with the old at some crucial points, so that acceptance of the new involves destruction of the old. Because there is no fully logical way to reason from one system to another system incompatible with it, Kuhn also insists that one cannot make a purely logical decision between them.[66] In writing his essay on combustion Lavoisier implicitly sensed both of these aspects of his relation to Stahlian phlogiston theory: the first by portraying himself as constructing a new edifice rather than attempting to reconstruct the old; the second by not attempting to refute the phlogiston theory logically, but simply offering another system which he believed could explain the same phenomena more naturally, with fewer internal contradictions.

From the fact that the old system and the new must be incompatible, Kuhn has inferred that the scientist who moves from one to another must do so by some sort of holistic shift. In his original discussion of this phenomenon in *The Structure of Scientific Revolutions*, he wrote that "the new paradigm, or a sufficient hint to permit later articulation, emerges all at once, sometimes in the middle of the night, in the mind of a man deeply immersed in crisis. What the nature of that final stage is—how an individual invents (or finds he has invented) a new way of giving order to data now all assembled—must here remain inscrutable and may be permanently so."[67] Following Norwood Hanson, Kuhn likened the change of perception a scientist undergoes in such situations to a Gestalt switch. There are enough ambiguities in Kuhn's discussion so that it is difficult to pin down his position precisely, but he conveys the impression that, like others in analogous situations, Lavoisier must at some point have experienced a sudden, Gestalt-like shift in his perception of the phenomena he had been investigating. "After discovering oxygen," Kuhn writes, "Lavoisier worked in a different world."[68] The outcome of Lavoisier's progression does appear to have placed him in a conceptual world so fundamentally different from that in which he started that, when the beginning and end points are compared, they seem to be separated by a holistic shift. Lavoisier's movement between these points, however, did not resemble so simple a process. From the odyssey we have followed we can see that he endured long years during which he found no resting place between the conceptual world of phlogiston and the new conceptual world he anticipated but could not yet visualize in complete form. Since these two worlds were logically incompatible, but for long stretches of his voyage he could not entirely do without either of them, he was constrained to live with incoherence. Sometimes he was, no doubt, uncomfortable with this halfway position, as we have seen he was with inconsistencies within his own formulations; but he was probably not able, from that position, to perceive all of the incompatible elements between the two systems that could be easily traced once the replacement system was complete and tight. There were times, for example, when he used the term "matter of fire" to refer to his own conception, times when he used it as a synonym for phlogiston, and times in which it is not entirely certain which he meant. Clearly he could not, while in midstream, always keep the two worlds apart.

If the Gestalt switch model is highly suggestive, it is misleading, I think, precisely because of the simplicity which allows it to function in the way it does. One can view all at once all of the visual details present in a Gestalt figure, so that one sees it all at once as one or another form. A conceptual structure is so much more complicated that one cannot perceive its details all at once, but must inspect them over a period of time. As we have seen, Lavoisier had to work on one part of his system after another. A failure to find a solution to a problem forming one facet of the structure could force him not only to put up with inconsistencies within the whole for long periods of time, but even sometimes to contemplate changing his course back toward the system from which he had set out. The process was so prolonged, so dense, and so complex that it is inadequately characterized by words such as "switch" or "shift." The idea of a "passage," which may be as brief or as long as circumstances demand, appears more suitable. Fortunately, since it can be broken down into smaller portions, a passage is also less inscrutable. These comments are not, however, intended to be yet another criticism of the overall structure of Kuhn's view of scientific revolutions. The framework he proposed twenty years ago has proven resilient enough not to crack under the stress of repeated attacks, and will undoubtedly dominate discussion for years to come. Lavoisier's course does suggest that there is room for further articulation of the nature of those events that Kuhn locates at the core of a scientific revolution. If his views on the process by which the first individual makes the transition from one conceptual framework to another are less well developed than his account of the processes leading toward and from it, that is because there have been available very few historical descriptions of the fine structure of those personal transitions. If Lavoisier's experience were to prove representative of what those who initiate such revolutions undergo, then the substitution of the image of a passage for that of a switch would not undermine but enrich the structure of Kuhn's scientific revolutions.

VII

Where did respiration fit in the synthesis of his views on combustion as Lavoisier was pulling the other elements of his edifice together? For a short time it seemed that he might again put off treating that connection. He was well aware, as he began to compose his essay, that respiration was an integral part of his system, but he was not ready to bring it immediately into the picture. "There is no time here," he wrote after introducing the four general laws of combustion and calcination, "to show the analogy which exists between animal respiration, combustion, and calcination; I shall return to it later in this memoir."[69] He almost forgot to do so. Having completed his discussion of the subjects summarized above, he ended with a paragraph stating that "circumstances have permitted me here to present only an overall view of the system,"[70] and that he would deal with the parts in later memoirs. He must, however, have remembered his intention to include respiration, and have decided that it was too central to his whole system to leave out. Crossing out his two concluding paragraphs, he inserted the following:

> I announced above that the theory presented in this memoir could serve to explain a part of the phenomena of respiration, and it is with that that I shall terminate this essay.
>
> I showed in the memoir that I read at the public meeting of last Easter that pure air, after entering the lungs, comes out again in part in the state of fixed air. In passing through the lungs the pure air therefore undergoes a decomposition analogous to what takes place in the combustion of *charbon.* Now in the combustion of *charbon* there is a disengagement of matter of fire; therefore there ought equally to be a disengagement of matter of fire in the lungs, and it is this matter of fire which is distributed with the blood throughout the animal economy and *distributes the heat there* [before continuing the paragraph, Lavoisier changed the phrase here italicized to "supports a constant heat"] of around 32½ degrees on the Réaumur thermometer. This idea, which is supported by facts and by constant analogies, may perhaps appear risky; but before rejecting or condemning it, I ask one to consider that the heat of animals depends on the decomposition of the air in the lungs, that there are no warm animals except those that respire regularly, and that this heat is the greater the more frequent the respiration is, that is to say, that there is a constant relationship between the heat of the animal and the quantity of air which enters, or at least which is converted to fixed air in, the lungs.[71]

In concise but powerful form Lavoisier thus described respiration as a combustion analogous to that of *charbon,* converting pure to fixed air, and releasing the heat which maintains the constant temperature of warm-blooded animals. The phenomena associated with the process conformed admirably to his four "laws" of combustion. Respiration released matter of fire; it took place only in pure air, and consumed the pure air; and it produced a particular acid, in this case fixed air. The simplicity and coherence of this theory lend it the character often associated with those flashes of insight in which a scientist suddenly sees, in a single mental act, the solution of a difficult puzzle. Lavoisier himself referred to the theory in this passage as an "idea," and an idea is something that often occurs to someone as a unit. Through the record of his private thoughts and his investigations, however, we can see that the origin of this idea was quite different. The idea stated so simply here was the product of a long evolution, and it was composed of elements which themselves only gradually became clear. Its lineage is traceable to the two notes of 1774 and early 1775,[72] in one of which Lavoisier had suggested that respiration consumes a portion of the air, in the other of which he had described the process as a conversion of common air to fixed air. The subsequent development of his conception of the composition of the atmosphere had enabled these once-divergent views to merge. The description of the role of respiration in releasing matter of fire is also an amplification of ideas expressed in rudimentary form in those first two notes. The line of descent between the initial notes and the finished statement was, however, not a direct one. As we have seen, in the intervening years Lavoisier had connected his investigation of respiration to the calcination of mercury. In that way he had strongly advanced one facet of what became the above statement, the absorption of pure air in respiration, but at the expense of the remaining elements—the conversion to fixed air and the release of matter of fire. In the final stage of development he had retrieved these ideas, so that Lavoisier's progress was a roundabout one, bringing him, in a sense, back to his starting point; but he returned there bringing with him crucial insights that he had acquired along his "detour."

The clarity and the broad scope of Lavoisier's present statement contrast sharply with the tentative, limited statement he had made only a few months before in his memoir on respiration about the possibility that respiration may convert the pure air absorbed to the fixed air released. At first glance it may appear that Lavoisier was now claiming that he had already set forth in that memoir the view he now presented. Close reading suggests, however, that he asserted only, in the first sentence of the above paragraph, to have shown then that a part of the pure air which enters the lungs is converted to fixed air. As the second sentence implies, he was now able to *account for* that change by the analogy to the combustion of *charbon*. What had been in the spring only a hypothesis about the change of one air into another in respiration had become a comprehensive, functional theory of respiration. It is hardly accidental that Lavoisier reached this clear picture of respiration in the same essay in which he presented his first clear interpretation of the combustion of *charbon* itself. Because he had from the beginning viewed respiration as integral to his plan of investigation of the processes that fix and release airs, a clarification of any of these processes illuminated the others. Once he had established that both respiration and the combustion of *charbon* absorb and release the same airs, then an explanation of the conversion underlying that particular exchange was almost bound to further his understanding of both processes. The culmination of this mutually reinforcing interaction in the almost simultaneous construction of a strong theory of the combustion of *charbon* and of respiration was therefore the most predictable outcome of his endeavor.

Not only did Lavoisier recover from his earliest ideas about respiration the view that the process releases the matter of fire which maintains the heat of animals, but he devoted the bulk of his statement to the physiological significance of the release and to supporting arguments for its reality. As his paragraph reveals, however, he did not have any new evidence in favor of this interpretation, but merely articulated the commonsense idea adumbrated already in the note of February 1775, that there is a relation between the warmth of animals and their respiratory activity. It seems evident that his new emphasis on respiration as the source of animal heat derived from the shift from an analogy with calcination, which normally does not emit heat in manifestly sensible quantities, to an analogy with combustion processes, which do; and to the recent strengthening of his conceptions of the role of matter of fire in general, especially his interest in its absorption or release in chemical changes.

Lavoisier did not state that the process which occurs in the lungs is the combustion of *charbon,* but that pure air undergoes there a decomposition *analogous* to that form of combustion. This cautious comparison, stopping short of an actual identification of the two processes, can be interpreted in more than one way. Everett Mendelsohn has implied that Lavoisier was not quite ready to state that the formation of animal heat was "itself a chemical process." He places Lavoisier's formulation as the penultimate step in a long historical development. Physiological processes, long viewed as "vital" phenomena, only analogous to those of physics and chemistry, were on the way to being treated as identical with the latter; and Lavoisier was here on the threshold of making that final transition.[73] That view appears reasonable if one is treating Lavoisier's statements simply as stages in a larger trend. There is no evidence, however, that Lavoisier was himself locating his views within such a broad setting. From the fine structure of his own development it appears clear that he described the respiratory decomposition as analogous to the combustion of *charbon* in the same sense that chemists habitually reasoned by analogy from one chemical process to a similar one whose properties were less fully characterized. He could state only that respiration produced an analogous decomposition because he had no direct evidence that a *matière charbonneuse* is present in the lungs and that its combustion was the cause of the conversion of pure air to fixed air. The analogy between the two processes was that both cause this same conversion. At this point he might similarly have described the combustion of candles as analogous to that of *charbon,* since candles too produced the same change, but the wax which is consumed was not known necessarily to be composed of *matières charbonneuses*. We might object that the conversion of pure air to fixed air is, according to Lavoisier's new theory of the combustion of *charbon*, sufficient grounds for deducing the presence of a *matière charbonneuse;* but that interpretation was still itself too new and too insecure to provide a firm basis for such deductions.

Lavoisier referred back to his analogy further on in the paragraph, when he asserted that his theory of respiration "is supported by facts and by constant analogies," the latter referring evidently to the properties respiration shared with the combustion of *charbon*. Later, however, he decided to rest his case on the "facts" alone, and not the analogy, so he rewrote the sentence which had begun "This idea, which is supported by facts and by constant analogies, may perhaps appear risky . . . " to the following:

> This idea [might appear] perhaps risky at first glance, but before rejecting it or condemning it, I ask one to consider that it is supported by two constant and incontestable facts; that is, on the decomposition of the [pure] air in the lungs and on the disengagement of matter of fire which accompanies every decomposition of pure air, that is to say, every passage of pure air to the state of fixed air.[74]

The change that Lavoisier made here implies both that he had originally viewed the analogy to the combustion of *charbon* as part of the evidence for his theory of respiration, and that he subsequently decided his case would be stronger if he relegated the analogy to a mere comparison. He now supported his theory by the "facts" that pure air is decomposed in the lungs, forming fixed air, and that such decompositions always release matter of fire. That is, from the observed conversion of pure air to fixed air in respiration he could identify the process as a member of a general class of such decompositions, all of which released heat. He was no longer relying on the analogy to one specific combustion which respiration only resembled. We may note, however, that the status of the conversion of pure air to fixed air in the lungs had undergone a remarkable transition in Lavoisier's mind. Only four months earlier he had presented that idea hesitatingly as a possible alternative to the theory that the pure air is absorbed in the blood and replaced by an equal quantity of fixed air. He was not then so confident of this alternative as to perceive it as an "incontestable fact." The intervening mental transformation is also a measure of how far the comparison between respiration and combustion had displaced from his thinking the comparison to calcination that had once so captured his imagination. His growing confidence in his theory of respiration as a whole is perhaps reflected in his adding to the phrase that it appears "perhaps risky," the qualification "at first glance."

Lavoisier's first "theory of respiration," that the absorption of pure air into the blood causes the red color of arterial blood, had vanished with scarcely a trace. (Perhaps a silent residue remained in his inconspicuous qualification that the pure air which enters the lungs comes out "in part" as fixed air.) Where had that idea gone? We have already considered the gaping flaws in the theory itself. Perhaps after gaining some distance on it, Lavoisier had been able to see how unsatisfactory it was, despite its attractions; or it may have simply been that the strong development of the alternative theory made the first theory irrelevant to him. Since he never again mentioned the first theory publicly, we have no way of knowing what he came to think of it. His behavior was, in fact, typical; for scientists regularly discard theories in which they have lost either confidence or interest, without afterward explaining why they have done so.

The demise of Lavoisier's first theory of respiration in favor of the one presented in his essay on combustion has recently been described as a "choice" Lavoisier is supposed to have made between two "sites of respiration"[75]—between the idea that the combustion occurs in the blood during the circulation and the idea that it occurs in the lungs. To put the issue that way is, as should now be obvious, to misunderstand the alternatives that he entertained; for the process that he envisioned as taking place within the blood was not the same process that he presumed to occur in the lungs. From the time that he wrote out his first two notes on respiration, whenever Lavoisier had thought about a conversion of ordinary, or pure, air to fixed air, and a release of heat, he had taken it for granted that the lungs were the site of this process. This was the simplest and most obvious assumption to make. The starkly uncomplicated way in which Lavoisier perceived the conversion is revealed in the fact that to his original statement ". . . there ought equally to be a disengagement of matter of fire in the lungs," he added in the margin of his text ". . . in the interval between inspiration and expiration."[76] Evidently he imagined that the pure air breathed in in one inspiration was immediately changed into the fixed air breathed out in the next expiration. At this stage in the development of his theory Lavoisier had drawn no further inferences about the process difficult to reconcile with a combustion located in the lungs.

Lavoisier introduced his description of respiration at the end of his essay in a way that suggested it was an application of his theory of combustion, and it has mostly been viewed that way ever since. All that we have learned of his progression to this point, however, belies the idea that he first completed his theory of combustion and then extended it to respiration. His essay on combustion taken as a whole appears as a new conception of "general combustion" embracing within a unified framework all three of the specific types of processes—combustions, calcinations, and respiration—that he had been studying. His "theory of combustion," he wrote early in the paper, explained "all the phenomena of combustion, of calcination, and even a part of those which accompany respiration."[77] In a passage already quoted he referred to "the analogy which exists between animal respiration, combustion, and calcination." In order to understand Lavoisier's position we must keep in mind that the particular combustions he had investigated—those of phosphorus, sulfur, charcoal, candles, and pyrophor—differed as much from typical calcinations as either of these categories differed from respiration.

Like other terms in eighteenth-century chemistry, "combustion" was gradually acquiring a broader meaning abstracted from its original applications. In literal combustions bodies burned with a visible flame, and conspicuously emitted heat. Combustible bodies had, of course, always been known to differ greatly in their degree of inflammability, ranging from those which "burn with a brilliant, very luminous flame, accompanied by smoke and soot," to those which burn only with difficulty, "without sensible flame, only becoming reddish." Some substances would not even burn by themselves. "One must borrow a foreign fire and cause it to penetrate the body" one wished to burn.[78] On that basis the concept could be extended to calcinations, as when Macquer termed them "slow combustions." With the phlogiston theory Priestley had built a theoretical bridge between combustions, calcinations, and respirations. Lavoisier now built a corresponding but stronger bridge, by showing that the three processes shared the same four laws. Lavoisier chose to *define* combustion by these four laws, even though two of the three processes so included did not sensibly display the central phenomenon, the emission of heat and light. What direct observation could not affirm he could now infer theoretically, through his conception of pure air as a combination of a base with matter of fire. The absorption of pure air, as in calcinations and the combustion of phosphorus and sulfur, or its conversion to fixed air, as in the remaining processes, must release matter of fire, even though the slowness of some of these processes makes the phenomenon difficult to perceive. In the case of calcination this was nearly a pure inference. Lavoisier admitted that the phenomena defining combustion "are extremely slow and difficult to grasp in the calcination of metals." The traditional identification of combustion and calcination had probably been made easier by the fact that a few metals, such as zinc, actually burned. In the case of respiration there was no heat immediately traceable to the inferred combustion, but Lavoisier could offer indirect evidence by adding the accessory hypothesis that respiration is the source of that heat which maintains the warmth of the body. Far from being a new area of application for a theory of combustion previously established around purely chemical operations, respiration was one of the three pillars upon which Lavoisier erected his general conception of combustion.

VIII

When he had written the first draft of his essay on combustion, Lavoisier knew that, notwithstanding the "contradictions" that he professed to see remaining for future resolution, he had reached the goal so long pursued. Now he was in a great hurry to establish his achievement publicly. Without waiting for the Academy to open, he had a fair copy made and took it to Condorcet for his signature on September 17.[79] When the Academy reassembled for its traditional reopening on St. Martin's Day, November 12, Lavoisier was ready to present his paper—an auspicious occasion, as it turned out, for the celebrated American scientist and statesman Benjamin Franklin was the honored guest. By foresight or good luck Lavoisier had included in his text a flattering reference to Franklin's views on matter of fire.[80]

How did Lavoisier's challenge strike his audience? According to a report in the medical journal *Gazette de santé*, his reading of the memoir "created a sensation." Hearing about it through this and another brief extract, Guyton de Morveau wrote Macquer, who had heard the paper directly, for more news about the situation. Macquer reassured him. "A great weight has been lifted from my stomach." His fear that Lavoisier had something devastating to reveal had been exaggerated. As Macquer summarized the argument, Lavoisier had claimed that the matter of fire is not contained in combustible bodies, but is a constituent part of the air. In combustions the matter of fire is disengaged from the air, leaving "only that which he calls *the base of the air*, which he admits is entirely unknown to him. You can judge whether I should have been so afraid."[81]

Historians have generally treated such reactions mainly as evidence that tradition-bound chemists failed to recognize the significance of Lavoisier's attack.[82] Such judgments are themselves, however, colored by later events. Macquer's criticism that Lavoisier could not identify the base of pure air was reasonable. Lavoisier's confidence that it existed was based on the weight gains associated with combustions and calcinations, and on the coherence of the entire system he was proposing. For chemists who were hearing about his system for the first time, and who habitually relied on qualitative tests to identify a substance, this base of pure air would naturally appear to be an undefined, hypothetical entity.

If the phlogiston chemists were relieved that Lavoisier had not overwhelmed them, that may also have been because he had been careful not to try to force them into a corner. He did not claim to have destroyed the phlogiston theory, even admitting that if one accepted its premises one could explain the phenomena of calcination and combustion "in a very fortunate manner." What he asserted was that one could dispense with the phlogiston theory and explain the same phenomena, with "fewer contradictions," by means of his own theory: but he stressed repeatedly that he was presenting only a "hypothesis," and not even a "rigorously demonstrated" one.[83] Astutely he made no reference to the phlogiston views of his colleagues, his only mention of them being to credit Macquer for the concept of calcination as a slow combustion. Lavoisier evidently understood human nature well enough to know that he could not make chemists who had worked productively for many years within the phlogiston framework abandon their long-nurtured views overnight. He promised to develop the consequences of his "system" in future memoirs.[84] He was probably resolved to win them over gradually, by presenting his case strongly but without demanding capitulation, until they would have time to see for themselves what gains he could continue to make with his views.

If Lavoisier was gentle with his French colleagues, he was equally sparing of his distinguished English contemporary. In contrast to the memoir on candles, which he had not yet made public, his combustion memoir made no explicit criticisms of Priestley's theories. The implications for Priestley's approach were veiled in general references to "the doctrine of Stahl."[85] Perhaps Lavoisier hoped that if he avoided treating Priestley as the principal spokesman for the theoretical system he opposed, Priestley might come to realize for himself that he should escape from the ruins of the old edifice; or else, if he anticipated that they must eventually clash, he did not rush toward that unhappy event. When he did read his memoir on candles, on December 6, he had softened the rather harsh passage about the entanglement of Priestley's phlogisticated air in Stahl's edifice to read, "Since I am about to combat the doctrine of Stahl on phlogiston with a series of experiments, the objections which I shall make against that doctrine will fall equally on the phlogistication of air supposed by M. Priestley."[86]

5

Collaboration and a Move toward Plant Chemistry

At the end of 1777, Lavoisier appeared poised for a strong forward thrust in his scientific enterprise. He had closed the major gaps in his theoretical structure. He had made the break with the prevailing theory of combustion toward which the course of his investigation had long been carrying him. He had announced a series of further experiments that he planned to direct against the phlogiston theory, and had predicted the opening of a limitless new field in the chemistry of acids. He had indicated that he or his associates were continuing the investigation of respiration. Although he had already delivered much, he had promised even more. There was much unfinished business on his agenda, from weak spots in the experimental evidence underlying his sturdy theoretical superstructure, to the application of his theories to a broader range of chemical phenomena. Instead of moving ahead vigorously with this well-defined, highly promising program of research, however, Lavoisier carried out fewer experiments of his own, and wrote fewer original scientific papers, during the next four years than at any other comparable period in his career. The reasons for this lapse are not easy to establish. It has sometimes been assumed that the press of his financial and other nonscientific affairs left him no time for his research; and that he was more concerned during these years to consolidate and systematize what he had already accomplished than to develop his investigations further.[1] Both factors may have played a part, but the arguments for those explanations have not been developed, and they are not, on the face of it, persuasive. Throughout his professional life Lavoisier was able to carry on simultaneously a range of activities that, as Henry Guerlac puts it, "is hard for lesser talents and less rigidly disciplined personalities to comprehend."[2] There were times, between 1777 and 1781, in which new outside responsibilities probably did preempt Lavoisier's entire working time, but it is hard to account for the whole four years in that way. Nor was there any necessary incompatibility between systematizing the work already done and extending the research onward. In the following account some additional factors will be suggested, but the situation remains somewhat mysterious. As we shall see, in spite of his reduced scientific pace, these years were not barren of significant developments within the research program that Lavoisier had sustained so much more actively over the four years that preceded them.

The view that Lavoisier was engaged during these years primarily in formulating his system instead of further experimentation is based largely on a manuscript, written probably sometime during 1778, which appears to be a plan for a second volume of his *Opuscules physiques et chymiques*. In the four-paragraph introductory statement Lavoisier wrote that he intended "to give an account of the general system conceived fifteen years ago, deposited at the Academy ten years ago, and meditated on since then." There followed titles for twelve chapters, which indicate that he planned to begin with his conception of the aeriform state, the formation of acids, and matter of fire, and then proceed to apply these principles to each of the combustion processes he had examined experimentally.[3] The manuscript, however, represents a preliminary idea; he could have written it out in a few minutes. There is no evidence that he began to elaborate on it earlier than about 1780, so that it is hard to establish that he spent much of the intervening time working in that direction.

There is reason to suppose that a large proportion of whatever time Lavoisier could spare for research activity during these years went into a collaborative effort with a rising star in the Parisian chemical firmament, Jean-Baptiste Michel Bucquet. Three years younger than Lavoisier, Bucquet had turned from the study of law to medicine at the age of sixteen, in 1762; but while working toward his degree at the Faculty of Medicine he also managed to find time for the ardent study of chemistry. Like Lavoisier, he learned the elements of the subject from the celebrated Rouelle. He also became an enthusiast for natural history, and spent several years learning botany. After obtaining his medical license in 1768, he conceived of a grand design to teach a course that would connect together chemistry and natural history. Quickly acquiring a reputation as a brilliant teacher, Bucquet also began to implement his design in systematic textbooks. In 1771 he put out *Introduction to Natural Bodies Drawn from the Mineral Kingdom*, followed in 1773 by *Introduction to Bodies Drawn from the Plant Kingdom*. The second book was not only the most complete and methodical treatise available on plant analysis, but the first one based on the new order of analysis by solvents taught by Rouelle. Bucquet's pedagogical talent was soon recognized by his appointment, in 1775, as professor of pharmacy. The next year he acquired a still more prominent position, succeeding Augustin Roux as teacher of the public chemistry course of the Faculty of Medicine.[4]

Bucquet often gave lecture demonstrations of chemical operations, and since they sometimes went wrong in front of his large audiences, some people regarded him as a chemist with more knowledge than practical skill. In his own laboratory, however, he was known as an able experimentalist. During the early

1770s he presented a large number of memoirs at the Academy based on his own investigations. Few of them were published, but his contributions were well respected by his colleagues.[5]

A lucid, careful thinker, Bucquet knew the chemical literature well, kept up with, and evaluated critically the new developments in the field. He was eclectic but selective, and distrusted theories that lacked full experimental support. He was particularly interested in the new chemistry of airs, for which, following Macquer's lead, he reintroduced Joan Baptista Van Helmont's old term *gas;* and he was more concerned with their operational characterization than with the theoretical interpretation of their composition. He preferred to test disputed issues in the laboratory rather than to deduce answers from theory.[6] On the other hand, he showed little of the driving creative imagination of Lavoisier. Just as his textbooks covered the existing state of chemistry methodically rather than advance it, so in his special laboratory investigations he mostly cleared up uncertainties left by the more pioneering work of others. In his extensive study of fixed air, for example, his main achievement was to remove doubts that the fixed air obtained from limestone by dissolving it in an acid really derived from the limestone. He did this by calcining the limestone alone in a closed vessel and showing that it still yielded fixed air. In January 1778, Lavoisier and Macquer reported to the Academy that Bucquet had "confirmed and completed the theory of Black . . . [and] that he destroys the last reasonable objections that one can make against that system."[7]

Lavoisier and Bucquet began to collaborate in the spring of 1777, an auspicious time in the careers of both men. One of Lavoisier's laboratory notebooks consists of a series of chemical operations intended for lecture demonstrations. The first of these, dated April 10, is in the handwriting of Bucquet, whereas the remaining ones, dated between then and November 27, appear to be in Lavoisier's hand. The reasons for Lavoisier's participating in preparations intended probably for Bucquet's course are not clear. Berthelot suggests that Lavoisier was "completing his personal education."[8] That explanation is not entirely convincing, for Lavoisier had had, early in his career, substantial experience with conventional analytical methods. Nevertheless Bucquet's methodical approach may have been useful to him. Lavoisier had specialized for four years so strongly in pneumatic techniques that he might have felt a need to strengthen his skills in more general procedures. On the other hand, since these demonstrations may well have been intended for the public chemistry course that Bucquet was giving for the first time, Lavoisier may have contributed his knowledge of operations Bucquet had not previously demonstrated.

Whatever may have been their original motivation for working together, Bucquet could offer Lavoisier talents and experience complementary to his own. His breadth of knowledge of mineral analysis, of plant and animal chemistry, of anatomy and physiology greatly exceeded that of Lavoisier. His precise, critical thought, his penchant for finding the weak points in conclusions thought by others to be well established, could provide a salutary check on Lavoisier's conceptual formulations; while his methodical approach to experimentation could counteract Lavoisier's tendency to make do with experiments that had turned out imperfectly. Less innovative but more thorough than Lavoisier, Bucquet was in a good position to help him reinforce the structure of his newly fashioned "edifice." Bucquet was, however, by no means the subordinate partner in the cooperative effort that developed between the two; it is clear that, even as Lavoisier attracted Bucquet into his scientific enterprise, he himself began to be drawn into the orbit of Bucquet's interests.

The range of experimental investigations on which Bucquet and Lavoisier collaborated was apparently very extensive. According to Fourcroy's eulogy of Bucquet,

> He carried out with Lavoisier an immense series of researches on the conduction of heat in different fluids; on the production of the artificial sulfur of Stahl; on liver of sulfur made with pure alkali and with alkalies neutralized with fixed air; on the reciprocal decomposition of nitre and different vitriols; on the combinations of cinnabar with many other substances; on the combinations of corrosive sublimate with many other bodies; on the analysis of Prussian blue; on fulminating gold, etc.[9]

In September 1777, they presented to the Academy the abstracts of fifteen memoirs representing experiments they had performed jointly. Shortly afterward they made an attempt to determine the products of the combustion of inflammable air.[10] Of special significance to both men was a convergence of Lavoisier's interest in respiration with Bucquet's interest in asphyxia and in the means to revive persons who had been suffocated.

Asphyxiation was a very old problem. Throughout history people had suffocated in mines, in rooms heated with charcoal, and in the vicinity of wine fermentation vats. Physicians had long been concerned about the symptoms of suffocation and how one might attempt to revive the victims. Autopsies on those who had died under such circumstances had revealed that the lungs were smaller than normal but filled with blood; that the left cavity of the heart was empty, whereas the right was engorged. The remedies to which physicians resorted were divided into two classes: one was to use stimulants such as cold water, friction, moderate heat, sharp odors, vinegar, or spirits of ammonia to restore the "extinguished vital force"; the other was bleeding to relieve the plethora of blood in the lungs, the right ventricle, and certain other blood vessels. The new chemistry of airs obviously provided an opportunity to reexamine the circumstances of asphyxia more scientificially, to explain it in terms of the chemical properties of the airs, and to attempt to deduce a rational therapy based on chemical theory. When Sage dramatically revived the bird Lavoisier had asphyxiated with fixed air in front of the emperor, by means of volatile alkali, he became convinced that he had discovered such an explanation and therapy. Fixed air, he claimed, asphyxiated by the effects of its acidity in the lungs, and volatile alkali counteracted these effects by neutralizing the acidity. Sage carried out further experiments to support his conclusion, and embarked on a campaign to establish volatile alkali as the sole effective therapy for asphyxia.[11]

To Bucquet, Sage's claim appeared to be a chemist's theory that took no account of the accumulated experience of medicine. As a physician "who, although a zealous amateur in chemistry, and convinced of the advantages [chemistry] can procure for the art of healing, has witnessed the errors that that science has imported into medicine too often not to be on guard against it,"[12] Bucquet felt strongly motivated to examine the question for himself by asphyxiating animals with specific gases, and testing on them the efficacy of volatile alkali and the other methods ordinarily applied for suffocated humans. With characteristic thoroughness he embarked on a long, systematic series of experiments. As the asphyxiating gas he utilized the fixed air produced from limestone, the vapor from glowing charcoal, and inflammable air. Into each of these he placed birds, rabbits, guinea pigs, and frogs. For each situation he utilized multiple animals, varying the length of exposure in the gas and the degree of asphyxiation produced. He observed the visible symptoms, and attempted to revive each type of animal with several of the agents customarily used, and with Sage's volatile alkali. On the animals that died he performed autopsies. Between the spring of 1777 and early 1778, he carried out experiments on about two hundred animals. He found that fixed air from limestone asphyxiated animals more rapidly than charcoal vapor, presumably because the latter contained some ordinary air, and that inflammable air acted most rapidly of all. Although the behavior of the animals and the autopsy findings differed for the three gases, in each case the lungs were diminished in size and gorged with blood. Bucquet concluded from their condition that these gases could not penetrate into the lungs, and that the animals therefore suffocated in the same way that they would in a vacuum. He found that the three classes of animals were affected quite differently. Birds died very promptly, quadrupeds somewhat more slowly, with variations according to their age and condition. Frogs endured for very long times. Bucquet attributed these differences to their natural habitats. Birds normally lived in "very pure air"; quadrupeds in air "more charged with exhalations"; frogs often lived in swamps and ditches, which disengage inflammable gas, and they spent part of their lives in a state of hibernation, which is itself a "veritable asphyxiation." With respect to his original question, Bucquet showed that volatile alkali was no more effective than other stimulants; whether they were able to revive the animals or not depended upon the degree of asphyxiation.[13]

Bucquet's study was typical of his scientific approach. The experiments were not novel; as we have seen, Priestley and Lavoisier themselves had often tested the effects of new airs on animals; and others, including Torbern Bergman, had more specifically examined asphyxiation with animals. Bucquet was, however, more methodical than anyone else had been, and he amassed so much evidence that those who reviewed his work were convinced that he had made a decisive contribution.[14] Because the questions involved were so controversial and important, many members of the Parisian scientific and medical establishments attended Bucquet's experiments. He claimed that more than eighty persons in all had assisted with one or more of them.[15] None, however, was more assiduous in his assistance than Lavoisier. Bucquet mentioned simply that Lavoisier had "been present at my [experiments] and found that the animals that I suffocated were in a state of asphyxiation at least as complete as was the bird revived by volatile alkali" by Sage after Lavoisier had placed it in fixed air in the demonstration for the emperor.[16] Lavoisier, who wrote the report on Bucquet's book for the Academy of Sciences, remarked in it that he himself "had been a witness to the majority of the experiments of M. Bucquet, and can certify that they were made with great care and attention."[17] Lavoisier must therefore have been with Bucquet for a very large number of experiments, an indication that he was very interested in the investigation. Such interest was hardly surprising, considering the obvious connection to his own interest in applying his theory of respiration to practical questions about the salubrity of the air. Since the experiments involved his own operational specialty, the handling of different species of airs, Lavoisier could obviously contribute more to the investigation than the mere testimony that the animals had truly been asphyxiated. Reciprocally, from Bucquet's autopsies he could learn something about the internal aspects of respiration previously inaccessible to him. Spending so much time in this way, however, must have cost him much of the very limited time he had available in general for laboratory work, and may account for his apparently having done so little in late 1777 and early 1778 to further his own lines of experimental investigation. The situation suggests that he placed at least as high priority on Bucquet's work as he did on his own research program.

During the course of Bucquet's investigation of asphyxia Lavoisier became sufficiently involved in the problem to take some initiatives of his own. Besides testing specific gases isolated in the laboratory, Bucquet wished to examine the composition of the atmosphere in special localities. On January 22, 1778, Lavoisier wrote in his laboratory notebook,

> M. Bucquet being occupied with experiments on asphyxia, and needing to extend them to a great number of airs, I thought it would be interesting to test that of swamps.
>
> Consequently M. Lelong, M. Fourcroy, and I descended into

> the moats of the Bastille, to the bank of the river, climbed up again, and established ourselves on the stream or moat full of water which flowed there. The bottom of this moat was muddy; when one touched the bottom large bubbles arose, and the mire was black at the bottom. In less than two hours we collected around twenty pints of this air, but a large twelve-pint bottle having broken, we were reduced to twelve pints.[18]

After this adventure Lavoisier and his colleagues returned to the laboratory and tested their swamp air in the usual ways. It appeared to be "mephitic," and to contain some fixed air. By mixing it with various proportions of dephlogisticated air they composed an atmosphere "very close to that of common air." These results puzzled Lavoisier, for in a similar expedition to another part of the same moat he had collected the characteristic inflammable air of swamps. He could not explain the difference, but thought "in any case one ought to be very skeptical of the quality of the inflammable air from swamps."[19]

The nature of swamp air was of particular concern to Bucquet because of the experiments with frogs. He was, he believed, the first person to observe their special capacity to survive in inflammable air. With these considerations in mind he and Lavoisier together attempted to compose a gas which would have the same properties as swamp air. By combining liver of sulfur and pyrophor in a closed vessel they were able to collect under a bell jar a gas which burned slowly with a blue flame, just as did the air often collected from swamps. In the discussion of swamp gas in his book on asphyxia, Bucquet reported, on the basis of Lavoisier's experience in the moats of the Bastille, that one could not always be sure that the gas collected from swamps was the inflammable air of swamps.[20]

As the above account suggests, by then not merely was Lavoisier assisting Bucquet in his numerous experiments with animals; but by contributing his expertise in the handling and testing of airs, he was becoming an active participant in Bucquet's enterprise. Those historians who view Lavoisier as an ambitious, self-aggrandizing personality may be surprised to see him here devoting such effort to support the work of his colleague when, busy as he is assumed to have been then, he might have been expected to reserve his restricted research time to the pursuit of his personal scientific interests.

On the other hand, Lavoisier did obtain some benefits from his collaboration for his own interests. A week after the Bastille outing, on January 27, he and Bucquet carried out on a guinea pig a test similar to those Bucquet had been conducting on the effects of asphyxiating gases, except that the air to which they exposed the animal was dephlogisticated air. According to an account Lavoisier gave several years later, their purpose was to determine whether it was necessary for the health of an animal that respirable air be present in the same proportion as in the normal atmosphere. At three o'clock in the afternoon they put one guinea pig in a bell jar filled with the dephlogisticated air, and began comparing the frequency of its inspirations with that of another guinea pig in open air. Lavoisier had to leave after fifty minutes, but Bucquet or someone else continued the observations. By five o'clock the enclosed guinea pig was breathing very slowly and had fallen on its side. Finally it died. By then Lavoisier had probably returned, and he tested the air remaining in the jar. It was still "very dephlogisticated"; a candle burned with a large, crackling flame. The guinea pig had therefore died not by consuming all of the available dephlogisticated air, but from prolonged exposure to it. Bucquet performed the usual autopsy. The skin of the animal was enflamed. The right auricle and ventricle were gorged, and the lungs were collapsed but also engorged with blood. According to Lavoisier's later account they concluded that dephlogisticated air alone is toxic, and that animals require a "just proportion" between respirable air and mophette. This experiment was the only one of those on which he worked with Bucquet that Lavoisier recorded in his own notebook, an indication that he regarded it as a part of his own research program rather than of Bucquet's project. The similarity to the experiments in which he was only helping Bucquet suggests, however, that their collaboration was reaching the point at which their individual research interests were partly merging into shared interests.[21]

In his book on asphyxia, Bucquet renamed fixed air "acid of chalk," and gave a careful rationale for his choice. He wrote that "Lavoisier and I believed that we could give [that name] to this acid." Lavoisier added a footnote to his memoir on respiration saying that he would henceforth call fixed air "acid of chalk" or "chalky acid," and that in the elastic state he would designate it "aeriform chalky acid." In the several memoirs he had written but not yet published he replaced the words "fixed air" in most (but not all) of the places it appeared, as well as the term "mephitic acid" that he had previously attempted to substitute, by one or another of these variations of the new term. Only in his memoir on the combustion of candles did he mention that he did so "in imitation of Bucquet."[22] These statements leave some ambiguity over which of the two men invented the new term. Most likely they were by now working so closely together, and exchanging ideas in conversation so freely, that neither was sure who had originated it.

II

On April 8, 1778,[23] Lavoisier read for a second time the memoir in which he had originally demonstrated, in April 1775, that mercury precipitate reduced without charcoal disengages not fixed air, but the "air itself entire," or "the purest portion of the air." For the occasion he made some revisions in the text that have attracted widespread attention from historians. Most prominently, he altered the language in which he had described that air, calling it now "the most salubrious, the most pure portion of the air," and air "in an eminently respirable state." Fastening on to this last phrase, he again referred to the air later in his memoir as "eminently respirable air." At the same time he deleted references to it in the original version as "common air," and eliminated the experimental description that it reacted to the nitrous air test in the same manner as common air. When he reread the memoir he also brought to the meeting the apparatus with which he had carried out the experiment three years before, to give his audience a better "idea of the operation."[24]

Historians have tended to treat with suspicion the textual changes Lavoisier made.[25] The implication seems to be that he sought to represent himself as having clearly understood in 1775 that the air released from the mercury calx is a specific portion of the atmosphere when, in fact, he had then still not distinguished it unambiguously from ordinary air. If one couples this suspicion with acceptance of Priestley's charge that Lavoisier had obtained the idea for the experiment from him in the first place, then one creates an image of Lavoisier as one who is known to have had an "occasional tendency to allow the work of others to pass as his own."[26] There is, however, no solid evidence that in making these changes he was attempting to rewrite history. He would have been naive to do so, since the original article was readily available in the prominent *Journal de physique*. His motivation was probably simpler. By the spring of 1778, when his new theoretical edifice had solidified, the experiments on mercury calx would have come to appear to him as one of the decisive experimental foundations on which he had erected it. Yet, when he looked back on the paper which reported these experiments from the vantage point he had since attained, the descriptions of the air he had identified in it would have appeared confused, ambiguous, and inconsistent. The embarrassment of allowing such flaws to remain, in what he could now anticipate might someday be regarded as a classic paper, is obvious. Since the paper had yet to appear in the Memoirs of the Academy, chronically two to three years late in publication, he had a convenient opportunity to avoid that outcome. He took this opportunity not only to correct the description of "eminently respirable air" which has drawn so much comment, but also to incorporate the understanding of the composition of fixed air that he had recently gained. Where he had originally concluded with a provisional acknowledgment of Priestley's view that fixed air is a combination of common air and phlogiston, he now wrote a replacement paragraph in which he concluded that the experiments detailed in the memoir demonstrated fixed air to be "the result of the combination of eminently respirable air with the *charbon*."[27]

The day after reading his revised memoir Lavoisier left Paris for an extended expedition connected with his role as director and a commissioner of the Gunpowder Commission. A central concern of the commission since its formation in 1775 had been to find new sources of crude saltpetre to use in the manufacture of gunpowder. With another member of the commission, Jean-Baptist Clouet, Lavoisier spent three months traveling through the provinces of France in search of such sources.[28] Soon after his return he turned his attention back to his personal scientific concerns, reading at the Academy on July 18 the memoir submitted the previous September, "The combination of matter of fire with evaporable fluids, and the formation of elastic aeriform fluids."[29] This paper was based on the experiments he had carried out with Laplace more than a year earlier. There is no direct evidence that Lavoisier found time during the remainder of 1778 to resume active experimental investigations. If he did so, it was probably as a continuation of his collaboration with Bucquet. As their scientific partnership deepened, the two chemists conceived of a grand plan to repeat a large number "of the experiments carried out up until the present day; it was necessary to reconsider them under a new point of view."[30] This brief reference to the project, made by Lavoisier later on, seems to indicate that he and Bucquet intended to reexamine the whole body of accumulated chemical investigations of the past, in order to assimilate the observations that generations of older chemists had made into Lavoisier's new theoretical framework. Such an ambitious project would demand the extraordinary energies both men possessed, as well as the talents of each of them—Bucquet's encyclopedic knowledge, critical acumen, and systematic approach were as crucial as Lavoisier's theoretical powers. It is not clear when they decided to merge their individual investigative pathways into this common plan. Possibly the joint abstracts they submitted to the Academy in September 1777 were already first steps in such a venture; but it is equally probable that the larger goal emerged only afterward, as their first common efforts proved fruitful and they grew closer in spirit as well as in work.

III

The earliest experiment recorded in Lavoisier's laboratory notebooks after his return from the saltpetre expedition did not take place until eight months later, on February 16, 1779.[31] On that day he undertook to repeat the experiment of the summer of 1777 in which he had attempted unsuccessfully to produce acid of sugar by mixing sugar with nitrous acid. To judge from the abstract of a memoir on acids he had submitted to the Academy that September, no line of investigation had then appeared more promising or urgent to him than the extension of his theory of acids in this direction. That it took him a year and a half to return to the question is a measure of how far he had been diverted by other matters.

In the new experiment Lavoisier arranged a retort, intermediary receiver, and pneumatic jar to collect the airs in the same manner as in the first experiment. He took extra care, however, to make his lutes strong and tight enough to resist the eroding effects of the nitrous acid that had caused him trouble the first time. He mixed in the retort two ounces of nitrous acid with four gros of sugar and two ounces of water. To avoid the decomposition of acid of sugar that had spoiled his first experiment, he applied heat to the retort with extreme care, removing it altogether as soon as the sugar dissolved. As the temperature in the retort rose from forty to forty-five degrees Réaumur, the solution began to boil, and reddish vapors passed "in abundance." He lost the first 12 cubic inches of the evolved air, and collected the remainder, amounting in all to 305 cubic inches, in five separate portions. The first portion proved to contain "the purest and strongest nitrous air I have ever obtained" (he estimated afterward that 42 out of the 45 cubic inches was nitrous air, the remainder fixed air). From time to time he heated the retort gently, just enough to keep the reaction going. When larger proportions of inflammable air and fixed air began to come over he discontinued the operation.[32]

After disconnecting the apparatus, Lavoisier found in the retort "2 ounces, 6 gros, and 18 grains of a very strong, very concentrated, odorless acid, having all of the properties that M. Bergman describes" as those of acid of sugar. In the intermediate bottle was an acidic fluid having the odor of nitrous acid. By saturating this fluid with strong fixed plant alkali (potash), then finding how much nitrous acid was required to saturate an equal quantity of that alkali, he determined how much nitrous acid had distilled over. Subtracting that quantity from the original 2 ounces, he determined that 1 ounce, 4 gros, 15 ⅓ grains of nitrous acid had entered into the reaction. On the basis that nitrous acid is composed of equal volumes of nitrous air and of pure air he calculated that 183 cubic inches of nitrous air would have been released, and that 183 cubic inches of pure air, amounting by weight to 1 gros 30 grams, had combined with the sugar to form acid of sugar. He had measured 190 cubic inches of nitrous air in the collection jars, a far better agreement with the calculated volume than in his first experiment. To reach that agreement, however, he had in the meantime had to revise the proportions of pure air and nitrous air in nitrous acid from those he had given in his memoir of 1776.[33]

Lavoisier had now attained his main purpose; he had changed sugar into acid of sugar, and in such a manner as to support his conception that the acid consisted of a particular base combined with the base of pure air. To solidify his gain, he did the experiment once again on the following day, changing the proportions of sugar to nitrous acid. He used 3 gros 2 grains of sugar in place of the previous 4 gros, again with 2 ounces of nitrous acid and of water. He carried on the distillation in the same way as before, but "pushed this experiment a little further," with the result that more of the acid distilled over. After the operation 1 ounce, 7 gros, 28 grains of acid of sugar remained in the retort, but since some water had splashed over from the intermediary bottle, he considered that weight unreliable. In the same way as before he collected the air in several fractions—six this time instead of five—and analyzed for nitrous air, fixed air, and inflammable air as in the previous experiments. He also calculated the quantity of nitrous acid whose pure air had combined with the sugar, and again calculated an equivalent amount of nitrous air released which closely matched the amount determined by analysis of the collected airs.[34]

This second experiment was no clear improvement over the first, was in fact probably less reliable. In neither case were the quantitative results certain enough to establish with precision the proportions of pure air and sugar in acid of sugar. Nevertheless, both experiments had succeeded in the sense that they were both interpretable consistently in terms of Lavoisier's conception of the composition of acid of sugar.

Considering how little time he had devoted to his long-standing research program recently, Lavoisier achieved in these two days of concentrated effort a remarkable triumph. For the first time, he was able to extend his theory of acids experimentally beyond the small group of common mineral acids on which he had built his theory in the first place. He had taken a bold first step into that "immense field of chemistry" that he had so grandly foreshadowed in the abstract deposited for the past seventeen months with the secretary of the Academy. Now he acted quickly to write the memoir that he had so long before implied was already nearly completed.

The most prominent feature of Lavoisier's paper "On the formation of acids in general, and of the acid of sugar in particular" was the new term he introduced to designate his conception of the base of pure air:

> The base of the most pure air being so essential to the formation of acids that they could not exist without it, I shall in the future call it the *acidiform principle.* This designation will eliminate periphrases, will make my manner of expression more rigorous, and will avoid the ambiguity . . . of the word *air*. That name has, in fact, through modern discoveries become generic, and it expresses, moreover, substances in the state of elasticity, whereas here it is a question of considering them in the state of combination, and in the liquid or solid form.[35]

His adoption of this term *acidiform principle* for the base of pure air has been viewed by historians, with good reason, as signifying that Lavoisier had now made his theory of acidity, and the role of that principle in it, the centerpiece of his entire theoretical structure.[36] Consequently, although he had originally defined that portion of the atmosphere whose base it forms in physiological as much as in chemical terms—that is, as the *respirable* portion of the atmosphere—it might appear that he had now reached a purely chemical definition of that air. It was now the combination of matter of fire with a base defined by the chemical property common to that class of substances which the air formed when it entered into other combinations. At one level this was certainly the direction in which Lavoisier had moved. At another level, however, he counterbalanced this move by the name he began, at about the same time, to attach to the air into which the acidiform principle enters. As we have seen, he had for a long time had difficulty settling on a suitable name for this central object of his attention. In the present paper, as in his memoirs of the past three years, he had most often either retained Priestley's term "dephlogisticated air," even though it expressed a theoretical framework he no longer accepted; or called the air "pure air," although that phrase still reflected his earlier uncertainty over whether the air was common air itself or a specific component. As noted above, in his revised memoir on the reduction of mercury calx, he tried out the phrase "eminently respirable air." This term must have appealed to him, because in the manuscripts he had still awaiting publication he substituted it for the other terms he had originally written.[37] Thus, while coining for the base of this air a term that reflected his most prominent chemical theory, he reaffirmed with his term "eminently respirable air" that the most characteristic property of the elastic fluid itself was still its physiological one. (Sometime afterward, at the suggestion of Condorcet, he substituted for this phrase the more compact term "vital air," which sustained the characterization, although in less vivid form).[38]

After introducing the term *acidiform principle* in the present paper, Lavoisier reviewed briefly the application of his theory to the common acids, repeated that a vast new field of chemistry lay at hand, enumerated the various types of chemical operations required to combine the acidiform principle with different classes of substances, and then turned to the example he wished mainly to discuss, drawn "from an experiment well known for several years from the memoirs of M. Bergman."[39] He then described in full detail the first of the two experiments he had recently carried out, and summarized the second as an effort to assess the effects of changing the proportions of sugar and nitrous acid. The immediate conclusion he drew was that

> M. Bergman and all those who have written on this subject have therefore been in error when they regarded the acid in question as the result of the decomposition of the sugar. It would appear certain, on the contrary, that this acid is formed by the combination of the sugar, in its entirety, with about one-third of its weight of the acidiform principle.[40]

With this satisfying conclusion Lavoisier had met the main objective of his investigation, and fulfilled the title of his paper. Instead of ending there, however, he went on to write:

> I thought that this same procedure might in addition provide a means to perform a more complete and certain analysis of sugar than those which have been carried out up until now. In this regard I have nothing entirely complete to offer, but I believe nevertheless that I should add here an experiment of the same type as the preceding, leaving for another memoir to return to the consequences that can result, whether for the analysis of sugar, or for that of plant matters in general.[41]

He went on to describe an experiment similar to the preceding two, except that he applied somewhat more heat, and collected a larger proportion of fixed and inflammable air relative to the quantity of nitrous air. He described nothing remaining in the retort. After determining the quantity of nitrous acid consumed in the same way as in the other experiments, he interpreted what had happened in the operation by comparing it with those two.

> One saw from the preceding experiments that [the nitrous acid] began by combining with the sugar to form a particular acid with it, and in the experiment in question here we learn that, if after the acid of sugar has been formed one raises the heat to the degree of a moderate fire, it is almost entirely resolved into fixed air, or chalky aeriform acid, and inflammable air. Now, what is chalky acid? I have shown elsewhere that it is a result of the combination of *matière charbonneuse* with the acidiform principle; from which it follows, that sugar is composed of a little inflammable air and much *matière charbonneuse*. This latter joins with the acidiform principle furnished by the nitrous acid and forms with it the great quantity of aeriform chalky acid that one obtains near the end of the operation. I propose to clarify by new experiments the obscurities that this type of analysis still leaves.[42]

A reader of this paper would naturally be led to assume that, after carrying out the first two experiments in which he changed sugar to acid of sugar, Lavoisier had realized that by carrying the operation further he could decompose the sugar, providing a new method for analyzing that substance. It is rather startling for us to find, then, that the experiment he reported was not a new one he had devised for this purpose, but the first, unsuccessful effort he had made in the summer of 1777 to produce acid of sugar![43] As well as any other event in his long trail of investigations, this one reveals Lavoisier as the master improviser, salvaging a flawed experimental operation by finding a new way to interpret it after the fact. Only after he had attained through the later experiments the objective which had eluded him in the first one could he view this one not as an effort to form acid of sugar that had failed because the sugar decomposed, but as an analysis of sugar by decomposition. We may recall from Chapter 1 that, as far back as 1774, he had pondered about how he might develop new means to analyze plant matters. He had expected even then that they would release fixed air and inflammable air, and that they would leave a residue of *charbon*, but he did not then know what the composition of *charbon* was.[44] He may have kept in mind ever since then this projected investigation, without getting around to doing anything about it. Now, five years later, something prompted him to perceive that in his first, unsuccessful effort to produce acid of sugar he had in his hands a solution to the questions he had then been asking. As predicted, the sugar decomposed to form fixed air and inflammable air. With his new understanding of the composition of fixed air, however, he could now establish the relationship between these products and the *charbon* he had previously regarded as a residue of the decomposition process.

Within the present paper on the theory of acids, Lavoisier's discussion of a method for the analysis of sugar appeared as a digression. Returning to his main topic, he repeated that what he had just established about the composition of acid of sugar would apply to "a great number of animal and plant substances." He summarized his results in five points which were also a restatement of his theory of acidity. Undoubtedly buoyed by the first major experimental advance he had made in many months, he presented his manuscript at the Academy for the signature of Condorcet, but did not read it at that time. Sometime afterward he added to his summary, in the margin of his manuscript, a sixth point which related not to the principal subject of his paper but to the analysis of the sugar:

> 6. That it is quite probable, especially according to the last experiment that I have just reported, that the *matière charbonneuse* is preformed in the plant matters, and that it is not in any way the work of the fire, as chemists have thought up until now.[45]

In his note about plant analysis in 1774, Lavoisier had himself referred to *charbon* as a residue of decomposition, in keeping with the view he here rejected. As we have seen, however, the meaning of the term *matière charbonneuse* had long since begun to drift away from the original sense of charcoal as the tangible substance left after plant substances were burned, and had taken on attributes of a principle that could exist in combination with other substances. Lavoisier was therefore not introducing an entirely new conception of *matière charbonneuse*, as he supposed he was, but only completing a gradual transition that had been under way for many years. Having done so, he naturally did not compare his position with the ambiguous intermediate stages; but contrasted it with the opposite pole, the original definition of *charbon* from which the transition had begun.

After hurrying to write up and obtain the official signature on his paper on acids, Lavoisier appeared to be in no rush to read it at the Academy. Over the summer he gave three other relatively minor papers. In one he completed his demonstration of the composition of vitriolic acid by reducing it with mercury to volatile sulfurous acid. The other two, one on the "vitriolization of iron pyrites," the second on the properties that distinguish the air from other elastic fluids, he did not even publish afterward.[46] Perhaps one reason that he delayed presenting a paper that was obviously far more significant than these was that he was not satisfied with the way he had written it. Evidently put together quickly because of the importance of the experimental results, it may well have appeared to him not to have related these results adequately to their broader context. At any rate, he rewrote the paper extensively, substantially shifting its emphasis while retaining its basic structure. The three experiments, which he had recounted in detail in the original version, he now reduced to summary descriptions of the procedures and results. At the beginning he added several paragraphs placing his theory of acids within a historical setting as the last of several successive stages in the analysis of natural bodies by decomposition. He also extended his discussions of his own theory. In keeping with these changes, he changed the title of his paper from "On the formation of acids in general, and of the acid of sugar in particular," to "General considerations on the nature of acids, and on the principles of which they are composed."[47] Where his paper had originally been a report of research on a specific acid, framed within his general theory, it now became the fullest statement of his general theory, illustrated by the latest example he had investigated.

Within this revised format Lavoisier retained his description of the analysis of sugar; but he modified the paragraph with which he introduced that topic:

> Independently of the light that this type of experiment sheds on the nature of acids, it furnishes a new means to proceed toward the analysis of animal and plant substances; and, although in this regard I have nothing entirely complete to offer, I shall give an account of the first attempt of that sort that I have made on sugar.[48]

Here Lavoisier was carrying his transmutation of the actual course of his investigation a subtle but critical step further. Not only had he redefined a failed effort to produce acid of sugar as an analysis of sugar, but he had now represented that operation as the deliberate starting point for a new field of investigation. If we regarded scientific papers as historical narratives, we would have to view Lavoisier as playing quite loosely with the facts; but this is not their intended role. If Lavoisier had not intended this experiment to be the beginning of a new area of research when he performed it, nevertheless he made it potentially just that when he came retrospectively to view it as such.

IV

On November 17, 1779, Lavoisier finally got around to reading his memoir on acids to the Academy.[49] In his typical manner he announced in it that he planned to follow it up with further memoirs extending his results to many other cases. After acid of sugar he "proposed to show successively in different memoirs that, by analogous procedures, one can join the same [acidiform] principle to animal horn, hair, animal lymph, wax, essential oils, expressed oils, manna, starch, arsenic, iron, and probably a great number of other substances from the three kingdoms, and thus convert them into true acids." The method of analysis by which he had determined the composition of sugar, he implied, could apply also "to a great number of animal and plant substances."[50] Thus the pursuit of his theory of acids was leading him from the circumscribed arena of mineral and pneumatic chemistry within which he had achieved his momentous successes, into vast uncharted domains of plant and animal chemistry, even as his realization that he had a new method for determining the composition of plant and animal substances was reinforcing the same trend. He was, however, on the verge of entering a far more complex and uncertain field of analysis, one with which he had had relatively little experience. Sugar he could procure in what was regarded as pure form, because it was a commercial product. Moreover, the exceptionally able analyst Torbern Bergman had provided him with knowledge of a specific acid derived from sugar, and directions for how to produce it. To go beyond that, Lavoisier would have to face the intensely demanding task of isolating from the plant and animal substances he enumerated the poorly defined acids they were thought to be capable of yielding. The very talented and far more experienced Carl Wilhelm Scheele had been following that quest for years, and had yet to duplicate his great success with tartaric acid. If Lavoisier appeared confident that he could make headway in so difficult an area, it must have been because of his scientific partnership with Bucquet. No French chemist was more knowledgeable about plant analysis than Bucquet. He had himself carried out analyses of animal substances, such as lymph and blood, and according to Fourcroy, "no one had ever described animal chemistry more extensively" than Bucquet did in his course lectures.[51] It is, in fact, very likely that Bucquet encouraged Lavoisier to set his sights on this daunting investigative pathway, and that Lavoisier counted on Bucquet's support to help him across its pitfalls. By this time, however, it was too late for that.

Always in frail health, Bucquet exacerbated his condition by the strenuous pace of his activity. He suffered from intense migraine headaches, gastric upsets, and insomnia. In April 1779, he became very ill, with terrible pains, convulsions, and extreme weakness. After two months he recovered somewhat, and in the fall he attempted to carry on with his course at the Faculty of Medicine. He was, however, so weak that he arose from his bed only with great effort, delivered his lecture by pure force of will, and returned exhausted to bed to rest for the next effort on the following day. Finally, on January 24, 1780, at the age of thirty-three, Bucquet died.[52]

In a manuscript for an introduction to a projected general treatise on chemistry, Lavoisier wrote a little later, in connection with the reassessment of all past chemical investigations that he and Bucquet had planned to carry out together,

> We had only just begun it, but death has cut down this indefatigable chemist who embraced all at once every part of the science of chemistry, who formulated a precise picture of that science, who reexamined its gaps. I have lost the help of this companion of my work, and I acknowledge that I have not had the courage to undertake such an extended work alone.[53]

Even allowing for the conventions of French eulogistic writing, this passage rings true as an expression of Lavoisier's sense of deprivation. It is only occasionally that we can penetrate the formality of his writings and the discipline he imposed on his activities to find such evidences of inner warmth and vulnerability. If he had carried out so little in the way of laboratory investigations over these past two years, that may have been in part because he had so completely merged his research plans with those of Bucquet that the turmoil of Bucquet's last year thoroughly disrupted them; and his death left a scientific and personal void that Lavoisier could only gradually refill.

* * *

On February 12, 1780, Lavoisier asked Condorcet to sign a new draft of his memoir on acids. This copy contained numerous small additional changes. While keeping most of the extended discussions of the preceding version, Lavoisier had also restored some of the language and experimental details he had previously deleted from the original paper. In one place, however, he made a novel modification. The sentence which he had written "I shall henceforth give to dephlogisticated air in its state of combination and of fixity the name acidiform principle," he changed to read, "I shall henceforth designate dephlogisticated air or *eminently respirable air* in its state of fixity by the name of acidifying principle, or, if one prefers the same signification in a Greek word, *by that of oxygen principle*." The phrases italicized here he placed in the margin, because there was not enough space for them between the lines, and Condorcet interrupted the vertical line, that he customarily used to indicate what portions of a manuscript his signature covered, so as to show that it included these words.[54] In the text Lavoisier changed the other references to "acidiform principle" into "acidifying or oxygen principle." Slipped this way into the third draft of his memoir, a year after he had introduced "acidiform principle" into the first draft, this change has the appearance of a casual afterthought. We obviously wonder whether Lavoisier thought of it himself, or whether someone who heard him talk about the acidiform principle suggested to him that the Greek version would be more imposing. Whatever the circumstances, this added touch had fateful consequences for the entire language of modern chemistry.

Part 2

Heat, Water, and Respiration 1781–1785

All of the major lines of investigation Lavoisier carried out during the years 1781–85 were extensions of problems defined by the new conceptual structure he had established during the previous decade. The best-known events of this period were the quantification of his matter of fire through the method of calorimetry that he devised together with Laplace, and the demonstration through synthesis that water is composed of inflammable air and vital air. These two developments deeply influenced almost every area of Lavoisier's research enterprises, including especially his theory of respiration.

During these years Lavoisier continued the quantitative approach to chemical operations that had already proven so effective in building his theoretical structure. Now, however, he began to encounter increasingly difficult experimental problems. Moreover, his objectives required him to strive not merely for quantitative results, but for results accurate enough to use as bases for complex further calculations. The laboratory records for the period afford illuminating examples of his efforts to cope with these challenges. We shall therefore in Part 2 examine in considerable detail Lavoisier's experimental procedures and the quantitative inferences he derived from his results.

As in Part 1 the focus remains on Lavoisier's theory of respiration, together with those aspects of his general chemical investigations that impinged most directly on it. I have not described fully his efforts to establish the composition of water, even though the consequences of those investigations were crucial to his views on all aspects of the chemistry of life, because that dramatic story has been given special attention elsewhere, and because it is too complex to incorporate within the confines of this volume. On the other hand, I have treated extensively his effort to establish the quantitative composition of fixed air, because that investigation is generally overlooked in historical treatments of Lavoisier, because it illuminates his scientific approach particularly well, and because its outcome was crucial to the subsequent development of his theory of respiration.

6

The Importance of Melting Ice

The chemical edifice he had put in place by 1780 afforded Lavoisier far more potential directions for further work than he was in a position to pursue in the near future. Almost every area of application for his theoretical structure stood in need of intensive investigation. At the same time he was more than ever overburdened with extrascientific responsibilities.[1] Under such circumstances we may wonder if even this tightly organized person may have found it difficult to establish a clear order of research priorities, especially after losing his closest collaborator. Whether or not he attempted to devise a systematic plan, the external evidence suggests that contingent events impinged strongly upon Lavoisier's choices as he began, during 1781 and 1782, to regain the earlier momentum of his experimental activity.

In 1781 Lavoisier encountered a book which covered a range of chemical and physical investigations remarkably similar to those he had pursued from 1772 to 1777. His friend the Baron Philippe-Frédéric de Dietrich published in 1781 a French translation of Carl Wilhelm Scheele's *Chemical Treatise on Air and Fire,* which had first appeared in German in 1777.[2] In it Scheele, who had actually written the book two years earlier,[3] had shown, independently of Lavoisier, that "atmospheric air must be composed of two different kinds of elastic fluid." He too observed that various combustible substances, including candles, phosphorus, and pyrophor, absorbed only a certain proportion of the air in an enclosed space. By distilling nitrous acid Scheele obtained both Priestley's nitrous air and a colorless air in which candles burned more brightly than in ordinary air. When added to the residue left after combustion this air reconstituted atmospheric air. Scheele named the new component "fire air." It was obviously equivalent to Priestley's dephlogisticated air and Lavoisier's "eminently respirable air." Scheele, an analytical chemist of unmatched skill and tactical imagination, had thus made on his own a large proportion of the crucial experimental discoveries that Priestley and Lavoisier made. Like Lavoisier at that time, Scheele did not use his conception of an atmosphere made up of two species of elastic fluid to dispense with phlogiston. Instead he devised a modified phlogiston theory, according to which the phlogiston given off from a burning combustible body combines with fire air to form fire itself. The fire then escapes through the walls of the vessel, accounting for the observed loss in volume of the air enclosed within the vessel.[4]

After completing his description of the experiments by which he believed he had proven that air consists of two "immediate principles," and explicating his concept of fire, Scheele wrote, "Now I shall go further and see if a still deeper decomposition of the air is possible." Rather surprisingly, the method by which he hoped further to decompose the components of air was through respiration. He placed a rat in a jar covered with a bladder and left it for thirty-one hours, by which time the animal had died. Then he inverted the jar over water and punctured the bladder. Only about two ounces of water rose into the jar. Next he himself breathed as long as he could into and out of a bladder. The air contained in the bladder afterward had "the same characteristics" as that in which the rat had respired. Each contained only "one-thirtieth part of aerial acid, which I precipitated with limewater, and a burning candle was immediately extinguished in it." When Scheele kept a few flies for several days under a glass jar inverted over water, until they too died, lime-water absorbed much more—"around one-fourth"—of the residual air, and a flame also went out in it. In the most novel of his experiments, Scheele found that germinating pea seedlings had the same effect on the air as did the flies.[5]

Scheele attributed that portion of the air absorbable by limewater at the end of these experiments to the transformation of air into aerial acid. What Scheele called aerial acid was obviously the same as what Lavoisier was then calling "chalky aerial acid." Scheele was now "curious to know whether it might not be the fire air which is transformed into aerial acid." To test this possibility he mixed one part of fire air with three parts of the air in which the pea seedlings had grown, and in which they would no longer grow, from which he had removed the aerial acid. The seedlings once again grew as in ordinary air. When they stopped growing again, he could once more remove a fourth of the remaining air with limewater. "It is, therefore," he inferred, "the fire air which is transformed into aerial acid." When he himself breathed into such reconstituted air, very little aerial acid formed, just as when he had breathed into a bag of ordinary air. Finally, Scheele repeated all these experiments with pure fire air. Once again his own breath produced "very little aerial acid," whereas flies produced so much that when he afterward inverted the jar in which they had stayed over limewater, the water gradually rose until it nearly filled the vessel. Seedlings did not grow well in pure fire air, but he believed that they too converted some of it into aerial acid.[6]

Scheele abruptly interrupted his description of this sequence of investigations at one point with an opinion supported by a highly interesting experiment:

> I believe that one must attribute the effect which animals provided with lungs have on the air to the blood present in the pulmonary blood vessels. The following experiment caused me to draw this conclusion.
>
> It is known that if freshly drawn blood stands in the open air it acquires a beautiful red color on its upper surface, and that, if the lower portions come into contact with the air, they too become red. Does the air itself undergo a change here? I filled one-third of a jar with freshly drawn ox blood, covered it tightly with a bladder, and shook the blood frequently. Eight hours later I found no aerial acid in this blood, nor that the volume had diminished. The flame of a candle was, however, immediately extinguished.[7]

Because he had carried out the experiment during the winter, he believed that the change produced in the air could not have been due to putrefaction; besides, putrefaction would have produced aerial acid. Scheele thus found that the blood had exerted the same effect upon the air as he and the rat—that is, the animals with lungs—had done. They removed the fire air, as shown by the fact that a candle would not burn in the residue, but they failed to convert it to aerial acid. Therefore, he inferred, those changes which the lungs produce on the air must actually occur in the blood within the lungs.

Scheele was now faced with the problem of explaining why, although both plants and animals consume fire air, only plants and animals without lungs convert it to aerial acid. "It is the fire air," he wrote, "by means of which the circulation of the blood and sap in animals and plants is maintained. It is, however, a remarkable circumstance that the blood and the lungs do not have the same effect upon fire air as do insects and plants, because the latter transform it into aerial acid, and the former into spoiled air."[8] By "spoiled air" Scheele meant the residual air which was neither absorbed in limewater nor able to support combustion and respiration. It was obviously equivalent to Lavoisier's *mophette*.

We need not follow in close detail the theory Scheele concocted to make sense of this "remarkable circumstance." It involved the idea that "all acids originate from fire air," a view curiously prefiguring the theory Lavoisier developed shortly afterward; but Scheele maintained that fire air itself is a combination of a "mild acid" with phlogiston. When fire air enters plants it attracts phlogiston, and its acid appears as aerial acid. Phlogiston, Scheele argued, is absorbed in the lungs, making the blood corpuscles more fluid, so that they appear brighter red. He left to others to explain what becomes of the phlogiston "during the course of the circulation of the blood." Because the blood has less affinity for phlogiston than do plants and insects, "the blood cannot change air into aerial acid; it is changed only into an air which is intermediate between fire air and aerial acid, that is, a spoiled air."[9] These ideas were not tightly argued, and suggest that as a high theorist Scheele's talent was not up to his splendid gifts as an experimentalist.

One of the great "might have beens" in the history of science is the impact that Scheele's book would have had if it had appeared when he wrote it. Aware of Priestley's early work, and of Lavoisier's first steps into the problems of combustion and calcination through a copy of the *Opuscules* which Lavoisier sent him, Scheele had more than kept pace with them experimentally. He had probably discovered his "fire air" before Priestley discovered "dephlogisticated air" and Lavoisier discovered "the purest part of air."[10] Conceptually he was also in some ways ahead of them. Although, like Priestley, he maintained a place for phlogiston, he had clearly formulated and experimentally supported the view that there are two species of elastic fluid, of which only one is absorbed in combustions and in respiration, while Lavoisier was still uncertain whether "the air itself entire" or some portion of it is absorbed. While Lavoisier was still searching for the relation between the composition of fixed air and common air, and Priestley was arguing that the fixed air which appears during combustion and respiration is already present in the atmosphere and merely displaced from it when the air becomes loaded with phlogiston, Scheele interpreted the formation of fixed air—his aerial acid—as a transformation of fire air, a kind of acidifying principle. By the time Scheele's book came out in 1777, however, Lavoisier had independently reached all of these positions, had based them on the more persuasive foundation of weight measurements, and was freeing them from the ubiquitous web of phlogiston explanations. By the time English and French translations of Scheele's treatise appeared, in 1780 and 1781, the opinions he had expressed were more than half a decade old. Priestley wrote a commentary in 1780 on the differences between Scheele's views and his own, retaining, among other things, his earlier belief that the fixed air formed in combustions and in respiration is merely separated from the atmosphere.[11]

Lavoisier and his colleague Claude-Louis Berthollet reviewed Dietrich's French edition of Scheele's treatise in manuscript, and presented a verbal report on it to the Academy in August 1781. They were then asked to make a more detailed analysis of Scheele's experiments. This request Lavoisier fulfilled on his own, with a memoir entitled "Reflections on calcination and combustion, on the occasion of a work entitled *Chemical Treatise on Air and Fire*." He read the memoir to the Academy on December 1 and 7.[12] Lavoisier was obviously struck by the correspondence between Scheele's experimental investigations and his own, and found it necessary repeatedly to call attention to the fact that he had carried out his simultaneously with or earlier than the date of the original publication of Scheele's book in 1777. Scheele's theoretical interpretations of his results Lavoisier could easily dispose of. If Scheele had measured the weight changes in his combustion reactions, he would have had no need to resort to the idea of a combination of phlogiston with fire air escaping through his vessels in order to explain the "loss" of air; he would have realized, as Lavoisier himself had, that the losses are completely accounted for in the weight gain of the combustible. "The question today," he asserted,

> is no longer to know what becomes of the air in combustions, calcinations, and other analogous operations; it is quite clear that it combines with the residue, and that one finds in it, or in the aeriform fluid that forms, all the matter introduced into the experiment. The whole problem is reduced to that of knowing whence derives the matter of fire—the heat and the flame: whether it derives from the body which burns, or from the air without which no combustion can take place. That is the state of the question, in the light of the modern discoveries on that subject.[13]

Scheele's theories, in other words, were no longer relevant to the present stage of development of these chemical problems—a stage reached largely, Lavoisier implied, through his own work. Nevertheless, Scheele's book was still of great interest to physicists and chemists "because of the multiplicity of experiments it contains, because of the simplicity of the apparatus, and because of the precision of the results which he has obtained in many circumstances."[14] With his admiration for Scheele's experimental ability, it is not surprising that Lavoisier took very seriously Scheele's investigation of respiration:

> M. Scheele has tried, as M. Priestley was the first to do, and as I did after him, to enclose animals in given quantities of air, and to examine the effects which take place. He has recognized, as I did (Mémoires de l'Académie, année 1777, p. 185), that the volume of the air is not reduced very much by the respiration of animals; that a portion is converted to fixed air, and that a diminution of volume takes place [when alkali or limewater is added, Lavoisier omitted to say] exactly proportional to the quantity of vital air originally contained in the atmospheric air.
>
> Bees exert upon the vital air the same action as other animals which respire do. If one encloses bees in a given quantity of air, the vital air is found at the end of a certain time to be converted into fixed air, and afterward the bees perish if one does not renew the air. The time in which the bees can live in a given quantity of air is almost exactly inversely proportional to the number of these insects.
>
> If, according to M. Scheele, one places ox blood in a measured quantity of common air, its volume is neither increased nor dimin-

> ished, but a considerable portion of the vital air is converted into fixed air. This very remarkable result throws a great light on the phenomena of respiration, because respiration produces exactly the same effect on the air.

Here Lavoisier inserted another reference to his memoir on respiration of 1777, in order to indicate that he had already demonstrated this effect of respiration by then. He continued,

> M. Scheele has repeated these same experiments, substituting vital air for that of the atmosphere. He has himself attempted to breathe that air, and he has observed that after fifty-six inspirations and expirations it had not diminished at all in volume; he adds that it contained little fixed air.
>
> Vegetation has an action on the air still more marked than that of animals. This type of experiment appears to belong exclusively to M. Scheele.

Lavoisier went on to describe some details of Scheele's experiments with pea seedlings, noting especially the "peculiarity that the vegetation of peas, according to M. Scheele, makes little progress in vital air." Then he curtly dismissed Scheele's explanation of his observations on respiration as consequences of Scheele's initial presuppositions. He remarked that "by supposing that the air is dephlogisticated in the lungs, M. Scheele separates himself from all the rest" of the phlogistonists, who believe, with Priestley, that the air is phlogisticated there. "In fact," Lavoisier judged, "the latter opinion is scarcely more supportable than the former."[15]

Lavoisier's reaction to Scheele's treatise was clearly complex and ambivalent. The "reflexions" he wrote in response to it betray an evident mixture of respect; of apprehension lest the remarkable series of investigations belatedly made available to French readers might make his own discoveries appear less original; of condescension toward theoretical efforts which, however they might have appeared in 1777, were now in his estimation thoroughly outmoded; and of special interest in what Scheele had to report about respiration. Lavoisier portrayed Scheele's work on respiration as best he could as a "confirmation" of his own, and as a worthy generalization of his own results to include insects and germinating seedlings. He barely mentioned that Scheele had found that "animals with lungs" produce very little fixed air. There is good reason to believe from a later comment,[16] however, that Lavoisier in fact felt that this finding constituted enough of a challenge to his own conclusions so that he might have to mount further evidence against it.

Finally, Scheele's single experiment on ox blood obviously struck Lavoisier as crucial. Assimilating Scheele's conclusion to his own viewpoint, Lavoisier misstated, perhaps unconsciously, Scheele's description of the outcome. Scheele had inferred that the changes in the air caused by blood were the same as those caused by respiration in the lungs because in his experiments both processes absorbed fire air and *neither* produced aerial acid. Lavoisier, apparently grasping at Scheele's statement about the identical effects of blood and respiration, reported that Scheele had found that "a considerable portion of the vital air is converted [by the blood] into fixed air." That is, Lavoisier represented Scheele as having shown that blood exerts the same effects as Lavoisier himself had found respiration to do.

We can readily appreciate why Scheele's experiment on blood so excited Lavoisier. The analogy he had drawn in 1777 between respiration and the combustion of *charbon* had already implied that there must be in the lungs some substance equivalent to a *matière charbonneuse* to combine with vital air. Ox blood was a standard source for charcoal derived from "animal substance."[17] The view Lavoisier had reached by 1779, that *matières charbonneuses* are constituents already present in plant and animal matters, rather than products of the heat which reduces these matters to charcoal, implied that blood would contain *charbon*. Therefore, when Scheele's experiment and the conclusion he derived from it drew Lavoisier's attention to the close connection between the action of blood and of the lungs on the atmosphere, it was probably quickly apparent to him that the blood can serve as the source of *charbon* which takes part in a combustion reaction with vital air. Moreover, as a source which flows through the lungs and is renewed by nutrition, the blood would be able continually to replenish the *matière charbonneuse* lost in the process. There is no way to determine whether such reasoning first occurred to Lavoisier by reading Scheele's account, or whether Scheele's experiment appeared to confirm an idea he had already had. In either case, the language in which Lavoisier singled out Scheele's experiment in his report, evaluated in the light of Lavoisier's subsequent writings on the subject, leaves little doubt that Scheele's brief account induced him either to begin, or to advance along, such a line of thought.

We should note also that Lavoisier's interest in Scheele's experiment was far different from his old use of an analogy between respiration and calcination to explain the red color of arterial blood. Although the color change apparently prompted Scheele to make the experiment in the first place, and Scheele incorporated an explanation for the arterial color in his version of the phlogiston theory of respiration, neither of these aspects of Scheele's description attracted Lavoisier's attention. For him the sole significance of Scheele's contribution was the demonstration of the effects of the blood on the air. His own newly emerging views about the connection between respiration and the blood had, therefore, little essential connection with his earlier speculation.

II

Although his review of Scheele's book probably stimulated Lavoisier to renewed thought about respiration in 1781, it did not shape the immediate course of his revived experimental activity. During that year he was preoccupied with a "long and difficult" series of experiments he was pursuing with Laplace, on the expansion of metals and glass between the freezing and boiling points of water.[18] He was, therefore, devoting his limited research time to problems associated with the nature of heat. Such studies were related indirectly to the experiments he and Laplace had undertaken in 1777, but his reasons for turning back to this area after a four-year lapse were probably external. In the intervening years his partnership with Bucquet seems to have displaced the collaboration he had begun with Laplace. Bucquet's death left him in need of someone else with whom to carry on the joint research efforts on which he so obviously thrived, and may have induced him to renew his association with Laplace. A further incentive to return to studies on heat was that at just this time news of major developments in the theory and experimental investigation of heat was reaching Paris from England and Scotland.

Joseph Black had discovered the concepts of latent heat and specific heat by 1760, but because he did not formally publish on the subject at that time, his views, like those on respiration, became known only gradually through his lectures and through associates who studied directly with him. A brief account of his ideas on heat appeared in 1772 in French, and Lavoisier probably read it, but it is most likely that they did not strongly impress him then. During the 1770s a former student of Black, William Irvine, developed a theory of heat based on Black's discoveries, but including a concept of "absolute heat" differing from Black's ideas. Adair Crawford, an Ulster Scot who heard Irvine lecture at Glasgow, then developed a method for measuring specific heats (which, following Irvine, he called "heat capacities") by mixing two different substances which were initially at different temperatures. From the final temperature of the mixture and the respective masses of the substances he could calculate their respective specific heats. Applying this method to airs, he found that the specific heat of fixed air was much lower than that of dephlogisticated air. Ordinary air was intermediate, although closer to dephlogisticated air. Crawford also determined that arterial blood had a slightly greater specific heat than venous blood did. Using these differences of specific heat, Crawford elaborated Priestley's phlogiston theory of respiration into an explanation of the formation and distribution of the heat in warm animals.[19]

Crawford published these views in England in 1779, in a book entitled *Experiments and Observations on Animal Heat*. It was quickly sold out, and copies were soon afterward almost impossible to procure. His ideas reached French scientists mainly through Jean Magellan, who wrote a commentary on them that appeared in May and June 1781 in the journal *Observations sur la physique*. Crawford's theories, as transmitted through Magellan, apparently stirred intense "agitation" in the French Academy of Sciences, and it was undoubtedly through this source that Lavoisier learned of them.[20] It will, therefore, be convenient to present Crawford's theory of animal heat here by means of Magellan's succinct summary:

> Atmospheric air has much more *specific heat* than the air expired from the lungs of animals, because the latter is *phlogisticated*, and in large part *fixed.*

From measurements purporting to show that the specific heat of ordinary air is sixty-nine times that of fixed air, Magellan then made a calculation showing that when common air is converted to fixed air a great amount of heat must be released.

> Therefore, the heat which is distributed within the animal body at each inspiration, in consequence of this conversion or transmutation of *common air* to *phlogisticated air* and to *fixed air*, must be very considerable. . . .
>
> The specific heat of the blood which passes from the lungs into the arteries is to the blood in the veins . . . approximately as 100 to 89. . . .
>
> From experiment one knows that all animals which have lungs have much warmer blood than those without lungs. It is even a general rule that the blood of those which have lungs is the warmer, the larger their lungs are.
>
> The quantity of the *specific heat* of a body is diminished by the addition of *phlogiston*, and augmented by its separation.

This last proposition Magellan supported with tables showing that the specific heats of metallic calces, which according to the phlogiston theory are metals deprived of their phlogiston, are higher than those of the corresponding metals themselves.

> It is from these propositions, established by the author upon a great number of experiments, that he has concluded that *animal heat* derives from the heat of the air which the animals respire. But one should see, in its original form, the reasoning and the proofs upon which Doctor Crawford has established this doctrine, which seems as well established as a theorem of Euclid.[21]

Further on Magellan pointed out that it was to "Doctor Priestley" that one owed the "discovery of the use of respiration," which is "to discharge excess phlogiston from the animal economy." Crawford had now demonstrated that "it is to the same process that one must attribute *animal heat.*"[22]

If Lavoisier did not take Magellan's advice to read Crawford's rare book, then he would have had to infer from the above propositions the actual outline of Crawford's theory. The discharge of phlogiston into the air in the lungs, and the conversion there of common air to fixed air, decreased the specific heat of the air, so that it released "absolute heat." Because the specific heat of the blood increased as it became arterial in the lungs, the blood could absorb this heat without increasing its temperature. Passing through the body, the blood became venous as it received phlogiston, its specific heat decreased again, and it released the heat throughout the animal.[23]

Everett Mendelsohn, who has treated in detail Crawford's theory of animal heat as it originally appeared, considers "the theories as expounded by Lavoisier and Crawford" by 1780 to be "conceptually almost identical."[24] There were, in fact, convergent elements in their thought, and both brought in a few similar supporting arguments. It is only, however, by restricting attention narrowly to theories of "animal heat" that one can view their concepts as similar. Lavoisier was constructing not an independent theory of animal heat, but a theory of respiration. The release of heat in an animal was for him a concomitant to a respiratory process conceptually inseparable from his views of "combustion in general." Crawford's theory was, on the other hand, tied to Priestley's phlogiston theory of respiration.

Magellan's interpretation of Crawford's experiments and ideas not only excited the French scientific community generally, but induced Lavoisier and Laplace to change the direction of their investigation of heat. Crawford's method of "mixing" to determine specific heats stimulated them to carry out similar experiments. Most of the sophisticated theoretical considerations on which they based their experiments were formulated by Laplace, and show clear connections with Magellan's discussion. Some of the experiments Lavoisier and Laplace carried out were explicit repetitions of Crawford's mixing experiments.[25] This derivative work was, however, only a small part of their new research plan; for Crawford's work served in a broader sense as the catalyst through which they finally came to appreciate the central importance of the concepts of Black that lay behind it. The main thrust of their investigation was a highly original use of the concept of latent heat to devise a method for achieving what Lavoisier had wished to do in 1777, but which he had not then known how to go about. With an ice calorimeter, the idea for which apparently also came from Laplace,[26] they had finally at hand the means to determine the actual quantity of heat released during any physical or chemical process that could be arranged to take place inside it.

The "machine" which Laplace invented, and Lavoisier had constructed, utilized in two ways the latent heat of fusion of water. First, heat released within the innermost chamber melted some of the ice contained within an immediately adjacent space that almost completely surrounded it. The ice which melted ran down through a funnel into a jar. All of the heat was in this way consumed in changing the state of the ice, none in raising the temperature. "The weight [of the water] exactly measures the heat disengaged from the [experimental] body, because . . . all of the heat is arrested in the internal layer of ice." The other way in which the method depended upon latent heat was that a second outer surrounding layer of ice protected the internal layer from any effects of outside heat. So long as this ice cover remained, it absorbed all external heat without increasing in temperature, so that this heat could not penetrate to the inner layer.[27]

Elegant in principle, the calorimeter also proved practical, although it required rather special conditions to function well. The exterior temperature had to be above zero Réaumur, otherwise the temperature of the external ice layer could fall. When, on the other hand, the outside temperature was far above zero, it proved impossible to prevent the colder inside air from sinking through the inner ice chamber and out through the funnel. Warmer air then entered through the top of the machine and "deposited some of its heat in the ice of the internal chamber." The higher the temperature, the more rapidly this circulation took place. Consequently, when Lavoisier and Laplace began their first experiments with the new apparatus, in July, this problem interfered so much that they had to postpone further research until winter. It was best, they learned, "to operate only when the external temperature does not rise above three or four degrees."[28]

In their first successful experiments, which they carried out between November 1782 and the end of January 1783, Lavoisier and Laplace measured the specific heats of mercury, lime, slaked lime, oil of vitriol, iron, and a few other substances, by the quantity of ice they melted in falling from their initial temperature to zero. This method they afterward presented as an alternative to the method of mixtures Crawford had used;[29] but this use of the calorimeter was, at least for Lavoisier, of secondary importance compared with the main purpose for which they had developed the method. In the famous joint memoir on heat, he and Laplace pointed out a few months later that the method of mixtures, while adequate for specific heats,

> is almost impossible to use for the heat absorbed or produced by [chemical] combinations, and it is completely insufficient to determine the heat evolved by combustion or respiration. The observation of these phenomena being the most interesting part of the theory of heat, we have thought that a method appropriate to determine these quantities with precision would be of great utility in that theory, because without its aid one can form only vague hypotheses about their cause; hypotheses about which it would be

> impossible to test the agreement with experiment. It was that consideration which first motivated us to occupy ourselves with the problem.[30]

III

For combustion and respiration experiments it was essential to be able to change the air within the calorimeter. To this end Lavoisier had a second "ice machine" built (see Figure 2). Two tubes inserted into its lid allowed one to blow atmospheric air through the inner chamber with a bellows. In order that this air not impart extraneous heat into the calorimeter, such experiments could be carried out only when the external temperature was "very little different from zero."[31]

On January 28, 1783, Lavoisier performed the first combustion experiment in this calorimeter, burning a candle and weighing afterward the quantity of ice melted. The operation was apparently successful, but Lavoisier did not consider the result reliable, because the outside temperature was a little too high.[32] He and Laplace may have begun with the combustion of a candle because it was the easiest process to carry out inside the apparatus. His general theory of combustion gave him ample reason to be equally interested in the heats evolved by combustion and by respiration; but the character of the remainder of the investigation suggests that at this time the heat of respiration was Lavoisier and Laplace's central concern. That concern is traceable to the view Lavoisier himself had developed in his memoir on combustion, in which he had presented respiration as the source of animal heat. Undoubtedly, however, Crawford's theory of animal heat reinforced the priority Lavoisier and Laplace now placed on measuring the heat of respiration. In an undated letter which, if one places it to fit within the sequence of events recorded in the laboratory notebooks, was written on Sunday morning, February 2, 1783, Laplace expressed to Lavoisier the urgency of getting on with the respiration experiments and detailed the procedures they should follow. "The weather is so favorable for our experiments just now," he wrote,

> and we have so little reason to expect similar conditions during this year, that it is essential to take advantage of it to carry out our experiments on the respiration of animals. I entreat you, therefore, if you can count sufficiently on the reliability of M. Gingembre, to engage him to perform the experiment on the guinea pig this evening.[33]

Laplace went on to indicate how the guinea pig should be placed on cotton to protect it in the wire basket inside the calorimeter, how it should be kept from escaping from the basket by covering it with an iron grill, and how one should renew the air in the basket only as much as necessary to support its respiration. He believed that the animal could be safely left in the calorimeter

MÉMOIRE SUR LA CHALEUR

Figure 2. Drawings of ice calorimeter, and of apparatus for measuring effects on atmosphere of respiration and combustion. *Left.* Cross section of ice calorimeter, with cover removed. Ice packed in outer chamber *a* insulates calorimeter. Ice packed in inner chamber *b* is partially melted by heat produced in combustion or respiration. Resulting water drains through stopcock *yk*, collecting in basin *P*. In respiration experiments, animal is suspended in mesh basket in center of calorimeter, shown also separately on right. *Upper right.* Bell jar used to measure absorption of vital air and formation of fixed air in combustion, and for the respiration experiments in a closed system. Marble basin *M* contains mercury, in which bell jar *B* is immersed. Dish *C*, floating on mercury, contains charcoal for combustion experiments. *ED* indicates level of mercury at beginning. *E'D'* indicates level at end of combustion, or period of respiration. *E''D''* indicates level after addition of caustic alkali. Lavoisier, *Oeuvres*, 2: Plate 2.

for five or six hours. After leaving the calorimeter overnight, one would "carefully weigh the water which will have drained out. It will be essential," he added,

> to repeat this experiment at least two times, and to preserve the animal with care, in order to determine afterward the quantity of fixed air that its respiration produces at a temperature of zero. This experiment, if well done, will irrevocably establish the cause of animal heat, concerning which the experiments of M. Cra[w]ford, although very ingenious, still leave some uncertainty. I believe that it will be good to repeat the experiment on the combustion of a candle when the temperature will be one or two degrees, in order to be able to determine by that means the quantity of heat which is released in the change of dephlogisticated air into fixed air.

Laplace ended his letter by expressing his disappointment that the distance to the Arsenal, where Lavoisier planned to carry out the experiments, made it difficult for him to follow them. "Nevertheless, if I am able, I shall be at the Arsenal at six or seven o'clock this evening."[34]

This important letter shows that although Lavoisier took the direct responsibility for performing the respiration experiments, Laplace was deeply interested and involved in them. There is no evidence that Lavoisier was less interested, but perhaps he was so busy that Laplace had to press him to find the time to carry them out in the midst of his other activities when the right weather conditions arrived. The letter might also seem to imply that Laplace was the dominant partner in designing the investigation; but it is more likely that his directions were a form of memorandum reminding Lavoisier of procedures they had previously discussed.

In conjunction with their later account of the ensuing investigation, we can infer from Laplace's letter how he and Lavoisier anticipated at the beginning that they would "establish irrevocably the cause of animal heat." They intended to measure the quantity of heat an animal would produce during a given time period, then to measure how much fixed air the same animal would produce at the same temperature over the same time. By comparing the quantity of heat the animal produced with the heat emitted by a burning candle in producing the same quantity of fixed air, they would be able to judge whether the heat released in the conversion of vital air to fixed air is adequate to account for the heat actually released by the animal. It is clear from the letter that they expected in advance that the answer to this question would be affirmative.

Apparently Lavoisier was not able to take up Laplace's plea on the day he received his letter; but the weather remained favorable the next day, and this time he moved to put their plans into action. On the morning of February 3 the temperature stood at 1½ degrees. At 8:12 am Lavoisier (or perhaps the aforementioned M. Gingembre) put a guinea pig, whose internal temperature was 20 degrees, into the "machine." Because they "were afraid that there was not a sufficient renewal of air in the machine to sustain the respiration of the animal," they blew air through it with a bellows at 8:25, 9:00, 9:17, and 11:00. By then the outside temperature had risen to 2½ degrees, but it afterward went back down to 2 degrees. After ventilating the calorimeter once more at 12:41 pm, they removed the animal at 1:40 and found that its internal temperature was still 20 degrees. The animal had been inside the calorimeter for a total of 5 hours and 28 minutes.

Afterward they let the melted ice drain out of the machine until 3:00 and collected 6 ounces, 3 gros, and 47 grains of water; but because they believed that the machine had probably not been "sufficiently" drained during the hour and 20 minutes they had allowed for it, they estimated "the quantity of water produced at 7 ounces, or at least at 6 ounces 7 gros." The correction was evidently based on intuition.[35]

On "the evening of the same day," Lavoisier and Laplace "repeated this experiment with the same guinea pig. The temperature of the animal was 20½ degrees. It was very lively and healthy, so that it had not suffered at all from the morning session." When they put the animal back into the machine at 9:28 pm, the external temperature was 2½ degrees. It was probably a measure both of their interest in the experiment and of the lengths to which they had to go to operate under weather conditions cold enough for their calorimeter that they continued the experiment right through the night, staying around to work the bellows at 11 o'clock, midnight, 1:00 am, and 4:00 am, and removing the animal finally at 8:04 in the morning. It had been in the calorimeter this time for 10 hours and 36 minutes. However Lavoisier and Laplace may have felt by then, the guinea pig "had not suffered, and was looking healthy." Draining the calorimeter until 9:50 am, they collected 14 ounces, 2 gros, and 22 grains of water. Deciding once again, however, that the machine had not drained sufficiently, they believed "one could raise the quantity of water produced to 14 ounces and 5 gros."[36] We may infer that after they had assured themselves in the first experiment that the guinea pig could easily withstand long exposure to the calorimeter, they had probably doubled the length of the second experiment so that the drainage problem would introduce a proportionately smaller error into the result.

With these two experiments, carried out over a marathon twenty-four-hour vigil, Lavoisier and Laplace began[37] what Mendelsohn has called "the most important group of experiments in the history of metabolic-heat studies."[38]

February 4 was slightly colder than it had been the day before, the temperature in the evening being only one degree. This was "very favorable weather" for the calorimeter, so they pressed on, repeating the measurement of the heat released by a candle. Immediately after lighting the candle they placed it in the machine and, ventilating it constantly with the bellows, kept it burning for thirty minutes. The candle lost 64½ grains in weight, and after allowing the calorimeter to drain for five hours, at 2:00 am they collected 1 pound 4 gros of water. This amounted, Lavoisier noted, to 1 pound, 2 ounces, 4½ gros per gros of candle consumed. Although the result was "a little feeble by comparison to the experiment of January 28," Lavoisier had more confidence in it because it was performed at a temperature closer to zero.[39]

The next day the temperature was about the same, and Lavoisier and Laplace turned to the combustion of *charbon.* They had to resort to an ingenious trick to know the amount consumed. Placing a piece of glowing charcoal in a crucible on a scale weighted on the other side so that it would balance when the charcoal weighed exactly 1 ounce, they blew on the burning pieces with a bellows until that moment occurred. Then they "enclosed the charcoal on the spot in the machine," and continued to blow on it through the ventilation tubes. The experiment lasted thirty-two minutes. "During that time a rather thick and smoky vapor with a charcoal odor emerged from all of the joints of the machine." They thought that the vapor must be due in part to some drops of water having fallen on the charcoal. When the experiment ended, at 10:30 pm, the charcoal was entirely consumed, leaving only a few cinders. After the machine had drained until 7:00 am, they collected 6 pounds, 3 ounces, and 2 gros of water. Even though this was during the middle of the night, "the weather had become warmer" by then, "and the thermometer was at +4 degrees." That was enough to cause some of the melting by convection to which they had earlier discovered their machine was susceptible. For this reason they suspected that "1 ounce and 2 gros were due to the machine during the night." Accordingly, they reduced the amount derived from the combustion of charcoal to 6 pounds 2 ounces.[40] As we have already seen, Lavoisier regularly made such corrections in his data from guesses about sources of small errors he could not directly measure.

Lavoisier recorded no more calorimetric experiments in his notebook for about two weeks following these intensive three days. It may well be that the warmer weather which was already setting in by the time they finished this last one prevented them from going on. On February 21 they returned to these experiments, doing the heat of combustion of phosphorus, of the detonation of nitre, and another trial of the combustion of *charbon.* Two days later they did another measurement on nitre and on phosphorus, and one on the heat of solution of iron in vitriolic acid. On February 28 they measured once more the heat produced by a candle, burned this time for twenty minutes. Lavoisier made another typical "correction" of the weight loss, from the 69¾ grains they actually measured, to 69½ grains, because "there was a small amount of time lost [between lighting the candle and] putting it into the machine." Later that day they repeated again the heats of combustion of nitre and of sulfur.[41] With that, so far as the notebook record informs us, these combustion and respiration experiments with the calorimeter ended. Although Lavoisier and Laplace may have performed a few others not recorded there, it is unlikely that they did many more, for they wrote afterward that the mildness of that winter had not permitted them to make a large number of them.[42]

On a date which Lavoisier did not record, but which, if the notebook is not further out of order at this point, was sometime between February 5 and March 14, he and Laplace performed the following experiment:

> Respiration of animals
>
> In a special apparatus, of which we shall later give a special description and drawing, we placed a small guinea pig in order to maintain it continually in good health by continually supplying it with fresh air at the rate of about 30 pints per hour. We left it in the apparatus for exactly nine hours. The air which we furnished it was forced, on leaving, to bubble through two bottles containing caustic fixed plant alkali.
>
> The quantity of fixed air which we found combined in the first bottle was 15 grains, and the quantity found in the second phial was only 3 grains. That makes 18 grains in all, which is equivalent to about 26 cubic inches. Now 26 cubic inches of dephlogisticated air corresponds to about 11¾ or 12 grains. Thus in this observation the animal produced no more than 6 or 6¼ grains of *matière charbonneuse*.[43]

In this experiment Lavoisier returned to the "effects" of respiration upon the atmosphere which had occupied him in 1777, but with crucial innovations in purpose, conception, and procedure. He now took for granted, in fact his method relied upon, the qualitative effects he had then established. His aim now was to measure the amounts of each of the substances involved in the conversion of "vital air"—or, as he even yet sometimes called it, dephlogisticated air—to fixed air during a given time interval. For this objective his old method, in which the animal breathed in a closed vessel over mercury, had serious deficiencies. Although it had permitted a direct measurement of both airs involved, as the new method did not, the composition of the air in which the animal breathed had become progressively more "noxious"; respiration had become increasingly abnormal, and the animal could live less than an hour in it. Here Lavoisier and Laplace had devised a method which obviated these drawbacks by continually replacing the vital air the animal used up and removing the fixed air it produced. The guinea pig was thus able to breathe, under normal conditions, for over nine times as long as the former experiments had lasted. They were in this way measuring the process at its presumed normal, rather than a disturbed, rate, and with greater accuracy, because the quantity of fixed air produced over the extended time would be proportionately greater.

The penalty they had to pay for these advantages was that without a closed chamber they could not determine the quantity of vital air consumed by the usual means of the change in the total volume of air present. They could directly determine the fixed air formed in an open system, because they could absorb it in caustic alkali and measure the quantity as the increase in the weight of the absorbing bottles. From that result they calculated indirectly the weight of the vital air used up, but the result depended on several assumptions and uncertain values. From other experiments Lavoisier estimated that the density of fixed air was about 7⁄10 of a grain per cubic inch,[44] from which he figured that the volume of fixed air equivalent to the 18 grains collected in the alkali was 26 cubic inches. Next he assumed that the volume of vital air absorbed was equal to that of the fixed air formed. This assumption was no doubt based on his prior respiration experiments in closed chambers, in which the volume had changed very little until he removed the fixed air. Then, assuming a density for vital air between 0.45 and 0.46 grains per cubic inch, based on measurements which are not identified in the notebook,[45] he reached his figure of 11¾ to 12 grains of vital air consumed. Finally, assuming that all of the vital air consumed is combined with *matière charbonneuse* to form the fixed air, he subtracted the calculated weight of vital air from the measured weight of fixed air to obtain his figure for the amount of *matière charbonneuse* the animal must have provided to convert the vital air into fixed air. Besides these particular assumptions his calculation rested on his fundamental conviction that all of the matter that enters into a chemical change can be accounted for in its products.

In this case the result turned out to be so low that Lavoisier did not believe the basic measurement on which the calculation depended could be accurate. "Perhaps," he thought, "there is reason to believe that some fixed air remained in the bell jar" in which the animal had been placed.[46]

There are few clues to illuminate how Lavoisier and Laplace may have been led to devise this important advance in the techniques for studying respiration. One can suppose that a straightforward analysis of the requirements for an effective quantitative measurement could have yielded the experimental design they followed. From the desirability of making the measured product as large as possible one could infer the necessity for extending the time over which the product is produced. From that requirement one could readily infer that the air must be renewed, since the animal would not otherwise survive through the experiment. This requirement would rule out the standard means for measuring the quantities of the vital air absorbed and the fixed air produced by the volume changes in a closed chamber. Having no means to measure the volumes of airs entering and leaving an open system, they were left with only the method of the weight gain in alkali to determine the fixed air. Lavoisier and Laplace *could* have proceeded through such strictly logical steps to their solution. The logical steps, however, are easier to arrange in place after the solution is reached than when one is still searching for the way. There is a remarkable coincidence between the elements of the solution of this problem and the features of their method for measuring the heat released in respiration. There too the necessity for a large enough quantity of heat to measure accurately had dictated an extended period of time, which had required in return that the air be regularly renewed. There too the product to be determined was "trapped" in a manner which resulted in a weight measurement. A final coincidence is that, six years having elapsed since Lavoisier's earlier respiration experiments, he and Laplace reached this solution during just those weeks in which they had been carrying out the calorimetric experiments. If, as Thomas Kuhn has argued, scientists commonly solve problems by perceiving that, in ways not always specifiable in every detail, they are *like* other problems which have been solved,[47] then we may imagine that, deliberately or tacitly, they may have to some extent modeled this experiment on the preceding calorimetric ones.

Lavoisier's record of this respiration experiment tacitly reveals that his conception of the process had undergone a significant change. As we have seen, in 1777 he had described respiration as "analogous to the combustion of *charbon*. Now, however, in calculating the quantity of *matière charbonneuse* "produced by the animal," he was assuming that the process occurring in the lungs was not merely similar, but identical, to that which takes place when charcoal or some other substance containing *matière charbonneuse* is burned. Lavoisier must have made this mental transition either by the time he and Laplace took up the new investigation of respiration, or at least so near the beginning of the investigation that he could not have derived his new view from its results.

We can only guess at the factors which may have induced this conceptual development. Perhaps it was the outcome of nothing more than the passage of time. As one grows accustomed to one's own new ideas, one is apt to drop qualifications or cautious modes of expression contained in the original formulations. Or, perhaps the continued evolution of Lavoisier's conception of *matière charbonneuse*, differentiating the theoretical substance more clearly from its prototypical physical manifestations, had eliminated the need to think of the substance consumed in respiration as only analogous to that matter. The only more specific intervening event that might have led Lavoisier toward the literal identification of these processes was Scheele's experiment on the absorption of vital air by ox blood. The reasoning that I have suggested Lavoisier might have gone through in response to Scheele's observation could at the same time have convinced him that the blood was the source of the substance contributed by the animal to the conversion of vital air to fixed air, and that that substance was actually *matière charbonneuse*. The conceptual change was, in any case, subtle enough so that Lavoisier might have made it almost without noticing it; for in eighteenth-century chemistry the distinction between analogous processes and the same process occurring under different circumstances was much less sharp than it later became. Nevertheless this mental step has recently been treated as a great turning point in the overarching relation between vital and chemical processes.[48]

Extending the time period by renewing the air was not the only approach Lavoisier and Laplace tried in order to measure the quantities of air respired. To obtain a direct measure of the volume of vital air absorbed they reverted, on May 5, to an experiment of the old type, in a closed bell jar over mercury. They utilized dephlogisticated air, evidently to allow the animal to breathe as long as possible within the limitations of this arrangement. To increase the accuracy of their measurement they used a new eudiometric adaptation of Priestley's nitrous air test, devised by the Abbé Fontana, to determine the proportion of impurities in the dephlogisticated air. In this method one added to the sample air successive smaller portions of nitrous air until the volume of air had contracted as far as possible. The original 4 parts of dephlogisticated air contracted to 0.63 parts, so that it contained about 15 percent impurities. Filling the bell jar with the dephlogisticated air, and marking the level of the mercury, "we introduced, through the mercury, two sparrows, who did not appear to suffer . . . by their passage through it." After an hour, they removed the birds, who "had begun to appear languid and to respire hurriedly." They then introduced two other birds into the jar, but these began to suffer after a few minutes, and they had to take them out at the end of a quarter of an hour. The small decrease in volume resulting directly from the respiration they estimated from the slight change in the height of the mercury and the diameter of the jar. Next they absorbed the fixed air by pipetting a layer of caustic alkali onto the surface of the mercury in the jar, and marked the new level of the mercury, correcting for the thickness of the alkali layer. They then determined the volume of vital air at the beginning and end of the experiment from the weights of water required to fill the bell jar to the respective marks. They found in this way that the "quantity of vital air consumed was 21.84 inches." Despite the care with which they had made the basic measurements, however, they found afterward that they had forgot to observe the temperature and barometric pressure during the experiment, so that they could not reduce this volume to standard conditions; an omission "which," Lavoisier noted wryly, "detracts from its precision."[49]

On May 12 Lavoisier and Laplace repeated the same type of experiment, using a guinea pig instead of the sparrows, and a bell jar affording about three times the volume of dephlogisticated air they had previously used (see Figures 3–6). They employed dephlogisticated air produced at the same time as that which had served on the last experiment.

> We filled a bell jar with it, and, having placed it over the mercury, we were able to introduce a guinea pig, which remained in it for an hour and a quarter. At the end of that time, since it seemed

> to be starting to suffer, we removed it in the same way that it had entered; that is, through the mercury. The animal did not appear to have suffered very much during all these operations.

They determined the volumes in the same manner, from the weight of water needed to fill the space; but since there had been substantial differences between the internal and external levels of the mercury, they made corrections for the changes in the pressure. Being "curious to examine whether the dephlogisticated air we had employed contained a sensible quantity of fixed air," they placed a sample of it in a column over mercury and added caustic alkali. From the resulting decrease in volume Lavoisier estimated that the initial 248 cubic inches of dephlogisticated air had contained 8 cubic inches of fixed air, and only 240 cubic inches of "vital air." The corrected volume of the air remaining in the bell jar after the experiment was over and they had added caustic alkali was 200.5 cubic inches. Out of this reduction of 39.83 cubic inches, 8 cubic inches represented the fixed air originally present, so that the "quantity due to the respiration" was 31.83 cubic inches.[50] This was a result in which they apparently had strong confidence.

On the same day they returned to the new type of experiment in which they renewed the air. Refining their initial effort, however, instead of simply ventilating the chamber with outside air, they directed dephlogisticated air into it to replace the vital air consumed.

> We placed a guinea pig under a bell jar immersed in mercury and containing ordinary air. A tube had been attached, through which air entered, and another through which it left. The entry tube was adapted to the dephlogisticated air apparatus. The exit tube was immersed into a two-necked bottle of caustic alkali, and the air was again forced, upon leaving that bottle, to pass through a second bottle of caustic alkali. The animal remained in that situation for 2 hours and 35 minutes, after which we reweighed the bottles. The first had increased by 51 grains. The second had increased by only half a grain at the most.[51]

One week later, on May 19, they carried out another experiment using the same procedures.

> The guinea pig had been in the apparatus for three hours, and during that time the weight of the first bottle had increased by 63 grains, and that of the second by 8 grains.

Now they introduced an additional operation to preclude, at least partially, the source of the error they suspected in the initial experiment of this type, namely that some fixed air may have remained in the respiration chamber instead of passing into the alkali bottles:

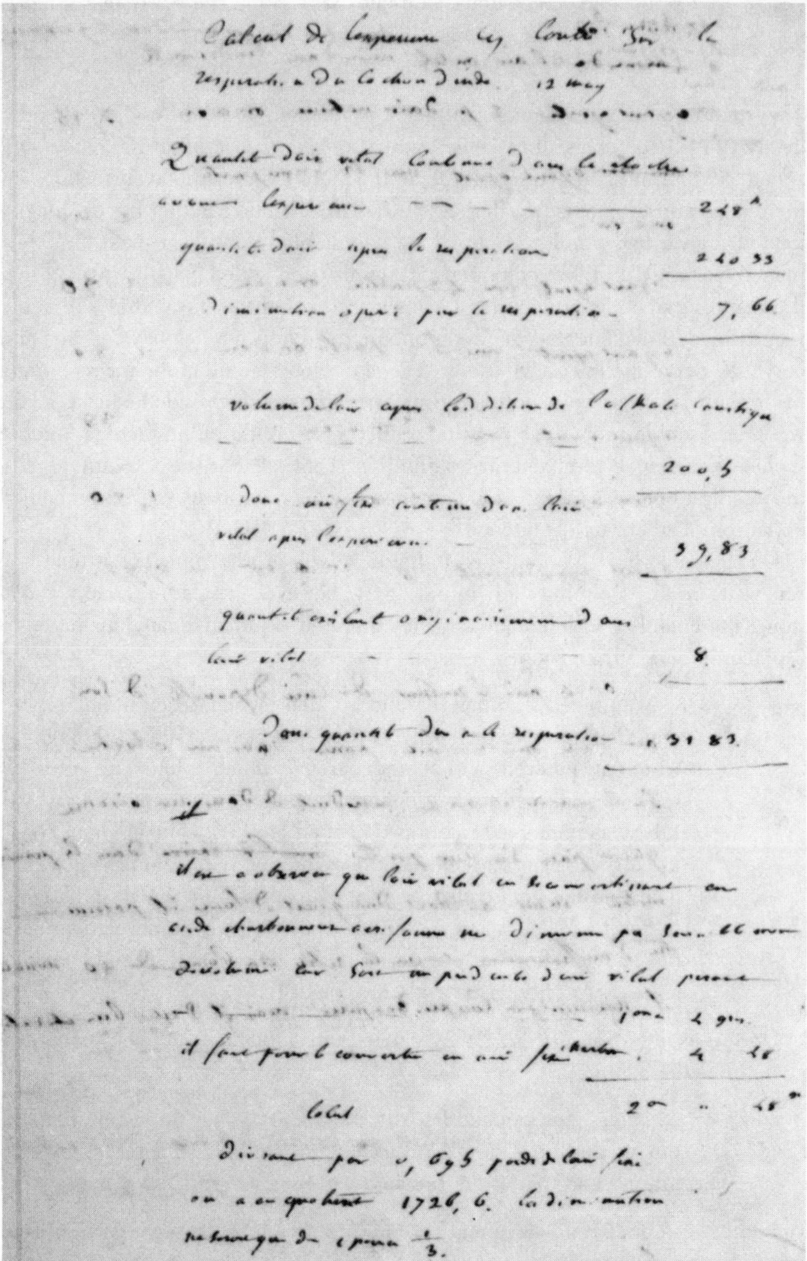

Figures 3–6. Lavoisier's laboratory notebook record of respiration experiment on guinea pig carried out on May 12, 1783. Transcriptions of the

Calcul de l'expérience cy-contre sur la
respiration du Cochon d'Inde 12 May

Quantité d'air vital contenu dans la cloche
avant l'expérience – – – – – – – – – – – 248 P.

quantité d'air après la respiration 240 33

diminution operé par la respiration 7,66

volume de l'air après l'addition de l'alkali caustique
– – – – – – – – – – – – – – – – – – 200,5

donc au fin contenu dans l'air
vital après l'expérience 39,83

quantité existant originairement dans
l'air vital – – – – – – – – – – – – – 8

donc quantité due a la respiration 31 83

il est a observer que l'air vital en se convertissant en
acide charbonneuse aeriforme ne diminue pas sensiblement
de volume. Car un pied cube d'air vital pesant
– – – – – – – – – – – – – – – – – 1 ounce 4 gr.

il faut pour le converter en air fixe charbon 4 48

total 2 on 48 gr

divisant par 0,6 g 5 poids de l'air fixe

on a en quotient 1726,6. la diminution
ne seroit que de 1 pouce 1/3.

---

notebook pages are on facing pages. The experiment begins on p. 43 (Figure 4) and continues on p. 45 (Figure 6) of the notebook. Page 42 (Figure 3), the left-hand page facing initial page of the experiment, contains the calculations of the quantity of vital air consumed and fixed air produced, derived from the results at the time of the experiment. Page 44 (Figure 5) contains the revised calculations made later, after Lavoisier inferred that water is also formed in respiration. Lavoisier, *Cahiers*, R-8, ff. 43–45, Archives of the Académie des Sciences de Paris.

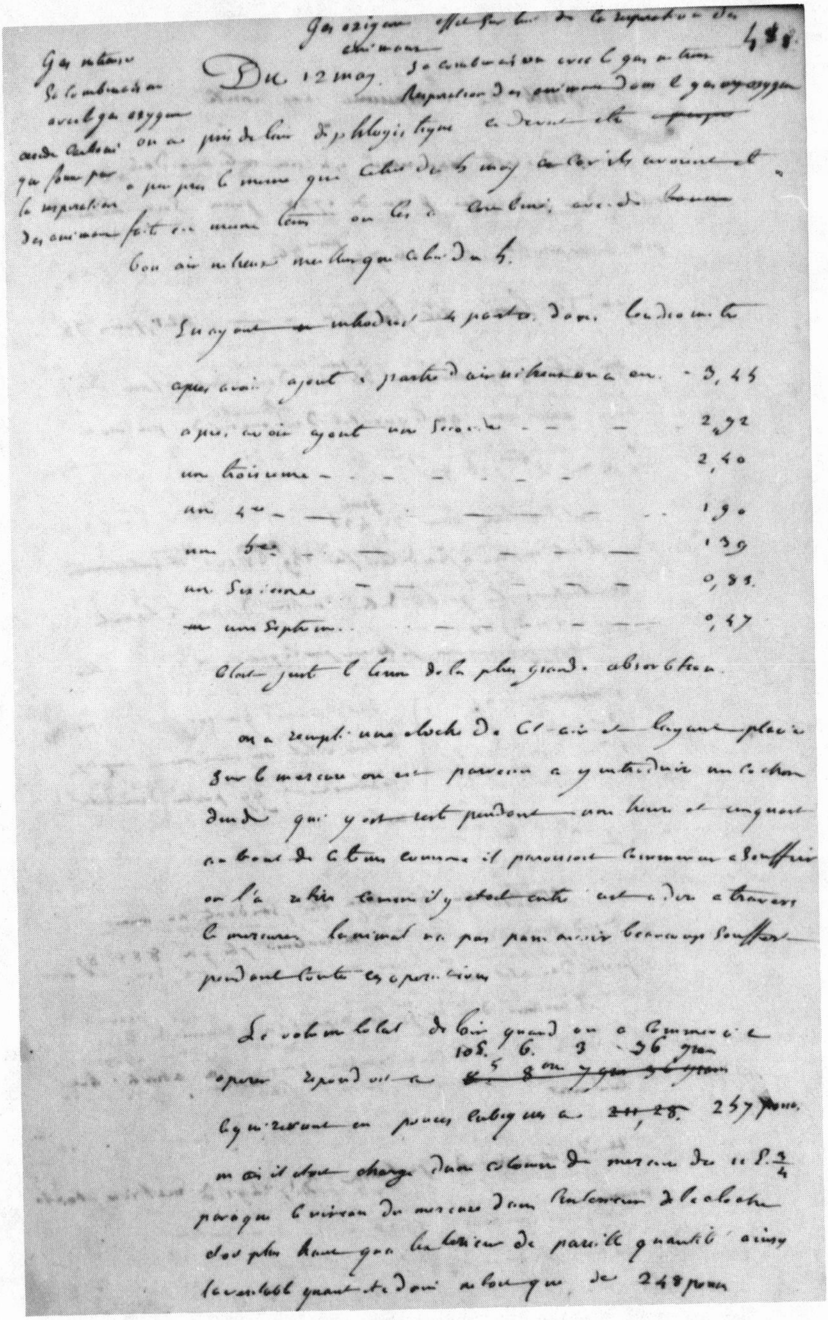

Figure 4.

Gas nitreux
Sa combinaison
avec le gas oxygene

Gas oxigene effet sur lui de la
respiration des animaux

Du 12 May — Sa combinaison avec le gas nitreux
Respiration des animaux dans le gas oxygène

acide carbonique
formé par
la respiration
des animaux

on a pris de l'air dephlogistiqué ce devoit être à peu près le même que celui du 5 May, car ils avoient été faits en même tems on les a combiné avec de bon air nitreux meilleur que celui du 5.

En ayant —introduit 4 parties dans l'eudiometre
après avoir ajouté 1 partie d'air nitreux on a eu – – – 3,45
après avoir ajouté une seconde – – – – – – – – – – 2,92
une troisième – – – – – – – – – – – – – – – – – 2,40
une 4me – – – – – – – – – – – – – – – – – – – 1,90
une 5me – – – – – – – – – – – – – – – – – – – 1,39
une sixième – – – – – – – – – – – – – – – – – – 0,83
– une septième – – – – – – – – – – – – – – – – 0,47

C'etoit just le term de la plus grande absorbtion.

On a rempli une cloche de cet air et l'ayant placé sur le mercure on est parvenu a y introduire un cochon d'Inde qui y est resté pendant une heure et un quart. Au bout de ce tems comme il paraisoit commencer à souffrir on l'a retiré comme il y étoit entré, c'est-à-dire à travers le mercure. L'animal n'a pas paru avoir beaucoup souffert pendant toutes ces operations.

Le volume total de l'air quand on a commencé a
10. £ — 6. — 3. — 36 grains
opérer repondoit a ~~8^5~~ – – – – ~~8^ou~~ – – – ~~7 gros~~ – – ~~36 grains~~
Ce qui revient en pouces cubiques à ~~211,28.~~ – 257 pouces on ~~ait~~ il etoit chargé d'une colonne de mercure de 11 £.3/4 parceque le niveau du mercure dans l'intérieur de la cloche etoit plus haut que l'extérieur de pareille quantité. Ainsy l'available quantité d'air ne soit que de 248 pouces.

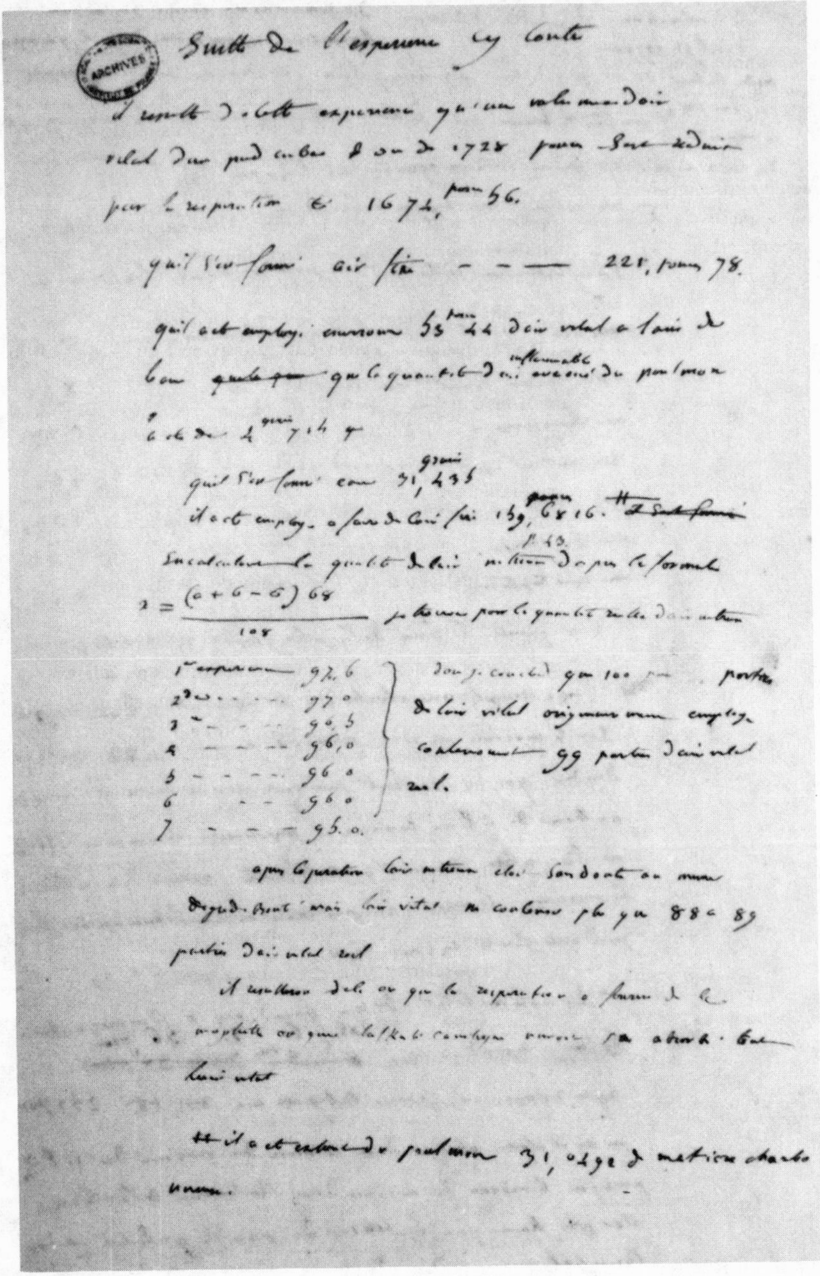

Figure 5.

Suitte de l'expérience cy contre

il resulte de cette expérience qu'une volume d'air vital d'un pied cube ou de 1728 pouces s'est reduit par la respiration en 1674, pouces 56.

qu'il s'est formé air fixe – – – – – – – – 228. pouces 78
qu'il a été employé environ 53 pouces 44 d'air vital a faire de l'eau ~~que le qu~~ que la quantité d'air inflammable evacué du poulmon a été de 4 grains 715 gr.

qu'il s'est formé eau 31, grains 435

il a été employé a faire de l'air fixe —159, pouces 6816 ~~il s'est formé~~ -11-

En calculant la quantité de l'air nitreux p.43 d'après la formule

$$x = \frac{(a + b - c)\,68}{108}$$

je trouve pour la quantité réelle d'air nitreux

1er experience	97.6
2me ex – – – –	97.0
3me – – – – –	96.5
4 – – – – –	96.0
5 – – – – –	96.0
6 – – – – –	96.0
7 – – – – –	95.0

d'ou je conclus que 100 parties de l'air vital originairement employées contenoient 99 parties d'air vital réel.

après l'opération l'air nitreux étoit sans doute au même degré de bonté, mais l'air vital ne contenoit plus que 88 à 89 parties d'air vital réel.

Il resulterais de la ou que la respiration a fourni de la mophette ou que l'alkali caustique n'avoit pas absorbé tout l'air vital.

*Il a été extrait du poulmon 31, 0492 de matières charbonneuses.

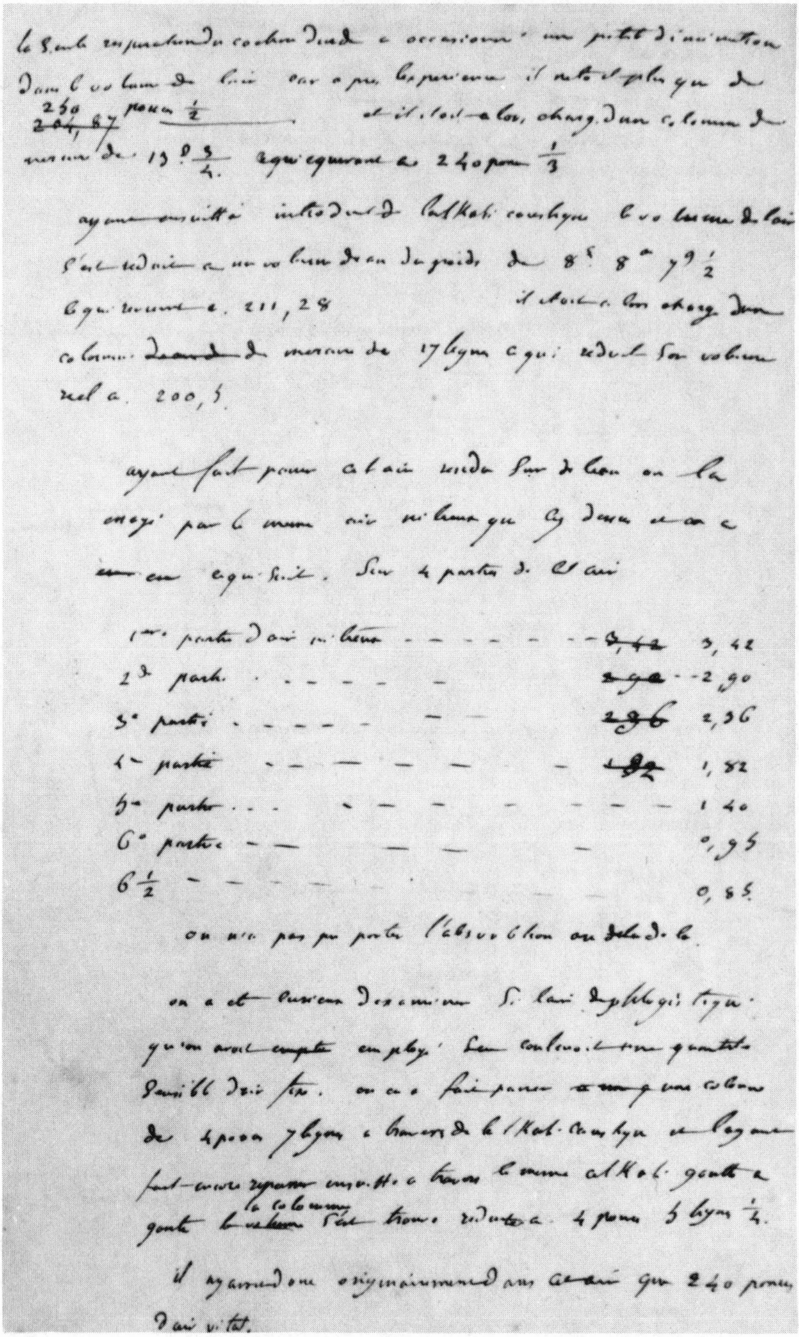

la seule respiration des cochons d'inde a occasionné une petite diminution dans le volume de l'air car après l'experience il restoit plus que de 250 pouces 1/2 et il etoit alors chargé d'une colonne de mercure de 13 l. 3/4 ce qui equivaut a 240 pouces 1/3

ayant ensuite introduit de l'alkali caustique le volume de l'air s'est reduit a un volume d'eau du poids de 8 o 8 gr 79 1/2 ce qui revient a 211,28 il etoit alors chargé d'une colonne de mercure de 17 lignes ce qui reduit son volume reel a 200,5.

ayant fait passer cet air vicié sur de l'eau on l'a essayé par le meme air nitreux que ... ce qui suit. sur 4 parties de cet air

1re partie d'air nitreux	3,42
2e partie	2,90
3e partie	2,36
4e partie	1,82
5e partie	1 40
6e partie	0,95
6 1/2	0,85

on n'a pas pu porter l'absorbtion au dela de la.

on a été curieux d'examiner si l'air dephlogistiqué qu'on avoit employé ne contenoit une quantité sensible d'air fixe. on en a fait passer une colonne de 4 pouces 7 lignes a travers de l'alkali caustique et l'ayant fait ensuite ... a travers le meme alkali goutte a goutte la colonne s'est trouvée reduite a 4 pouces 5 lignes 1/2.

il n'y avoit donc originairement dans cet air que 240 pouces d'air vitié.

Figure 6.

la seule respiration du cochon d'Inde a occasionné une petite diminution dans la ~~volume de~~ l'air, car après l'expérience il n'etoit plus que de 250 pouces ½ ~~204.87~~ et il etoit alors chargé d'une colonne de mercure de 13^{l} ¾ ce qui equivaut a 240 pouces ⅓

ayant ensuitte introduit ~~d~~ l'alkali caustique le volume de l'air s'est reduit a un volume d'eau du poids de 8£ 8^{g} 79½ ce qui revient a 211,28 il etoit alors chargé d'un colonne ~~deau de~~ de mercure de 17 lignes ce qui reduit son volume réel a 200,5.

ayant fait passer ~~pass~~ cet air residu sur de l'eau on l'a essayé par le même air nitreux que cy dessus et on a – eu ce qui suit. Sur 4 parties de cet air

1er partie d'air nitreux – – – – – – – –	~~3,42~~	3,42
2e partie – – – – – – – – – – – – – –	~~2,90~~	2,90
3e partie – – – – – – – – – – – – – –	~~2,36~~	2,36
4e partie – – – – – – – – – – – – – –	~~1,82~~	1,82
5e partie – – – – – – – – – – – – – – – – – – –		1,40
6e partie – – – – – – – – – – – – – – – – – – –		0,95
6½ –		0,85

on n'a pas pu porter l'absorbtion au ~~dela~~ de la.

on a été curieux d'examiner si l'air dephlogistiqué qu'on avoit ~~comple~~ employé ~~s'en~~ contenoit une quantité sensible d'air fixe. On en a fait passer ~~a un q~~ une colonne de 4 pouces 7 lignes a travers de l'alkali caustique et l'ayant fait encore repasser ensuitte a travers le même alkali goutte a goutte la colonne ~~le volume~~ s'est trouvée reduit a 4 pouces 5 lignes ¼.

il n'y avait donc originairement dans cet air que 240 pouces d'air vital.

> In order that less fixed air remain in the bell jar, which has a capacity of 300 cubic inches, at the end of the experiment we passed through it a large quantity of air, which must have carried off the greater part of the fixed air.

While they were improving the experiment in this way, however, something else went wrong:

> The guinea pig suffered much during the last half hour, in spite of the fact that the current of air was considerable. No doubt this malaise derived from the fact that it was half immersed in the mercury. It died a half hour after it was taken out of the bell jar.[52]

Later the same day they placed a candle in a closed bell jar over mercury, lighted it by means of a piece of phosphorus and a hot iron, and kept it burning for "a very long time." Using the same methods as in the respiration experiments carried out in closed chambers, they measured the volume of air before and after the burning and after they had added caustic alkali. The corrected values for these three volumes were, respectively, 202, 175, and 75.8 cubic inches. The weight of the candle decreased by 21.3 grains.[53] The fact that the volume decreased by a fourth as much during the burning as it did in the absorption in alkali—in contrast to respiration where the first of these decreases was very small—ought to have alerted them to the possibility that in burning candles something else in addition to the conversion of vital air to fixed air might take place. Lavoisier did not, however, record any interpretative comments concerning the processes involved.

On May 24, Lavoisier and Laplace performed a similar experiment on the combustion of charcoal in dephlogisticated air. Beforehand they had calcined the charcoal in a crucible and kept it in a closed bottle until they were ready for it. Placing 6 gros 19.6 grains of this calcined charcoal under a bell jar, inverted, as in the preceding experiments, over mercury, they ignited it by means of small pieces of tinder and phosphorus. Measuring and correcting the volumes of air inside the jar in the usual manner, they obtained for the beginning 205.2 cubic inches; after the combustion 173 cubic inches; and after absorption in alkali 75.0 cubic inches. The quantity of charcoal burned was 17.2 grains. These results were remarkably similar to those for the burning candle, although Lavoisier made no note of their resemblance. For this experiment, unlike that for the candle, he added a set of calculations which incorporate an interpretation of the chemical change that had taken place.[54] Since these calculations reveal one obvious difficulty that Lavoisier noticed at the time, and a deeper one that apparently remained hidden to him, it will be useful to reproduce his summary in full:

Total quantity of air reduced in the experiment	205.2 [cubic inches]
Quantity absorbed spontaneously by the combustion of *charbon* and before the addition of caustic alkali	32.2
Quantity absorbed afterward by the addition of caustic alkali	98.0
Remaining from the 205.2 cubic inches of dephlogisticated air	75.0

The amount of charcoal consumed was 17.2 grains, but since there was a little bit of water given off in this experiment, we do not believe more than 15 grains should be counted. Thus 15 grains of charcoal and 130 2/10 cubic inches of dephlogisticated air give 98 cubic inches of fixed air.

130.2 [cubic inches] of dephlogisticated air will contain 1/24 of fixed air, that is to say, 5.4. Thus 124.8 of dephlogisticated air + 15 grains of charcoal give 92.6 of fixed air.

124.8 [cubic inches] of dephlogisticated air at 0.45 [grains per cubic inch] weighs	56.16
Charcoal	15
Total	71.16
92.6 of fixed air at 0.72 [grains per cubic inch] weighs	66.67
Difference	5.49 [*sic*]

There seems to be a portion of the weight lost.

The "little bit of water given off" Lavoisier must have noticed as moisture that collected in the bell jar. Since he believed water was an element, he had to assume that it had been contained as such in the charcoal. Unable to measure it, he made one of his customary guesses at how much to deduct for it, in order to arrive at the figure of 15 grains of *charbon* consumed. He counted the total decrease in the volume of air in the bell jar during the combustion and the absorption with alkali (32.2 cubic inches + 98.0 cubic inches = 130.2 cubic inches) as the quantity of dephlogisticated air that combined with this *charbon.* For the quantity of fixed air formed, however, he counted only the 98 cubic inches absorbed by the alkali. From both of these figures he subtracted 5.4 cubic inches to account for the fixed air he had found his dephlogisticated air to contain as an impurity.

Lavoisier then tried to draw up a balance sheet for the chemical change. To do so, he converted the volumes of dephlogisticated and fixed air to weights, applying the same estimates of the densities of these airs that he had used to convert weights to volumes in the respiration experiment in an open system. The results did not add up well. The weights of the dephlogisticated air and *charbon* consumed differed from that of the fixed air by almost one-third of the weight of *charbon*. (The "difference" was not quite as bad as he thought, because he had also made an error in subtraction—it should have been 4.49 grains).

Lavoisier did not indicate what he thought might have caused "a portion of the weight [to be] lost." We can see, however, a major discrepancy in his interpretation of the results. Having already deduced in 1777 from his general theory of combustion that the combustion of *charbon* consists of its combination (or the combination of *matière charbonneuse*) with dephlogisticated air to form fixed air, he allowed here for nothing else than that process. In this case, however, a major proportion of the dephlogisticated air disappeared before he added caustic alkali. Since the combustion had taken place over mercury rather than over water, one could not correctly ascribe this loss of dephlogisticated air to the formation of fixed air that had been absorbed in some other way. Nor was it consistent with his treatment of analogous situations to assume that the volume decreases in the conversion of dephlogisticated air to fixed air itself. His interpretation of the respiration experiment in an open system assumed that the volume remained the same. Nevertheless Lavoisier here treated the 124.8 cubic inches of dephlogisticated air that disappeared as combined in the 92.6 cubic inches of fixed air formed. On one side of his balance sheet he took into account the total decrease in volume; on the other side he included only the volume absorbed in caustic alkali. In this case, unlike some of the other ambiguous situations we have examined, Lavoisier seems to have been genuinely confused. At this time, however, he had no means available to resolve the confusion; the most he could have done, even if he recognized the problem, was to say that there was something else going on that he could not explain.

It is not immediately evident whether Lavoisier and Laplace performed this experiment on the combustion of charcoal in the first place as part of their investigation of respiration, or as an end in itself. Laplace's letter concerning the respiration experiments suggests that it was not part of their initial plan, according to which they intended to compare respiration with the burning of a candle. Lavoisier had ample independent reason for attempting the experiment. As long ago as 1774 he had wished to carry out just such a combustion in a closed jar over mercury, in order to ascertain what *charbon* contributes to the composition of fixed air.[55] Afterward, having solved this problem theoretically, he needed more than ever an experimental confirmation that the fixed air formed in the combustion of *charbon* is a combination of the *charbon* with the base of dephlogisticated, or vital, air. Whatever may have been their motivation to do the experiment, after the fact Lavoisier and Laplace incorporated it as a crucial piece in the argument for their theory of respiration.

IV

Lavoisier and Laplace presented the conclusions they reached through their investigation of respiration as part of the classic "Memoir on heat" which they read at the Academy during the meetings of June 18 and 25, 1783.[56] Three out of the four articles into which they divided their paper dealt with the general theory of heat, the theory underlying the calorimetric method, the description of the practical method, and the whole range of measurements they had undertaken. The calorimetric respiration experiments were embedded within the latter under the heading "results . . . on the combustions of bodies and animal heat." The combustions included those of *charbon*, phosphorus, and vitriolic ether, and the detonation of nitre.[57] After summarizing the two experiments they had carried out on the guinea pig in the calorimeter, they converted the results to a common base of ten hours:

> According to the first, the quantity of ice the animal can melt during ten hours is twelve ounces four gros; the quantity by the second experiment is, in the same interval, thirteen ounces, six gros, twenty-seven grains. The average of these two results is thirteen ounces, one gros, thirteen and a half grains.[58]

Article 4 of the memoir, entitled "On combustion and respiration" is, according to Guerlac, the only portion which it is certain that Lavoisier wrote.[59] This subtitle embodies an ambiguity which pervades the entire section. On the one hand, Lavoisier was discussing combustion in the sense of his earlier memoir on "combustion in general"; that is, the role of vital air, fixed air, and especially of heat in processes of this class. At the beginning he enumerated, as he had in the older paper, "combustion, respiration, and the calcination of metals" as the categories included within the general process; and it was probably only because the ice calorimeter was not suitable to study a process requiring an outside source of heat that he excluded calcination from the remainder of the discussion, leaving "combustion and respiration" as the prime examples. The article was, however, also a comparison between respiration and the particular form of combustion involving *charbon*. These two topics are so intimately interwoven within the article that it is easy to overlook when Lavoisier was moving from one theme to the other. When he wrote, in the opening paragraph, that Crawford had, in his book of 1779, "presented an explication very similar" to that which Lavoisier had himself given in his memoir on combustion in 1777, he was referring to a characteristic common to all three forms of combustion, that "pure air [vital air] is the principal source of the heat." Lavoisier then stressed the way in which their views differed—in his own theory the heat disengaged is previously combined in the pure air, whereas Crawford considered "heat free in the pure air." He summarized Crawford's conclusion that it is the difference between the specific heats of pure air and common air which accounts for that released in combustions, "such as that of phosphorus." Considering the measurements of these specific heats "too delicate" to draw conclusions without many repeated experiments, he ended this segment of his discussion by saying that until such experiments may be performed, "we limit ourselves to comparing the quantities of heat which are disengaged in combustion and in respiration with the corresponding alterations of the pure air, without examining whether this heat comes from the air, or from the combustible bodies and the animals which respire."[60] In all of this, therefore, Lavoisier was addressing the general theory of combustion, rather than the special relation between respiration and a particular form of combustion. As he proceeded in his discussion, however, the latter theme came to the fore and gradually crowded out the more general theme. It is one more manifestation of the inextricable mingling of Lavoisier's ongoing investigation of respiration with the development of his overall view of combustion.

In his introductory paragraph Lavoisier mentioned that when in combustions vital air is converted to fixed air, it is "by the addition of a principle which we shall, in order to avoid all discussion of its nature, name the *base of fixed air*." In his description of the combustion of charcoal he described this base as "a principle furnished by *charbon*."[61] Thus Lavoisier had now come to distinguish the underlying constituent of *charbon*, and of other substances which produce fixed air from vital air, so sharply from the physical *charbon* itself that he needed to identify the former with a term that expressed not its common source, but its presence in the uniform product of its combustion. Lavoisier evidently wished to avoid "discussions of its nature" because the "principle" was not known except in its combinations with other substances.

Lavoisier described in great detail an experiment to determine the quantity of vital air consumed and of fixed air formed in the combustion of charcoal. The experiment was, in fact, the previously discussed experiment of May 24 in his laboratory notebook; but he had new calculations based on this data that significantly altered the results. Deciding that the dephlogisticated air contained only 1/57, rather than 1/24, of fixed air, he made a smaller deduction for that impurity. The figures he presented for the three volumes involved, corrected for temperature and pressure, differed by only small amounts from those in the notebook: 202.35 cubic inches (instead of 205.2) at the beginning, 170.59

(instead of 173) after the combustion, and 73.93 (instead of 75.0) after absorption in alkali. In estimating the amount of *charbon* consumed, however, he made a larger change. No longer taking into account the "water given off," he argued instead that to the measured loss of 17.2 grains one should *add* a correction for the cinder the charcoal contained. In the experiment, he claimed, "there are 18 grains of *charbon* consumed, including the cinder." The basis for his reasoning is far from clear, since the weight of whatever cinder was present would have remained constant during the combustion.[62]

Substituting eighteen grains of *charbon* for the fifteen grains he had assumed in the original calculation substantially changed the outcome of his new calculation of the proportions in which *charbon* and pure air combined in fixed air. One ounce of charcoal, he now found, consumes 4,037.5 cubic inches of pure air and produces 3,021.1 cubic inches of fixed air. Converting the volumes to weights, he concluded that "one ounce of *charbon,* in burning, consumes 3.3167 ounces of pure air and forms 3.6715 ounces of fixed air."[63] He had not reduced the original calculation to a base of 1 ounce of *charbon,* but if he had done so the corresponding figures would have been 3.74 ounces of pure air and 4.45 ounces of fixed air.

Making these changes did not help Lavoisier to resolve the difficulties we have found in the original results. The difference between the volume of pure air consumed and of fixed air formed remained as large as before. He now apparently accounted for this difference merely by assuming that in the conversion process the volume is diminished. "If we designate the volume of pure air consumed by unity," he wrote, "its volume after the combustion will be reduced to 0.74828."[64] He made no effort, however, to reconcile this reduction with his earlier assumption that there is little or no change in the volume.

In making these changes, moreover, Lavoisier only augmented the difficulty he had noticed in his first calculation, that "a portion of the weight [was] lost." If we add his figures for the pure air and *charbon* consumed (3.3167 ounces plus 1 ounce), the total of 4.3167 ounces differs from the weight of fixed air formed, 3.6715 ounces, by almost two-thirds of the weight of *charbon* involved. In his public presentation of the results Lavoisier simply glossed over the discrepancy. Following his statement of these figures he wrote "In ten parts of fixed air, therefore, there are about nine parts of pure air and one part of a principle furnished by *charbon;* . . . but a determination so delicate requires a larger number of experiments." His treatment of the situation appears singularly careless. Hardly alluding to the large weight loss incurred, he was estimating the quantitative proportions of fixed air by means of a rough calculation which—without acknowledging or defending such an inference—attributed the discrepancy to an assumption that somewhat less than one-third of the *charbon* burned had been incorporated into the fixed air. Such an assumption would accord with his new description of fixed air as a combination of pure air, not with *charbon* itself, but with a principle furnished by *charbon*. Yet the only additional constituent of *charbon* of which he seemed to be aware was the very small proportion of cinder. As a quantitative determination of the substances entering into this combustion and of their proportions in the product, this experiment was a fiasco, and it is no wonder that Lavoisier omitted presenting the results in the form of a balance sheet. Fortunately for him, he did not, for his immediate purpose, need to use the results in that way. He was primarily interested only in establishing the heat disengaged in the combustion of a given quantity of *charbon*, or in the formation of a given quantity of fixed air, by comparing the result of this experiment with that of the combustion carried out in the calorimeter. The combustion of one ounce of *charbon*, he concluded, melts 6 pounds 2 ounces of ice; or, in the formation of 1 ounce of fixed air, it "can melt 26.692 ounces." He and Laplace presented their results "with great circumspection," Lavoisier wrote, because they had made only one experiment on the heat evolved by that combustion, "and although it was made under quite favorable circumstances, we can nevertheless not be entirely sure of its precision until we have repeated it several times."[65] From the above discussion it is evident that they had even more reason than they admitted to be circumspect.

Lavoisier made similar calculations for the other combustion processes they had examined. In absorbing 1 ounce of pure air, phosphorus can melt 68.634 ounces of ice. It was remarkable, he emphasized, that this amount was "almost two and a third times as much as when it [pure air] is converted to fixed air" through the combustion of *charbon*. In the detonation of nitre, on the other hand, "the quantity of heat which develops [from the combination of 1 ounce of pure air to form nitrous acid] can melt 3¼ ounces of ice"; that is, less than one-eighth of the heat formed in the conversion of the same amount of pure air to fixed air.[66]

Finally turning directly to the question of "the alterations which the respiration of animals causes to pure air," Lavoisier described first an experiment carried out on a guinea pig. This was the experiment of May 12, in which he and Laplace had placed the animal in dephlogisticated air in a closed jar and measured the change in volume produced by the respiration and by absorption with alkali. Here too the volume of the pure air that disappeared was larger than that of the fixed air that formed. Again he assumed that the volume of the air "had been a little bit diminished" in the process. He noted, however, that this decrease was proportionately less than in the combustion; the ratio was 1 to 0.814 in place of 1 to 0.74828. "That difference could derive in part from errors in the measurements," he surmised, "but it might also be caused by something we had not at first suspected." When they had introduced the animal into the bell jar, a little bit of air, clinging to the body of the animal, might have been introduced along with it. "Therefore, the air would appear less diminished by the respiration than it actually was."[67]

His interpretation of these results is a double display of the way in which Lavoisier's strong theoretical structure now dominated his evaluation of the experimental situation. Having accepted an unexplained diminution in the volume of the air during the combustion of charcoal in order to maintain his view that the process consists of the combination of *charbon* with the base of pure air, he extended the same interpretation to the outcome of this respiration experiment; going further, he ascribed the difference in the degrees of diminution in the two cases to extraneous factors in order to maintain his theory that in respiration the identical process takes place. These were eminently reasonable judgments. If there was no theoretical justification for assuming that the volume of the pure air diminished in changing to fixed air, neither was there any theoretical obstacle to that move. The earlier assumption—which he still held when he performed the first respiration experiment of this series, in the open system—that the volume of pure air consumed is about equal to that of the fixed air formed, was merely an empirical generalization. In the subsequent experiments carried out in the closed system Lavoisier was attempting, more deliberately than ever before, to measure the respective volumes involved. When these experiments, for charcoal, respiration, and for a burning candle as well, all seemed to reveal a marked diminution, the new results would naturally appear to him to supersede the earlier observations. As to the difference between the two ratios of 1 to 0.814 and 1 to 0.74828, in view of the experimental uncertainties one might expect in a first effort to make such a quantitative comparison between respiration and the combustion of charcoal, this difference was in fact so minor that to treat it as he did was the most appropriate response. If Lavoisier had abandoned a major theoretical commitment every time he encountered such an experimental discrepancy, he would long since have been forced to give up his enterprise.

From the weight of fixed air the guinea pig had produced during the hour and a quarter it had been under the bell jar, Lavoisier extrapolated that in ten hours it would have evolved 212.576 grains. In order to justify this procedure he had to contrive a rationale for treating the respiratory rate over the shorter period as normal, even though the composition of the air had been changing over that time. At the beginning the animal was breathing "pure air"; at the end, he suspected, it was breathing the fixed air "deposited by its own density in the lower part of the bell jar where the animal was, [and which] would displace the pure air to the top." The fixed air was probably "also itself harmful to the animal." He reasoned that at the beginning the animal, breathing pure air, "perhaps" produced more fixed air than it would in ordinary air, whereas, breathing fixed air toward the end, it produced less. One "could assume without sensible error that the quantity of fixed air produced [over the entire hour and a quarter] is the same as that which the animal would have produced in atmospheric air."[68] The assumption that the animal was at the end breathing in a layer of fixed air was based on the explanation Lavoisier had devised in 1776 for the fact that a sparrow had died in an atmosphere still containing four-fifths "pure air,"[69] and it rested on the further assumption that airs separated into layers according to their relative densities. The assumption that animals respire more rapidly in pure air than in common air was based on no more than the analogy that other combustions take place more quickly in it. Even if all these assumptions were valid, he had no basis for inferring that the elevated consumption at the beginning and the diminished consumption at the end would compensate one another with no "sensible error." Looking back over time we need no special insight to perceive the frailty of these assumptions, for they turned out to be wrong. For Lavoisier, who did not have that advantage, they must have seemed so plausible as to raise little question. Otherwise it is hard to see why he would have relied as heavily upon the result of this type of experiment as he did upon the results of the experiments in which the atmosphere was continually renewed; for those experiments had obviated the whole problem. Probably his confidence in the assumptions was due in large part to the fact that the extrapolated result came out reasonably close to the 236.667 grams which he calculated for the experiment with an open system that he and Laplace had carried out on May 19. That experiment he now described as one in which they had "determined directly the quantity of air produced by a guinea pig when it respires the air of the atmosphere itself."[70]

To the notebook description of the experiment of May 19 they added two features which indicate their awareness of the necessity to control for possible interfering factors. In order to prevent the "vapors of respiration" from being deposited in the caustic alkali bottles, where they would add to the weight measured as that of fixed air, they reported, they had used a tube curved in such a way that these vapors would condense before reaching the bottles. To demonstrate that none of the fixed air measured in the bottles derived from the current of atmospheric air itself, they had repeated the experiment without the guinea pig, and found "no increase at all in the weights of the bottles."[71]

Lavoisier mentioned only briefly the result of a "third experiment made on a guinea pig in dephlogisticated air." The quantity of fixed air it produced, extrapolated to ten hours, was 226 grains. When we consider that the experiments were carried out in two different ways, using different guinea pigs, the three results were in remarkably good agreement. Lavoisier took their average, 224 grains, as representing the amount that still another guinea pig, in the calorimeter experiment, had produced during the ten hours it had remained there. He acknowledged that, since the above experiments "had been carried out at a temperature of fourteen or fifteen degrees, it is possible that the quantity of fixed air might be a little less than at the temperature of zero degrees which existed in the interior of our machines." They hoped, in order to increase the precision of the comparison, to measure in the future the fixed air produced at the lower temperature.[72] From the letter of Laplace quoted earlier in this chapter we can see that they had at the beginning planned to measure the "quantity of fixed air that [the guinea pig's] respiration produces at a temperature of zero." That they had not done so in the meantime is most likely due to the fact that by the time they reached this phase of their investigation it was already late spring, and such outside temperatures were no longer attainable. Much has been made of this temperature difference as a major flaw in Lavoisier and Laplace's method. Hindsight makes for easy judgments; we know that within the temperature range in question the respiratory rate increases linearly as the temperature decreases. That knowledge was gained, however, by means of the tradition that Lavoisier and Laplace's pioneering investigaton initiated. At the time, although Crawford already believed that respiration increased as the temperature decreased, there was no compelling evidence that this was a significant effect. That Lavoisier and Laplace were aware of the potential problem was mostly due to their own unproven but penetrating insight, that respiration may produce more or less heat in compensation for variations in the rate at which heat is lost to the surroundings.[73]

The principal goal of Lavoisier's investigation of respiration was to compare the heat produced in respiration with that produced in the combustion of charcoal. To do so he needed to establish a common measure of the two processes. Of the three possible measures, the quantity of *charbon* consumed, that of pure air consumed, and that of fixed air formed, the latter was obviously the most accessible one, the only quantity directly measured in all of the relevant experiments. Having estimated, from three of the respiration experiments, that in ten hours the guinea pig formed, on the average, 224 grains of fixed air, he calculated from the single set of experiments on charcoal that, in producing this same quantity of fixed air, the combustion of *charbon* would have melted 10.38 ounces of ice. The guinea pig itself would actually have melted, according to the average of the two calorimetric respiration experiments extrapolated to ten hours, "13 ounces." Since the animal had had the same internal temperature when they removed it from the calorimeter as it had when they put it in, the ice melted represented the heat produced "during the same interval of time by the vital functions of the guinea pig." Suggesting that the 13 ounces should perhaps be decreased "by an ounce or two," because "the extremities of the animal were cooled even though its interior remained the same; and furthermore because the vapors which its internal heat had evaporated melted a small quantity of ice in condensing again," he concluded:

> After diminishing the quantity of ice by about two and a half ounces one will have the quantity melted by the effect of the respiration of the animal on the air. Now, if one considers the errors inevitable in these experiments, and in the assumptions from which we began in order to make the calculations, one will see that it is not possible to hope for more perfect accord between these results. Thus, one can regard the heat which is disengaged in the change of pure air into fixed air by respiration as the principal cause of the conservation of the heat of the animal, and if other causes concur to sustain it, their effect is inconsiderable.[74]

This famous comparison, the climactic point in Lavoisier's investigation of respiration, stands at the heart of his argument that respiration really *is* a form of combustion of *charbon.* Historians have reacted to the claim in widely divergent ways. Some, such as McKie, accept without comment Lavoisier's argument that the "figures of 10½ and 13 ounces showed as much agreement as could be expected in the circumstances."[75] Guerlac notes that there was "a significant discrepancy: more heat was produced by the guinea pig than by the burning of carbon";[76] but in his very brief account of Lavoisier's physiological work he does not analyze further the situation at this stage. Mendelsohn suggests in a footnote that "the authors presented their results with some hesitation, since their figures for the heat liberated in the combustion of carbon were based on only one experiment. The guinea pig melted 13 ounces of ice in 10 hours, and only by allowing correction factors to account for 2½ ounces do they come within range of the theoretical 10.38 ounces which they expected." He mentions also two criticisms of their procedures made by others—that not all of the melted ice drained out, and that the conditions in the calorimeter were both extreme and different from those in the respiration experiment—but he declines to "scrutinize the computations involved."[77] Culotta judges Lavoisier's conclusions very harshly. "They obtained more heat from the respiring guinea pig than from the oxidized carbon. Lavoisier offered the feeble rationale that chilling effects of the ice increased the heat output of the guinea pig. Of course, were this true, the animal would have consumed more oxygen." In a footnote Culotta adds, "Lavoisier reduced the figure two ounces as an allowance for the low temperature in the calorimeter which forced the animal to produce more heat in order to maintain its constant body temperature. He knew of course that this was not an answer to the dilemma."[78] Applying a strict presentist criterion, J. R. Partington concludes that "since the heat of combustion of charcoal found by Lavoisier and Laplace is quite wrong the agreement is purely accidental."[79] Clearly the question of whether Lavoisier was making a reasonable judgment when he called the agreement "as perfect as one could expect in these experiments" calls for more comprehensive consideration.

In estimating that one could decrease the measured heat production of the guinea pig by "about 2½ ounces," and thereby achieve the most "perfect accord" that could be expected, Lavoisier was obviously indulging in rhetorical exaggeration. He was well aware that such exact agreement would be fortuitous. In presenting the calculations for the ice which charcoal had melted while producing a given quantity of fixed air, he had pointed out that one could not be certain of the exactitude of an experiment performed only once, and added, "We have already said, and we cannot insist too much on that subject, that it is less the result of our experiments, than the method which we have used, that we are presenting."[80] That very experiment provided one of the essential figures for the comparison in question between combustion and respiration. So too did the single seriously flawed experiment on the effects of the combustion of charcoal on the air. Furthermore, the final "corrections" with which he embellished the outcome were typical of those he had made in the data of the individual experiments, from guessing at how much melted ice had failed to drain, to first subtracting and later adding a corrective factor to the weight of *charbon* consumed. We should keep in mind that (at least if my view that Laplace wrote his letter at the commencement of the investigation is valid, and probably even if it is not) Lavoisier and Laplace had carried out these experiments with the aim of demonstrating the agreement they now believed they had found. Given the inevitable experimental uncertainties about which they had to make subjective judgments in order to obtain any meaningful conclusions, we can hardly doubt that, consciously or unconsciously, these judgments were influenced by the outcome they sought. If they had completed their comparison utilizing the original calculations concerning the combustion of charcoal that Lavoisier had entered in his laboratory notebook, they would have reached the result that in forming 224 grains of fixed air *charbon* can melt 8.5 ounces of ice, rather than the 10.38 ounces they calculated after modifying their assumptions. The comparison of 8.5 to 13 would have afforded them a far weaker argument for the identity of the two processes. On the other hand, it is evident that they did not shape their results with the single-minded intention of making them approach the desired agreement. For example, they based their "average" of 224 grains of fixed air formed in ten hours of respiration on three experiments chosen from at least five recorded in the notebooks. They discarded not only the first one, that was so anomalously low that Lavoisier had immediately suspected it, but also one whose extrapolated result would have given 199 grains in ten hours. Had they replaced the largest result of the three experiments they used by this one, their final average figure for the ice melted by the guinea pig would have been slightly below 12.5 ounces, reducing the "error" by almost one-quarter. The interplay between observation and expectation was complex, and we cannot reasonably infer that Lavoisier and Laplace took undue license with their data.

One cannot adequately evaluate the strength of Lavoisier and Laplace's demonstration that respiration is the same as the combustion of *charbon* if one restricts attention, as most historians have, to the narrow question of whether the difference between 10.38 and 13.0 constitutes a significant discrepancy. Underlying the comparison is an unstated presupposition that the heats of combustion of different combustible bodies differ significantly enough so that they are characteristic of the respective substances. Moreover, even granting this condition, one cannot judge how close the agreement must be in order to establish that the same combustion process is occurring in two given situations unless one knows what general magnitude of difference to expect in the heats released in different processes. There was little prior evidence to go on for either count, since Lavoisier and Laplace were themselves gathering the first data of this kind ever obtained. They did, however, have results for three forms of combustion, those of phosphorus, charcoal, and nitre. In consuming 1 ounce of pure air, phosphorus could melt 68 ounces of ice, charcoal 29.3 ounces, and nitre 3 ⅔ ounces.[81] By comparison with these figures, the difference between 10.3 and 13 would appear small enough to discount. Given the uncertainties in the experimental data, Lavoisier and Laplace were justified in concluding that the agreement was sufficiently close to support strongly their view that these were measurements of the heat of the same combustion process. On the other hand, we can see that the degree of agreement they achieved depended upon some further assumptions that were themselves uncertain, and that by making other plausible assumptions one could easily reach a result which would appear far less favorable to their conclusion. What they had been able to provide was a result compatible with a theory they had previously embraced, that reinforced their confidence in its correctness, and that added a new dimension in which respiration could be quantitatively compared with combustion. In the long run what was most important about these experiments was not the agreement between the two results, but that they had demonstrated the feasibility of measuring the quantities of heat released in both processes. In 1777 Lavoisier had doubted whether such measurements could be made.

Although the heat released by respiration and by the combustion of charcoal dominated Lavoisier's discussion in this memoir, he did not rest his case for the identity of the two processes entirely on that property. An equally important argument was that all, or nearly all, of the vital air an animal consumes is converted into fixed air. To support this position he had to refute the results of Scheele, as well as some earlier observations of Priestley, indicating that animals produce "very little fixed air and a great quantity of phlogisticated air." In "a great number of experiments, examined with all possible care," Lavoisier asserted, "we have constantly observed that the change of this gas [that is, vital air, which Lavoisier still only rarely referred to as a gas] into fixed air is the most considerable alteration which it undergoes in the respiration of animals."

He detailed only one such experiment—probably the only one described in the memoir which is not recorded in the notebooks. After a guinea pig had respired extensively in "pure air" and they had removed the fixed air with caustic alkali, they had introduced birds to respire in the residue, again removed the fixed air, and in this way "we succeeded in converting a great part of the pure air we had employed into fixed air. That which remained of the air had about the same goodness as it ought to have, on the supposition that the conversion of pure air into fixed air is the sole effect of respiration on the air. It appears certain to us that if respiration produces other alterations in pure air, they are inconsiderable."[82] For a scientist as devoted as Lavoisier was to quantitative measurements and completed balance sheets for chemical operations, this was a curiously vague, inconclusive demonstration. His inability to prove rigorously that respiration can convert *all* of the pure air supplied to an animal into fixed air may have been one of the main reasons that he left open the possibility that the process may cause, in small amounts, "other alterations of the pure air." He also stated, always with a similar reservation, that the change of "pure air into fixed air" is the "principal" cause, the "prime" cause, or the cause "at least in great part" of the heat released.[83]

Lavoisier thus consistently expressed the identification of respiration and the combustion of *charbon* with a qualification; but a qualification is not a hesitation. I do not believe that Lavoisier harbored any doubt at all that the conversion of pure air to fixed air which characterized respiration was the manifestation of a literal combustion of "a principle furnished by *charbon*." There was, in fact, nothing about that identification incompatible with the possibility that some other process involving the consumption of pure air might, to a small extent, take place concurrently. Concluding the article with a three-page discussion of the concept of respiration at which he had now arrived, he stated, without equivocation, that

> respiration is thus a combustion, a very slow one, to be sure, but otherwise perfectly similar to that of *charbon*. It takes place in the interior of the lungs, without releasing visible light, because the matter of fire set free is immediately absorbed by the moisture of these organs. The heat evolved during this combustion spreads into the blood which traverses the lungs, and from there it is distributed through the whole animal system. Thus the air which we breathe serves two objects equally necessary for our survival. It removes from the blood the base of fixed air, an excess of which would be very harmful; and the heat which the combination deposits in the lungs makes up for the continual loss of heat which we experience to the atmosphere and surrounding bodies.[84]

In this passage Lavoisier stated publicly for the first time that, except for its slowness, respiration is *perfectly* similar to, not merely analogous to, a combustion of *charbon.* From the public record alone, we might readily assume that the measured correspondence between the heats released in the two processes had *led* Lavoisier to this stronger position. From the record of the investigation itself it has become instead evident that those results probably confirmed the theoretical position he had already reached.

Lavoisier continued to describe the combustion here without qualification as happening in the lungs. Contrary to what some historians have suggested, he had up until this point, at least publicly, never entertained any other possibility for the site of a respiratory *combustion.* Of the process involved he now stated for the first time specifically that "it removes from the blood the base of the fixed air." As far as we can surmise from the evidence available, there is no reason not to suppose that this elaboration of his theory reflects the influence on him of Scheele's experiment on ox blood. Lavoisier's use in this situation of his new term "base of fixed air" suggests that the sharper separation he was now making between physical *charbon* and the underlying principle involved both in respiration and combustion facilitated the association of that principle with the circulating blood.

Immediately following his newly strengthened statement of what respiration *is,* Lavoisier addressed himself for the first time to a problem implicit all along in his assumption that the heat is produced in the lungs; how is it that this heat appears evenly spread through the interior of the animal body?

> The animal heat is almost the same in the different parts of the body. This effect appears to depend upon the following three causes: the first is the rapidity of the circulation of the blood, which transmits the heat it receives in the lungs promptly out to the extremities of the body; the second cause is the evaporation which the heat produces in the lungs, and which diminishes the degree of their temperature; finally, the third relates to the increase observed in the specific heat of the blood when, by contact with the pure air, it loses the base of fixed air it contains. A part of the specific heat [Lavoisier here does not use "specific heat" in the same sense as in the remainder of the passage] released in the formation of fixed air is thus absorbed by the blood, its temperature nevertheless remaining the same; but when, during its circulation, the blood comes to take up the base of fixed air again, its specific heat diminishes, and it releases the heat; and since this combination takes place in all parts of the body, the heat which it produces aids in keeping the temperature of the parts remote from the lungs almost the same as that of the lungs themselves.[85]

Perhaps because he now had a sense of the measurable magnitudes involved in the respiratory production of heat, Lavoisier was more aware than when he had formulated his theory in 1777 that its localized formation in the lungs posed a difficulty in terms of the measurable uniformity of the temperature in the interior of the body. Perhaps also Crawford's theory to deal with this problem had drawn his attention to it even as it led him to include Crawford's solution among his own. Neither of the other two explanations he invoked was trivial. The effect of the rapid circulation—which could have been drawn almost straight from William Harvey's description of the way in which "the hot blood, sent through the arteries to the whole of the body, warms all the farthest parts"[86]—was obvious and important. The supposed cooling effect of the evaporation of moisture in the lungs was undoubtedly suggested by the earlier experiments he had carried out with Laplace on the cooling action of evaporating volatile liquids. These speculations should, however, be kept in due proportion. As Mendelsohn has observed, the problem of the distribution of heat was for Lavoisier a "secondary question," and "remained an unsolved problem."[87] His "explanation" clearly displays the character of the tentative suggestions a scientist often puts forth when his solution for a given problem raises another problem he has not yet examined in detail. The passage as a whole gives the impression that he had simply juxtaposed all of the plausible ideas he could muster on the subject.

As usual when he indulged in such conjectures, Lavoisier quickly brought the discussion back to what he considered that he had actually established:

> Nevertheless, whatever may be the manner in which the heat of the animal is restored, its primary cause is that heat evolved from the formation of fixed air. Thus, we can establish the following proposition: *whenever an animal is in a permanent and undisturbed state; when it can live for a prolonged time in the milieu which surrounds it, without suffering; in general, whenever the circumstances in which it exists do not sensibly alter its blood and its humors, so that after several hours the animal system undergoes no sensible variation, the conservation of animal heat is due, at least in large part, to the heat which the combination of the pure air respired by animals with the base of fixed air provided by the blood supplies to it.*[88]

In reducing his conclusions to a basic proposition he would stand on, Lavoisier displayed his habitual prudence. He left out of it the physiological speculations which have fascinated so many others, limiting his theory to the most immediate inferences he had drawn from the experimental investigation. Moreover, he framed and qualified the theory by his grasp of the fundamental condition which has in more recent times been called the "steady state" of the organism. The fact that within this basic proposition the only internal physiological feature he retained was that the blood supplies the base of fixed air may mean that by now that idea appeared to him to follow so directly from this fundamental condition that it seemed to him unquestionable; or it may reflect as well that among the "influences" of his contemporaries on Lavoisier's conception of respiration, only the work of Scheele penetrated to the inner core of his position.

After recapitulating the argument that "independently of all hypotheses" about the nature of the heat involved in combustion itself, the identity of the quantities of heat produced in the combustion of charcoal and in respiration demonstrated that "the change of pure air to fixed air by respiration" is the cause, "at least in great part, of the conservation of animal heat,"[89] Lavoisier closed with an extraordinarily profound look ahead:

> In order to complete this theory of animal heat, we would still have to explain why, although in environments greatly varying in temperature and density, animals always maintain approximately the same heat, and yet without converting pure air to fixed air in quantities proportional to these differences; but the explanation of these phenomena involves the increases and decreases in the evaporation of the humors, their alteration, and the laws according to which heat is transferred from the lungs to the extremities of the body. Thus, before we occupy ourselves with that subject, we must wait until analyses, clarified by a great number of experiments, have made us familiar with the laws of the transmission of heat in homogenous bodies, and in its passage from one body to another of a different type.[90]

This passage is astonishingly perceptive; it took the less acute followers of Lavoisier nearly half a century to catch up with it. The judgment contained in it casts Lavoisier, perhaps as fully as anything else he wrote, as the master of "the art of the soluble."[91] More than any of his contemporaries involved in the question of respiration, and to a degree seldom surpassed by scientists in any field at any time, Lavoisier understood what problems he could solve with the means available, and what problems he could only delineate for future solution.

* * *

Lavoisier's otherwise lucid discussion of the results of the investigation of respiration reported in the "Memoir on heat" leaves unclear some key questions about the logic underlying the experiments. What, precisely, did he and Laplace seek to verify when they set out to compare the heat released in respiration with that released in the combustion of charcoal? What did they accept as given, or previously established, and what did they regard as the theory or hypothesis being tested? What did they consider afterward to be the conclusions reached by means of the experimental demonstration? The paragraph immediately following Lavoisier's argument that the two results, 10.38 and 13 ounces of ice melted, were as close as could be expected, beginning with the sentence "Respiration is thus a combustion . . . perfectly similar to that of *charbon*," implies that they had arrived at this statement as the outcome of their experiments. Without delving into the matter in detail, historians have generally accepted such an interpretation.[92] If that is so, the reasoning on which they based the experiments should be reducible to something like the following sequence. Respiration is known to be the source of animal heat; respiration and the combustion of charcoal have been shown to be similar, in that both processes convert vital air to fixed air; if respiration and the combustion of *charbon* are also alike in all other essential respects, then an animal should release the same quantity of heat, while forming a given amount of fixed air, as charcoal does. The hypothesis, therefore, would be the identity of respiration and the combustion of *charbon;* the testable deduction would be that an animal and charcoal produce the same quantity of heat in equivalent circumstances. Verification of the latter prediction would then corroborate the hypothesis. There are indications, however, that Lavoisier and Laplace may also have viewed the situation the other way around. The paragraph describing the experimental result itself ends with the sentence "Thus, we can regard the heat which is disengaged in the change of pure air into fixed air by respiration as the principal cause of the conservation of the heat of the animal." This same idea reappeared again within the proposition, quoted above in full, in which Lavoisier underlined what the experiments had established. If these statements are taken as the conclusion reached through the investigation, then we may infer that what they accepted as given beforehand was that respiration is identical to the combustion of *charbon.* The hypothesis they were testing would then be that respiration is the source of animal heat.

Laplace's letter written before they commenced the experiments, stating that they would "establish the cause of animal heat," supports the view that it was this line of reasoning with which they had, in fact, begun. We need not choose between these alternatives, however, for Lavoisier and Laplace may not themselves have sorted them out; or they may have looked at the problem sometimes in one of these directions and sometimes in the other. Thought is so rapid, compared with the time that a complex experimental investigation requires, that the investigator has opportunities to explore the problems under study from many angles, to consider and reconsider what is at stake. During the course of such an investigation the scientific reasoning that accompanies it can be too subtle and fluid, too replete with hidden assumptions and tacit steps, to be captured by a static linear chain of hypothetical-deductive logic. The central objective may shift, means and ends be interchanged; and the set of interconnected propositions under study is not necessarily divided strictly into givens and hypotheses. It is evident from his earlier published discussions of respiration that Lavoisier entered this investigation having previously concluded that respiration is both a combustion like that of *charbon*, and the source of animal heat. The success of the investigation made him more certain of both conclusions, and led him to further explorations of their implications. Had the experimental outcome been unfavorable, he and Laplace might have been pressed to scrutinize the logic of their position more rigorously, in order to decide which, if any, of their propositions they might be forced to relinquish; but in the event, such an analysis did not become necessary.

7

Water Divided

The "theory of animal heat" which Lavoisier elaborated in the "Memoir on heat" in June 1783 was both the culmination of a decade of intermittent thought and experiment on the subject and a program for more intensive future research. Confident that other scientists, whom he encouraged to repeat these experiments, would "be led to the same result," he was, all the same, aware that the data he and Laplace had gathered needed further verification; and beyond confirmation of the basic result, the methods they had established invited broader extension. "We propose for ourselves," Lavoisier wrote, "to repeat and vary these experiments by determining the heat regenerated by diverse species of animals, and by examining whether in all of them that quantity of heat is constantly proportional to the quantities of fixed air produced by respiration. Birds would appear to be preferable to quadrupeds for this type of experiment, because for the same time and for an equal size they produce a greater quantity of fixed air."[1] Thus, if we take Lavoisier at his word, he and Laplace were ready to embark on a comprehensive series of investigations paralleling those they had just completed. Although, as we shall see, they did make a start on the plan outlined here, they never came anywhere close to completing it. During the following year Lavoisier made a major advance with his theory of respiration, but it was in a quite different direction from what he had in mind at this point. His progress came not directly out of a systematic continuation of the respiration experiments, but from collateral developments in his other lines of research. The next phase of his involvement with respiration illustrates beautifully the way that unpredictable scientific events can wrench an ongoing investigation onto a different course, which nevertheless appears afterward as a perfectly logical extension of the earlier pathway.

There is evidence that during the time Lavoisier was carrying on the previously described investigation of respiration he had also been seeking a means to test Scheele's conclusion that the respiratory action of the lungs is due to the blood passing through them. The record of the experiments he may have undertaken is, however, so fragmentary that we can recover only a glimpse of his activity on this front. In December 1782 he had placed some ox blood in a bell jar over mercury and left it until May 1, 1783, in order to find out what airs the fermentation of the blood would generate. "There was a very abundant evolution of elastic fluid," two-fifths of which was absorbed in caustic alkali, leaving a residue in which a candle was extinguished. Lavoisier was apparently encouraged enough to place another portion of the blood into the bell jar to continue the experiment,[2] but no traces of its subsequent outcome have survived. The fact that the airs evolved included fixed air, the product of respiration, may have interested him. Yet it is difficult to see how such a result could have been very relevant to his theory; Scheele had stressed the importance of distinguishing the action of fresh blood on the air from products owing to its own decomposition.

In July—that is, shortly after they had presented the results of their respiratory experiments to the Academy—Lavoisier and Laplace were engaged in another experiment with ox blood which was more obviously aimed at confirming Scheele's view. Lavoisier's laboratory notebook does not contain a direct record of the investigation, but he entered into his notebook, on July 19, a draft of a letter to Laplace describing the situation at that point.

> To Monsieur de La Place
>
> I have found it necessary, monsieur my dear colleague, to make a change in the procedure for our experiment with ox blood, because it was extremely difficult to place the thermometer into the vessel which contained the blood when it was under the bell jar. Therefore I decided to fill my bell jar with another quantity of dephlogisticated air, and I introduced into it a layer of ox blood in the same way that we introduce caustic alkali. This layer was thick enough so that the bulb of the thermometer could be immersed in it.
>
> The mercury bath was at 20⅑ degrees of the thermometer; before being introduced into the fixed air the ox blood was at 20³⁄₁₁ degrees. Two or three minutes after the blood had been introduced into the dephlogisticated air the thermometer which had been immersed in it was at 21⅓.
>
> I removed the thermometer several times from below the bell jar and it seemed to me that the ox blood maintained quite constantly a temperature of one-half to three-quarters of a degree higher than that of the mercury bath. Since the difference is very small, one cannot place complete confidence in the result of this experiment. It will be necessary to repeat it on a similar quantity of ox blood and to arrange things in such a way that the heat acquired is not lost so easily to surrounding bodies.

> A remarkable circumstance, of which there can be no doubt, is that the ox blood, far from increasing the volume of dephlogisticated air, diminishes it by a small amount. That decrease takes place during the first minutes, and the next morning it was no greater. You see that M. Fontana was wrong. I am leaving immediately, so that for fifteen days I shall not have the pleasure of seeing you.[3]

From this description it seems clear that Lavoisier was looking for evidence that the ox blood was consuming vital air and producing heat; that is, that respiration itself was taking place in blood withdrawn from the animal. It would be all too easy to dismiss this experiment as an ineffectual footnote to an otherwise auspicious investigation of respiration, a wasted step revealing only that Lavoisier's view of the physiological aspects of the process was nearly as oversimplified as that of Priestley or Scheele. In 1783, however, there was no way for Lavoisier to apprehend how remote he was from approaching the internal process of respiration. It was a bold, direct attack on the problem, one which he and Laplace would have no reason to think could not succeed. One of the triumphs of eighteenth-century experimental physiology had been the recent demonstrations, by Lazzaro Spallanzani, that gastric juice removed from the stomach and placed in contact with food can reproduce digestion.[4] Whether or not Lavoisier and Laplace were conscious of the parallel, there was no *a priori* reason why blood withdrawn from the blood vessels and placed in contact with vital air could not similarly reproduce respiration. We have no evidence about how long Lavoisier and Laplace may have persisted in the attempt. The lack of any other recorded experiments, or references to such experiments in Lavoisier's later publications, suggests that nothing more definite came out of it. On the other hand, even the equivocal evidence he here reported to Laplace, fitting his presuppositions as it did, may have been enough to reinforce his conviction that the blood contains the base of fixed air which combines with vital air in respiration.

By the time Lavoisier sent the news of this experiment to Laplace, they had both been caught up in another event of momentous significance. Laplace read the first section of their joint memoir on heat at the Academy on June 18. Six days later, Lavoisier recorded in his notebook,

> In the presence of MM. Blagden, du Sejoin, Laplace, Vandermonde, Fourcroy, Meusnier, and Legendre one combined in a jar dephlogisticated air with inflammable air extracted from vitriolic acid. The two airs entered through a tube, and at the moment they came together they burned right inside the jar. One burned in this way 50 or 60 pints of inflammable air, and consequently at least 20 pints of dephlogisticated air. The experiment did not succeed

> perfectly, because it was necessary to relight it several times. One had in the jar for a result 2 gros 33 grains of pure water which did not redden tincture of tournesol [an acid indicator].[5]

The following day Laplace completed the reading of the memoir on heat at the Academy as scheduled, but the announcement he and Lavoisier had to make must have overshadowed even this landmark investigation. Describing the experiment they had just completed, they concluded that "water is not a simple substance; it is composed, weight for weight, of inflammable air and vital air."[6] The two collaborators were participating in one of the most dramatic scientific developments of the era. Water, since antiquity one of the primordial elements, was so no longer. The story of the syntheses which so abruptly altered the traditional status of water, carried out first by Henry Cavendish in England, then independently in Paris by Gaspard Monge as well as by Lavoisier and Laplace, has been recounted in close detail, and needs no reiteration here.[7] The result, however, cast new light on almost every domain of Lavoisier's ongoing research endeavors. We shall follow mainly those aspects which collectively impinged upon his conception of respiration.

The initial effect of the discovery of the synthesis of water upon Lavoisier's investigation of respiration was undoubtedly to divert him from it. The new result was so "extremely important for chemical theory" that it demanded further verification and extension. The subject dominated much of his research effort through the summer and fall. Prompted by a suggestion Laplace made to him in September, that the inflammable air evolved when a metal dissolves in dilute acid probably arises from the decomposition of the water, Lavoisier now sought to complete the demonstration of the composition of water by decomposing it directly with substances having greater affinity for the vital air in water than inflammable air has. Three such substances were iron, zinc, and *charbon.* He began with iron. Introducing a small amount of iron filings and water into a jar filled with mercury and inverted over a basin of mercury, he observed that "from the first day" the iron began to lose its metallic luster, to undergo calcination, and that in proportion to this change inflammable air collected in the jar. The water was therefore being decomposed into dephlogisticated air, which united with the iron, and inflammable air, which was freed. There was now, in Lavoisier's view, "irrefutable" proof that water is not a simple substance.[8]

As usual when he had reached a decisive point in the investigation of a key phenomenon, Lavoisier foresaw a "vast field of experiments" opening out ahead of him. One of these was the continued investigation of solutions of metals in various acids, exploring further Laplace's view that the inflammable air given off derives under some circumstances from the water, under others from the acids. Another direction in which the new "field" led him was back to his earlier concern with the composition and reactions of plant and animal substances. As we have seen, he had established in 1779 that sugar contains inflammable air and *matière charbonneuse;*[9] and in a few subsequent experiments on the fermentation of sugar and other plant or animal matters he had observed that they evolve fixed air. The knowledge that water can be decomposed now prompted him to attempt to reinterpret processes involving such substances. He focused particularly on the fermentation of sugar, (known then as "spirituous" or "vinous" fermentation because its most characteristic product was traditionally known as "spirit of wine").

After its annual fall vacation, the Academy reconvened on November 12, and Lavoisier read at this meeting a memoir on the general progress of his investigation of the decomposition and recomposition of water. An "extract" of his memoir appeared in December in Abbé Rozier's *Observations sur la physique.* In spite of the fact that Lavoisier appears in the third person in the extract, Guerlac has shown, from an identical unpublished manuscript in Lavoisier's hand, that he himself wrote it.[10] He concluded with a summary of the ideas which were guiding him as he began a new study of fermentation:

> After attending to the effects of the decomposition of water in the solution and calcination of metals, M. Lavoisier reported on several experiments on spirituous fermentation which he had undertaken from the same point of view. Although he acknowledges that he has not yet obtained absolutely decisive results, he nevertheless believes it justifiable to suspect, and even to believe, that the formation of the "vinous" part [that is, the spirit of wine] is due to the decomposition of water. In that operation the dephlogisticated air contained in the water joins with the *partie charbonneuse* of the substance of the sugar, and forms fixed air, which is evolved throughout the time that the fermentation lasts. At the same time the inflammable air, modified and combined with another portion of water by means of an intermediary not yet known, forms the "spirituous" part [the spirit of wine]. In the same way, in considering the processes of vegetation, he was led to believe that it is probably the inflammable air contained in the water to which the inflammable matter of plants is due. These assertions will no doubt appear rather bold at first sight; but, independently of the proofs contained in this first memoir, M. Lavoisier promises to develop them in succession, and he ends his memoir with this modest conclusion: it is that, if the decomposition of water in a multitude of operations in nature and in art is not rigorously demonstrated, it is at least exceedingly probable.[11]

This summary report is notably vague concerning the actual experiments Lavoisier had performed on fermentation. As we saw in Chapter 1, this phenomenon had been one of the first subjects he had pursued as part of his general research program on the fixation and release of airs in 1773. He had, however, broken off his experiments on fermentation, because he saw that in order to explain the formation of the acid in the late stages of the process he needed first to know more about acids in general.[12] As we have seen, that study occupied him for six years. As far as can be discerned from his records, he did not return to fermentation until 1781. In October of that year he examined the fermentation of cane sugar in water. Placing them in a distillation flask on which he had marked volume levels with a diamond, he waited two days for the sugar to begin fermenting. Finally a few bubbles began to appear. He covered the flask with a dried membrane, beneath which he tried to collect the air which was evolving. Then he either ended the experiment inconclusively, or omitted to write down the rest of it.[13]

There are no records of any further experiments up until the time Lavoisier read the memoir summarized in the above passage. It appears, therefore, that although he had retained his interest in fermentation over all these years, Lavoisier had made little progress in his investigation of the subject. When he reported that he had undertaken "several experiments on spirituous fermentation" from the point of view of the decomposition of water, he might have been referring to new experiments never recorded in his notebooks or otherwise reported in detail; but it is likely that he had in mind only these scattered earlier attempts. It would be in keeping with his style to resuscitate older experiments when some new consideration renewed his interest in them, and to treat them then as though they were part of his current research efforts. He need not have got very far in such investigations to propound the theory presented in the above passage; for it rested on little more than his theory of the decomposition of water, what he had learned by 1779 about the composition of sugar, the common observation that fermentation produces fixed air and spirit of wine, and the assumption that the highly inflammable spirit of wine contains inflammable air. The fact that he thought that spirit of wine consists of a combination of inflammable air with "another portion of water by means of an unknown intermediary" suggests that he had not yet investigated its composition in detail. More significant than whatever experiments he may have carried out was that he expressed the intention, in this revealing passage, to add another research domain to his ongoing enterprises; and that this new area would direct his attention particularly to the composition of sugar and of inflammable plant or animal substances, as well as to the process of fermentation.

II

December brought cold weather and the opportunity to resume the calorimeter experiments of the previous winter. It was again Laplace who stirred Lavoisier to get on with these investigations, and who urged him as well to focus on respiration. As a letter to this effect which he sent Lavoisier during the month indicates, Laplace was probably more worried than Lavoisier that their theory of respiration rested on too few experiments:

> Sunday
>
> Monsieur and very dear colleague
>
> Take advantage of the favorable weather we are having for our experiments. Please have *charbon* burned in one of our machines, and repeat the experiment twice. Have three sparrows respire in it, then a guinea pig, and repeat these experiments as many times as possible. I believe that if the agreement which we found in our first experiments is upheld in these, our theory of respiration will be sufficiently established.

After suggesting that in the "other machine," the one without openings for renewing the air, Lavoisier begin with measurements of the specific heats of metals, Laplace added,

> Please do not lose any time, and if you have need of my assistance I shall be there whenever you let me know about it. If you can complete the experiments on *charbon* and on the guinea pig between now and Thursday, that would please me very much; for I shall not conceal from you that I have some concern about our first experiments.[14]

On December 14, Lavoisier began an intensive series of calorimetric measurements, a good part of which followed the line Laplace had admonished him to take up. In this second round they were particularly concerned to measure with greater precision the quantity of ice melted during the processes under study. To attain this objective they allowed the calorimeter to drain for a much longer time—for as much as fifteen hours—following the experiment.[15] This strategy must have restricted them more than ever to days on which the outside temperature was close to zero Réaumur, because at warmer temperatures the extended drainage time would only enhance the error caused by the passage of air by convection through the inner ice chamber of the calorimeter. The winter of 1783–84 must have been colder than the preceding one, however, for they were able to begin experiments on at least thirteen days over the next two months. For several of them the external temperature was one degree,[16] just the optimal condition for operating the "ice machine."

Beginning, as Laplace had requested, with the combustion of *charbon*, for which they had been able to perform only a single experiment the year before, Lavoisier obtained on December 14 only an "uncertain" result. On the eighteenth, with an outside temperature of one degree, he repeated the experiment.

Burning "very pure, well-calcined *charbon* of black alder" wood, he found that 96 pounds, 7 ounces, 2 gros of ice melted for each pound of *charbon* consumed. That result was so close to the 96 pounds 4 gros per pound of *charbon* measured in the experiment of the preceding winter that it must have strongly reassured Lavoisier and Laplace about the reliability of their method. Turning, on December 22, to the respiration of a guinea pig, Lavoisier performed two experiments, using different animals, and obtained quite different results. The amount of ice the first guinea pig melted, extrapolated twenty-four hours, was 1 pound, 15 ounces, 32 gros. The second melted nearly twice as much, or 2 pounds 13 ounces. This divergence made Lavoisier and Laplace realize how much the respiration of animals varies "according to their size, vigor, and the state of their health."[17]

Then, departing from Laplace's schedule for verifying the "first experiments" on respiration, Lavoisier extended the range of combustion measurements to include inflammable substances derived from plant and animal matter. On December 31 he did two experiments with candles. It is unlikely that he was resorting to this merely as a familiar and convenient combustion reaction; for reasons hinted at in the passage quoted above from his memoir on the decomposition of water, and which will become clearer below, he was becoming particularly interested in the combustion of wax. First he burned a single candle for one hour, ventilating the calorimeter frequently, and found that it melted 9 pounds, 1 ounce, 3 gros of ice per ounce of candle consumed. In a second experiment in which three candles burned together, however, the corresponding figure was 8 pounds, 5 ounces, 2 gros. This difference in the two results, amounting to "one-fourteenth," caused Lavoisier and Laplace to ponder which one they should "choose" as the more accurate. The second would seem at first to be more reliable, since the three candles had melted "triple" the quantity of ice that the single one had. Reflecting, however, that the combustion in this case might have been so rapid that the ventilating air current had removed some heat from the calorimeter, they decided on an "average" result closer to that of the first experiment. The fact that they regarded a discrepancy of one part in fourteen as serious enough to require a special explanation suggests that they were increasingly confident of the accuracy of their basic measurements of the ice melted.[18]

On New Year's Day they filled a lamp with olive oil and burned it for an hour in the calorimeter. Three days later they burned mutton tallow in another lamp, and found that it melted, per ounce consumed, 7 pounds, 10 ounces, 1 gros of ice. The outside temperature was 3½ degrees, however, and they thought that "that quantity [of ice] is too large, because the thermometer was too high and we had to ventilate [the calorimeter] for an hour with air at + 3 degrees, which must have melted some ice." Accordingly they did the experiment over on January 7, when the temperature was down to 1 or 1½ degrees, and obtained this time a result of 5 pounds, 15 ounces, 6 gros per ounce of tallow, "that is, a little less than *charbon*" produces. Afterward they concluded, however, that this result was too low, because tallow inevitably burns with smoke, so that a portion of its *charbon* is carried away without burning.[19]

Returning now to the subject of Laplace's special concern, Lavoisier attempted to measure the heat produced by six sparrows. Since Lavoisier had stated in the memoir on heat that birds would be more suitable than quadrupeds for future respiration investigations, they probably considered this to be a particularly important experiment:

> I placed six sparrows into a small holder and then put them into the machine during the evening. I did not take them out until the next day, after twelve hours. The external temperature was at + 1. After two hours I looked to see whether the birds were suffering and found them in good condition.
>
> The quantity of ice melted was found to be 1 pound 2 ounces, but when I removed the birds, two were dead, and one died during the day. Since I do not know at what hour the first two died, the experiment is uncertain; but it is rather likely that they died very near the end.
>
> In the evening I put the other three birds back in the machine, where they remained for 12 hours. They were removed in good health.
>
> The quantity of ice melted was 7 ounces 2 gros, the thermometer being at + ½. This experiment is quite exact.[20]

Despite the active respiration of birds, the accuracy Lavoisier attributed to the second half of this experiment did not derive from a larger quantity of ice melted, since the amount was less than that attained the year before in some of the experiments with guinea pigs. Lavoisier's assurance probably rested upon the more complete drainage of the melted ice for which they were now waiting, and upon the ideal temperature conditions for the experiment.

The discovery of the composition of water affected Lavoisier's calorimetric experiments, as it did every area of his current scientific activity. He and Laplace incorporated into the new series a measurement of the heat of "the slow combustion of hydrogen and the recomposition of water." The preparations for the measurement were extraordinarily tedious. Three weeks were required to set up the apparatus, and the combustion itself lasted for eleven and a half hours. The heat of combustion turned out to be smaller than they had expected. Along with all of the heats of combustion, Lavoisier and Laplace were measuring, in the other calorimeter, the specific heats of twenty different substances, including metals and their calces, ordinary and vital air, and several heats of solution. The new series of calorimetric experiments apparently ended in late February, most likely, once again, because of warmer weather.[21]

III

While they were pursuing the new series of calorimetric combustion experiments, Lavoisier and Laplace probably intended to carry out afterward a complementary series on the quantities of vital air these processes consumed and of fixed air formed, just as they had done the year before. In March 1784, shortly after finishing the winter's work with the calorimeter, they did begin a set of combustion experiments of this type. First they burned wax, in the form of a candle, in dephlogisticated air, measuring the decreases in the volume of the air caused by the combustion and by the addition of caustic alkali to the remaining air. Next they carried out a similar experiment on the combustion of *charbon* in dephlogisticated air. Then they "enclosed a guinea pig in a large flask in order to measure the quantity of fixed air produced by its respiration." They renewed the air continually during the eight hours and thirty minutes the animal remained in the flask, and forced the outgoing air through two bottles filled with caustic alkali. Finally they burned phosphorus, the combustion of which they had also measured once more in the calorimeter, and determined the amount of dephlogisticated air it absorbed.[22]

The parallels between these experiments, the preceding calorimetric ones, and the combination of the two they had carried out the previous year suggest that Lavoisier and Laplace began these, as before, in order to determine the quantities of heat released for a common measure of combustion, and to refine their comparison between the heat of respiration and that of the combustion of *charbon;* if so, however, that objective somehow dissipated along the way. The new series duplicated only a portion of the combustion processes studied in the calorimetric series, and included only one of the two types of animals they had utilized in the calorimeter. The single respiration experiment stood isolated and incomplete. Of the two caustic alkali bottles used to absorb the fixed air produced, the second showed an anomalous weight *loss* after the experiment, and Lavoisier did not bother to compute the total weight of fixed air absorbed.[23] As far as surviving records show, Lavoisier and Laplace never utilized either these experiments or the preceding calorimetric measurements to compute new values for the comparative heats of combustion and respiration.[24]

It appears rather surprising that they did not follow through on Laplace's urgent plea to repeat the earlier experiments in such a way as to gather the data which might confirm the "agreement" of the first results on which they had based their theory of respiration. Possibly the new experiments they did carry out were sufficiently in accord with the older ones to relieve Laplace's anxiety, so that it became unnecessary to complete the entire plan. Conversely, the large difference they had found in the heat released by two guinea pigs over a given time period may have forced them to recognize that, with their present methods, they could not hope to reach a concordance between the heats of combustion and respiration more precise or reliable than the one they had already published. Another contributing factor was that during the spring of 1784 the composition of water again dominated Lavoisier's research concerns. Typical of the impact of this preoccupation on his investigative course was that, while omitting to use the results of his latest combustion experiments on wax and on *charbon* to recalculate heats of combustion, he utilized "deficits" he now perceived in the amount of fixed air formed relative to the materials consumed in those experiments, in order to calculate the quantities of "water formed" during the process.

Although, in these and other types of experimentation Lavoisier pursued during the first half of 1784, the composition and decomposition of water was a predominant motif, some of the experiments served more than one purpose. They incorporated efforts to determine the composition of *charbon*, to arrive at an accurate measurement of the proportions of the constituents of fixed air, and to develop analyses of inflammable plant and animal substances. These several objectives were so closely interwoven within the procedures of the experiments that in some of them it is impossible to pick out which may have been at the time the main objective. This coalescence of several goals within the same group of investigations was probably due to the fact that the new conception of water as a combination of inflammable air and vital air prompted all at once the reinterpretation of a wide range of phenomena involving water or substances containing inflammable or vital air.

One of the most significant opportunities that the discovery of the composition of water afforded Lavoisier was to reassess his problems concerning the combustion of charcoal. We may recall that in the crucial but troublesome experiment performed on May 24 of the previous year, he had at first attributed moisture that appeared during the combustion to water contained in the charcoal. In the published account of the experiment, however, he had ignored this complication. He wrote that account only a very short time before he learned that inflammable air and vital air can combine to form water. The new discovery now made it possible to consider that moisture arising during a combustion such as that of charcoal may have been formed in the process. During the following October or November, while he was attempting to complete the demonstration of the composition of water by decomposing it with iron, he found out from Charles Blagden that Priestley had recently reduced minium (lead calx) to metallic lead in inflammable air. Whereas Priestley interpreted this result as further confirmation of the phlogiston theory, identifying inflammable air with phlogiston itself, Lavoisier assumed that the inflammable air must have removed vital air from the calx, forming water with it. Priestley's experiment therefore only "confirmed more and more for me the opinion I held that water is a composite body."[25] The experiment also reminded him of an observation he himself had made many years before and recorded in his *Opuscules* in 1774. After reducing minium with charcoal, he had found that the total weight of the products, including the elastic fluid disengaged, was 1 gros 44 grains less than the weight of the materials employed. Having noticed that a few drops of water had collected in the recipient during the operation, he had suspected that "a portion of water in the minium separated during the reduction." Repeating the experiment with identical quantities, he had been able to collect only 24 grains of water; but he believed that the density of the elastic fluid formed may have been greater than he had assumed in calculating its weight, and that this factor, together with the water, might account for the deficit.[26] When he turned back to these results in 1783, he explained the situation quite differently. The charcoal must have furnished inflammable air, which combined with *principe oxygine* contained in the minium, to form the water.[27] The experiment was thus equivalent to Priestley's, except for the source of the inflammable air.

The main point Lavoisier now saw in this old experiment was a further proof for the composition of water; his explanation incorporated, however, a new conception also of the composition of charcoal. He was now describing that substance as a combination of "true *matière charbonneuse*" and inflammable air.[28] Whether this insight emerged specifically from his reexamination of the old experiment, or whether he was merely applying to that situation a clarification which had occurred to him sometime earlier during the months since the discovery of the synthesis of water, we cannot determine. In the latter case, his resuscitation of the results of work performed a decade before probably provided retrospectively the first confirmatory evidence for the conception. We have seen that in November he was also, in the light of the composition of water, considering sugar and spirit of wine as substances containing inflammable air. There is no way to ascertain the order in which he developed these interpretations, or even whether they emerged in series rather than in parallel. Whatever may have been the detailed stages in the growth of these ideas, they were by the end of 1783 merging in Lavoisier's mind into a general view of inflammable plant substances as combinations of *matière charbonneuse* and inflammable air. That viewpoint was undoubtedly reawakening his earlier interest in the analysis of plant and animal matters, and probably explains why he began to feature substances such as wax and olive oil in his combustion experiments that winter. The same general interest may have led him, at the beginning of the following March, to distill coal (known in French as *charbon de terre*) in order to determine the quantity of inflammable air which that substance could yield.[29]

IV

The further development of Lavoisier's views on *matière charbonneuse*, plant and animal substances, and ultimately on respiration was enmeshed more tightly than ever within the framework of his research on the composition of water. In 1784 his occupation with the latter subject took on a new direction imparted by his participation in a commission appointed by the Academy, to examine the prospects for aviation excited by the recent balloon ascents of the Montgolfier brothers and the Charles brothers. Appointed in July 1783, the commission would normally have expired in December, when it reported its findings. Lavoisier, however, intervened to reconvene the commission to investigate "the most economical means to produce inflammable air on a large scale," in order to advance the alternative of filling balloons with inflammable air. At the same time Jean-Baptiste Meusnier, a highly talented mathematician serving as an engineer in the army, finished reading a report to the Academy on the engineering of a stable hydrogen balloon. Impressed with his imaginative theoretical analysis of the problems of flight, Lavoisier asked Meusnier to join him in experiments on the generation of inflammable air. Since they had "strong reason to believe that inflammable air existed in great abundance" in water, Lavoisier and Meusnier decided to use water as their source, and as a consequence they "gradually found ourselves engaged" from "another point of view" in the question of the analysis and synthesis of water.[30]

Previously, as described above, Lavoisier had been able to decompose water slowly, in small amounts, with iron filings. He and Meusnier decided that the only way to make the operation rapid would be to carry it out at a very high temperature. For this purpose they designed the famous "gun barrel" experiment (see Figure 7). Detaching a four-foot iron gun barrel from its breech, so that it formed a tube open at both ends, they inserted it in an inclined position through a furnace so that its central portion could be surrounded with glowing coals. From a funnel connected to the elevated end of the barrel they could allow water to flow into the barrel at a rate controlled by a stopcock. As the water passed through the red-hot central portion of the barrel, it vaporized. The lower end of the barrel connected, through tubing, with a bell jar over water, where they could collect any air which evolved from the operation. In two experiments carried out with this apparatus in March, they found that large quantities of inflammable air passed out of the gun barrel. Examining the gun barrel afterward, they observed that its inner surface had taken on the appearance of a calx of the metal. In subsequent experiments, in order to prove that the inflammable air was derived from water which disappeared during the operation, they inserted between the gun barrel and the bell jar a coiled tube, or "serpentine," descending through a cold water bath. Here any water vapor escaping decomposition condensed and collected in a recipient bottle. Another

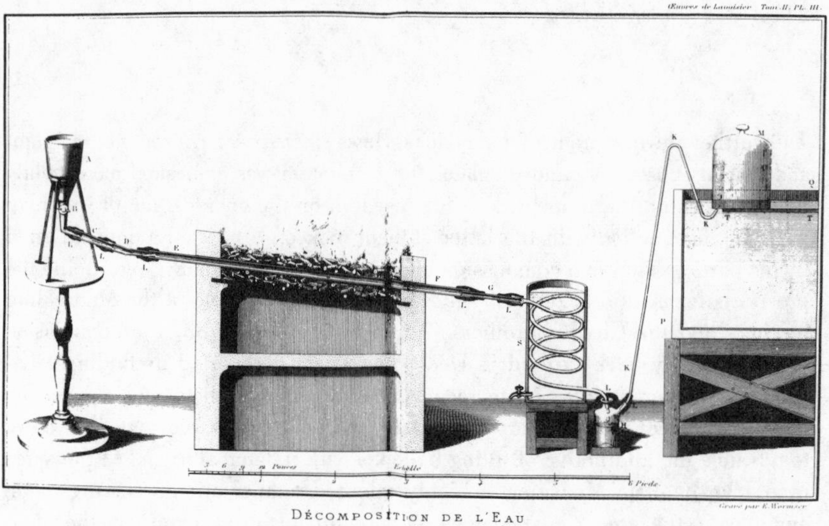

Figure 7. Apparatus used by Lavoisier and Meusnier for "gun barrel" experiments to decompose water. On left, at *A*, the funnel with stopcock *B* allows water to enter the gun barrel at a controlled rate. The sloping barrel, *EF*, passes through a charcoal fire. The coiled tube, *S*, is cooled by surrounding water to condense any undecomposed water, which collects in bottle *H*. Pneumatic jar *M*, at right, collects airs produced by the decomposition of water. Lavoisier, *Oeuvres*, 2: Plate 3.

modification they later made was to line the barrel with copper, which did not react with water, and to place the iron within it in the form of filings. This change enabled them to verify more conclusively that during the process the iron gained weight, and also made it possible for them to use the same gun barrel more than once.[31]

Quickly successful in their quest for a means to produce large amounts of inflammable air, Lavoisier and Meusnier now took advantage of their new apparatus to elucidate further the processes by which water can be decomposed. According to Lavoisier's theory, the decomposition of water by iron was equivalent to an ordinary calcination, only that the dephlogisticated air derived from the water rather than from the atmosphere. To support this view they deemed it essential to show that all combustible and calcinable substances, and no others, decomposed water. They tested a "large number of incandescent bodies, principally metallic substances," and the results were "in accord" with this exception. "Knowing, moreover, from the most common operation in metallurgy that the principle in *charbon* has an even greater affinity for dephlogisticated air, since it can remove it from iron," Lavoisier concluded that *charbon* ought to be especially suitable to decompose water. When brought into contact with water, *charbon* should "burn without the aid of air."[32]

To test this deduction, Lavoisier and Meusnier on April 10 introduced into the copper-lined gun barrel 4 gros 15⁴⁄₁₀ grains of charcoal which they had previously deprived of its inflammable air by heating it to incandescence for two and a half hours in a closed crucible. They were able to fill nine vessels with the mixture of inflammable and fixed air evolved when they passed water through the gun barrel, and stopped the operation after three hours and fifteen minutes, when "the operation was no longer giving off much of anything." Emptying the gun barrel, they found all the charcoal gone except for 6 grains of cinders.[33] The experiment was thus highly successful. "This experiment," Meusnier and Lavoisier asserted at the Academy on April 21, "demonstrates the first example of a complete combustion carried out without air, and permits no further doubt concerning the true principle of respiration and combustion"—that is, that it is dephlogisticated air—or concerning the identification of that principle with "that which water deposits when it forms inflammable air."[34] In other words, the fact that *charbon* formed fixed air with the substance it attracted out of the water further confirmed the identity of that substance as dephlogisticated air; at the same time, if one assumed the composition of water, the result confirmed that it was dephlogisticated air which combined with *charbon* in respiration and in combustion.

In qualitative terms the experiment was decisive. Now that multiple tests had sustained the general theory of the composition of water, however, Lavoisier and Meusnier believed that they should use the gun barrel experiments to subject the theory to the more critical examination of rigorous quantitative measurement.[35] In keeping with Lavoisier's overall analytical approach, they hoped to determine as exactly as possible the balance between the substances consumed and those produced. For that objective the *charbon* experiment presented very complicated problems, arising from the variable mixture of inflammable and fixed air which it produced. As Meusnier, who recorded the experiment in Lavoisier's notebook, remarked:

> It is evident without further examination, that the aeriform products in this experiment must be equal in weight to the substances consumed; but in order to demonstrate that by the facts and by calculation, it would have been necessary to absorb all of the fixed air immediately in fixed alkali, in order to determine its weight accurately.[36]

"We ought to have passed the aeriform products through two successive flasks filled with caustic alkali," Meusnier lamented at another point in his analysis of the experiment, "but we were not equipped to do that."[37] The unfortunate consequence was that the fixed air was partially absorbed in the water of the basin in which the collecting flasks were immersed, and that the proportion lost this way would vary inversely with the time required for filling each flask. Since the rate of filling had decreased over the course of the experiment, the amount of fixed air absorbed on the way would have varied also, introducing, as Meusnier noted with understatement, "some uncertainty" in the results.[38]

We might expect that the obvious lesson for Lavoisier and Meusnier to draw was that the experiment was faultily designed, and that they would have to repeat it after adding the appropriate bottles to intercept the fixed air. Instead Meusnier embarked on an extraordinarily elaborate computation in order to estimate, from three samples of the mixture of inflammable air and fixed air taken at intervals during the operation, the total amount of fixed air which had probably been lost in the water bath during the collection of the air in each of the nine flasks filled during the experiment. That they should have chosen this tedious and uncertain option suggests a characteristic of Lavoisier's research not often mentioned by historians. By the standards of his day Lavoisier utilized exceptionally complex apparatus, often specially constructed for a particular type of experiment. His ample personal financial resources enabled him to provide himself with far more costly equipment than most chemists could afford. Yet he undoubtedly could not make unlimited outlays. I suspect that it was in part the expense of repeating such experiments, in part the limited time he had available for research, which led him, in this as in other cases, to attempt to rescue the results of an imperfect experiment by calculated or estimated corrections; and that similar limitations probably induced him, in this and other cases, to make the same experimental results do for a variety of purposes. In this instance the calculations necessary to compensate for the experimental deficiencies were so intricate that they filled fourteen pages in the laboratory notebook.[39]

For our purpose it would be superfluous to follow through these lengthy computations, even though they reveal in a most fascinating way the kinds of assumptions Lavoisier and Meusnier made concerning the nature of the processes and the accuracy of their measurements. In the course of the analysis, however, Meusnier was led to make a subsidiary calculation which is directly relevant to our story. At one point, in order to calculate, from the quantity of dephlogisticated air consumed in the experiment, the quantity of fixed air which *should* have been produced, he returned to the experiment on the combustion of *charbon* which Lavoisier had carried out on May 24 of the previous year. We have already seen, in the preceding chapter, the original calculations Lavoisier and Laplace had made at the time, and the loss of material upon which Lavoisier had remarked, but from which he had then drawn no significant inferences. In the light of the new knowledge of the decomposition of water, however, this result looked quite different. If we first turn back to pages 180–82 to review the older calculation, we can readily appreciate the intellectual shift which had taken place by the time Meusnier made the following revised analysis of the "Experiment performed by M. Lavoisier on the combustion of *charbon* in dephlogisticated air, May 24, 1783."[40]

Meusnier followed Lavoisier's original protocol in correcting the measured volumes of dephlogisticated air at the beginning of the experiment, the total volume immediately following the combustion, and the volume remaining after absorption of the fixed air, to standard temperature and pressure. Converting the volumes to weights, he then found that 62.49 grains of dephlogisticated air had been employed, whereas 68.60 grains of fixed air was produced. The difference, 6.11 grains, represented the "*charbon* [which had] entered into the fixed air"; but the amount of *charbon* actually consumed had been 17.20 grains, so that 11.09 grains had "disappeared."[41] This "deficit" was about twice what Lavoisier had calculated. Part of the difference was due to Meusnier's having used different figures for the densities of the two airs, and his omitting the deduction Lavoisier had made for fixed air contained in the dephlogisticated air at the beginning. The rest of it was because Lavoisier had "corrected" the quantity of *charbon* consumed from 17.20 to 15 grains, because "a little bit of water [was] given off." Whereas Lavoisier had then considered the appearance of this water a minor side effect, the source of an error whose magnitude he simply guessed at, Meusnier now accepted the deficit as measured, and attempted to explain it in terms of the formation and decomposition of water. There were, he thought, two ways to account for the 11.09 grains of *charbon* lost:

> What is that part of the *charbon?* If it were the inflammable air of the water, the quantity which has just been determined would by itself suffice to bring about the combustion of 55.45 grains of dephlogisticated air, and the loss of weight would [therefore] have been considerably greater.
>
> Let us therefore envision this operation from a different point of view and regard the deficit of 11.09 grains as the result of the water formed by a very small quantity of inflammable air contained in the *charbon*, as follows:

Inflammable air contained in the *charbon*	1.848
Dephlogisticated air which has served to burn it	9.240
Sum corresponding to the water formed	11.088[42]

Meusnier calculated these values for the inflammable air and dephlogisticated air by assuming that inflammable air forms one-sixth of the weight of the water. This proportion had been established as a result of the experiments of the preceding year on the synthesis of water from the combustion of the two airs, and confirmed by "scrupulous measurements" of the density of the inflammable air produced in the recent gun barrel experiments utilizing iron.[43]

Recalculating the results of the experiment of May 24 on the basis of the second alternative quoted above, Meusnier showed that "it will follow from this way of looking [at the problem] that nearly the whole of the *charbon* will be capable of entering into the composition of the fixed air":

Dephlogisticated air consumed, as before	62.49 grains	
The same employed in forming water	9.24	
Dephlogisticated air converted to fixed air	53.25 grains	53.250 grains
Charbon consumed	17.200 grains	
Inflammable air contained in the *charbon*	1.848	
Actual *charbon*	15.352	15.352
Total [of substances consumed], corresponding to fixed air formed		68.602 grains

The quantity of fixed air calculated from the volume of air absorbed in caustic alkali being 68.60 grains, the total of substances consumed and produced balanced perfectly, a persuasive confirmation of this "manner of viewing" the combustion. The conclusion had further consequences for the composition of fixed air itself:

> This viewpoint seems more natural, and causing nearly all of the *charbon* to enter into the fixed air, it gives quite different proportions between the dephlogisticated air and the *principe charbonneux* which constitute chalky acid [fixed air].[44]

Meusnier expected to verify his interpretation further by showing that with new proportions for the composition of fixed air based on it he could work out a consistent balance of reagents and products for the present experiment on the decomposition of water by *charbon*. He ended up instead with an "impossible result," a calculated total volume for the inflammable air produced which exceeded the total volume of the vessels in which they had collected the evolved air. That outcome aroused in Meusnier "a mistrust of the results of the experiment of May 24 which has supplied us with some of the givens for this calculation; I fear that the volume of air after the combustion and prior to the absorption may have been raised higher than it should have been, because of the heat resulting from the combustion which one was perhaps not able to allow enough time to dissipate." Meusnier therefore turned to the more recent experiment on the combustion of *charbon* which Lavoisier had carried out only a few weeks before. Originally, while seeking suitable data in Lavoisier's notebooks, Meusnier had passed over this experiment, because Lavoisier had not recorded the heights of the mercury in the bell jar, figures required in order to correct the measured volumes to standard pressure. Assuming now, however, that Lavoisier had used the same bell jar for this experiment as he had for the earlier one of May 24, Meusnier estimated the mercury levels and carried out the calculations. By this time he had utilized the averaged results of the two most recent water decomposition experiments using iron to revise the proportion of inflammable air in water from one-sixth to 1:5.629, and he used the new ratio in his further computations.

For the combustion experiment in question, Meusnier found,

the dephlogisticated air consumed weighed	47.52 grains;
the *charbon* consumed was	18.30 grains;
giving a total of	65.82 grains.
Since the weight of the fixed air calculated from its volume was	58.80 grains,
there remained a deficit of	7.02 grains.

This deficit was smaller than that of the experiment of May 24, Meusnier reasoned, because Lavoisier had used calcined *charbon* containing less inflammable air. The 7.02 grains, he assumed, represented water containing 5.7729 grains of dephlogisticated air and 1.2471 grains of inflammable air (1.2471:7.02::1:5.629). Subtracting the quantity of dephlogisticated air accounted for by this water from the total dephlogisticated air consumed, he calculated that 41.7471 grains had entered into the fixed air. By subtracting the quantity of inflammable air in the same water (1.2471 grains) from the weight of the charcoal employed (18.3000 grains), he computed the weight of *charbon* in the fixed air (17.0529 grains), and arrived at the ratio of *charbon* to dephlogisticated air in fixed air. At the same time he had established the composition of the charcoal itself (18.3000 grains of charcoal consisted of 17.0529 grains of *charbon* and 1.2471 grains of inflammable air). When Meusnier utilized the composition of fixed air determined in this experiment to recalculate the results of the decomposition of water by *charbon*, the problem which had prompted his lengthy digression, and uncovered other sources of error, he came up with a plausible outcome.[45] He and Lavoisier therefore came to have "more confidence" in the recent combustion experiment than in the one of the previous May; but Lavoisier seldom discarded the data from any experiment, and in this case he nevertheless reported with caution, in a subsequent publication, the results of the earlier experiment along with those of the later one.[46]

I have presented these calculations and the accompanying reasoning in part because they reveal with remarkable clarity the manner in which Lavoisier and his collaborators proceeded in such situations, adjusting assumptions to results and results to assumptions, in order to wrest coherent conclusions from the limited number of experiments they were in a position to perform and the imperfect quantitative measurements which they often obtained. This instance also shows beautifully how the need for a particular piece of data, the composition of fixed air, in a particular experimental situation, prompted them to reevaluate older results from a new point of view, causing as well a reinterpretation of the process which had been under examination in the earlier experiments. When Lavoisier had performed the experiment of May 24, 1783, he was thinking of the combustion of *charbon* as a simple conversion of the "principle" contained in it to fixed air, and any water appearing in the process was an accidental source of error. By the time he carried out a similar experiment in March 1784, he had available the general knowledge that *charbon* contains inflammable air as well as the principle which enters into fixed air; but if the sequence in which I have reported the above events is historically valid, it was not until Meusnier required the accurate composition of fixed air for a particular computation that he and Lavoisier were led to work out in detail the consequences for the combustion of charcoal—that is, to *treat* the process quantitatively as one involving both the formation of fixed air from the *matière charbonneuse* in charcoal, and the formation of water from its inflammable air.

The foregoing interpretation might at first glance appear refuted by the fact that the combustion experiment carried out in March 1784 includes calculations of the deficit between the fixed air formed and the dephlogisticated air consumed, and that the deficit is regarded as due to "water formed." On this assumption the compositions of water and fixed air are calculated.[47] These computations are independent of the corresponding ones Meusnier carried out on the same data in early April. My inference that Meusnier's calculations were germinal to this approach to the combustion of charcoal must assume that the calculations adjoining the experimental protocol itself were added later. The format of the pages involved suggests that the relevant calculations might have been inserted afterward, for the ink is browner and slightly lighter than that of the rest of the record of the operations and results. The decisive evidence rests, however, on the ratios of inflammable air to water implicit in the calculations of the composition of water. As we have seen, up until early April Lavoisier was assuming a proportion of one to six. By the end of the calculations related to the experiment of April 10, Meusnier had switched to the ratio of 1:5.629. When Meusnier and Lavoisier reported their new series of decomposition experiments on water with the gun barrel to the Academy, on April 21, they stated that they had derived from the aggregate of the results a more "rigorous" value for the proportions of inflammable air and dephlogisticated air in water. They were now estimating "that water contains about one-seventh of its weight" of inflammable air.[48] Lavoisier must subsequently have refined the value once again, however, because in his memoir on the composition of fixed air, written sometime after June 7, 1784, he utilized a ratio of 1:7.623. It is this ratio which is used in the calculations in Lavoisier's notebook accompanying the combustion experiment of March, calculations which he published without alteration in the memoir on fixed air.[49] He must, therefore, have added those calculations to the experiment sometime after the events we have just followed. Lavoisier's reinterpretation of the nature of the combustion of *charbon* was, at least in part, a by-product of the strenuous effort of his collaborator Meusnier to salvage one of his flawed combustion experiments in order to consolidate his theory of the composition of water.

V

In his summary paper on the composition of water, Lavoisier had hinted, in December 1783, that he was becoming interested in the decomposition of that substance by "the operations of nature," as well as by chemical procedures, and that the operations of nature he had principally in mind were fermentations and "the processes of vegetation."[50] In both instances his new conception of water stimulated him to revive an old interest. We have seen that he had attempted his first fermentation experiments in the months just after setting out his general program, early in 1773, to investigate the processes that fix or release airs. His interest in vegetation went back even further. During the late 1760s he had taken up the question of the transmutability of the elements, focusing particularly on the long-debated claim that water can be transmuted into earth. The primary basis of this claim was the famous seventeenth-century experiment of Joan Baptista Van Helmont, who had placed a willow tree in an earthen vessel containing dried earth, watered it for five years with rain water, found at the end of that time that the weight of the earth remained unchanged, and asserted that "one hundred and sixty-four pounds of wood, bark and roots had come up from water alone."[51] In the intervening century and a half several other well-known scientists, including Robert Boyle, had repeated variants of this experiment. In his first memoir on water, read to the Academy in 1770, Lavoisier thoroughly reviewed the literature on this subject and concluded that all the experiments were indecisive. He also pointed out that, since "plants are not composed only of water and earth, [but] contain also oils, resins, saline and odoriferous constituents, acid and alkaline juices, etc.," then if water were indeed the sole source of the matter contained in plants, one would have to conclude that water "is changed into as many particular substances as one can discover in all the plants with which we are acquainted, a supposition which is not confirmed by any experiment."[52] As with so many chemical phenomena, this question of the relation between water and the formation of plant substances appeared to Lavoisier in a wholly new light after he knew that water can be decomposed. What had seemed totally implausible to him when it applied a transmutation of elements might be quite reasonable in terms of the decomposition of the water and the recombination of its constituents with other substances.

Lavoisier's renewed interest in vegetation was probably reinforced also by an important recent investigation of the chemical aspects of the phenomenon by Jean Senebier. Of the prominent investigators of respiration during the preceding decade—Priestley, Scheele, and Lavoisier—only Lavoisier had up until then restricted his attention to the exchanges of *animals* with the atmosphere. Priestley and Scheele had each studied the effects of both animals and plants on the surrounding air. As is well known, Priestley was the first to discover that plants can "restore" air "vitiated" by animals breathing in it.[53] Not all of Priestley's results were consistent, however, and Scheele's observations seemed opposed to them.[54] Between 1779 and 1782 Jan Ingenhousz and Jean Senebier resolved the contradictions by demonstrating that plants "dephlogisticate" air only when exposed to sunlight. Senebier went on to show that the source of the "pure air" plants release is fixed air which they absorb. In 1782 Senebier published a three-volume treatise which integrated all these investigations into a coherent viewpoint.[55]

Lavoisier took up the question of vegetation again in the spring of 1784 in the modified, extended version of his memoir on the composition of water. His new view of the composition of water provided him with an alternative to Senebier's interpretation of the process by which plants evolve pure air. "Nature," he wrote, "furnishes us with a great number of means" to separate the constituents from water:

> Water is the great reservoir in which [nature] finds the matter for the combustibles which she is continually forming before our eyes, and vegetation appears to be her grand method. If we bring together the experiments of MM. Van Helmont, du Hamel, Vallérius and Tillet [Van Helmont's demonstration that plants convert water into their own substance, and later versions of the experiment], with those performed recently by MM. Ingenhousz and Sennebier [*sic*], it becomes evident that, on the one hand, water is the principal agent of vegetation, and on the other hand, that during its course vegetation habitually evolves a great quantity of vital air through the vessels of the leaves. Water therefore decomposes in plants through the action of vegetation; but it decomposes in the inverse order from that which we have observed up until now [in chemical operations]. In fact, in vegetation it is the

> vital air which becomes free, [whereas in chemical operations it is the inflammable air], and it is the aqueous inflammable principle which remains combined in order to form the *matière charbonneuse* of plants, their oils, everything they contain which is combustible. These different substances appear at present to be no more than modifications, not yet identified, of the inflammable principle of water.[56]

This passage shows how Lavoisier's interest in the composition of plant substances was expanding, beyond their chemical analysis and their usefulness as a class of combustible substances, to embrace the natural physiological processes through which they originate. It contains, however, an idea so startling at first glance that I tried for a while to persuade myself that Lavoisier had not expressed himself clearly. If the *matière charbonneuse* were "no more than" a modification of the "inflammable principle," then "the base of fixed air" could not be a permanent, independent entity. This would seem difficult to reconcile with the whole thrust of Lavoisier's analytical procedures—more akin to Priestley's tendency to view various substances as qualitative modifications of one another than to his own efforts to separate substances into distinct constituent "species." The above statements, however, cannot readily be dismissed; they evidently amplify, in fact, the statement in the earlier, summary version of his memoir on water, that "it is probably the inflammable air contained in the water to which the inflammable matter in plants is due"; and they may also fit somehow into the framework of a question he pondered at the beginning of the present memoir: "Are there several species of inflammable air? Or rather is that which we obtain always the same, more or less mingled, more or less altered by the union with the different substances it is capable of dissolving?"[57] Moreover, this viewpoint has affinities with, if not a direct connection to, an earlier speculation Lavoisier had offered in 1777, that the fixed air formed in the combustion of a candle may be "nothing but inflammable air which is disengaged from the candle . . . plus the eminently respirable air in which the combustion takes place."[58]

The idea that *matière charbonneuse* and all other combustible plant substances are modifications of the "inflammable principle" (by which Lavoisier now meant that principle which, when combined with matter of fire, forms inflammable air) might also seem to be a reversion toward a phlogiston-like theory, in that Lavoisier was postulating that different inflammable substances owe their inflammability to a single "principle of inflammability";[59] but we need not necessarily draw such drastic inferences. We have seen that for nearly a decade Lavoisier had gradually been augmenting the distinction between tangible charcoal and the principle contained in it which enters into the composition of fixed air. He had, however, yet to obtain that principle itself, free from its combinations. Its identity was therefore uncertain, and it is not so surprising after all if his new view of the composition of water led him to entertain the conception that the principle of *matière charbonneuse* is embodied in some modification of the inflammable principle.

It is possible that some of the experiments Lavoisier performed during the spring of 1784, for example the distillation of coal, were somehow efforts to verify that *matière charbonneuse* is a modification of the inflammable principle. There are no discernible traces of such an aim, however, in either the procedures or the comments upon individual experiments. More probably he did not actually expect to be able to confirm his conjecture experimentally, for he implied in the quoted statement that nothing but "nature's operations" could effect this modification. He considered it impossible to decompose water by chemical means in such a way as to combine the inflammable principle with another substance, while releasing the vital air, because the inflammable principle has "a greater affinity for the *principe oxygine* than for any other substance."[60] His theoretical conception may therefore have had no detectable consequences for the research program he was carrying on, during which he appeared always to treat combustible plant substances as combinations of inflammable air and the base of fixed air in stable proportions. That this probably was his position is supported by his discussion of spirituous fermentation in the paragraphs immediately following the previously quoted passage.

Lavoisier had revived his long-standing interest in spirituous fermentation mainly because it "is another means to decompose water by the wet way." At the time he wrote his extended memoir on the composition of water he was pursuing his investigation of fermentation, but he had not yet completed it, so that he included in his discussion only a "succinct summary" of his experiments. Recalling that he had shown earlier, in 1779 in fact,[61] that sugar contains *charbon* "already formed," he asked himself why, since *charbon* decomposes water "in the dry way," it would not also "decompose it by the wet way." That is, since dry *charbon* combined with the *principe oxygine* of the water vapor in his gun barrel experiments, he expected that when sugar ferments, the *charbon* contained in the sugar ought similarly to combine with the *principe oxygine* of the water in which the process occurs, forming the "enormous quantity of fixed air which is disengaged." The inflammable air thus set free would then form "the spirituous part, the spirit of wine."

> The decomposition of the water in spirituous fermentation thus takes place by means of a double action. On the one hand, the *matière charbonneuse* tends to combine with the *principe oxygine;* on the other hand, this same *matière charbonneuse* tends to combine with the inflammable principle of the water.

Although these statements are somewhat ambiguous, it is clear from his discussion as a whole that he considered spirit of wine, like other inflammable plant matters, to be composed of *matière charbonneuse* and the inflammable principle. "Another very remarkable circumstance in the spirituous fermentation," he noted, was that

> if one carefully collects the products, one sees clearly that in adding together the weights of the fixed air disengaged, that of the portion of the sugar which remains undecomposed, and finally, the spirituous part, one has a product much greater than that of the sugar composed, whereas on the contrary one finds an equal loss in the weight of the water.

It is not immediately obvious why Lavoisier stated this relationship in this unusual way as "a very remarkable circumstance," since it amounts to the balance between reactants and products he always expected to find in any chemical process. At any rate, he announced that he planned to continue his investigation, which "ought to provide the subject of a special memoir directed uniquely toward that topic."[62] Thus his effort to multiply the ways to decompose water was leading him back to the phenomenon of fermentation that had fascinated him ten years before. His progress in this decade on other fronts now appeared to provide the means he had then lacked to confront this complicated problem.

8

Fixing the Composition of Fixed Air

Lavoisier did not immediately carry out his pledge to make fermentation the subject of a further special investigation; he nearly always had more research plans in mind than he could pursue at any given time. In the weeks after he had completed his work on the composition of water he turned instead to another problem which had similarly been embedded in that work as a subsidiary problem. The task which he now elevated into the central objective of investigation was to determine the exact composition of fixed air. As we have just witnessed, Meusnier had reassessed Lavoisier's earlier combustion experiments with charcoal in order to obtain the proportions of *charbon* and dephlogisticated air for his analysis of the results of the decomposition of water by *charbon.* After he had reinterpreted the first experiment, the troublesome one of May 24, 1783, Meusnier had computed proportions for fixed air which amounted to about 78 percent dephlogisticated air and 22 percent *charbon.* From the more recent experiment of March 1784, in which he had greater confidence, he arrived at values near to 71 and 29 percent, respectively. (The actual data recorded in the notebook are 41.7471 grains of dephlogisticated air and 17.0529 of *charbon* in 58.8000 grains of fixed air.)[1] This second result was reasonably close to the values of 72.125 and 27.875 which Lavoisier calculated for his memoir on water from the data of the old experiment on the reduction of lead ore by charcoal, the same one whose results he had dusted off when he heard about Priestley's reduction of lead ore in inflammable air.[2] Despite this agreement, Lavoisier felt that there were so many sources of uncertainty in the combustion experiments on *charbon* that it was "necessary to multiply the experiments."[3] Perhaps Meusnier's concern to establish the proportions of dephlogisticated and inflammable air in water "with rigor," by "comparing together at one time the results of numerous experiments,"[4] influenced Lavoisier to raise his standard of rigor also for fixed air. For this purpose he began a new series of combustion experiments on May 10.

Even though he and Meusnier had been able to account for the deficits observed in the combustion experiments on ordinary charcoal by ascribing them to the formation of water, Lavoisier decided to attempt to eliminate experimentally a condition which "might throw some doubt on our conclusions" because of the fact that "the formation of water might appear theoretical, and it is not yet generally accepted by all physicists and chemists." To do so they sought out an "absolutely pure *matière charbonneuse* from which the last portions of inflammable air which it might contain" had been removed. What they used was *charbon de Bourdenne*, employed ordinarily in making gunpowder. As an added precaution they calcined this material for two hours in a luted crucible before placing it in the combustion chamber. In the first experiment they did not weigh the *charbon* remaining after the combustion. Lavoisier, who apparently did all of the calculations based on the experiments himself, was therefore obliged to derive the quantity of *charbon* consumed from the difference between the 34.655 grains of fixed air formed and the 25.157 grains of dephlogisticated air used up (both of these quantities being calculated in turn from the corrected volume changes). "Thus, *charbon* burned, 9.506." These figures yielded a composition of fixed air consisting of 72.6 percent dephlogisticated air and 27.4 percent *charbon*.[5]

That outcome was probably near to Lavoisier's expectation, as will be seen below; but the lack of a measured quantity of *charbon* consumed precluded checking the validity of the assumption incorporated into the calculation, that all of the *charbon* and dephlogisticated air consumed entered into the fixed air. They therefore repeated the experiment, this time duly weighing the *charbon* before and after the combustion, on May 17. They obtained the following:

Dephlogisticated air consumed	70.65 grains
Charbon consumed	21.30
Total of substances consumed	91.95
Fixed air	92.26
Error	0.31

This was, in fact, an impressively small difference between the substances consumed and the product. When Lavoisier determined the composition of fixed air from these quantities, however, the outcome, 76.834 percent dephlogisticated air and 23.165 percent *substance charbonneuse*, diverged considerably from the results based on earlier experiments. Having noticed that "a little air had escaped underneath the bell jar during the combustion," he recalculated the results on the "supposition" that four cubic inches of dephlogisticated air had in this way been lost. The "error," or difference between the measured and calculated consumption of *charbon*, now became larger (the total of substances consumed decreasing to 90.0516 grains), and Lavoisier tried to eliminate the new discrepancy by working backward to a smaller value for the density of fixed air used to compute its weight from its measured volume. He was encouraged that the resulting density was closer to the density of fixed air found by the Abbé Fontana than was the figure he had previously applied. Nevertheless, when he recalculated the composition of fixed air on this basis, the outcome was only slightly changed (to 76.4 and 23.6 percent).[6] The situation thus remained unsatisfying.

Apparently frustrated in his attempts to solve his problem by burning highly purified *charbon*, Lavoisier next tried to reach his goal by means of the combustion of a wax candle. He performed the experimental operations on June 1. Taking for granted by now that the candle produced both fixed air and water, he resorted to the type of calculation that Meusnier had made for the combustion of ordinary charcoal; that is, he treated the deficit between the total quantities of the substances consumed and the fixed air produced as a measure of the water formed. He found the wax to be composed of 87.035 percent *charbon* and 12.965 percent inflammable air, "and for the composition of the fixed air" he arrived at the figures of 71.78 percent dephlogisticated air and 28.22 *charbon*. He encountered no obstacles during his calculations, and the close accord between this result and that reached earlier by Meusnier must have made this for him a far more persuasive experiment than the preceding ones using purified *charbon*. Since it relied on his theory of the composition of water, however, it was still vulnerable to the objections of those who might not accept that theory. Lavoisier perceived in the data a strong argument in support of his theory:

> If one wished to suppose that no portion of the candle was employed to form water, and that all of the deficit was water contained originally in the wax, one would have an absurd result, because all of the wax would be nothing but water.

The measured deficit, that is, was 21.52 grains, almost equal to the 21.75 grains of wax consumed. Lavoisier treated the deficit as composed of 2.824 grains of inflammable air derived from the candle and 18.696 grains of dephlogisticated air. If it were instead preformed water, the entire 21.52 grains would have had to derive from the 21.75 grains of wax.[7]

In spite of this argument, which he did not use publicly, Lavoisier still wanted to establish the composition of fixed air on results independent of his theory of water. He therefore tried once more, on June 5, the combustion of purified *charbon*. The results confronted him with further difficulties, which he struggled to resolve by repeatedly revising his assumptions. At the beginning of the experiment the volume of dephlogisticated air in the bell jar, corrected to standard temperature and pressure, was 187.676 cubic inches. During the combustion this volume decreased by 3.219 cubic inches, leaving a corrected volume of 184.460 cubic inches. The corrected volume remaining after the fixed air had been absorbed in caustic alkali was 73.825 cubic inches. Subtracting the latter from the *original* volume (187.676 cubic inches), he obtained for the volume of dephlogisticated air entering the reaction 113.851 cubic inches. Using the figure 0.47317 for the density of dephlogisticated air, he converted this volume to a weight of 53.871 grains. Now, subtracting from the volume left just after the combustion (184.460 cubic inches) the 73.825 cubic inches left following the addition of caustic alkali, he calculated that 110.635 cubic inches or, at a density of 0.7, 77.444 grains of fixed air had formed.[8]

The small loss in volume which had ensued during the combustion itself Lavoisier thought he could account for by the difference in density between dephlogisticated air and fixed air, so that he did not have to regard that decrease as representing anything else formed from the dephlogisticated air. Assigning, therefore, all of the dephlogisticated air consumed to the fixed air formed, he subtracted the 53.871 grains of dephlogisticated air used from the 77.444 grains of fixed air, and determined that 23.753 grains of *charbon* had entered the fixed air. Here the first difficulty entered, because the measured loss in the weight of the *charbon* was only 11.55 grains. Putting aside that discrepancy for the moment, Lavoisier worked out the composition of fixed air from the weights of the two airs. The result was 69.561 parts of dephlogisticated air and 30.439 of *charbon* in 100 parts of fixed air, clearly in his view a deviation from the results of earlier experiments. Trying a different value for the density of fixed air, he reached only a still more aberrant result. Obviously puzzled, he wrote, "I do not see how to reconcile this experiment with the others except to suppose that I did not allow [the bell jar] to cool for a long enough time after the combustion to obtain the true spontaneous absorption." Seeing no other way to go, and perhaps influenced by the fact that Meusnier had suspected the same source of error in the original combustion experiment of May 24, 1783, Lavoisier adopted this possibility and, as he had so often done before, made a "correction" by simply guessing at a figure which seemed more reasonable than the actually measured one. "I shall suppose," he decided, "that the fixed air after the combustion had not been sufficiently cooled, and that in place of a reduction of around 4 cubic inches, it had undergone one of 10 cubic inches." This was a less sophisticated way to approximate such an error than Meusnier or Laplace might have tried, but Lavoisier did not have their mathematical expertise. If his intuitive estimate was valid, then the volume of fixed air formed should have been 103.851 cubic inches in place of the 110.635 cubic inches he had used in the first calculation. (Lavoisier apparently reached the new figure by the rather absurd operation of substracting from 100.635 cubic inches, not 6 cubic inches, but 10 minus the exact measured absorption, 3.219 cubic inches!) Applying the new volume, equivalent to 72.176 grains of fixed air, in place of the original volume which had yielded a figure of 77.444 grains, Lavoisier found a calculated consumption of 18.305 grains of *charbon*, and for the composition of fixed air 74.64 percent dephlogisticated air and 25.36 percent *charbon*.[9]

This result was not much better than the first one. The alteration had overcorrected the composition of fixed air; for it is evident that Lavoisier was aiming for a preselected target:

> In effect the experiment on the combustion of *charbon* made by M. Meusnier with water gives for the composition of fixed air
>
> | | |
> |---|---|
> | *Charbon* | 29 |
> | Dephlogisticated air | 71 |
> | | 100 |

Moreover, the new calculated value for the *charbon* consumed (18.305 grains in place of 23.573), while somewhat closer to the measured value of 11.55 grains, was still much too far off to leave any promise that they could by such methods be reconciled. This recalcitrant situation led Lavoisier to reflect that "perhaps there is in the same manner in all of the experiments on the combustion of *charbon* more *charbon* burned than I think, and the error arises from the fact that it has attracted moisture before being weighed." Readily adhering to his own suggestion, he wrote, "I am proceeding on the supposition that in all of my experiments there was more *charbon* burned than the weight of the *charbon* determined afterward indicates, and I thus calculate":

> | | |
> |---|---|
> | Dephlogisticated air employed | 53.871 [grains] |
> | Fixed air produced, 108 cubic inches at 0.695 | 75.060 |
> | Thus, *charbon* burned | 21.189, |
> | From which one derives for the composition of one hundred parts of fixed air | |
> | Dephlogisticated air | 71.77 |
> | *Charbon* | 28.23 |
> | Total | 100.00.[10] |

At last Lavoisier had arrived at a composition very near to that which he was so clearly seeking. How had he attained the desired result? The key number in the above calculation was the 108 cubic inches he chose for the volume of fixed air produced. This quantity was in between the original corrected value of 110.635 and the figure of 103.851 he had derived by making the additional "correction" for inadequate cooling. He gave no justification for the intermediate figure he now substituted for those; and since he was only guessing in the first place about the source and size of the "error" in the original figure, it is not unreasonable for us to infer that when he saw that his first alteration had changed the final result by too much, he had chosen a new, smaller correction deliberately intended to make the composition of fixed air come out as he thought it should.

From the compelling evidence of his laboratory notebooks we can see that every experiment Lavoisier had utilized to establish the quantitative composition of fixed air had been in one way or another problematic. He was nevertheless satisfied enough with them to put together a memoir on the subject. Going back to each of his earlier combustion experiments involving *matière chabonneuse,* he refurbished their results by adding calculations based on the assumption that water as well as fixed air formed, and utilizing his latest ratio of 1:7.623 for the proportion of inflammable air in the water. The oldest of the experiments using charcoal, that of May 24, 1783, which Meusnier had already worked over, now yielded, as might be expected from Meusnier's suspicions about it, deviant values: 76.5497 percent *principe oxygine,* and 23.4503 percent *substance charbonneuse.* By this time Lavoisier was able to give a new explanation for the inadequacy of that experiment, based on his conclusion that the *charbon* absorbed moisture after the combustion. The figure obtained for the amount of that substance consumed was not the true quantity.[11] The experiment of March 1784 which Meusnier had preferred to the preceding one now reinforced that preference by yielding from the new calculation the proportions of 71.602 *principe oxygine* to 28.399 *matière charbonneuse pure.* Lavoisier justified placing "more confidence [in this experiment] than in the others" of similar type not simply by the fact that it gave the desired outcome, but by the retrospective observation that "the *charbon* had remained for a shorter time under the bell jar before being weighed; it did not have time to absorb much moisture, so that the result must be much closer to the truth."[12] Applying the same recalculations to the combustion experiment carried out during March on wax, he obtained a slightly less satisfactory result—69.675 percent dephlogisticated air and 30.325 *substance charbonneuse*—even though the composition of the wax itself came out very close to the result of his most recent experiment on wax.[13] Before drafting his article, Lavoisier once more altered the calculations accomanying his final experiment on purified *charbon.* Changing the value of the fixed air formed from 108 to 109 cubic inches, he now came out with 71.112 parts of dephlogisticated air to 28.888 of *substance charbonneuse.*[14]

With his recalculations apparently completed, Lavoisier started the article itself, using the title "Combination of the oxygen principle with *substance charbonneuse.*" After writing a paragraph about the strong affinity of that substance for oxygen, and beginning a discussion of the efforts he and Laplace had made to "comprehend the circumstances of that combustion" by carrying it out in vital air,[15] he discarded this first attempt and started over under the title "Memoir on the formation of the acid called fixed air or chalky acid, and which I shall henceforth designate by the name of acid of *charbon.*" This change suggests that in the process of organizing his thoughts to write out his results he subtly shifted his sense of the main purpose of the investigation. It was a study not of the properties of a particular combustible body and the combustion process it underwent, but of the composition of the product of the combustion. With this orientation settled, he went on to write out the complete memoir in essentially one step. He made small changes as he went, or afterward in the margins, to clarify or qualify his views; but did not need to make further alterations in his data, his organization, or his basic arguments. After the fair copy had been made he added a few more small changes and submitted it for publication.[16] As we have seen, Lavoisier did not always reach the completed stage of a manuscript with such ease. Some of them he struggled with through several successive versions, altering the boundaries of the investigation, changing emphasis, developing or suppressing ideas along the way, before he reached a statement he regarded as definitive. In this case, however, he was building upon methods and conceptual structures with which he had been long familiar.

Except for the first two experiments performed in May on purified *charbon de Bourdenne*, which were obviously faulty, Lavoisier included in his memoir on the formation of fixed air all of the combustion experiments he had carried out on charcoal and on wax since the spring of 1783.[17] He even incorporated a summary version of Meusnier's intricate calculations connected with the gun barrel experiment, recasting them so that the composition of fixed air, actually determined along the way to the composition of water, appeared instead as the final outcome of the procedure.[18] He repeated a description of the experiment on the reduction of minium by charcoal, retrieved from his *Opuscules* of 1774, which he had just published in his memoir on water, now slightly altered to make its central outcome appear also to be the confirmation of the composition of fixed air.[19] He stitched these diverse investigations together in his memoir in such a way that the most recent ones, performed with the immediate objective of establishing the precise proportions of fixed air, as well as the earlier ones carried out originally with other objectives in mind, all now seemed to be parts of an integrated investigation supposedly aimed from the beginning at that goal.

Lavoisier began his account of the investigation with the "first experiment, performed with M. Laplace,"[20] and gave the impression that he was describing the rest of them in the sequence in which he and his collaborators had done them; but he was actually organizing them into a rational reconstruction that superseded their true chronological order. He described the two experiments utilizing ordinary charcoal, indicating that the result of the second of them "must come very near to the truth"; he then invoked the possibility that some doubts might be cast on it, by those who did not accept his theory of the composition of water, as the rationale for repeating the experiment with highly purified *charbon de Bourdenne*. He reported only his final version of the calculation performed on the results of the last of the three of these which he had carried out. Despite the difficulties which he had encountered with that experiment, he presented it as "that which appears to me to merit the greatest confidence." Continuing, he wrote that "after having examined the combination of pure *substance charbonneuse* with the oxygen principle, and having proven that it produces nothing but fixed air, . . . we were curious to see what would take place in the combustion of more highly composed bodies. We decided to begin by burning wax, because it is not volatile, it gives off little smoke in burning, and it exists in a solid and concrete form."[21] The logic of proceeding from the simpler to the more complex situation was flawless. As we have seen, however, Lavoisier had not actually followed such a progression. He had carried out the first of the two experiments on wax in March, just preceding the second experiment on charcoal, which was only subsequently interpreted as involving the formation of water; and had performed the second of the wax experiments midway in his latest experimental series, at a point at which his experiments with *charbon de Bourdenne* had bogged down.

Lavoisier made an equally smooth transition to the next section of his memoir: "After having thus assured ourselves that the combustion of different species of *charbon,* whether it contains inflammable air or not, and the combustion of wax [all] gave the same results, . . . it remained for us to examine what would take place if one obtained the oxygen principle from somewhere else than in the air; for example, in the water, and in metallic calces."[22] There followed the description of the experiment on the decomposition of water by charcoal in the gun barrel, then of the reduction of mercury and of lead calces by charcoal. The first of these, far from having followed all of the direct combustion experiments on charcoal in ordinary or dephlogisticated air, had come in the middle, as part of an investigation of the composition of water rather than of fixed air, and had probably provided the turning point in Lavoisier's interpretation of the combustion of charcoal. Of the experiments on metallic calces, at least one of them—that on lead ore—dated from 1774!

By now we can hardly avoid viewing Lavoisier's memoir on the formation of fixed air as a perfect illustration of Peter Medawar's trenchant dictum that scientific papers do "not merely conceal but actively misrepresent the reasoning that goes into the work they describe."[23] In Lavoisier's presentation a set of experiments carried out intermittently, replete with shifting objectives and interpretations, with groping efforts to wrest strong conclusions from weak data, with trails followed, left, and picked up again, had become transformed into a single-minded, strictly progressive, brilliantly conceived and executed investigation moving with undeviating stride toward the solution of one critical problem. To say all this is not to find fault with Lavoisier; for, as Medawar's pronouncement implies, Lavoisier was only doing what scientists do regularly. If a scientific paper obscures the historical course of the investigation on which it rests, that is because it is not meant to reveal that course in a literal sense. If historians are sometimes misled about the function of such a paper, scientists seldom are. They understand very well that their colleagues have taken twists and turns on the way to reach the resolutions they are reporting, and that these vicissitudes are most often not relevant to the end results. They expect a scientific paper to convey the most persuasive and economical case for its conclusions that its author can devise, even at the expense of its veracity as a historical account of the work. That Lavoisier was able to do just this with exceptional skill was as important to his success as was his experimental and intellectual skill in reaching his conclusions in the first place.

Even if concealing the actual historical record of the investigation only conforms to the normal functional role of a scientific paper, nevertheless Lavoisier's concealment of the full extent to which he had had to manipulate his data in order to make them fit his purpose might seem to be a real shortcoming in his memoir. He did acknowledge that the disagreement between the calculated and measured consumptions of *charbon*, leading to the inference that the absorption of moisture had prevented a true measurement of the quantity, had "obliged" them to "deduce the weight of the *charbon* burned" from the weight of fixed air formed; but he did not mention the rough adjustments to some measurements of the fixed air formed, made because of the suspicion that inadequate cooling had distorted the immediate results. He did admit in general that uncertainties over such factors as impurities in the *charbon* made it necessary to rely on multiple experiments; but he said nothing about the revisions and guesses he had had to make in reducing the data of the crucial third experiment with *charbon de Bourdenne*, in order to get out of it the result he needed.[24]

Only in once instance, that of the gun barrel experiment, which was less central to his case for the composition of fixed air, did Lavoisier openly discuss the fact that he had arranged the results in such a manner as to simulate an exact balance between the substances utilized and those produced. This discussion, though directed at one specific situation, reveals, I believe, much about his attitude toward the quantitative methods he practiced in general, and especially toward his notorious habit of reporting his results to far more decimal places than could possibly be meaningful. Following a table of the weights of the fixed air and inflammable air produced in the experiment, plus the air contained in the vessels, he noted that the total of 2 ounces, 6 gros, 71.320 grains was exactly that of the materials employed—"a striking confirmation of the exactness of the theory." He had, in fact, given precisely the same total for the *charbon* and water consumed, after making deductions for the cinder and for a portion of oxygen which "remained attached to the gun barrel." One might ask, he continued, "how it is possible that one would have arrived in this manner at a result which agrees to nearly a thousandth of a grain, and might make of this very exactness an argument for believing that the experiment has been stretched to fit the calculations." Lavoisier explained that all of the quantities given "are very exactly those which were written down directly in the [laboratory] notebook at the time of the experiment." When these quantities were added up, there was a deficit of 1 gros 29.380 grains. After considering the possible sources of the deficit, he and Meusnier had attributed it to oxygen which had probably penetrated through the seam of the copper lining of the gun barrel and combined with the iron composing the barrel itself. There were probably also other small sources of error. The precise balance shown was therefore an artifact. "Far from regarding the above results as rigorously exact, therefore, I believe them, on the contrary, susceptible of some modifications; but if one supposes several grains, or even gros, of difference, the accord between theory and experiment would be no less striking."[25]

The view Lavoisier expressed here was, I believe, characteristic of his general attitude toward the quantitative measurements in his investigations. We have observed him repeatedly making intuitive estimates of the nature and magnitude of an error just as he did here; and have repeatedly found him writing out the totals of several measurements to the number of places corresponding to the most accurate measurement included, rather than to the least accurate. In following such practices he was not beguiling himself into believing that his results were accurate to the degree that these long numbers might seem to signify. In the present memoir, although he left the calculated results, as well as the immediate measurements, for each individual experiment in the form of such long numerals, in the end he approached very cautiously the question of how closely he had actually established the composition of fixed air. At first he hesitated to draw any firm conclusion. "These multiple experiments seem to leave no doubt about the nature of *acide charbonneux*," he wrote, "and they leave only very little, even, concerning the proportions in which the two principles enter into its composition." With that he simply ended the memoir. On second thought, he became more confident, crossed out the last half of the sentence, and wrote instead that fixed air is an aeriform acid "composed of around twenty-eight parts of *matière charbonneuse* and seventy-two of the oxygen principle."[26] This was an eminently realistic evaluation of the overall result he had achieved by combining the outcomes of his varied experimental efforts.

We can only surmise why Lavoisier kept publishing individual measurements which, to our eyes, present a misleading claim to extreme accuracy, even though he understood their limitations. The most plausible explanation is that, lacking formal statistical methods for determining the probable errors in his experimental results, and lacking the conception of significant figures which has become second nature to a later age, he would have been uncertain about how many places he could eliminate from his numbers without losing information; that he therefore habitually played it safe by retaining the measured values exactly as he had recorded them; and that he would not have expected eighteenth-century readers to interpret the significance of these figures in the way that twentieth-century readers do.

While these considerations may be able to account for the manner in which Lavoisier *presented* his data, they may not appear to excuse the way he altered his calculations and assumptions until he had made as many of the experiments as possible yield results as close as he could manage to the composition he finally accepted. Was this not an egregious example of "fudging the data"? It was certainly manipulation. In an era, however, in which we are increasingly prone to suspect that scientists sometimes "cheat," we should guard against the temptation to catch one of the old masters at it too. We commonly accept as inevitable that every phase in the gathering, selection, and use of data is "theory laden," and that if it were not so experimentation would be aimless. In this particular case there was no formal theory inducing Lavoisier to favor the outcome of seventy-two parts oxygen to twenty-eight of *charbon*. What he appeared to be seeking was the convergence of the results of the different experiments around some common figure. Probably sensing intuitively the range within which the point of convergence would fall, he clearly made assumptions which aided him in getting his results to conform as well as possible to that range. There are times when such treatment amounts to cheating. There are other times when it amounts to mastering the data instead of allowing the data to master the scientist. In the hands of a person with the insight of Lavoisier, such means cannot lightly be characterized as shady practices—especially in view of the fact that for the problem at hand he came out with a value which has held up extraordinarily well.[27]

A further potential criticism is that Lavoisier did not continue the investigation long enough, or he would have obtained experimental results beyond reproach and not been forced to resort to expedient maneuvers with his data. I have already suggested that the costs of carrying on such experiments may well have restricted him, as did the extremely limited time his many other responsibilities left him for scientific research.[28] Moreover, we are easily swayed by the modernity in much of Lavoisier's experimental approach to overlook that he operated under quite different conditions from his nineteenth- or twentieth-century counterparts. The experimental operations described in the memoir on fixed air appear deceptively simple. We can easily forget how tedious they were to prepare, when pieces of apparatus which composed a system required to be airtight had to be joined together by luting; when the source of heat was a charcoal furnace whose management demanded a skill and patience hardly credible to those who routinely use Bunsen burners; when each air and other reagent had to be produced by methods which involved further rounds of the same tedious kinds of preparation. The modern expectation that, after carrying out many preliminary experiments to establish the optimal conditions for measuring a given phenomenon, one then performs "definitive" experiments for publication is a standard Lavoisier could not always afford to maintain, even though, as we shall see, he recognized the principle and on certain critical occasions he did his utmost to live up to it. If he made do in this and other situations with relatively few experiments imperfectly carried out, he had probably done the best he could under the circumstances.

In publishing his conclusions regarding the composition of fixed air Lavoisier again introduced a new name for the object of his investigation. His title, "Memoir on the formation of the acid called fixed air or chalky acid, and which I shall henceforth designate by the name of acid of *charbon*," announced his intention loudly. The change in name was part of his continuing effort to clarify the distinction between a persisting chemical entity and the substances whose composition it entered; between "that which one is accustomed in common usage to designate as a compound of *substances charbonneuses*, aqueous inflammable air, a small portion of earth, and a little fixed alkali," for which he would retain the word *charbon*, and the characteristic substance in *charbon* freed of the other adhering materials. The purified substance he now proposed to call *substance charbonneuse*. He was not entirely consistent in his new nomenclature. Acid of *charbon* should have been named acid of the *substance charbonneuse* to conform with his other choices. In addition, as in other similar situations, he had difficulty remembering to use his own new names. In the first draft of his memoir he not only fell into using the simpler term *charbon* for what he had designated as *substance charbonneuse*, but reverted quickly to the old familiar "fixed air," or to the term "chalky acid" that he and Bucquet had tried to introduce several years before. He corrected many of the lapses on the first draft, and caught a few more on the fair copy, but even in the final published version some of the older terms slipped through.[29] Despite the trouble he experienced trying to break his entrenched linguistic habits, however, he seemed by now finally to have resolved the conceptual ambiguity that had persisted for nearly a decade. The suggestion he had so recently made in his memoir on water, that *substance charbonneuse* (there called *matière charbonneuse*) may be formed by the inflammable principle, had vanished without trace or explanation. Although he did not explicitly define *substance charbonneuse* as an unchangeable entity, he described acid of *charbon* as a combination of the oxygen principle and *substance charbonneuse* "in the same way" that vitriolic and phosphoric acid are combinations of that same principle with sulfur and with phosphorus.[30] He thus implied that *substance charbonneuse* has the same status as sulfur and phosphorus.

This further evolution of Lavoisier's conception of the nature of these three related substances was, in a sense, merely the continuation of a trend he had been pursuing for a long time. The stimulus toward this culminating phase perhaps came from the experience of working with types of *charbon* which he regarded as highly purified; or the definiteness of the quantitative composition of fixed air determined in several ways may have enhanced his sense that its constituents were both fundamental, stable entities. The formerly rather abstract "base of fixed air" had become for him as concrete as the fixed air which contained it. He could therefore express the nature of the air in a more fundamental way by abandoning the familiar label based on its very general physical character in favor of one based on its composition. The name acid of *charbon* accorded both with his general theory of acids and with the practice of distinguishing a given acid from other acids by identifying the specific "base" from which it is derived.[31]

We have noted that in the course of Lavoisier's investigations during the first half of 1784 one problem after another emerged from the status of a subordinate part of another principal problem to become an independent research goal, and that sometimes what had been at a certain point the main problem took on in turn the role of a supporting analytical tool. Thus the composition of fixed air had to be established as a means to determine the composition of water in certain experiments. Later the composition of water entered into the calculations necessary to determine the exact composition of fixed air. Fermentation too was developing into an area of investigation for its own sake after serving as a means to study the various ways water is decomposed. Still embedded in the work Lavoisier had completed on these various problems by the summer of 1784 was another potentially autonomous experimental problem. By then he had in the course of his combustion experiments determined the proportions of the inflammable principle and of *substance charbonneuse*, not only in charcoal, but also in wax and in spirit of wine. Here were the foundations for a systematic exploration of the composition of organic substances; but despite his prior interest in that topic, these analyses had apparently not yet coalesced for him into an explicit research program.

9

Water and Respiration

Throughout 1784 Lavoisier was preparing to conduct a new set of experiments which would establish as accurately as possible the composition of water, and which would disarm opposition to his theory of its nature. He intended to repeat, with added precautions based on his previous experience, the method of decomposition in an iron gun barrel; and he planned a large-scale synthesis of water, for which he was having two new calibrated gasometers built in order to measure precisely the quantities of vital air and inflammable air utilized. By the end of December he had received the new equipment, and he and Meusnier, who continued to collaborate with him on the project, were beginning elaborate preparations for what Lavoisier had planned so carefully to be a conclusive demonstration. With over thirty people present, including commissioners appointed by the Academy at Lavoisier's request to oversee the experiments, and all of the chemists of the Academy, Lavoisier and Meusnier carried out simultaneously a decomposition and a synthesis experiment on February 27 and 28, 1785.[1] The decomposition operation incurred a loss of 2 gros 3 grains of material, which could be ascribed either to escaping inflammable air or water vapor, so that the result was indecisive. They could infer from it only that "in order to form 100 pounds of water no less than 81, or more than 87, pounds" of vital air is required. The synthesis experiment, performed with extraordinary care to eliminate all sources of error they could detect, yielded a far closer balance between matter consumed and formed. After making various corrections Meusnier calculated that a total of 5 ounces, 4 gros, 20½ grains of inflammable and vital air had produced 5 ounces, 4 gros, 51 grains of water. The discrepancy was a mere 30½ grains. "It follows from the ratio between the vital air and the inflammable air used," according to the only direct report of this experiment to be published, "that water contains, per 100 pounds, 15 pounds of inflammable air and 85 pounds of vital air."[2] This result Lavoisier regarded as definitive. Thereafter he settled on the proportions of 85 to 15, writing in his *Traité élémentaire de chimie* in 1789 that "we have reason to believe that it is exact to nearly one part in two hundred."[3] He was wrong, of course; but he and Meusnier had done everything that the skilled chemical analyst and the sophisticated mathematician together had it in their power to do, to achieve the most reliable result then attainable.

These experiments on water are justly regarded as Lavoisier's climactic investigative achievement in the realm of general chemistry. They formed, however, only one facet of his multiple activities during the period. Throughout his career he had been deeply concerned to apply his scientific knowledge to matters affecting the public welfare. As we saw in Chapter 4, no sooner had he clarified his theory of respiration in the spring of 1777 than he drew on it to dramatize the need for proper ventilation in public buildings. This was more than a gesture on the occasion of the Emperor Joseph II's visit to the Academy, for Lavoisier persistently pressed for attention to this problem. When he became a member of a commission appointed in 1780 to devise plans for new prisons, he stressed in its report that it was urgent to provide more fresh air in the densely packed existing prisons, and to design the new ones so as to assure an adequate circulation.[4]

It may have been in part because of his interest in public health that Lavoisier was elected in 1782 to the Royal Society of Medicine. Although he did not afterward participate in its affairs as actively as he did in those of the Academy of Sciences, he did from time to time prepare reports to the society on topics for which he could bring his scientific expertise to bear on medical questions.[5] His new association with the medical world undoubtedly further stimulated his interest in applying his theory of respiration to the problem of the salubrity of the air in crowded places. Early in 1785 he prepared a paper on that subject to present at a meeting of the Society of Medicine. He entitled it originally "Memoir on the alterations which take place in the air in the ordinary circumstances of society."[6]

In keeping with the occasion Lavoisier offered a broad review of his concept of the atmosphere and his theory of respiration, as starting points for examining the practical questions on which he wished to focus attention. Initially he must have conceived of his paper as an updated version of the one he had delivered at the Academy in 1777 in the presence of the emperor; for he began by copying with little change the two introductory paragraphs in that paper setting forth the view that airs constitute one of the three general states of matter.[7] From then on, however, his new memoir diverged from the earlier one, as he first developed these physical concepts more fully, and then added more recent information concerning the quantitative composition of the atmosphere.

Having summarized the "knowledge that physics and chemistry can provide for medicine on the constituents of the air which we respire," Lavoisier turned to the central questions on which he wished to fix the attention of his medical audience: "What are the alterations that this air undergoes during different conditions of society? What is their influence on the respiratory organs? What disorders in the animal economy can result from these alterations, and what methods are there for preventing or remedying them?" Before addressing himself directly to these practical problems, however, he had to describe the effects of respiration itself on the air. Beginning with the most common knowledge, he reminded his listeners that an animal can respire for only a limited time in a given quantity of air. On the basis of the comparative sizes of humans and the animals he had used in his experiments, he estimated that a human can survive for only about an hour in four cubic feet of air. Next he described the changes in the chemical composition of a given volume of the atmosphere produced by an animal respiring for as long as possible in it. This discussion will shortly become our central concern in the present chapter, but for now we shall pass on to the next stage of his argument. From the relatively small change he found in the proportion of vital air to mophette in air "exhausted" by respiration, compared with that in normal air, he concluded that this proportion can vary only within narrow limits if the air is to remain respirable. The obvious consequence was that when people gathered in numbers sufficient to alter the air within an enclosed area, serious problems could arise. Before moving on to that practical aspect of his talk, however, Lavoisier digressed to ask what might be the effect of a greater than normal proportion of vital air in the atmosphere. Choosing the extreme case, he reported publicly for the first time the experiments he and Bucquet had carried out together seven years earlier on guinea pigs placed in pure vital air. These animals, he stressed, had died long before the air had been "completely vitiated"—that is, when it still consisted mostly of vital air—and the autopsies showed signs of fever and inflammation. The animals had therefore succumbed not to a lack of respirable air, but because of the toxic effect of pure vital air.[8]

After establishing to his satisfaction that "salubrious air" must not differ greatly from the 27 parts of vital air in 100 parts of ordinary air that he then took to be the composition of the atmosphere, he finally focused on the central point of his lecture: in public places such as theaters and hospitals, "where a great number of people assemble, and especially if the air circulates slowly there," it was important to determine how far the air becomes altered. He had himself made some preliminary measurements for that purpose. In the lowest dormitory of a general hospital, where the most people were confined in the least space, he had taken two samples of air at the point which he regarded as "the most unhealthy." The air drawn at the bottom of this room differed only slightly from normal air, but that taken from near the ceiling "had suffered a much more considerable alteration." He found for the composition of 100 parts of this air 18½ parts of vital air, 2½ of fixed air, and 79 of mophette, compared with 27 parts of vital air, 1 of fixed air, and 72 of mophette in open air on the same day. Not satisfied with a single case, he had then tried the same test on the air in a crowded theater. He chose the palace of the Tuileries, where the

Comédie Française was then playing to a full house. Carrying a pneumatic flask filled with water up into the balcony, he collected one sample of air from a vacant box. To collect his lower sample he descended into the orchestra pit with another pneumatic jar. He was so afraid that he would attract attention and disrupt the performance, however, that he slipped in hurriedly a few minutes before it ended, hastily collected the air, and departed. When he afterward examined this air and found "no sensible difference from outdoor air," he decided that the reason was that he had obtained it too close to the entrance. The air from the box, however, was substantially altered, the proportion of vital air being diminished by a fourth of its normal amount. As he incorporated these tests into the first draft of his manuscript, he admitted, quite realistically, that "these experiments were not carried out with as much care as I would have wished." Such measurements, he asserted, ought to be repeated many times. The task was too large for one individual to carry out on his own, and he advocated that the government undertake the task, in order to obtain "precious knowledge" for the future construction of buildings in which large numbers of people will assemble.[9]

Despite the inadequacies he acknowledged in these efforts to test the salubrity of the air in public buildings, Lavoisier did not defer drawing broad conclusions from them. The difference between the composition of the air at the bottom and the top of the two enclosures he had examined he interpreted in keeping with his earlier conception that the atmosphere tends to separate into layers according to the densities of its constituent airs. Thus the lighter mophette would be expected to collect at the top, where the tests in fact seemed to show that its concentration was the greatest. If the ventilation is adequate, a circulation will ensue, the mophette escaping at the top and being replaced by fresh air that enters from below. If the design of the building does not permit such a circulation, however, then a crowd of people in it will soon vitiate the air. Extrapolating his earlier estimate that one person can survive for only an hour in four cubic feet of vital air, he calculated that in a theater measuring thirty by twenty-five feet, and thirty feet high, an audience of a thousand people would render the air completely mephitic within five to six hours, if the air were not renewed by circulation.[10]

Lavoisier did not restrict his concern to the graver consequences of unventilated buildings for public health, but took on also the subtler penalties that such situations exacted. To the above discussion he added in the margin of his first draft that his calculations explain why, when a hall is crowded, "the attention of the audience cannot be sustained beyond two or three hours." By the end of that time their physical suffering so overpowers their mental state that the unfortunate lecturer who may be scheduled to address them last will find that "the interest of his subject is not communicated to the audience; he does not attain their goodwill, or even their attention, and for his effort he does not receive the tribute of applause and recognition on which he might have counted under more favorable circumstances."[11] Perhaps it has not been duly appreciated that in the midst of his many preoccupations Lavoisier found room to try to alleviate the risks of public speaking. He wrote on the subject with such feeling, in fact, that he must himself have experienced the humiliation of putting an audience to sleep.

Lavoisier had a fair copy of his manuscript prepared, and presented it to a public session of the Royal Society of Medicine on February 15, 1785.[12] In his first draft he had planned to announce that the practical questions he had posed concerning the alterations of the air and their effects formed "the objective of a work which I have undertaken, and of which I shall attempt today only to give a very succinct idea." Persuading himself that he was in the first stage of an extended venture, he later strengthened the second half of this sentence to read ". . . of which I shall report successively to the society in a number of memoirs." As with similar assertions about research in progress, Lavoisier did not, in fact, follow up his promise; nor did he succeed in getting the government to carry out the multiple measurements of the quality of the air in public places that he deemed essential. These failures to follow through probably did not matter as much as he thought they would, however, for the combination of his theory of respiration and the few rough tests he had carried out was enough to provide a strong general argument for well-ventilated buildings.

II

We may now return to that section of the original draft of this memoir in which Lavoisier described the quantitative effect of respiration on the air and the inference which could be drawn therefrom:

> Air which has thus been respired by humans or by animals for as long as possible is found to be diminished by about one-sixtieth of its volume. That is to say, the 1,728 cubic inches which comprise one cubic foot are reduced to about 1,700. Submitted afterward to a chemical analysis, this air is found to be composed as follows:

Vital air	173 cubic inches
Fixed air	300
Atmospheric mophette	1,227
	1,700

By weight this gives:

Vital air		1 gros	9.858 grains
Fixed air		2	64.500
Atmospheric mophette		7	64.065
Total	1 ounce	3	66.423

This result can provide matter for a great number of very important reflections. First of all, one sees that the atmospheric air exhausted by respiration, although diminishing in volume by one-sixtieth, acquires an augmentation in absolute weight of 49.529 grains per cubic foot. [The manner in which Lavoisier reached this last figure will be discussed below.] The air thus extracts a ponderable substance from the lungs of animals, and this substance combined with the vital air converts it to fixed air. As for the atmospheric mophette, it is in no way altered, and it comes back out of the lungs in the same weight and the same volume that it had entered them.

I should point out that all of the results have been measured on the respired air after it had been cooled and had deposited the excess of moisture with which it was charged on leaving the lungs.[13]

Deciding that the statement "and this substance combined with the vital air converts it into fixed air" required more explanation, Lavoisier substituted for it, in the margin of the manuscript:

> but since one finds afterward in the air only one-third of the vital air originally contained in it, and one finds a corresponding quantity of fixed air in its place, it results from this that the ponderable substance which has been extracted from the lungs by the act of respiration has been added to the vital air and has transformed it into fixed air.[14]

This discussion has the appearance of a report on a recent set of experiments, and of conclusions drawn rather directly from them. In fact, however, Lavoisier reconstructed the "result" from old data obtained within a different problem setting. To arrive at the data exhibited in the above tables he combined measurements he had obtained in the first experiment on a bird in 1776, in which he had taken into account the "two effects" of respiration and which he had reported in his original memoir on respiration in 1777,[15] with figures for the composition of normal air presumably obtained in later analyses. In the introductory section of the manuscript presently under discussion he gave as the composition of normal air by volume,

Vital air	484 cubic inches
Mophette	1,227
Fixed air	17
Total	1,728 cubic inches, or one cubic foot[16]

The composition of air "respired as long as possible," as shown in the passage quoted above, was based on this composition of normal air, together with the simple observations from the old respiration experiment that the volume of air in the jar at the end of the experiment was "one-sixtieth" less than at the beginning, and that caustic alkali further reduced this volume by "one-sixth." In 1776 he had derived no further quantities from these two figures; at that time he was attempting only to establish qualitatively that respiration consumes vital air and produces fixed air. Now he was able to retrieve from those old quantitative notations, together with more recent values he had come to accept for the composition of the atmosphere, a calculated composition for the residual air of the original experiment. The 1,700 cubic inches representing the volume of the air after the bird had died in it he obtained by subtracting one-sixtieth from a cubic foot (1,728 − [1,728/60] = 1,699.2). One-sixth of the latter value yielded 283 cubic inches of fixed air formed. Adding this to the 17 cubic inches of fixed air that he included in the composition of normal air gave the 300 cubic inches of fixed air contained in the cubic foot of vitiated air. The quantity of mophette in this air he fixed by assuming, as he argued in the text, that the same quantity of mophette which enters the lungs emerges again from them. Finally, his figure of 173 cubic inches of vital air remaining was simply the difference between the total of 1,700 cubic inches and the sum of the other two constituents. The "chemical analysis" to which Lavoisier claimed to have submitted this respired air was thus far less direct than his discussion would, on the surface, suggest.

To convert these volumes to weights, Lavoisier used the density values of 0.47317 grains per cubic inch of vital air, 0.69500 grains per cubic inch of fixed air, and 0.46811 grains per cubic inch of mophette. The first two of these were the same values he had used in the final calculations for his memoir on fixed air the previous year. From density measurements of normal air made by de Luc, Lavoisier adopted for the weight of a cubic foot of normal air the figure of 1 ounce, 3 gros, 16.894 grains.[17] It was by subtracting that quantity from the 1 ounce, 3 gros, 66.423 grains that he calculated for the weight of 1,700 cubic inches of the residual air that he arrived at 49.529 grains of weight gained per cubic foot of air during the respiration. When we consider the multiple assumptions and approximations involved in these calculations, we may reasonably conclude that Lavoisier found this gain in weight because he was looking for it.

Comparing Lavoisier's discussion of respiration in the present passage with his previous treatments of the subject, we can see that he was here restating the bare essentials of the same theory he had formulated several times before, but supporting it in a new way. For the first time he was attempting to derive his theory of respiration, as he had previously derived his theories of the combustion of phosphorus, sulfur, and *matière charbonneuse*, as well as of the calcination of metals, strictly from balance sheet considerations. His calculation resembled in form the effort he had made in 1783 to establish the weight relations pertaining to his single flawed combustion experiment on charcoal, at a time when he regarded that also as a simple conversion of vital air to fixed air.[18] In the memoir on heat he had not attempted such a calculation for respiration, but had interpreted the respiration process, as he had done since his memoir on combustion of 1777, by analogy to the experiments with charcoal. What he appears to have been doing here, whether consciously or not, was to free his theory of respiration from dependence on that analogy, by deducing it solely from the quantitative results of a respiration experiment. He refrained even from identifying the "ponderable substance" he inferred to have been extracted from the lungs as a *matière charbonneuse*. However uncertain the quantitative data on which he depended may have been, the form of argument he adopted was clearly more rigorous than those on which he had previously based his theory.

Historians can apply different standards of judgment to Lavoisier's new proof for his theory of respiration. Each has its own validity, but depending on which we choose we shall arrive at very different evaluations. If we demand quantitative accuracy by presentist standards, then we must dismiss the conclusions on the grounds that the composition of the atmosphere on which he based his calculations—twenty-seven parts of vital air per hundred—was far from the mark. We may, on the other hand, relax our criteria so as to expect him only to have utilized the best evidence attainable at the time. As we have seen, he had made many efforts to determine this proportion accurately, ever since he began to view the atmosphere as composite. He had revised his estimate repeatedly as new methods came into play. During 1783 he had gone over the whole question again, examining carefully the different techniques that had been proposed for utilizing Priestley's nitrous air test as a measure of "the quantity of vital air contained in a given quantity" of any sample of air. After ascertaining by trial and error the proportions of nitrous air and vital air required to saturate each other, he devised a formula for determining the quantity of vital air from the contraction obtained when he added nitrous air in excess of this saturation amount. In three trials he obtained the closely concordant values of 25.3, 25.0, and 25.2 percent of vital air in ordinary atmospheric air. In spite of this agreement, he accepted as valid the value of twenty-seven parts per hundred that he had found from the combustion of pyrophor in 1777, "in Paris," because he thought it likely that the proportions varied with the season and location.[19] Perhaps it was because he was utilizing the composition of air in connection with a respiration experiment also performed in Paris in 1777 that he based the present calculations on the proportion of twenty-seven parts of vital air rather than on the twenty-five parts that his more recent nitrous air tests indicated. Lavoisier expected that the precision of measurements of the composition of the air would be improved in the future, especially since he knew that Henry Cavendish was working to perfect the eudiometric methods in use. We can, in summary, judge that in the present situation Lavoisier based his calculations on a reasonable assessment of the best available information on the composition of ordinary air.

Even if we apply an evaluation according to contemporary rather than presentist standards, however, we may wonder why Lavoisier relied on one of his earliest respiration experiments, in which he had recorded the volume changes rather casually, instead of drawing upon the later experiments of the spring of 1783, in which he had been more attentive to the quantities of vital air converted to fixed air and had improved his techniques for measuring them. The most likely reason was that none of the more recent experiments was as suitable for the particular objective of this memoir. He was concentrating his attention on the alterations that respiration produced in normal air. All the respiration experiments he and Laplace had carried out in ordinary air in 1783 utilized their new open system, which permitted them to measure the fixed air formed with greater accuracy, but provided no basis for inferring the quantity of vital air consumed, now that he could no longer assume equal volumes of the one and the other. All the experiments in closed systems which could provide the basis for such an inference they had carried out in pure vital air, a condition less relevant to Lavoisier's present purpose. We might ask why Lavoisier did not carry out a new experiment designed specifically for the use for which he needed the results. Aside from the fact that he habitually mined as much information from experiments previously performed as his ingenuity allowed him to do, he was probably not in a position to mount another experimental effort during the period he wrote this manuscript, because his resources were already extended by the preparations under way to carry out the large-scale experiments on the composition of water. In short, Lavoisier did not exert himself to attain the best possible data for his calculations, because he was not engaged in a new research venture concerning respiration itself. It was probably only in the course of composing a background discussion for his measurements of the salubrity of the air in public places that he perceived the possibility of using experimental information he had readily at hand in order to provide a new justification for his theory of respiration.

Even though limited to new calculations based on old data, Lavoisier's reformulation of the essential theory was impressive. If one trusted the data and his use of them, then the result was the firmest argument for the theory that he had yet devised; and the data as he presented them contained implicitly a strong incentive to trust the outcome. Although he did not report it, the composition of fixed air can readily be derived from his result, and he would most likely have tried out the calculation. The figure he would have reached—about seventy-four parts of vital air to twenty-six parts of the "ponderable substance"—would fall well within the range of the results he had obtained in his laborious efforts to establish those proportions through the experiments on charcoal and wax. To realize that from his old experiment on respiration he could derive a result consistent with those results must have been highly satisfying. As Karl Popper emphasized in his classic *The Logic of Scientific Discovery*, consistency "can be regarded as the first of the requirements to be satisfied by *every* theoretical system, be it empirical or non-empirical."[20] Lavoisier's new treatment of his theory of respiration could survive that fundamental test.

Lavoisier's restatement of his theory of respiration can be viewed as part of an advanced stage in what philosophers of science call "the context of justification." With it he could replace the reasoning which had originally led him to the discovery, or the justifications he had previously given for the theory, by a stronger argument for the conclusion he had long since reached. Some philosophers of science are now questioning, however, whether the context of justification can be meaningfully separated from the context of discovery.[21] Their position seems borne out by the situation under discussion, for if Lavoisier's new treatment was at first intended as a process of justification, it appears to have become afterward the occasion for a further layer of discovery.

III

The fair copy made from Lavoisier's first draft of the memoir on alterations of the air retained intact those paragraphs deriving his theory of respiration from weight considerations. He may have presented it in that form at the Society of Medicine. At some point, however, he crossed out the first paragraph and the weight tables following it, and wrote in their place, in the margins of the manuscript, a new statement incorporating a major revision in his theory:

> If one considers the air which has thus been respired by an animal for as long as possible in terms of its quantity, one finds it sensibly diminished in volume. That diminution, as I propose to show elsewhere, is caused by the fact that there emanates from the lungs of animals a small portion of inflammable air which, combining with the vital air, forms water. This theory of the for-

mation of water is supported by experiments that I have already presented to the Academy of Sciences and that will be published shortly. From them it results that in almost every combustion there is a formation of water, and the agreement which is here again encountered between the effects of combustion and those of respiration proves more and more that these operations have a great analogy.

However that may be, if one takes a cubic foot of air exhausted by the respiration of an animal and submits it to chemical analysis, one finds it composed approximately as follows. I say approximately, because great variations are found in the quantity of fixed air.

This air contains,

Of vital air	173
Fixed air	200
Atmospheric mophette	1,355
	1,728

This gives, by weight

Vital air		1 gros	14½ grains
Fixed air		1	66
Atmospheric mophette	1 ounce	0 gros	26 grains
	1	3	34½[22]

Lavoisier retained the paragraph in his original text beginning with the sentence "This result can provide matter for a great number of very important reflections," but heavily modified the remainder of it. It now read,

> One sees in the first place that atmospheric air acquires from the effect of respiration an augmentation of its absolute weight, not counting that which is due to the water which has formed and which is deposited. The air thus extracts from the lungs a ponderable substance, which combines with a portion of the vital air to form fixed air. This matter is *substance charbonneuse*. One of the principal functions of respiration therefore is to extract a portion of the *matière charbonneuse* continuously from the animal economy by way of the lungs.[23]

It can hardly escape our notice that these paragraphs embody the first recorded trace of a very important advance in Lavoisier's theory of respiration. Like certain crucial earlier developments, this step appeared in the form of a marginal revision added to the early draft of a memoir, suggesting once more an intimate connection between the formulation of prior conclusions on paper and the emergence of further insights. The passages do not directly state how the new view occurred to him; but they do provide enough clues to reconstruct the general direction of thought that may have led him toward it. Since it is most likely that Lavoisier worked on his manuscript during the same period that he was making preparations for the large-scale experiments on the composition of water, and in their aftermath, he would have been more than normally predisposed to perceive in other situations the possibility that processes involving the formation of water were also occurring. There is no further evidence to suggest, however, that this concurrent activity provided any more than a background conditioning effect. In the absence of clear channels between the statement of the revised respiration theory and some other event, we can only look to the previous version of the paragraphs themselves as the most proximate source for the ensuing insight.

Before proceeding, we must dispose of one superficially probable interpretation. These passages do not confirm the view generally accepted by historians, that Lavoisier was forced to the revised theory by a discrepancy between the quantity of vital air consumed in a respiration experiment and the quantity accounted for in the fixed air formed.[24] As we have seen, the calculation he had just made had worked out quite well. Moreover, because he had derived the quantity of vital air in the residual air from the difference between the fixed air present in it and the total remaining volume, he did not have an independent measure of the vital air consumed through which he might have been able to detect such an anomaly. The opening paragraph of the revised discussion, in which he ascribed the diminution in the volume of the respired air to the formation of water, may seem to imply otherwise; but a diminution in volume could not have served to establish a deficit, because Lavoisier well knew that material balances are based on weights, not volumes. In the first version he had already pointed out that the volume decreased, but stressed that the weight increased in the same process. In the "Memoir on heat" he had reported the especially large decreases in volume that occurred during the respiration experiments of 1783 without seeking a theoretical interpretation.[25] The decrease in volume attending the respiration during the experiment which had served as the basis for his present discussion most likely attained the significance that Lavoisier attributed to it in the second version only as a consequence of his realization, for other reasons, that water may form in respiration.

Further evidence against the possibility that the quantitative results of a respiration experiment forced Lavoisier to modify his theory can be seen in the revision of his calculation of the composition of the residual air that he included in his statement of the revised theory. It is, in fact, difficult to make sense of the change he made, for he appeared to base the new calculation on an assumption that the volume after the respiration was the same as the starting volume (1,728 cubic inches), even though in his text he retained the observation that the volume was diminished. Whatever he might have had in mind, it is nevertheless evident that the formation of water did not enter into the calculation.

If we then ask what in the first draft might have pointed Lavoisier toward the new insight, we cannot give a certain answer; but there are two features of the original treatment, either one of which, or both together, would have been suggestive. First, the quantitative calculations that he added to the older respiration results resembled closely the calculations he had carried out during 1783 and 1784 on the results of his combustion experiments on charcoal. We have seen that with those charcoal experiments he had also attempted first to interpret the measured weight and volume changes in terms of the conversion of vital air to fixed air alone, but had been driven to conclude that water also formed from inflammable air contained in the charcoal. Afterward he had come to expect water to form, not only in these combustions, but also in those of substances such as wax and oils. Scientists commonly approach a given problem by seeing it as somehow *like* another problem they have solved. As Lavoisier now modeled his calculations for interpreting respiration on a type of calculation he had formerly applied to a combustion process he had come to regard as essentially identical to respiration, it would seem almost inevitable that sooner or later it would occur to him that the same added complication he had encountered there might pertain also here. The second suggestive feature of his original discussion was that he put into it the very observation that would most readily facilitate an inference that water really does form in respiration. That is, he commented that the air leaving the lungs was charged with an excess of moisture, which deposited when the air cooled. At the time he inserted this remark he apparently had in mind only to alert the reader that he had avoided a complication that might otherwise have interfered with his volume measurements; but the observation provided a natural conceptual bridge to the idea that this moisture is a product of the act of respiration itself. If these two aspects of Lavoisier's discussion did open for him a mental pathway to the new insight, we cannot ascertain whether he reasoned in a temporal order paralleling this reconstruction, or in the inverse order, or if the whole picture fell into place for him at once. Whatever the ultimate fine structure of his creative mental act might have been, the driving power behind it seems not to have been a specific quantitative deficit he had to resolve, but the suggestive power of the analogy between respiration and the combustion of charcoal.

The foregoing interpretation accords with the character of Lavoisier's revised statement itself. The theory of the formation of water in respiration, he wrote explicitly, is "supported by experiments I have already presented to the Academy of Sciences," and that were now in press. The memoir in question was undoubtedly that on the formation of fixed air, or acid of *charbon*, written the previous summer and still awaiting publication in the chronically late Memoirs of the Academy.[26] In that memoir, we may recall, Lavoisier had treated the combustion of various forms of charcoal and of wax as including the formation of both fixed air and water. He now stressed, as though it were the most significant consequence of the new theory, that it strengthened the analogy between respiration and these combustions.

The guidance that the analogy between respiration and the other combustions offered Lavoisier in this situation illustrates what has recently been called the "interaction" concept of analogous reasoning. According to this view, once an identification by analogy has been established, further development of either side of the analogy is apt to stimulate a corresponding development of the other.[27] Such developments not only modify the nature of the two entities likened to each other, but can shift the reference points of the comparison, as well as the degree of identification between them. The development just discussed temporarily reversed, in both of these respects, the trend of Lavoisier's thought over the preceding five years. As we saw earlier, the abstraction of a *matière charbonneuse* from its common association with tangible charcoal had facilitated the identification of respiration with a generalized combustion process involving that principle. Between 1777 and 1783 Lavoisier had come to regard the relation between them as not only an analogy, but an identity. The revision of his respiration theory, however, involved a reversion to the relation of analogy between respiration and other specific processes; for it was the combustion of particular substances, such as charcoal itself, or wax or oil, to which he was comparing respiration in the main statement of his modified theory. That viewpoint may have lasted, however, not much longer than it took Lavoisier to write it out, because a little further on, as we have seen, when he subordinated the formation of water and fixed his attention on the formation of fixed air he reidentified the "ponderable substance" that forms it as *matière charbonneuse*. Tacitly he now envisioned respiration as divisible into two combustions, one identical to that of *matière charbonneuse*, the other to that of inflammable air. These are only slightly different ways of viewing the same situation, and to distinguish them may seem to be mere hairsplitting; but they are worth examining when we can find them in a document which captures a creative scientist at such a germinal moment during the formation of a significant conceptual advance. It may, more commonly than we suppose, be by wandering through such subtle nuances that scientists nudge themselves along toward larger changes. Only a minute fraction of these nuances ever pass beyond the head of the thinker onto paper. Our access is normally limited to records written at intervals very much longer than those between successive thoughts about the same problem. It is the cumulative effects of the small creative touches that have been added in the meantime that lend to scientific creativity the appearance of a much smaller number of more sharply delineated mental leaps.

Deliberately or inadvertently, when Lavoisier rewrote the three paragraphs in his draft memoir to incorporate a revised theory of respiration, he subverted the original force of the discussion. The quantitative argument he had given for his basic theory was no longer conclusive, since it neglected the formation of water. Not surprisingly, Lavoisier deleted the quantity he had calculated for the weight gain of the air and had used as proof that a ponderable substance from the lungs had combined with it, and did not replace it with another figure. What had been a more rigorous, quantitative justification for the old theory became a preliminary qualitative description of a new theory.

IV

Sometime after substituting the revised theory of respiration for the old one in his memoir on the alterations of the air, Lavoisier realized that his argument for it was not good enough. The analogy to other combustions was only suggestive, and the mere observation that the volume of the air diminished during respiration was not conclusive. A full quantitative justification, equivalent to the now outmoded one he had recently worked out for the old theory, was needed. Such a calculation, being more complex, ought to be based on more accurate measurements than could be extracted from the respiration experiment of 1776. He turned, accordingly, to one from the more recent series, that carried out on a guinea pig on May 12, 1783, in vital air. In light of the new circumstances, this experiment also afforded the advantage over the earlier one that the volume decrease in question was proportionately almost twice as large. On the blank left-hand page facing the original record of the experiment he summarized the volume changes that had occurred. The initial, corrected, volume of 248 cubic inches of vital air had diminished during the respiration to 240.33 cubic inches, a decrease of 7.66 cubic inches. Caustic alkali reduced the volume to 200.5 cubic inches. Subtracting the latter from the quantity remaining after the respiration gave 39.83 cubic inches of fixed air present in the residual air; but since he had determined that 8 cubic inches of fixed air had existed in the original vital air as an impurity, the quantity of fixed air formed by the respiration was only 31.83 cubic inches. Thus far Lavoisier was merely reviewing the situation as he had analyzed it before in 1783. We may recall that at the time he reported this experiment in the "Memoir on heat," he had referred the change in volume during the respiration to a simple, unexplained decrease in the volume of vital air as it is transformed to fixed air. With the aid of the knowledge of the composition of fixed air that he had gained since then, however, he was now in a position to subject that assumption to a quantitative test. From the density of fixed air (for which one can show that he utilized a figure of 0.50 grains per cubic inch) he calculated the weight of a cubic foot of vital air to be 1 ounce 4 gros. On the basis of combining proportions of seventy-two parts of vital air to twenty-eight of *matière charbonneuse* (again not stated, but implicit in the calculation), he found that 4 gros 48 grains of the latter would combine with the cubic foot of vital air. Adding their weights together he found that a cubic foot of fixed air should weigh 2 ounces 48 grains. Then dividing this weight by the density of fixed air (stated as 0.695 grains per cubic inch), he concluded that its volume would be 1,726.6 cubic inches, only 1⅓ cubic inches less than the initial 1,728 cubic inches of vital air. "It is to be observed," he wrote in recording this calculation in his notebook, "that in being converted to aeriform *acide charbonneuse*, vital air is not sensibly diminished in volume."[28]

The impact of this inference is not immediately evident from this notebook page alone. Only when we are aware of the time and circumstances under which he wrote it does its meaning become clear. At the time he carried out the experiment he could not have performed such a calculation, because he did not know the combining proportions of fixed air. The fact that he also based the calculation on a density of 0.50 grains per cubic inch of vital air enables us to infer that he actually carried it out during the course of rewriting his memoir on the alterations of the air, because in the first draft and fair copy he listed the value of 0.47317 and only then switched to the figure of 0.50.[29] Thus it appears evident that, after he had concluded on other grounds that water forms in respiration, and that the decrease in volume is due to that process, it became important to eliminate the possibility he had once accepted, that the conversion of vital air to fixed air could itself explain this decrease. Having done so, he had set the stage to reinterpret the original experiment on the assumption that some of the vital air consumed forms water.

Conforming to the convention that he had already been following in his memoir on the alterations of the air, Lavoisier converted the volume changes summarized from the experiment of May 12, 1783, to the base of one cubic foot of vital air. To work out a balance sheet, however, he then had to reconvert all the volumes to weights. That done, he used the proportions of fixed air established during the intervening year, and those for water just established during his most recent decomposition experiments, to derive the quantity of vital air accounted for in the fixed air. The difference between this quantity and the quantity of vital air consumed gave him the quantity of the latter left to form water. From the proportion of vital air in that water he deduced in turn the amount of inflammable air required to form it. On the next blank page in his notebook Lavoisier outlined the results of these calculations:

> Continuation of the experiment opposite
>
> It results from this experiment that a volume of one cubic foot, or 1,728 cubic inches, of vital air was reduced by respiration to 1,674.56 cubic inches.
>
> That 221.78 cubic inches of fixed air formed.

> That about 53.44 cubic inches of vital air was employed to form water.
>
> That the quantity of inflammable air evacuated from the lungs was 4.715 grains.
>
> That 31.435 grains of water formed.
>
> That in forming fixed air 159.6816 cubic inches [of vital air] was employed.

Below a calculation of the purity of the vital air employed, he completed this tabulation with the statement

> 31.0492 of *matières charbonneuses* was extracted from the lungs.[30]

This brief summary, inobtrusively inserted in Lavoisier's notebook without even a title to indicate its significance, thus represents a historical landmark, the earliest quantitative demonstration that water forms in respiration. Because no details of the calculations are given, however, we shall not analyze it further, but turn instead to a slightly revised, somewhat fuller account of it that he wrote out afterward.

After working out these calculations, Lavoisier rewrote the entire section dealing with his theory of respiration in his memoir on the alterations of the air. He replaced both the original paragraphs and the earlier marginal additions with an expanded discussion occupying six separate pages. Recapitulating briefly the experiment on the guinea pig on which he based his new inferences, he then reproduced, with some modifications of detail, the calculations he had entered in his laboratory notebook. Based on an initial volume of one cubic foot, or 1,728 cubic inches, of vital air, the volume remaining after the respiration corresponded to 1,672¾ cubic inches, representing a decrease of one thirty-second of the original volume. The further reduction produced by adding caustic alkali was 229½ cubic inches, which represented the fixed air formed in the respiratory process. The final remaining residue, which he put down as 1,443⅔ cubic inches, was "very pure vital air." Again converting the volumes to weights, he arrived at the following quantities for the vital air remaining and the fixed air formed:

Vital air	1 ounce	2 gros	1¾ grain
Fixed air		2	15
	1	4	16¾

This quantity, he noted, represented a gain in weight of 21.87 grains. This augmentation of the absolute weight, he asserted, could only be *matière charbonneuse* extracted from the lungs "by the act of respiration."[31]

So far he was following the same argument that he had made in the original version of this section, except that the numbers were different because he derived them from the experiment of 1783 in place of that of 1776. Then, however, he extended the same form of argument to include a quantitative justification for his new theory that water too forms in respiration:

> But one must consider that this increase in weight, which appears to be only 21.87 grains, is actually much greater than one would at first believe; in fact, in the experiment which I have just described, only 229½ cubic inches of fixed air formed. Now, according to very exact results, which I have discussed elsewhere, 100 parts by weight of fixed air are composed of 72 parts of vital air and 28 of *charbon*. The 229½ cubic inches of fixed air obtained would therefore contain
>
> | | |
> |---|---|
> | Vital air | 114.84 grains |
> | *Charbon* | 44.66 |

If, as is probable, Lavoisier used for the density of fixed air the figure 0.695, the 229½ cubic inches would weigh 159.5 grains, from which the above values would immediately follow from the composition of fixed air Lavoisier mentioned. That composition, as we have seen, was the one he had reached during his investigation of fixed air during the previous spring. "The 114.84 grains of vital air," he continued, "amount [in volume] to 229⅔ cubic inches." (That this calculated volume of the vital air consumed was nearly identical to the volume of the fixed air produced must have been, for Lavoisier at this point, only a coincidence, for he did not remark on it.)

> If, therefore, the vital air had been employed only to form fixed air, the quantity remaining after the operation would have been
>
> | | |
> |---|---|
> | 1,728 − 229⅔ | 1,498⅓ |
> | The quantity found was only | 1,443⅔ |
> | Deficit | 54⅔[32] |

Lavoisier's compressed statement here can be made less cryptic by expanding it somewhat. Having converted the volume of fixed air formed to a weight, in order to calculate, from the proportions by weight of vital air and *charbon* in it, the weight of vital air which must have entered this fixed air, he had then reconverted this weight back into a volume of fixed air to find out how much the initial volume of vital air ought to have decreased in supplying that quantity. Subtracting this amount, 229⅔ cubic inches, from the initial 1,728 cubic inches, he found that 1,498⅓ cubic inches of vital air ought to have remained after the fixed air was removed. In fact, after the addition of caustic alkali the final volume was only 1,443⅔ cubic inches, or 54⅔ cubic inches less than expected.

When Lavoisier made this calculation he had already inferred on other grounds that water forms in respiration; and the object of the calculation was clearly to demonstrate a quantity of vital air unconsumed in forming fixed air, that was therefore available to form the water. Nevertheless, when he came to the point of drawing that conclusion, he wavered; for he realized that the result could be interpreted in another way. In the next paragraph of his draft he equivocated. "It is therefore evident," he wrote,

> that not all of the vital air which has entered the lungs comes out again in an elastic state, and it follows either that a portion of the vital air unites with the blood, or else that it combines with a portion of inflammable air to form water. I shall discuss in other memoirs the grounds one could invoke in favor of these two opinions.

He went on to state that "the same experiment repeated in common air gives analogous results"—evidently a reference, chronologically very misleading, to the original respiration experiment of 1776. Then he wrote, "But without involving myself in purely theoretical considerations," he would examine the composition of the air after it had been breathed in as long as possible.[33]

It thus appears that, having lost confidence in the force of the conclusion he had been approaching all this time, he decided to postpone the resolution of the question to some future time. Afterward, however, he recovered his nerve and decided to indicate his choice, even while acknowledging some uncertainty about it. To the end of the above paragraph he added, in the margin of the draft:

> But in supposing, as there is some reason to believe, that the latter [opinion] is preferable, it is easy to determine, in accord with the above experiment, the quantity of water which forms by respiration and the quantity of inflammable air which is extracted from the lungs.[34]

He began this "determination" by setting out in a slightly different form the calculation of the deficit, designated now "the portion employed to form the water," decided the repetition was unnecessary, and eliminated it. He then went on to show the final stage in the demonstration, the estimation, from the composition of water, of the quantity of inflammable air.

> Now since 85 parts by weight of vital air and 15 of inflammable gas must be employed to form 100 parts of water, it comes out that with 54⅚ cubic inches of vital air that are found to be missing 32¼ grains of water must have formed, and 4⅚ grains of inflammable gas were discharged from the lungs of the guinea pig.[35]

Lavoisier now based his justification for the formation of water in respiration on an experimental discrepancy between the measured quantity of vital air consumed in a respiration experiment and the quantity accounted for in the observed quantity of fixed air formed. By a rigorous quantitative argument resting on these weight relations he supported the conclusion that the missing vital air combines with inflammable air. We should note, however, that the 54⅔ or (54⅚ reached in the alternative calculation) cubic inches difference upon which he relied for this argument represented only about one twenty-seventh (or less than 4 percent) of the two volumes compared. In many similar situations he had either disregarded such a small disagreement or made an adjustment for some suspected experimental error in order to eliminate it. This calculation therefore reinforces the evidence against the accepted historical interpretation that some new experimental result forced Lavoisier to realize that his previous theory was inadequate. Only after inferring for other reasons that respiration forms water did he go back to an old experimental result to find a discrepancy he had not previously noticed in it. Lavoisier did not modify his theory to cover an observed deficit; he uncovered a deficit to make place for his modified theory.

The alternative "opinion" Lavoisier had raised, that "a portion of the vital air unites with the blood," does not signify, as some historians have supposed, that he persistently harbored the view that a part of the respiration may take place in the blood. In spite of the superficial similarity of this statement to the idea he had entertained in 1777, that the vital air combines with the blood, the two suggestions were based on entirely different considerations. The earlier idea was inspired by the qualitative analogy between the color of mercury calx and that of arterial blood; the new one was an acknowledgment that the deficit of vital air he had identified in order to support his theory of the formation of water was subject to a different interpretation. He was not in either case posing alternative sites for equivalent processes. In the present situation, if the "missing" vital air did unite with the blood, it would be to take part in some entirely unknown process; for if it merely combined there instead of in the lungs with *matière charbonneuse* to form fixed air, it would ultimately reappear and not be missing. Since he left this idea totally undeveloped, and did not return to it, it seems most likely that after temporarily seeing it as a potential objection to the thrust of his argument, he simply put it aside. As for his "preferred" theory, he assumed as before the simplest location for the process. The water formed where the vital air and the inflammable principle were most likely to come into contact: in the lungs.

Lavoisier inserted the folded pages on which he had written out his new justification for the formation of water in respiration into the original fair copy of his memoir on alterations of the air, crossing out the corresponding passages it replaced. He made minor modifications in the remainder of the copy and published the paper in that form in the Memoirs of the Society of Medicine.[36]

His revised theory of respiration thus became almost a paper within a paper. The unity of the original draft was sacrificed to the new views Lavoisier developed in the course of writing it. The history of the construction of this memoir thus explains the anomalous character of the published version, in which Lavoisier introduced this very important theoretical advance inconspicuously in the midst of a paper on the practical effects of respiration, for which the new feature of his theory was irrelevant.

We cannot establish precisely when Lavoisier wrote this new section of the memoir. He must have done so at least two weeks after he had read the paper at the Society of Medicine, for the calculation utilized the proportions of inflammable air and vital air in water that he derived from the grand synthesis experiment of February 27–28. The Memoirs of the Society of Medicine were even more laggard than those of the Academy of Sciences, so that although his paper was included in the volume for 1782–83, that volume did not appear until 1787. I feel that he probably wrote the section containing his new respiration theory much closer to the time he read the paper than to the time of publication. It does not seem to reflect any information that he acquired later than the spring of 1785, nor does it give evidence of having been stimulated by subsequent investigations in any other area. In keeping with the interpretation I have given of the manner in which each version of the theory of respiration stimulated the next step, I would expect that the entire development took place over a relatively short time.

* * *

Between 1783 and 1785 Lavoisier did not significantly increase his knowledge of respiration through further experimentation. Nevertheless, in the reflected light of the progress he was making in other experimental investigations, he greatly advanced his respiration theory. The most decisive clarification derived from the theory of the composition of water, a discovery which sooner or later affected his understanding of every chemical phenomenon associated with plants and animals with which he dealt. The discovery of the synthesis of water did not impinge immediately upon his theory of respiration, but spread toward it through the intermediary of other chemical processes. First it was the combustion of charcoal that he was able to view in the new light as a more complex phenomenon than he had formerly supposed. Then he extended the same form of explanation to the combustion of wax and other "organized bodies." By the time it occurred to him that respiration too fell into this category of processes that form both fixed air and water, his experimental progress in the other areas had provided him with new analytical means to support the idea. Not only could he bring to bear the theory of the composition of water itself, but the new, more precise (as he thought) determinations of the composition of fixed air and of water enabled him to carry out with confidence the calculations by which he could buttress his new theory of respiration with quantitative arguments. New experiments on respiration itself were not essential, because with these new conceptual and analytical tools he was able to reinterpret respiration experiments already performed from a perspective that had been beyond his horizon during the spring of 1783 when he carried out the last series of them. All of the later developments were at that time totally unpredictable for Lavoisier. The continuing experiments on respiration he intended to pursue at the time he wrote the memoir on heat would, if he had carried them out under the circumstances that then existed, have gone in a quite different direction. Yet, by the time he reached the revised theory of 1785, it appeared a natural extension of his earlier theoretical position.

It may be one of the special marks of a scientific thinker as penetrating—and as fortunate—as Lavoisier that unforeseen developments so regularly permitted him to expand his previous theoretical positions rather than undermined them. Sometimes later events preserved or enhanced his conclusions even while removing some of the experimental pinions on which they had earlier seemed to rest. It should be evident, for example, that the new respiration theory seriously weakened Lavoisier and Laplace's demonstration that the combustion of *matière charbonneuse* is the source of animal heat. If the combustion of inflammable air was involved as well, then one would not expect a respiring animal to produce the same quantity of heat as the combustion of charcoal does in forming a given quantity of fixed air. There should be a surplus of heat due to the concurrent process. Much later, Lavoisier asserted that he and Laplace had recognized in the first place that animals disengage more heat than ought to result from the quantity of fixed air they formed during the same time.[37] There is no evidence from the available documents, however, that this difference entered into the considerations that led him to modify the theory. It was, rather, a convenient retrospective explanation for a discrepancy that Lavoisier had earlier regarded as insignificant.

Meanwhile, what of Laplace's earlier concern that Lavoisier ought to repeat those calorimetric and combustion experiments on charcoal and on animals "as many times as possible," in order to ensure that their theory of respiration was "sufficiently established"? The record is silent. I suspect, however, that the continuation of that investigation remained one of the unfulfilled intentions of a very busy man with far more creative scientific ideas than he could test to exhaustion. Lavoisier kept his calorimeters around year after year, in the hope that he would someday be able to extend his investigation of heats of combustion to other processes; but year after year he was too preoccupied with other things to get around to it.[38] If he had been able to take up this work again he would probably have included further respiration experiments. I doubt, however, that their omission seriously worried him. By 1785 he was probably so sure of his basic theory of respiration that he felt little need for further calorimetric demonstration. No longer collaborating formally with Laplace, he was freer of his younger colleague's more cautious attitude. His confidence in his theory was dependent not on any single decisive proof, but on all of the accumulating investigations and conceptual developments that concurred in support of his conception. There were no major contradictory phenomena to explain away. He must have had the sense that everything fit so well into a coherent pattern that he simply could not be on the wrong track.

Part 3

Lavoisier in the Plant Kingdom 1785–1789

With the completion of his experiments to determine the proportions of the constituents of fixed air, and the large-scale operations to establish the proportions of water, Lavoisier had by early 1785 established to his satisfaction the main experimental foundations for the general system of chemistry that he had been constructing for over a decade. During the next four years he worked vigorously and effectively to gain acceptance for his general chemical principles; but that task now took the form of campaigning to win new converts, devising a nomenclature to express the new concepts, founding a journal to promote them, and writing an elementary textbook to synthesize and teach them. In his laboratory life he was free for the first time to shift his attention toward other ventures. During the next four years he directed most of his experimental activity toward the chemical composition or processes of plants. His interest in each of the three problems he took up—fermentation, vegetation, and the composition of plant substances—grew for him out of his prior interests, especially his preoccupation with the operations that decompose water. Gradually, however, the investigations changed character, so that the chemistry of plants became increasingly his central objective. By 1788 he was mobilizing all of his investigative talents and knowledge to clarify one of the "most striking and extraordinary operations of all those that chemistry presents us"—that is, the mysterious process of fermentation.

Lavoisier applied to these areas within plant chemistry the same experimental methods he had developed during his studies of combustion and respiration. The phenomena he now took on were, however, more complex than those which he had so brilliantly analyzed with these methods. In plant chemistry he ran into the most intractable experimental difficulties he had ever faced in his long scientific career. Some of them he never did resolve. In following the details of his struggles with these problems, we can acquire insights concerning his scientific approach that are not so evident from the earlier investigations in which technical success came more readily. Moreover, in spite of the practical obstacles he only partially overcame, the conclusions he drew from, or to some extent imposed on, these investigations were of fundamental significance.

His studies in plant chemistry not only pressed Lavoisier's experimental methods to the limit, but induced him also to make more explicit than before the foundation for, and the expression of, the basic principle underlying all of his chemical investigations: that is, the assumption that the weight of the products of any chemical change must equal the weight of the substances that enter into it. These investigations therefore hold as much interest for our understanding of the general structure of the "chemical revolution" as for our knowledge of the foundations of the special area of plant chemistry.

10

The Composition of Inflammable Plant Substances

When Lavoisier envisioned a vast new field for the analysis of plant and animal matters in 1779, he had been generalizing from his experience with a single plant substance, commercial sugar. When he returned to the subject in 1785, the prototype substances he utilized were spirit of wine, olive oil, and wax. Neither his earlier nor his later choices were derived from judgments about their importance as constituents of plant matter, or from knowledge that their compositions were broadly representative. In both instances he was led by contingent circumstances to utilize these particular substances. He had originally distilled sugar with nitrous acid to elucidate its relation to "acid of sugar," in support of his general theory of acidity, and found that by modifying the same process he could identify qualitatively the principles composing the sugar. By 1785, however, he no longer doubted that plant substances were composed qualitatively of the inflammable principle and *matière charbonneuse*, or these two together with the oxygen principle. What now interested him was to determine the quantities of these constituents, just as he had been concerned with the quantitative proportions of the constituents of fixed air and of water. To determine these principles rigorously in plant substances, however, he had to burn them completely in a closed chamber, as he had done with charcoal. With the procedures available to him he could not do that for sugar. The three inflammable substances he had already employed in his combustion experiments were far more likely prospects for such treatment.

Just as he had at first ascertained the composition of fixed air merely as a by-product of his study of the combustion of *charbon*, had then found that he needed to establish the proportions more accurately in order to use them in his calculations concerning the composition of water, and only after all that taken up the determination of the precise composition of fixed air as an end in itself; so did Lavoisier at first burn "inflammable plant matters" as examples of combustion, or as a way to determine the composition of fixed air, and only afterward come to view the determination of the quantitative composition of these plant substances as his main goal. In another transposition of ends and means typical of scientific investigation, the solutions of the problems of the composition of water and fixed air now provided him with all the general methods and principles he needed to make the analysis of plant substances his central research object. That Lavoisier "invented" the combustion method of organic analysis was therefore in part the unplanned outcome of the fact that he had previously utilized plant materials in his study of combustion. The treatment of these substances as combinations of *substance charbonneuse* and inflammable principle, the general methods for burning them in closed chambers and for calculating from the airs consumed and formed the original constituents of the substances, had all been worked out in performing the same operations on various forms of charcoal. The combustion of charcoal itself Lavoisier had regarded as the combustion of *matière charbonneuse* containing some inflammable principle as an impurity, but it could also be viewed as the analysis of a substance derived from plants. Once he shifted the focus of his attention all that remained to be done, as Lavoisier put it afterward, was "to determine with precision the quantities of water and of *acide charbonneux* formed during the combustion of the diverse substances, in order to infer the quantities of inflammable air and *principe charbonneux* which they contain; that is the object which I have proposed for myself in regard to some of them."[1]

Spirit of wine seemed particularly well suited to serve as the central material object through which Lavoisier entered this transition in his research program. A prominent product of the distillation of plant materials ever since the late Middle Ages, ubiquitous in chemical laboratories because of its special solvent properties in addition to its more traditional qualities, spirit of wine burned so readily and so completely that it was sometimes referred to as the "inflammable liquid." In his first public presentation of combustion experiments carried out on it, Lavoisier suggested in the fall of 1784 that it was almost inevitable that sooner or later he would have included it in his older program of investigating combustion processes. "The experiments that I have undertaken on combustion in general," he wrote, "and about which I have already talked to the Academy many times, naturally led me to examine what takes place in the case of spirit of wine." For the first experiments of this kind, he went on, he used his "ordinary method," introducing a spirit of wine lamp into a glass jar inverted over mercury.[2]

Since Lavoisier did not indicate when he had carried out this experiment, and since he commonly went back to his older laboratory records for results which he reported as though they represented recent work, it is possible that this too was a retrospective account of an operation performed at an earlier stage of his research. There are, however, no surviving records of such an experiment previous to the time he described it,[3] and there are reasons to infer that he became especially interested in this particular combustion only after the discovery that water can be synthesized. Then the subject took on a new significance, because there were striking observations in the older literature which could now be seen as evidence that water forms as spirit of wine burns.

"According to Boerhaave," Lavoisier noted—and therefore according to one of the standard authorities for eighteenth-century chemists—if one holds a cold piece of porcelain in a spirit of wine flame, drops of nearly pure water condense on it.[4] This was, however, only a casual observation compared with the study of that phenomenon that the French chemist Claude-Joseph Geoffroy reported to the Academy of Sciences in 1718 (see Figure 8). The original objective of Geoffroy's investigation had been to improve on the tests which were then available to evaluate commercial *eau de vie* and spirit of wine. *Eau de vie*, the product of a distillation carried out with fewer rectifications than were required to produce spirit of wine, was graded according to the proportion of inflammable liquid to "phlegm" (the traditional term for the watery fraction of a distillation). Good spirit of wine, on the other hand, was regarded as nearly free of phlegm. The first test Geoffroy devised was to ignite the sample in a metal cylinder surrounded by circulating water to prevent the temperature of the sample from rising. After the "inflammable liquid" had burned off, he could determine from the level of the liquid remaining in the cylinder the proportion of phlegm the sample contained. His results demonstrated, he claimed, "that there is no spirit of wine without phlegm, and from which I cannot extract a considerable quantity." By burning a spirit of wine lamp under a distillation flask with openings at top and bottom, he was able to collect in another way the phlegm "that one can extract from spirit of wine." This phlegm was "absolutely insipid"; did not turn tincture of violets red, so that it was not acidic; and had the same density as water. It could, Geoffroy wrote, "pass for elementary water." In each of his tests he weighed the spirit of wine and the water he obtained from it, and found that in some cases the latter amounted to more than half of the former.[5]

Lavoisier introduced his own experiments on spirit of wine with a brief summary of Boerhaave's observation and Geoffroy's results.[6] Although it is possible that Lavoisier learned of Geoffroy's article only after the fact, I think it more plausible that he had long known about this thorough quantitative investigation, so similar in approach to his own. As the above description shows, Geoffroy believed, as all chemists then did, that water is elementary. The water must therefore have been present all along, and his results simply indicated that all spirit of wine, no matter how often rectified, still retained a large proportion of the water from which distillers attempted to separate it. Until 1783 Geoffroy's results would have had the same meaning for Lavoisier. As soon as he knew about the composite nature of water however, it would have appeared to him self-evident from Geoffroy's experiments that the combustion of spirit of wine is one of those processes in which water is formed. During the era in which Lavoisier was seeking out all the means he could find to decompose or recompose water, such knowledge was a powerful inducement for him to investigate the

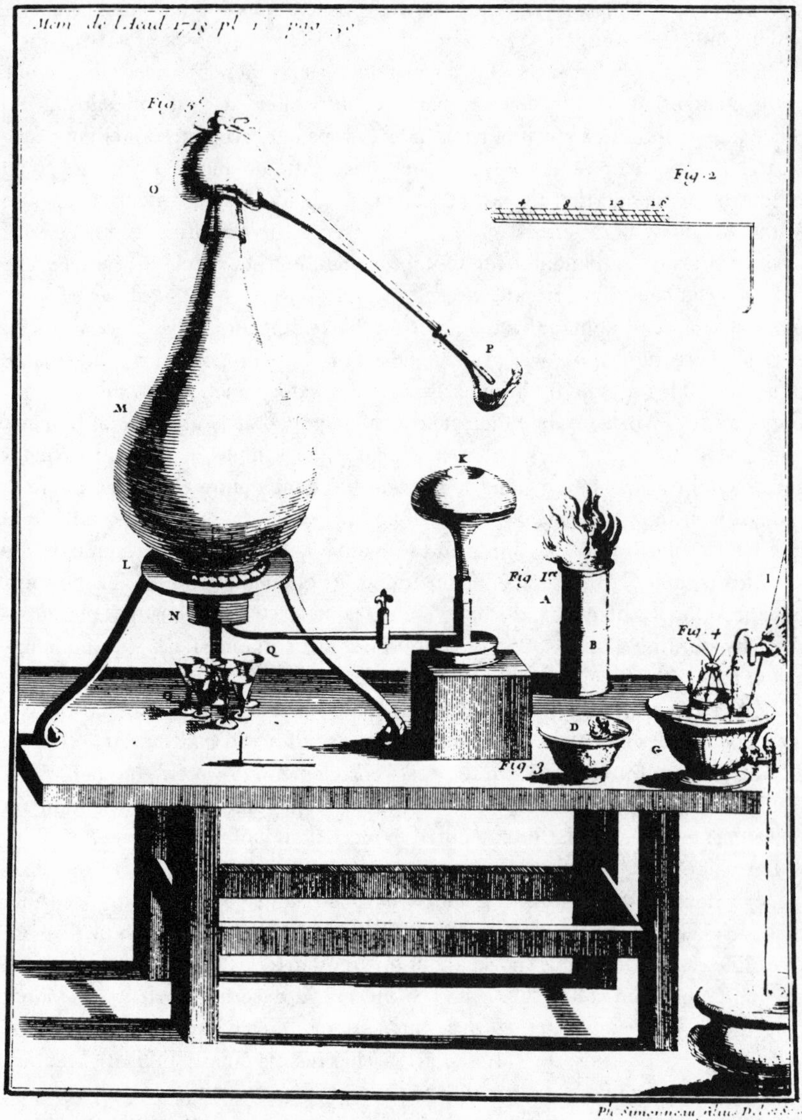

Figure 8. Apparatus used by Claude-Joseph Geoffroy for experiments on spirit of wine. Figure 1 is the metal cylinder in which he burned spirit of wine; Figure 4 shows the same cylinder immersed in circulating water. Figure 5 shows the apparatus in which he burned spirit of wine under a distillation flask. *K* is the spirit of wine lamp. The spirit of wine burns at the end of tube *Q*, inserted through the open bottom of distillation flask *M*. Glasses, *O*, catch the liquid formed in the flask which does not pass over into receiver *P*. Geoffroy, *Mémoires de l'Académie des Sciences*, 1718, page 50, Plate 1.

phenomenon for himself. When he began his own experiments, he reported, "I anticipated a considerable diminution in the volume of the air [and] . . . production of water."[7]

Even though he expected water to form in this combustion, Lavoisier was unprepared for the quantity he obtained. "What surprised me very much," he related, "is that the weight of this water was found to be greater than that of the spirit of wine that I had burned." He did not say how he had measured this water, but the lack of any indication that he calculated it indirectly implies that he may have obtained a rough estimate by collecting what he could of the water that actually appeared inside the inverted jar. The startling outcome of the experiment prompted him to seek a way to measure the quantities more accurately by operating on a large scale. To this end he consulted his current collaborator, Meusnier, a man as adept at devising experimental methods as he was at the mathematical analysis of experimental results, who designed for him a "very simple apparatus" (see Figure 9). It contained an ordinary spirit of wine lamp, whose flame burned at the base of a metal chimney. The vapor arising from this flame traversed the chimney without condensing, because an insulating sand jacket kept the chimney at high temperature. The vapor then descended through a coiled tube, eighteen feet long if extended, inside a cylinder filled with ice water; the cooled vapor condensed there and flowed out at the bottom into a bottle.[8] Their method can be viewed as a highly refined adaptation of the second method Geoffroy had used seventy-five years earlier to collect the water given off in the same process.

No laboratory notebook records of the experiments Lavoisier carried out with this apparatus exist, but there is a surviving loose data sheet, dated September 3, 1784, containing the measurements made during one such experiment. On that day he burned 8 ounces, 7 gros, 64 grains of spirit of wine and received 10 ounces, 2 gros, 57 grains of water,[9] representing an increase, as he observed in his report of the experiments, of about one-eighth of the original weight.[10] On the day after this experiment, "MM. Lavoisier and Meusnier read the report of their experiments on the combustion of spirit of wine and its transmutation into water" at the Academy. It was another one of those special occasions on which a royal visitor was present, this time Prince Henry of Prussia.[11] In all likelihood this report was the fair copy of the manuscript from which the above description of the experiments is taken. If so, the secretary recording the minutes of the meeting was misled by the title of Lavoisier's paper. What Lavoisier actually said was:

> In a less enlightened century one would have been able to present this experiment as a transmutation of spirit of wine into water, and the increase in the weight would have made it appear even more marvelous. Today, reduced to its proper significance, this proves nothing except that something else is added to the

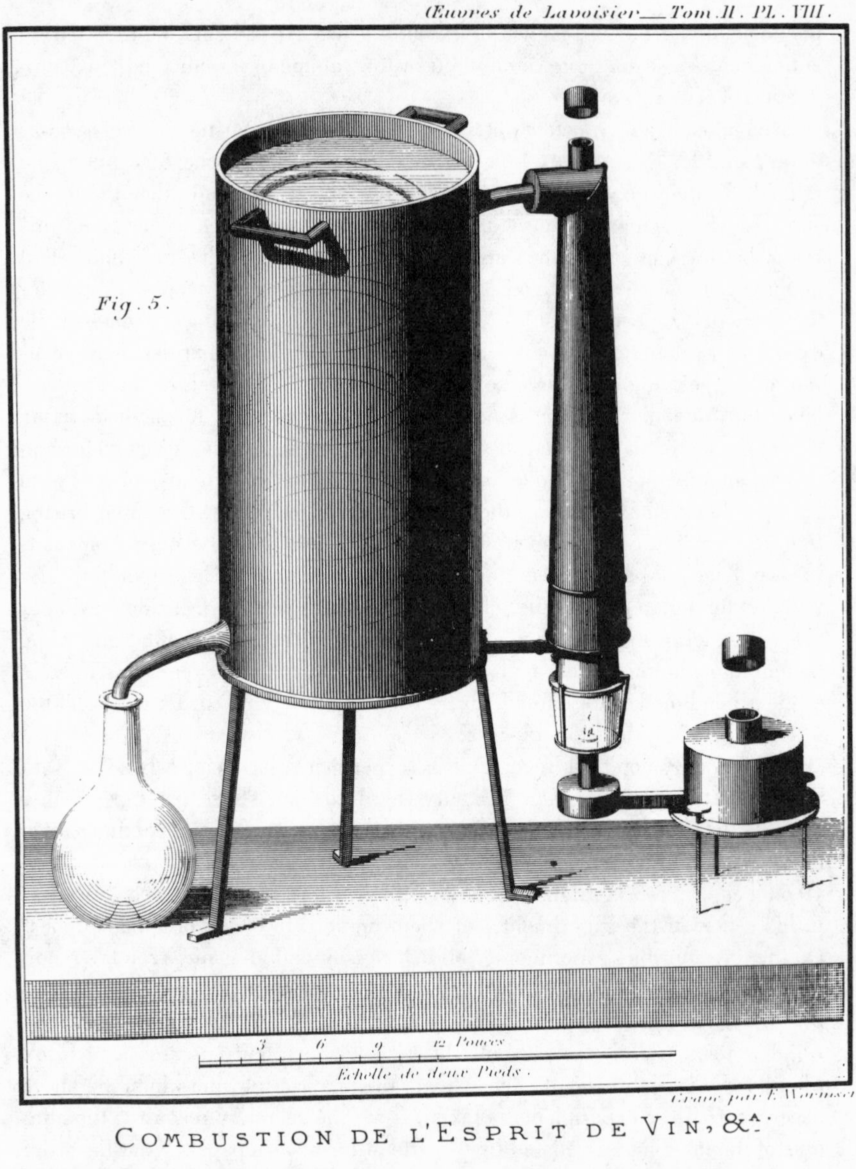

COMBUSTION DE L'ESPRIT DE VIN, &A.

Figure 9. Apparatus designed by Meusnier for Lavoisier's large-scale experiments on combustion of spirit of wine. The spirit of wine lamp is on right side. The insulating chimney is the narrow tube on right side of main apparatus. The large central vessel on the tripod contains the coiled condensing tube surrounded by cold water. On the far left is the jar in which condensed vapor collects. Lavoisier, *Oeuvres*, 2: Plate 8.

> spirit of wine during the combustion, that this something is the air, and that the result is water.[12]

The central point of the experiment, as Lavoisier then saw it, was that it supplied another proof that water is not a simple substance, but one composed of the air and the inflammable principle.

It may have been for the benefit of the princely visitor that Lavoisier simplified his interpretation of the process, referring to the constituent added to the spirit of wine generally as "the air" rather than specifically as the "oxygen principle," and neglecting the formation of fixed air which went unmeasured in this experimental procedure. Perhaps also the occasion influenced Lavoisier and Meusnier to repeat the experiment "in the presence of the prince," and to set up as well the gun barrel apparatus, with which they had earlier decomposed water, in one of the offices of the Academy where members and guests could view it after the meeting.[13] It was, however, probably not purely to impress his audience that Lavoisier inserted a passage into his manuscript, which he eliminated probably before he read it, asserting:

> If I had announced, before making this experiment public, that without mixing any tangible substance with the spirit of wine it would be possible to convert it into water, not merely pound for pound, but with a considerable excess in addition, I would have been met with nothing but incredulity. Nevertheless, this marvel is, in a certain sense, taking place at this very moment, under the eyes of the Academy.[14]

Lavoisier must really have felt that this "very extraordinary result" was a sort of marvel, even if he could provide for it a perfectly natural explanation.

Charles Gillispie has observed that "scientists have sometimes written that Lavoisier formulated the law of conservation of matter. The reality was simpler. He assumed it. It was for him . . . a precondition but no finding of his science."[15] The above passages help to elucidate Gillispie's viewpoint by suggesting how simple, yet how deep, Lavoisier's feeling was about this principle. To have thought that spirit of wine could become heavier through some kind of transmutation would have been for him to revert to a past age which believed literally in marvels. He could imagine no way appropriate to his own enlightened era to explain such a gain in weight except as the addition of another substance. His explanation was simply an application of the general, assumed principle that nothing is created or lost in a chemical change.

Lavoisier did not publish this report of his experiments on spirit of wine independently, but tacked most of it onto the end of the published version of the memoir on the decomposition and recomposition of water that he had read at the Academy the previous spring.[16]

II

The record does not tell us precisely how or when Lavoisier's combustion experiments on spirit of wine ceased to be for him primarily a form of proof for the composition of water and became instead a means for determining the quantitative composition of spirit of wine itself. There need not have been any particular external stimulus, since the analysis of plant substances had long been one of his general goals, and since he had already carried out such a determination for wax as a subsidiary aspect of his determination of the composition of fixed air. The pursuit of this objective using spirit of wine as his subject may have been a natural coalescence of present occupations and past ambitions. Nevertheless, Lavoisier could not simply have drifted onto this new course during an ongoing investigation without planning to do so. The conditions necessary to carry out such a determination with spirit of wine differed so much from those attending the previous combustion experiments as to require a new, deliberately planned experimental arrangement. At some point Lavoisier must have made a distinct decision to orient his investigation of spirit of wine in another direction. He probably reached this watershed sometime after the meeting of September 4, 1784, in which he still appeared to fix his attention on the composition of water, and sometime long enough before mid May of 1785—the date of the first recorded experiment of the new type—to allow for the conception, design, construction, and some early trials of an apparatus incorporating a significant technical innovation. Since he was, as we have seen, preoccupied experimentally for most of this period, up until the end of February, with the large-scale water experiments, we might surmise that there was a hiatus in the spirit of wine experiments during the winter. When he took them up again in the spring, having carried off these dramatic demonstrations of the composition of water, he was less disposed than he had been up until then to view every phenomenon he could as yet another "proof" for his theory of water. He was in a position to formulate other research objectives, or to implement previously defined objectives that had been thrust aside.

In trying to adapt the combustion of spirit of wine to his new purpose, Lavoisier faced a formidable obstacle. He could not use the large-scale apparatus of Meusnier, because it was an open system. For an analysis the "primary condition" was "to carry out the combustion in closed vessels, in order not to lose anything and to be able to determine the quantity of the aeriform substances before and after the combustion." If he reverted to his ordinary method, the quantity of spirit of wine he could burn under an inverted bell jar filled with common air would be too small to attain accurate results. If he increased the available supply of oxygen by filling the jar with vital air, however, the spirit of wine would burn so rapidly that it would vaporize, and "when the fluid is reduced to a vapor it explodes with vital air. I could not therefore risk introducing a spirit of wine lamp under a jar of vital air."[17]

"This difficulty at first caused me some trouble," Lavoisier acknowledged in a sentence in the first draft of his memoir which he later eliminated, "but I succeeded in conquering it." He did so by designing a closed system comprising two interconnected inverted pneumatic vessels (see Figure 10). The first was the usual bell jar over mercury, in which the spirit of wine lamp burned. It contained common air. The second vessel, over water, was filled with vital air, from which he could from time to time replace the vital air used up in the first vessel. A valve on the tube connecting the two chambers remained closed until the flame in the bell jar began to subside. Then he opened the valve. The level of mercury in the bell jar, which had been rising, descended again, while the level of water in the second vessel rose until the pressures in the chambers returned to equilibrium, forcing vital air into the bell jar. During the course of the combustion he repeated this operation two or three times. Finally the ac-

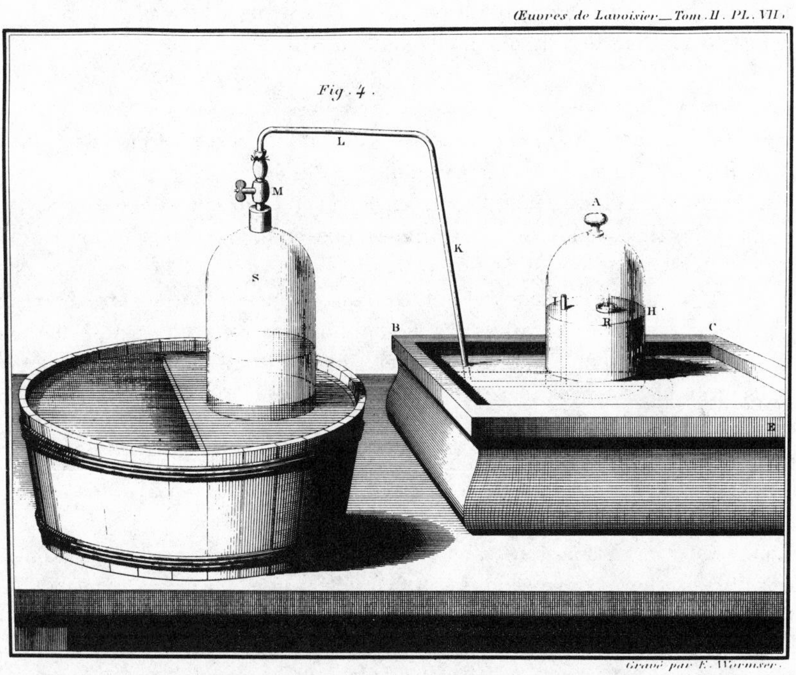

COMBUSTION DE L'ESPRIT DE VIN, &c.ª

Figure 10. Lavoisier's apparatus for burning spirit of wine in a closed system. *BDEC* is the marble basin containing mercury. Bell jar *A*, on right, immersed in mercury, is the combustion chamber, filled initially with ordinary air. *R* is the spirit of wine lamp, floating on mercury. On left, jar *S*, containing vital air, is immersed in water. Vital air is supplied intermittently to replenish that consumed in *A*, by opening valve *M*. Lavoisier, *Oeuvres*, 2: Plate 7.

cumulated fixed air extinguished the flame. He absorbed the fixed air in the usual way in caustic alkali.[18]

Although this procedure obviated the dangerous explosions Lavoisier had feared, the experiments he performed in this way did "not always succeed, and . . . [were] often thwarted by small accidents. One of the most frequent is the fracture of the bell jar; the heat of the flame warms the top of it so strongly that it breaks."[19] As was often the case, Lavoisier's ambitious experiments were stretching to the limit the technical capacity of the equipment of his time.

"Of the quite large number [of these experiments] that I have performed," Lavoisier later commented, "there is only one of them with which I am fully satisfied."[20] His laboratory notebook, however, contains only two such experiments, including the one which satisfied him. These two were almost certainly the last two that he carried out. Given his general tendency to overstate the number of experiments he did, I suspect these two were the only ones that he carried to completion. Perhaps all the others he attempted ended in the destruction of the bell jar, leaving him no data to record.

On May 14, 1785, Lavoisier ignited a lamp containing 7 gros 29.8 grains of spirit of wine in the bell jar. According to the loss in the weight of the lamp, 1 gros 62.5 grains was consumed. This was about one-fortieth of the quantity he had burned in the one recorded experiment with Meusnier's apparatus, so that in spite of the modification of his standard method Lavoisier was constrained to operate on a very small scale. From the changes in the levels of the mercury in the bell jar and the water in the flask supplying vital air, he computed the weights of vital air consumed and of fixed air produced, but he carried out no further analysis of these results.[21] Evidently he was not satisfied with the experiment. The only clue he left to the fault he may have found with it was the comment in his notebook that "the air surrounds the spirit of wine so that some of the latter has dissolved in it, and consequently the consumption of the spirit of wine has not been as great as it appeared to be."[22] It is possible that he made some adjustment to the lamp to lessen this effect when he repeated the experiment on May 16, for the measured consumption of spirit of wine (1 gros 21.5 grains) was almost one-third smaller than in the previous one. On the other hand, he may have convinced himself that this source of error was unavoidable but minor. Later on he thought that, although he could not rule out the possibility that some spirit of wine was "vaporized by the heat, independently of the portion burned," the quantity so lost "could not be very large," or it would have detonated.[23] At any rate he performed a fuller analysis on the data. First he computed the quantity of vital air consumed and of fixed air produced, in the normal way, from the volume of the enclosed air before and after the combustion and after adding caustic alkali. As usual in such operations, he could not collect the water produced under the bell jar, so he calculated it in his standard manner as the quantity necessary to make the products balance the materials consumed:

Weights of materials employed		
Weight of vital air	1 gros	32.4
Weight of spirit of wine	1	21.5
Total	2	53.9
Fixed air obtained	1	23.28
Water formed	1	30.62[24]

Evidently satisfied that these results were "quite exact," he moved on to the combustion of olive oil, using the same apparatus and experimental procedure.

Because olive oil was not easily volatilized, Lavoisier did not encounter the difficulties he had had with spirit of wine. He could assume that the decrease in the weight of the lamp represented "rigorously the quantity burned." The main drawback, he felt, was that he was able to burn only a small amount of oil (actually a little less than two-thirds of the weight of the spirit of wine in the second experiment). He would have preferred to operate on a larger scale, but since he thought that would require an "extremely complicated apparatus,"[25] he contented himself with the outcome of a single experiment performed with the means at hand.

As in the preceding experiment, Lavoisier used the measured loss of weight of the substance burned and the changes in volume in the vessels to calculate the amount of water formed. He chose, however, a more elaborate method than he had applied to the result of the spirit of wine experiment. Instead of establishing a simple balance between the materials consumed and produced, he broke the balance down into the constituents of these materials—the vital air, inflammable air, and *matière charbonneuse*—establishing the quantities of vital air and of inflammable air available to form water, and adding these together to obtain the calculated weight of water. Although more complicated, this route afforded an independent calculation of the proportions of water, which Lavoisier could use in turn to check the reliability of the experimental measurements. He summarized these calculations as follows:

Recapitulation of the combustion of the oil	
Vital air employed	58.94 grains
Oil burned	18.30
[Total of substances consumed]	77.24 grains
Quantity of *matière charbonneuse* employed to form fixed air	15.706 grains
Quantity of vital air employed for the same means	40.388
Total [of fixed air]	56.094 grains[26]

The first of these two totals was the sum of two measured quantities. The second total was itself the measured quantity. Lavoisier obtained the weight of the fixed air formed by multiplying the reduction in volume caused by absorption in caustic alkali times the density of fixed air (0.47317 grains per cubic inch). He then used the proportions of vital air and *matière charbonneuse* in fixed air which he had established the year before (72:28) to calculate the quantities of these two constituents in the product.

By subtracting the vital air determined in this way to have been used in forming the fixed air from the total of the "vital air employed," Lavoisier obtained the quantity which must have formed water; and by subtracting the quantity of *matière charbonneuse* required for the fixed air from the total of "oil burned," he obtained the quantity of inflammable air which must have entered into the water:

> According to this supposition, there would remain to form water
>
> | | |
> |---|---|
> | Vital air | 18.552 [grains] |
> | Inflammable air | 2.594 |
> | Total | 21.146 water formed |
>
> This approaches, to within a very small fraction, nearly the proportions required to form water according to previous experiments.

That is, the proportion of vital air to inflammable air in water which he had accepted since the large-scale decomposition experiment of the year before was 85 to 15, whereas the proportion reached independently through the above experiment was about 87 to 13 (Lavoisier did not actually give this figure). That was indeed impressively close. Lavoisier nevertheless believed that the agreement could be made even closer if he assumed a small source of error in the measurements:

> If, in order to make this result conform [to the composition of water], it were necessary to suppose the quantity of oil burned to be greater by a quarter of a grain, there would be nothing to be surprised at, because there were several pieces of white iron on the plate of the lamp which made it appear to be heavier, and which made the quantity of oil burned seem less.
>
> Moreover, since the water obtained was slightly acidic, it would not be surprising if there was a slight excess of vital air employed.[27]

As we shall see further on, Lavoisier kept these ideas in mind. Meanwhile, he decided to go back to the results of the preceding spirit of wine experiment to recalculate the water formed there in a manner more like what he had just done for the olive oil experiment. In a small space left at the bottom of the page on which he had written the original balance calculation, he crowded in the following:

> Beginning with the supposition that 100 parts by weight of fixed air contain 28 of *charbon* and 72 of vital air, the 95.28 grains of fixed air above are composed of

Charbon	26.6784
Vital air	68.6016
Total	95.2800

Having run out of space on that page, he continued on the facing left-hand page he normally left for later additions:

Total quantity of vital air employed	1 gros	32.4
Quantity employed to form fixed air		68.6
Therefore employed to form water		35.80
Which supposes for inflammable air		6.02
Total of water formed		41.8[28]

Close examination of Lavoisier's calculation shows that, although similar in form to the calculation for the olive oil experiment, it was based on different assumptions. For the olive oil, he had derived the quantity of inflammable air from the difference between the total weight of the substance burned and the weight of the *matière charbonneuse* in the olive oil, as determined from the fixed air produced. Here he had calculated the inflammable air from its proportion in water, as derived from his recent large-scale water synthesis experiment. This procedure therefore provided no check on the experiment from two independent determinations of the composition of water. Why had he proceeded differently in the two cases? The method he followed for the olive oil experiment assumed that olive oil is composed entirely of *matière charbonneuse* and inflammable air. The close approximation between the composition of water he derived in the course of the calculation and the values for it that he already accepted confirmed this assumption. For spirit of wine, however, he probably did not make that assumption, because he expected that it might contain some water already formed.

More conspicuous on Lavoisier's data sheet than these tacit suppositions is the stark discordance between the end results of the calculation and the result he had reached in his earlier simple balance computation. The original one had shown that 1 gros 30.62 grains, or 102.62 grains, of water had formed. The new calculation came out to less than half of that quantity. If, as suggested above, he carried out the second calculation in the manner he did because he suspected that spirit of wine contained water, then we can expect that he would be prepared to view these divergent outcomes as a verification of that suspicion. On the other hand, the fact that he referred to both results as "water formed" suggests that he had not clearly perceived in advance that the two calculations would arrive at measures of water of different origins. There is evidence, moreover, that as he undertook to write up his investigation for a memoir on the subject, and therefore had to interpret the experiment more fully, he was at first uncertain what these results meant.

In the first draft of this memoir, entitled "On the combination of the oxygen principle with spirit of wine, oil, and different combustibles," Lavoisier described the immediate results of the experiment on spirit of wine in a verbal format that followed closely in form the original balance sheet he had entered in his notebook.

> The weight of the spirit of wine which I was able to burn in this experiment was 32.7 grains.
>
> The quantity of vital air consumed by the combustion was 220.235 cubic inches, weighing 1 gros 32.4 grains.
>
> The quantity of fixed air, or *acide charbonneux*, which formed was 95.28 cubic inches, weighing 1 gros 23.28 grains. [Lavoisier copied this data from his notebook erroneously. The statement should read "was 137.094 cubic inches, weighing 95.28 grains, or 1 gros 23.28 grains." The error remained in the published version, but does not affect the outcome.]
>
> Finally, the quantity of water formed was 41.8 grains.[29]

If we compare this presentation with the original tabulation (see above, p. 273), its anomalous character leaps out at us. The values for the vital air and fixed air are identical to those in the notebook; but the quantity of spirit of wine burned is only one-third as much; and the quantity of water formed is not that of the original balance calculation, but the far different result of the second method of calculation. How had Lavoisier put together this hybrid representation of two different balance sheets? We cannot ascertain precisely what he was *thinking*, but what he *did* was to accept as the correct quantity of water formed the figure reached from the quantity of vital air available to form it, rather than the figure derived from the overall balance of substances entering into and produced in the process. The reason for his choice is fairly obvious; for that method was based on his theory of the formation of water, an interpretation of the chemical change involved as the combination of inflammable air assumed to be contained in the spirit of wine, with vital air present in the combustion vessel. The other figure was an empirical one, based only on the more general principle of the equality of the products with the substances entering a chemical change. To arrive at the figure of 32.7 grains for the spirit of wine consumed, he had simply subtracted from the measured consumption the difference between the two calculated results for the quantity of water formed (102.62 − 41.8 = 60.82; 93.5 grains − 60.80 = 32.7 grains of spirit of wine). What did the difference between those two calculated results represent? Lavoisier may already have had in mind what it was, but the calculations assumed only that it was present originally in the fluid burned, that it either burned or was vaporized along with the spirit of wine, and that it did not appear among the products attributable to the combustion of the spirit of wine itself.

On the basis of this formulation of the material balance, Lavoisier went on to calculate the composition of the spirit of wine:

> If one supposes, as I have established elsewhere, that water is formed of 856 parts of vital air and 144 of inflammable air [there is no explanation given for this slight deviation from the 85:15 ratio that he used most of the time after the large-scale water experiment], one finds that the 32.7 grains of spirit of wine that were burned in that experiment are composed as follows:

Charbon	26.68
Inflammable air	6.02
Total	32.7[30]

Lavoisier had already obtained these values for the quantities of inflammable air and of *matière charbonneuse* during the course of the second method of calculating the quantity of water formed that he recorded in his notebook. The *matière charbonneuse* was derived from the quantity and composition of fixed air; the inflammable air from the vital air left over to form the water. Now, by interpreting the total of these two substances as making up the spirit of wine burned, he had reached for this substance the goal, expressed in the introduction to this draft, to "determine with precision . . . the quantity of inflammable air and of *principe charbonneux*" that such combustible substances contain.[31]

Lavoisier was not satisfied with this solution for much longer than it took him to write it out. Before writing anything more, he crossed out the composition of the spirit of wine, together with the paragraph introducing it. He also replaced the value of 32.7 grains of spirit of wine in the balance statement preceding that paragraph with one approximating the original measured consumption (not 1 gros 21.5 as in the laboratory notebook, but 1 gros 18 grains. Perhaps he reduced the amount slightly to take into account his suspicion that a small amount of spirit of wine vaporized.) In place of the statement "The quantity of water formed was 41.8 grains," he put "The quantity of water existing under the jar after the combustion was 1 gros 27.12 grains," followed by the explanation that he could not collect and weigh that water, so that he had calculated it. Allowing for the same small reduction he had made in the spirit of wine consumed, this was the quantity of water he had calculated in the notebook from the overall balance, but had labeled at that time "water formed." Then he rewrote the composition of spirit of wine as follows:

Charbon		26.68
Inflammable air		6.02
Water		57.30
Total	1 gros	18.00 grains[32]

These alterations reveal transparently the manner in which Lavoisier changed his point of view in the very process of expressing it on paper. The larger result for the quantity of water that he had in the first place calculated from the overall balance of materials as "formed" in the combustion, he now treated as water simply present at the end of the combustion. The smaller quantity calculated by the second method now represented the true amount formed. The difference between them must therefore represent water not formed in the process. If not formed then, it must have been present already in the spirit of wine, and merely vaporized. That is how he now represented the composition of the spirit of wine. It contained not only *matière charbonneuse* and inflammable air, but water as well. A little further on in the draft he gave verbal expression to his conception by listing the quantity as that which "existed in the spirit of wine before the combustion."[33]

We are here surprisingly close to the nascent[34] moment of an issue that came to pervade all of organic chemistry for more than half a century. In his first set of combustion analyses undertaken with the main objective of determining the quantitative proportions of the constituents of plant substances, Lavoisier was confronted with the necessity to choose between alternative ways to represent how these constituents compose the substance. He chose one, quickly abandoned it, and chose another in its place. For many years afterward uncertainties reigned about similar choices.

What conceptual distinction underlay Lavoisier's decision? What did it mean to choose between excluding this preformed water from, or including it in, the composition of spirit of wine? We immediately think of the problem in terms of differences between chemical combination and solution, but we risk assuming several layers of conceptual development that lay still in the future. Did Lavoisier mean only that water existed in the spirit of wine in the old sense that Geoffroy had had in mind: that is, simply that one could never rectify distilled spirit of wine enough to free it entirely of the water which accompanied it? Or did he now envision spirit of wine as an entity that included water in some more intimate combination? The very representation of the water as a definite proportion of the total composition would seem to us to imply the latter, but we must not assume that Lavoisier was explicitly aware of all the implications embedded in his representation. Nor should we project backward onto his view of the situation his later statements on the subject; for he may not yet have formulated them. Since he did not leave a discussion of the grounds for his choice at this time, we have only a decision embodied in a change in the way he *proceeded.* This change may have been the outward manifestation of a conceptual shift of which he left no verbal trace; but it may have been that to change the visible representation of the situation in his text was all that he decided to do, that no deeper mental transformation lurked behind it. When we regard the history of science as a history of ideas, we are predisposed to attribute change to conceptual shifts, and to assume that procedures change as a consequence of those shifts. More often than we commonly appreciate, I believe, the procedural changes are germinal. Acting as precedents, the procedures the scientist adopts, without necessarily thinking out thoroughly the grounds for doing so, shape future modes of investigation whose conceptual implications may unfold gradually only in the aftermath.

Scrutinizing, independently of Lavoisier, the discrepancy between the two quantities of water at which he arrived through what he regarded initially as two methods for calculating the same quantity, we may notice another way to resolve the anomaly, which would have preserved the original designation of both quantities as water formed in the combustion. One might have retained the larger figure as the true measure of the total amount of the water formed, and inferred that the smaller figure represented that portion of the water arising from the combination of oxygen, supplied from the vital air in the vessel, with a portion of the inflammable principle available in the spirit of wine. The remainder of the oxygen necessary to saturate the inflammable principle would have had to come from the only other substance consumed, the spirit of wine itself. This line of reasoning would lead to the conclusion that spirit of wine is composed of *matière charbonneuse,* inflammable air, and oxygen. Why did Lavoisier disregard this alternative? The only answer that can be gleaned from the surviving record is that it apparently did not occur to him. The structure of his experiment; the way in which he brought his data to bear on the calculation of the quantity of water involved in the process; the manner in which the anomaly arose and his response to the difficulty; the traditional view of spirit of wine as normally containing water, passed along from a time in which that water was considered elementary and therefore necessarily preformed, all concurred to guide him toward a solution utilizing the idea that water existed in the spirit of wine. Nothing either in the contingent circumstances of the experiment, or in his general theoretical structure, would direct his attention to the possibility that spirit of wine contains oxygen. He was, after all, assimilating this situation to other combustions he had dealt with in the past, and treating the spirit of wine as a preeminently combustible body. Combustible bodies in general, his system taught, did not *contain* oxygen; they combined with oxygen derived from other sources. The representation of this particular substance as containing water in its composition in turn so shaped his approach to the composition of plant substances in general that, as we shall see, he later had great difficulty coming to see the situation in another way; and Lavoisier's orientation toward the question of whether water preexisted in plant and animal substances resonated through much of the controversies about organic composition for decades to come. Seldom do the records of scientific research reveal more clearly the way in which the local circumstances of a germinal investigation can induce a mental pattern that long outlasts the circumstances themselves.

After substituting the table which included water in the composition of spirit of wine for the original table without it, Lavoisier added a second table reducing the same composition to the base of one pound of spirit of wine. He then began a discussion apparently intended to show that the proportion of water to spirit of wine he had previously obtained in his large-scale combustion experiments was compatible with the composition he had now established. At the bottom of the page, however, he broke off, and drew a line through the entire page, thus discarding his table of composition for a second time. He had evidently decided to make another major change. This time the alteration involved not the way of viewing the composition of spirit of wine itself, but the way of depicting that composition on paper. In order to do so he had first to introduce five symbols to stand for the substances involved:

▽ water	ch *substance charbonneuse*
🜁 vital air	▽̶ fixed air

Then, he went on, if one assumes the proportions he had previously established for the composition of fixed air and of water, "One can make the following calculations":

$$\overset{S}{\nabla}\ 90\text{ grains} + 🜁\ 104.4\text{ grains} = ▽̶\ 95.28\text{ grains} + \nabla\ x$$

(He used the traditional symbol $\overset{S}{\nabla}$ for spirit of wine. The symbols he introduced were, in fact, adaptations of such traditional chemical symbols to newly defined substances. The weights used were the same as those in his revised balance statement, except that he showed them as grains rather than as gros and grains.)

> This equation does not assume anything except that the weight of the matter is the same before and after the combustion, which is demonstrated equally by reason and by facts. It follows from it

> that [He then crossed out this revealing statement and continued directly from the equation itself];
> from which one easily deduces
>
> $\nabla = 99.12$ grains
>
> If one then substitutes for the 95.28 grains of fixed air in this equation the quantity of oxygen principle and of *matière charbonneuse* which enter into its composition, one will have
>
> $\overset{S}{\nabla}$ 90 grains + $\triangle$ 104.4 grains = $\triangle$ 68.60 grains
> + ch 26.68 grains + ∇ 99.12 grains

Lavoisier went on to deduce, from the weights shown in this equation, the quantity of vital air left over to form water, the quantity of water actually formed in the combustion (which now came out to 42.12 grains instead of 41.8, because he went back to his standard proportions of eighty-five parts oxygen to fifteen of inflammable air in water), and finally the quantity of water which "existed in the spirit of wine before the combustion." For these deductions, however, he reverted to verbal description and a conventional tabular format. Following that he showed the composition of spirit of wine in the familiar manner.[35]

The sentence just following the first of the two equations, which Lavoisier eliminated, makes clear what these expressions meant to him. They were nothing more than a new way to represent the principle he had always assumed, that the total weight of matter before and after a chemical change is the same. It is to us, however, immediately obvious both that the new representation must have had some significance for Lavoisier deeper than he stated in his draft, and that it is the germinal point for another trail that traverses the whole of modern chemistry.

It would be beyond the bounds of this book to elucidate the origins of Lavoisier's customary tabular form of representing the same principle. Gillispie has pointed out that those who are prone to see social factors shaping science suggest that Lavoisier drew his balance sheet approach to chemistry from financial accounting practices, and point to similar accounts he kept for the input, labor, purchases, and yields of the experimental farm he established on his country estate. Others, including Gillispie himself, who prefer to see scientific practices derive from past scientific practices, find the source of Lavoisier's method in the work of Joseph Black.[36] Both types of explanation are customarily given at too general a level to be convincing. Lavoisier utilized the balance sheet form regularly, and assumed the principle behind it, from the famous 1770 memoirs on water onward.[37] The sources of his conviction and practice must be sought in a richer study than has yet been carried out of his training and experience before 1770, including his work as an analytical chemist and his extensive knowledge of the older chemical literature.[38]

If the roots of Lavoisier's balance sheet approach were deep, and perhaps intuitive, the above effort to represent that approach in a dramatically different form appears deliberate and traceable to more immediate influences. It is well known that he greatly admired the precision and rigor of mathematics, and we might therefore ascribe these equations to a desire to enhance the appearance of his methods by glossing them over with the aura of a mathematical form. There are grounds, however, to suggest a more specific source and a stronger reason for his approach. It must be more than a coincidence that he thought of it at a time when he had been collaborating closely with two mathematicians over a period of four years. He must have been impressed by Laplace's use of algebraic equations to provide the theoretical foundations for their joint memoir on heat. More immediately germane to the present situation, however, were the algebraic methods Meusnier used to help him design and interpret his own experiments. A particularly cogent example is an analysis Meusnier wrote out on four sides of a loose folded sheet for Lavoisier for an experiment planned to decompose water by means of spirit of wine in the gun barrel apparatus. After setting up algebraic expressions for the weights of the constituents of spirit of wine, fixed air, and water, in which he designated the inflammable air of the preformed water in the spirit of wine as the unknown, x, Meusnier derived further expressions for the quantities of fixed air and inflammable air that the decomposition would yield. He then advised Lavoisier on how the proportion of water required to spirit of wine used, as well as the amounts of the aeriform products, would vary with the quantity of water existing in the spirit of wine. From his calculations Meusnier was able to recommend to Lavoisier not only the proportion of water to spirit of wine he should use, but also the most effective and least costly method to absorb the expected quantities of fixed air.[39] Such analyses must have led Lavoisier to realize not only the general usefulness of algebra to chemistry, but the flexibility that algebraic representations of chemical changes might lend to the kinds of calculations he himself customarily made on his experimental results.

If such experiences may have inspired Lavoisier to attempt to exchange the balance sheet for the equation, in what sense was the expression Lavoisier formulated in this draft an equation? It contained the mathematical symbol for equality, it included knowns and an unknown, and Lavoisier made a simple substitution in it of one expression for the quantitatively equivalent expression. In algebriac fashion he "solved" for the unknown. Thus it did display attributes of an algebraic equation. It was, however, a very limited form of equation. Unlike those that Meusnier worked out for him, it included no variables or algebraic coefficients allowing for the insertion of different constants. Lavoisier formulated it not as a generalized solution, but as the representation of a specific set of data. It remained, in effect, a chemical balance sheet in the image of mathematical symbols. Lavoisier's chemical equation, in this nascent form, was only analogous to an algebraic equation. We should reiterate, however, that once a connection by analogy has been made, it can be suggestive of further development. The analogy between an algebraic equation and Lavoisier's principle that the weights of material before and after a chemical change are equal could suggest ways of analyzing chemical changes which the conventional balance sheet could not.

As mentioned above, Lavoisier presented the composition of the spirit of wine itself, the object of the investigation, as an ordinary table. In the revised pages of the draft following the equations, he gave three forms of the table: for the actual amount of spirit of wine burned, for 1 pound, and for 100 pounds. With the slight alterations caused by going back to the ratio 85:15 for the constituents of water, the computation for one pound of spirit of wine was:

Charbon		4 ounces	5 gros	68 grains
Inflammable air		1	0	71
Water		10	1	5
Total	1 pound	0	0	0

As in other cases, Lavoisier presented these results with what appears to our eyes a specious claim to minute accuracy, even while acknowledging in his manuscript, "I do not pretend that this is a rigorous method for analyzing spirit of wine." He called attention to two causes of uncertainty: the vaporization of the spirit of wine, and the fact that he could not collect and measure the water formed in the experiment. He even suggested that there might be included in the composition of spirit of wine a very small quantity of some "other principles which escape this type of analysis." Almost in the same breath, however, he maintained that he had "reason to believe that the results are quite exact."[40] In the ambivalence of his own attitude toward his results we see here another manifestation of the constant tension between Lavoisier's abiding faith in the fundamental principle that the weights of materials before and after an operation are the same, and his frequent inability fully to verify it; between the paramount importance he placed on precise quantitative results, and the difficulties he encountered in achieving them.

III

Just as the experiment on olive oil had caused Lavoisier far less trouble than those on spirit of wine did, so was the interpretation of the results less problematic for him. As seen above, he had already in his notebook calculated that the results were consistent with the assumption that olive oil is composed entirely of *matière charbonneuse* and inflammable air. His subsequent finding that spirit of wine contains water did not prompt him to raise the possibility that olive oil also does. In the draft of his memoir he entered the results essentially as he had recorded them in the notebook, then represented the material balance in an equation corresponding to the one he had devised for spirit of wine. (The symbol for oil was ○°○.) He solved similarly for *x*, the quantity of water formed, justified that procedure again by invoking the principle that "the weight of material contained in the jar is equal before and after the combustion, which I regard as obvious," and similarly substituted the constituents of fixed air for fixed air itself in a second equation. Then, apparently remembering the remark in his notebook that the result of the experiment could be made to conform more closely to his previous results for the composition of water if one supposed "the quantity of oil burned to be greater by a quarter of a grain" than the weighed quantity, he replaced the figure 18.6 grains that he had at first used in his equation and text by 19 grains. Rather disingenuously, he did not mention in his text that he was making such a correction, but simply removed the statement "the quantity of oil burned in this experiment was found to be 18.6 grains," and wrote instead "the quantity of oil burned was not very large, it was exactly 19 grains."[41] If we recalculate the proportions of water from these revised results for the olive oil experiment, we find that Lavoisier achieved his end; for the proportion between the vital air (18.552 grains) available to form water and the inflammable air (3.2940 grains), as calculated from the difference between the new total for oil consumed and the *matière charbonneuse* in the fixed air, comes out almost exactly to the 85:15 ratio he obviously sought. We shall see a little further on how determined he was to preserve that exact conformity.

In the draft of his memoir Lavoisier moved from the discussion of olive oil to a final section on the combustion of wax. "The same method applied to the candle," he wrote, "has given me the exact quantity of water that formed during the combustion."[42] His next sentence indicated that the method was not actually quite the same, for with a candle he needed only the ordinary single inverted jar to carry out the combustion. The discussion nevertheless conveys the impression that this examination of wax was a continuation of the same recent investigation that had resulted in the preceding sections on spirit of wine and olive oil. What he actually did was to dig out the two combustion experiments on wax that he had carried out the year before and published in his memoir on the composition of fixed air.[43] Then he had already calculated the composition of wax, but only along the way to a determination of the proportions of fixed air. Now he recast that old data to fit his present objective. Once again, therefore, he was constructing a coherent single investigation on paper by joining the results of experiments carried out as parts of separate investigations.

Although the data from these older experiments remained the same, the results Lavoisier now derived from them were much modified, not only because he used them for a different purpose, but because intervening developments had altered the conditions under which they were to be interpreted. Originally he had derived from these experiments values for the composition of fixed air that deviated significantly from the 72:28 ratio he ultimately accepted as the best expression of the combined results of all of the experiments performed to that end. Reworking these data now, he had to accept those proportions as given, with the consequence that other values he had previously calculated could no longer hold. Previously he had treated the overall deficit between the wax and vital air consumed, and the fixed air formed, as the measure of the water formed. From a value for the composition of water that he later discarded, he had derived the quantity of vital air contained in that water, and used the difference to determine the composition of fixed air. Now he could no longer immediately assume that the deficit in the overall balance was the water formed, because from the established composition of fixed air he could calculate independently the quantity of vital air available to form water and, from the established composition of water, the amount of water that could in this way be formed. That is, just as in the experiment on spirit of wine, there were two methods to compute the same quantity; but by the time he carried them out on the data from the wax experiments, he had learned to give precedence to the second of these methods. When he made these calculations, he found that "one cannot entirely attribute the deficit to the water which has formed." The actual deficit was 22.297 grains, whereas the amount of water that could have arisen in the process was only 21.082 grains.[44]

This was hardly a discrepancy of the order of magnitude that he had encountered with spirit of wine, and if he had not encountered that other one first it is unlikely that Lavoisier would have seen in this very small one reason to doubt that the two results represented the same quantity. The prior experience had, however, sensitized him to the possibility that there might be additional water preexisting in such a combustible body, and he wondered, therefore, if the same situation applied to wax. "That difference would be very well explained," he wrote, "if one supposed that 1.215 grains of water existed in 21.9 grains of wax, and it was on that idea that I at first fastened." (Since the section on wax has been lost from the original draft, we cannot tell whether or not Lavoisier had still been holding this "first" view when he wrote out his initial analysis of the situation). When he carried out the same recalculations on the data from the second of the two old experiments on wax, however, the discrepancy he detected was in the opposite sense. The quantity of water determined from the overall balance was 0.278 grains *less* than that calculated from the quantity of vital air available. This tiny difference must be due to "errors inevitable in this type of experiment." This outcome led him to think that the first discrepancy too might represent only an experimental error; but he found it difficult to make up his mind. "It is not at all decided," he admitted in his manuscript, if water enters into the composition of the wax, no more than in the case of oil. Whatever the case may be, in the state of incertitude in which the difference between these two results leaves us, and until I have been able to obtain more certain foundations, I shall give the composition of the wax as it results from each experiment.

. . . .

Composition of a hundred pounds of wax according to the first experiment

Substance Charbonneuse	80 pounds	0 ounces	1 gros	53 grains
Inflammable air	14	7	0	22
Water	5	8	5	69
Total	100			

Composition of a hundred pounds of wax according to the second experiment

Substance Charbonneuse	85 pounds	1 ounce	7 gros	15 grains
Inflammable air	14	14	0	57
Total	100[45]			

Lavoisier's plan simply to report two divergent results, implying not only different quantitative values for the composition of wax, but qualitatively different interpretations of its composition, appears strangely indecisive. It seems quite out of character with his usual tendency to nudge his data as necessary to meet his theoretical needs. In this case the discrepancies were minor compared with others he had readily discounted. His exceptional response to this situation provides a very revealing insight into the relation between scientific theory and experiment, because his split decision clearly derived from the fact that his theoretical position itself did not provide the unequivocable guide through experimental difficulties for him here that it so often did. He had just previously concluded that spirit of wine contains water in its composition. There was no possiblity of ascribing the major discrepancy in that case between the two calculations for water formed to experimental error. On the other hand, he had concluded that olive oil contains only inflammable air and *matière charbonneuse,* and the experimental results provided a nearly perfect fit with that interpretation. When he came to wax, therefore, he had one precedent for each of the possible inferences to be drawn from the ambiguous outcome of his calculations. The combination of unclear theoretical direction and equivocal experimental evidence left Lavoisier stranded on the fence.

Sometime after the fair copy of his memoir had been made, Lavoisier changed the value he accepted for the density of vital air from 0.47317 to 0.5 grains per cubic inch. The reasons for this alteration were probably unrelated to these combustion experiments, but it required him to recompute all of their results, because he had based the weights of vital air he utilized in the calculations on the measured volume change multiplied by the density. When he did the calculations for spirit of wine over, the only effect was to alter the final proportions somewhat. For olive oil, the situation was more delicate. As we may recall, it had been particularly important to him that the proportions for water deducible from this experiment come out in exact accord with his established ratio of 85:15. In order to attain that fit he had corrected the measured weight of 18.6 grains of oil to 19 grains. The alterations required by the new density for vital air now threatened to upset the concordance he had reached. By examining the various alterations he made in the values shown in his equation for the combustion of olive oil (which I have not reproduced, because viewed by itself it is only confusing), one can glimpse his efforts to hold onto that agreement. The previous quantities he had figured for the vital air in the water (18.569) and inflammable air (3.276) were in fact precisely in the desired proportion. Now, after making the necessary change in the equation for the quantity of vital air consumed, he replaced these two numbers for the constituents of the water with the figures 21.4062 for the vital air and 3.7776 for the inflammable air.[46] These numbers add up to the total quantity of water derived from the overall balance of materials before and after the combustion, and they too are precisely in the ratio 85:15. Lavoisier must have obtained them therefore by utilizing that ratio to calculate the quantities of these constituents in the total quantity of water. Unfortunately this quantity of vital air deduced this way is less than what he would have obtained by subtracting from the total of the vital air consumed the quantity accounted for in the fixed air. If he had taken that value for vital air (it would have been 21.89 grains) and obtained the inflammable air (3.29 grains) by subtracting it from the weight of the water, in order to satisfy the balances, the proportions for water would have come out to about 87:13. To us, that does not appear much further off than Lavoisier often came out, but it clearly was not close enough for him. It was to eliminate about the same magnitude of discrepancy that he had previously raised his estimate of the olive oil burned. It was necessary to adjust the results again. He made two further changes in the data. He increased the quantity of olive oil consumed again, to 19.25 grains, and he changed the volume of fixed air produced from 80.711 to 79½ cubic inches. Recalculated on that basis, the numbers for the inflammable air (4.05) and the vital air (22.94) contained in the water both upheld very nearly the desired ratio (22.94:4.05::84.96:15.04), and allowed the other balances to come out right.[47]

From a long distance, Lavoisier's actions in this situation may appear trivial or inappropriate: trivial, because the corrections involved were minor compared with the inaccuracies expected in such an experiment carried out only once; and inappropriate because he trimmed the observed quantities in order to obtain and preserve a desired fit. To the former criticism one can reply that the question of how much accuracy one can expect to extract from a given experiment is a matter for subjective judgment until there exist other independent checks, and that Lavoisier was so much closer to the circumstances than we can be that we should be reluctant to judge the effort superfluous. Regarding the second, it is not self-evident that the quantitative values which stood closest to the empirical measurements were necessarily the most reliable determinants of the quantities relevant to the results. From his experience with a type of experiment of which he was the sole master, Lavoisier had abundant reason to suspect that there were always liable to be unknown factors interfering with his measurements. The composition of water was one of the quantitative values he had worked hardest to establish, and, of the constants on which he relied, probably the one in which he currently placed the most confidence. If he therefore "corrected" measured values so that they would produce the same outcome for water, he probably did not doubt that the resulting figures for the olive oil burned and the fixed air produced were closer to the real amounts than were the untouched figures recorded in his laboratory notebook. That he carried out these manipulations not to misrepresent his results to others, but to satisfy himself, is clear from the fact that neither in any of the versions of the calculations nor in the text of the memoir he was preparing did he mention that the quantities representing the vital air and inflammable air in the water were in exactly the desired proportion. It was, however, probably that hidden agreement that led him to state publicly, "I have reason to think that the results I am about to present leave nothing to be desired with respect to their accuracy."[48] In following Lavoisier through the subtle maneuvers behind that assertion, we are not exposing a minor scientific fraud. We are witnessing the way in which a dauntless explorer contrived to maintain the integrity of his enterprise as he eased himself past another of the countless experimental pitfalls strewn along his path.

For the composition of wax the change in the density for vital air added no new problems for Lavoisier. On the contrary, it relieved him of the dilemma he had been facing. By increasing the total weight of vital air consumed, this change provided for a larger quantity of vital air left over from the amount accounted for in the fixed air. Now the quantity of water into which he calculated this vital air could enter fell only 0.5 grains short of the quantity present after the combustion according to the overall balance method. That was no longer enough to worry about, and Lavoisier consequently escaped from his quandary over whether wax does or does not contain water. It is possible, of course, that he made the decision first that wax does not contain water, then altered the density of vital air as necessary to eliminate the discrepancy. That interpretation entails the corollary, however, that he created for himself the previously described difficulty for olive oil from which he then had to extricate himself. It would have been cavalier for Lavoisier to alter a constant that he used very often in his analyses on no other grounds than to make one particular result come out as he wanted it to. The most plausible interpretation is that a change he made coincidentally happened to solve this problem. At any rate, he rewrote the section on wax to show both experiments leading to a composition containing only *matière charbonneuse* and inflammable air, and left no hint of his recent indecision.[49] From a presentist viewpoint we can regard this development as fortuitously unfortunate, for it drew him away from the "correct" inference that wax and oils do contain small proportions of oxygen. The significance of these first analyses of their kind lies, however, not so much in the correctness or incorrectness of their results in detail as in the demonstration of the general power of the method.

In order to incorporate the changes due to the new density for vital air, Lavoisier rewrote a large portion of the fair copy of his memoir. The chemical equations that had embellished his first two drafts did not survive this further revision; for he put the newly recalculated results back into standard balance sheet form. We can only speculate whether he found the new equations impracticable or cumbersome, whether he feared they might distract readers from the main objective of his paper, whether someone else dissuaded him from using them, or whether he just felt more comfortable with the familiar representation. Whatever his reasons for withdrawing this bold innovation, privately he did not give up the connection he had made between the principle that the matter before and after a chemical change is the same, and the usefulness of algebraic equations.

* * *

There is no record of when, or if, Lavoisier read at the Academy the memoir whose formation we have followed in this chapter.[50] It was published in the Memoirs for 1784, appearing actually in 1787. It is reasonable to suppose that he wrote it not long after carrying out the experiments on spirit of wine and olive oil, in the late spring of 1785. As the first account of the combustion of several plant substances to establish their quantitative composition, this paper is justly regarded as the historical starting point for that mode of elementary analysis around which the field of organic chemistry eventually emerged. It was not, however, necessarily Lavoisier's intention, when he carried out the experiments incorporated in this memoir, or even when he began to write it, to produce the first analyses of the elementary composition of organic substances. The title of the paper suggests nothing of the kind. It refers only to "the combination of the oxygen principle with spirit of wine, oil, and different combustible bodies." In the first paragraph he referred back to his earlier discovery that the water produced by burning spirit of wine weighs more than the spirit of wine. He then completed his introduction of the subject of his paper by writing, "I have since recognized that this phenomenon was a constant feature of almost all combustions, that one equally obtains from oils and from wax a considerably greater weight of water than of the combustible which has been consumed." He therefore appeared to be taking as his subject area combustible bodies in general, although he could not really have meant to include all types of combustible bodies. Only after writing out this paragraph, or perhaps even after writing all of the draft, did he add the qualification that this phenomenon "takes place constantly in the combustion of all plant and animal matters."[51] (In the fair copy this was changed to the slightly more modest, but still grossly exaggerated, claim that he had recognized the phenomenon in "a great number of plant and animal matters.")[52] The domain of his investigation now appeared to be plant and animal substances, but it still unfolded only gradually in the discussion that the main objective was to determine the quantitative composition of three such substances rather than to show how much water each combustion produced. All of these idiosyncracies of the memoir suggest that Lavoisier did not set out on this investigation with the clearly defined purpose of performing the first combustion analyses of plant substances, but only gradually came to appreciate that this was the main significance of what he had achieved. That is the way of many innovative ventures in the history of science.

11

Nature's Operations

Viewed from a distance, Lavoisier appears to have made, around 1785, a distinct transition in his research interests. The repertoire of problems concerning combustion and respiration that had occupied him for a dozen years gave way to a research program oriented around the chemistry of plants. From close range, however, the questions on which he had focused until then, especially his recent fixation on the composition of water, seem to interpenetrate so intimately with the investigation of substances and processes from the plant domain that it is hard to tell where the former ended and the latter began. Ends and means remained subtly interchangeable. Lavoisier himself regarded the same investigations sometimes as the continuation of his study of combustion; sometimes as part of his primordial program to identify the "airs" given off by various substances; sometimes as further examples of the processes which compose and decompose water; and sometimes as an examination of "nature's operations." He came only slowly to reorganize his views of the divisions of his enterprise. As his perspective shifted, plant substances and processes came to seem more than just further opportunities to elucidate the general problems he had already been studying; and the solutions he had already reached for these problems came to appear more as the source for methods to apply in order to establish a new chemistry of plants. The mingling of purposes during this period of reorientation characterized especially the next stage in his study of fermentation.

As he set out to pursue more persistently the problem of fermentation on which he had already made several abortive starts, Lavoisier's first need was to establish the conditions most suitable for studying the process. The usual spirituous fermentation, which was nearly synonymous with wine making, began with the freshly expressed juice of grapes, or other ripe fruits. When allowed to stand at a temperature between ten and twelve degrees Réaumur, the juice began after a time to ferment spontaneously, disengaging bubbles at an increasing rate. Macquer defined fermentation, in accord with these characteristics, as "an intestine movement which excites itself, with the aid of heat and appropriate fluidity, between the integral and constituent parts of certain highly composed bodies." Since all of the fermentable plant juices have a sugary taste, sugar itself was considered "very susceptible to fermentation."[1] Lavoisier decided to use not these juices, but sugar alone, for his study of fermentation. As he recalled several years later, he wished to determine the "constituent principles of the fermentable body"; but "a rigorous analysis of the highly composed fruit juices would be impossible. I chose the simplest of all the bodies susceptible of fermentation, sugar, with whose nature I had already been familiar."[2] A more specific motivation at the time was his idea that in fermentation the *substance charbonneuse* contained in sugar decomposes water, forming fixed air with the oxygen principle and releasing the inflammable air to form, somehow, the spirit of wine. The sugar he used was cane sugar, because sugar cane was the source from which sugar could be extracted most abundantly, in purest form.[3] It was not yet evident that the sugar so obtained was a different species from the sugar contained in grape juice.

Although the advantage of using sugar to reduce fermentation to its simplest possible form was clear to Lavoisier in principle, he found it not so easy in practice to induce the sugar to ferment. In 1781, as we have seen, he had already attempted to do so at least once without success.[4] A measure of his subsequent difficulties is suggested in a manuscript found among his papers, but evidently written by someone else familiar with his work. In this "Collection of facts concerning fermentation and its different effects," the author reported that "purified sugar yielded no ardent spirit and did not ferment at all during a long and closely followed experiment of M. Lavoisier lasting more than a year."[5] There is no record in Lavoisier's notebooks specifically identifiable as the experiment in question here, so that we cannot tell just when he carried it out, or what procedures he followed. Since the manuscript also alluded to his experiments on spirit of wine discussed in the preceding chapter above, it is reasonable to infer that he experienced this arduous failure during the period between 1783 and 1785 when his public statements indicate he was turning his attention to the subject.

On May 30, about two weeks after finishing his combustion experiments on spirit of wine and olive oil, Lavoisier began an experiment evidently intended to find the way around the stubborn obstacle he had encountered. Despite the ordinary characterization of fermentation as a spontaneous "movement" of the fermentable substance, it was generally known that sometimes another substance stimulated the fermentation. Macquer, in fact, defined a "ferment" as "a substance actually in fermentation, or which has a very great disposition to ferment and which one uses to determine or excite the fermentation of another body." The examples he gave were the froth of fermenting beer, and a "*pâte* of well-leavened flour."[6] Earlier in the century Boerhaave had listed "yeast, fresh flowers of malt liquor or wine which are thrown up to the top whilst they are in the act of fermentation" as ferments.[7] It was clearly the need for a stimulating agent that Lavoisier had in mind now as he "dissolved four ounces of sugar in two pounds of water in order to make various tests on the substances most suitable to excite fermentation."[8] He did not, however, utilize the commonly recognized "ferments," undoubtedly because their own complexity would seem to run counter to his desire to simplify the process. Instead he chose iron filings, the very pure *charbon de Bourdenne,* and cream of tartar. Of these three, the rationale for cream of tartar is the most obvious. This solid, acidic salt was deposited from fermenting wine after the first, most active, stage was finished.[9] Lavoisier might well have supposed that its prior presence with the fermentation juice could activate the process. The composition of cream of tartar had also been worked out, so that if it proved to excite fermentation he would have a relatively simple chemical system to study. The choice of iron filings is less easy to explain, although it might have had something to do with the widely known property of plant acids to dissolve them, and especially the fact that tartaric acid formed with them an unusual soluble tartar.[10] A possible theoretical reason for using *charbon de Bourdenne* is that Lavoisier might have hoped that it would add to the water-decomposing action of the *matière charbonneuse* in the sugar itself.

Lavoisier placed two ounces of his solution of sugar and water into a twelve-cubic-inch jar filled with mercury and inverted over mercury. To two other equal portions of the solution he added respectively the iron filings and the *charbon* and placed them similarly over mercury.

In the first jar, "from May 30 until June 24 there was no appearance of the formation of air. During the day of June 24 one introduced a little cream of tartar. By the twenty-ninth a very small portion of air had been produced." There had been, meanwhile, only slightly more activity in the solution containing *charbon,* but more striking results in that containing iron filings. Bubbles of air had begun to form after a few days, and by June 11 they equaled at least half the volume of the solution. By June 29 their total volume was more than twice that of the solution. Lavoisier then tested the air that had formed. "This air detonated lightly, with a sound like barking. It precipitated limewater weakly, and caustic alkali absorbed about one-twelfth of it." These tests thus indicated that the air contained a little fixed air and inflammable air. Lavoisier noticed also that "the water had a sugary taste, mingled with the taste of iron. The iron had not become rusted." From these observations he inferred that "the oxygen has separated from the inflammable air to unite with the sugar and form acid of sugar, which dissolved the iron." To verify this interpretation he precipitated the iron from the solution with fixed alkali.[11]

Lavoisier's hope of fermenting sugar with one of these simple agents was obviously dashed. The cream of tartar and the *charbon* excited little activity at all, and what the iron filings excited was not a usual spirituous fermentation.

It produced, not fixed air and spirit of wine, but fixed air, inflammable air and, as he thought, acid of sugar. This outcome apparently diverted him from his original purpose in devising the tests. His subsequent actions suggest that what mostly fixed his attention by the end of the experiment was that although the sugar to which he had added the iron filings did not ferment, it decomposed water in another way, combining with its oxygen principle. A feature of this process which probably particularly impressed him was that it represented a combustion taking place without contact with the external air, since it had occurred in a jar filled with mercury. Circling back to his long-standing preoccupation with the decomposition of water, he next tried out whether he could obtain the same effect by placing sulfur in water with iron filings. "It appeared," he concluded from this experiment, "that the sulfur becomes vitriolic acid at the expense of the water. It would, however, not be impossible that an iron calx and inflammable air formed; but in any case it is certain that there is a decomposition of the water and that the inflammable air is due to that decomposition."[12]

II

It is difficult to identify a directing thread in Lavoisier's experimental activities during the second half of 1785. The laboratory record is unusually sparse, and gives evidence only of rather sporadic additions to lines of investigation with which he had already been concerned for varying lengths of time.[13] It may well be that he was even busier than normal with other activities. In June he brought together all of the results of his previously published work on combustion for his "decisive attack" on the defenders of the phlogiston theory. In the same month he announced that he had repeated some experiments by Henry Cavendish on the combination of nitrogen and oxygen brought about by an electric spark.[14] During the second half of the year, however, he presented no more memoirs based on new work. Serving as director of the Academy for the year 1785, he became deeply involved in a reform of its organization.[15] Planning and implementing that change must have occupied much of his energy. It is also possible that after reaching the culmination of the long drive to establish his theory of combustion he needed some time to refocus his priorities and build up momentum for another set of experimental objectives.

Among the few experiments in the notebooks for the period between June 30 and the end of the year there were only two which relate to the issues we have been following. Lavoisier carried out one experiment on acetous fermentation, the process which he regarded, along with Macquer, as a further stage in spirituous fermentation, producing an acid. Lavoisier found out that acetous fermentation will not take place without contact with external air. On Christmas

Day he got out the ice calorimeter and made a single measurement on the heat released during the combustion of olive oil.[16]

During the first three months of 1786 Lavoisier returned to the decomposition of water by means of *charbon.*[17] The novel feature of his new investigation was that he carried out the critical experiment in the absence of air. From the situation we can surmise that he was pursuing a line of enquiry which had opened up with his observation that sugar decomposed water without air, and which he had continued with the similar experiment using sulfur. Since he had already theorized in the spring of 1784 that, when sugar ferments, it is the *charbon* contained in it which decomposes the water, this action of sugar on water would be expected to turn his thoughts again to the action of *charbon* on water. It may also have been this conjunction of observation and inference which led him to think about Priestley's experiments on charcoal. During an extensive study of the formation and properties of charcoal, Priestley had long ago shown that when charcoal is made from wood, inflammable air is released, in larger quantities the more strongly it is heated. Later he discovered that charcoal exposed to air gradually regains weight, and that by subjecting it to heat in an earthen retort he could again expel air from it. The weight which the charcoal had gained back, Priestley thought, might derive either from the air itself or from moisture. "It may . . . be determined whether the air expelled from charcoal by heat, be the air which it had imbibed, or that which was formed by the decomposition of the charcoal by means of water," Priestley reasoned. "For this [latter] will be inflammable air, whereas the other . . . will be partially phlogisticated." The air he obtained turned out to be about one-tenth fixed air. Some of the rest of it "was inflammable, burning with the lambent blue flame, which shews that moisture had been imbibed by the charcoal."[18] From Lavoisier's viewpoint, of course, this appearance of inflammable air meant not that charcoal was decomposed by water, but that water was probably decomposed by charcoal. He himself had, as we have seen, obtained both fixed and inflammable air by passing water across charcoal in the gun barrel. In his experiments as well as Priestley's, however, both water and ordinary air had been present as possible sources of the airs produced.

Lavoisier now decided that in order to prove conclusively whether the water or the air was the source of the fixed and inflammable airs it was necessary to carry out comparative experiments with the *charbon* exposed separately to the one and the other. He therefore calcined *charbon* in "perfectly dry air" and obtained only a little fixed air and mophette. "When, on the contrary, I protected the *charbon* from contact with the air, but soaked it in a little water," both fixed air and inflammable air were rapidly produced. By repeating that operation "a great number of times," he was able to volatilize all of the *charbon.* Collecting and measuring the airs, he was able to construct a balance sheet from which he worked out that the oxygen contained in the fixed air was in exactly the same proportion to the inflammable air produced as in the composition of water. "Strictly speaking," Lavoisier wrote afterward in reporting the experiment, the operation had been "not an analysis of the *charbon* at all; . . . it is really an analysis of the water; and from it there results only the proof that the oxygen has more affinity with the *charbon*, when the latter is glowing red, than with the inflammable air, as we have already demonstrated."[19]

The preceding is only a plausible reconstruction of the reasoning which may have led Lavoisier to this experiment. The role of Priestley's investigations is derived from Lavoisier's published account of the background for his own; but as we have seen repeatedly, Lavoisier was prone to replace the actual sequence of events with a more logical one. The connection I have suggested between the outcome of the fermentation experiments and the decomposition of water by *charbon* is only an inference based on the parallels between them and between both of them and his previously expressed theory of fermentation. Lavoisier himself did not explicitly draw such a connection. If the reconstruction is nevertheless valid, then we can see Lavoisier setting out into the uncharted, "mysterious" chemistry of fermentation but doubling quickly back to more familiar territory to come up with a somewhat tighter proof for the decomposition of water by *charbon*. That conclusion was, as he seemed to acknowledge in the above passage, merely a confirmation of what he had already shown. Afterward, however, he saw that with the same point of view he could venture forth again toward the chemistry of plant substances. From that stage onward the balance of his interconnected interests began to tip more decisively in the direction of "nature's operations."

The experiment with *charbon* and water, "into which only two substances enter, clarified for me," Lavoisier wrote, "the much more complicated distillations in which one also obtains considerable quantities of fixed air and inflammable air. I have repeated, from that point of view, some of the principal experiments reported by Doctor Hales in his *Vegetable Staticks*."[20] The experiments to which he referred were among the many Stephen Hales had performed on diverse processes which he found either gave off or absorbed air, and which had so heavily influenced Lavoisier when he first became interested in combustion in 1772. What Lavoisier had particularly in mind here were operations Hales had carried out on a series of plant materials which he placed in a retort connected to a large receiver inverted over water so that he could collect the air driven off when he heated the retort. A typical experiment was the following:

> *As to vegetable substances,* from half a cubicke inch, or 135 grains of heart of *oak,* fresh cut from the growing tree, was generated 108 cubick inches of air, i.e. a quantity equal to 216 times the bulk of the piece of *oak,* its weight was about 30 grains, ¼ part of the weight of 135 grains of *oak.*[21]

In two experiments of this kind Hales tested the quality of the air. That from this particular operation caused a live sparrow placed in it to die instantly. The air generated from peas caused a lighted candle to "flash." At that time there was no conception that different species of airs exist, and Hales was generally content to prove that "the great quantities of air which are thus obtained from these several substances by distillation are true air, and not a mere flatulent vapour." That is, he showed that, after being generated, they remained permanently elastic. To explain how the air could be compressed as drastically as it must be in substances which yield many times their own volume of it, he assumed that the particles of air must be able to switch from their elastic to an inelastic or "fix'd state." From the weights of the air generated he concluded that "air makes a very considerable part of the substance of vegetables, as well as of animals." Because solid substances appeared to give off more air than liquids did, he inferred that the air in a "fix'd state" is the "band of union" responsible for the cohesion of the bodies in which it inheres.[22]

Lavoisier's published description of the investigation of plant substances which he began by repeating Hales's distillation experiments is the sole source of information on the subject. It should therefore be quoted in full (continuing from the two sentences quoted at the beginning of the above paragraph):

> I submitted various species of plants and wood to distillation in a pneumaticochemical apparatus, and I observed, first, that in all of these distillations one obtained a mixture of fixed air and inflammable air. Second, that the quantity of the aeriform product varied greatly, according to the species of plant subjected to the distillation, and according to the manner in which one carried out the distillation. Third, that in a great number of plants the proportion of fixed air and inflammable air was nearly constant; that there was slightly more than two parts of carbonized inflammable air [that is, of inflammable air containing some *charbon* "held in solution"], to one part of fixed air, that is to say, that the nature of the aeriform products and their proportions were almost the same as in a simple distillation of water and *charbon.* Fourth, that it was not the same in plants which contained preformed oil; that in the distillation of the latter there is disengaged a very large excess of inflammable air which is due not to the decomposition of the water, but to that of the oil itself.
>
> Such great uniformity in the results indicated an identity in the cause which produced them, and I had no doubt after that, that a great part of the inflammable air and the fixed air which were disengaged when one distills plants over an open fire was the effect of the decomposition of the water; that the *matière charbon-*

neuse was preformed in the plants, as I had declared in 1778 [actually 1779], and I now viewed the decomposition of plants by fire as no more than a play of affinities of the oxygen contained in the water, which separates from the inflammable air to join with the *charbon* and form fixed air.

Although these conclusions appeared to me to be tightly linked with the facts, and reason seemed to me unable to attack them, I nevertheless believed that I should not adopt them without confirming them further by new experiments; and this is how I reasoned. If the inflammable air and the fixed air which plants give off in distillation really do derive from the decomposition of the water by the *charbon;* if, as I have shown elsewhere, *charbon* is not able to bring about the decomposition except at a degree of heat much greater than that of boiling water, it follows that if one removes from plants most of the water which enters into their composition by means of a low heat maintained for a long time, they should no longer give off fixed air or inflammable air when one afterward distills them over an open fire; or, at least, the quantities ought to be considerably reduced. If, on the other hand, one exposes them suddenly to a brusque fire, in such a way that the *charbonneuse* portion is exposed and heated sufficiently before the water has had time to escape, one will obtain a much more copious aeriform product. The experiment did not refute what the theory had predicted for me. Wood shavings exposed brusquely to an ardent fire gave me very abundant aeriform products, as M. Priestley had already observed, because the *matière charbonneuse* had been brought to incandescence before the water had time to disengage; when, on the other hand, I employed only a gentle fire continued for a long time, which I raised only gradually and by degrees, water passed over in the distillation, the shavings became completely dry, and when I afterward increased the intensity of the fire I obtained hardly any fixed air, and much less inflammable air.[23]

Without independent evidence of the actual course of Lavoisier's investigation, we are left in doubt not only about whether the operational and mental events took place in the elegant form of his logical reconstruction, but also about when he completed the distillations of plant materials that he described here. That could have taken place up until near the middle of November 1786, the time at which he was prepared to read at the Academy the memoir based on them. They were, however, similarly described in a surviving rough draft of an earlier version of the same memoir. This draft is undated, but may well have been written as early as the late spring or summer of 1786.

The title of his draft, "On the air which one extracts from plants when one decomposes them by distillation over an open fire," signifies what Lavoisier felt at the time was the main thrust of the investigation:

> These experiments, or rather the consequences which result from them, completely reverse the system that Hales, and after him *all the physicians had formed* [Lavoisier then crossed out the phrase here italicized and wrote instead more realistically] a large number of physicians had formed about the texture of plants.

The "enormous quantity" of air disengaged in the distillation of plant matter had persuaded these people "that the air was an element of [these] bodies, that it was that which held together the other elements." His experiments should now force them, however, to recognize that the air is a product of the operation, and that it consequently does not even exist in the plants. He could "not resist pausing" over the remarkable circumstance that the old chemists had imagined in plants a substance which did not exist there, whereas they had not recognized that *substance charbonneuse* really did preexist in plants.[24] Lavoisier clearly enjoyed the irony of this double reversal that he had imposed on the older ideas of plant composition, but his overthrow of Hales's "system" was largely a rhetorical triumph. Hales had presented his ideas concerning the fixation of air in plant substances sixty years earlier, long before distinct species of air were recognized, and before most of the specific plant substances known in Lavoisier's time had been identified. Lavoisier was, however, able to bring a similar argument to bear on a more contemporary issue:

> Some modern chemists have regarded the plant acids, such as tartaric acid, acid of sugar, acid of vinegar, and formic acid as composed of fixed air and inflammable air in different proportions, because these acids distilled over an open fire or treated with nitrous acid give off a great quantity of these airs; but these airs are, like those which one obtains from all plant substances, a product of the operation. They are the result of the decomposition of the water by the *charbon* of the plant.[25]

Although Lavoisier did not name the chemists who held the view that plant acids are composed of fixed air and inflammable air, he almost certainly had in mind his younger colleague Claude-Louis Berthollet, and the versatile Italian scientist, the Abbé Fontana. One of Berthollet's first scientific investigations, in 1776, had been the chemistry of tartaric acid. He dealt mostly with the properties of the many salts formed by that acid, but he also produced from it with heat a large quantity of fixed air, together with a little oil. Berthollet suggested that the acidity of plant acids is due to fixed air. Fontana tested Berthollet's conclusion by distilling all of the plant and animal acids known at the time and collecting the airs they yielded in a pneumatic flask over mercury. Tartaric acid, acid of vinegar, formic acid, and acid of sugar—exactly those named by Lavoisier—as well as various acidic fruit juices, all gave off large quantities of fixed air and some inflammable air. Fontana believed that he had proven that all of these acids were composed essentially of fixed air, which "is the acid principle of all of these bodies." The inflammable air he thought derived from the oil which the acids also yielded by distillation. Extending his research to other plant substances such as sugar, gums, and resins, Fontana was able to obtain fixed air and inflammable air from them also, sometimes by distillation alone, sometimes by distilling the substance with nitrous acid.[26]

Fontana published his very extensive series of experiments in two articles in the *Journal de physique* in July and September 1778, that is, a few months before Lavoisier reported to the Academy his first analysis of sugar, carried out similarly by distillation with nitrous acid, and yielding also a little inflammable air with a large amount of fixed air. At that time Lavoisier had enthusiastically projected a "completely new pathway opening up" for the application of the same methods to other plant and animal substances;[27] but Fontana had already energetically entered that pathway. Covering a broad range of plant substances, Fontana discovered an impressive uniformity in their composition, in the fact that each yielded fixed and inflammable air, while at the same time the differing proportions of the two constituents distinguished the substances from one another. It is quite possible that Lavoisier never extended his own investigation beyond sugar because he soon afterward saw that Fontana had preempted the field.

Fontana's interpretation of his results did not go unchallenged. Almost as soon as the first of his two memoirs, dealing primarily with formic acid, appeared, Nicolas Deyeux, a Parisian pharmacist, published a critique of several aspects of the investigation. Although "it is not impossible to believe that fixed air forms the base of certain acids," Deyeux wrote, it is very difficult to be persuaded that a substance with properties as distinctive as those of formic acid "contains no other acid than that of fixed air." "Finally," he added,

> need we repeat here what has already been said so many times? That is, that it is difficult to judge the composition of a substance by means of the results one obtains when one utilizes fire for the analysis. Is it not for the fixed air which M. l'Abbé Fontana has obtained in his experiments the same as for the oil, the fixed alkali, and the volatile alkali which we obtain every day when we

> distill a plant or an animal substance over the open fire? Just as it would be absurd to say that these different products existed as such in the composition of the body which one has distilled, so it would perhaps be equally absurd to believe that the fixed air which appears during the decomposition of formic acid preexisted in that acid.[28]

In another passage Deyeux referred to the fixed air as the "debris" of the acid from which it came. He was thus applying to the situation a standard argument against accepting the products of a distillation analysis as constituents of the substance analyzed. Deyeux had no basis on which to suggest how fixed air might be formed during the process. Eight years later, however, Lavoisier was in an excellent position to give a very specific explanation of that process, based on his knowledge of the combustion of fixed air and of water. It could be understood as a combination taking place between the *matière charbonneuse*, which he regarded as a true constituent of the plant substances, and oxygen derived from water, releasing from the water the inflammable air which also appeared in the analysis.

It was not fortuitous that Lavoisier mentioned the plant acids to illustrate the questions about composition he believed applicable to plant substances in general; for by 1786 the investigation of this class of substances had become the forefront of plant chemistry. Scheele's brilliant series of discoveries of one plant acid after another had not only doubled the number of known acids of all kinds, but made these acids the largest and best-defined group of substances derivable from the plant kingdom. Lavoisier himself had not participated in this line of research, however, except for his reinterpretation in 1779 of the composition of acid of sugar and its relation to sugar itself. He could therefore offer only a general explanation of the composition of these acids in keeping with his own principles.

In his draft memoir Lavoisier pointed out that when plant materials are fermented they also yield fixed air and inflammable air, through the same process as when they are distilled. When treated with nitrous acid or oxygenated marine acid, the vital air from the acid combines with the *substance charbonneuse* to form the fixed air. His attention was thus centered on the products of decomposition and how they formed, rather than on the composition of the plant substances themselves before they are subjected to such operations.[29] There is, however, one passage, a portion of the account of his investigation, the published version of which is quoted above, that reveals his conception of that composition at the time he wrote this draft:

> I no longer doubted that the inflammable air and the fixed air which are disengaged when one treats plants by the open fire are a result of the decomposition of the water. I have proposed since

> 1778 [1779] that the *substance charbonneuse* that one extracts from plants, whether by combustion or by distillation, was not at all the product of the fire, that it existed completely formed in the plants, and that the fire only separated it from the volatile materials with which it had been joined. There exists therefore in the plants everything necessary in order to form fixed air and inflammable air.

Afterward he made explicit what this last sentence implies, by adding in the margin, "since there exists in them *matière charbonneuse* and water."[30]

Although one could argue that Lavoisier meant only that in plants there is water in addition to particular substances containing *matière charbonneuse*, the simplest and most direct interpretation is that he thought the substances obtainable from gross plant matter are themselves composed of *matière charbonneuse* and water. This idea seems to underlie his whole discussion in the draft, even though he gave no more than this bare statement of the conception itself. For the existence of the *matière charbonneuse* he referred back to his memoir on the acid of sugar. At that time, however, he had thought that the other constituent was simply the inflammable air that came off when he reacted sugar with nitrous acid. How he came to believe instead that the other constituent is water can be inferred from the most recent development of his investigation of plant substances. As we have seen in the preceding chapter, the circumstances surrounding his combustion analyses of spirit of wine had led him to the view that this particular plant substance contains preformed water. As he moved, a year later, toward a conception that would include the composition of plant substances in general, that prominent precedent undoubtedly influenced him. The circumstances of the present investigation reinforced the same inclination. He began by proving, in a more rigorous manner than before, that *charbon* decomposes water. For this demonstration he used charcoal moistened with water. This process then became the model through which he sought to understand the decomposition of other plant substances. The fact that they not only produced inflammable air and fixed air, but did so in the same relative proportions as did *charbon* and water, strengthened his sense that the processes were strictly analogous. The only significant difference he perceived was that the plant substances already included the water that he had to add to the *charbon*. Perhaps not fully aware of the extent to which this comparison had shaped his reasoning and excluded alternative points of view, Lavoisier assumed without further argument that the essential constituents of plant substances are *substance charbonneuse* and water.

Having compared the distillation of *charbon* and of plant matters, and the forms of fermentation, through their common property of decomposing water,

Lavoisier sought to assimilate these processes more fully into his chemical system by extending his concept of combustion to include them:

> If by combustion one means the combination of *matière charbonneuse* with oxygen to form fixed air, then a kind of combustion takes place in closed vessels when one heats plant or animal matters in them over an open fire, but in this case this combustion is done by means of the water, and without a release of flame and light, in contrast to those which take place in the air, which is always accompanied by flame and light. The same is true for vinous and putrid fermentations; one can regard them as true combustions, since there is a combination of *charbon* and oxygen.[31]

Near the end of his draft memoir, sensing perhaps that he was expanding the use of the term combustion so far beyond its commonplace meaning that he might not be understood, he qualified his usage by defining two types of combustion. Those combustions which require air, which take place "with a burst and with light," he designated "ardent combustions." The other, "more tranquil," type he called "obscure combustion." He accompanied these new terms with several starts toward a discourse on the need to revise the language of chemistry in order to keep up with the advance of the science.[32] (These ideas, expressed in the draft in fragmentary form, have a special interest as a preliminary form of what eventually developed into Lavoisier's well-known discussion of the relation between science and language in his *Elementary Treatise of Chemistry*.)

In 1777 Lavoisier had defined combustion not only by explaining ordinary combustions in terms of his oxygen theory, but by generalizing to include the features those processes had in common with calcination and with respiration. Now, almost a decade later, he generalized the concept further by incorporating processes that took place in the absence of air. When he began his study of combustion, such an application would have appeared self-contradictory, for the presence of air was an essential condition for combustions. By 1786, however, his theoretical structure was strong enough to unify processes that were, in terms of their directly observable properties, very unlike. This later development has attracted less than its share of historical attention, since Lavoisier's general chemical system is regarded as having been essentially completed by then. Neither Lavoisier nor his theoretical structure, however, had become rigidly fixed. He and his theory of combustion were still flexible enough to grow and change as he applied it to an ever-widening range of phenomena. Moreover, the circumstance that it was in order to include special processes that plant substances undergo, and even, as we shall see, the physiological process of germination, that he expanded his fundamental chemical theory illustrates once again that Lavoisier did not merely apply a finished system of general chemistry to plant chemistry; for the special problems he encountered in plant chemistry in turn induced a significant new development of his general chemical theory.

It was not only fermentations that Lavoisier incorporated into his extended definition of combustion. Responding to his own question, how did vinous and putrid fermentation differ, he declared:

> There exist in nature three operations which differ extremely little from one another, the germination of seeds, vinous fermentation, and putrid fermentation. The same seed which, when moistened with a small amount of water, produces a plant putrefies when isolated from contact with the air . . . ; diluted with a little more water and mixed with a ferment, it yields a spirituous liquor. In all three cases the water is decomposed.

The only difference between the last two is that in putrid fermentation the inflammable air is given off, whereas in vinous fermentation it remains "engaged in the combination to form the spirit of wine." He then went on to consider the third case:

> Finally, in germination and vegetation it is not by means of the *matière charbonneuse* that the water is decomposed; this happens through a force with which we are not yet acquainted. At this point I know only that many seeds cannot vegetate without air, that they cannot vegetate in mophette, or probably in any air that is not respirable. In vegetation the inflammable principle of the water remains engaged in the combination. It forms the combustible part of the plants and probably their *matière charbonneuse*.[33]

This discussion echoes Lavoisier's remarks on vegetation in his memoir on water of the spring of 1784, and shows among other things that he still entertained the idea he had formed then, that in nature's operations the inflammable principle might be the source for *matière charbonneuse*.[34] His new treatment of the subject, however, displayed significant changes of emphasis. Whereas he had earlier mentioned vegetation in the most general terms as a process that decomposes water, he now narrowed his focus to the limited process of germination. Where he had once simply juxtaposed vegetation and fermentation as two natural operations that decompose water, he now sought to tighten the parallels between germination and two forms of fermentation until they appeared as variants of the same process. It is conceivable that Lavoisier developed his ideas in this direction on his own, but more likely that he was influenced by a chapter on germination in Jean Senebier's three-volume work on the effects of light on plants. "I believe," Senebier wrote in 1782, "that germination is produced by fermentation pushed up to a certain point." To make his case, he enumerated as many similarities as he could find between these processes. Seeds themselves are very fermentable. Germination and fermentation both require moisture and heat; but if there is too much water, the seeds putrify instead. Fermentation and germination both require "the presence of air." Just as fermentation will not take place in fixed air, so "seeds do not germinate either in fixed air or in inflammable air." The odor of germinating seeds is like that of fermenting seeds. Putrid fermentation differs from those two processes in that it releases inflammable gas. Senebier drew numerous other parallels between fermentation and germination, relating particularly the chemical composition of the contents of germinating seeds to the composition of fermented liquids.[35] Despite major differences in detail, Senebier's salient argument that germination is a form of fermentation strikingly prefigured Lavoisier's position. Since Lavoisier gave indications elsewhere of familiarity with Senebier's work, it is a reasonable inference that this chapter may have been the main source for Lavoisier's ideas on the subject. If so, he astutely picked out from Senebier's discursive discussion just those features most conducive to a treatment of germination within his own theoretical framework.

Compared with his panoramic statements about vegetation in 1783 and 1784, Lavoisier's description of germination in this draft memoir suggests also that he was moving toward a concrete investigative approach to the problem. Though he mentioned "forces with which we are not yet acquainted," he fixed on specific conditions under which seeds would or would not germinate. The tone of the passages seems to invite experiments to elucidate further the conditions set forth. Depending on when this draft was written, Lavoisier was, in fact, either readying himself for, or had already launched into, what was for him a new field of experimentation. In either case, the links he perceived here between germination, fermentation, and combustion explain why he found himself, during the summer of 1786, in the unaccustomed role of growing plants in his laboratory.

III

On August 6 Lavoisier began a set of twelve simultaneous tests of the germination of garden cress and maize seedlings under varied conditions. He placed the seedlings under jars inverted over mercury. Each type of seed he subjected to six different circumstances. In two jars the mercury filled the entire space so that the air was excluded. In two others common air filled the space left above the mercury. One of each of these pairs he exposed to light at a window, the other he left in the laboratory covered with a linen cloth. Lavoisier left the jars for ten days, then tested the air contained in each. The experiments were not uniformly successful. In three of the jars containing cress seeds so much air was generated that the jars overturned. The cress seeds kept without air or light produced about ten cubic inches of air which extinguished a candle and emitted "a very strong odor of fermentation." The air produced by the seeds without air but exposed to sunlight was three-fourths fixed air, and the other one-fourth was "lightly inflammable." The maize seeds under each of the experimental conditions generated only about a cubic inch of air which extinguished a candle.[36]

Meanwhile Lavoisier had begun on August 10 a second set of experiments on cress seeds, comparing the growth of seedlings germinated in pure vital air and in ordinary air. To moisten the seeds he placed them on pieces of cotton soaked in water. Observing closely the course of their development, he found that the seedlings in "dephlogisticated air," as he sometimes even yet called that gas, grew "much more rapidly." By the end of the fifth day they were "almost twice the size" of those in ordinary air. He "could not judge definitely" whether there had been an absorption or production of air in either jar, because the amounts of the one or the other had been too small. He suggested, however, that "there was more likely absorption than production." Afterward the growth ceased in both jars, the plants began to wither and turn yellow, and the volumes of air sensibly diminished. He waited ten more days before testing the air in the two jars. That in which the ordinary air had been placed permitted a candle plunged into it to burn "as well as in ordinary air," whereas in the jar originally containing vital air the candle "burned better than in ordinary air but less well than in ordinary vital air."[37] In his notes of this experiment Lavoisier left no trace of the surprise which it must have caused him. Several years earlier he had reported to the Academy Scheele's observation that seeds do not germinate well in pure vital air, and Lavoisier himself accepted the view that vegetation requires fixed air. However he may have explained to himself the luxurious development of the seeds placed in vital air, he must have attained little satisfaction from his examination of the changes which the germinating seedlings had produced in the surrounding air. In this respect the experiment was as inconclusive as the first set.

On the fifteenth of August Lavoisier began still another group of germination experiments. He placed eight sunflower seeds in a jar without air but containing water soaked up in a sponge, forty or fifty cress seeds in a second jar under the same conditions, and some cress seeds in pure mophette. After a month none of these seeds had shown any signs of germinating.[38] On the eighteenth he had in addition placed

> under a large bell jar filled with common air an earthenware plate over which I had spread a thin layer of well-moistened cotton. I allowed water to run under the cotton and sowed on top of it sunflower, nasturtium, and cress seeds. The water was raised into the jar by means of a siphon, and I marked the level of the water.
>
> On the evening of the 19th the germination began. By the

morning of the 20th all of the little sprouts had formed, and the radical was beginning to extend downward. There was only an almost insensible decrease in the volume of the air.

On the 25th the absorption of the air was much more noticeable. The germination of the cress was very abundant and the vegetation very nice. The stems of the plants were pale, the foliage was green, and all of them had at their tips a drop of water, which disappeared from most of them by slipping down along the stem to fall onto the cotton. The nasturtiums did not have a noticeable germination, but they were on the verge of it; and some of the sunflowers had begun to germinate.

On the following days the vegetation of the cress made little progress, and it was soon almost entirely arrested, just as happened to the same plant sown on cotton in the open air. The two differed only in that the latter had grown a little taller. This circumstance could be due to the fact that the roots did not have enough space to spread out in [in the jar], whereas they were perfectly free in the control experiment.

During the last days of the month the nasturtiums began to develop, and their stems grew rapidly up to the top of the jar. Several leaves developed at their extremities. Two sunflower seeds had also germinated, but they did not raise themselves very high. At the same time the volume of the air had been decreasing by larger amounts.

The 13th [of September]. Since the vegetation did not appear to be making further progress, and I was afraid that fermentation might set in, I made a mark on the jar at the level of the water.

The barometer was at 28 inches ½ line, and the thermometer at 14 degrees.

The second mark was about one inch and 6 lines above the first, which gives by measuring [the volumes] an absorption of about ⅕.

Having determined this decrease more precisely from the weight of water I found

[blank space left on page]

This air extinguished candles completely. It contained a very slight portion of fixed air. I recognized by means of caustic alkali that it was of ——[39]

The record of the experiment breaks off abruptly at this point, and no further experiments on vegetation are entered. The striking contrast between Lavoisier's meticulous observations of the development of the plants from their seeds and his aborted examination of the air remaining in the jar at the end suggests that he probably undertook this investigation with high expectations which were not fulfilled. For all his scrupulous attention to comparative conditions and controls, he was not able to determine marked differences in the quantities or qualities of the airs produced which he could relate to the various conditions to which he had subjected the seeds.

We cannot fully reconstruct Lavoisier's reasons for setting up each of the individual experiments in this series on vegetation; but his general aim must have been to confirm his theory that vegetation decomposes water. In taking up this research he was obviously stimulated by the observations of Priestley, Ingenhousz, and Senebier, as well as by Senebier's theory of germination; but his experiments were different from those of his predecessors. Senebier had included a few general observations that he had made to support his speculation; but the central investigation showing that fixed air is converted to vital air he had carried out with mature green leaves.[40] Priestley too performed his experiments on vegetation mainly with parts of developed plants (aside from his well-known experiments on the "green matter" which forms in water).[41] Only Scheele had specifically examined the changes which germinating seeds produce in the air. As we have seen, Lavoisier had reported in 1781 on Scheele's observation that germination alters the air in the same way that respiration does, a finding which Lavoisier regarded as a new and significant discovery.[42] That very result, however, raises a puzzling question concerning Lavoisier's own experiments five years later. If germinating seedlings convert vital air to fixed air, whereas green leaves in the sunlight convert fixed air to vital air, then Lavoisier appears to have arranged some of his experiments in such a way that these two opposing effects would be most likely to mask one another. By allowing the seeds not only to germinate, but to develop as far as they would into young plants, he was precluding the possibility of obtaining results representing either process alone. Moreover, if he were familiar with the difficulties his predecessors had encountered over the interference of decay processes with the results of vegetation itself, it is hard to see why, in some instances, he waited for days after the plants stopped growing and began to wither before he examined the resulting air.

The most plausible explanation for these apparent aberrations is that Lavoisier was entering a field of investigation new to him, and that he was struggling to learn how to study vegetation with the experimental techniques which had served him so well in so many investigations of the effects of other processes upon the air. The very care with which he noted the stages in the physical development of the seedlings hints at the newness of the phenomena to him. If he had not yet learned to conduct such experiments with the same skill he had acquired in other areas of investigation, that is not really surprising. He himself acknowledged later that the "first experiments I have made on this subject" had not "yet presented to my eyes evident results." He planned to repeat the experiments, but not until the following year, presumably when the season would again be suitable for germinating seedlings.[43] There is no evidence that he ever carried out this intention.

Just as silence can speak more loudly than words, so empty spaces can sometimes tell as much as writing on a page. The place Lavoisier left blank in the laboratory record of his final experiment on vegetation, for the analysis of the air he never recorded, bears witness to the fact that even this most resourceful of experimentalists could not always bring his plans to fruition. The significance of his attempt lies not in the distance by which it fell short of his aims, but in the unique evidence it provides of how vigorously Lavoisier's interests in the processes of plant life were expanding.

Three days after he had ended the last of these experiments on vegetation, Lavoisier returned to the problem of spirituous fermentation. Sometime since his unsuccessful fermentation experiments of the summer of 1785 he must have abandoned the idea of seeking a simple chemical substance to activate the fermentation of sugar; for he now resorted to the chemically mysterious but practically effective "ferment," beer yeast. He assembled an apparatus consisting of a large glass distillation flask, in which the fermentation was to take place, connected by means of siphon tubes successively to two bottles containing caustic alkali for absorbing the fixed air evolved, and then to a bell jar over water intended to collect any air which passed through the caustic alkali bottles. On September 16 he began the preliminary operations. He weighed the distillation flask by suspending it directly from the arm of his balance in place of the usual cup. He then introduced 2 pounds 8 ounces of sugar dissoved in 12 pounds of water, "verified" that the total weight of the flask and contents equaled its original weight plus that of the sugar and water (the two quantities actually differed by a little less than an ounce), and prepared to add 1 pound 4 ounces of yeast in liquid form.[44]

Intending to measure the quantity of fixed air produced from the weight gained by the alkali bottles, Lavoisier weighed these bottles and their contents, then connected the several vessels with the siphon tubes and luted all of the joints. Everything was ready by 11:15 on the morning of September 18. He mixed the yeast into the sugar solution. "By half past one [in the afternoon] the fermentation was already under way, and in spite of the two intermediary vessels, air passed into the [final pneumatic] jar. That was the air of the vessels [that is, the air present within the apparatus at the beginning]. The first jar has been broken." Lavoisier replaced it with a bell jar. "The fermentation proceeded rapidly through the day and the following night: a large quantity of yeast was driven out [of the distillation flask] in the form of a froth, and passed into the intermediate vessel. I was obliged to disassemble the apparatus several times" in order to retrieve this yeast. He had in fact to open it up six times for that reason, and to collect and weigh the froth each time, in order to ascertain the quantity of yeast lost from the distillation flask. "Afterward the fermentation became less tumultuous, although continuing to go rapidly." Only a small additional quantity of yeast passed over into the intermediate vessel, "but because there was not enough caustic alkali to absorb all of the fixed air, much of [the latter] passed into the bell jar. One could not measure its quantity, the portion absorbed by the water being unknown, but by adding together the losses of weight one will be able to evaluate it."[45]

Three days later, while the fermentation was still going on, Lavoisier weighed the distillation flask and the caustic alkali bottles. From the gain in weight of the latter he calculated the portion of the fixed air absorbed there, but, as his earlier comment indicates, this did not represent the total. To obtain that figure he deducted from the overall loss in the weight of the distillation flask the aggregated weight of the yeast he had gathered from the intermediary vessel. By October 14, "the evolution of fixed air was very much slower." He repeated the weighings, this time not bothering with the saturated caustic alkali bottles, but calculating only the total "weight of fixed air disengaged," as before, from the loss in the weight of the distillation flask, after making allowance again for the substance which had passed "at different times" into the intermediary bottle.[46]

Lavoisier had finally attained an active fermentation of sugar—far more active than he was prepared for. Not having made provision to keep the yeast from being driven out of the flask by this activity, he was forced into the tedious operation of taking the apparatus apart repeatedly, collecting, and weighing the substance lost in this way. Not having provided sufficient absorption capacity for the fixed air in alkali, he was unable to utilize the most reliable method for determining the quantity evolved, and had to fall back on an indirect calculation utilizing only his basic principle that the weight of the substances present after the reaction must equal those present at the beginning. The calculation was not unreasonable as a first approximation, but it depended on a small difference between two large measurements of the heavy distillation flask, and left him with no check on his assumption that all of the weight loss in the distillation flask beyond that which he could account for in the substances he gathered from the intermediate vessels represented the fixed air produced. For an experiment which occupied him for as long as this one did it may seem surprising that Lavoisier did not break off the operation as soon as he saw that it was not going according to plan, and start over with more adequate arrangements. We have already seen, however, that it was characteristic of Lavoisier that once he had set up an experiment he carried on with it as best he could even after recognizing flaws in its design or execution, and attempted to save as much as he could of the results by making additional assumptions in his calculations. In the present case, he continued the same fermentation operation for another six months.

IV

While his fermentation experiment went on and on, Lavoisier rewrote his draft memoir "On the air which one extracts from plants when one decomposes them by distillation over an open fire," in order to present it at the public meeting of the Academy to be held on November 15. Much of the content of the paper remained the same, but he gave it a new title: "Reflections on the decomposition of water by plant and animal substances."[47] This alteration was more than stylistic. It suggests that what he had made the main point before, the reversal of the conclusions Stephen Hales had drawn from distillations of plant materials, was really a secondary historical footnote, and that the investigations described in the paper were in fact continuations of his quest to identify processes that decompose water.

Among the refinements Lavoisier made in this new draft, one is particularly interesting in that through successive revisions he raised a particular experimental strategy to the level of an important general principle. To establish that the source of the difference between the weight of the *charbon* he had subjected to successive distillations until it disappeared, and the weight of the fixed and inflammable air produced, derived from the water decomposed in the process rather than from the air, he had in a subsequent experiment "taken the greatest precautions to isolate [the *charbon*] from contact with the air." The simple description of the experimental procedure he then modified, making a somewhat more general comment. "It was evident that this matter, thus altered and extracted from the atmosphere, could not be anything but air or water, / but in order to know to which of these two the formation of the aeriform fluids is due, it was necessary to vary the conditions of the experiment." He then went on to describe how he had isolated the *charbon* from the air. Finally, he replaced that description, and the portion of the above statement following the solidus, with

> In an experiment whenever several causes or several circumstances become entangled in producing an effect, one can discover to which of these causes to ascribe the effect only by removing successively each of these causes except for one, and by interrogating each one separately, so to speak, according to this principle, which is that of a sound analysis.[48]

In elevating this particular problem to an illustration of the principle of sound analysis, Lavoisier demonstrated his sure grasp of the function of what later came to be called control experiments.

In his original draft Lavoisier had restricted his attention to plant matter, but he did include a brief statement that "all that I have just said about plant substances applies to animal substances." In the margin he added the bare hint of a qualification, "with slight differences."[49] As his new title implies, he now wished to generalize his subject so as to incorporate animal substances more fully. To do so, however, he had to specify the nature of the qualification. To the preceding statement he added:

> The *acide charbonneux* that one extracts from them is in the same way the result of the decomposition of water, but since these substances are more composed than plants, since they contain mophette, the phenomena they present by distillation are more complicated, and they form through the combination of the mophette with inflammable gas a particular product which is volatile alkali, as M. Berthollet was the first to announce.[50]

Claude-Louis Berthollet, a frequent visitor to Lavoisier's laboratory, and next to Lavoisier himself the most capable investigative chemist in Paris, had in fact announced less than a year before this that animal substances contain mophette, and are therefore "much more composed than purely plant substances." Like Lavoisier, Berthollet had been stimulated several years earlier by Torbern Bergman's discovery of acid of sugar. He had applied Bergman's method of distillation with nitrous acid to animal matters, and shown that they as well as plant substances yield acid of sugar. Continuing to orient his research around animal substances (which were understood by this time not to mean strictly substances derived from animals, because plants too contained in smaller quantities substances whose properties were very similar to the substances considered typical of animal matter), Berthollet arrived by 1785 at a position in which he could explain that volatile alkali, the characteristic distillation product of animal substances, did not exist as such in the substances, but was a product of recombination during the operation.[51] Berthollet's work on animal substances thus complemented Lavoisier's work on plant substances. Together they provided a new basis for understanding not only the common features of the composition of plant and animal chemistry, but also the essential difference between them.

Almost as a parenthetical remark, Lavoisier inserted on the left margin of this second draft of his memoir after his discussion of animal substances,

> One will perhaps ask me if the oils that one extracts from plant and animal substances by distillation over an open fire were already formed in these substances, or rather if they are the product of the operation. I would respond that my experiments have not yet resulted in any decisive knowledge in that regard, but that since in the last analysis oils are all composed of *charbon* and inflammable gas, it is very possible that they are formed during

> the distillation by the combination of the inflammable gas from the water with an excess of the *charbon* that is contained in the plant.[52]

The question of whether the oils received by distilling plant matters are contained in that matter or are a product of the decomposition process was one of the oldest, most difficult problems in the long tradition of analysis by distillation. It had been debated over and over since the sixteenth century, the level at which the question was asked gradually shifting as conceptions about the nature of chemical composition in general changed. Lavoisier now found himself able to redefine this question in terms of his new understanding of the constituents of plant substances. If substances comprising the intact plant matter are composed of *matière charbonneuse* and water, then the formation of oils in the process of distillation can be understood on the same general principles of recombination by which he had been able to understand the decomposition of plant matter to yield fixed air and water or inflammable air. Although not able to *answer* the age-old question, in addressing himself to it he caught the first glimpse of the great potential power of his new principles of plant composition to explain the transformation of one plant substance to another.

Of all the topics included in the first draft of his memoir, that which changed most when he rewrote it was his discussion of vegetation. He dropped completely the original passages describing germination and the two forms of fermentation as very similar processes, the conditions for germination, and the possibility that in vegetation the inflammable principle forms *matière charbonneuse*. In their stead, he "terminated" his new draft with some quite different "reflections relative to vegetation." Whenever one decomposes a substance containing two "principles," one can do so by attacking either one of the two principles, or as the old chemists had described it, by one or the other of its different *latera*. In all combustions water is decomposed through the *latus* of its oxygen, which combines with the combustible body. In vegetation, however, nature decomposes water through the other *latus*, so that the oxygen is set free, while the inflammable principle remains "engaged to form the plant." To understand "this great operation which nature appears to have surrounded up until now with a thick veil," he continued,

> one must know that there can be no vegetation without water, and without fixed air, or *acide charbonneux*. These two substances mutually decompose during the act of vegetation through their analogous *latera*. The inflammable principle separates from the oxygen to unite with the *charbon* in order to form oils, resins, and to constitute the plant. At the same time the oxygen which becomes free combines with light to form vital air.[53]

Claiming that time would not permit him to describe the experiments on which these assertions were based, but that he planned to discuss them in "other memoirs," he suggested only that they were based partly on his own experiments and partly on those of Priestley and Senebier.

In making this revision Lavoisier achieved a historic advance. By synthesizing his view that vegetation decomposes water with the cumulative outcome of the investigations of Priestley and Senebier, that in sunlight plants absorb fixed air and emit vital air, Lavoisier had arrived at the first general statement of the fundamental relation between the exchanges of plants with the atmosphere and the formation of the substances which compose them. How he attained this insight is less self-evident. Despite his suggestion that his conclusion rested in part on his own experiments, it seems unlikely that the inconclusive experiments he had carried out on germination had led him to it. Perhaps, however, by immersing him more deeply in the subject, these experiments induced him to take a broader view of the problem. Surmounting his initial enthusiasm for the seductive idea that germination was little more than a kind of fermentation that decomposes water, he had come to realize the necessity to include in an interpretation of vegetation all of the gaseous exchanges known to take place. Putting aside Senebier's idiosyncratic view of germination, and incorporating Senebier's larger investigative contribution to the theory of vegetation instead, Lavoisier found that the overall picture fit together exceedingly well. It also rendered superfluous the idea he had harbored since 1783, that vegetation may form *matière charbonneuse* from inflammable principle, because the fixed air that plants absorb became the obvious source for the *matière charbonneuse* they contain. He thereby lost a conception which had clearly held some fascination for him, that in nature there might be some deeper transmutations of the principles that he treated as fundamental entities in chemical operations; but in return he was able very successfully to unveil one of nature's grand operations as conforming to those same principles.

There is an interesting parallel between these stages in Lavoisier's thought about vegetation and the stages he had gone through ten years earlier in his interpretation of respiration. In both cases a fixation on an attractive analogy had temporarily caused him to neglect one of the two processes he already knew to be occurring. Then it had been the comparison between respiration and the calcination of mercury that made him resistant to incorporating the formation of fixed air into his theory. When he accepted that both of the two "effects" of respiration must be accounted for, he reached a far more coherent theory than he had had while he excluded one of them from consideration.[54] Now it had been the comparison between germination and fermentation that held his attention on the feature he believed to be common to both, the decomposition of water. When he accepted that there was a "double decomposition" involved in vegetation, here too he attained a more integrated theory than he could formulate while he omitted the absorption of fixed air from his scheme. When one is studying a complex phenomenon it is often advantageous to resolve it into simpler components which one can then analyze separately. Sometimes, however, the opposite is true. The simpler components may be only fragments of an integrated system of which one can make better sense by treating it as a whole. In his study both of respiration and of vegetation Lavoisier encountered such situations, and each time he had to learn by trial and error the level of integration most accessible to theoretical interpretation.

In reworking his manuscript on the distillation of plant substances to prepare it for presentation at the open meeting of the Academy he lost some of the unity of its original subject matter. In recompense he infused into it a number of insights of considerably greater scope than his initial discussion. The word "reflections" that he added to the title suggests the more diffuse character of the new version. These were, however, uncommonly profound reflections.

There was not enough time at the meeting of the Academy of November 15 for Lavoisier to entertain the public with his "Reflections." The first opportunity he had to present the memoir to his colleagues was in February 1787, when he read it in installments, one of them on February 21.[55] By then he was becoming involved in a project that was about to change the language in which he discussed this and all other facets of his research enterprise.

12

Language, Organic Composition, and Fermentation

During the first half of 1787 Lavoisier's most urgent scientific business was the preparation of a new chemical nomenclature. He worked on it together with his Parisian colleagues Berthollet and Fourcroy, but especially with Guyton de Morveau, of Dijon, whose earlier proposals for reform provided the starting point for this endeavor. At the beginning of March Morveau was in Paris. "We are taking advantage of this circumstance," Lavoisier wrote to Meusnier, "in order to work with him on a chemical nomenclature. That is, at present, perhaps the most pressing matter of all for the advancement of the sciences." Lavoisier and his collaborators prepared for this reform with great care, not only in working out their system, but in publicizing it. Before presenting it in detail, Lavoisier read at a public session of the Academy on April 18 a "memoir on the necessity for reforming and perfecting the chemical nomenclature," in which he stressed the close connection between the clarity of the language of a science and its concepts. Organizing a meticulous campaign to win over the members of the Academy at the start, he and his associates displayed their new system in tables placed in the hall of the Academy, so that academicians could become familiar with them, and so that "we can receive advice and perfect our work through discussion." On May 2 Morveau followed with a more specific description of the terms the reformers had settled on for naming the simple bodies, and illustrative examples of the way they designated compound substances by names which directly expressed their composition. In the following weeks other associates gave papers on topics related to the new nomenclature. On August 29 Morveau and Lavoisier brought the campaign to a climax by presenting the complete set of tables of old and new names which were printed later the same year in the *Méthode de nomenclature chimique*, jointly composed by Morveau, Lavoisier, Berthollet, and Fourcroy.[1]

It would be beyond the scope of this study to summarize the general need for reform of the terminology of chemistry or the overall system which the reformers introduced.[2] Here I shall discuss only the changes involving those four substances which figured so prominently both in Lavoisier's investigation of respiration and the analysis of plant and animal substances.

For the substance which stood at the heart of these phenomena, Morveau and Lavoisier merely consolidated the transformation he had introduced a decade earlier when he proposed the word "oxygen" to express its characteristic property of forming acids. We have seen, however, that in the intervening period Lavoisier had continued to use a variety of other terms for that substance in a gaseous state, including especially "vital air" and even "dephlogisticated air." Such mixed usage was not compatible with the uniform system at which the reformers now aimed. Their resolution of the case was that "vital air is oxygen gas." The justification which Morveau gave for finally abandoning Lavoisier's "vital air," along with Priestley's "dephlogisticated air," is particularly revealing:

> When one changed the name of dephlogisticated air to that of vital air, one no doubt made a choice more conformable to rules, by substituting for an expression based on a mere hypothesis an expression drawn from one of the most striking properties of that substance, and which characterizes it so essentially that one ought not to hesitate to use it whenever one would simply need to indicate the portion of the atmospheric air which supports respiration and combustion; but it has now been well demonstrated that that portion is not always in the gaseous, or aeriform, state, that it decomposes in a great many operations and lets go of a greater or less quantity of the light or caloric which are the principles which constitute it as vital air.[3]

The logic of the nomenclature, Morveau went on, requires that a substance be designated in such a way that the first term in its name indicates its most simple state. Therefore the word "oxygen" took precedent, and in keeping with their general practice, they added the word "gas" to indicate the combination of oxygen with caloric.

In thus dispensing with his own term "vital air," Lavoisier and his associates deliberately submerged one of the main historical roots of his interest in that part of the atmosphere "which we respire." The demands of a thoroughly systematic nomenclature, expressing the *chemical* properties of substances, identified oxygen as a strictly chemical entity, and by implication made combustion a purely chemical process. Lavoisier's theory of respiration therefore appeared afterward to reduce the physiological process to a chemical one, suppressing the fact that his conception of combustion itself had emerged from mutual comparisons of the physiological and the chemical processes. Historians, looking back through the filter of this same modern nomenclature, have, perhaps, been conditioned in the same way to view the origins of Lavoisier's theory of respiration as an *application* of a previously formulated chemical theory of combustion.

The physiological character which oxygen lost in the new nomenclature surreptitiously reappeared in the naming of another gas. What Priestley had called phlogisticated air and Lavoisier called mophette could now be identified as a portion of the atmosphere which can enter specific chemical combinations to produce nitrous and nitric acid, as well as ammonia. To correspond with the naming of oxygen, Fourcroy proposed "alkaligen," a term expressing the prediction that the substance would eventually be found to exist in the fixed alkalies as it had already been found in volatile alkali. Because that was an uncertain prospect, however, and because it was hard to think of a name which would express the double property of entering into acids and bases, the reformers settled for a term which expressed no chemical property at all, but a physiological one. "In these circumstances, we believed that we could do no better than to select that other property of phlogisticated air, which it so clearly manifests, that it does not support animal life, that it is truly nonvital." They named the gas *azote*—"without life."[4] If vital air was gone, its trace remained in this mirror image of the remaining portion of the atmosphere as one which lacked its essential physiological property.

The rationale for giving up "inflammable air" was a simpler one, based on identifying the principle with its most characteristic chemical property. "The property of inflammability does not belong to it exclusively," Morveau explained; "whereas it alone can produce water by its combination with oxygen." Consequently they named the inflammable principle *hidrogen,* for "engendering water," and inflammable air became hydrogen gas.[5]

The new nomenclature settled at long last the lingering ambiguity over the designation of fixed air and of the constituent which formed its base. "No other entity," Morveau commented, "has received as many names as this gas to which M. Black originally gave the name of fixed air." Lavoisier had contributed more than his share to the profusion of shifting names. Here the general principles of the new system made a stable solution look so easy that we may wonder how Lavoisier could have had so much difficulty for so long finding a satisfactory language with which to express the relationships involved.

> When one has seen fixed air form through the direct combination of *charbon* and vital air, by means of combustion, the name of this gaseous acid is no longer arbitrary; it derives of necessity from its radical, which is pure *matière charbonneuse.* It is, therefore, "carbonic acid," its compounds with bases are "carbonates"; and, in order to lend still more precision to the designation of this radical, by distinguishing it from the *charbon* of ordinary usage, isolating it in thought from the small portion of foreign matter which it ordinarily contains, and which comprises its cin-

> der, we shall adopt the modified expression "carbon," which indicates the pure essential principle of *charbon*, and which has the advantage of specifying [that principle] with a single word, in such a way as to preclude all ambiguity.[6]

As we have seen, Lavoisier had already attempted to make these distinctions by designating the pure principle as *matière charbonneuse*, or *substance charbonneuse*, and the gas as *acide charbonneux;* but he himself had not been able to handle such clumsy terminology consistently, and had lapsed frequently into using *charbon* sometimes to mean the crude substance and sometimes the pure principle. Now the elegantly simple device of dropping the *h* from *charbon* achieved this aim, allowing the nomenclature to catch up with the conceptual clarification Lavoisier had reached several years earlier. Although English translations of French writings in the new terminologies prolonged some of the old confusion by translating carbon part of the time as charcoal, and even the French authors themselves occasionally still slipped up, we shall henceforth simply use the word "carbon" in the sense that Morveau defined it in the above passage.

In his preliminary memoir on nomenclature Lavoisier introduced the famous pragmatic definition of what later came to be called a chemical element. "We are content to regard here as simple, all substances which we cannot decompose: everything which we obtain as the ultimate result of a chemical analysis."[7] By this criterion carbon, oxygen, hydrogen, and azote were all simple substances. At first Morveau did not actually lend them all that status. Oxygen, hydrogen, and azote he placed in a first category of "substances which approach most closely to the state of simplicity," whereas carbon went into the next category of "acidifiable bases or radical principles of acids" which had not yet been decomposed, but which, he implied, were more likely to be found later to have constituent parts than were substances in the first category.[8] By the time Lavoisier wrote his *Elementary Treatise of Chemistry* a year later, he had become more consistent with his own definition, placing all four within a much longer list of "simple substances."[9] Thus, by the standards of the new system of chemistry, carbon, hydrogen, oxygen, and azote became not merely constituents common to plant and animal substances, but their principal *elementary* constituents. The quest which plant and animal chemists had pursued for nearly two centuries ended through a combination of new methods, new conceptions, and a new definition of what was to be regarded as elementary.

II

During the spring of 1787, sometime after he and his colleagues had worked out the new nomenclature, Lavoisier wrote an additional section to insert into the draft of his memoir "Reflections on the decomposition of water by plant and animal substances." He had asserted, we may recall, that experiments analogous to those described in the memoir itself showed, contrary to the views of some modern chemists, that plant acids, "like all plant substances, do not contain fixed air already formed." That point, he now saw, required further development "to render it more intelligible." He did not address himself to it directly, however, but shifted the discussion from plant acids to sugar, the plant substance on which he had "made the greatest number of experiments." To begin, he stated clearly the conception of the composition of plant substances to which he had previously only alluded in passing:

> In the analysis of sugar that I made I have recognized that this substance, and all those analogous to it, are composed of nothing but water and *charbon*. The small quantity of other principles ["such as earth," he added in the margin] are not essential to sugar; they do not form a constituent part. Sugar is therefore nothing but water rendered solid by combination with carbon, *carbonated water*. . . .
>
> One of the principal operations of vegetation is to join the carbon to the water.[10]

On the basis of this composition, Lavoisier wrote, one could predict the types of alterations that sugar undergoes. If heated gently, much of its water is separated from it, but a small quantity of the carbon combines with hydrogen from the water to form "syrupy acid," or in the new nomenclature, pyromucic acid, and several other products result from similar recombinations of the constituent principles of the sugar. With greater heat similar recombinations occur, but in different proportions, so that the quantities of the products differ. The easiest way to "change the proportions of the principles in sugar" was by "addition"; that is, a substance such as nitrous acid, by giving up its oxygen to the sugar, converts it, depending on the proportions used, to one or another of tartaric, acetous, or oxalic acid. Similarly, he argued, one obtains these acids from spirit of wine by causing the oxygen from oxygenated muriatic acid to combine with some of the hydrogen in the spirit of wine, leaving the remainder of the hydrogen combined with the carbon in "the requisite proportions to form oxalic or acetic acid." Berthollet was thus mistaken to conclude, when he obtained these acids from plant substances, that they existed there. He had instead formed them from the plant materials.[11]

After giving these explanations of the products to which plant substances can give rise, Lavoisier added,

> In accordance with these reflections, one ought to regard plant substances as a triple combination of oxygen, hydrogen, and carbon, a combination of little solidity that a very slight heat can al-

> ter and destroy. Then the oxygen and the hydrogen combine with one another and form water, which is disengaged, carrying along with it a little hydrogen and carbon combined in an oily or soapy state, and the *charbon* remains alone.[12]

The passage is remarkable not only becuse it contains probably the first written statement of a conception of composition that became a leitmotiv of thought in early nineteenth-century organic chemistry and biology, but because it appears to contradict the conception with which Lavoisier began this supplement to his memoir. There he had not described sugar as a triple combination of these constituents, but viewed two of them as combined in water, which is in turn combined with carbon. This is not a mere contradiction, however, for in these paragraphs we may be following a trace of the mental pathway along which Lavoisier moved from the one to the other. We must be cautious, however, for two reasons. First, although the character of the passage suggests that Lavoisier may have been making this conceptual transition even as he wrote it, such a document inevitably presents a very incomplete record of the many times and ways in which a person must think about such a problem. As we shall see, Lavoisier later recalled that he had reflected on this question for years before making up his mind. Second, there is a page missing from the manuscript in between the two quoted passages, and the last phrase of the page preceding the gap, "but are the oxygen and the hydrogen . . . ,"[13] suggests the possibility that on the lost page he might explicitly have discussed the question.

With these reservations in mind, we can still reconstruct, on the basis of the information that is available here, a plausible account of what led him to his new conception. We have seen that it was not that his view that sugar and other plant substances contain carbon and preformed water rested on any general demonstration, but that the local circumstances of his investigations of plant composition had predisposed him to think about them in that way. It was, however, a new thing for him to apply this conception to explain the many alterations that substances such as sugar undergo when heated. It is quite possible that the very process of enumerating these decompositions, especially those occurring at a low heat, impressed him with the instability of the substances so subject to them, and that along the way it struck him that a triple combination could explain this instability. It would be much harder to imagine "carbonated water" undergoing such alterations so readily, because in order to decompose water, as he had found in the many experiments in which he had done so, one had to apply far more drastic treatment.

We need not assume that, at the time Lavoisier wrote the above passage suggesting that one should regard plant substances as triple combinations, he had yet perceived that this conception implied the rejection of his conception of them as combinations of carbon and water. Initially he may merely have been devising an *ad hoc* hypothesis to deal with a particular phenomenon. Whether we assume that Lavoisier acquired his new insight between the time he wrote the first and the second passages quoted above; or that he had had the idea before and only incorporated it here for the first time into his writing, this passage appears close enough to the nascent form of an idea so that we may reasonably infer that it was the ease with which plant substances are altered or destroyed at low temperatures, and the multiplicity of their products, that first attracted him to this conception of composition.

After this digression on sugar as a prototype for understanding the composition of plant substances, Lavoisier returned, in the new section he was writing, to topics he had already included in the previous draft of his memoir. They required some modification in the light of his new discussion. Where he had attributed the carbonic acid that animal matters yield to the decomposition of water contained in them, he now said instead that "the carbonic acid . . . is not preformed in them, they contain only the materials"[14] from which the carbonic acid is formed. He had already maintained that the oils obtained by distilling plant matters are formed in the process. Now he added a qualification, that he meant only "empyreumatic oils." The oils one can procure by simply expressing them obviously exist as such in the plant.[15] The most important addition he made to his discussion of oils was to deal with a weighty objection to his explanation of their formation. The objection was most likely one that he himself had thought of. He had argued that they form in the decomposition of substances such as sugar as a portion of the carbon of the latter joins with its oxygen to produce carbonic acid, leaving the hydrogen to combine with another portion of the carbon to form the oil. Then he acknowledged that

> one could, it is true, object that if this explanation were accepted it would follow that upon distilling water over *charbon* a portion of oil should form. This difficulty, which had at first appeared serious to me, has seemed to me to disappear by the following considerations. Although the sugar is composed of hydrogen, of oxygen, and of carbon, and consequently it contains the principles of water, as well as those of oil, and finally those of carbonic acid, it does not actually contain oil or water or carbonic acid. It is a triple combination, the resultant of which has properties very different from the various mixts which can form with its constituent principles combined two by two. Thus, although water plus *charbon* contains all of the same principles as sugar, it is certainly not sugar. It follows that the least heat, that which is only just above that of boiling water, is enough to decompose the sugar ["and to recombine two by two its principles which had formed a triple combination," he added in the margin], and at that temperature it

> can form oil. The decomposition of water by *charbon* requires, on the other hand, a red heat, and this heat not only is higher than that at which empyreumatic oils form, but is even enough to decompose them.[16]

Through this revealing passage we can visualize Lavoisier identifying an anomaly in his own prior explanatory framework, recognizing it for an important problem, wrestling with it, and resolving it in a manner that strongly reinforced the conception of plant composition he had only shortly before formed for himself. If we assume not that this conception had first occurred to him in the course of writing the paragraphs preceding this one, but that it entered his mind sometime before he began to organize his thoughts on paper, then we can even surmise that the conception may have originated while he was contending with the objection about the formation of oils. Whether the reasoning whose lucid outcome is displayed in this passage was the source of this conception, or merely solidified it, in either case it captures a powerful creative mind at work. The capacity for self-criticism and the willingness to alter general ideas that had been central to his thinking in order to meet a difficulty that he perceived in a specific deduction made from them, illustrated so well here, help to explain why Lavoisier was so outstanding a theoretician. He achieved far more in this instance than to "dissipate" an objection, as he afterward put it; for in doing that he was also exploring a fundamental new way to interpret the composition and transformations of plant and animal substances.

Further evidence that Lavoisier was making the mental transition between two conceptions of the composition of plant substances as he wrote this insertion for his memoir was that he afterward rewrote it so as to eliminate the traces of the transition. Moving the statements about the "triple combination" forward from those points in the original version where they had entered his discussion as interpretations of special problems, he replaced the opening description of sugar as "carbonized water" with the following general statement:

> The most rigorous analysis [of sugar] reveals ultimately nothing but water and *substance charbonneuse,* in other words, oxygen, inflammable principle, and *substance charbonneuse.* The very small quantity of other principles which can be contained in it does not appear to be essential to sugar, it does not form one of its constituent parts; but the important point would be to know the order in which these principles are joined to one another, and here is the idea which I have formed. First of all, there appears to be in the sugar a portion of oxygen and of inflammable principle combined in the state of water, which is not essential to the constitution of the sugar and which forms in some way its water of crystallization; but the sugar contains in addition a great quantity

> of oxygen and of inflammable principle joined to *substance charbonneuse*, which appear to form a triple combination. That combination, which is created by vegetation, and which art is apparently not able to imitate, is very common in the plant kingdom. It is known in general under the name of "saccharin body," of "mucous body," etc. The *substance charbonneuse* is in considerable excess in this type of combination; with regard to the inflammable principle and the oxygen, these two principles are in nearly the proportion necessary to compose water. There is only a slight excess of oxygen. Thus, although sugar, and the plant substances in general, contain the materials of fixed air, those of oil, and those of water, they do not actually contain any of these substances already formed, because these principles are not combined in them two by two, but, as I have already stated, form a triple combination.[17]

This paragraph, which appeared in the published version of the memoir, is another historic landmark: the first general theoretical statement that plant substances are composed of the three constituent principles that have ever since been accepted as their most important elements. It is notable also in that, even as he formulated this generalization, he had already been led, by the considerations that are more visible in his earlier draft, to go beyond the simple identification of these constituents and to define the central question as the "order in which the principles are joined together." His answer was the starting point for debate and investigations that occupied his successors throughout the formative era of organic chemistry.

There is reason to believe that, in spite of the cogent reasoning by which he reached it, Lavoisier had trouble accepting his own answer. In his *Elementary Treatise of Chemistry* he wrote in 1788,

> I had proposed formally, in my first memoirs on the formation of water, that this substance, regarded as an element, is decomposed in a great number of chemical operations, notably in vinous fermentation. I supposed at that time that water existed already formed in the sugar, whereas I am persuaded today that it contains only the materials necessary to form water. One can well understand that it had to cost me something to abandon my first ideas; moreover, it was only after several years of reflections, and after a long series of experiments and observation on plants, that I made up my mind.[18]

At first sight this account may appear incompatible with the interpretation I have given that Lavoisier made this conceptual change within the length of time that he took to draft a portion of a memoir. We need not, however, dismiss either view. To reconcile them we need only infer that he went through this mental transition more than once. We sometimes assume that after having a new insight the person who has had it inhabits a different conceptual world. As Gruber has pointed out, however, that person may choose not to follow where the insight would lead.[19] Lavoisier may well have thought of the possibility that the three principles in plant substances existed in a triple combination well before he wrote the draft in which that idea first appeared, but rejected it because he did not want to give up his older concept with its connections to his preoccupation with the decomposition of water. In that case the arguments he framed in the passages discussed above could not have led him to the idea in the first place, but instead forced him to reconsider it and to decide that he must give preference to it. Alternatively, or in addition, there is evidence, as we shall see, that even after publishing this view, he subsequently had doubts about it as he found a new reason to return to that concept of a "carbonized water" to which he had formerly been so attached.

In the very discussion in which he adopted the new view in general, Lavoisier retained a residue of the old. In passing he noted that spirit of wine, unlike oils, is composed of hydrogen, carbon, and water. Thus, for the substance whose investigation had most influenced him earlier to assume that water exists in plant substances, he retained that view. The transformation of his general theoretical framework, however, reduced spirit of wine from the paradigmatic model of a pattern of composition, to an inconspicuous anomaly within his conception of a triple combination of principles. Oils were anomalous in another way. They contained only carbon and hydrogen; but this anomaly is traceable, as we have seen, to the fact that his experimental data lent themselves to the conclusion that no oxygen was present. For animal substances Lavoisier had no hesitation about extending his new general conceptions. These substances, he wrote, "are equally the result of a triple combination of oxygen, hydrogen, and carbon. They contain neither water, nor carbonic acid, nor oil already formed, but all of their elements." As with plant substances, a slight heat suffices to cause these elements to recombine, forming those three substances as decomposition products. The phenomena are more complicated, however, because there exists "a fourth principle in animal matters"—that is, the azote.[20] Perhaps he could more readily apply his new conception of composition to animal matters than to spirit of wine, because not having investigated them himself, he had fewer predispositions to overcome. In any case, the distinction he drew here between the three principles, or elements, characteristic of plant substances, and the four of animal substances, became the standard way to differentiate them.

In those passages in which Lavoisier explained the various alterations of plant substances in terms of additions, subtractions, and recombinations of their constituent elements, he speculated rather freely for one who ordinarily kept his reasoning under tight control. He offered only qualitative descriptions of processes whose outcomes depended upon purported quantitative relations between the composition of the substance altered and the composition of its products. At this level of discussion he could all too easily explain almost any observed change. His explanations were, however, admirably clear. If he gave unusually free rein to his imagination here, it seems evident that the reason was that he had caught the vision of a whole new way to approach the long-standing problems of plant and animal chemistry, and that his enthusiasm carried him further than usual beyond what he could immediately confirm. It was, in fact, a prescient vision. For the first time in the history of these fields of investigation, the transformations of characteristic plant and animal substances could be reduced consistently to the reassortments of unchanging constituents. Lavoisier's speculations therefore opened a new era.

That Lavoisier made this grand vision public in a discussion tucked so inconspicuously within a memoir bearing the narrow title "Reflections on the decomposition of water by plant and animal substances" strikes us as incongruous. We might have expected him to organize the memoir around the large subject rather than the more limited one. By following the steps in the construction of this memoir we can understand how the local circumstances in his intellectual pathway led him to formulate these ideas when the memoir had already taken shape, and to insert them at a place within it where they connected with a point he had made in a discussion oriented around different themes. As in his memoir "on the alterations of the air," he ended up with a kind of paper within a paper. Perhaps, however, there was a deeper reason for the mold into which he fitted these ideas. Lavoisier had crossed the frontier of the domain of plant chemistry mainly in search of more processes to exemplify combustion and the decomposition of water. While exploring these boundary regions he was also being drawn toward more general questions at the heart of plant and animal chemistry themselves; but his sense of what his central scientific enterprise was seems not yet to have caught up with the direction of his latest interests. At this point he may still have thought of his views on the composition and transformations of plant and animal substances as sidelights growing out of the continuation of the research program that had dominated his scientific career since 1773. The new interests were, however, rapidly outgrowing that subordinate status.

III

Lavoisier's steady drift from a research program centered on the problem of combustion toward one organized tacitly around the problems of plant chemistry is most discernible in his experimental activity during the first half of 1787.

The cluster of problems at which he directed his main effort was not in itself new. Fermentation, the combustion of carbon and of spirit of wine, and the analysis of sugar were all by now familiar topics. It is possible that he had no central objective linking them, that he was simply pursuing his earlier efforts on several independent problems associated through conceptual and methodological overlaps. There are good circumstantial reasons to infer, however, that these four problems were coalescing in his mind into an overriding concern to mount a climactic attack on the most complex of them, the phenomenon of fermentation. The composition of spirit of wine, of carbonic acid, and of sugar were all essential to a full description of fermentation, since all three substances were involved in that process. The one new investigation he took up in this period, the conversion of spirit of wine to ether, may appear unrelated; but Lavoisier, in fact, viewed that process as in some sense an extension of spirituous fermentation. Just as the mild, sweet substances that undergo fermentation became volatile and inflammable in forming spirit of wine, so did the latter become even more so in changing to ether.[21]

The first experiments of this group Lavoisier carried out on yeast, on February 20. Having procured from a brewer six to eight pints of beer yeast in the form of a fluid *pâte*, he tried to filter it. He succeeded only after heating the yeast, obtaining a deeply colored filtrate resembling beer. A second filtration yielded a lighter colored liquid. Both liquids precipitated limewater weakly, and were very slightly acidic.[22] In these operations Lavoisier might either have been seeking clues about the composition of yeast, or trying to extract from it a ferment which would not produce the froth that had so inconvenienced him in the long fermentation experiment which was still going on. In either case this brief exploration does not appear to have uncovered anything particularly significant.

On March 19 Lavoisier attempted to carry out a new combustion of charcoal, in a bell jar filled with vital air over mercury, in order to determine once again the proportions of vital air and *charbon* in fixed air (even as he was devising the new nomenclature he was still privately utilizing a mixture of the new and the old). The experiment failed, and he tried again one week later. He used *charbon de Bourdenne*, well calcined in order to reduce it as nearly as possible to pure carbon. This time the combustion went very well. The 18.2 grains of *charbon* with which he began left only a very small residue of 0.29 grains consisting of pieces of *charbon*, and 0.47 grains of cinder. None of the problems which had afflicted each of the experiments from which he had pulled together his memoir on the composition of fixed air in 1784 interfered with the smooth outcome of this new effort. Then he had been unable to use his direct measurements of the loss in weight of *charbon* because he suspected the residue had gained weight by attracting moisture. Now he obviated that problem by the simple expedient of drying the residue just before he weighed it. The total of the substances consumed:

Vital air	45.421 grains
Charbon	17.440
Total	62.861,

came out so close to the quantity of carbonic acid formed, 62.281 grains, that he had to assume only a mere 0.58 grains of water formed. The result had been, therefore, the nearest he had ever come to a pure combustion of carbon. Making only very minor adjustments in his final calculations, he ended up with a "composition of fixed air, according to this experiment," of

Vital air	71.837
Charbon	28.163
Total	100

This result, confirming so closely the average proportion of 72:28 which he had extracted from the aggregate of his more problematic previous analyses, must have been particularly heartening to Lavoisier.[23]

It may well be that Lavoisier had returned to the composition of fixed air simply because of a lingering dissatisfaction with the experiments on which he had based his published conclusion, or an uncomplicated desire to improve all of his important quantitative measurements from time to time. His renewed interest in the problem may also, however, have been linked to his growing interest in fermentation and the analysis of plant and animal substances, for both of which an accurate knowledge of the combining proportions of carbon and oxygen in carbonic acid could become crucial.

On the same day that he carried out this very successful analysis, March 26, Lavoisier distilled spirit of wine in nitrous acid (nitric acid in the new nomenclature), in order to convert the spirit of wine to ether. He connected the retort with three receivers, the first one to collect the ether, and the last two, containing caustic alkali, to trap the fixed air formed. From the weight changes in each of these vessels he estimated the quantity of spirit of wine consumed and the quantities of the products of the reaction. Also on this day he recorded briefly another experiment on the combustion of spirit of wine, using the serpentine apparatus designed by Meusnier.[24]

Meanwhile the fermentation experiment he had begun back in September of the previous year was still going on. On April 27 he weighed the distillation flask in which it was taking place once more, but made no calculation of how much additional fixed air had formed. A few bubbles were still forming in the liquid, but he poured it out of the flask and filtered it to collect the portion of the yeast which had settled to the bottom. There is no indication that he carried out any further analyses based on the overall result, or that he obtained after all these months anything from the experiment except experience which would help him to control the conditions more effectively in subsequent experiments. He began another fermentation experiment, in fact, on the same day that he ended this one. Placing 2 pounds 9 ounces of sugar, 10 pounds 4 ounces of water, and 4 ounces, 0 gros, 58 grains of yeast in a glass bottle, he inserted in its mouth a stopper containing a long glass tube, and luted them together. He weighed the bottle together with its contents. The yeast he was using was a rather dry *pâte*. To determine the amount of moisture it contained he further dried and weighed a small portion of it. The *pâte* was difficult to mix into the fermentation solution, but after a few hours it was sufficiently disaggregated so that the liquid became frothy and began to disengage bubbles of air.[25] To judge from Lavoisier's procedure, it appears that after his failure to collect all of the fixed air in caustic alkali in the previous fermentation experiment he decided this time to simplify the operation by carrying it out in a single bottle, allowing the fixed air to escape, and relying from the start on the weight change of the bottle to determine its quantity. In this way perhaps he hoped also to avoid the troubles he had had before with yeast drawn over into the collection bottles.

While this fermentation was going on, Lavoisier went ahead with his investigation of the properties of yeast. On May 4 he took a pound of yeast *pâte*, dried it over a low fire until it was reduced to a yellow powder weighing a little over four ounces, heated it further until it again softened into a *pâte*, and then put it into a retort. He connected the retort to a receiver with three openings, one of them connecting to a collection bottle below, the other to a second bottle containing caustic alkali. He then distilled the yeast in the traditional manner, gradually increasing the heat and collecting the products in four fractions. Throughout the operation an air was disengaged, a result, Lavoisier inferred, of the decomposition of water by *charbon* (carbon), contained in the yeast. The caustic alkali bottle increased in weight, presumably because the distillation released carbonic acid. At the end of the distillation a residue of *charbon* remained in the retort. While the second and third fractions were being collected, solid volatile alkali was deposited on the walls of the receiver.[26] In this operation Lavoisier appears to have been seeking to identify qualitatively the constituents of yeast. In view of his general conception of the composition of plant and animal substances it probably did not surprise him to find in these products evidence that yeast contains hydrogen (the air disengaged), carbon, and azote (combined with hydrogen in the volatile alkali). The fact that the yeast yielded azote would indicate that, although derived from a plant, it was an "animal matter" in the sense that this designation had come to apply to a class of substances, whether from plants or animals, which contain a "fourth principle" in addition to those characteristic of plant substances.

On June 5 Lavoisier weighed the bottle in which the fermentation begun on

April 27 was still going on. The contents of the vessel had lost over that time 1 pound, 3 ounces, 7 gros, 62 grains. On June 12 he weighed it again. In this interval it had lost only about 2 gros more. Probably deciding that the fermentation was about over, he prepared to analyze the fermented liquor by distillation. To collect the products he devised an elaborate apparatus consisting of a series of connected vessels (see Figure 11). The crystalline alembic and head which he selected for the distillation he connected through an extension tube to a "three-point matras," that is, a flask with openings at the top, the bottom, and on one side. This flask was joined through a friction fitting with a bottle below it, and connected from its side opening to a series of five additional bottles. The second and third bottles, left empty, were surrounded by ice. The fourth bottle contained distilled water, the fifth was empty, and the sixth contained caustic alkali. This last bottle communicated with a pneumatic bell jar. Before beginning the distillation he weighed each of the vessels and the extension tube.[27]

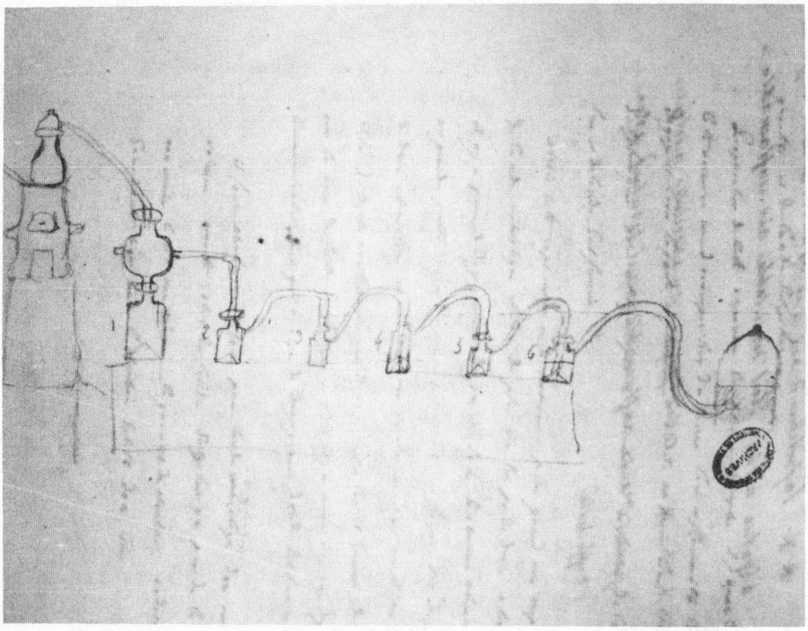

Figure 11. Lavoisier's sketch of apparatus for analysis begun June 5, 1787, of products of fermentation. On the far left is the distillation flask on a furnace. 1 is a three-point matras; 2, 3, bottles surrounded by ice; 4, bottle containing water; 5, empty bottle; 6, bottle containing caustic potash. On the far right is a pneumatic vessel. Lavoisier, Cahiers, R-12, Archives of the Académie des Sciences de Paris, f. 167.

Clearly Lavoisier had planned with great care an arrangement which would enable him to separate products of differing volatility and solubility in water, as well as any carbonic acid and other gases which might be released. He bestowed as much care on the operation itself. To "avoid accidents," he placed the alembic in a sand bath and raised the heat of the fire very slowly. It took him six hours to bring the liquid to the boiling point. After three more hours a first fraction of spirit of wine had collected in bottle 1. He poured it into another bottle and weighed it. Adding 12 grains to the measured weight because he had lost a little in the transfer, he estimated that this fraction weighed 10 ounces, 0 gros, 50 grains. Reconnecting bottle 1 to the matras (an operation greatly facilitated by the fact that he had utilized a friction connection rather than the conventional luting), he distilled for four and a half hours more and obtained 14 ounces, 7 gros, 47 grains more of liquid. This second fraction was a very watery spirit of wine with an odor of yeast. A piece of paper dipped in it would hardly burn. A third fraction weighed 4 ounces, 6 gros, 36 grains. Meanwhile a very small amount of pure spirit of wine collected in the cooled bottle 2. By weighing the alembic at the end of the operation he determined the decrease in the weight of the fermentation liquid. He measured also the increase in weight of the caustic alkali, which was very small (as expected, since the carbonic acid produced during the fermentation itself had been allowed to escape from the fermentation bottle). Apparently no gas passed into the pneumatic chamber, since he recorded no change in its volume. From all these measurements Lavoisier "recapitulated" the products of the spirituous fermentation as follows:

	[pounds]	[ounces]	[gros]	[grains]
1st portion of spirit of wine, including that which remained in the funnel, and the loss during the transfer		10	0	60
2d portion		14	7	50
3d portion		4	6	36
Pure spirit of wine remaining in bottle 2		0	0	38
Increase in weight of caustic alkali in bottle 6		0	0	18
Quantity [of carbonic acid?] estimated to have remained in extension tube		0	0	8
Increase in weight of stoppers		0	0	32
Total	1	14	0	26

	[pounds]	[ounces]	[gros]	[grains]
Weight of the liquid consumed in the distillation	1	14	1	30
Loss			1	4

This was a satisfying verification that he had carried out the operation and weighings precisely, accounting for nearly all of the material separated from the fermentation fluid. It was, however, not an adequate representation of the products of the distillation, for the spirit of wine was obviously mixed with water, and he had not identified the substances left in the fluid at the end of the distillation. To determine how much spirit of wine his fractions included, he measured their specific gravities with a hydrometer he had designed for such use. He matched the measured specific gravities to the specific gravities of known mixtures of spirit of wine and water. In this way he estimated that the first fraction contained slightly less than eight parts of spirit of wine to nine of water, and the weaker second fraction five parts of spirit of wine to eleven of water.[28]

To analyze the fluid left in the alembic after the distillation, Lavoisier evaporated the 2 pounds, 1 ounce, 0 gros, 28 grains of "noticeably acidic" liquor over a sand bath and a very gentle heat for eight days. Near the end it had an odor of vinegar. Then, in order not to lose any products, he was "obliged" to distill the remaining liquid. He obtained three watery products, the first two acidic, the third yellowish and containing a small amount of solid material. The residue remaining in the retort was "a little decomposed and a little carbonaceous." He regarded it as "partly decomposed sugar." On the basis of these further analyses Lavoisier wrote out a second form of summary of the products separated from the fermentation fluid:

Recapitulation

Quantity of fermented liquid analyzed	3 pounds	15 ounces	1 gros	58 grains
Products obtained				
Spirit of wine in 1st product		4	0	69.3
Spirit of wine in 2d product		3	4	33.5
Spirit of wine in bottle 2				38.0
Spirit of wine evaporated			1	4.0
Spirit of wine absorbed in stoppers				24.0
Total of spirit of wine		7	7	24.8

	[pounds]	[ounces]	[gros]	[grains]
Residue of the distillation, sugar partially decomposed giving sirupy acid by distillation			4	36.0
Water, with a little vinegar in solution	3	6	5	69.2
Total	3	15	1	58

It is evident from the exact balance between the weight of the fluid analyzed and the products that Lavoisier had estimated those quantities he could not directly measure, so as to make it come out even. Since he had analyzed only a portion of the fluid which had undergone fermentation, he next converted the essential totals from the preceding table to those which the entire fermenting solution would have yielded:

Spirit of wine	1 pound	7 ounces	5 gros	18.80 grains
Residue of distillation		1	5	30.85
Water, containing a little vinegar in solution	10	3	4	39.10
[Total]	11	12	7	16.75[29]

From the initial quantities of sugar, water, and yeast he had used, and with the estimate of carbonic acid evolved which he could obtain from the decrease in the weight of the fermentation bottle over the time of the fermentation itself, Lavoisier had all he needed in order to complete an overall balance sheet of the substances present before and after the fermentation. There is no indication in his notebook, however, that he drew up such a balance at the time he completed the experiment.

Lavoisier's reason for taking up the subject of fermentation in 1784 had been that it was one of "nature's operations" for decomposing water. He had had in mind then that some of the *matière charbonneuse* contained in sugar combines with the oxygen of the water to form fixed air, while the remainder combines with inflammable air to compose the spirit of wine. He had already claimed that spring to have found that the weight of the sugar and water consumed is equal to the weight of the products. Judging from the fact that in 1786 and 1787 he was still struggling to work out suitable experimental conditions for analyzing the fermentation process, his earlier assertion must have been based on very general considerations. Now that he was in a position to establish such an overall balance with some reliability, however, his goal had grown more ambitious. As he had done for the combustion of spirit of wine, oil, and wax, he wanted not only to show that the materials present before the fermentation reaction were equal in weight to those present afterward, but to balance their constituent elements as well. At a time when he was learning to visualize the various alterations of sugar and other plant substances in terms of additions, subtractions, and recombinations of their elements, spirituous fermentation undoubtedly came to appear to him as an exemplary opportunity to examine such changes in more specific detail. For such purposes it was an urgent matter to know the quantitative composition of sugar. That is undoubtedly why, a few days after carrying out the above analysis of the products of fermentation, he began a series of experiments on sugar intended to discover a method by which he could attain that knowledge.

IV

The main obstacle Lavoisier faced in his effort to analyze sugar has already been suggested. The combustion methods with which he had been able to determine for the first time the proportions of carbon, hydrogen, and oxygen in several plant substances depended upon their being readily inflammable, burning completely in a closed space, so that he could decompose them entirely to carbonic acid and water. Sugar unfortunately did not have this property. He had therefore to look for other means to decompose it, if possible still by some form of oxygenation so that he would end up with these same two products. The general direction of his thought at this time is, I think, indicated by a passage in the final version of his memoir on the decomposition of water by plant and animal substances.

> Allow me, before I leave this subject, to make the observation that there are four principal ways to oxygenate plant and animal substances. One can oxygenate them by combustion in free air; by distillation over an open fire, with the aid of the water they contain; by any fermentation, whether vinous [spirituous] or putrefactive; finally, by their combination with the acids to which oxygen is only weakly bound, such as nitric acid or oxygenated muriatic acid. These three types of oxygenation produce analogous effects, with the sole difference that in oxygenation by the air there is a release of caloric; in that by water [in which type Lavoisier apparently included oxygenation both by distillation and by fermentation] there is a release of hydrogen; in that by nitric acid there is a release of nitrous gas.[30]

On the surface Lavoisier devised this classification to elucidate the new distinction he was making between "ardent combustion" and "obscure combustion." The passage probably also reflects, however, a pragmatic preoccupation with the problem of how to analyze those plant and animal substances that were recalcitrant to the method utilizing the "ardent" form of combustion.

On June 6, 1787, Lavoisier wrote in his laboratory register, "I have attempted to combine sugar with concentrated sulfuric acid. As soon as one heats the mixture the sugar is decomposed. One obtains at the same time a moderate quantity of inflammable air and of sulfurous acid." It is not clear whether he was referring to an experiment which he had just carried out, or reflecting on an earlier one. In either case he was engaged in an effort to decompose sugar by one of the methods of "obscure combustion" outlined in the preceding paragraph. The reaction with sulfuric acid was analogous to the one with nitric acid which he had mentioned as his example of oxygenation by "acids to which oxygen is only weakly bound." In comparing the results of this experiment with those of a similar one using dilute sulfuric acid, he perceived an anomaly. His description of the difficulty is worth quoting in full because the passage offers a precious glimpse of Lavoisier reasoning privately in immediate response to a puzzling situation:

> The explanation of this experiment would seem to be simple. In that situation a decomposition of the sugar takes place. The inflammable air is disengaged and leaves the *charbonneuse* part at the bottom. At the same time the sulfuric acid is attacked by the *charbon*. It forms fixed air and sulfurous acid.
>
> But this explanation does not hold up anymore when one employs vitriolic acid diluted by more than its weight of water. Then there is no disengagement of gas at all. The sugar is in part carbonized. What happens then to the inflammable air of the sugar? There are two possibilities. Either the sugar does not contain any, or else it is destroyed as soon as it is evolved; and in that case it would form water with the base of the sulfuric acid. But there is here still an insurmountable difficulty. That is, that there is no disengagement of sulfurous acid.
>
> One must carbonize sugar by vitriolic [Lavoisier then crossed out vitriolic and wrote] sulfuric acid in a large vessel, then absorb the sulfuric acid by alkali, and examine the neutral salt and the quantity of *charbon*. One will no doubt discover what renders *charbon* soluble in water.[31]

We may note in passing that these paragraphs reveal Lavoisier once more mingling in his private notes the old and the new nomenclature, at the very time when he and his associates were publicly campaigning to sweep out terms which they regarded as residues of the past. Here he utilized alternately the new terms sulfuric and sulfurous acid, and the traditional name for the first of these, vitriolic acid. In one case, but not the other, he crossed out "vitriolic" and replaced it with "sulfuric." He continued to use the comfortable old term "inflammable air," which should now have been hydrogen gas, and he fell back on the old ambiguous usage of the words *charbon* and *charbonneuse* even though he had devised new terms to obviate that ambiguity. If it is true that revolutionary changes in science imply new uses of language which make it impossible for those who have adopted the new and those who remain in the old to communicate fully with each other, then Lavoisier's tendency to cross over that language barrier in the midst of a single chain of thought raises interesting questions about whether he also crossed over in the thoughts themselves. Even revolutionaries may continue to live partly within the old regimes they believe they have overthrown.

The next day Lavoisier carried out an experiment based "on the consequences of the above views." After weighing a retort he placed in it 6 gros of sugar and a mixture of "half sulfuric acid and half water" weighing altogether 2 ounces, 1 gros, 52 grains. He adapted a tube to the retort (the tube must have connected to a pneumatic vessel, although this is not directly mentioned), and began to heat it. The first air he collected he assumed to be the air contained in the vessels at the start.

> Then the mixture darkened and swelled up, while scarcely disengaging any air. After I had increased the fire a little, sulfurous acid was disengaged in white vapors, and at the same time air passed over in a more regular manner; then I believed that I should remove the retort.

Again weighing the retort, he found that it had lost 3 gros 4 grains, which he attributed to the sulfurous acid formed. Then he broke open the retort and detached the blackish material that he found in it, estimating that he lost 12–15 grains of it in the process. The black material was pulpy in consistency. When he mixed it with water and let it stand for a while "the *charbon* fell to the bottom." He washed the *charbon* three times, filtered, dried, and weighed it, but did not enter the result in the space he left in his notebook for that purpose. To find out whether the sulfuric acid had been "changed in its nature by its combination with the sugar," he saturated a portion (presumably of the liquid left in the retort, although the record does not say so), with calcareous earth. A precipitate of selenite formed, confirming the presence of sulfuric acid; but because the supernatant liquid was still slightly bitter, Lavoisier suspected that it also contained some other salt. Filtering out the selenite, he added vitriolic acid to the remaining solution, obtaining nothing but an odor of nitrous acid. With fixed alkali, however, he formed a grayish precipitate.[32] When he examined the airs that he had collected during the experiment, Lavoisier found that the first portion, which he had thought to be the ordinary air contained in the vessels, "extinguished a flame on the spot, which one had not expected." The next portion was "true inflammable air." Later during the course of the experiment he collected "a few cubic inches of inflammable air which burned with difficulty."[33]

It is doubtful that these results resolved for Lavoisier the questions which had stimulated him to perform the experiment. Most likely he had chosen the mixture of half sulfuric acid and half water as a borderline situation between the divergent phenomena he had observed with concentrated and dilute sulfuric acid. The result was closer to that for concentrated acid in that some sulfurous acid and some inflammable air formed; but that outcome did not assure that the same thing would happen when the sulfuric acid was diluted "with more than its weight of water." Moreover, even if all of the weight loss was, as he suggested, due to sulfurous acid, less than one-fifth of the sulfuric acid would have been converted. Fixed air must not have formed in quantities large enough to measure. The analysis of the situation seems, therefore, to have remained incomplete. Neither did the experiment move him very far toward a quantitative analysis of the composition of sugar, even if he recorded somewhere else the quantity of *charbon* contained in the black material. Among other uncertainties, the inflammable air he collected was not all pure. Although we cannot tell what Lavoisier's own reaction to the outcome was, from a distance it appears only to have confronted him with further complications.

One indication that Lavoisier may have left this experiment with the feeling that oxygenation by acids was not immediately promising for the analysis of sugar was that two weeks later he turned to distillation, the only feasible alternative left in his list of combustion methods. In order to collect the gaseous products he set up an arrangement similar to what he had used for his analysis of the products of fermentation. The distillation retort led into another bottle with three openings, one connected with a jar underneath it, the other to four more flasks of which bottles 3 and 5 (see Figure 12) contained caustic alkali. The end of the series was again a pneumatic vessel. As usual he weighed each vessel before beginning the analysis.

He then

> lighted [the fire] at noon and proceeded [to increase it] very slowly. At 1:30 PM the sugar began to melt, and soon afterward to turn brown, but without disengaging air. At the same time a yellow acid passed over, the color of a gold solution, and the last portions of which were more brownish.

A second more deeply colored acid passed over later. He weighed both acids. Meanwhile, however, the sugar swelled up so much that he had to stop the operation. He started over with a larger retort and about the same amount of

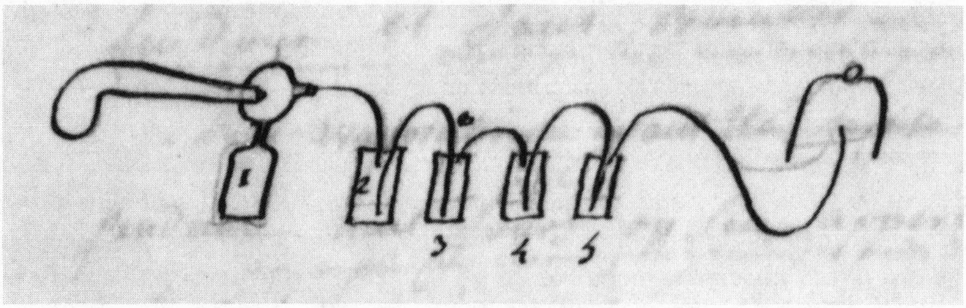

Figure 12. Lavoisier's sketch of apparatus for distillation analysis of sugar. On the far left is the distillation retort; 1–5 are collecting bottles, 3 and 5 containing caustic alkali. On the far right is a pneumatic vessel. Lavoisier, Cahiers, R-12, Archives of the Académie des Sciences de Paris, f. 185.

sugar. This time there was room enough for the expansion of the sugar, but while that substance was still incompletely carbonized the retort broke, and his second attempt therefore also ended abruptly. He nevertheless weighed the yellow acid which had again appeared, and found also that the jars containing caustic alkali had gained about 22½ grains in weight. There was overall, however, "in this operation a quite considerable amount of material missing, which it is difficult to explain." About all he could salvage from this abortive experiment was to examine the yellow acid more closely. It turned out to be an acid known as syrupy acid, which Scheele had recently obtained from milk sugar. In the new nomenclature it was pyromucic acid.[34]

Trying once more, Lavoisier went back to a retort smaller even than the one he had used in the initial experiment, probably to decrease the chance of another breakage. To avoid the problem of swelling he did not introduce the sugar itself into the retort, but placed there 1 ounce, 5 gros, 15 grains of "*charbon* of well-carbonized sugar." By raising the heat, with careful control, over a long time, he managed to bring the retort to the point at which it began to soften, "without breaking it." During the operation some inflammable gas passed over, but there is no indication that he measured it. Of the two bottles containing caustic alkali one gained 1 gros 50 grains, the other "only 14 grains" in weight. From the change in weight of the retort during the operation he estimated that of the *charbon* originally placed there 6 gros remained at the end. In the first bottle he collected 3 gros 60 grains of the syrupy acid, together with a heavy oil and a few grains of one that floated on top.[35] Lavoisier apparently did not draw up a balance sheet of the operation, no doubt because the small amounts of products, the lack of a measure of the inflammable gas, and uncertainty over what had been lost in carbonizing the sugar prior to the distillation rendered the results unsuitable for such a calculation. Thus his third attempt to overcome the technical obstacles frustrating his analyses was no more successful than the first two. His need to know the composition of sugar was, however, no less pressing, and in the absence of any promising alternatives he persisted with yet another distillation on July 19.

From the weight of the retort he now selected, which was intermediate between the one he had used in the first trial interrupted by the swelling of the sugar and the one which had broken in the second trial; and from the weight of the sugar (2 ounces, 4 gros, 52½ grains), which was about a third of the amounts used in each of the first two trials, we can surmise that the only way Lavoisier now saw to try to obviate the troubles which had ruined the prior efforts was a judicious compromise between these conditions: that is, a retort small enough to lessen the risk of breakage, but large enough to contain the swelling of the least amount of sugar from which he could hope to obtain enough of the products to measure reliably. Nevertheless he was again forced to stretch the technical limits of his apparatus. Near the end of the operation, as the syrupy acid and a thick oil began to come over into the first receiver, he "pushed [the fire] to the point of melting the retort, but the experiment did not fail." Its success, however, was very limited. "The vessel being broken, one lost the syrupy acid." Moreover, although he separated the gases evolved into several fractions, and measured them, the result "is not rigorously exact because of the great quantity of air in the vessels, which have a very large volume, so that each air is mixed with the preceding." Even the determination of the *charbon* in the retort was not without its problems. The quantity remaining, according to the change in the weight of the retort, was 6 gros 48 grains; but "as the *charbon* still contained water, since it yielded inflammable air, one could suppose that only 6 gros 36 grains of *charbon* actually remained."[36]

After four tries at analyzing sugar by distillation and one attempt by oxygenation with acid, Lavoisier must have felt very far from his goal. Perhaps for relief, he turned his attention to another phenomenon, the conversion of spirit of wine to ether. In order to characterize that transformation he had to know the composition of ether. Here he had even worse luck. If the problem with sugar was that it was not easily combustible, that with ether was the opposite. On July 27, he recorded,

> Combustion of ether
>
> I had prepared an ether lamp to be ignited under a bell jar of common air, with the intention of supplying the dephlogisticated air gradually as the combustion proceeded.

In other words, he utilized the same apparatus which had earlier worked so well for spirit of wine.[37] Now, however, "at the moment when the phosphorus was ignited there was an explosion and the bell jar was broken into a thousand pieces. Fortunately I had taken precautions against accidents." Lavoisier was apparently daunted enough not to repeat the attempt, but not too intimidated to utilize what remained of the apparatus that same day for a new analysis of spirit of wine. That operation went smoothly.[38]

Lavoisier's laboratory notebooks contain only one experiment performed between July 19, 1787, and March 1788. Very probably he did, in fact, no more than that, for he was during these months extremely busy in a new realm of activity. Elected to the first Provincial Assembly of Orléanais, he left Paris for Orléans for September 14–22, and again in October. It was on October 27 that he carried out an experiment on prussiate of lime; but he could have had little time for sustained research, because he was also occupied with a commission report on hospitals, a report on ironworks, and other duties for the Academy. When he had finished these, he went back to Orléans, where he took a very active part in the second session of the Assembly.[39] He must have been forced, therefore, to leave his current central research problems, fermentation and the analysis of plant and animal substances, in a state of suspended aspiration.

V

It may have been because he had no time for further experiments that Lavoisier decided, sometime after completing those described in the preceding sections, to use the results he had already in hand as best he could to "prove" his original contention that spirituous fermentation is "a phenomenon of the decomposition of water."[40] As he often did when he had a topic in mind that he considered to be of general interest, he aimed at a paper to present at the next open meeting of the Academy, probably the annual November meeting marking the end of the Academy's vacation.[41]

As he also customarily did on such occasions, Lavoisier shaped his presentation somewhat to cater to his audience. "The fear of fatiguing the attention of the public for too long" prompted him in the memoir he wrote to "suppress the details of the experiments and to present only the results."[42] His tactic also unfortunately makes it difficult for the historian to ferret out the manner in which he arrived at the results he described. There is enough data to establish that he based his analysis primarily upon the fermentation operation that he had carried out between April 27 and June 12; but not all of the figures he included in the account of the experiment given in his memoir are readily identifiable with those in the original laboratory records; and although some of the sheets on which he recorded intermediate stages in the reduction of the data survive, I have not been able to ascertain in detail how he derived all of his calculations. Nevertheless it is possible to follow his general approach.

In the fermentation experiment on which he relied for this memoir, we may recall, Lavoisier omitted the apparatus for collecting fixed air, probably because in the previous experiment it had proven inadequate to the task. Accordingly he could now calculate the quantity of fixed air only indirectly, by subtracting the weight of the fermentation bottle at the end of the experiment from its weight just after he had filled it with the fermentation mixture. That amount, 1 pound, 4 ounces, 1 gros, 40 grams, he utilized without change during his calculations, and he retained it in the text of his memoir. About the other product, spirit of wine, he was less certain. As we have seen, by distilling a portion of the fermented liquid and analyzing the various fractions he had concluded that there had been 1 pound, 7 ounces, 5 gros of spirit of wine formed. Subsequently he must have doubted that outcome, however, for in the first balance sheet of the experiment he drew up, he used the quantity 1 pound, 12 ounces, 4 gros, a figure whose source is not obvious. The sum of the spirit of wine and fixed air formed, plus 1 ounce of yeast and 3 ounces of undecomposed sugar he estimated to be present at the end, added up to 3 pounds, 4 ounces, 5 gros, 40 grains, which he took as the total of the materials, other than water, after the operation. The total quantity of sugar, water, and yeast that he had put into the flask at the beginning was 13 pounds, 1 ounce, 0 gros, 58 grains. Subtracting the former from the latter gave 9 pounds, 12 ounces, 3 gros, 18 grains of "water fallen back"—that is, of water that remained in the flask at the end. In other words, he calculated the quantity of water present at the end as the amount necessary to balance the materials present before the operation with those present or accounted for at the end. The initial quantity of water he had added, however, was 10 pounds, 4 ounces, so that there was 7 ounces, 4 gros, 54 grains "missing."[43] It was, in fact, probably Lavoisier's aim in constructing this balance to reveal that missing water; for if water were decomposed during fermentation, as he supposed, then there must be less present at the end than at the beginning. We may note that this small difference between two large quantities depended heavily on the assumption that all of the weight lost by the bottle represented fixed air given off, as well as various assumptions he must have made during his indirect calculation of the quantity of spirit of wine.

In the next stage of his analysis of the experiment, Lavoisier did change some of the assumptions on which he had based this first calculation. He returned to his original figure of 1 pound, 7 ounces, 5 gros, 18 grains for the spirit of wine formed, he decided to neglect the yeast, and he reduced his estimate of the undecomposed sugar to 1 ounce. He must have made these adjustments with some qualms, for they reduced the already small negative water balance by more than half. Fortunately for his conception of fermentation, the new calculation still left 3 ounces 7 gros of "missing" water that he could maintain had been decomposed in the process.

At some point in his investigation of fermentation Lavoisier had decided to use the phenomenon as the occasion to revive his effort to express in the form of equations the principle that no material is gained or lost in chemical operations. The first manifestation of this intention is on the data sheet in which he showed the result of his revised balance calculation as follows:

> 3 ounces 7 gros of water + 2 pounds 8 ounces sugar = 1 pound 7 ounces 5 gros 18 grains spirit of wine + 1 pound 4 ounces 2 gros carbonic acid[44]

This was enough to attain his original purpose, the demonstration that fermentation is a process which decomposes water. Now, however, he undertook the further task of breaking his equation down into the quantities of carbon, hydrogen, and oxygen comprising the four substances involved. By this time he had available analyses of the quantitative composition of each of the four substances appearing in his equation. Those for the composition of water and carbonic acid he regarded as firmly established. For spirit of wine he still had only one reliable result. As we have just seen, for the analysis of sugar he was in the midst of serious unresolved difficulties. Accordingly, he began with the other three. From the quantities produced and the composition of the spirit of wine and carbonic acid he computed the following totals for their elements:

Hydrogen		4 ounces	1 gros	24.16 grains
Oxygen	1 pound	11	3	6.69
Carbon		12	2	41.15

Although he represented the breakdown of the quantities in balance sheet format, he maintained the aura of the mathematical equation by referring to the figures for water and sugar as the "left-hand side" (*premier membre*), and the spirit of wine and carbonic acid as the "right-hand side" (*second membre*); and he designated the above totals as the "right-hand side simplified," that is, as a redistribution of the quantities on this side of the equation. From these totals he subtracted the quantity of hydrogen and oxygen represented by the 3 ounces 7 gros of water on the left-hand side (in keeping with his established 85:15 ratio for the proportions of water, these were 3 ounces, 2 gros, 25.2 grains of oxygen and 4 gros 46.8 grains of hydrogen). The remainder represented the composition of the other member of the left-hand side, the sugar.[45] (That result is shown in the paragraph below).

What Lavoisier had in effect done at this point was to utilize his fermentation results to attain the goal that, to judge from his laboratory records, still eluded his more direct efforts; that is, as a means to determine the composition of sugar. As we shall see, there is reason to infer that a little later he came to see that conclusion as the principal outcome of this computation. In the present context, however, he viewed the situation somewhat differently. He treated the result as a "calculated" result for sugar, that he could check against an "experimental" result. In spite of what appears from a distance the completely unsatisfactory state of his efforts to analyze sugar through other methods, he somehow managed at this time, "by combining successfully" the two procedures he had used—analysis by distillation and by acids—to come up with a result for the composition of sugar that he considered "very satisfying."[46] However he may have accomplished this (I have found no record of the methods he used), he arrived at a result somewhat different from the preceding. On his data sheet he represented them side by side:

Sugar (2 pounds 8 ounces)	Calculation (pounds,	ounces,	gros,	grains)	Experiment (pounds,	ounces,	gros,	grains)
Oxygen	1	8	0	53.49	1	7	3	42
Hydrogen		3	4	49.36		3	5	36
Carbon		12	2	41.15		12	6	66[47]

The discrepancy between these two results was not large enough to discourage Lavoisier. On the contrary, he regarded the fact that they differed by "no more than an eighth" as independent evidence for the accuracy of all the foundations on which he had constructed his analyses of the fermentation operation—that is, the compositions of water, carbonic acid, and spirit of wine that he had previously determined. In order to demonstrate this conclusion more fully, he reversed his approach, taking the independent analysis of sugar as the given. Embarking on an extraordinarily complicated procedure, he then "supposed successively that all of the substances in the preceding equations were known except for one, and I thus verified each of my results, the one through the other."[48] Why Lavoisier thought it would strengthen his case for the mutual consistency of his analytical results to treat each one in turn as the unknown is far from clear; especially when the reliability of the respective "knowns" differed so sharply. One almost suspects that he had become so enamored of thinking about chemical balances as mathematical equations, in which one could readily interchange knowns and unknowns, that he grossly overtreated the problem.

Lavoisier's enthusiasm for the application of the mathematical equation to his own science was now growing to such proportions that he planned to organize his entire memoir on fermentation as an object lesson on that theme. He intended, he wrote, to present "the reasoning which had directed" the experimental operations, and to "discuss the method of the operation," rather than to describe the operations themselves in detail. In chemistry, as in all other sciences, he declared, reasoning must "proceed from the known to the unknown by means of a veritable mathematical analysis, and . . . all scientific reasoning implicitly contains true equations."[49] (In his classic statement of scientific methodology in his far better known "Preliminary Discourse" for the *Elementary Treatise of Chemistry,* Lavoisier reiterated this phrase one year later: "I have imposed upon myself the rule of never proceeding except from the known to the unknown." There, however, he transformed the sense of the phrase so as to suggest that he proceeded always from direct sense experience and experimental observation toward the immediate deductions he could draw from them.[50] The above phrases are more revealing of the source and meaning of his idea; it grew out of the formal distinction between the knowns and the unknowns in an algebraic equation.) To illustrate this mechanism of scientific reasoning, he took a "simple" example, the procedure a chemist carries out in a conventional analysis to identify an unknown salt. After describing the operations, he asserted that the chemist tacitly forms an equation in which one might represent the unknown base as x and the unknown acid as y, and solves for these unknowns. "This reasoning, the thread of which is so easy to grasp in a simple operation," he maintained, "is the same in the most complicated operation, and I am going to apply it to spirituous fermentation, one of the operations of nature and of art about which the least is known up until now."[51] Lavoisier actually followed through with this plan only in a rather nominal way. Although he applied the word equation liberally in his discussion of the fermentation results, he represented them in the form of the same balance sheets he had always relied on before he had seen the new mathematical light.

After describing the fermentation process in general terms, explaining why he used sugar instead of more complex fruit juice for his experiments, giving the proportion of water to sugar that he had found most effective (4:1), and summarizing the visible phenomena that accompany a typical fermentation experiment, he presented the data from "one of the experiments of this type that succeeded best for me."[52] The materials which entered the process were:

Distilled water	10 pounds	8 ounces	0 gros
Very pure sugar	2	8	0
Dried beer yeast			3
	13	0	3

The materials afterward were:

Water containing a small portion of plant acid or vinegar	10 pounds	4 ounces	1 gros
Pure spirit of wine, freed as much as possible of water	1	7	5
Carbonic acid	1	4	2
Dry yeast			3
	13	0	3

From the quantities of spirit of wine and carbonic acid given, it is clear that this was the experiment of April 27–June 5, and that these tables represented in somewhat altered form the balance he had established in the second of the two calculations summarized above. Although it is not evident what rationale he used to change the quantities of water at the beginning and end of the experiment, we can see that the difference between them—3 ounces 7 gros—is the same quantity of water he had previously calculated to be consumed. We might, therefore, in light of the notebook record, very well amend his optimistic statement to read, "This is the only one of the experiments of this type that succeeded for me." In language borrowed from mathematics he continued, "Now in this equation sugar is the only constituent part that is unknown"; but "there is nothing simpler than to substitute all of these [known] values in the preceding equation and to deduce that of sugar by calculation." After giving the result—the same composition for sugar that we have seen on his data sheet—he went on, "One will understand that I must have been eager to verify this calculation through the way of experiment, and to that end I undertook an analysis of sugar far more exact than those which had been made up until now."[53] He gave no details of this analysis of sugar beyond the statement already quoted above that he had combined the procedures of distillation and treatment by acids, and that the outcome differed by only one-eighth from the "calculated" value.

When Lavoisier had worked out the composition of sugar by "calculation" from his fermentation equation, he was struck by the fact that the proportion of hydrogen to oxygen in sugar was very nearly the same as in water. On the data sheet in which he recorded the composition of the 2 pounds 8 ounces of sugar used in the operation, he noted that "in order to form water" from the quantity of hydrogen present in it, it would require 1 pound 4 ounces out of the 1 pound 8 ounces of oxygen. There was, therefore, "a slight excess of oxygen." (Lavoisier actually wrote "of hydrogen," but this was obviously a simple slip.)[54] This near coincidence seems to have enticed him to give up his newly acquired conception of sugar as a triple compound of carbon, hydrogen, and oxygen; for in his memoir he wrote, "One will no doubt be surprised to see that, in the last analysis, sugar is composed almost entirely of nothing but oxygen, hydrogen, and carbon, or in other words, of water and carbon with a slight excess of oxygen. I admit that I myself had difficulty getting used to this idea, but the experiments are, in this respect, decisive." As so often in similar situations, he promised another memoir soon, devoted entirely to the analysis of sugar.[55] If, in the light of these statements, we examine the values he arrived at for the composition of sugar derived from "experiment" (see his table reproduced in Figure 13), we find that the hydrogen and oxygen are given as almost exactly in the proportions of water (57:10::85:15). Given that the analytical efforts he had made on sugar had fallen far short of the decisiveness he attributed to them here, it is not unlikely that his reversion to the concept that sugar is a combination of water and carbon provided a convenient guide for him to extract a coherent result out of those troubled experiments.

The results of all of the calculations in which he had treated each of the members of the fermentation equation in turn as the unknown, Lavoisier compressed into a table in which he compared the composition of each of the four substances derived in that manner with its composition as obtained from independent analyses. In the fair copy of his memoir the table appeared as in Figure 13.[56] He was obviously very proud of this table. It would enable one, he wrote,

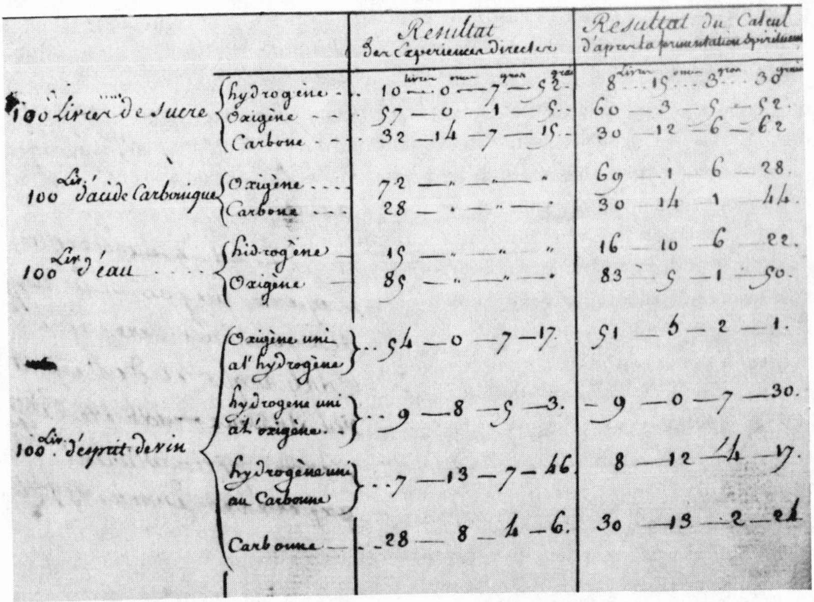

		Resultat des Experiences directes	Resultat du Calcul d'apres la fermentation spiritueuse
		livres onces gros grains	livres onces gros grains
100 livres de sucre	hydrogène	10 — 0 — 7 — 52	8 ... 15 ... 3 ... 30
	Oxigène	57 — 0 — 1 — 5	60 — 3 — 5 — 52
	Carbone	32 — 14 — 7 — 15	30 — 12 — 6 — 62
100 Liv. d'acide Carbonique	Oxigène	72 — " — " — "	69 — 1 — 6 — 28
	Carbone	28 — " — " — "	30 — 14 — 1 — 44
100 Liv. d'eau	hidrogène	15 — " — " — "	16 — 10 — 6 — 22
	Oxigène	85 — " — " — "	83 — 5 — 1 — 50
100 Liv. d'esprit de vin	Oxigène uni a l'hydrogène	54 — 0 — 7 — 17	51 — 5 — 2 — 1
	hydrogène uni a l'oxigène	9 — 8 — 5 — 3	9 — 0 — 7 — 30
	hydrogène uni au Carbonne	7 — 13 — 7 — 46	8 — 12 — 4 — 17
	Carbonne	28 — 8 — 4 — 6	30 — 13 — 2 — [illegible]

Figure 13. Table of "calculated" and "experimental" results for composition of substances involved in fermentation of spirit of wine, as shown in Lavoisier's manuscript memoir "Sur la fermentation spiritueuse," Fiche 1452, Archives of the Académie des Sciences de Paris, p. [12].

"to judge the degree of precision at which chemistry has already arrived, and what remains to be done in order to reach the final degree of perfection that it can attain."[57]

Because this table bears a superficial resemblance to those tables Lavoisier later published in the chapter on fermentation in the *Elementary Treatise of Chemistry*, we should stress that this one, unlike those, is not a balance sheet of the materials taking part in a fermentation operation. It is simply a listing of the compositions, per hundred parts, of each of the four substances involved in fermentation. As he neared the end of the first draft of his memoir, Lavoisier became aware that he had, in fact, drifted away from his initial intention. He caught himself up with the comment:

> But I notice that I have become so interested in conveying the method that I followed, and the results to which they have led me concerning the nature of the substances which participate in the fermentation or result from it, that I have, in a sense, lost sight of the main object of the memoir, to give an explanation of the phenomenon of spirituous fermentation.[58]

This is, I believe, a very revealing remark. I have pointed out in a number of places that in Lavoisier's scientific investigations means and ends seem often to undergo subtle interchanges, so that it is not always clear what his central purpose was at a given time. His realization here that he had almost inadvertently exchanged his means and his ends not only supports that generalization, but shows that occasionally the investigator himself became confused about it. Although he probably read this passage to the Academy, he afterward rewrote it to eliminate the implication that he had not written strictly according to plan. "After having conveyed the method that I have followed in my work," he now began the same paragraph, "nothing remains for me to do except to establish the theory of the [fermentation] operation."[59] His revision reveals something as interesting as did the original. Lavoisier evidently did not want to appear in print as someone who could forget his aim and have to call himself back into line. The cool logic of his published writings has contributed to the image of Lavoisier himself as a cool, detached person, one whose every move sprang from carefully reasoned motives.[60] The above paragraph as he first wrote it allows us a hint of a more spontaneous personality behind that facade. One can find similar hints in parts of other first drafts that did not survive his critical editorial eye. If his published work so seldom betrays spontaneity, it is probably because his conception of the objectivity of science led him to suppress most of these personal touches as he worked his drafts into their final form.

The theory of the phenomenon of fermentation that Lavoisier had to remind himself to include in his memoir was that this process was "the effect of a double decomposition. . . . About half of the carbon . . . of the sugar joins with the oxygen of the water to form carbonic acid; . . . at the same time, the other half of the carbon . . . joins with the hydrogen of the water and a portion of undecomposed water to form the spirit of wine." Thus, nearly three years after declaring that fermentation is one of the operations of nature that decompose water, Lavoisier finally felt the satisfaction of verifying his claim through "a multitude of circumstances which permit no further doubt that matters take place in this way."[61]

As he neared the end of his draft memoir, Lavoisier sensed that in solving the problem of fermentation he was approaching that pinnacle of achievement toward which the long, arduous research trail on which he had embarked fifteen years before had been leading him. In a burst of personal pride he finished by appraising with no false modesty the position he had attained:

> This ensemble of proofs which sustain and mutually support one another [he had in mind mostly the concordance between the "calculated" and "experimental" values for the composition of the substances involved in fermentation] give to the modern theory of chemistry, to that which I dare to call my own, a degree of certitude to which it is impossible to refuse assent. I have had the satisfaction to see, through the correspondence which I maintain with a large number of the physicians and chemists of Europe, that every day new converts are made, that the majority of those who are not yet persuaded are at least shaken, and I dare say that among those who hold to the old opinions without reserve or modification there are probably none who have taken the trouble to study the question in depth.[62]

Lavoisier had come a long way in the decade since he himself first dared to break openly with the "old opinions."

For all of the bravado with which he presented his "proofs" of the nature of fermentation as the fulfillment of his entire chemical system, there are hints in his memoir of an uneasy awareness that the ground under him was less firm than he made it out to be. While stressing how small the differences were between the "calculated" and "experimental" values in his table, he acknowledged obliquely that he was not really satisfied with these results. In his initial draft he wrote, "New research carried out with still more precise apparatus will lead to still more certain results, and I have not given up hope of arriving at the degree of precision which one could reasonably desire, even before the publication of this memoir."[63] (He subsequently crossed this passage out and restated the same idea in smoother but somewhat less revealing form.) Given Lavoisier's habit of understating his difficulties in public accounts of his experiments, we may view this statement as a thinly veiled admission of serious problems that he had not yet solved, and that he was gambling on being able to clear up before he committed his conclusions to the permanent public record.

There was only one specific experimental obstacle that Lavoisier discussed in his memoir:

> One of the principal causes of the slight errors that remain to be corrected might derive from the fact that we do not yet know how to analyze with precision the quantity of water that carbonic acid in the aeriform state can hold in solution. In that regard I have had to incorporate suppositions that are not yet supported by rigorous experiments, and this is one of the points that I would apply myself to clarify if it did not present almost insurmountable difficulties.[64]

Clearly he was skirting a potentially damaging situation. If this error were really as "slight" as he supposed, it would introduce only minor inaccuracies; but the quantity involved could be a critical factor. He had calculated the water deficit on the assumption that the entire weight loss of the fermentation bottle represented "pure carbonic acid." There is another data sheet on which he treated this 1 pound, 4 ounces, 1 gros, 40 grains of loss as "fixed air saturated with water," and allowed for 2 gros 27.20 grains of water.[65] A quantity of that magnitude was safe; but, as his passage implies, he had no strong experimental support for his estimate. If the proportion of water "dissolved" in the carbonic acid happened to be much larger than he supposed, the deficit left for him to attribute to water decomposed in the operation could be reduced dangerously close to the vanishing point.

Lavoisier's allusions to possible sources of small errors obviously only touched the surface of the problems he had experienced in the investigations on which he was relying for the conclusions he presented in his memoir. His account of the fermentation operation itself seems almost contrived to divert attention from the actual procedure he had followed in the experiment he was using for his data. "I suppose," he wrote, "that one has employed an apparatus arranged so as to allow nothing to escape, such as modern chemistry employs."[66] His listeners would hardly guess that in precisely the experiment he reported he had omitted such an arrangement and allowed the aeriform product to escape. If we could query him on this point he would undoubtedly have replied that he had established, in a preceding experiment in which he did collect the aeriform product, that it was "pure carbonic acid," although experimental difficulties had prevented him from measuring it accurately. He had preferred the data from the present experiment because he had more confidence in its quantitative results. The combination of one experiment in which he established the qualitative nature of the product and of another in which he determined its quantity therefore led to the same effective outcome as if he had been able to combine all of these elements into a single experiment. It would probably have appeared perfectly justifiable to him to talk in terms of an experiment he would like to have been able to carry out—and still hoped to carry out before his memoir was published—in the confidence that it would have led essentially to the same results. As he regularly did, Lavoisier was constructing on paper a somewhat idealized investigation that he might have carried out but for contingent complications.

Lavoisier decided to forego his grand table of the experimental and calculated compositions of water, sugar, carbonic acid, and spirit of wine when he read the memoir at the Academy, because "it would not be understood at all in a lecture."[67] It is not certain that he actually gave the lecture. There is no specific record concerning it in the minutes of meetings of the Academy. It is, however, quite possible that this was the unnamed memoir that he read at the meeting of November 14, 1787.[68] Whether or not the public ever had the opportunity to hear his memoir on fermentation, he must sooner or later have become dissatisfied with what he had written, for the memoir was never published.

* * *

It is easy to form the impression that Lavoisier's memoir on fermentation was a failure, but difficult to define the grounds on which to declare it a failure. We cannot rely on the incorrectness of the conclusion, for by such standards many of the most significant achievements in the history of science are failures. Nor is the fact that Lavoisier himself did not publish it an adequate reason; for that decision itself might have been a mistake, or he may simply have neglected to do anything about it. We may sense that, beyond such external criteria, the memoir displays some intrinsic breakdown in the quality of his reasoning, the use of his evidence, or his judgment about the state of his experimental foundations. Somehow he appears to have stretched his own methodological canons near to the breaking point. Not only did the central contention of his theory rest on a dangerously small deficit in the balance between much larger quantities, but at least two of those quantities themselves rested on indirect measurements and further assumptions. He had not carried out the fermentation experiment on which he based his case according to the procedures that he himself prescribed. He conjured up out of what appear to us to have been largely unsuccessful attempts to analyze sugar a set of values for its composition that he treated as a reliable independent check on the composition derived from the fermentation operation itself. We are tempted to view this memoir as evidence that Lavoisier was straying beyond rational reconstruction toward misrepresentation; that he was laying claim to an achievement he had not reached.

Viewing the memoir as a lapse from standards Lavoisier had previously maintained, we can find explanations for such behavior in his personal situation.

He had attained success after success in his overall research program. He had become the unchallengeable leader of French chemistry and attracted a coterie of devoted followers. His influence and prestige had now spread abroad as well. Distracted by his participation in the heady political developments of a rapidly changing national situation, yet anxious to cap the edifice of his chemical system by conquering the most complex chemical phenomenon he had taken on in a way that would display his methods to particular advantage, might not Lavoisier have lost a measure of that prudent self-criticism that had for so long protected him from damaging errors? Confident by now that he had changed the face of chemistry more extensively than any other single person in the entire history of that science, he may well have acquired a touch of hubris. Had the intrepid investigator at last overreached himself?

If we judge that he did, we must still face the question, in what way did Lavoisier's treatment of fermentation differ from the approach that had yielded so many "successful" scientific memoirs? If he forced questionable data to fit a preconceived notion that fermentation decomposes water, how does that differ from the practices I have elsewhere described as essential to maintain the integrity of his theoretical structure in the face of so many unavoidable experimental pitfalls? If he somehow pulled together out of several individually unsuccessful analyses an "experimental" composition of sugar, is that really different from the brilliant manner in which he drew out of a series of flawed combustion experiments on charcoal the "correct" proportions of carbon and hydrogen in fixed air? What emerges from such comparisons is that there are no strict methodological rules by which to demarcate successful from unsuccessful investigations. If we conclude that in his memoir on fermentation Lavoisier went astray, the distinction between his actions in this case and in that of his successes rests only on matters of degree. The experiments on which he relied for his composition of sugar were only more deeply flawed than those on which he relied for the composition of fixed air. His reliance on a small deficit for the critical conclusion that water is decomposed in fermentation was not different in kind from his reliance on a small deficit to establish that water is formed in respiration; but the conclusion was more vulnerable because there was so little corroborating evidence for it. There was no escape from the types of decisions Lavoisier made to reach the conclusions he formulated in his memoir on fermentation. Throughout his career he had to make similar decisions, and each one carried the risk that he could be wrong. We can only sense in this case that the risks were larger, and that he had provided himself with fewer safeguards.

As historians we too must take risks if we are to evaluate the quality of the scientific work of our subjects. We accept the proposition that the observations scientists make cannot be totally independent of the theories which guide them. Neither can our interpretations of past events be totally independent of what they did or did not afterward lead to. If we escape the crude presentism of judging simply on the basis of whether the theory of fermentation Lavoisier presented in this memoir was "right" or "wrong" according to what is believed today, we may still be entrapped in subtler hindsight effects. There is no way I can be certain that I would have perceived Lavoisier's memoir as intrinsically unsuccessful if he had published it and it had been favorably received by his contemporaries.

In another sense we may judge the memoir no failure at all, for Lavoisier's decision not to publish it suggests that he learned something from it. It may well be that the experience of writing, and perhaps of presenting, it exposed to him the gaps in his position that he had not previously perceived. Through the chastening effects of recognizing that he had overreached, he may have become prepared to handle the problem more effectively the next time around.

13

The Trouble with Sugar

Among the tactics that Lavoisier and his recently acquired followers devised to overcome the remaining opposition to their new chemical system was to publish a French translation of Richard Kirwan's *An Essay on Phlogiston,* together with commentaries rebutting Kirwan's position. When he wrote his book in 1787, Kirwan had adopted a modified phlogiston theory, according to which "inflammable air, before its extrication from the bodies in which it exists in a concrete state, was the very substance to which all the characters and properties of the phlogiston of the ancient chymists actually belonged." The controversy between his view and the "*antiphlogistic* hypothesis," as he designated Lavoisier's theory of combustion, is, he wrote, "at present confined to a few points, namely, whether the *inflammable principle* be found in what are called phlogisticated acids, vegetable acids, fixed air, sulphur, phosphorus, sugar, charcoal, and metals."[1] Kirwan organized his argument in separate chapters dealing with each of the common mineral acids, the dissolution of metals, and the precipitation of metals by each other. The "few points" of controversy actually encompassed the general issue of the nature of combustion, the inflammable principle, and the composition of every major class of substance, and are therefore beyond the boundaries of our present subject. Kirwan's case intersects our story, however, because he illustrated the application of his views to plant substances with the example of acid of sugar.

Within Kirwan's theoretical framework sugar was "a compound of fixed air with a much larger proportion of inflammable air and some water, all condensed to a degree of which we are ignorant." Acid of sugar consisted "of this peculiar basis, stripped of its superadded phlogiston, and united to a large proportion of fixed air in a condensed state: the saccharine acid does not therefore preexist in sugar, but is formed by the operation that exhibits it." Kirwan maintained that the antiphlogistic theory was inadequate to explain "the analysis and production of the vegetable acids." He based this claim mainly on a critique of the analysis of sugar and acid of sugar which Lavoisier had incorporated into his memoir of 1779 on the nature of acids.[2] Kirwan began by casting doubt on the reliability of the analytical results upon which Lavoisier had based his interpretation of the composition of the two substances. Adding up the figures Lavoisier had given for the sugar, nitrous acid, and water with which he had begun the distillation that produced acid of sugar, and the weights of the substances Lavoisier had mentioned as present at the end, including the weight gain of the "intermediate bottle" used as a receiver, Kirwan claimed that the difference between the two totals:

Original weight	2,602
Total of products	2,502.952
Loss	99.048,

"represented a loss so considerable that it were superfluous to enter into an account of the quantity of nitrous acid decomposed."[3] Since the quantity of nitrous acid consumed had served as the basis for determining the quantity of oxygen contained in the acid of sugar, Kirwan was implying that Lavoisier's conclusions about the composition of the latter were invalid.

Kirwan's representation of Lavoisier's experiment was a blatant misuse of another person's figures in order to make them appear discredited. On the surface, a loss of 99 grains of material, when compared with the significant weights involved in Lavoisier's calculations—288 grains of sugar, and 103 grains of nitrous acid—seems so large as to make any conclusions about the addition or subtraction of constituents seem gratuitous. On the other hand, it represented less than 4 percent of the total of the substances Lavoisier had weighed before and after the experiment. If Kirwan's criticism were cogent it would be, therefore, by raising reservations not about Lavoisier's analytical accuracy, but about the wisdom of drawing conclusions from small differences between large aggregates of measured quantities. In fact, however, Lavoisier had not made the overall balance calculation which Kirwan constructed from his results. His determination of the quantity of nitrous acid decomposed rested on a titration of the nitrous acid found in the intermediate bottle, to find out how much of the acid originally placed in the retort with the sugar had not combined with it.[4] It may well be that Lavoisier's reputation for being less than rigorously accurate in his use of the balance sheet grew in part out of such inappropriate interpretations of his data by his opponents.

Kirwan buttressed his criticism with a string of arguments. For example, according to him, Lavoisier "infers from this experiment that sugar is a *sort* of charcoal, which uniting with the oxigenous principle of the nitrous acid, decomposes that acid, lets loose the nitrous air, and forms the saccharine acid." Kirwan objected that, if this were so, then "the acid of sugar and fixed air should be one and the same thing, since both are composed of the oxigenous principle united to charcoal."[5] Again Kirwan was misrepresenting Lavoisier, who had, it is true, written that acid of sugar is "nothing else but the sugar in its entirety combined with the acidifying principle or oxygen"; but who had also concluded that sugar itself is composed of "a little inflammable air and much *matière charbonneuse*."[6] I cannot go fully into Kirwan's position here, because his arguments depended upon his own theories regarding the composition of nitrous acid, a manifestation in turn of his particular conception of phlogiston and inflammable air. One of his criticisms is, however, interesting because it might have been suggestive to Lavoisier:

> If the saccharine acid consisted of sugar undecomposed, and barely united to the oxigenous principle, then it should be formed by treating sugar with the black calx of manganese, or with dephlogisticated marine acid; for both these substances contain abundance of the oxigenous principle, and easily give it out; yet after various trials, neither Mr. Scheele nor Mr. Morveau were able to form a particle of the saccharine acid, by means of either of these substances.[7]

As is well known, Lavoisier's wife translated Kirwan's *Essay* into French, and Lavoisier, de Morveau, Laplace, Monge, Berthollet, and Fourcroy divided up the task of writing chapter-by-chapter refutations of Kirwan's arguments. The collaborators must have carried out these assignments with great dispatch; for the *Essay* appeared in 1787 and they finished their commentaries by the end of that same year. On January 26, 1788, they asked the Academy for a commission to evaluate the work for publication.[8]

The response to Kirwan's chapter on acid of sugar was given to Antoine Fourcroy, a logical choice, since of Lavoisier's associates Fourcroy had specialized more than anyone else in the chemistry of plants and animals. He opened with a general summary of the state of plant chemistry which reflects clearly Lavoisier's recently formulated conceptions:

> Although we do not yet have any very positive knowledge of the diverse principles which form plant matters, modern experiments have nevertheless made it clear that these principles are much simpler and less numerous than one formerly believed, since on final analysis one separates from plants nothing but the base of inflammable gas, which we call hydrogen, the *charbon* which preexists in it, oxygen, or the acidifying base of vital air, azote, or the base of azotic gas, water, and some earths. It is with these five or six primitive substances, which appear very simple, or at least whose constituent elements cannot yet be isolated, that the work of vegetation produces the extracts, insipid mucilages, sugar, the fixed, volatile, and aromatic oils, gluten, starch, coloring matter, the various acids, etc.[9]

This remarkable paragraph compressed into one succinct statement Lavoisier's theory of the composition of plant substances, an allusion to the new definition of a chemical element, some samples of the changing nomenclature, a theory of vegetation, and a sketchy classification of plant substances reflecting recent advances in plant chemistry.

Turning to the specific question of the composition of sugar, Fourcroy asserted that "the most exact analyses" had not uncovered anything in it except hydrogen, carbon, water, and a small amount of alkaline earth. There was nothing whatever to prove that it contained "carbonic acid already formed; M. Kirwan makes that claim without positive proof. Everything indicates, on the contrary, that this acid, which is disengaged by the action of the fire or of fermentation, forms at the very moment of its disengagement."[10] Fourcroy's argument provides a nice example of the obstacles to full communication which arise between scientists reasoning within different general conceptual frameworks. Fourcroy's "carbonic acid" was Kirwan's "fixed air." For Fourcroy the difference was merely one of nomenclature, but the constituent principles of Kirwan's fixed air were dephlogisticated air and phlogiston.[11] The explicit debate over whether fixed air exists as such in sugar or is formed in its analysis therefore covered an implicit disagreement over the nature of the entity they were discussing. The fact that Fourcroy included water, rather than oxygen, among the "primitive constituents" respectively of sugar and of plant substances in general suggests that he was influenced by the shift back to this conception that Lavoisier had recently made at the time he calculated the composition of sugar from the fermentation equation in preparing his memoir on fermentation.

In the new chemical system acid of sugar became oxalic acid. Fourcroy dismissed Kirwan's view of the composition and the formation of oxalic acid from sugar on several grounds, including the objection that "one cannot demonstrate the presence of carbonic acid in oxalic acid."[12] The details of his arguments, as particular manifestations of a more general rejection of explanations embedded within the phlogiston framework, need not divert us here. More important to us is Fourcroy's reply to the criticism of Lavoisier's experiments and conclusions of 1779. Fourcroy did not actually answer Kirwan's charges, but declared them irrelevant:

> The objections that M. Kirwan makes . . . relative to the formation of oxalic acid do not appear to us to be as strong as he believes. To reply to them precisely, we shall remark in the first place that the memoir of M. Lavoisier on that acid, printed in the volume [of the Memoirs of the Academy of Sciences] for 1778, from which M. Kirwan takes the majority of his arguments, is very far removed from the most exact knowledge that modern discoveries have taught us about the nature of plant substances. If a per-

> son were to rely only on works written ten years ago to learn about our theory, he would risk attributing to us inaccuracies and even errors that experiments which have continued without interruption since that epoch have gradually eradicated.[13]

This comment was somewhat unfair to Kirwan. It is true that, at the time Fourcroy wrote it, Lavoisier's memoir was almost ten years old. If we take into account, however, that the volume of the Memoirs of the Academy in which it was printed was not actually published until 1780, the period in question diminishes to seven years at most. During this time Lavoisier had written nothing to indicate that he retracted anything he had stated about sugar and acid of sugar in that memoir. As an expression of the pace at which Lavoisier's supporters felt they were advancing their field, however, the remark is most illuminating. Never before in the history of chemistry would a chemist have claimed on principle that an article published only ten years earlier by the leader of his own school was already remote from "modern discoveries."

In his effort to relegate Kirwan's criticisms to an outmoded stage of Lavoisier's research, Fourcroy reported on Lavoisier's current position regarding the composition of sugar:

> M. Lavoisier has carried out more exact research on sugar, and he would no longer say today that sugar enters as a whole into the composition of oxalic acid, or that it is *charbon* which forms the base of the sugar. His new researches on sugar, analyzed by spirituous fermentation, show that this plant substance contains, per hundred pounds, about 8 pounds of hydrogen, 60 pounds of oxygen, and more than 30 pounds of carbon.[14]

The composition that Fourcroy gave for sugar was, in fact, exactly what Lavoisier had worked out from the April 27–June 5 fermentation experiment and used for the table of "calculated" values in his memoir on fermentation. He had compared it there with the "experimental" value obtained from analyses of sugar by distillation and by oxygenation with acids. Fourcroy, however, gave only the fermentation result, and referred to it as the result of an analysis by fermentation—that is, as Lavoisier's most "exact" *experimental* result. This shift suggests that at the time Fourcroy wrote this section of the reply to Kirwan, either he or Lavoisier had decided that the result obtained by the distillation and oxygenation experiments was less trustworthy than the one that Lavoisier, in his memoir on fermentation, had regarded as a calculated result.

After the passage just quoted, Fourcroy continued, "It is not the whole [of the sugar] which enters into the composition of oxalic acid: the sugar is decomposed, just as is the nitric acid which serves to form" with it the oxalic acid. Carbonic acid is disengaged, because some of the carbon of the sugar combines with oxygen from the nitric acid. The oxalic acid therefore "contains less carbon than the sugar," and this explains why the sugar loses weight "on becoming an acid." (Kirwan had used the fact that Bergman and others had obtained less oxalic acid by weight than the sugar they consumed as an argument against Lavoisier's interpretation of the relation between the two substances.)[15] Oxalic acid is another compound formed of carbon, hydrogen, and oxygen. "In order to have a more exact knowledge of oxalic acid, we lack only an exact knowledge of the proportions of these principles which enter into its composition." Fourcroy concluded by asserting that "our doctrine on this point, as on all others, is the simple result of experiments." The remaining plant acids, he added, contain the same three principles, differing only in their proportions.[16]

In the light of the experimental situation underlying Fourcroy's refutation of Kirwan, we can see that his interpretation of the conversion of sugar to oxalic acid was less solidly supported by quantitative data than he might have wished. Since he acknowledged that the proportions of carbon, hydrogen, and oxygen in oxalic acid were unknown, his claim that it contains less carbon than the sugar from which it derives was unsubstantiated—it was merely required in order to interpret the situation according to the French chemists' conception of the composition of plant substances. Neither was the composition of sugar as firmly established as Fourcroy implied. Even as Fourcroy publicly extolled their "doctrine" as "the simple result of experiment," Lavoisier must have been in private acutely aware of the insecurity of the very experimental foundation on which his associate based that boast.

II

Lavoisier was still preoccupied with affairs related to the Provincial Assembly during much of the first two months of 1788. Having at its last adjournment been appointed to an interim commission on finances, he spent part of February in Orléans.[17] According to his laboratory notebooks he was not able to resume experimentation until the second week in March. From the evidence that is available it is reasonable to infer that during the time that did remain to him for scientific thought and investigation during the first half of this year, his paramount concern was to improve on the treatment of fermentation that he had attempted in his memoir on that subject.

There is only a sparse bit of evidence to intimate that Lavoisier may have tried, or even contemplated trying, new experiments on fermentation itself at the time. A loose sheet, whose placement in his laboratory notebook indicates that it might have been inserted during the spring of 1788, contains on its front side three measurements of the weights of different distillation flasks, and a notation concerning quantities of water and sugar to use. On the back side are three tabulations of initial quantities of the constituents of a fermentation mixture. The second of these, captioned "comparative experiment in the open air," is a tantalizing suggestion that he thought of comparing the effects of fermentation in a closed vessel and in the open air, and may be connected with his earlier classification of fermentation as one of those "obscure combustions" that obtain oxygen from water rather than from the atmosphere.[18] There are no further details, however, to indicate that he actually carried out any such experiments. If he did begin them, he probably did not complete them.

In view of the statement in his memoir that he hoped to obtain more accurate fermentation results with a "more precise apparatus," even before his paper went to press,[19] it may appear surprising that Lavoisier did not pursue his declared intention more vigorously. There are three possible explanations, all of which may have played a part. The first was that he might have had too little time. The second was that sometime during this period he ordered an apparatus to be especially built for fermentation experiments, and he may have been waiting for it to be completed. The third is that he may have felt that it was even more urgent to remedy his lack of a reliable independent analysis of sugar than to overcome the shortcomings in his previous fermentation experiments.

While biding his time about further experiments on fermentation itself, Lavoisier returned again and again to the only previous one in which he seemed to place confidence, that of April 27–June 12, 1787, in a dogged effort to squeeze out of it the information he needed to verify his theory of the operation. His critical problem was to find some way around the incompleteness of that experiment. He needed either an independent composition for sugar, in order to determine from its carbon content how much of the weight loss to ascribe to the carbonic acid disengaged; or else to generate the latter from some alternate assumptions, and to use the quantity of carbon in the carbonic acid, along with the rest of the balance between the products and the "materials" of the fermentation, to recalculate the composition of sugar. The trouble with the latter approach, as he indicated in his memoir, was that an accurate determination of the water dissolved in the carbonic acid presented for him "insurmountable difficulties." The trouble with the former was the sorry state of his attempts to analyze sugar by other methods.

Since most of the data sheets on which Lavoisier carried out his herculean computational efforts are undated, uncertain in their order, and most likely incomplete, it is not possible to reconstruct the entire sequence of his attempts to escape from this dilemma. We can, however, identify at least three distinct stages in his progress. The first of these is recorded on that group of sheets which utilize approximately the same values for the composition of sugar that he reported as the "result of direct experiment" in his memoir on fermentation. It is possible, in fact, that he had worked these out even before he wrote the memoir, but did not include their results in his discussion there. I think it more likely, however, that he did these further analyses on the same data sometime afterward—the most plausible period for them is between mid November 1787 and mid March 1788.

In these further calculations, Lavoisier determined the quantities of the constituent principles in each of the four substances of the fermentation equation from his independent analyses of their composition, just as he had done for the memoir itself. Instead of using each set of three of them to derive a calculated composition for the fourth, as he had done there, however, he relied on the "experimental" compositions of all four to determine how much of the weight loss during the fermentation to assign to the carbonic acid disengaged. (In the earlier calculations, we may recall, he had supposed that all of this loss was carbonic acid.) The calculation was based on the carbon balance before and after the operation. The former was represented by the carbon in the sugar decomposed, together with a small amount he allowed for the carbon in the yeast. (He apparently estimated the latter by assuming that the dry weight of the yeast consisted mostly of carbon, together with a very small proportion of mophette.)[20] To this total of 13 ounces, 4 gros, 5.1 grains, he added an estimate of the carbon in the syrupy acid which had appeared in the fermentation liquid afterward,[21] to obtain the round number of 14 ounces of carbon before the operation. The known quantities of carbon afterward consisted of that contained in the spirit of wine (based on the amount of that product he had determined through the complex procedures carried out at the end of the fermentation experiment and on the composition of spirit of wine established in his memoir on the combustion of that substance), plus a "nearly carbonaceous residue" found in the bottle. This total was 8 ounces, 3 gros, 31 grains. He then set up the following balance:

Carbon before the operation	14 ounces	0 gros	0 grains
After the operation	8	3	31
Loss of carbon	5	4	41

Using his standard proportion of twenty-eight parts carbon to seventy-two parts of oxygen, he then computed that this loss represented 1 pound, 3 ounces, 7 gros, 12.8 grains of "fixed air formed."[22]

That quantity was so close to the total loss in the weight of the bottle, 1 pound, 4 ounces, 7 gros, 40 grains, that it appeared to confirm that the quantity of water "dissolved" in the fixed air was very small—not enough to threaten the overall balance from which he had earlier verified his theory that water decomposes in the operation. Now, however, he calculated the quantity of water consumed in a new way, one that depended upon his recent return to the view that sugar is a combination of carbon and water. Originally he had counted as the water present before the operation only what he had put in as water. This time he added to that quantity the amounts he assumed the sugar and the yeast contained:

Natural water	10 pounds	4 ounces	0 gros	0	grains
Water of the sugar	1	9	6	36.9	
Water of the yeast		3	5	58	
	12	1	4	22.9	

Once he had introduced this conception, it followed that all of the oxygen present in the fermentation mixture was contained, in one or another of these three categories, in the form of water. Consequently the oxygen which combined with carbon to form the carbonic acid must have derived from the decomposition of some of this water. With these presuppositions, he simply calculated from the proportion of oxygen in water that, in order to supply the oxygen, 1 pound, 0 ounces, 6 gros, 59.8 grains of water was "destroyed" in the operation.[23] Lavoisier also calculated the water "deficit" in another way. Still assuming, as he had all along, that the oxygen in spirit of wine is combined with part of the hydrogen as water, he added the amount of water in the 1 pound, 7 ounces, 5 gros, 18 grains of spirit of wine he had found produced in the operation to the quantity of water found afterward by distillation and to the small quantity of water he had just shown to be carried off with the carbonic acid. Subtracting this total, 11 pounds, 2 ounces, 2 gros, 52 grains, from the total before the operation, left a decrease of 15 ounces, 2 gros, 42 grains [*sic*]. This result differed by less than one-tenth from the preceding quantity calculated from the oxygen in the carbonic acid; but Lavoisier noted that "this calculation should be recomputed, because I have not taken into account the remaining yeast and the carbon removed in the vinegar"[24] (that is, in the small quantity of acetic acid which he believed had formed during the operation). There is no record of his having repeated the calculation with these corrections.

The magnitude of the water decomposed during the operation now appeared considerably larger than it had when derived from the overall balance equation (about 1 pound, compared with 3 ounces 7 gros), and might seem to have strengthened the support for Lavoisier's theory of fermentation. That theory had, however, taken a peculiar turn in the new calculation. Inherent in the previous balance calculation was the assumption that the water which fermentation decomposes is external to the sugar. Now he appeared to make no distinction between that water and the water that he considered part of the constitution of the sugar itself. Since the latter quantity (1 pound, 9 ounces, 6 gros, 36.9 grains) was more than enough to account for the water he now calculated to have been decomposed, it now appeared ambiguous whether the process he envisioned was a decomposition of "natural" water, or an internal decomposition of the sugar. As in an analogous earlier situation, since we do not know what Lavoisier had in mind, we cannot tell whether his conception of the process had shifted, and he changed the mode of calculation to reflect the change; or whether he merely devised a new procedure whose conceptual implications were still tacit.

In addition to the preceding calculations, Lavoisier made some computations intended to convert the weights actually used in the experiment to a base of 500 pounds of material before and after the operation. In doing so he does not appear to have introduced any new assumptions, although the data sheets involved are too fragmentary for us to be certain.[25] He left no commentary on the outcome of the preceding efforts to establish the detailed balance of the fermentation equation, so that we cannot tell whether he was for an appreciable length of time satisfied with them. The conclusions embodied in them were so heavily dependent on the very shaky "experimental" composition for sugar that he had put together from the analytical attempts of the previous summer, however, that this work must sooner or later have driven him to accept that he must find a better way to establish that composition. When he returned to his laboratory in the spring of 1788, the analysis of sugar became, in fact, the primary item on his research agenda.

III

The first experiments recorded in Lavoisier's laboratory notebook during 1788 were certain key demonstrations of the new chemical system, such as the decomposition of water with iron, made on March 12, in an unsuccessful effort to convert the Chevalier Landriani to his views. The second of these experiments involved the well-known reaction of charcoal with red oxide of mercury to produce carbonic acid.[26] One month later, on April 12, Lavoisier again utilized red oxide of mercury, but this time he combined it with sugar. Placing 1 ounce, 5 gros, 64 grains of sugar together with 6 ounces, 7 gros, 40 grains of the oxide of mercury into a small retort, he connected the latter to a two-necked receiver leading in turn to a vessel containing caustic alkali. As soon as he began to warm the retort, a large amount of a liquid the color of syrupy acid passed into the receiver, together with a white vapor, "a great abundance of azotic gas, perhaps a little carbonic acid gas, but no trace of oxygen gas." Although he removed the two coals which he had ignited to heat the retort, the reaction continued very rapidly, making the whole apparatus very hot.[27]

Although Lavoisier did not write down the rationale for this experiment, his reasoning seems self-evident. The previous summer he had already attempted to oxygenate sugar by reacting it with a substance which easily gave up its oxygen, but he had then considered using only acids for this purpose. A similar result could, however, be expected by means of an oxide of a metal which readily yields its oxygen. The fact that the red oxide of mercury possesses this property had been, as is very well known, crucial to the discovery of oxygen and to the clarification of Lavoisier's theory of combustion. Then the oxide of mercury had proven valuable just because it could be reduced without charcoal. Now, however, it might prove equally valuable because of the ease with which the carbon in charcoal could attract its oxygen from it. The fact that he had just utilized this reaction during the demonstrations for Landriani may have been the immediate stimulus which prompted him to realize that the carbon in sugar too might readily attract the oxygen from red oxide of mercury. The vigor of the reaction he obtained, in spite of having employed only half as much sugar as the smallest amount he had tried in the earlier attempts with sulfuric acid, must have nourished the hope that he might finally have found the way around the obstacles that had blocked all his efforts to analyze sugar accurately. The present experiment was itself obviously not satisfactory. It had got out of control, and he had obtained from it not even a significant amount of the carbonic acid which ought to be the measure of the carbon in the sugar. At the end of his record of it he put down, "One will recommence this operation." Accordingly he began a second such experiment on April 18, using about the same quantity of sugar, but twice the amount of the oxide of mercury. He intended to collect the products in three intermediate bottles plus the caustic alkali bottle. The operation must again have gone badly, however, for he recorded only the initial weights of the substances used and of the collecting bottles, and did not even put down the outcome.[28] On April 29 he tried once more.

For the experiment of April 29 Lavoisier used 6,000 grains of red oxide of mercury, or one and a half times as much as in the first experiment, but only about half as much sugar as in the earlier one (500 grains, or 6 gros 6 grains, in place of 1 ounce, 5 gros, 64 grains). Most likely he was seeking to ensure that the carbon would be completely oxygenated by tripling the proportion of oxide to sugar, while making the operation easier to control by using less sugar. To increase the capacity for absorbing the carbonic acid produced he added a second caustic alkali bottle. He did not describe the course of the operation itself, but it must have gone smoothly, for he carried out extensive calculations to reduce the data in order to represent the substances consumed and produced. By carefully collecting the remaining oxide of mercury and the metallic mercury in the retort, the receiver, and the connecting tube, and weighing all portions of the apparatus before and after the operation, he was able to account for all but a very small deficit in the oxide originally used. For determining the proportion of carbon in the sugar, however, the important measurement was the quantity of carbonic acid disengaged. This he obtained from the increase in the weights of the receiver, which had been filled with water at the beginning, and of the two caustic alkali bottles. The total turned out to be 2 gros 61 grains.[29] This result must have been a major setback for Lavoisier. Assuming the proportions of 28 carbon to 72 oxygen, the carbon contained in this product amounted to only about 11 percent of the weight of the sugar consumed (the residue of carbon left after the operation weighed only 6 grains). According to his fermentation analysis, however, carbon makes up about 30 percent of sugar. He would therefore have had to conclude either that something drastic had gone wrong in this experiment, or that the results and assumptions on which he had based his previous estimate of the composition harbored some gross error. During the following weeks he considered both alternatives.

The outcome of the preceding experiment probably induced Lavoisier to defer his goal of a complete analysis of the composition of sugar until he could find another means to resolve the more immediate discrepancy concerning the proportion of carbon contained in it. With that end in mind he turned once again—at a date not specified, but undoubtedly close to the time of the above three experiments—to the action of sulfuric acid on sugar. Perhaps because of the troubles he had encountered the year before when he tried to carry out this reaction in a closed system in order to collect the gaseous products, he did not attempt now to oxygenate the sugar to carbonic acid, but simply carbonized the sugar in an open vessel. He mixed 3 ounces, 3 gros, 56 grains of sugar with an unspecified quantity of sulfuric acid diluted with an equal proportion of water. He heated the mixture until the "material had been reduced to carbon." After washing, this carbon weighed 1 ounce 1 gros. When he tried to calcine the carbon in a medicinal phial in order to dry it, however, the phial broke and he lost the contents. Trying again with the same quantity of sugar in 8 ounces of concentrated sulfuric acid and 3 ounces of water, he had better luck.

> I heated gently, and after a few moments all of the carbon of the sugar separated out. Sulfuric acid fumes arose. When I judged that all of the carbon had been disengaged I poured everything into a large glass full of water.
>
> The carbon was thoroughly washed and dried in the air. It then weighed 1 ounce, 3 gros, 2 grains.
>
> I dried it in a sand bath at a temperature above that of boiling water. A slight odor of sulfuric acid was emitted. Afterward the carbon weighed only 7 gros 67 grains. There were about 6 grains lost in transferring it. I had used 2,000 grains [of sugar]. The carbon is 577 [grains]. Carbon [:] sugar [=] 10,000 [:] 2,885.

In the margin Lavoisier added,

> Since the carbon had not been calcined over a strong fire, I assume that it would have lost 17 grains more, which would have reduced the proportion of carbon in sugar to 28 [parts per hundred].[30]

If we lean too heavily on modern knowledge of the complexity of the products of the action of acids on sugar, we can all too quickly dismiss this simple experiment as a makeshift retreat by Lavoisier in the face of his inability to devise a workable combustion method for sugar. For Lavoisier himself at this difficult point on his path, however, it was a logical move. In the explanation he had put in his notebook the summer before for the products he had observed when sulfuric acid combined with sugar, he had already worked out a partial theoretical basis for this experiment, in that he had inferred that the substance separated out was the *matière charbonneuse* of the sugar, released when the sulfuric acid either disengaged hydrogen gas or combined with the hydrogen to form water. His earlier position appears to leave one major source of uncertainty, for he had then considered that concentrated sulfuric acid might also be "attacked by" some of the carbon, forming carbonic acid. Since he did not make any provision for measuring carbonic acid in this experiment, his result would appear vulnerable to an undetected loss of the substance he was determining. He must somehow have satisfied himself that under the conditions of the experiment no carbonic acid is produced. At any rate the outcome of this experiment was probably very welcome to him. At a time when his distillation analyses of sugar had not worked out at all, and his oxygenation analyses with oxide of mercury were confronting him with very anomalous results, this determination of the proportion of carbon in sugar at least provided him with a figure close enough to the one calculated from his fermentation experiment to allow him to believe that he had acquired one solid foothold toward the broader solution he sought.

In this experiment we also see Lavoisier engaging in his common practice of guessing at a source of error which he could utilize to improve the result in the direction of a desired outcome. Why he favored exactly 28 parts of carbon per 100 of sugar is hard to fathom, unless he was entertaining the possibility that the total quantity of hydrogen and oxygen in sugar might correspond to the quantity of oxygen alone contained in carbonic acid. Soon afterward, however, he had cause to doubt what had appeared up until then as the well-established composition of carbonic acid itself.

On May 9 Lavoisier placed in a glass retort a mixture of red oxide of mercury and charcoal (of unspecified type, but necessarily one which he considered to be pure enough carbon to exclude a significant amount of hydrogen). His motive is not recorded; but in view of the anomalous result he had encountered ten days before when he heated the same oxide with sugar, he was probably trying to find out what had gone astray then, by testing the general method in a situation in which he could directly measure how much carbon was available to be oxygenated. As in the corresponding experiment with sugar, he used 6,000 grains of red oxide of mercury, to which he added 3 gros 36 grains (252 grains) of charcoal. He heated the mixture until "the charcoal burned . . . and a large quantity of carbonic acid was disengaged." He did not collect this carbonic acid, however, but attempted instead to calculate the quantity of oxygen which had entered into combination with the carbon, from the difference between the initial weight of the mercury oxide and that of the mercury he recovered afterward from the apparatus. To achieve this he had to make a number of assumptions concerning the quantities of impurities such as the "gray calx" (oxide of lead), metallic lead, and oxygen remaining in the residue after the operation, and to carry out a second distillation on the residue mixed with additional charcoal. Adding up all the amounts of liquid mercury he could collect from the retort, the neck of the retort, and the receiver, and adding a small amount for the mercury which would have adhered to the "gray calx," he calculated that altogether 7 ounces, 7 gros, 16 grains of the metal had been formed. The residue in the retort weighed 1 ounce, 7 gros, ½ grain. Assuming that the proportion of oxygen in the residue must be less than it had been in the original oxide of mercury, where it had amounted to only about one-sixteenth of the total weight of the oxide, he inferred that no more than 40½ grains of this residue could consist of oxygen. "That being supposed," the residue would contain 1 ounce, 6 gros, 32 grains of the metal. The total amount of mercury "obtained" at the end of the experiment was, therefore,

	1	6	32
	7	7	16
Total	9 ounces	5 gros	48 grains

Subtracting this total from the 6,000 grains of red oxide with which he had begun, he obtained for the quantity of oxygen which the oxide must have contained 5 gros 48 grains, or 408 grains. (The figure given in the notebook is 4 gros 48 grains, but from the calculations themselves one can easily tell that this was a mistake in copying. Lavoisier's 4s and 5s were very similar.) From this figure he deducted the 40 grains of oxygen he assumed to have remained in the residue, and one-tenth of the weight of the residue itself (about 100 grains) to account for impurities in the red oxide, and arrived at the figure of 269 grains for the quantity of oxygen "employed to form carbonic acid." To reach the corresponding figure for the carbon employed, he deducted from the original weight used 12 grains which remained at the end, and one-twentieth of the original weight for impurities in the charcoal. That left 228 grains for the carbon contained in the carbonic acid. "That would be," he commented at the end, "46 percent carbon, and no matter what error one assumes, it cannot be less than 40."[31]

Lavoisier must have written that final conclusion with a feeling of consternation. Of all the combining proportions he had worked to determine with precision, there were few which he must have regarded by then as more firmly established than that there are 28 parts of carbon to 72 parts of oxygen in carbonic acid. How could he reconcile those numbers with an experiment which seemed to require at least 40 parts of carbon in 100 of carbonic acid?

The first action Lavoisier took in response to this disturbing situation was to recalculate the result of the latest experiment in another way; that is, to determine the total weight of the carbonic acid from the difference between all of the materials consumed and the total of the remaining substances, instead of from its oxygen content, the difference between the total weight of the red oxide and the weights of the metal and the oxygen in the remaining residue. Adding together the original weight of the red oxide and the charcoal, he obtained for "the quantity of matter employed, 8 ounces, 7 gros, 59½ grains." The total weight of the mercury found after the operation was 7 ounces, 7 gros, 40 grains. "Thus the matter employed to make carbonic acid," obtained by subtracting the second of these quantities from the first, was 1 ounce, 19½ grains, or 595½ grains. The amount of carbon which would have entered into this carbonic acid he got by deducting the 12 grains left in the retort from the 252 grains he had used. Subtracting this 240 grains from the 595½ grains, he obtained for

> oxygen 355½ grains, from which is to be deducted one-tenth for the mophette, leaving 320 grains. That is very nearly oxygen 57, carbon 43. This calculation appears to me to contain nothing hypothetical, unless it is the evaluation of the mophette.[32]

The one-tenth of the weight of the oxygen (or 35 grains, which he subtracted from both the total figure of 595½ grains carbonic acid and from the 355½ grains oxygen, to yield the ratio of 320/560, or 57 percent oxygen) represented the quantity of azote estimated to form the nitric acid assumed as an impurity in red oxide of mercury.

The outcome of the recalculation, we can readily see, was only to confirm that this experiment yielded values for the composition of carbonic acid radically different from those Lavoisier had previously accepted. He was now in a serious predicament. If his old figures were incorrect, then many other inferences he had built on them must also be reconsidered. The compositions he had published for spirit of wine, olive oil, and wax would all be wrong, as well as some of the calculations of the composition of water which were dependent on the composition of carbonic acid. Even the revised theory of respiration would be affected. The very small difference between the quantity of oxygen consumed and the quantity contained in the carbonic acid formed, in the experiment on which he had based his conclusion that hydrogen is also burned, would be converted into a much more impressive deficit if this new result were to take precedence. We have no way of knowing how extensively Lavoisier thought about the implications of his immediate analytical dilemma; nor is it easy to see, from our distance, why it was that he apparently decided at this point to place more trust in the single new result than in all of the earlier results which he had managed to make converge around the 28:72 ratio. His choice is particularly surprising in view of the fact that the earlier combustion experiments had involved direct measurements of the carbonic acid produced, whereas the latest one included no such check on the quantity calculated indirectly from the differences between those quantities he did measure.

Lavoisier then went back to the data from his analysis of sugar with red oxide of mercury of April 29, determined, in spite of its anomalously low yield of carbonic acid, to salvage from the results a calculation of the proportions of carbon, hydrogen, and oxygen in sugar. Remarkably enough he began by simply discarding the measurement of the carbonic acid produced. He took as a *given*, the value of 28 parts carbon per 100 of sugar which he had got out of the analysis of sugar by carbonization. Then he utilized the determination of the oxygen disengaged from the red oxide during the experiment of April 29 as a basis for calculating the carbonic acid and water formed during that analysis. From the difference between the weight of the red oxide employed and that of the mercury recovered, he estimated that the amount of "oxygen disengaged with azote" from the red oxide was 6 gros 15 grains. It is, he reasoned,

> clear that the 6 gros 15 grains, or 447 grains, of oxygen was employed to form carbonic acid and water. Now the quantity employed to form carbonic acid is determined by the quantity of carbon combined in the sugar. Now there was 140 [grains] of it combined, thus only 134 was employed to make carbonic acid, which gives for the corresponding quantity of oxygen, according to the proportion of 43 to 57—177.63 grains of oxygen.

Lavoisier based these calculations on the quantity of 500 grains of sugar he had used in the experiment. He derived the figure of 140 grains for the carbon from the assumed proportion of twenty-eight parts carbon per hundred of sugar. He subtracted 6 grains for the carbon left in the retort at the end of the operation. Then, as the proportion of "43 to 57" indicates, he applied his newly revised values for the composition of carbonic acid to calculate the amount of oxygen which would combine with the 134 grains of carbon. He continued,

> Thus out of the 447 grains of oxygen from the oxide (from which one-tenth is deducted) [for the azote he assumed to be mixed with the oxygen], there has been employed

to make carbonic acid	177.63
to make water	224.37
Total	402.00 [= 447 − (447/10)]

Having thus obtained the quantity of oxygen which must have formed water by subtracting that contained in the carbonic acid from the total consumed, he concluded, "But 224.37 grains of oxygen employed to form water supposes 39.6 grains of hydrogen in the sugar." This last figure he had obtained from his well-established proportions of 15:85 for the hydrogen and oxygen in water. Knowing now the quantities of carbon and of hydrogen in the sugar, he obtained the oxygen contained in it by subtracting these two quantities from the total weight.

Carbon	140		Carbon	28.00
Hydrogen	39.50	or, per	Hydrogen	7.92
Oxygen	320.41	hundred	Oxygen	64.08
	500			100.00[33]

This result must have been satisfying to Lavoisier, because it came out fairly close to the proportions from the fermentation experiment (carbon 30; hydrogen 8; oxygen 60). That convergence may also have reinforced his preference for the new values for the composition of carbonic acid. If he had carried out the calculation with the old proportions of 28:72, the composition of sugar would have come out to 28 parts carbon, 2.02 parts hydrogen, and 69.97 parts oxygen in 100 parts sugar—a result which would only have thrown further confusion on the situation.

Here again Lavoisier had chosen to improvise with the results of highly imperfect experiments instead of trying to improve the experiments until they yielded unproblematic results. In this case the suggestion that time or expense limited his capacity to repeat the experimental work does not seem to apply, because at the time he was already beginning to expand his use of the oxide of mercury method to analyze other substances. Why did he not rather put his first priority on perfecting the analysis of sugar? I think that there is no strictly logical explanation. Perhaps the way he proceeded had by now become entrenched in his scientific style. After so many years of experience with experiments based on similar techniques he must have acquired a great deal of confidence in his ability to judge what facets of a given experimental result he could rely on, and what *ad hoc* manipulations he could safely incorporate to compensate for results which he had reason to distrust. Maybe he had even come to enjoy shoring up weak experiments by ingenious handling of the data. That approach had served him well often enough so that it would hardly be fair to reproach him that it did not guide him infallibly toward modern accepted values.

Lavoisier must have had high hopes that red oxide of mercury might provide a general method to analyze the plant substances he could not burn directly in oxygen gas; for in the very face of the unsatisfactory result of his analysis of sugar of April 29 with that method, he went ahead to make preliminary tests for applying the method to a variety of gums and resins. On May 4 he made a series of "trials on the proportions of red oxide of mercury to employ in order to burn the gums and resins." He used seven different substances. For sandarac he found that "with twelve parts of red oxide [to one of sandarac] a little carbon and a little oil remained. With eighteen parts there is a little oxide in excess." With other substances the quantitative relations were somewhat different. For gum mastic, for example, "with eighteen parts, carbon and a little resin remain. With twenty-four parts a very small amount of oxide and a little carbon remain." He recorded corresponding results for gum benjoin, gum lac, and three other similar substances.[34]

On May 20 Lavoisier carried out a full experimental operation on sandarac. On the basis of the preliminary test he mixed 6,000 grains of the oxide with 300 grains of sandarac, a proportion slightly greater than that which he had found just gave an excess of oxide. He utilized the familiar apparatus, a retort for heating the mixture, connected to a receiver containing water, two caustic alkali bottles, and a pneumatic jar to capture other gases. "The operation . . . took place with great rapidity," the bell jar filling quickly. Removing the jar in which the first portions of air collected, he received the remainder in a second jar. After 193 cubic inches had entered this jar, "the operation suddenly stopped, and a quantity of air which I estimated to be 1/20 cubic inch passed backward [toward the retort]. I augmented the fire quickly by opening the flues, and the air began again to pass outward, some of which had previously reentered, and some of which derived from the operation. The two together made a total of 47 parts. Through the whole course of the experiment the air which passed through was accompanied by a large quantity of white vapor which condensed and appeared to be water." The air which collected in the bell jar just before the break in the operation turned out to be "a heavy and oily hydrogen gas." He measured the gain in weight of the alkali bottles, and collected and weighed the mercury found in various parts of the apparatus. Some portions of the mercury were "impregnated with oil."[35] Lavoisier made no calculations of the composition of sandarac in his notebook, and he apparently carried out no further analyses of plant substances by means of oxide of mercury. We cannot tell whether he regarded this as a promising beginning but never had an opportunity to follow it up, or whether the complications he encountered in this experiment discouraged him from pursuing the method.

On the same day that he performed this experiment on sandarac, Lavoisier again confronted the nagging question of the composition of carbonic acid. At the end of the calculation earlier in the month which had prompted him to adopt the ratio of 57 parts oxygen to 43 of carbon, he had remarked that the only hypothetical factor which entered his procedure was the estimate that one-tenth of the "oxygen" in red oxide of mercury was actually azote. Now he decided to check that supposition by analyzing the oxide he had been using. He did not specify the method that he employed for this purpose, but he most likely reduced the oxide by heating it without charcoal, and tested the gas it yielded eudiometrically. In his notebook he wrote:

> Note of 20 May
>
> examination of that oxide of mercury [having been] made, it yields no mophette, or azotic gas, at all. Therefore one must calculate according to the figures of 355.5 oxygen and 244 grains of carbon. [That is, one must use the value of oxygen as measured, without deducting one-tenth for mophette.] This gives:

Oxygen	59.30
Carbon	40.70
Total	100.00[36]

Rounding off the much-revised composition of carbonic acid to sixty parts oxygen and forty parts carbon, Lavoisier then began to recalculate older results for other substances on the basis of these latest values. On July 1 he went back to the combustion experiment on spirit of wine of May 16, 1785, from which he had derived the composition of that substance published in his memoir on the subject.[37] When he substituted the ratio of 60:40 for the old one of 72:28 the proportions of the constituents of spirit of wine came out very differently from what he had previously accepted:

	Calculation of July 1, 1788	Composition as based on 72:28 ratio
Carbon	40.76	28.52
Hydrogen	7.88	7.87
Preformed water	50.71	63.60
	100.00[38]	100.00

The form in which he put the calculation down in his notebook is of special interest, because it shows that privately he was coming more and more to think about chemical balances as algebraic equations. In contrast to the original calculation, which was in standard balance sheet form, the one he now added below it looked like this:

Calculation of July 1 on this same experiment

93.5 $\overset{S}{\bigvee}$ + 110.317 oxygen = 95.280 carbonic acid + 108.537 water

The spirit of wine is composed of one portion of preformed water, of hydrogen, of carbon. Therefore I can say:

x preformed water + *y* carbon + *z* hydrogen + 110.317 oxygen
= 95.280 carbonic acid + 108.537 water
= 38.112 carbon + 57.168 oxygen + 108.537 water

Upon subtracting the carbon from both sides, this reduces to:

x water + *z* hydrogen + 110.317 oxygen = 57.168 oxygen + 108.537 water

and upon subtracting the oxygen common to both sides, one has:

x water + *z* hydrogen + 53.149 oxygen = 108.537 water

From which one derives *z* hydrogen = 7.97
x water = 464.6

Lavoisier then departed from the algebraic format to state that from the proportions of water (85:15) and of carbonic acid (60:40) one could calculate the composition of spirit of wine.[39] It is still not evident that Lavoisier was able to do anything with his equations that he had not already done with his balance sheets, but obvious that the appearance of a more rigorous form of mathematics appealed to him.

The renewed attention Lavoisier gave to the composition of spirit of wine was undoubtedly in preparation for a renewed effort to establish the equation for fermentation. On the same day that he wrote out the above, he began to construct a new detailed account of the substances present before and after the fermentation. As usual, he relied on the experiment of April 27–June 12, 1787. The formulation was too extended to represent in the form of an equation, so that he resorted again to an intricate tabular format. This time he converted the experimental quantities to a base of 100 pounds of sugar and 400 pounds of water. His motive for redoing what he had already worked out several times before seems to have been that he now regarded the new composition for sugar that he had derived by combining the carbonization and red oxide of mercury experiments as more accurate than the composition on which he had relied for his earlier calculations. The change from the older proportions, 32.8 carbon, 57 oxygen, 10 hydrogen per 100, to the new values of 28 carbon, 64.08 oxygen, 7.92 hydrogen would obviously force a substantial revision in the balances of the constituent elements within the equation. As can be seen in the table he now prepared, the composition he used for sugar is essentially identical to his latest analytical result:

Calculation of July 1, 1788
Materials of the Fermentation

Water	400			
Sugar	100			
Beer yeast				
Water	7	3	6	60
Dry Yeast	2	12	1	28
Total	510	0	0	16
Details				
Water 400 pounds				
Hydrogen	60 pounds	0	0	0
Oxygen	340	0	0	0
Sugar 100 pounds				
Hydrogen	8	0	0	0
Oxygen	64	0	0	0
Carbon	28	0	0	0

I have omitted here the complicated breakdown of yeast into its constituent elements and the redistribution of the weights of the elements contained in the table to group the oxygen, hydrogen, carbon, and azote together and display the totals of each element.[40]

This data sheet included only the materials present at the beginning of the data sheet. In the corresponding previous balances he had drawn up, Lavoisier had usually listed the products on a separate page. Either he did not complete the second half of this one on July 1, or else the page containing it is missing. Its absence is unfortunate. Since the composition of sugar incorporated in the first half assumes the 60:40 ratio he had recently adopted for carbonic acid, it would be very interesting to know if he utilized, or intended to utilize, these same proportions for the carbonic acid itself, and to use the composition for spirit of wine that he had just calculated on that basis.

Lavoisier accepted for almost two months the change he had been impelled to make in the composition of carbonic acid, but it is hard to believe that he ever felt comfortable about it. Almost as soon as he had made the above calculations based on the 60:40 ratio, he came to have serious qualms about abandoning the old figure of 72:28 on the grounds of a single experiment. During the next three days he thought over the conditions under which he had carried out his analysis of carbon with oxide of mercury, and concluded that it was not so decisive a result as he had up until then taken it to be. In his notebook he wrote down:

> Reflection of 4 July
>
> It should be noted, with respect to this result, that the quantity of carbon remaining could have been greater than I estimated it; [and] that one must deduct [from the initial quantity of carbon] the cinder, the alkali, etc. [contained as impurities in the charcoal]. It is therefore perhaps not on 240 grains of carbon that one must make the calculation, but perhaps on 200. For a sizable quantity of it was blown [into a powdery state in which it] could have been confused with the gray calx. On supposing that this view is correct, one would have:
>
> | | |
> |---|---|
> | Oxygen | 395.5 |
> | Carbon | 200.0 |
> | Total | 595.5 |
>
> that is, per hundred
>
> | | |
> |---|---|
> | Carbon | 33.6 |
> | Oxygen | 66.4 |
>
> One can see that it is possible to reconcile [the result with the old ratio]. There was, in addition, a portion of water formed, which consumed a certain portion of the oxygen. That circumstance [permits one to make the two figures] approach still closer.[41]

Lavoisier evidently picked the figure 200 out of the air, since he had no quantitative estimate of how much of the carbon he could account for by the factors he mentioned. The main significance of his reflection was undoubtedly that he was coming to realize that the experiment was too problematic to justify giving up the ratio on which he had previously relied. There are no further comments on the subject in his notebook, but when he described the formation of carbonic acid in his *Elementary Treatise of Chemistry* a few months later, he mentioned only his older combustion experiments as the basis for determining its composition, and he stated without qualification, "It requires seventy-two parts of oxygen by weight to saturate twenty-eight of carbon."[42]

We may recall that Lavoisier's notebook contains *two* combustion analyses of spirit of wine carried out in 1785, one performed on May 14, the other on May 16. It was on the second of these two, the only one with which he had at that time been "fully satisfied,"[43] that he had based his published composition, and on which he had also carried out the recalculation of July 1, 1788. He also went back to the May 14 experiment, even though he had previously regarded it as less reliable, and completed another calculation of the composition of spirit of wine from its results. But whereas he had dated the reevaluation of the May 16 experiment, he did not date these new calculations based on the May 14 analysis. Nor did he comment on the composition he was assuming for carbonic acid; but the computation in fact incorporates the old ratio of 28:72. It is tempting to infer that he may have made this reassessment soon after he decided to revert to those values. The outcome:

Preformed water	63.949
Carbon	29.154
Hydrogen	6.897
	100.00[44]

was so close to the original results of the May 16 experiment (see above, p. 371 right side) that Lavoisier's confidence in both experiments must have become greater than it had been at the time he carried them out. He was, in fact, probably well satisfied by then that he had reliably established the composition of spirit of wine. His calculations in the *Elementary Treatise* can be shown to be based on an assumed composition of sixty-four parts preformed water, seven parts hydrogen, and twenty-nine parts carbon,[45] very nearly the average of the results of these two older experiments.

Sometime probably soon after these developments, Lavoisier continued on two blank pages in his laboratory notebook the fermentation balance he had begun on July 1 on a separate sheet. The table for the materials present before the operation was identical to the one he had written on July 1, except that he omitted the breakdown to the constituent elements. Below that he gave the following table of the products:

Products after fermentation				
Dry spirit of wine	57	11	1	57.6
Residue of sugar	4	1	4	2.7
Dry yeast	1	6	0	50.0
Water and vinegar	397	9	0	28.7
Carbonic acid saturated with water	49	4	1	21.0
	510	0	0	16.0[46]

Although Lavoisier did not indicate the source of these figures, they can be shown to be derived by directly converting the results of the experiment of April–June 1787 to the base of 100 pounds of sugar before the operation.

This new balance sheet contains some particularly interesting features. First, at this stage Lavoisier did not attempt to calculate the dry carbonic acid, as he had previously done from his older composition of sugar, but simply represented the weight loss as "carbonic acid saturated with water." Second, the negative water balance was now only 3 pounds, compared with 96 pounds of sugar consumed, and even this very small deficit took no account of the water contained in the carbonic acid. For a third significant feature of his new calculations, we must look back at the table of July 1, to notice that Lavoisier represented the sugar there as a combination of hydrogen, oxygen, and carbon—not of carbon and water. We are left wondering whether this was merely an alternative form of accounting, adopted because he was highlighting the balance of the elementary constituents in the entire fermentation equation, or whether he may again have been thinking of sugar as a triple combination of these three principles. If the latter were the case, then we could find in the new analytical result a rationale for his changing his mind yet again. It was, we remember, his calculation of the composition of sugar from the fermentation equation itself, when the proportions of hydrogen and water had come out very close to their proportions in water, that apparently prompted him during the previous year to switch back to his older conception of sugar as carbonized water.[47] The new composition did not fit this conception very well (64:8::89:11 instead of 85:15), so that in adopting it he may at the same time have loosened his attachment to his old idea.

Following the general balance between the materials and the products of fermentation, Lavoisier gave a "detail for spirit of wine," reducing the total weight of that product to the weights of its constituent parts, carbon, hydrogen, and water.[48] This tabulation is particularly interesting, because by working backward one can show that it is based on a composition for carbonic acid of 69.6 parts oxygen to 30.4 parts of carbon.[49] This suggests that Lavoisier may have worked it out, and therefore have done the work on his fermentation equation recorded on these notebook pages, sometime after July 4, during that period when he had come to think that he could make the proportion based on the red oxide of mercury experiment "approach" the old ratio "still closer" than the proportion of 66.4:33.6 which he calculated on that day, but before he decided to go back entirely to the old figure of 72:28.

Unless some additional pages have been lost, it appears that in early July Lavoisier left his new fermentation calculations unfinished. There are some surviving notes containing additional derivations based on the preceding tables that he might have made at anytime after he readopted the 72:28 ratio; but he may not have carried these out until the fall. If that is the case, then the most probable explanations for the delay are that he was still not satisfied with his analysis of sugar; and that he hoped that when his new fermentation apparatus was ready he would be able to obtain more precise data concerning the operation itself. Since he planned to trap and weigh the carbonic acid in caustic alkali, he would then not have to resort to indirect methods to compute it, and he would have enough information to provide independent checks on the calculated balances.

IV

While waiting for his new fermentation apparatus, Lavoisier began an effort to extend his analyses of the composition of plant and animal matters to substances containing azote. On July 16, he distilled a "copious" amount of horn in a retort. He did not state what animal the horn came from; but that material had in general been regarded traditionally as a paradigmatic "animal matter," because it yielded an abundance of volatile alkali when distilled.[50] In the light of Berthollet's recent investigations of animal matter this property meant that horn contains a large proportion of azote, which combines with hydrogen during the distillation to form ammonia. Lavoisier combined the customary distillation procedure with his standard methods for measuring the gaseous products—in this case a series of receivers including one empty bottle, a bottle half filled with water, two bottles containing alkali, and a pneumatic jar. In his usual way he weighed each piece of the apparatus (except the pneumatic part) before the operation. During the distillation ammonium carbonate collected in solid form in the neck of the retort, the first bottle, and connecting tubes. After he had maintained the operation for 6½ hours, he began to increase the fire in order to distill off a heavy oil which had collected in the retort; but the oil was not able "to pass over, because the ammonium carbonate was blocking the end [of the retort]; the oil which had been volatilized fell back onto the horn, which had swollen up and become porous. I extinguished the fire immediately and allowed [the apparatus to cool]." The increase in weight of the second, third, and fourth bottles gave him the quantity of carbonic acid disengaged. Because of his inability fully to separate the products of the distillation, however, the weight changes of the retort and the first bottle gave only quantities representing mixtures of ammonium carbonate, oil, and water. The result, therefore, was of little use for determining the quantities of these constituents of the horn. Perhaps for this reason he did not bother to record the nature or quantity of the gas which entered the pneumatic jar.[51]

Lavoisier tried again on July 28, following the same general procedures. He ran into similar complications:

> I applied the fire by degrees and then increased it. At first pure water passed over, collecting in the receiver as it was distilled. Then ammonium carbonate, partly liquid and partly solid, crystallized on the interior surface of the receiver, combined in part in the state of a soap with the oil which was beginning to disengage. At the beginning of the distillation of the oil, the lute which joined the retort to the receiver became detached. I stopped the operation at once, and took advantage of the situation to change the tube connecting the receiver to the first [alkali] bottle, which was beginning to fill up with solid ammonium carbonate in spite of the care I had taken to cool the receiver with a wet linen.
>
> . . . .
>
> When the apparatus had been reconnected, I relit the fire under the retort, and the distillation continued; but I was forced to stop it because the horn was swelling up and was already descending into the neck of the retort. I stopped the fire and weighed the retort after it had cooled.

Again Lavoisier had had to end the operation prematurely, and without achieving usable results. Although he accounted at the end for 11 ounces 6 gros of the 12 ounces of horn with which he had begun, he had still not been able to separate the products sufficiently to determine their individual weights. The increase in the weight of the first bottle, for example, represented the total of the "salt and oil which passed into it," while the loss in weight of the retort was made up of the "water, oil, and salt" which passed out of it.[52]

In a third effort to overcome his technical problems, Lavoisier distilled another two pounds of horn on August 6, utilizing a more elaborate apparatus and extended procedures. He added a second empty receiving bottle and a third alkali bottle. "The experiment succeeded reasonably well," he thought afterward. "There was only one lute which failed, but I reconnected it so quickly that the loss was not significant. Just as with the preceding experiment, it was necessary to stop this one before it was completed, because the horn swelled up considerably." He was able this time to separate sufficiently the ammonium carbonate formed and the oil, so that he regarded the total quantity of ammonium carbonate collected as containing only "a small quantity of oil." In the retort he was left again with a mixture, of "a quantity of horn in a carbonaceous state mixed with oil"; but he thought he could separate the constituents of the mixture by redistilling this "carbon" of horn. He placed it in a second retort connected to a receiver, two alkali bottles, and a pneumatic jar. After he had maintained the distillation for five hours, the retort broke, and he had yet again to break off the operation unfinished. There was still a little salt and oil in the retort and connecting tube, but after completing his weighings he estimated it at only around thirty-three grains. He had obtained about three gros of carbonic acid in the alkali bottles. In the pneumatic jar he had collected four portions of "hydrogen gas containing much oil in solution." Because of the melting of the retort, however, he could "not rightly evaluate the weight of the gas. It might even be possible that a hole having formed in the bottom of the retort, a little bit of carbon had fallen into the fire. In order to be rigorous, it would perhaps be more prudent to begin the operation over."[53]

To judge from the exceptionally meticulous character of these entries in his laboratory register, Lavoisier must have begun these experiments on horn with the idea that they were very important, and to have performed them with special care. Since he did not directly state their objective, we cannot be certain how much he felt he had accomplished at this point. His results did support qualitatively the view that animal matter is composed of carbon, hydrogen, oxygen, and azote, since the products he obtained—ammonium carbonate, oil, hydrogen gas, and carbonic acid—collectively contained these same four principles. That outcome would not have seemed to him much of an advance, however, because he had already described the existence of these four principles in animal matter as a foregone conclusion. To judge from his procedures in this experiment, his previous analyses of plant substances, and his general chemical approach, he was undoubtedly searching for a method to determine the quantitative proportions of the four principles in this representative animal substance. If so, he clearly had not reached his goal. Like so many distillers before him, he had attained only a partial decomposition of the substance being analyzed. In the third experiment, however, he had made some progress toward a further resolution of the mixed products. Even while he considered how he might persist in this direction, he took on other related problems in plant analysis.

On August 18 Lavoisier distilled five varieties of cloves in order to find out how much essential oil each type yielded. Cloves had long been a prominent source of oils favored for medicinal purposes, and the character of Lavoisier's investigation suggests that he may now have been casting around among the repertoire of plant substances traditionally subjected to distillation, in order to identify suitable objects for analysis.[54] There is no indication that he followed up this exploratory set of experiments.

I have described Lavoisier as satisfied enough with the composition of sugar at which he had arrived in April, in spite of the improvised analytical results from which he derived it, so that he moved on to other investigative problems. Later events will confirm his willingness to build other conclusions on those figures. That does not mean, however, that he had given up trying to improve on the empirical foundations for the composition. In August, in fact, he tried still another method to oxygenate the sugar. Although he regarded red oxide of mercury in general as the most suitable of the metallic oxides for this purpose, because the mercury had so little affinity for its oxygen, there were others which "could, up to a certain point, fulfill the same object." Among these was the black oxide of manganese.[55] In early August he had distilled some of this oxide with nitre, probably in connection with an independent line of investigation. On August 21 he tried a distillation of the black oxide with sugar. As usual, he heated a mixture of the two substances in a retort connected to an empty receiver, two alkali bottles, and a pneumatic jar. The experiment succeeded better than some recent ones, in that he was able to continue it until nothing further was evolved. The alkali bottles showed the expected weight gain from the carbonic acid disengaged. In the pneumatic jar, however, he collected mostly azotic gas. That outcome could only have confronted Lavoisier with a new complication, since he did not consider azote to enter into the composition of sugar, and probably did not expect the oxide of manganese to be a source of it. That same afternoon and evening he distilled some of the black oxide alone, and obtained azotic gas along with oxygen gas. The result with sugar must therefore have been caused by impurities in the oxide. Lavoisier also returned on this day to the investigation of horn which he had left in an unfinished state two weeks before. He attempted again to redistill the carbon remaining in the retort after the initial distillation of horn, employing this time the carbon left from the second of the original series of three experiments. The alkali bottles became saturated with carbonic acid, and he collected in the pneumatic jar a mixture of carbonic acid, atmospheric air, nitric acid, and a little hydrogen gas. On August 22 he distilled a mixture of starch and manganese (probably he meant the oxide of manganese) and collected several portions of hydrogen gas in the pneumatic jar, along with the carbonic acid in the alkali bottles. On the twenty-third he placed milk in four bell jars over mercury, two of them containing atmospheric air, the other two oxygen. After eight days he found in one jar a mixture of carbonic acid and azote. On the twenty-fourth he once more distilled a mixture of black oxide of manganese and sugar. He must have used a purer oxide, for he obtained this time hydrogen gas with no azote. There remained a considerable residue in the retort which he apparently did not analyze further. He began a similar analysis of gum copale, but did not record any data beyond the initial weighings. On the twenty-sixth he again distilled the black oxide by itself, and on the twenty-seventh he continued his efforts of the twenty-first to analyze the carbon left over from his attempted analysis of horn. This time he distilled the residue in nitric acid.[56]

Lavoisier seems to have pursued these experiments during the last week of August with unusual intensity, for he was occupied with one or more of them almost every day. Unless there is some coherent thread of progress which escapes me, however, he seems to have been groping rather frantically for an opening which he could not find. Turning from one to another of his related lines of inquiry, he carried out one indecisive experiment after another. The fragmentary nature of this section of his laboratory register, in contrast with the systematic detail he had put down a few weeks before when he began his analyses of horn, seems almost symbolic of a dissipation of hope for a significant advance in his investigation of plant and animal matter. It must therefore have been with some relief, as well as anticipation, that he took delivery in early September of the new fermentation apparatus with which he expected to confirm his analysis of the process which had for so long fascinated and challenged him.

In the *Elementary Treatise* Lavoisier wrote that the study of fermentation "demands special apparatus, designed uniquely for this type of experiment." The one he described there he had "adopted definitively after having successively made a great number of corrections" (see Figure 14). Its arrangement was similar in principle to the apparatus he had already put together regularly for various operations which produce carbonic acid and other gases. It consisted of a matras, or long-necked distillation flask, in which the fermentation took place, a receiving bottle with three openings, of which one was attached to a bottle below it, and another through a long connecting tube to two caustic alkali bottles and a pneumatic jar. The special features incorporated into the

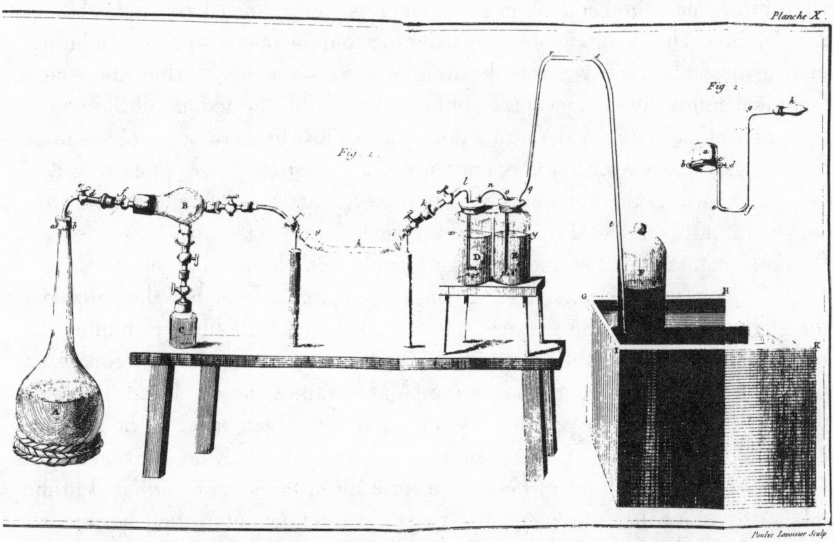

Figure 14. Fermentation apparatus described by Lavoisier in his *Elementary Treatise of Chemistry.* On the far left is fermentation flask *A*. *B* and *C* are bottles intended to trap foam driven over in fermentation; *h* is a horizontal tube containing deliquescent salt to trap water formed in fermentation. *D* and *E* are caustic alkali bottles to collect vapors or gases which pass through preceding vessels. Lavoisier, *Traité élémentaire de chimie* (Paris: Cuchet, 1789), 2: Plate 10.

equipment appear to have been designed particularly to overcome the difficulties Lavoisier had run into in his long fermentation experiment extending from September 1786 to April 1787. The jar beneath the receiver was arranged to facilitate collecting any yeast froth which might be driven over from the matras. The tube connecting the receiver to the alkali bottles included a long section filled with a deliquescent salt to absorb the water carried off with the carbonic acid. Regarding the alkali bottles, he wrote, "Of the small portion not absorbed in the alkali of the first bottle, none will escape the second bottle." He must therefore have provided them with a large enough capacity to avoid the mischance which had befallen him in the earlier experiment, when the carbonic acid had evolved so rapidly that the alkali bottles could not absorb all of it. There were valves inserted between each piece of the apparatus, "in such a way that we can close off its two extremities and weigh each piece separately at any time during the experiment."[57]

The fermentation apparatus was probably built by Nicolas Fortin, who had been making scientific equipment for Lavoisier since 1783. It was elegantly designed and beautifully crafted. The glass bottles were supported on a special wooden platform and connected by precisely turned brass fittings. The valves were brass, and the sections of the apparatus were joined by airtight thumbscrew joints. The latter enabled Lavoisier to avoid the onerous process of luting, and to dissemble and reassemble the pieces very quickly.[58] Altogether these technical refinements must have eliminated much of the tedium of the operation, as well as reduced the errors due to gases lost in the process of weighing the separate pieces while the operation was in progress. There is no record of the date at which the apparatus was delivered,[59] and my inference that Lavoisier had it at his disposal by September comes from the fact that he carried out then a fermentation experiment using apparatus which fits its description.

On September 9, Lavoisier set up the new apparatus, weighed the parts, put the sugar solution in the matras, and the alkali in the bottles. Retaining the ratio of sugar to water of 1:4 which he had used in the older experiment on which he had more recently based the balance tables, he employed 3 pounds of sugar with 12 pounds of water. On the morning of September 11 he added 1 ounce, 7 gros, 8 grains of yeast. In doing so, he estimated, he lost 6 grains of water and 2 grains of sugar, because a little bit of the solution adhered to the tube with which he introduced the yeast. The fermentation then began, but even this specially constructed equipment was not quite trouble-free:

> A few bubbles began to be disengaged at 1 o'clock, but since I noticed that the liquid did not descend in the tubes, I suspected that there was a leak somewhere. It was not until 3:30 P.M. that I discovered it and repaired it. Since the disengagement had been very slow, I assumed that no more than twelve to 15 cubic inches

> of air [Lavoisier here wrote "perhaps sixteen" between the lines] had been lost, . . . and that it was perhaps only the air of the vessels. That judgment was made by means of the time it took for the tubes to be filled.

Taking extra care, Lavoisier marked the height of the alkali in the bottles with strips of paper.[60]

By September 20, 210 cubic inches of common air had filled the pneumatic jar. On that day Lavoisier added a third alkali bottle to the apparatus. He added a fourth bottle as a "precaution" on October 3, even though the third bottle was not yet saturated. On October 8 "an accident occurred to the apparatus, causing liquid in the bottles to flow back into the tube containing the deliquescent salt, and about half an ounce of liquid was lost." At this point he weighed all of the relevant parts of the apparatus again. There the record stops.[61]

All of the procedures Lavoisier described in his notebook support the impression that he undertook this experiment in a manner befitting what he could expect to be a definitive analysis of fermentation; yet there is no indication that he carried the process to completion, that he determined how much spirit of wine it had produced, or that he did anything further with the data that he did gather. Moreover, as far as we can tell, he never had another opportunity to use the "uniquely" designed apparatus which he described with such justifiable pride in his *Elementary Treatise*.

Sometime while this fermentation reaction was under way, Lavoisier took up again the analysis of horn, still determined to wrest a quantitative result from the products he had collected in the earlier experiments. To determine how much ammonium carbonate had formed in the distillation of August 6, he titrated the salt he had removed then from the apparatus with dilute sulfuric acid. From the loss of weight which ensued he estimated how much carbonic acid was driven off in the saturation reaction. Tenaciously seeking a way to analyze further the volatile oil he obtained in the distillation of horn, he poured concentrated sulfuric acid on some of it, attempting to reduce it to carbon. It merely dissolved. He was no more successful when he tried to reduce the oil to carbon with nitric acid. Trying next to oxygenate the oil by boiling it in fuming nitric acid, he obtained only two bitter nitrous salts. Repeating the experiment on oil of turpentine, he added "lightly fuming" nitric acid, which failed also to reduce this oil to carbon. Finally, by adding two parts of fuming nitric acid and one of sulfuric acid to a little oil of turpentine distilled twice, he obtained nitrous vapors which left behind a residue of porous carbon.[62] Despite this limited success he was still a long way from a general method for determining the quantitative composition of horn. He continued through September and October to distill a few more plant and animal matters, including horn again, wax, oil, and ivory. In November he attempted to analyze starch and meat by distillation.[63] None of these efforts yielded interesting results. The final entries in the last surviving laboratory notebook Lavoisier kept have the appearance of an investigation gone sterile, just as the arduous efforts of his predecessors for more than a century to determine the constitution of plant and animal matter through distillation analyses had done long before he took his turn at it.[64]

14

Plant and Animal Chemistry in the New Chemical System

While he was bogged down in his troubled search for adequate general methods to determine the composition of sugar and other plant and animal matters, Lavoisier was finally bringing to completion another grand project he had long planned, a general treatise describing the entire new system of chemistry. The exact schedule on which he wrote it cannot be established, but he must have spent a large part of the year 1788 on it. Daumas suggests, from the character of the manuscript of the *Elementary Treatise* which has survived, that Lavoisier was able to write out the final version with very few revisions.[1] By September he was far enough along to enter negotiations for publication, and he was finished by the end of the year.

Of the seventeen chapters comprising part 1 of the *Elementary Treatise of Chemistry,* over five are devoted to plant and animal chemistry. These portions differ sharply in character from the chapters on caloric, the atmosphere, combustible bodies, and acids. For those general topics Lavoisier was able to reformulate into a systematic presentation experiments and conclusions he had reached long before, and refined to a high degree. For plant and animal chemistry, on the other hand, he had to extract conclusions as best he could from investigations which were far from finished. If, as seems reasonable, Lavoisier reached these sections by the early fall of 1788, he was, as the foregoing discussion indicates, confronting major unsolved problems in each of the major areas of the subject on which he had to write. The *Elementary Treatise* therefore undergoes in these chapters a transition from polished textbook to almost a preliminary progress report.

The conception of the composition of plant and animal matter that Lavoisier formulated in the *Elementary Treatise* was a more methodical version of the ideas he had already expressed in his memoir "On the decomposition of water by plant and animal substances." Having finally made up his mind on the question over which he had vacillated for so long, he reaffirmed that plant substances contain carbon, hydrogen, and oxygen in a triple combination, and that animal substances contain azote in addition. In some statements he included phosphorus and sulfur as further constituents of animal matter. He also described in a similar way the decompositions and conversions which these substances undergo as additions, subtractions, and recombinations of their simple constituents.[2] He fitted these views, however, into a classification of plant and animal substances which integrated them into his general chemical system. The plant and animal classes corresponded exactly to those of the mineral kingdom except that, in place of the simple combustible bases of the latter, they contained composite bases. Ordinary simple combustible bases, such as sulfur, phosphorous, and carbon, he pointed out, are able to combine not only with oxygen, but with one another, forming sulfides, phosphides, and carbides. The foundation for all plant substances was the particular combination of two simple bases, hydrogen and carbon. "When hydrogen and carbon join together . . . there results a particular combination known as an oil, and that oil is either fixed or volatile, depending on the proportions of hydrogen and carbon." Fixed oils, he thought, contain an excess of carbon, which can be separated, whereas volatile oils contain the two principles in a "more exact proportion . . . not susceptible of being decomposed." As he remarked in his discussion, he had already demonstrated in 1784 that oils were composed of carbon and hydrogen. Empirically he had little to add to that earlier work, but it now played a new role within his conceptual system. The double base of carbon and hydrogen was defined as the equivalent in plant chemistry to the simple combustible, or "acidifiable," bases in mineral chemistry.[3]

Lavoisier developed his entire classification scheme for plant and animal substances around this equivalence, by treating them all as products of the oxygenation of composite bases; that is, as "acids and oxides of double and triple bases." The oxides of the plant kingdom were sugar, the various species of gums, and starch. "These three substances possess a radical composed of hydrogen and carbon combined into a single base, and brought to the state of an oxide by a portion of oxygen; they differ from one another only in the proportions of the principles which compose the base." By acquiring a further quantity of oxygen these oxides passed to the plant acids, of which there were already thirteen known. These were distinguishable only by their proportions of carbon and hydrogen, and by differences in their degree of oxygenation.[4]

Extending these same ideas to "the acids and oxides of three and four bases" which he thought characteristic of the animal kingdom, Lavoisier had to rely more on hope than on existing analytical knowledge. There were six known animal acids—lactic, saccholactic, bombic, formic, sebacic, and prussic. Although he thought that each of these acids had a base composed of azote, phosporus, hydrogen, and carbon, he had very little evidence for the claim: only the general knowledge that prussic acid, and perhaps gallic acid, contain azote. For the animal oxides he was even vaguer.

> The oxides of the animal kingdom are still less known than those of the plant kingdom, and their number is still undetermined. The red part of the blood, the lymph, almost all of the secretions are true oxides, and it is from this point of view that it is important to study them.[5]

The classifications that Lavoisier devised for plant and animal materials depended upon quantitative criteria, differences in the proportions of the simple principles comprising their bases, and in the proportions of oxygen added to these bases. Nevertheless, as he acknowledged repeatedly, he had not actually determined these proportions. Of the plant acids, he wrote, "We know what the principles that comprise them are, and I have no doubts in that regard, . . . but the proportions are still unknown."[6] Concerning animal substances he admitted "that their composition is not yet known very exactly. We know that they are composed of hydrogen, carbon, azote, phosphorus, and sulfur, all carried to the state of an oxide by a greater or lesser quantity of oxygen; but we are absolutely ignorant of the proportions of these principles."[7] How then did he arrive at a classificatory sysytem based on proportions he did not know? He did have one prominent example from which to generalize. He had analyzed an oil and found only carbon and hydrogen in it. He had worked out the proportions of carbon, hydrogen, and oxygen in sugar; and from his early investigation of the acid of sugar he knew that oxalic acid is obtained by oxygenating sugar. It seems evident, however, that the main force of his argument rested on an analogy between plant and animal substances and those of the mineral kingdom on which he had constructed his fundamental theories of oxygenation and acidification. By defining composite bases as "radicals" analogous to the simple combustible bases of mineral chemistry, he extended the general principles of his new chemistry throughout the three realms of chemistry. His forceful precedent deeply influenced the succeeding era.

The *a priori* aspect of Lavoisier's views on the composition of plant and animal substances is most evident in the nomenclature he proposed for the plant oxides and acids. Drawing another analogy, to the terms "extractoresin" and "resinoextract" which his old teacher Guillaume Rouelle had coined to classify plant substances soluble in both water and alcohol according to the relative degree of their solubility in these two solvents, Lavoisier listed the following names:

hydrocarbonaceous oxide	hydrocarbonous acid
hydrocarbonic oxide	hydrocarbonic acid
carbonohydrous oxide	oxygenated hydrocarbonic acid
carbonohydric oxide	carbonohydrous acid
	carbonohydric acid
	oxygenated carbonohydric acid

"It is probable," he wrote optimistically, "that this variety of language will be sufficient to indicate all of the varieties which nature presents us, and that as the plant acids become better known, they will arrange themselves naturally, and as if by themselves, in the framework which we have just presented."[8]

II

Believing, as he did, that his analysis of the fermentation process would provide the climactic demonstration of the power and precision of his system of chemistry, Lavoisier undoubtedly planned to make the chapter on spirituous fermentation one of the highlights of his *Elementary Treatise*. If, however, he had expected to have new and more accurate experimental data available to him in time to write this section, his hopes must have been dashed by the disappointing outcome of the first trial of the new apparatus. Before he could carry out another effort, he probably reached the point at which he could no longer put off completing that chapter. He was, therefore, forced to fall back on the same old experiment whose results he had been working over for more than a year.

To prepare the complete balance of the substances taking part in the fermentation operation, and their constituent elements, which he wished to include in his discussion of the process, Lavoisier began with the tables he had constructed in July. His first additional move was to repeat, with the new composition for sugar, the calculation of the quantity of dry carbonic acid formed, by means of the carbon balance. The tabulation, which he wrote out on another separate page, was as follows (as in the July tables themselves, these figures represent not the actual weights determined in the experiment itself, but those weights converted to a base of 100 pounds of sugar):

Calculation for the fixed air

Carbon of the spirit of wine	16 pounds	11 ounces	5 gros	63.50 grains
Carbon of the yeast		6	2	29.50
Carbon of the vinegar		10		
Carbon of the residue of the sugar	1	2	2	52.8
	18	14	2[*sic*]	1.80

This total represented all of the carbon at the end of the experiment, except for what the carbonic acid contained. As this enumeration shows, he was now taking into account the yeast and "vinegar" at the end, a factor he had reminded himself to include after an earlier calculation in which he had neglected them.

The quantity of carbon at the beginning was the 28 pounds in the sugar, plus 12 ounces, 4 gros, 59.00 grains that he estimated for the yeast. The difference between the two totals gave the carbon in the carbonic acid:

	28 pounds	12 ounces	4 gros	59.00 grains
−	18	14	2	1.80
	9	14	2	57.20

Then, using the ratio of 72:28 for the proportion of oxygen to carbon in carbonic acid, he computed the oxygen and added it to the preceding figure to obtain, for the weight of the carbonic acid formed, 35 pounds, 5 ounces, 4 gros, 19.14 grains.[9]

The outcome of this calculation differed sharply from the corresponding result of his earlier work on the problem, and must have come as something of a shock to the intrepid calculator. Previously he had come out with only a minor difference between the weight of the dry carbonic acid and the total weight of carbonic acid "saturated with water." In the calculation of July, however, he had determined that the latter quantity was 49 pounds, 4 ounces, 1 gros, 21.0 grains. The difference, 13 pounds, 14 ounces, 5 gros, therefore amounted to almost a third of that total. Whereas he had once passed off his inability to make a rigorous calculation of the water "dissolved" in the carbonic acid as the source of a "slight error," now he had to acknowledge this quantity as a major factor. In the *Elementary Treatise* he wrote that the carbonic acid "carries with it in addition a quite considerable portion of water, which it holds in solution."[10] What effect did this development have on the water balance so essential to his theory of fermentation?

Knowing now how much carbonic acid had formed in the operation, Lavoisier was in a position to compute the amount of water present at the end by subtracting the total weight of the products of the fermentation from the total quantity of the materials he had included in the original fermentation mixture. He carried out such a computation on another piece of paper. Although these pages are not dated, we can safely guess that he would have been anxious enough to know the outcome so that he probably did the calculation as soon as possible after the preceding one. The quantities at the end were:

Carbonic acid	35 pounds	5 ounces	4 gros	19.14 grains
Spirit of wine	57	11	1	58
Acetic acid	2	8	0	0
Residue of sugar	4	1	4	2.[0]7
Yeast	1	6	0	50
	101	0	2	57.21

Subtracting this total from the 500 pounds of starting material, he found "therefore [for] water, 398 pounds, 15 ounces, 5 gros, 14.79 grains left at the end of the operation." If we turn to his table of starting materials from July 1, we can see that there were initially 400 pounds of water as such, plus 7 pounds, 3 ounces, 6 gros, 60 grains contained in the yeast, which could be separated by drying it. There was, therefore, still a deficit of nearly 9 pounds, that he could ascribe to water decomposed in the operation. He began to calculate the quantities of hydrogen and of oxygen present in the 398 pounds of water,[11] probably as a step toward establishing the "Details" balance sheet of the elements contained in the materials and products of the fermentation.

The satisfaction Lavoisier may have felt at this confirmation of the water deficit was short-lived, for he had reached it by making a simple error. The total weight of the starting materials was not 500 pounds, but, with the yeast included, 510 pounds. When he corrected this quantity in his tabulation, the quantity of water left was 408 pounds, 15 ounces, 5 gros, 14.79 grains.[12] The deficit that his theory required had, therefore, suddenly vanished!

From simple, unlabeled, innocent-looking tabulations on untitled data sheets we can thus unlock the cognitive steps which led Lavoisier to a result of momentous consequence for the theory of fermentation that had guided his investigation for four long years. Unless he were to challenge his own result by changing his assumptions and doing the calculation another way, that theory was no longer tenable. There is no evidence that he resisted the outcome in such a way. These pages are, however, silent about how Lavoisier reacted to the news they bore him. Was he confronted all at once with the apparent overthrow of all that he had striven so mightily to prove? Or had he already decided for other reasons that fermentation does not decompose water after all and, like so many scientists before and after him, found that the same experimental evidence that had once seemed to support his theory now supported a decision to abandon that theory? We have no very firm clues on the basis of which to choose between these possibilities. Lavoisier himself did not directly say what had caused him to change his mind. In a review of the *Elementary Treatise*, however, his protégé Armand Seguin offered the following explanation: "M. Lavoisier had been persuaded by earlier experiments that water is decomposed during vinous fermentation. A deeper familiarity with the nature of plant substances leads him here to different conclusions; and after having observed more accurately, he has corrected his ideas on this subject."[13] We must be cautious about inferring too much from so general a statement. Seguin was, however, probably working in Lavoisier's laboratory during the period in which Lavoisier made this transition,[14] and his viewpoint may therefore reflect at least an outward familiarity with the circumstances under which it took place.

The order of events that Seguin's account suggests is that Lavoisier first changed his mind on the basis of general considerations about the nature of plant substances, and afterward made new observations that confirmed "different conclusions." Before considering the way in which Lavoisier may have reached those conclusions, we should amend Seguin's version of the second phase in this development. Lavoisier did not make new experimental observations that confirmed his new conclusions. If he "observed" more accurately, that can mean only that in the light of those conclusions he perceived more accurately the results that he could derive from experiments already made.

The most probable point of reference for the assertion that Lavoisier had acquired a "deeper familiarity with the nature of plant substances" is his idea that they consist of triple combinations of their constituent elements. If that conception was the source for Seguin's allusion, then it would appear that when, after backsliding for a time to the view that sugar contains water, Lavoisier reaffirmed that plant substances contain only the elements of water, it followed as a direct corollary that fermentation does not decompose water. Such an interpretation finds support in a portion of a passage in the *Elementary Treatise* already quoted in full in Chapter 12. "I had proposed formally, in my first memoirs on the formation of water, that this substance, regarded as an element, is decomposed in a great number of chemical operations, notably in vinous fermentation. I supposed at that time that water existed already formed in the sugar, whereas I am persuaded today that it contains only the materials necessary to form water."[15]

In another passage in the *Elementary Treatise*, he pointed out that the quantity of sugar decomposed was sufficient to account for the alcohol, carbonic acid, and acetic acid produced. "It is, therefore, not necessary to suppose that water is decomposed in this operation; unless one supposes that the oxygen and hydrogen are in a state of water in the sugar, which I do not believe."[16] Here, too, Lavoisier seemed to associate together these two ideas in his rejection of both of them. The explanation that his view that fermentation decomposes water was dependent on his view that sugar contains water does not fit, however, with the experimental reasoning by which he had previously attempted to support his theory, for it was by establishing a balance between the weight of the sugar consumed and the products of fermentation that he had tried to demonstrate, in his earlier data sheets and in his memoir on fermentation, that one must invoke a loss of some water in order to complete the balance. Had that water come from the sugar itself, it would not have caused such a deficit. To complicate matters further, we recall that at an intermediate phase in his analysis of the situation he included the water in the constitution of the sugar as part of the total water present at the beginning, so that he appeared to make no distinction between the external and the internal water.[17]

Can we find a coherent interpretation of the way in which Lavoisier gave up his theory of fermentation that reconciles these apparent contradictions in his thought? There is, I think, no prospect of isolating a discrete sequence of hypothetico-deductive reasoning ending with a refutation. Rather, he must somehow have clarified a situation that he had not quite thought through in the beginning. His theory that fermentation decomposes water had not, in fact, specified whether the water was internal or external to the sugar, and he may himself have been vague enough on that point so that he sometimes looked at it one way, sometimes the other, and sometimes both ways at once. During the periods in which he thought of sugar as a triple combination, he would have had no choice but to look for the decomposed water outside the weight of the sugar consumed. During the periods in which he thought of sugar as containing water, he was not forced into that position. It may well be, in fact, that his revival of the latter view smoothed his passage across a conceptual divide that appears from its two end points to demand a single mental leap. The calculation in which he aggregated the water of the sugar with the external water might have permitted him to view fermentation as a decomposition internal to the sugar without yet requiring him to give up the view that water is decomposed. Later, when he again left behind him the concept of sugar as carbonized water, he could no longer have it both ways; but if he had already reached the position that the sugar itself is the source of all the elements of the fermentation products, then the remaining mental step involved in abandoning the decomposition of water was a much smaller one. Although we can distinguish logically between rejecting the concept that sugar contains water and rejecting the concept that fermentation decomposes water, Lavoisier may not have separated these steps clearly in his own mind.

This interpretation of Lavoisier's mental passage still does not allow us to ascertain whether he had completed it at the time the calculation described above revealed to him that there was no water deficit after all. All that we can say is that if that result did not induce him to "correct his ideas," as Seguin put it, then it at least harmonized very well with a correction he was already making.

In the *Elementary Treatise* Lavoisier wrote that "the effect of fermentation reduces" to

> separating the sugar, which is an oxide, into two portions; to oxygenating one of them at the expense of the other in order to form carbonic acid from it; to deoxygenating the other in favor of the first, to form of it a combustible substance, which is alcohol: so that, if it were possible to recombine the two substances, alcohol and carbonic acid, we would recompose the sugar.[18]

Out of the demise of his old theory, therefore, Lavoisier had salvaged an interpretation of fermentation that became the germinal conceptual foundation for the modern treatment of the subject. The decomposition of water was no longer relevant.

There is another way to look at the conceptual transformation Lavoisier made. If we restrict our attention to spirituous fermentation alone, his problem appears to have been to establish whether water was or was not decomposed during that particular process. In the beginning, however, he was not looking at fermentation alone. He had identified fermentation in 1784 as one of nature's operations for decomposing water; that is, he grouped it with those processes whose shared feature was the main source of his interest in them. Between 1784 and 1788 he had to learn to see fermentation independently of the class of phenomena in which he had placed it. He had, in other words, to rearrange the boundaries between the categories into which he had divided his conceptual world. The adjustment he made was facilitated by the fact that at about the same time that he was having to give up his theory of fermentation, the new classification of plant substances that he was devising for the *Elementary Treatise* provided an alternative theoretical framework into which he could assimilate fermentation. As a plant oxide, sugar now belonged for him to that class of double bases which contained oxygen that they might give up, but which could also acquire a further quantity of oxygen. In order to explain fermentation he had only to extend this view to visualize both processes taking place at once. He could, therefore, remove fermentation from the class of operations that decompose water without leaving it in limbo as a peculiar process unrelated to others within his chemical system. He transferred it from one order of phenomena that interested him to another order that he was just at that time expanding to encompass the plant kingdom. In the recounting, these conceptual moves appear straightforward and logical; but to make them in the first place required a high level of creative genius.

As the final step in making his fermentation data ready for the *Elementary Treatise,* Lavoisier compiled a new set of tables showing the detailed balances of all of the elements contained in each substance present before and after the operation, and a "recapitulation" in which he grouped the individual quantities by element rather than by substance. These tables have been widely admired (see Figure 15). They appear amply to fulfill Lavoisier's aspiration to display the state of precision his methods had achieved by applying them successfully to one of the most complex phenomena known to chemistry. The paragraphs in which he described how he had reached these results have become even more famous:

> This operation is one of the most striking and extraordinary of all which chemistry presents to us, and we must examine whence come the gaseous carbonic acid that is disengaged, whence the inflammable spirit which is formed, and how a sweet substance, a plant oxide, can be transformed in this way into two such different

substances, of which one is combustible, the other distinctly incombustible. One can see that, in order to reach a solution for these two questions, it is necessary first to know well the analysis and the nature of the substances able to undergo fermentation; for nothing is created, either in the operations of art, or in those of nature, and one can state as a principle that in every operation there is an equal quantity of material before and after the operation; that the quality and the quantity of the [simple] principles are the same, and that there are nothing but changes, modifications.

It is on this principle that the whole art of making experiments in chemistry is founded. One must suppose in every case a true equality or equation between the principles of the bodies one examines, and those which one obtains through the analysis. Thus, since the must of the grape yields gaseous carbonic acid and alcohol, I can say that *must of grape* = *carbonic acid* + *alcohol.*
It follows from that that one can arrive in two ways at a clarification of what happens in vinous fermentation: first, by determining carefully the nature and the principles of the fermentable body; second, by observing carefully the products which result from the

TABLEAU des réſultats obtenus par la fermentation.

liv.	on.	gr.	gr.			liv.	on.	gr.	gr.
35	5	4	19	d'acide carbonique compoſées	d'oxygène..........	25	7	1	34
					de carbone........	9	14	2	57
408	15	5	14	d'eau compoſées	d'oxygène..........	347	10	»	59
					d'hydrogène........	61	5	4	27
57	11	1	58	d'alkool ſec, compoſées	d'oxygène combiné avec l'hydrogène.	31	6	1	64
					d'hydrogène combiné avec l'oxygène.	5	8	5	3
					d'hydrogène combiné avec le carbone.	4	»	5	»
					de carbone........	16	11	5	63
2	8			d'acide acéteux ſec compoſées	d'hydrogène........		2	4	»
					d'oxygène..........	1	11	4	»
					de carbone.........		10	»	»
4	1	4	3	de réſidu ſucré compoſées	d'hydrogène........		5	1	67
					d'oxygène..........	2	9	7	27
					de carbone.........	1	2	2	53
1	6	»	50	de levure ſeche compoſées	d'hydrogène........		2	2	41
					d'oxygène..........		13	1	14
					de carbone.........		6	2	30
					d'azote............			2	37
510	»	»	»			510	»	»	»

Figure 15. Tables containing Lavoisier's balance sheets for fermentation as published in his *Elementary Treatise of Chemistry*. Lavoisier, *Traité élémentaire de chimie* (Paris: Cuchet, 1789), 1: 143–148.

RÉCAPITULATION *des résultats obtenus par la fermentation.*

		liv.	on.	gr.	gr.
liv. on. gr. gr. 409 10 » 54 d'oxygène.	de l'eau	347	10	»	59
	de l'acide carbonique	25	7	1	34
	de l'alkool	31	6	1	64
	de l'acide acéteux	1	11	4	»
	du résidu sucré	2	9	7	27
	de la levure		13	1	14
28 12 5 59 de carbone.	de l'acide carbonique	9	14	2	57
	de l'alkool	16	11	5	63
	de l'acide acéteux		10	»	»
	du résidu sucré	1	2	2	53
	de la levure		6	2	30
71 8 6 66 d'hydrogène.	de l'eau	61	5	4	27
	de l'eau de l'alkool	5	8	5	3
	combiné avec le carbone dans l'alkool	4	»	5	»
	de l'acide acéteux		2	4	»
	du résidu sucré		5	1	67
	de la levure		2	2	41
2 37 d'azote				2	37
510 » » »		510	»	»	»

Matériaux de la fermentation pour un quintal de sucre.

		liv.	onc.	gr.	gr.
Eau		400	»	»	»
Sucre		100	»	»	»
Levure de biere en pâte, composée de	Eau	7	3	6	44
	Levure seche	2	12	1	28
TOTAL		510	»	»	»

Détail des principes constituans des matériaux de la fermentation.

		liv.	onc.	gr.	grains.
liv. onc. gr. grains. 407 3 6 44 d'eau composées de	Hydrogène	61	1	2	71,40
	Oxygène	346	2	3	44,60
100 l. de sucre composées de	Hydrogène	8	»	»	»
	Oxygène	64	»	»	»
	Carbone	28	»	»	»
liv. onc. gr. gr. 2 12 1 28 de levure seche composées de	Carbone	»	12	4	59,00
	Azote	»	»	5	2,94
	Hydrogène	»	4	5	9,30
	Oxygène	1	10	2	28,76
TOTAL		510	»	»	»

Récapitulation des principes constituans des matériaux de la fermentation.

		liv.	on.	gr.	grains.	liv.	onc.	gr.	gr.
Oxygène	de l'eau	340	»	»	»	411	12	6	1,36
	de l'eau de la levure	6	2	3	44,60				
	du sucre	64	»	»	»				
	de la levure	1	10	2	28,76				
Hydrogène	de l'eau	60	»	»	»	69	6	»	8,70
	de l'eau de la levure	1	1	2	71,40				
	du sucre	8	»	»	»				
	de la levure	»	4	5	9,30				
Carbone	du sucre	28	»	»	»	28	12	4	59,00
	de la levure	»	12	4	59,00				
Azote	de la levure					»	»	5	2,94
TOTAL						510	»	»	»

Après

> fermentation, and it is evident that the knowledge which one can acquire about the one will lead to reliable conclusions about the nature of the other, and reciprocally.[19]

Scientists and historians have singled out the last part of the first paragraph above as Lavoisier's only formal statement of what has since been named the principle of the conservation of mass.[20] Some have expressed mild puzzlement that he should have mentioned this fundamental law of nature only "in passing,"[21] in what is usually taken to be one of the more specialized chapters of his treatise. Knowing the earlier development of his interest in fermentation, we can now see why he did so. In his unpublished memoir on fermentation he had treated fermentation as both a difficult and a broad challenge to his methods. As he put it there, for a simple case there is no difficulty following a chain of reasoning in which an equation between the materials and the products of a chemical change is implicit. It is in handling a complicated case that it is most important to keep this principle firmly in mind. In addition to the principle itself, we see reflected here the association Lavoisier had been developing for the previous three years between it and the mathematical meaning of an equation. This succinct statement is, however, only an echo of the way in which he had attempted to apply to chemical problems the logical operations mathematicians performed on algebraic equations. Partington has pointed out that in the second of the above paragraphs Lavoisier called a chemical change publicly for the first time an equation.[22] Perhaps because of the gap between the private development of his views and this single, simplified textbook application, Lavoisier's chemical equation entered the field as not much more than the formalism of placing the substances present before and after a chemical operation respectively to the left and right of an equals sign and separating them by plus signs.

Whether represented as a balance sheet or an equation, Lavoisier's description of alcoholic fermentation signifies a major advance toward rigor in his handling of the processes involving plant or animal matter. We have seen that in the first flush of his recognition of the simple principles composing all of these substances he had speculated freely on the additions, subtractions, and recombinations of carbon, hydrogen, and oxygen which could explain the decompositions and other transformations of plant matter, a practice he reiterated in his more general discussions in the *Elementary Treatise*. Only in his study of fermentation did he reach beyond such qualitative, verbal description to give the first fully quantitative portrayal of a well-defined process within the domain of plant chemistry. It was a prototype for innumerable later accounts of other organic reactions by his successors.

The admiration which Lavoisier's fermentation equation has attracted from later generations of historians has been mingled with a readily understandable, wondering skepticism. Arthur Harden, a pioneer in a later stage of the investigation of alcoholic fermentation, wrote in 1911, "The research must be regarded as one of those remarkable instances in which the genius of the investigator triumphs over experimental deficiencies." The numbers contain serious errors, and "it was only by a fortunate compensation of these that a result as near the truth was attained."[23] Guerlac adds, "His data . . . were wholly unreliable, although the end result was correct."[24] Partington is even blunter: "All the quantitative data of this 'travail trés-penible' are erroneous, but the general conclusion is correct."[25] Fruton provides concrete specification for the same general view. "This agreement is all the more remarkable since all the analytical data must have been in error; the actual elemental compositions of sucrose and alcohol are very different from those given by Lavoisier. The alcohol was probably heavily contaminated with water, and he probably lost some of the carbon dioxide."[26]

Historical evaluation of Lavoisier's fermentation equation has not been facilitated by the vagueness of his own description of the analytical bases for the results he presented. Although he stated that his composition for sugar was derived from "a long series of experiments carried out in different ways and repeated many times," he gave no information about the nature of these analyses. The tables showing the balance between the starting materials and the products were, he said, "the results of my experiments just as I obtained them."[27] If this phrase seemed to imply that his results rested on multiple experiments, the tables have, for reasons that should now be obvious, the appearance of data derived from a single set of measurements.

The pathway of Lavoisier's investigation of fermentation that we have been able to follow removes some of the mystery about how he could have reached "correct" conclusions through "erroneous" results. As we shall see in a moment, however, it also introduces a paradox that has not generally been noticed. We may notice first that, although his tables show an exact overall balance of materials, none of the balances of the individual elements, except for carbon, is exact. This is what we would expect from the way in which he constructed them. The overall balance could not be otherwise, for Lavoisier calculated the quantity to be attributed to the escaping gases, a component of the total quantity after the operation, from the difference between the other quantities after the operation and the total quantity before the operation. For the experiment on which he based his calculations, he had no independent measurement of this component. Similarly, the carbon balance had to be exact, because he calculated the quantity of carbon in the carbonic acid from the difference between the carbon in the starting materials and that in the other products. The balances of oxygen and of hydrogen, which did depend upon the accuracy, or at least on the mutual consistency, of his independent analyses of the substances containing them, were not exact. They were, however, remarkably close (oxygen, 411 pounds before and 409 pounds afterward; hydrogen, 69 pounds before and 71 pounds afterward).

These near agreements are all the more surprising because Lavoisier's impressive-looking tables conceal a major incongruity. He retained even in the final version the proportions for sugar (carbon 28:hydrogen 8:oxygen 64) that he had extracted from the combined results of the carbonization and mercury oxide experiments of the previous April. Not only were the experimental foundations for that result somewhat questionable; but, as we saw, he derived this composition from them during the two months in which he considered the proportions of oxygen and carbon in carbonic acid to be 60:40. When he worked out the first half of his balance sheet, on July 1, he was still accepting these values, and he incorporated into it the same composition for sugar.[28] When he completed the second half of the balance sheet sometime later, however, he had returned to the proportions of 72:28 for carbonic acid, and he based the composition for spirit of wine that he included in that half, as well as for the carbonic acid itself, on that ratio. Thus he had put together in his equation for the operation compositions of substances on the two sides dependent on divergent values for a numerical factor critical to the calculation of these compositions.

It appears at first sight so improbable that Lavoisier would have overlooked such a discrepancy that one may perhaps doubt whether my interpretation of the course of events through which he reached those results is correct. I have found no alternative interpretation derivable from the surviving records which can obviate the above conclusion. It is always possible, of course, that he derived the same composition for sugar in another way which has left no trace in the available documents. Aside from such an unverifiable possibility, the most plausible explanation I can see for Lavoisier's apparent oversight is that his analysis of the situation was spread over so long a period of time that when he completed it he had forgotten how he originally calculated the composition for sugar. Had he corrected his result by recalculating the composition using the 72:28 ratio for carbonic acid, without making any other changes in the fermentation tables, the balances would have been less close. For oxygen the result might still have appeared reasonable (the change would have raised the total oxygen before the operation to 417 pounds, compared with 409 afterward); but for hydrogen the divergence would probably have appeared to him proportionally more serious (about 63 pounds before, compared with about 72 pounds afterward). The fact that even with the inconsistency he had grafted into his tables he was able to reach such near balances between each of the constituent elements involved in the chemical operation implies either that he was very lucky, or that he had become so skilled at shifting his assumptions to reach a desired outcome that no matter how his analyses had come out he would have been able to achieve the appearance of a well-balanced equation.

I have not been able to formulate a detailed explanation for Lavoisier's result which entirely eliminates chance good fortune from the outcome. Perhaps another historian with more mathematical experience can recover some secret in the surviving data sheets that has escaped me. In the meantime, however, it is possible, from his own characterization of how he proceeded, to suggest in a general way how he managed to shape so coherent an overall picture out of somewhat ill fitting pieces.

> I can regard the matter submitted to fermentation, and the result obtained after the fermentation, as an algebraic equation; and by considering each one of the elements of this equation successively as the unknown, I can deduce a value, and thereby correct the experiment through the calculation, and the calculation through the experiment. I have often profited by this method in order to correct the first results of my experiments, and to guide me in the precautions to take in order to repeat them.[29]

This general statement about his scientific method has received less attention than those ringing phrases of the "Preliminary Discourse" of the *Elementary Treatise* in which Lavoisier talked of submitting one's reasoning to the continual test of experiment; of conserving only the facts; and of reducing one's reasoning to such simple judgments that one never loses sight of the evidence which serves as their guide.[30] Compared with those well-known passages, which convey the aura of certainty to be expected of sound scientific method, the above passage suggests improvisation, tentative conclusions, doing the best one can under imperfect conditions. As our whole account of Lavoisier's investigative trail implies, however, it is this passage, rather than the ideologically oriented preface, which accords most realistically with his own practices.

We can see also that this methodological statement signifies a refinement of the approach Lavoisier had presented a year earlier in his memoir on fermentation. There he had worked out what he regarded as calculated values for each substance from the other experimental values; but he had simply juxtaposed them, leaving it to his audience to judge the closeness of fit between calculated and experimental values.[31] Although he withdrew the tables displaying this comparison ostensibly because they would not be understood, he may also have sensed a certain naiveté in this approach. Now, somewhat less candidly, but with more sophistication, he had, to judge from his own testimony, "corrected" the calculated and experimental values by one another. Differences such as he had once planned to display openly, he apparently suppressed by making his new tables reflect only the outcome of the adjustments he had had to make in order to merge the equivalents of those two columns he had once labeled "calculated" and "experimental."

If we cannot trace in full detail all of the maneuvers Lavoisier may have made to attain the impressive internal consistency of the balances in his final fermentation tables, we can at least outline how his approach may have influenced his crucial choice of the composition to accept for sugar. His statement that that result derived from "a long series of experiments carried out in different ways and repeated many times"[32] is outwardly misleading, in that few readers would suspect from it that all of these experiments were, in one way or another, unsuccessful. In conjunction with his more general statement about his method, however, this assertion may be quite suggestive; for it was the very absence of any single firm result that would have forced him to interpret whatever data he could glean from any of these experiments with an eye on their relation to whatever information any of the rest of them could supply. As we have seen, the manner in which Lavoisier derived the composition from the carbonization and mercury oxide experiments was so indirect that considerable latitude existed for shaping the outcome through the intermediate assumptions he had to make. At the time he carried out the calculations involved, the alternative result for sugar on which he probably placed the most confidence was that calculated from the fermentation balance itself.[33] The composition at which he arrived by combining the two other experiments was not identical to that one, but close enough so that it is reasonable to suppose that Lavoisier was guided during his calculations by the expectation that the result should be reasonably consistent with the result of the fermentation analysis. If so, then when he inserted the new result into the balances based on that same fermentation experiment, it would be assured in advance, regardless of the incongruity in his assumptions described above, that the balances, even for those two elements that relied on the compositions of each of the substances containing them, could not come out very far off. Undoubtedly he made further adjustments, possibly in the quantities of the minor products, that I have not identified. In any case, we have seen enough of his resourcefulness in similar situations so that we would expect him to be well prepared for this climactic test of his capacity to master uncertain experimental data.

If my interpretation of the means through which Lavoisier established his fermentation tables is valid, then the question naturally arises whether he represented the status of his results accurately in his *Elementary Treatise*. Unquestionably he created the impression that it rested on more extensive data than he had actually been able to gather. In addition to the optimistic description of the state of his analyses of sugar, he implied, without actually saying so, that his new specially designed apparatus, described in the second volume of the *Treatise*, was the same one that he had used for the fermentation experiments on which he based his tables.[34] Readers would therefore naturally assume that he had collected the carbonic acid in caustic potash rather than calculating it indirectly, as we have seen he did. In other words, in his typical fashion, he presented his investigation in the most favorable light he could, somewhat stretching the reality of the situation. I do not think, however, that he made fundamentally false claims for his results. As in other cases, he explicitly disavowed that the numbers which bore the appearance of minute precision actually represented such experimental accuracy:

> Although in these results I have carried the precision of the calculations down to grains, this type of experiment is still very far from being able to permit such great exactness; but since I operated on only a few pounds of sugar, and in order to establish comparisons I had to convert these to [a base of] one hundred pounds, I believed that I ought to allow the fractions to remain just as I calculated them.[35]

We can tell from his own data sheets, or by repeating his calculations, that that is just what he did. Perhaps he was misguided in doing so, but he was not attempting to mislead others.

The historical judgment that Lavoisier reached correct conclusions through erroneous results arises in part from misunderstandings about what conclusions he reached through the quantitative data he assembled. In the first place, he did not intend his balance sheets to represent a *verification* of the principle that the material present before the operation is equal to the material afterward. It is essential to the nature of a principle upon which the experiments themselves "are founded" that it stands of itself, prior to empirical proof. The language in which Lavoisier stated that principle in the chapter on fermentation thus conforms to the view, argued convincingly by Emile Meyerson fifty years ago, that he regarded it as an axiom, so basic and unquestionable that he was justified in utilizing it to correct analytical results that did not at first appear to conform completely to it.[36] His attitude in the application of the principle to fermentation was thus consistent with his approach throughout his investigative career. He preferred, when it was possible, to confirm experimentally that the materials and products of a chemical change did actually equal one another; but when that demonstration was not yet technically practical, he relied with complete confidence on the "axiom" to supply the missing information.

Just as Lavoisier did not rely on his balance sheets to prove that there was a quantitative equality of materials and products, neither did he derive from those quantitative results the qualitative nature of the equation. Spirituous fermentation was a familiar process when Lavoisier took it up. That its principal products were alcohol and carbonic acid (or rather spirit of wine and fixed air) was obvious from the start. Lavoisier recognized in his discussion that his verbal equation for fermentation was only a way to express the known process in accordance with the balance principle. "Thus," he wrote, "since the must of the grape yields gaseous carbonic acid and alcohol, I can say that *must of grape = carbonic acid + alcohol.*" For his measurements of the materials and products he claimed only that they "clarified" what takes place in this process.[37] The main contribution Lavoisier made to the equation itself was as much qualitative as quantitative. It was by choosing to experiment on the simplest fermentable material, in relatively pure form, that he was able to focus on the decomposition of a substance of known composition to form two other substances of known composition, and consequently to interpret a hitherto mysterious process in terms of the lucid principles of his new chemical system. Ultimately he did not employ his balance sheets to establish the nature of the fermentation equation, but used the fermentation equation to establish the balance sheets.

After stripping from Lavoisier's fermentation tables the achievements for which they were not responsible, we may be left wondering whether they were actually worth the tedious effort Lavoisier put into them, and the historical attention they have received. Emphatically they were—not because of what they directly proved, but because they opened up a powerful new way to *understand* this chemical process. As such, these tables provided the model not only for future investigations of fermentation, but for the formation of an entire new field of chemistry.

III

Before departing from those chapters of his *Treatise* in which Lavoisier organized as best he could the state of his knowledge of plant and animal chemistry, we should note that within the several chapters into which he divided his discussion, he harbored three different conceptions of the composition of plant substances. In the context of the decomposition of plant and animal matters by fire, he maintained the view that "neither oil, water, nor carbonic acid" exists in plant matters. They contain only the elements from which these substances can arise, in a state of "equilibrium."[38] When he listed the composition of alcohol, however, his older idea that this substance contained preformed water survived in defiance of his own generalization.[39] Moreover, when he classified plant substances as oxides and acids, he depicted them as double bases of carbon and hydrogen, or *radicals,* capable of various degrees of oxygenation. It is not clear whether or not he noticed the coexistence of these mutually incompatible ideas in his thought, but their presence there is readily understandable. Each originated in a particular problem, the circumstances of a particular investigation, or the effort to assimilate plant substances to the categories of a chemical system established first within the simpler chemistry of the mineral kingdom. That he did not choose between them is also understandable; for at this germinal stage these were simply different ways of visualizing a problem that lay still on the farthest horizon of the field he was making visible. With his usual acuity Lavoisier could foresee that the "order in which the principles are combined" was the central problem for future investigation, but he was not in a position to do more than outline options whose implications were left for his successors to explore.

IV

Lavoisier's description of his manner of work, in the paragraph about his use of algebraic equations in chemistry, may appear to be only partly true; while he did correct experiment by calculation and calculation by experiment, he omitted all too often to use the outcome of such procedures "to guide me in the precautions to take in order to repeat them." Certainly he was willing to publish his findings before he had been able to surmount all of the deficiencies he had discovered in his "first experiments," placing a heavy burden on the power of his calculated corrections. On the other hand, having published, he often returned afterward to try to improve on the experiments in question. These characteristics of his research style were especially prominent in his treatment of plant and animal chemistry in the *Elementary Treatise*. His deadline for writing these chapters must have come upon him while his research on the topics involved was bogged down among some of the most recalcitrant experimental obstacles he had ever confronted. Time and again he had tried new ways to analyze sugar, without turning up a notably effective method. In spite of extensive efforts, he had found no promising means to determine the proportions of the principles composing animal matter. His new fermentation apparatus had yet to yield a complete experiment to replace the data resulting from a single, less sophisticated older operation. He must have faced the decision of whether to omit these subjects from what he planned as his definitive survey of the new chemical system, or to go ahead with whatever results he had so far managed to procure. It was in keeping with his temperament, I believe, to go ahead; and with the astuteness of his judgment that he went ahead in such a manner that even with his improvised results and preliminary conclusions he was able to shape the future development of these fields.

Although he did not reveal the extent of his current experimental difficulties, Lavoisier did make it clear in his discussion of plant and animal chemistry that he considered himself to be at an early stage of ongoing research. He interjected in his discussion of plant and animal oxides and acids,

> I shall not dwell much on this matter, about which I have only recently formed clear and methodical ideas. I shall treat it more deeply in the memoirs which I am preparing for the Academy. The greater part of my experiments are complete, but it is necessary that I repeat and multiply them further, in order to be able to give more exact results for the quantities.[40]

Concerning his hypothetical classification of plant acids, he conceded that it was best provisionally to retain the old names, because "we are still far from being in a position to make a methodical classification." "I would reproach myself," he added, "for drawing conclusions too definitive from experiments which are not yet precise enough; but in conceding that this part of chemistry remains inadequate, I can add the hope that it will soon be clarified." The situation was even less advanced for animal matters. He could give only a "rapid glance" at them, he acknowledged, because their composition "is not yet known very exactly."[41]

Lavoisier conveyed the impression that he was hard at work to overcome these limitations. With regard to the plant oils, he wrote, "I am, moreover, occupied at this moment with experiments which will give a great development to this entire theory." He claimed to have a memoir giving more details about fermentation already in press, and promised further memoirs on the other subjects he discussed.[42] There is every indication that he was, indeed, planning to intensify his research efforts, for he was investing more heavily than ever in specially designed apparatus intended to cope with the difficult technical problems he had encountered in plant chemistry. An elaborate apparatus for the combustion of oils that he received near the end of 1788 reveals clearly how he hoped to overcome the limitations of his earlier experiments (see Figure 16). Probably adapted from the one Meusnier had designed for him to burn large quantities of spirit of wine or oil, the new one was connected to two long horizontal tubes to absorb the water in deliquescent salts, and in turn to a series of ten bottles for collecting in caustic alkali the large quantities of carbonic acid he expected. In this way he would be able to combine the advantages of the two types of experiment he had formerly been constrained to carry out separately. He would operate on a large scale and still be able to obtain all of the gaseous products, optimal conditions for determining the quantitative composition with greater precision. A new fermentation apparatus arrived in June 1789 (see Figure 17). From the modifications that it embodied we can readily see how Lavoisier planned to improve on his previous experiments on that problem (cf. Figure 18). He dispensed with the intermediate bottles for collecting the yeast froth that had spilled over in earlier experiments, evidently hoping instead to obviate that problem by inclining the fermentation flask, so that the froth would run down along one side of the neck instead of being carried over

Figure 16. Surviving apparatus intended by Lavoisier for large-scale combustion experiments on oil. The large copper cylinder on the table at near right probably contains a coiled tube in which vapors of combustion were to be condensed by the surrounding water. The horizontal tubes connected in series in the middle were to be filled with deliquescent salt for trapping condensed water vapor. The spherical bottles are caustic alkali bottles, connected in series, to collect fixed air. Apparatus on display in the Musée des Techniques of the Conservatoire des Arts et Métiers, Paris. Photograph by the author.

by the bubbling gases. In this way he also simplified the apparatus, eliminating a number of potential sources for leaks. He added a second horizontal tube to ensure that he could absorb all of the water vapor carried off in the carbonic acid, and provided for four caustic alkali bottles to make certain that none of the carbonic acid itself would be lost. Even more elegantly functional in appearance than the old, the new fermentation apparatus bore clear witness that Lavoisier had committed himself to do everything within his power to pursue his experiments until he could truly confirm his fermentation equation with a complete balance between experimentally measured materials and products of the operation. Seldom do the physical objects of scientific research reveal so transparently as do these products of Lavoisier's inventive genius and Fortin's expert craftmanship, the research strategies and goals they were designed to serve.[43]

Beginning in 1789 the rapidly spreading political changes commanded more

Figure 17. Surviving fermentation apparatus. This is a later modification of the apparatus described in the *Elementary Treatise*. The distillation flask, shown on the left, is inclined. Bottles for collecting foam are eliminated. Two horizontal tubes for collecting water, supported on a high wooden pedestal, are connected in series. On the right, four caustic alkali bottles in series end in an open tube intended to be connected to a pneumatic vessel. On display in the Musée des Techniques of the Conservatoire des Arts et Métiers, Paris. Photograph by the author.

and more of the time Lavoisier had hitherto been able to reserve for his laboratory. No laboratory notebooks have survived for the period after 1788, and no evidence exists that he was ever able to use the new apparatus he had acquired to pursue his objectives in plant chemistry. It is quite possible that he never carried out another fermentation operation, and never performed another analysis of plant or animal matter. What he had written in the *Elementary Treatise* as a preliminary summary of his first "methodical" ideas on these subjects became instead his final statement of them.

In 1792, when he was no longer in a position to pursue any of his scientific investigations, Lavoisier looked back at the accomplishments for which he hoped he would be recognized. He claimed "all of the theory of oxidation and combustion," and several other areas without qualification, but only "the first ideas concerning the composition of plant and animal substances."[44] He had had time

Figure 18. Surviving fermentation apparatus. The apparatus is identical to that described in the *Elementary Treatise*, but is viewed from the other side, with the fermentation flask shown on the right, the caustic alkali bottles on the far left. The pneumatic vessel is missing. The photograph shows well the brass valves and thumbscrew joints enabling Lavoisier rapidly to close off and disconnect the separate pieces. On display in the Musée des Techniques of the Conservatoire des Arts et Métiers, Paris. Photograph by the author.

only to make a start in this field, but it was one of the most auspicious starts in the history of science.

*   *   *

If we now stand back from our examination of the fine structure of Lavoisier's investigations in plant and animal chemistry in order to view their place within these fields in his own time, one of the most salient features we can observe is how limited the contact was between his research and the mainstream of prior or contemporary developments. For plant and animal chemistry this was a flourishing period, and French chemists took a prominent part. Particularly fruitful was the new "order of analysis" of plant substances taught by Guillaume Rouelle, which was based on the use of solvents to isolate individual substances from gross plant matter.[45] The earlier separation of wheat flour into gluten and starch by Iacopo Bartolomeo Beccari became the point of departure for the discovery of both types of substance in other plant materials.[46] Combining Beccari's discovery with his brother's solvent extraction methods, Hilaire Marin Rouelle characterized the green matter in plants, "vegetoanimal" matter, and other substances during the 1770s.[47] In 1773 Bucquet published the first textbook of plant chemistry to be oriented around the solvent methods.[48] Berthollet and Fourcroy worked to differentiate the various substances grouped under the general heading of "animal matter," and by 1785 Fourcroy had distinguished fibrin, albumin, casein, and gelatin.[49] In 1767 Louis-Claude Cadet had published what later appeared as a model analysis of bile, using the increasingly powerful repertoire of analytical methods based on the chemistry of acids and bases.[50] As we have already seen, Scheele opened up a whole new domain in plant chemistry with his discoveries of the plant acids.

Lavoisier had been personally associated in one way or another with several of the leading figures in these developments. The elder Rouelle was his first chemistry teacher, Bucquet his early collaborator, Fourcroy and Berthollet his later associates. Yet he himself did not participate broadly in any of these areas of investigation. They interested him only to the extent that they intersected his own research path. He took up the study of a plant acid in 1777 because its composition supported his theory of acidity. He became involved more extensively in the analysis of plant substances around 1785 not because this was a problem which had concerned other chemists for more than a century, but because the combustion of inflammable plant matters aided him in his investigations of the composition of water and fixed air. Even after he had committed himself to the analysis of plant and animal matter as his central field of research, he did not systematically absorb the latest developments in this active area, but used only those aspects which fit into the concerns growing out of his own previous work. The new array of plant acids attracted him because they fit so well into his theoretical framework; nevertheless, he made only a few fitful attempts to analyze any of them besides oxalic acid.[51] He was, of course, dependent in various ways upon the state of knowledge of plant and animal chemistry in his time. His choice of sugar as the substance on which to concentrate his analytical effort undoubtedly reflected indirectly the fact that sugar was just becoming widely recognized as a "universal" constituent of plants.[52] Berthollet's conclusion that animal matters contain azote became very important to Lavoisier, because it complemented his own description of the simple principles underlying plant and animal matter. His use of the newer knowledge of plant and animal chemistry was, however, narrowly selective. It is symptomatic of his restricted involvement in these contemporary events that when he began to analyze animal matter himself, he did not take up any of the newly characterized animal matters—fibrin, albumin, casein, or gelatin—which represented the forefront of current research. He used pieces of horn, one of the oldest known typical animal materials.

Perhaps Lavoisier did not enter more fully into the range of questions occupying others in plant and animal chemistry because he was not as experienced as the best of his contemporaries were in the sophisticated repertoire of qualitative analytical techniques these investigations required. He had specialized in quantitative methods, and chemistry was already too complex for an individual to be equally well versed in all phases of it. Perhaps his own agenda was simply too crowded to allow him to pursue all available avenues. In spite of the narrow focus of his entry into plant and animal chemistry, he was able, within the four years he devoted to it, entirely to change its shape. His success supports the view that crossing fields in science can often bring valuable innovations. The outsider to a given domain brings new ideas, transposes methods and concepts, in such a way that he is able to mount a fresh attack on problems which those inured to the customary approaches in that field have not had the imagination to solve. That characterization of the situation in plant and animal chemistry when Lavoisier took it up is, however, correct only up to a point; for the mainstream in which Lavoisier did not fully immerse himself included equally innovative and equally formative investigations. While Lavoisier contributed the key to future analyses of the elementary composition of organic compounds, his contemporaries contributed the foundations for the isolation and identification of those compounds upon which the elementary analyses could then be performed. The organic chemistry which matured during the next half century rested as heavily on the one as on the other.[53]

Part 4

The Animal Economy 1790–1792

While Lavoisier was preoccupied with plant chemistry, others were reacting to his theory of respiration. Crawford carried out comparative measurements of the heats of respiration and combustion similar to those of Lavoisier and Laplace, but introducing the method of water calorimetry. Priestley attempted to reconcile his phlogiston theory of respiration with later experimental findings. Followers of Lavoisier elaborated on the hypothetical mechanisms of respiration, medical implications, and the question of where the respiratory combustion occurs.

In 1790 Lavoisier again took up the experimental investigation of respiration. With the assistance of Armand Seguin he carried out extensive measurements of animal and human respiration under varied physical and physiological conditions. From this work he gained a more comprehensive conception of the physiological significance of respiration, connecting it with the other processes which maintain the overall balance of matter and of heat in the animal body. With Seguin he began an ambitious new research program to study all of these aspects of the animal economy. He began with digestion and with transpiration. Outside pressures again closed in on him, however, so that as his experimental goals grew larger, his opportunities to attain them became narrower.

15

Responses to Lavoisier's Theory of Respiration

When he had presented his paper on the alterations of the air due to respiration to the Royal Society of Medicine in 1785, Lavoisier had announced that he intended to "render successive accounts" of his further work on the subject. Over the next four years, however, he did not discuss respiration in any of his published memoirs, or in his *Elementary Treatise*. During all that time he made, according to his laboratory notebook, only one brief experimental effort to further his knowledge of the process. On April 12, 1786, he wrote down, "I tried to respire a volume of air equal to thirty pounds of water. It did not appear to me that there was a noticeable diminution of volume, but it was not possible for me to breathe this air for more than five minutes." Since the apparent diminution of the volume of the air in his earlier experiments on animals had posed both an anomaly for him and one of the clues that led him to revise his theory, it is easy to see why he wished to check further on the reality of the phenomenon. All that he got for his trouble in this test, however, was a headache. There is no indication that he followed up this or any other aspect of respiration for three more years. We can only guess whether he became too preoccupied with the analysis of plant and animal matter and fermentation to divert his limited laboratory time to respiration; or was unable to see what step he ought to take next in the development of his respiration theory; or came to be satisfied for a time with the theory as it stood in 1785. There is no reason to assume, however, that he ever abandoned his intention eventually to pursue the investigation further, for it was typical of his research style to shift tacks abruptly without losing sight of his steady overall course. In the *Elementary Treatise* he remarked, in an inconspicuous place, that he had "by design" avoided talking about "organized bodies," and that this policy had "prevented me from talking about the phenomena of respiration, of sanguification, and of animal heat. I shall return one day to these subjects."[1] The statement implied that he not only had kept in mind all along that he would take up again the problems with which he had previously been involved, but would expand his interest to related physiological problems. The phrase "one day" also suggests, however, that he did not yet have any immediate plans for getting started on such a research program.

While Lavoisier had nothing further to say about respiration his theory was attracting lively attention from others. Among his followers it was, as we would expect, readily accepted. Antoine Fourcroy, eager to apply the new developments in chemistry to physiology and medicine, had begun in 1781 to examine the medical effects of breathing vital air. Some physicians had argued, according to Fourcroy, that since vital air is the only respirable component of the atmosphere, consumptive patients, whose lungs were impaired, might be able to respire more easily in pure vital air than in ordinary air. Fourcroy found a transient improvement when such persons breathed vital air, but over a longer period their symptoms were aggravated. In order to explain these effects, and to learn how the action of vital air could be applied usefully in diseases, Fourcroy experimented with animals. "By causing animals to breathe atmospheric air and vital air comparatively," he claimed in 1789, he had "confirmed the doctrine of Lavoisier on respiration, and drew, with that scientist, several general corollaries concerning the use of the air in respiration, as well as in relation to the action of vital air in various diseases." He did not specify how his experiments "confirmed" Lavoisier's theory; it appears rather that he took the theory for granted and used it to interpret his observations. Two of his "corollaries" were merely restatements of Lavoisier's basic conclusion that vital air is converted to carbonic acid in the lungs, removing carbon from the blood and releasing heat which is distributed to all the organs. Fourcroy contributed only general supporting arguments such as that oviparous quadrupeds and snakes, which respire very little, also "have their blood at the same temperature as the environments they inhabit."[2]

Fourcroy stated as a third corollary a view which Lavoisier had assumed in a weak form during his investigation of respiration, but had never raised to a general principle. "Vital air being the portion of the air which alone serves for respiration, from which the animal heat derives, when one causes an animal to inspire it in a pure form, without the admixture of azotic gas with which it is united in the atmosphere, the animal should give rise to four times as much heat as is produced from atmospheric air." Pierre-Joseph Macquer had, according to Fourcroy, "presented the idea, as ingenious as it is true, that vital air should accelerate the vital movements and consume the reserves of vitality as strongly and promptly as it burns combustible bodies." Fourcroy had, he asserted, verified this prediction by experiment. "When one plunges an animal into a jar full of vital air, its respiration accelerates, its chest expansions increase considerably, its heart and arteries contract more forcefully and rapidly than in the natural state; it is soon in a febrile state; its eyes become red and protruding, perspiration flows from every part of its body, the temperature of all regions rises remarkably; finally, it is soon attacked by an extremely acute inflammatory fever which terminates in gangrene and a sideration whose principal source is the lungs." When Lavoisier and Bucquet had placed animals in pure vital air, the animals had died with signs of inflammation, from which Lavoisier had inferred that pure vital air is toxic. If these were the observations Fourcroy had in mind, however, he was interpreting them far more vividly than Lavoisier had done. Even if Fourcroy's description had been objective, moreover, such an experiment could have various interpretations; but he took it as direct verification that pure vital air accelerates respiration and all of the vital processes associated with it. On this dubious foundation he erected an edifice of explanations of the supposed deleterious effects of vital air on febrile diseases. Although contraindicated in such situations, he reasoned that vital air could be advantageous for treating various conditions in which pallor or other symptoms indicated that the respiration was too inactive. He went on to explain the good or bad effects of special environments on these states as due to local excesses or deficiencies of vital air in the atmosphere.[3]

Fourcroy's speculations fit into a typical eighteenth-century pattern of spinning broad systems of disease and treatment out of thin strands of empirical observation. The fact that enthusiastic followers of Lavoisier's "doctrine" also fell into such excesses serves to place in sharper perspective the disciplined restraint Lavoisier himself usually displayed when he confined his physiological and medical inferences to relatively brief suggestions clearly differentiated from what he treated as proven.

Not all French scientists accepted Lavoisier's "doctrine" with as little reservation as Fourcroy did. It was probably sometime during the years of Lavoisier's silence on the subject that the great mathematician Joseph Louis de Lagrange made his famous, though unpublished, objection to the view that the respiratory process Lavoisier and Laplace had described could take place in the lungs. Lavoisier's younger associate Jean-Henri Hassenfratz wrote in 1791 the only known summary of Lagrange's opinion:

> M. de Lagrange reflected that if all of the heat which is distributed through the animal economy were disengaged in the lungs, the temperature of the lungs would necessarily be raised so much that one would continually have to fear for their destruction; and the temperature of the lungs being so much different from that of the other parts of the animal, it would be impossible that no one had ever yet observed the difference. He believed that from that consideration he could conclude that all of the heat of the animal is disengaged not in the lungs alone, but rather in all of the parts where the blood circulates.
>
> He supposed, therefore, that in passing through the lungs the blood would dissolve the oxygen of the respired air, that this dis-

> solved oxygen would be carried by the blood into the arteries and from there into the veins; that during the course of the blood the oxygen would gradually leave its state of solution in order to combine in part with the carbon, in part with the hydrogen of the blood, and to form the water and the carbonic acid which is disengaged from the blood as soon as the venous blood departs from the heart to enter the lungs.[4]

Historians have sometimes assumed that Lagrange first expressed this view contemporaneously with Hassenfratz's article of 1791 supporting it.[5] Hassenfratz's account makes it evident, however, that Lagrange had voiced his opinion long before then, and that in the meantime the co-author of Lavoisier's theory, Laplace, had attempted to obviate the difficulty without giving up the view that the actual combustion occurs in the lungs:

> M. de Laplace, who had perfectly understood M. de Lagrange's objection, had sought long since [*depuis long-tems*] to resolve it by supposing that the oxygen, in combining with the blood, allows only a portion of its heat to be disengaged, and that the rest of the heat remains combined in the state of latent heat, and becomes sensible heat, that is, is disengaged, only during the circulation of the blood.[6]

Laplace's attempt to explain away the problem was not perceived as satisfactory, probably because, as Hassenfratz noted, "it was not supported by any facts, and appears to have only the remote analogy of the absorption of caloric by bodies which pass from the state of a solid to that of a liquid, and from that of a liquid to the elastic state."[7] Lagrange's opinion therefore remained as a strong challenge to the simple assumption Lavoisier had maintained ever since he first formulated his theory of respiration: that the combustion occurs at the point where the combustible substance and the oxygen are most likely to come together.[8]

Outside France, Lavoisier's theory of respiration was taken up even in some circles where his theory of combustion was still resisted. Adair Crawford, who was continuing his studies of the cause of animal heat, remained allied with Kirwan and Priestley in defense of a modified phlogiston theory.[9] Nevertheless, Crawford managed to incorporate Lavoisier and Laplace's strategy for demonstrating the equivalence of respiration and combustion into his ongoing investigation, and even to associate his own theory of animal heat with Lavoisier's conception of the respiratory process.

In the first statement of his theory in 1779, Crawford had depended entirely upon his measurements of the specific heats (he called them comparative heats) of arterial and venous blood, and of dephlogisticated, phlogisticated, and fixed air, in order to establish that in "the change which it undergoes in the lungs," "pure air" gives up some of its "absolute heat," and that the increased heat capacity of arterial blood compared with that of venous blood enables the former to absorb this heat, without giving it off as "sensible heat" until its passage through the circulation. Afterward he found that his measurements of these specific heats, especially those of the airs, contained major sources of error. Much of his subsequent research consisted of devising meticulous methods for making these measurements with "scrupulous attention to accuracy." By 1788, when he published an enlarged second edition of his *Experiments and Observations on Animal Heat,* he had learned that the differences in the heat capacities of the airs were less than he had formerly maintained, but were still sufficient to support his original theory.[10]

To this more rigorous repetition of his own investigation Crawford added a series of experiments based on the approach Lavoisier and Laplace had presented in their memoir on heat; that is, he compared the quantities of heat evolved by an inflammable body with that evolved by a guinea pig. Like them, he utilized two sets of experiments, in one of which he measured the heat production with a calorimeter, and in the other of which he measured the effects of the respective processes on the surrounding air. In each set, however, Crawford adopted procedures significantly different from those of Lavoisier and Laplace.

For the heat measurements Crawford avoided the ice calorimeter, because in 1781 he had found very suggestive evidence that animals respire more rapidly in a cold medium than in a warm one. When he had immersed a dog in warm water for fifteen minutes and afterward drew blood from its jugular vein, he observed that the blood was nearly arterial in color. Venous blood taken from a dog placed in cold water was, in contrast, "the darkest venous blood we had ever seen." Crawford supported his inference that this color difference was an indication that animals phlogisticate more respirable air in a cold than in a warm medium by showing that a guinea pig put in a jar of common air for a given length of time leaves that air "more phlogisticated," by the measure of Priestley's nitrous air test, when the air is cold than when it is warm. With this conclusion in mind, Crawford designed a water calorimeter, so that the animal might respire in it at the same temperature at which the respiratory exchange was to be measured. The calorimeter consisted, like that of Lavoisier and Laplace, of three concentric cylindrical chambers, the innermost one being where the combustion or respiration went on. The middle chamber was filled with water rather than ice, and Crawford protected the calorimeter from an exchange of heat with the exterior by packing the outer chamber with down rather than the ice of the Lavoisier-Laplace calorimeter. He measured the heat released in terms of the rise in the temperature of the water in the middle chamber. "The water, in the course of the experiment, was, at short intervals, gently agitated by a wooden rod for the purpose of rendering the diffusion of the heat uniform; and the temperature of the air in the room was augmented nearly in the same degree with that of the water."[11]

Burning a small wax taper in the calorimeter, Crawford found that "the temperature of the 31 pounds seven ounces of water was raised 2.1 degrees" Fahrenheit, and "the loss of weight in the wax taper was 26 grains." (These were English troy weights). A guinea pig left for two hours in the calorimeter raised the water temperature one degree. A piece of charcoal burned in it raised the temperature 3.1 degrees, while losing 56 grains in weight.[12]

Crawford's method for measuring the changes produced in the air by these combustions and by respiration was similar in principle to Lavoisier's method, but differed in execution. He too placed the combustible materials and the animal in inverted jars and determined the quantity of "pure air" consumed by the decrease in volume after he had absorbed the fixed air formed. Instead of introducing caustic alkali into the jar itself, he transferred the air remaining afterward into limewater bottles, then passed the residual air back into the original jars to measure the remaining volume. In the case of the guinea pig he utilized an apparatus in which he could displace the air through a "crooked tube" directly into a second inverted jar for this purpose, then return it through the same tube (see Figure 19). He carried out these operations over water rather than mercury, thereby incurring the risk that some of the fixed air would be dissolved in the water. In fact, he did not in this set of experiments measure the fixed air formed, but used the limewater only to remove it, in order to determine, by the decrease in volume, "the quantity of air changed" by the process. Thus, where Lavoisier and Laplace had invoked the quantity of fixed air formed as the common measure of respiration and the combustion of carbon, Crawford used, as the common measure of respiration and the combustion of wax and of charcoal, the quantity of "pure air" consumed—or, as he put it, "altered."[13]

It is most likely that Crawford began his experiments assuming that each of the three processes simply change pure air into fixed air, just as Lavoisier and Laplace had assumed in their memoir that the only product of respiration and the combustion of charcoal is fixed air. Along the way, however, Crawford noticed something which led him to change his view:

> When the wax taper was burned in the [calorimeter], . . . with a view to determine the heat which it produced, a considerable quantity of aqueous vapour was condensed on the inner surface of the interior vessel. But no vapour appeared when the experiment was made with charcoal. It is therefore probable that, in the former instance, a part of the pure air was converted into water; and

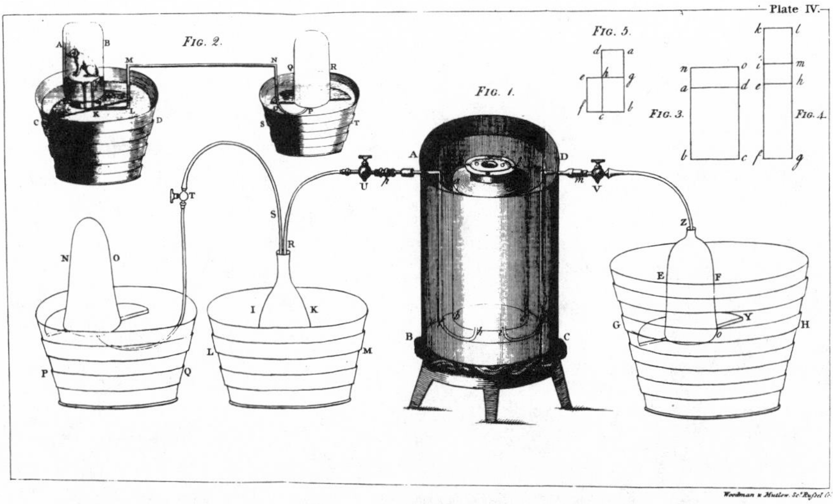

Figure 19. Apparatus of Adair Crawford for experiments on combustion and respiration. Figure 1 (below) shows the water calorimeter. The central chamber includes a glass-covered hole in the lid for observing combustion within. The middle chamber is filled with water; the outer chamber with down. The system of tubes and bottles (*NO*, *IK*, *EF*) is designed for measurement of the decrease of the volume of air during calorimeter experiment (not done in experiments described in text). Figure 2 shows the apparatus for separate measurement of consumption of "pure air" in respiration. After respiration the air in respiration chamber *AB* is displaced to chamber *QR*, where it is agitated with limewater, then returned to *AB* for measurement of decrease in volume. From Adair Crawford, *Experiments and Observations on Animal Heat and the Inflammation of Combustible Bodies*, 2d ed. rev. (London: J. Johnson, 1788), frontispiece.

> that in the latter, it was principally, if not entirely, changed into fixed air.[14]

Crawford then repeated the combustion and respiration experiments in inverted bell jars, but this time he measured the volume change both before and after absorbing the fixed air in limewater. He satisfied himself that the fixed air dissolved so slowly in the water over which the jars were immersed as not to affect these measurements. For the combustion of charcoal the ratio of the diminution before to that after absorption was 1:7, whereas for the wax taper it was 1:3.07, and for respiration nearly 1:3.5. Tacitly assuming that the small decrease before absorption in the case of charcoal meant only that when pure air is converted into fixed air it undergoes some contraction, Crawford reasoned that the additional decreases before absorption in the cases of the wax taper and respiration demonstrated that in both of these processes "part of the pure air . . . was converted into water." He supported this conclusion by calculating, from the densities of the airs involved, the weight relationships involved. In the respiration experiment 18.9 grains (English troy) of pure air disappeared, and 20.1 grains of fixed air formed. From the quantities of pure air consumed and fixed air formed in the combustion of charcoal he had calculated that the fixed air must have weighed one-fifth more than the pure air. On this basis he estimated that fixed air is composed of four-fifths pure air and one-fifth of a principle furnished by the charcoal. (He had not, in this experiment, measured the actual loss in the weight of the charcoal). Applying this composition of fixed air to the results of the respiration experiment, he concluded that "the quantity of pure air, changed into fixed air, was 16.08 grains [$20.1 \times 4/5 = 16.08$]; but the entire quantity of pure air, altered during the process, was 18.9 grains. It follows that 2.82 grains of this fluid were changed into water, and 16.08 grains into fixed air."[15]

Starting from Lavoisier and Laplace's theory of respiration as formulated in the memoir on heat, Crawford was thus led to revise that theory in the same sense that Lavoisier himself had afterward revised it. Crawford's argument for the formation of water was basically the same as Lavoisier's argument; both men calculated that more "pure air" is consumed than can be accounted for in the fixed air produced. It appears that Crawford reached this position independently of Lavoisier. The paper in which Lavoisier presented his modified theory to the Society of Medicine in 1785 did not appear in print until 1787, only one year before Crawford published his views in a long treatise on which he must have been working for some time. Crawford referred exclusively to the memoir on heat as the source of Lavoisier and Laplace's investigations and views. If my interpretation of the way in which Lavoisier reached the conclusion that water forms in respiration is correct, and if Crawford's own description of the way he reached it is faithful to the actual course of his investigation, then the two men's thinking converged in the same kind of experimental argument in order to support a conclusion which each had previously inferred from other considerations. Lavoisier had probably drawn the conclusion from a comparison between respiration and the combustion of charcoal, which he had, through a complex reassessment of previous experiments, come to treat as involving the formation of water. Crawford had drawn the conclusion from a comparison between respiration and the combustion of wax, which he had come to perceive as involving the formation of water through the incidental observation of condensed vapor in the calorimeter.

Crawford reduced the data from his respiration experiments so as to display comparatively the quantities of heat produced in respiration and combustion for the conversion of a common measure of "air," as Lavoisier and Laplace had done. Crawford's common measure, however, was that of the "pure air altered" rather than the fixed air formed; and his unit of heat was the amount that the temperature of a constant weight of water would have risen, rather than the quantity of ice melted.

> When equal quantities of pure air were altered by the combustion of wax and charcoal, and by the respiration of an animal, the quantities of heat communicated to 31 pounds seven ounces of water were as follows.
>
> | 100 ounce measures of pure air, altered | Degrees |
> |---|---|
> | by the combustion of wax imparted | 21 |
> | by the combustion of charcoal | 19.3 |
> | by the respiration of a guinea pig | 17.3 |
>
> From the foregoing experiments it appears, that the quantities of air altered being equal, more heat is produced by the combustion of wax than by that of charcoal, and more by the combustion of charcoal than by the respiration of an animal. These differences probably arise from the following causes: in the first instance, a considerable part of the air is converted into water, and more heat is produced by the conversion of pure air into that fluid than into fixed air. In the last instance, a part of the heat is carried off by the insensible perspiration.
>
> The results, however, approach so nearly to each other as to prove that the heat, in these processes, arises principally, if not entirely, from the conversion of pure air into fixed air, or into water.[16]

Opinions have differed over whether Crawford provided a more convincing demonstration of the equivalence of respiration and combustion than Lavoisier and Laplace had attained. Crawford himself believed that in substituting a water calorimeter for the ice calorimeter he had eliminated a central "inaccuracy" which the French scientists had already "suspected."[17] Recent historical accounts accept, or at least do not explicitly question, Crawford's claim. Goodfield has maintained, however, that the experimental method used by Lavoisier "has the advantage" that it depended upon measurements of the weight of ice melted, and "balances are more accurate than thermometers." The thorough historical analysis of Lodwig and Smeaton has shown that Crawford's method of water calorimetry gave better results in the hands of most experimentalists than did attempts to emulate Lavoisier and Laplace's use of the ice calorimeter, so that the water calorimeter eventually became standard. That was, in part, however, because others did not observe strictly the conditions under which Lavoisier and Laplace carried out their experiments.[18] The ice calorimeter proved far less versatile than the water calorimeter, but the results that its inventors obtained from it themselves were not necessarily less valid than those of the inventor of the water calorimeter.

Historical assessment of the relative accuracy of Crawford and of Lavoisier and Laplace in the measurements they made specifically concerning respiration is very risky. We may readily agree in principle with Crawford's assertion that Lavoisier and Laplace's results were affected by the fact that the animal must have respired more actively in their cold calorimeter than in the warmer respiration chamber. Yet Crawford's evidence that respiration in a cold medium is more rapid than in a warm one was largely qualitative; he could not, or at least did not, translate it into any figures which could be used to estimate how significant an error Lavoisier and Laplace might have incurred by ignoring the difference. Neither is it possible, in the absence of tests by the respective experimenters of the magnitudes of the errors inherent in their methods, to evaluate adequately whether the ice calorimeter or the water calorimeter provided more reliable measurements. Crawford was very experienced in making precise temperature measurements with sensitive thermometers, and he was alert to the need to apply correction factors. Lavoisier and Laplace's measurements of the quantity of ice melted were complicated by the problem of incomplete drainage, and their calorimeter was inaccurate when weather conditions varied more than a degree or two from the ideal. Crawford, on the other hand, had to manage the difficult operation of raising the temperature of the room in which he operated just enough to match the rising temperature of the water in his calorimeter. To analyze adequately the influence of these and other factors on the overall accuracy of results obtained two hundred years ago would not be much less difficult than to psychoanalyze historical figures we have never met.

Goodfield claims that Crawford's "results showed an even closer correspondence between combustion and respiration than those of the two Frenchmen."[19] It is difficult, however, to discern a significant distinction in the degree of correspondence in the respective results. Lavoisier and Laplace obtained heats for respiration and an equivalent measure of combustion which were near enough to support the view that the same underlying process was involved, yet acknowledged a divergence sufficient to induce them to give some explanation for the discrepancy—and so did Crawford. If Lavoisier's conjecture that the cooling of the extremities might account for the excess heat given off by his guinea pig was an unpersuasive, *ad hoc* argument, so was Crawford's assertion that the deficiency in the heat produced by his guinea pig was due to "heat carried away by insensible perspiration."

Judgments about the relative closeness of the correspondence that Crawford or Lavoisier and Laplace achieved are further clouded by the fact that they were not quite the same processes. When Lavoisier and Laplace concluded that respiration is identical to the combustion of *matière charbonneuse,* they were resting their case on the correspondence of heats produced by a common measure of what they regarded as *exactly* the same conversion, that of oxygen to fixed air. Crawford, however, was comparing the heat produced by processes he did not regard as identical; for wax and respiration produced water and fixed air, whereas he thought that charcoal produced only fixed air. If we restrict our attention to the two processes he did take to be the same, burning wax and respiration, then his two figures—21 for wax and 17.3 for respiration—correspond neither more nor less closely than do Lavoisier and Laplace's famous 10.3 and 13. Of course Lavoisier and Laplace's comparison would no longer hold the significance it originally had, for by this time Lavoisier too believed that respiration produced water. In order now to reestablish the correspondence between the heats of respiration and composition he would have had to carry out a more complex calculation, incorporating the relative contributions of the combustion of carbon and of hydrogen to the overall heat production of the animal. Either Lavoisier or Crawford might have attempted it, for both had measured the heat released in the formation of water from hydrogen and oxygen;[20] but, as far as is known, neither did.

In the light of the foregoing we can hardly credit Crawford with having confirmed Lavoisier and Laplace's theory in the sense of having made their demonstration more rigorous. He nevertheless did reinforce their position by reaching a similar outcome with different procedures. One of the most hallowed criteria for scientific validity is that experimental results must be repeatable. As Harry Collins has recently stressed, however, experiments repeated in different laboratories are almost never exact replicas of one another. The scientist repeating an investigation first carried out elsewhere generally seeks in some way to put his own design into the experiments. He not only wishes to avoid pure copying, but hopes that in some ways it will be a better experiment, so that it will be seen as a positive advance; or that at least it will avoid whatever pitfalls might inadvertently have been hidden within the original apparatus and procedures.[21] Even if the result is not an unequivocal improvement over its predecessor, the very fact that a variant method has led to similar results enhances confidence in the original conclusion.

In his conception of respiration as a chemical process Crawford remained poised between the phlogiston viewpoint of Priestley with which he had begun ten years before, and the theory of Lavoisier and Laplace which had inspired his later investigation of the problem. When discussing his experiments on the quantity of heat produced, he sounded much like Lavoisier minus the new nomenclature. Pure air is converted to fixed air and water. He assumed, with Lavoisier, that water is produced from the combustion of inflammable air and pure air (though he cited only Cavendish for the proof of its composition),[22] and that fixed air is formed from pure air and a "principle furnished by the charcoal." He considered this latter principle to be a "heavy inflammable air," a view which allowed him to maintain contact with the idea that combustible bodies give off inflammable principles loosely identifiable with phlogiston; but this was not so sharp a difference from Lavoisier's views, when we recollect that Lavoisier too had entertained the idea, in 1784, that the combustible principle in charcoal is inflammable air.[23] When Crawford discussed respiration in more general terms, however—as in describing his experiments on the effects of the temperature of the medium, for example—he used language such as "The quantity of air which an animal phlogisticates, in a given time, when it is placed in a warm medium, is less than that which it phlogisticates in an equal space of time when it is placed in a cold medium." He expressed the same idea somewhat differently when he wrote, "The air expired from the lungs of an animal is more phlogisticated in a cold than in a warm medium." Within the domain of his own theory of the manner in which heat is released during the circulation of the blood, he also held to the phlogiston framework. "The sensible heat of animals," he wrote, "depends upon the separation of absolute heat from the blood, by means of its union with the phlogistic principle in the minute vessels."[24] Such statements clearly descend from the theory of respiration which Priestley had developed in 1776. According to Priestley, phlogiston causes the dark color of venous blood and is separated from that blood as it passes through the lungs.[25] Crawford even adduced new evidence in favor of this view. His "ingenious friend Dr. Hamilton" closed off two adjacent sections of the jugular vein of a cat with ligatures, emptied one of the sections, and filled it with inflammable air. Then he allowed blood from the second section into it. "After an hour had elapsed, the blood being drawn from the vein, was found fluid, and had acquired a colour almost as dark as ink."[26] This inflammable air, obtained from iron filings dissolved in vitriolic acid, was a real substance exerting an observable effect on the blood, no matter how one explained it. The experiment, and Crawford's interpretation of it, however, were clearly inspired by a conception of the manifold chemical, physical, and physiological actions of phlogiston which held him rooted in the conceptual world that Lavoisier had long since rejected.

Crawford's theory of animal heat has recently been described as "almost too perfect and complete,"[27] and he has been linked with Lavoisier "in founding the oxidation theory of combustion and animal heat."[28] We should not overlook, however, the deep fracture splitting Crawford's views on respiration into fragments drawn from Lavoisier and fragments retained from Priestley. Unable to reconcile them, or unaware of the need to do so, he simply juxtaposed verbally ideas which belonged on opposite sides of the central theoretical chasm in the chemistry of his time. Even though contemporaries then, and historians since then, have seen Crawford's theory of animal heat as an ingenious synthesis, close inspection shows that it was fundamentally incoherent.

If Crawford slipped into and out of Lavoisier's theory of respiration at one level, he clearly and deliberately confronted Lavoisier over their divergent conceptions of the way in which heat is released in combustions. Crawford was uncommitted about whether heat itself is a substance or a force, and believed his theory independent of that issue. The conversion of *absolute* heat into *sensible* heat was, in his system, always due to changes in the heat capacities of the substances which contain it. In Lavoisier's view, on the other hand, the release of heat was, as Crawford put it, a chemical decomposition.[29] This divergence, of central importance for fundamental theories of heat and matter, was less crucial for the identification of respiration as a particular form of combustion; for whichever theory one adopted applied to both processes. Crawford's mechanism for the release of heat through the differing heat capacities of arterial and venous blood provided a very convenient means to explain how respiration could take place in the lungs even though the "sensible" heat is distributed evenly through the body. Lacking this explanation, Laplace had sought to attain the same end with his rather forced analogy to latent heat. Crawford's theory, based on meticulous measurements of the heat capacities of the airs exchanged in respiration, and of arterial and venous blood, might well appear to followers of Lavoisier's "doctrine" of respiration a more attractive way around the dilemma posed by Lagrange. Accepting it, however, entailed the disadvantage that one might purchase in the bargain Crawford's theory of combustion.

II

Crawford's revised treatise on animal heat came out during the time that the immediate followers of Lavoisier were at the peak of their campaign to convert the scientific world to the new system of chemistry. In France, Lavoisier had already won over the most important chemists, but he still faced opposition from such entrenched foes as the implacable editor of the most prominent scientific periodical of the day, *Observations sur la physique*. J. C. de Lamétherie not only wrote regularly skeptical editorial commentaries, but encouraged contributions from any quarter that might cast doubt on the validity of the new system. In England, Joseph Black was coming around, but Kirwan and Priestley were still in opposition. In Germany the ranks of the phlogistonists were still holding.[30] Besides writing the *Elementary Treatise* as a means by which students could be introduced to the new chemistry from the start of their training, Lavoisier founded with his supporters the *Annales de chimie* in order to provide a publication outlet favorable to investigations carried out in accord with their views.

Well-established chemists like Berthollet and Fourcroy, who had converted to Lavoisier's theories, were joined by younger men who became disciples of the new chemistry from the beginning. One of the ways in which such fledgling chemists served the cause was to write for the *Annales* reviews of current literature in the field. Particularly active in this respect were Jean-Henri Hassenfratz and Armand Seguin. Not surprisingly, when dealing with issues over which Lavoisier and his adversaries were contending, Hassenfratz and Seguin almost invariably supported the precepts of Lavoisier's chemistry. It would be interesting to know more about the extent to which Lavoisier may personally have orchestrated such activities. To judge from the internal evidence of the articles involved, I think he probably did not try to make writers like Hassenfratz and Seguin into mere spokesmen for his own positions. Both of them claimed, at least, to be expressing their own personal views. If they nevertheless followed closely the main outlines of Lavoisier's chemistry, that was more likely due to his intellectual domination of the group than to any direct control over what individuals within it wrote.

In the context of the contest which the people around Lavoisier were waging with those who still believed that the traditional phlogiston chemistry would prevail over its fashionable rival, Crawford's mixed views propelled his important new investigations into an intermediate zone, in such a way that both sides sought to make use of his work for their own ends. The phlogistonists in France found an ingenious, if devious, way to attack Lavoisier through Crawford. In August 1789 there appeared in *Observations sur la physique* a "Memoir on heat" by Léopold Vacca Berlinghieri. According to Berlinghieri, Crawford's theory of animal heat was untenable, because the quantity of heat which could be transferred from vital air to arterial blood in the lungs by means of the changes in their respective heat capacities was not large enough to make up for a great loss of heat which was required to evaporate the water vapor exhaled from the lungs. With Crawford's theory of animal heat thus "demonstrated" to be false, Berlinghieri reasoned that, since animal heat is a slow combustion, Crawford's general theory of combustion must also be incorrectly conceived. Swinging around then to his real target, Berlinghieri contended that "M. Lavoisier has devised on this subject [of animal heat and combustion] a theory which rests entirely upon that of Crawford." He went on to argue that since Lavoisier's theory of caloric incorporated the concept of specific heat derived from Crawford, Lavoisier's whole theory of combustion "falls with [the theory] of M. Crawford." Having demolished Crawford and Lavoisier, Berlinghieri announced that "I am now working to perfect" a new theory of heat, and promised a future essay on the subject.[31]

It fell to Hassenfratz to refute Berlinghieri in the *Annales de chimie*. The charges themselves were easy to dispose of:

> One sees that the entire objection that M. Berlinghieri makes to the theory of M. Crawford depends upon the supposition that the water vapor an individual gives off at each expiration has been drawn from the lungs in a liquid state. What proof does M. Ber-

> linghieri bring to support this hypothesis? None; and it is nevertheless with such a bold supposition that M. Berlinghieri wishes to destroy the connections between a myriad of facts through which M. Crawford and all those who have preceded and succeeded him have reached the same conclusion.

Had Berlinghieri examined the experiments which had led Crawford and other scientists to the theory of animal heat, Hassenfratz chided him, he would have learned that the exhaled water vapor originated from water already existing as vapor in the atmosphere, and from "water formed in the lungs by the union of a portion of the hydrogen of the blood with a portion of the oxygen gas of the inspired air." Since this latter process "disengages a large quantity of heat," the vapor "augments, in place of diminishing, the heat as M. Berlinghieri concluded." Hassenfratz wasted no time on Berlinghieri's further criticisms of Crawford's views on heat, because it was obvious to him that they were all deduced from his false hypothesis about the formation of exhaled water vapor, and because he saw through Berlinghieri's motive: "He appears to want to attack the doctrine of M. Lavoisier, to whose works I believe I should recommend those people who are not familiar with them."[32]

If Berlinghieri's loose arguments were readily dismissible, his tactic created a delicate situation for Lavoisier's followers. By stressing the dependence of Lavoisier's theory of heat on experiments and concepts derived from Crawford, the phlogistonists were forcing their challengers to defend Crawford; yet Crawford himself remained a phlogistonist, so that it was at the same time necessary for the Lavoisier group to maintain some distance from him. Hassenfratz did this by introducing his defense with a mixed opinion of Crawford.

> I am far from adopting the theory of M. Crawford in its entirety; but even in rejecting the hypothetical and conjectural in it, such as the determination of the comparative heat inherent in a body, no one would recognize more than I the clarity and skill with which he has made a great number of ingenious experiments, all appropriate to extend the bounds of our knowledge on a subject of such great interest as heat.[33]

Thus, Hassenfratz implied, Crawford has made important contributions, but he is not one of us. Moreover, this passage suggests that the theoretical contribution with which Lavoisier's followers credited Crawford was limited to the nature of heat itself.

The previously quoted passages referring to the theory of respiration and animal heat deliberately mention Crawford and "those who have preceded and succeeded him," and "Crawford and other scientists," as a way of denying Crawford any unique claims in this area. It was in keeping with this position that Hassenfratz directed his discussion of the evidence for the formation of water in the lungs away from Crawford, focusing on Lavoisier's discussion of the phenomenon:

> This formation of the water in the lungs appears to be demonstrated (1) by the proportion of carbonic acid expired, which is less than that which ought to be yielded in proportion to the quantity of oxygen gas which disappears; (2) by the quantity of the vapor given off, whose difference from that which atmospheric air contains is such that the quantity of oxygen included in the excess is almost equal to the excess of the quantity of oxygen absorbed over the quantity employed to form the carbonic acid.

Hassenfratz cited the memoir in which Lavoisier had presented the theory of the formation of water in respiration at the Royal Society of Medicine, in 1785, for details of "the experiments which led him to this conclusion."[34] We may recall, however, that in this memoir Lavoisier had based his conclusion on the first of the above two points. Although he had mentioned that there was an excess of water vapor exhaled, he had never expressed such a surplus quantitatively. If it were possible to measure the water vapor added to the air exhaled from the lungs, and to show that it contained just that quantity of oxygen necessary to account for the oxygen not utilized in the formation of carbonic acid, the result would indeed have been a powerful demonstration of the theory. There is no record, however, of either Lavoisier or anyone else's having attempted such an analysis, so that it remains unclear where Hassenfratz obtained the second of his two arguments.

Of all the followers of Lavoisier, it was Armand Seguin who attached himself most closely to his leader. Born in 1767, he was probably also the youngest of those who joined the Lavoisier circle during the 1780s. Seguin began to work in Lavoisier's laboratory sometime prior to August 1788, for Fourcroy reported then that "Seguin has made in Lavoisier's laboratory a discovery which can furnish another useful procedure" for obtaining pure oxygen gas from the oxides of manganese. Seguin apparently busied himself in general with investigations intended to strengthen the experimental supports for various points in Lavoisier's chemical system. Little is known of Seguin's scientific training, but it is quite possible that he acquired most of it from Lavoisier himself; for he wrote at the end of the summary of Lavoisier's *Elementary Treatise* which he published in the *Annales de chimie*, "I owe [to him] what little knowledge I may have."[35]

To the same volume of the *Annales* in which Hassenfratz deftly turned away Berlinghieri's attack on Crawford and Lavoisier in four pages, Seguin contributed a ninety-page article comprising part 1 of "General observations on caloric and its different effects, and reflections on the theory of MM. Black, Crawford,

Lavoisier, and Laplace on animal heat and on that which is disengaged during combustion; with a resumé of everything which has been done and written on that subject up to the present." This cumbersome title accurately reflects the character of Seguin's article. His analysis was obviously stimulated by the appearance of the new edition of Crawford's treatise. Seguin in fact followed closely the format of Crawford's book, summarizing its experiments and discussions in paraphrases of Crawford's own writing. While acknowledging and appropriating the useful in Crawford's work, Seguin, like Hassenfratz, also conspicuously drew attention to its shortcomings. The heading for the first chapter of his sixty-page second installment illustrates this maneuver very well: "Observations on the methods employed to determine the [heat] capacities of solids and liquids, and on the means to correct and to avoid in part the errors to which [the method] of Doctor Crawford is susceptible."[36] In the theoretical portions of his discussion Seguin offered elaborate interpretations of changes of state and combustion derived from Lavoisier's caloric theory. Obviously inspired by Lavoisier's treatment of that subject in the *Elementary Treatise*, Seguin extended Lavoisier's conceptions to provide detailed explanations of the mechanisms underlying various specific chemical transformations. Seguin displayed here a penchant for plunging with intricate expositions into areas of uncertainty where Lavoisier had prudently stopped with a brief, suggestive statement. For example, Lavoisier had given only a paragraph in the *Elementary Treatise* to the question of whether caloric may be a modification of light, or light a modification of caloric,[37] because he regarded the issue as unanswerable at the time. Seguin, on the other hand, spun out lengthy alternative explanations of particular processes, assuming first that caloric is elementary, and then that it is a compound of light and something else. All the while he acknowledged that such discussions ran the risk of "connecting supposition to supposition, and consequently of following a trail of illusions."[38] In these two ponderous articles Seguin unwittingly revealed himself as the quintessential overly eager apprentice, wielding tools forged by the master, but without the judgment and artistry which had enabled the master to construct with them a towering edifice.

Only in the last twelve pages of his massive discussion did Seguin directly take up respiration. There he began by setting straight the scientific priorities as he saw them. "It was M. Lavoisier who first announced [in 1777] that *animal heat* very probably depends on the decomposition of vital air." In 1779 Crawford had "adopted this opinion," and "assembled a series of experiments suitable to establish this conjecture." Summarizing briefly the evidence provided by Lavoisier's early investigations of the atmosphere and of respiration, together with such unqualified generalizations as that animals with lungs have temperatures higher than that of the surroundings, whereas animals lacking lungs have "almost the same temperature as the milieu," Seguin concluded that respiration is the principal cause of the augmentation of the temperature in warm-blooded animals, and that in the process "vital air changes in large part to carbonic acid gas." The "grand questions" still to be resolved, he believed, were, "How does this change take place? Where is the carbon necessary to the formation of this new gas found?" and "Does vital air undergo only this change?"[39]

Taking up the last question first, Seguin again credited Lavoisier, this time in a footnote, with being the first to suggest the answer "that water probably [also] forms during respiration; this conjecture is one of the most beautiful ideas with which that celebrated scientist has enriched the sciences." In his footnote Seguin quoted the entire section on that subject from Lavoisier's memoir on respiration of 1785. Evidently, however, Seguin felt that Lavoisier's "conjecture" was in need of confirmation, and he attempted to supply that need. "The discovery of the change of color" of the blood during its circulation, he declared, "has furnished the information necessary for the demonstration of Lavoisier's theory of respiration and animal heat." This was a strange, probably carelessly worded assertion, since the change in color of the blood had been known long before Lavoisier's theory. At any rate, drawing heavily from Crawford's book, Seguin went on to summarize Priestley's experiments showing that arterial blood "exposed to hydrogen gas takes on the deep, livid color of venous blood." He repeated almost word for word Crawford's description of the experiments of Doctor Hamilton which proved that finding more directly. "These experiments prove," Seguin claimed, "that the difference between the color of arterial and that of venous blood derives from hydrogen gas." One "can conclude, with M. Lavoisier and Doctor Crawford," he reiterated, "(1) that the change of color which the blood undergoes in the veins derives from its combination with this principle." He added two further conclusions as if they too followed from this demonstration: "(2) that in traversing the lungs the blood abandons part of the hydrogen it contains, and that it then takes on its bright red color; (3) that *animal heat* depends upon the decomposition of vital air."[40]

As can readily be seen, Seguin was juxtaposing arguments appropriated from Lavoisier and from Crawford. His particular assemblage of them into what he regarded as a proof for the theory of respiration is quite unconvincing. Treating Lavoisier's calculation of the missing quantity of oxygen consumed as mere grounds for *conjecture* that water is formed, Seguin loaded the whole burden of proving that conclusion on the color change produced in blood when hydrogen gas is mixed with it. He seems not to have noticed the fallacy of inferring from the evidence that hydrogen can darken blood experimentally the conclusion that hydrogen is the physiological cause of the change of arterial blood to venous blood. Nor did he stop there. Moving from "supposition to supposition," he confidently described the form in which hydrogen gas exists in the venous blood, and deduced from that form how it is that hydrogen and carbon can combine with oxygen in the lungs at a temperature much lower than is necessary for ordinary combustion.

> But since all of the hydrogen gas extracted from animal matter holds carbon in solution, it happens that the vital air which enters the lungs combines with the carbonated hydrogen [*hydrogène carboné*] released from the blood, and forms carbonic acid gas with the carbon and water with the hydrogen.
>
> If the carbon had not been divided, it would not have combined at all with vital air at the temperature of around thirty degrees; but, being held in solution, its molecules are dispersed, and have then a greater attraction for the oxygen.

To overcome objections that the hydrogen gas and vital air would not combine when there is no ignited body present, Seguin cited experiments by Priestley and Berthollet which "prove that hydrogen gas in a *nascent state*" can combine with vital air. Finally, he noted that his opinion differed from that of Crawford "only in that that celebrated scientist calls by the name of inflammable principle the substance which I have designated by the term carbonated hydrogen gas."[41]

In his treatment of respiration Seguin thus exhibited characteristics similar to those permeating his discussion of the theory of heat itself. Clever at lining up arguments, stout defender of Lavoisier's theories and priorities, Seguin lacked Lavoisier's ability to assess critically the degree of certainty attached to statements, inferences, and experimental demonstrations. What he had done with Priestley and Crawford's theory of respiration was simply to translate their "inflammable principle" into a substance assimilable to the conceptual framework of the new chemistry. His "carbonated hydrogen gas" corresponded to the "heavy inflammable air" which Crawford believed to be obtainable from all plant and animal matters.[42] Lavoisier had attributed the fact that he sometimes obtained an inflammable air whose specific gravity was greater than the usual type, to carbon dissolved in the latter;[43] Seguin must have been drawing on this conception to deduce the existence of his carbonated hydrogen in the blood. Whether he realized it or not, however, in transposing Crawford's theory into Lavoisier's chemistry, he had suppressed the connection between Crawford's explanation of the color change and Priestley's older conception that venous blood is "impregnated" with phlogiston. Left with what appeared to him the simple empirical finding that hydrogen is responsible for the color of venous blood, he elaborated from that slender basis not only the proof that water is formed in respiration, but a fundamental explanation, at the level of the molecular condition of the carbon and hydrogen in the blood, for the occurrence of the process under physiological conditions. Doubtless Seguin believed he was reasoning as Lavoisier would. What he lacked was Lavoisier's acute sense for how many inferential steps beyond the immediate experimental results one could take before becoming lost in a boundless speculative field.

Following his animated speculations about the mechanism of respiration, Seguin ended his long review with an extremely cursory summary of Crawford's measurements of the specific heats of arterial and venous blood, his evidence that an animal in a cold medium "consumes more air in a given time" than in a warm medium, and his experiments comparing the heat of combustion of wax and charcoal with that of respiration. Seguin's entire discussion of the latter topic was the following:

> Doctor Crawford has performed several experiments on the combustion of wax, of lard, of oil, and of charcoal, and he concluded that the quantity of *caloric* which is disengaged during the alteration of a certain quantity of vital air by the respiration of an animal is equal to that which is disengaged during the combustion of wax or charcoal in the same quantity of vital air.
>
> These experiments are done with care, but on very small quantities; they would perhaps he susceptible to some criticisms; but since they are not necessary to the conclusions which derive from this work, I shall content myself with having mentioned them.[44]

This facile dismissal of the experiments which, of all of Crawford's investigations, provided the most effective support for Lavoisier's theory that water is formed in respiration, and which constituted as well a major advance in the techniques of calorimetry—especially when contrasted with the way in which Seguin latched onto the color change of blood exposed to hydrogen—scarcely enhances our estimate of the scientific judgment of Lavoisier's new assistant.

On May 22, 1790, Seguin read a paper entitled "General observations on respiration and animal heat" to the Royal Society of Medicine, the same audience which Lavoisier had addressed on the topic five years before. The first portion of Seguin's presentation was a slightly refined version of what he had written in his review article concerning Lavoisier's original theory that vital air is decomposed in respiration, and concerning the color change produced in blood by hydrogen as the foundation for his explanation of the formation of water. The only significant additions he made were to announce that he himself had repeated Priestley's experiments on the color changes of blood in vital air and hydrogen, and to modify his argument that the physical state of the hydrogen and carbon in the blood enables them to combine with oxygen in the lungs. Instead of asserting that nascent hydrogen and dispersed carbon can be oxygenated without an igniting body, he now claimed that hydrogen in a fluid condition and carbon in a divided state can combine with oxygen "at the ordinary temperature of the atmosphere," instead of the much higher temperature they otherwise require.[45]

In the second half of his paper Seguin took up the question, "How does the temperature of each individual maintain itself at the same level from the center all the way to the extremities?" He obtained his answer from Crawford. After summarizing the experiments in which Crawford had found arterial blood to have a greater heat capacity than venous blood, Seguin clothed Crawford's explanation in the language of the new chemistry, including his own hypothetical "carbonized hydrogen."

> The attraction of the carbonized hydrogen for the oxygen being stronger than the combined attractions of the oxygen for the caloric and the carbonized hydrogen for the blood, the vital air decomposes during the inspiration, and then it abandons a portion of its specific caloric, which unites with the blood, whose capacity [for caloric] is augmented by the loss of a portion of its carbonized hydrogen; but the arterial blood, while circulating afterward, receives from the system, which is always in a more or less putrescent state, a certain quantity of carbonized hydrogen; and, during this change, its capacity being diminished, it abandons a portion of the caloric which it had absorbed in the lungs. This caloric is then carried along the surrounding humors, and raises their temperature in a nearly uniform manner. Thus, it is to the change of venous blood into arterial blood, and then of arterial blood into venous blood, that we must attribute the stability of the temperature, nearly constant, which one observes in all parts of our system.

Seguin mildly qualified his acceptance of this theory. It was not yet rigorously proven that the temperature of the body is perfectly constant from the center to the periphery, so that it was not certain that the explanation was necessary; but since the alternative "is not nearly so satisfying, I believe that one can admit what I have presented" until such time as experiments more precise than those of Crawford provided different results.[46]

We may note that, in addition to translating Crawford's theory into the language of the new chemistry, Seguin omitted all mention of what, in Crawford's own formulation, had complemented the measurements of the specific heats of arterial and venous blood; that is, the specific heats of the vital air and fixed air. These measurements were useless to Seguin's version, because they brought into the theory of animal heat the theory of combustion of Crawford, which Lavoisier's school rejected. As shown in the first part of the paragraph, Seguin substituted a mechanism based on Lavoisier's conception of caloric.

By eliminating the features of Crawford's theory of animal heat which were unacceptable in the chemistry of Lavoisier, and appropriating the remainder, Seguin thus produced a synthesis of Lavoisier's theory of respiration and Crawford's theory of the distribution of the heat yielded by this respiration. The most obvious question for us to ask is whether Lavoisier himself was behind this synthesis. We may recall that when Lavoisier had last addressed himself to the question, in 1783, he had briefly mentioned Crawford's theory as one of several means for distributing the heat produced in the lungs.[47] It would be plausible to see in Seguin's account Lavoisier's fuller development of, and stronger commitment to, a suggestion he had earlier made. Recent historians have assumed, though not without reservation, that Seguin generally spoke for Lavoisier.[48] As the above account of Seguin's previous writing suggests, however, we must be very cautious in equating Seguin's views with those of his teacher. Seguin showed a tendency to carry speculations based on Lavoisier's views to much greater lengths than Lavoisier ordinarily did. The above synthesis indulges in a degree of conjectural description of internal physiological processes that Lavoisier had up until then avoided. Moreover, in his longer review article Seguin had taken pains to convince his readers that he himself was contributing original opinions to the discussion of the nature of heat. He clearly perceived himself, however exaggerated the opinion was, as an independent scientific thinker. Until we can find positive evidence that Lavoisier accepted this synthesis of his theory with that of Crawford, it is safer to assume that Seguin was acting on his own initiative, and that Lavoisier's attitude toward the views of his disciple is unknown.

III

During 1790 the two chemists who had earlier done most to establish correspondences between respiration and combustion, Priestley and Lavoisier, each renewed his study of the process. Priestley was the first to present his findings, reporting them to the Royal Society on February 25. Still struggling to remold his pliable phlogiston to fit experimental developments which continually outdistanced the explanatory power of that venerable concept, he acknowledged that it had been necessary for him to revise his former view of respiration.

> I supposed, that in this animal process there was simply an emission of phlogiston from the lungs. But the result of my late experiments on the mutual transmission of dephlogisticated air and of inflammable and nitrous air, through a moist bladder interposed between them, and likewise the opinions and observations of others, soon convinced me, that, besides the emission of phlogiston from the blood, dephlogisticated air, or the acidifying principle of it, is at the same time received into the blood. Still, however, there remained a doubt how much of the dephlogisticated air which we inhale enters the blood, because part of it is employed in forming the *fixed* air, which is the product of respiration, by its uniting with the phlogiston discharged from the blood; for such I take it for granted is the origin of the fixed air, since it is formed

> by the combination of the same principles in other, but exactly similar circumstances.[49]

Forced to accept the evidence that dephlogisticated air combines with something else to form fixed air, Priestley had thus added to the roles of his phlogiston that of the other constituent of fixed air. To answer the question he had posed for himself, how much dephlogisticated air enters the blood, he compared the quantity of dephlogisticated air consumed, with the fixed air formed, by his own breathing. In order to do this, he too had first to determine the composition of fixed air. He did so by burning "charcoal of copper" in dephlogisticated air, repeating the experiment with wood charcoal in common air. The quantity of dephlogisticated air employed in forming the fixed air he estimated by the change in the volume of the air in which the combustion occurred, together with a determination of the proportions of dephlogisticated air in the volumes present before and after the experiment, made with his standard nitrous air test. The quantity of "phlogiston" in the fixed air he made equal to the loss in weight of the charcoals burned. Priestley was gallantly submitting the once purely qualitative phlogiston to the balance sheet criterion that Lavoisier had by this time made indispensable to chemical reasoning. From the combined results of three combustions he estimated that "about one-fourth of the weight of fixed air is phlogiston, and consequently that the other three-fourths are dephlogisticated air."[50] If we straddle the language barrier, we can see that this result was not far different from the 28:72 ratio for carbon and oxygen which Lavoisier had reached through a more painstaking investigation.

Priestley then proceeded to "ascertain how much fixed air was actually formed by breathing a given quantity both of atmospherical and of dephlogisticated air, in order to determine whether any part of it remained to enter the blood, after forming this fixed air." To do so, he "breathed in 100 oz m. [ounce measures] of atmospherical air, of the standard of 1.02, till it was reduced to 71 oz m. and by washing in water to 65 oz m., of the standard of 1.45." The "standards" referred to are measures of the reduction in volume produced by his nitrous air test. From these tests he could calculate the quantity of dephlogisticated air present before and afterward in the air he had breathed, and from the difference he could determine the quantity consumed. The quantity of fixed air formed he took to be the loss in the volume of the remaining air when he washed it in water. Repeating the experiment using dephlogisticated air to breathe in, he found in both cases that only one-fourth of the dephlogisticated air could have been employed in forming fixed air in the lungs. Consequently, "about three times as much entered the blood as did not."[51]

If we overlook the conceptual and language differences, Priestley's experimental result corresponded to the result from which Lavoisier had perceived in 1785 that not all of the oxygen consumed can be converted to fixed air. The proportion unaccounted for was, of course, dramatically larger. That Priestley could find only enough fixed air to account for one-third of the dephlogisticated air used was most likely due to the fact that he did not absorb the fixed air in alkali, but relied on his long-standing belief that washing air in water removes all of its fixed air. Remembering that Lavoisier had raised the possibility that the missing oxygen enters the blood, but dismissed it in favor of his theory that the oxygen forms water,[52] we can see Priestley as having now adopted Lavoisier's rejected alternative. Lavoisier's solution was not open to Priestley because, unlike Crawford, he still could not accept Lavoisier's theory of the composition of water;[53] but the alternative he embraced instead makes little sense. If dephlogisticated air is continually absorbed into the blood, what becomes of it? Unless it is removed from the body in some form, it must rapidly accumulate, an outcome obviously contrary to ordinary observation. No one could avoid all of the pitfalls lying in wait for those who pioneered in the study of the immensely complicated phenomenon of respiration. Lavoisier, more than any of his contemporaries, could sense when a conclusion he thought of might lead into a trap, and choose a more fruitful alternative. The less perspicacious Priestley marched on into the cul de sac.

At almost the same time that the hardy English veteran of respiratory investigations was returning to the fray to try to bring his theory up to date, a German newcomer was entering the lists from a very different conceptual direction, but bringing with him a conclusion which coincided in one crucial respect with Priestley's latest views. Christoph Girtanner was both a physician and a student of chemistry, and he drew on both backgrounds to conceive a grandiose scheme for a "universal physiology." Believing that the principle of irritability, defined experimentally by Albrecht von Haller forty years before, provided the basic principle upon which all of the bodily processes in health and disease could be explained, Girtanner tried to work out a complete account of the physiology and pathology of all organisms around the simple idea of the accumulation and depletion of irritability in all the parts of animals and plants which possessed that vital property. His views were similar enough to those of John Brown, who worked out a medical system on the principle of degrees of "excitability," so that Girtanner was accused of plagiarism. At any rate, attracted to Lavoisier's new chemistry, Girtanner decided that "oxygen is the principle of irritability," from which it followed that "the irritability of organized bodies is always in direct proportion to the quantity of oxygen which they contain." He based his claim on a diverse array of arguments, of which the most dramatic came from his medical experience. Mercury used in metallic form as a drug, he came to believe, had little effect on the body, whereas taken in the form of an oxide it causes symptoms which fit into his pattern for augmented irritability. Girtanner published a synthesis of the general principles of his system in *Observations sur la physique* in January 1790.[54]

If oxygen was essential for the irritability of all irritable parts of animals, then it must reach those parts through the circulation. "The blood which is oxygenated during its passage through the lungs," Girtanner wrote, "is deprived of this oxygen during the circulation, the oxygen having a greater attraction for the irritable fiber than for the carbon which is contained in the blood. In this process the caloric combined with the oxygen is set free; thence the animal . . . heat. The blood acts continually on the irritable fiber, and the fiber reacts on the blood."[55] When he read Seguin's review of the theory of animal heat and respiration in the *Annales de chimie,* Girtanner saw that the view that a carbonated hydrogen is oxygenated in the lungs, an idea Seguin seemed to associate with both Lavoisier and Crawford, was incompatible with his own conception of the physiological role of oxygen. He set out, therefore, to overturn the evidence for that view. Having gained from Seguin's treatment of the subject the impression that the main foundation for the theory that respiration takes place in the lungs was the belief that Dr. Hamilton's experiment had shown hydrogen to be the cause of the dark color of venous blood and its removal the source of the arterial color, Girtanner carried out a great number of experiments in which he exposed arterial or venous blood to oxygen, hydrogen, carbonic acid, nitrous air, and other gases. He noted the resulting color changes, and examined the changes in the composition of the gases in contact with the blood. Every one of his results he was able to assimilate to the conclusions that hydrogen is not the cause of the dark color of venous blood; that arterial blood is instead due to the presence of oxygen and venous blood to its absence; and that the dark color of venous blood derives from the carbon contained in it. From these and some other experiments in which he injected various gases into the jugular vein of an animal, he concluded that the blood acquires its arterial color from the oxygen it acquires in its passage through the lungs, and that the blood gradually gives up its oxygen during its passage through the body.[56]

That much Girtanner needed in order to sustain his own theory of irritability. As a system builder, however, he was eclectic enough so that he went on to incorporate as much as he could of Seguin's synthesis of Crawford's and Lavoisier's theories into a remarkably cumbersome theory of respiration. In a second memoir published in August 1790, he summarized his view as follows:

> During respiration one portion of the oxygen of the vital air combines with the venous blood, changing its deep color to a bright red one. A second portion of the oxygen combines with the carbon contained within the carbonated hydrogen gas which the venous blood exhales, and forms carbonic acid gas. A third portion of the oxygen combines with the carbon of the mucus, of which the lungs contain a great quantity, and which is continuously decomposing: that portion forms additional carbonic acid gas. A fourth

> portion of the oxygen combines with the hydrogen gas of the blood to form the water which is exhaled during respiration. The caloric which the decomposed vital air contained remains in part combined with the oxygen of the blood, whence derives the specific heat of arterial blood, which is greater than that of venous blood. Another portion of the caloric enters into combination with the carbonic acid gas. Finally, a third portion produces the temperature necessary for the formation of water by the combination of hydrogen gas and oxygen gas.[57]

Girtanner thus satisfied the needs of the several viewpoints assembled into his theory by simply assigning a portion of oxygen and a portion of caloric to cover each required function. The final sentence in his statement, concerning the third portion of caloric, enabled him to explain how water can be formed in the lungs without resort to Seguin's mechanism of dispersed carbon molecules and nascent hydrogen, an explanation he rejected as "hypothetical and entirely unconvincing."[58] Apparently he thought it more convincing to imagine that a local concentration of caloric in the lungs could enable the combination to occur at the temperature required to burn hydrogen in the laboratory.

A balanced evaluation of Girtanner's contribution to respiratory theory is not easy to make. He believed it to be founded firmly on the many observations and experiments he reported. His experiments on blood did effectively destroy the simplistic view of Crawford and Seguin that hydrogen causes the dark color of venous blood, and the results of some of these experiments provided reasonable support for his conclusion that oxygen is responsible for arterial blood. Many of the experiments, however, are vaguely described and unconvincing. His ability to make every one of them fit his theoretical position seems attributable more to his belief in the validity of his grand system than to the cogency of the analytical outcomes. The feature that his theory shared with that of Priestley was the inference that a portion of the inspired oxygen is absorbed into the arterial blood. Girtanner shared also with Priestley the conceptual blind spot which that conclusion entailed: how was "the great quantity of oxygen which the blood continually receives"[59] to be disposed of? Girtanner believed that it was used to accumulate irritability in all of the irritable fibers. If he had thought critically about the magnitude of oxygen involved, however, he should have realized that his solution was as incongruous as William Harvey had long ago shown it would be to assume that the blood propelled into the arteries by the heart is consumed to nourish these parts.

Within Girtanner's loosely conceived, thinly supported theory there was nevertheless embedded an insight of fundamental importance; that was that the physiological role of oxygen is somehow associated with the functions of the elementary parts composing an organism, and that if this is so, then in animals the oxygen must reach these parts through the arterial blood. He brought to this problem a perspective drawn from a conceptual and investigative tradition far removed from the chemical world in which Priestley, Crawford, or Lavoisier operated. The source of Girtanner's organizing idea of irritability, Albrecht von Haller, had focused attention on the fundamental properties of the ultimate "fibers" composing the fabric of an animal body, that is, on a level of organization below that of the visible organs with reference to which physiological functions were customarily described.[60] Approaching a respiratory theory that others had adduced from investigations of whole animals, Girtanner aimed to make that theory conform to the requirements of the elementary constituents of organisms. If the fit was forced, the outlook was farsighted. We can thus classify Girtanner all at once as an imitator, an uncritical assembler of all-encompassing systems, a dreamer who wished to reveal "the most hidden mysteries of physiology,"[61] and a prescient theorist anticipating the outlines of future development. Progressive enough to become one of the first German chemists to back Lavoisier's chemistry, he was alien enough from the spirit of that chemistry to construct vast speculations around a conception of irritability more protean even than the phlogiston Lavoisier was driving from the scientific arena.

16

Lavoisier's Return to Respiration

In 1790 Lavoisier began a new series of experiments on respiration. We cannot reconstruct the stages or timing of his investigation in detail, because no laboratory records of them exist, and Lavoisier's description is too general to establish the order of research, or even the procedures he followed in individual experiments. Nevertheless, it is evident that the work was very extensive. It included measurements made under at least a dozen experimental conditions. Lavoisier claimed, although probably with his usual overstatement, that "they were all repeated a great number of times."[1] The question naturally arises, how did he manage to carry out all this research during a period in which, according to the general view of historians, he had little time for his own scientific interests? His biographer Grimaux wrote that the revolution saddled him with many occupations which "unfortunately held him far from the laboratory." Each new day seemed to encumber him with further responsibilites. Lavoisier himself complained, in February 1790, in a letter to Joseph Black, "The condition of public affairs in France has, for the past year, slowed down the progress of the sciences for the time being, and has distracted scientists from their most cherished occupations."[2] Marcelin Berthelot has even considered it doubtful that Lavoisier kept any laboratory notebooks after October 1788, the last date recorded in the surviving ones, because he was "entirely occupied . . . from then on, by the commissions and administrative services of every type which were imposed on him."[3] Somehow, in spite of these obstacles, Lavoisier was able to return to his "cherished occupation." The chronology of his activities suggests, in fact, that he was less often interrupted by nonscientific events during 1790 than he had been the year before,[4] and he may have taken advantage of this letup to press forward with a research program he had long hoped to resume. Even then, however, he was able to complete this very time-consuming investigation only because of the eager assistance of Armand Seguin. Afterward Lavoisier attributed the success of the experiments largely to the "zeal, the patience, and the exactitude" of his enthusaistic young protégé.[5] Undoubtedly Seguin performed some of the experimental operations on his own while Lavoisier was busy elsewhere. The drawings by Madame Lavoisier of the respiration experiments carried out by Seguin, however, depict Lavoisier directing the operation himself.[6] If he could not always be present, it is nevertheless most probable that he designed the experiments and supervised their execution.

In some respects the respiration experiments Lavoisier carried out in 1790 were direct extensions of those he had last performed with Laplace in 1783 and 1784. The direction he now took, however, was quite different from what he would have done if he had been able to continue the work at the earlier time in the way he had planned to do. In 1783 he had envisioned repeating the comparative respiration and calorimetric measurements on other animals, to see whether the quantity of heat they give off is always proportional to the quantity of fixed air they produce.[7] Time alone seemed to have settled that question for him. He now took for granted that respiration is the source of animal heat, and fixed his attention on other aspects of the process. The central objective that he now had in mind was to measure the rate of human respiration under varied physiological conditions. In order to "guide" themselves in this work, however, he and Seguin first undertook a series of preliminary animal experiments, relying on the familiar subject of the earlier experiments, the durable, docile guinea pig.[8]

Time modified Lavoisier's approach in other ways as well. When he had last done respiration experiments he had thought that the sole product of the operation was fixed air, which therefore served as a convenient common measure for respiration and the combustion of *charbon*. Now he believed that there are two products for respiration, fixed air and water, the latter of which he had not been able to measure directly. Perhaps for that reason he measured respiration, as Crawford too had recently done, in terms of the consumption of oxygen, the constituent common to the two products. That change, however, raised a major new experimental problem. Although in closed systems it might have been possible to estimate the oxygen consumption from the loss in volume when the carbonic acid was removed, Lavoisier evidently did not consider such a procedure accurate enough for his purposes. Instead he decided to utilize eudiometric methods to determine the quantity of oxygen in the air before and after it was respired. We may recall that in 1785 he had been using a eudiometric adaptation of Priestley's nitrous air test to measure the quantities of oxygen in different samples of air in public places.[9] Sometime later, however, he had concluded that the method was too imprecise even to detect the difference between "the best quality of atmospheric air and the most harmful" air. The test contained, "as many as twenty sources of error."[10] Seguin took up the task of working out a better way. Afterward Lavoisier credited him with having developed the "simple convenient method for making the analysis of the air," without which "precise experiments on the effects of respiration" would have been impossible.[11]

The main requirement for a eudiometric determination of oxygen was to utilize a substance which would combine with all of the oxygen present in a given air sample. We may recall that back in 1777 Lavoisier had found that the combustion of pyrophor absorbed a greater proportion of oxygen from common air than any other substance he had previously tried.[12] Ordinary phosphorus also burned very vigorously and seemed to combine with all of the available oxygen. Several chemists, including Guyton de Morveau, Lavoisier, and Fourcroy, had utilized these substances to determine the proportions of oxygen and azote in the atmosphere. Seguin's present task was to devise a convenient eudiometric method utilizing one of these processes; that is, an arrangement which would allow them rapidly and reliably to analyze samples of air drawn from the respiration chamber.[13]

"In the first experiments which M. Lavoisier and I made on respiration," Seguin recalled, "we would determine . . . the volume of vital air which our respirable gases contained" by introducing 12–15 cubic inches of the gas into a small jar, 3 inches in diameter and 6 inches in length, filled with mercury. They then passed into the jar, which was presumably also inverted over a basin of mercury, a piece of phosphorus in an iron capsule, igniting the phosphorus afterward by means of a much smaller piece of heated phosphorus placed on the end of a curved iron rod. When all of the phosphorus was burned, they introduced another piece and heated it until it vaporized. If it did not burn, that assured them that the first piece had "totally decomposed the vital air"—that is, that it had separated the oxygen from its caloric and combined with the former. The method was very accurate, but very inconvenient. When the sample was nearly pure vital air the jar often became so hot that it melted. They switched from crystal jars to jars made of green glass, but these sometimes cracked. When the sample was ordinary air these accidents did not occur, but the need to introduce successive pieces of phosphorus made the operation annoyingly tedious. By chance they discovered an easier way. Needing to analyze 100 cubic inches of air, which they could not put into the jar all at once, they introduced a 20-cubic-inch portion and ignited the phosphorus. After the combustion, the residue of air was only 1 cubic inch. In order to shorten the operation, they decided not to clean the jar before adding the second 20 inches of air. They assumed they would have to reignite the remaining phosphorus in the jar. "We were very astonished," Seguin wrote, "when we saw that our phosphorus began to burn as soon as it came in contact with the small bubbles which we allowed to pass into the jar." They continued to pass the rest of the 100 cubic inch sample into the jar, bubble by bubble, so as to prevent the temperature from rising too high. All of it was consumed. Afterward Seguin realized that the result had surprised them only because they had failed to reflect on the fact that previously when they had removed the residue of unburned phosphorus at the end of an analysis, it had ignited spontaneously when it made contact with the outside air. On the basis of this experience Seguin devised a eudiometer using a tube 1 inch in diameter and 8 in length. After introducing the phosphorus into the tube, he heated it by simply pressing a glowing piece of charcoal against it on the outside of the tube. Then he introduced the air to be analyzed in small portions, so as to maintain a continuous combustion.[14]

Neither Lavoisier nor Seguin indicated just how they applied the new eudiometric method in the respiration experiments. Presumably they determined the proportion of vital air contained in the gaseous mixture at the beginning of the experiment by analyzing a sample. After determining the volume change during the experiment in the customary way by marking the change in the level of the fluid in the respiration jar, they could submit all, or a measured portion, of the remaining volume to a second eudiometric analysis.

Because Lavoisier wished to "continue experiments over a long time and on the same animal," he could not simply place it in a closed chamber and leave it there until it showed signs of distress, as he had done in 1783. Neither could he resort to the more complicated open system he had used then, in which the oxygen was continually replaced and the carbonic acid swept out through alkali bottles, because that method had permitted the measurement only of the carbonic acid. The guinea pigs could remain in a closed jar for a long time without suffering, he and Seguin found, provided they "absorbed the carbonic acid as fast as it forms." To do this they floated a dish containing the caustic alkali on the surface of the fluid in which the respiration chamber was immersed. If the experiment lasted several days they had also to replace from time to time the vital air consumed, by additional measured quantities of that gas. Now that he intended to measure the oxygen rather than the carbonic acid, Lavoisier could immerse the respiration jar over water rather than over mercury, since the solubility of carbonic acid in water did not matter. Besides being easier to manage and less costly, water was less likely to harm the animal when they had to pass it through the liquid. Thus, while similar in principle to his old respiration experiments, those which Lavoisier pursued on animals in 1790 were different from them in almost every detail.[15]

The most dramatic of the new experiments were those carried out on human respiration. "As painful, disagreeable, and even dangerous as these experiments to which one had to submit oneself are," Lavoisier reported afterward with a flourish, "M. Seguin wished them to be carried out on himself."[16] Unfortunately, there is very little description available of the apparatus or procedures they used for this bold undertaking. The well-known drawings by Madame Lavoisier show her husband carrying out two experiments with Seguin as the subject (see Figures 20, 21). In one of them he and his assistants are measuring Seguin's respiration "in repose," in the other "while performing work." The drawings suggest a general excitement attending these occasions, and reveal that Seguin breathed through a face mask into a tube. The details of the equip-

Figure 20. Lavoisier and Seguin carrying out an experiment on respiration with subject in repose, as drawn by Madame Lavoisier. Seguin is seated at the far left, breathing into a face mask. Lavoisier stands at near right, manipulating a pneumatic vessel. Madame Lavoisier is at far right, recording the results. The three others who assisted in the experiment, one of whom is taking Seguin's pulse, are not identified. From Edouard Grimaux, *Lavoisier, 1743–1794* (Paris: Félix-Alcan, 1888), facing p. 122.

ment portrayed for measuring the oxygen consumption are, however, fanciful, and useless for elucidating the methods used.[17] Lavoisier did not describe the apparatus when he summarized the experiments afterward at the Academy, because he had brought it along instead for his audience to see for themselves. He mentioned only that "at each expiration the air is forced to bubble through caustic alkali, where it deposits its carbonic acid."[18] The far end of the tube must have been connected to a pneumatic chamber, from which the volume and oxygen content of the remaining air could be analyzed.

On November 13, 1790, Lavoisier sent a letter to Joseph Black, in which he summarized with evident pride the progress that he had made up until then in his new study of respiration.

> During his stay in Paris M. Gullan witnessed several experiments which I have carried out on respiration. We have ascertained the following facts:
>
> 1. The quantity of vital air or oxygen gas that a man at rest and in abstinence consumes, or rather converts into fixed air or car-

Figure 21. Lavoisier and Seguin carrying out an experiment on respiration with subject performing work. Seguin is seated in the center, breathing into a face mask and working a foot treadle. Lavoisier stands on near left, gesturing to an assistant. Madame Lavoisier is on the right, recording the results. Others are not identified. From Edouard Grimaux, *Lavoisier, 1743–1794* (Paris: Félix-Alcan, 1888), facing p. 128.

bonic acid, during an hour is about 1,200 French cubic inches, when he is placed in a temperature of 26 degrees.

2. That quantity increases to 1,400 cubic inches under the same circumstances, if the person is placed in a temperature of only 12 degrees.

3. The quantity of oxygen gas consumed, or converted into carbonic acid, increases during the time of digestion, rising to 1,800 or 1,900 cubic inches.

4. By movement and exercise one reaches as much as 4,000 cubic inches per hour, or even more.

5. The temperature of the body is in every case constant.

6. Animals can live in vital air or oxygen which is not renewed, for as long as one needs, provided that one has taken care to absorb the carbonic acid gas in caustic alkali solution; so that this gas [oxygen] does not require azotic gas, or mophette, in order to be healthful and fit for respiration.

7. Animals to not appear to suffer in a mixture of fifteen parts of azotic gas and one part of oxygen gas, provided that one has

> taken the precaution to absorb the carbonic acid gas in caustic alkali as rapidly as it forms.
>
> 8. The consumption of oxygen gas and its conversion into carbonic acid are the same in pure oxygen gas as they are in oxygen gas mixed with azotic gas in the same proportions as . . . [ordinary] air.
>
> 9. Animals live for quite a long time in a mixture of two parts of inflammable gas and one of oxygen gas.
>
> 10. Azotic gas does not serve any purpose in the act of respiration, and it leaves the lungs in the same quantity and condition as it entered.
>
> 11. When by exercise and movement one increases the consumption of oxygen gas in the lungs the circulation accelerates, of which one can easily convince oneself by the pulse beat, and, in general, when the person is breathing without hindrance, the quantity of oxygen consumed is proportional to the increase in the number of pulsations multiplied by the number of inspirations.
>
> It is very appropriate, monsieur, that you should be one of the first to be informed of the progress which is being made in a pathway which you have opened up, and in which we all regard ourselves as your disciples. We are pursuing the same experiments, and I shall have the honor of imparting to you my further discoveries.[19]

This austere factual report fully justifies the pride with which Lavoisier forwarded his news to Black; for it reveals that within less than a year he had been able to make several fundamental advances in his knowledge of the respiratory process. From the questions he answered we can infer what his investigative priorities had been. The evidence that azotic gas plays no role in respiration can be viewed as confirmation of the basic claim he had been making since 1777, that oxygen gas is the only respirable portion of the atmosphere. The main thrust of his investigation, however, was not to strengthen the support for his theory itself, as Laplace had once urged him to do. There were no new experiments involving measurements of the heat produced, or comparing respiration and other combustion processes; nor did he report additional data for his conclusion that water is formed. Taking all these as given, he was exploring the manner in which the rate of respiration varies under different environmental and physiological conditions. Although he suggested in his account of these experiments that they had carried out the ones on animals primarily to prepare themselves for the human measurements,[20] the above enumeration of their results makes clear that they did not examine comparable conditions in the two cases. With the guinea pig they tested mainly the effects of breathing in different gases and varying proportions of oxygen and azote. With Seguin they tested the effects of different physiological states. The only overlap was that in both subjects they compared the rates at two external temperatures. This was a prudent approach; subjecting an organism to abnormal atmospheres, whose physiological effects were not known in advance, carried the greatest risk to the respiring individual. Such experiments were tried out on animals, Lavoisier's praise of the dangers to which Seguin was willing to expose himself notwithstanding. A human, on the other hand, could best vary his activity as needed to examine methodically the influence of exercise.

Lavoisier's letter to Black affirms that at this stage he was in direct control of the research, whether personally participating in the operations or closely directing them; for he referred to them as "my" experiments, and did not even mention a collaborator. His closing remark that he regarded himself as a disciple of Black was undoubtedly a gesture inspired by the fact that he was responding to a letter in which Black had praised and announced his adoption of Lavoisier's chemistry in his teaching.[21] There is no reason to doubt, however, that Lavoisier genuinely appreciated that Black's unpublished but well-known view that respiration resembles combustion had been a germinal stimulus to the whole line of investigation which he himself had afterward taken up. He might also have had in mind that Black's identification of fixed air had been the starting point without which no chemical investigation or theory of respiration could have been successful.

By the time he sent the news of his investigation abroad, Lavoisier had already incorporated much of the same information into a memoir on animal respiration, which he presented to the Academy on the same day, November 13, that he wrote Black. In the memoir he described, with a few numerical differences, and scarcely more detail, the same results that he had compressed into his letter. Although he wished to convey the general experimental approach he was following vividly to the academicians, by showing them the apparatus he used, he intended to defer the description of individual experiments to later memoirs, so that he could focus for this occasion on their broader significance.[22] He first considered omitting altogether the discussion of the animal experiments, which "fully confirmed" his earlier results, leaving them for Seguin to describe to the Academy in a memoir of his own. On second thought, however, he included a few of the highlights of the new work. "I have already pointed out," he wrote,

> that the azotic gas is only a purely mechanical agent in the act of respiration, and that this gas comes back out of the lungs in the same quantity in which it had entered. We have confirmed this fact by a great number of experiments, whose exactitude we can guarantee.[23]

We can only guess that it must have been through eudiometric analyses of the gases before and after certain respiration measurements that they were able to determine that the quantity of azotic gas present did not change. At any rate, this confirmation of his view led Lavoisier to predict that one ought to be able to substitute for the azote in the respired gas any other gas which was not itself harmful to the animal. They found, in fact, that a guinea pig placed in a mixture of hydrogen gas with oxygen gas, in the same proportion that oxygen is normally present in the atmosphere, remained for several hours without appearing to suffer.[24]

If this result only confirmed what Lavoisier had long asserted, the measurements of the respiration of a guinea pig in pure vital air provided a surprise. Knowing that combustion is the more rapid the purer the vital air in which it occurs, he claimed, "one had always thought" that the rate of respiration would be similarly dependent on that variable. "But the experiment has destroyed all those opinions founded on nothing more than analogy." He and Seguin had kept guinea pigs for several days in pure vital air, and in vital air mixed with azote in varying proportions. They found not only that the animals consumed in every case the same quantity of vital air as in normal atmosphere, but that their breathing, circulation, and temperature remained normal.[25] Lavoisier himself had never publicly asserted that the rate of respiration varies in proportion to the vital air in the atmosphere. The most he had done was to assume, in an experiment in which a guinea pig respired in a closed chamber filled initially with vital air, that the animal might have produced more fixed air than normal at first, and less than normal toward the end as fixed air accumulated.[26] His less cautious follower Fourcroy had, however, as we have seen, built a pathological system on the proposition that respiration and all associated vital processes accelerate in proportion to the amount of vital air in the atmosphere.[27] Such theories must have appeared hasty even to their authors in the light of Lavoisier's new finding.

In all of the new experiments dealing with the variation of the rate of respiration under specified conditions, Lavoisier restricted his attention to the consumption of oxygen, or, as he put it to Black, the conversion of oxygen to carbonic acid. It was only to simplify the comparisons, however, that he was leaving out the formation of water. When he considered what the average human consumption of oxygen might be, he brought the full theory back into play. He thought that one could approximate the amount of oxygen consumed as a cubic foot per hour, or 2 pounds, 1 ounce, 1 gros in twenty-four hours, from which, he asserted, it is "easy to conclude that a man consumes 2 pounds, 5 ounces, 4 gros of carbonic acid, and 10 ounces, 5 gros, 51 grains of water." From the established compositions of water and of carbonic acid he then calculated that this meant that "respiration removes 10 ounces 4 gros of carbon and 1 ounce, 5 gros, 51 grains of hydrogen in twenty-four hours."[28] Lavoisier never did provide the data on which these computations were based. He had not reported any new experiments in which both the oxygen consumed and the carbonic acid formed were measured, so that we may well ask what the source for this conclusion was. The proportion of water to carbonic acid differs widely from the proportions he had calculated in 1785, suggesting that he did not simply return to the same old experiment that he had used then. It would be particularly interesting to know how he reached this result, because the new proportion of water to carbonic acid—about 1:3.7—appears to be based on a much more convincing difference between the oxygen consumed and that represented in the carbonic acid formed, in whatever measurements he now utilized, than the difference on which he had originally relied for his revised theory of the formation of water in respiration. (The published version of the memoir gives the quantity of water formed as 5 gros 51 grams, which would represent a ratio of only 1:400, scarcely distinguishable from experimental error. That figure is, however, evidently a typographical error, resulting from the omission of the "10 ounces.")

II

All of his previous discussions of respiration Lavoisier had grafted into memoirs dealing also with other problems: the combustion of mercury, combustion in general, the measurement of heat, and the changes in the quality of the air in public places. In his "Memoir on animal respiration" he wanted not only to report on his new research, but to integrate all of his thought and work on the subject into a unified point of view. He began with a long introduction that mentioned cursorily the contributions of Boyle, Hales, Black, Priestley, and Crawford to the subject, and summarized succinctly the stages in his own prior investigation. Then he expressed, in a memorable passage, the conception of the process that he had reached:

> Thus, to confine myself to simple ideas that everyone can grasp, I would say that animal respiration is nothing else but a slow combustion of carbon and hydrogen, which takes place in the lungs, and that from this point of view animals that respire are veritable lamps that burn and consume themselves.
>
> In respiration, as in combustion, it is the air of the atmosphere which furnishes the oxygen and the caloric. In respiration it is the blood which furnishes the combustible; and if animals do not regularly replenish through nourishment what they lose by respiration, the lamp will soon lack its oil; and the animals will perish, as a lamp is extinguished when it lacks its combustible.[29]

This spare, lucid summation, elegant in its use of the lamp metaphor, was far more than a recapitulation of Lavoisier's earlier ideas on the subject. In his memoir on heat, he had already grasped the basic condition for the existence of a living organism; that it is an open system in continuous exchange with its surroundings, and that it must therefore maintain a balance between supply and consumption. Then, however, he had limited this point of view to respiration as a means to restore the heat lost to the exterior. Now he expanded the conception of balance to include the exchanges of the material substance of the body. Nourishment must supply the carbon and hydrogen burned in respiration, just as caloric from the vital air consumed must supply the heat lost from the body. In this way he greatly broadened the meaning of respiration. It was no longer a matter just of the combustion of carbon and hydrogen supplied from the blood; the substance of the animal itself was consumed in respiration. Nourishment and respiration were part of one large process encompassing much of the "animal economy."

Lavoisier's insight that an animal must maintain a balance between the tangible substances and the heat which enter it and leave it was a physiological equivalent to his chemical balance sheets. Conceptually they differed in that in chemistry he assumed an equality between the substances present initially and the products of a chemical change which had a beginning and an end, whereas in physiology he was envisioning a continuous process. It was the *rate* at which heat, carbon, or hydrogen is absorbed into the body which must equal the rate at which it is lost from it. If he measured this rate by the total quantities absorbed and given off over a given length of time, however, the two principles reduced to the same kind of operation. Like his chemical principle, the physiological idea was not new. It can be traced back as far as the earliest surviving record of a physiological experiment, attributed by an unknown ancient author to the Hellenistic physician Erasistratus. If one placed a bird or other animal in a pot without food, "and then were to weigh it with the excrement that visibly has been passed, he will find that there has been a great loss of weight, plainly because, perceptible only to the reason, a copious emanation has taken place."[30] In the early seventeenth century Sanctorius had utilized the same principle in the famous daily measurements he made on himself, his food, and his excretions.[31] That this simple idea was still far from universally understood at the end of the eighteenth century, however, is conspicuous in the way that it eluded both Priestley and Girtanner, when they proposed theories of respiration which left the oxygen absorbed into the blood simply accumulating in the animal body. Just as Lavoisier brought new vitality to the chemical balance principle by pursuing it persistently in all of his analyses, so he gave life to the physiological principle by keeping it consistently in mind as he developed his theory of respiration.

The passages quoted above remind us that, for all the growth that his theory of respiration had undergone, it was still rooted in the analogy to other combustions. The form of the analogy had, however, shifted. Now that he knew that respiration formed water as well as carbonic acid, he could no longer identify it simply with the combustion of carbon; but a lamp burned oil, a substance which, he had conveniently learned in the meantime, is composed entirely of carbon and hydrogen. A few paragraphs further on, as he formulated a concise demonstration of his theory of respiration, he switched the comparison to the burning of a candle, another substance composed of carbon and hydrogen. Describing first the fact that a candle burning in air consumes about half its oxygen and replaces it with carbonic acid and water, he added, "By adding the weight of the candle burned to that of the oxygen gas consumed, one obtains a quantity precisely equal to that of the carbonic acid and the water which have formed." He continued,

> The respiration of an animal under a glass jar produces exactly the same alterations in the atmospheric air: . . . a portion of the oxygen gas decomposes and forms carbonic acid and water.
>
> But oxygen gas can be converted to carbonic acid only by the addition of *charbon*. It can be converted to water only by the addition of hydrogen. This double combination cannot take place without the loss by the oxygen gas of a portion of its caloric. It follows that the effect of respiration is to exact from the lung, or rather from the blood which traverses it, a portion of carbon and of hydrogen, and to deposit in its place a portion of caloric, which instead of being disengaged in the form of free fire, as in combustion, is distributed with the blood, by the circulation, into all parts of the animal economy, and which supports the nearly constant heat that one observes in all animals that respire.[32]

By itself this was a brilliant restatement and qualitative justification of Lavoisier's theory of respiration. In its connections with the preceding description of the burning of a candle, and with the paragraphs likening respiration to a lamp, we can discern the continuing stimulation of metaphorical "interactions" on his thought. He was, in the first place, able to maintain the close identification between respiration and a particular combustion even after revising his theory of respiration, by shifting his point of reference from carbon to oil or wax. Beyond that, however, we can see that the analytical investigations he had carried out during the intervening years on the substances which comprised the other side of this form of the analogy might well have helped prepare him to broaden his conception of respiration so as to encompass the material balance of the animal. It was during his efforts to determine the precise composition of wax and of oil in 1785 that he had worked particularly to establish the weight balances between the combustibles and oxygen consumed, and the carbonic acid and water formed. The results of those efforts seem directly reflected in his statement above concerning the weights involved in a burning candle. Although the balance in animals may be implied in the commonplace fact that they do not ordinarily gain or lose weight, and that the substances consumed in respiration must come from the nourishment, Lavoisier had no specific knowledge that the carbon and hydrogen exhaled in the carbonic acid and water are furnished from the same quantity of those elements in the nourishment an animal receives. What he had was evidence that the same process is involved in respiration as in burning candles or oil, from which he could infer that there must be a supply of carbon and hydrogen equivalent to the wax of the candle or the oil of the lamp. It was, in a sense, by thinking of candles and oils as "nourishment" for a combustion that Lavoisier was able to connect the respiration of animals with their nutrition. It may have been because he had so often treated the combustion of these substances as an investigative problem of balancing the substances present before and after the operation that he could come to perceive in respiration the problem of how an animal maintains a balance between the consumption of substances in the lungs and the replenishment of these substances in nutrition.

Perhaps Lavoisier did not always regard these comparisons as mere analogies, but tended to think of respiration literally as the burning of an oil in the lungs. In the passage quoted above he may really have meant that "animals that respire are veritable lamps that burn," even though other parts of the same two paragraphs seem to separate respiration from such combustions. In a later portion of the memoir he wrote:

> I might go further . . . and show how there operates in the organs which secrete the chyle a veritable fermentation; how there is separated from the aliments by digestion carbonated hydrogen, which combines with the blood, in order to be evacuated afterward in the lungs. But I would be anticipating other memoirs in which I intend to develop the phenomena of nutrition.[33]

This extraordinary remark shows us how far Lavoisier allowed himself to speculate about the manner in which respiration, digestion, and nutrition form a complete chemical system. He needed only to invoke a special form of fermentation, producing the "carbonated hydrogen" from aliments—a process he may have imagined to be reducible to a chemical equation equivalent to the one he had established for alcoholic fermentation—in order to envision the entire passage of the combustible matter from the stomach through the blood to the place where it burned. The process was scarcely more mysterious than the passage of the oil in an oil lamp from its reservoir to the site of the flame. When we remember in addition that he thought oils were composed of carbon and hydrogen, and that all plant and animal matters were based on a radical containing carbon and hydrogen, we can readily imagine that in his mind he sometimes verged on identifying respiration literally with the burning of an oil lamp. Yet he characteristically drew back from his boldest conjectures. In the *Elementary Treatise* he had argued that plant and animal matter does not contain oil itself, but only its elements.[34] Here he prudently eliminated the above passage. He left it ambiguous whether his comparison between respiration and the lamp was a metaphor or something more, and he offered no description of the form in which, or the chemical process by which, the carbon and hydrogen of respiration enter the blood.

The writing and deletion of this passage are a fine example of the interplay between Lavoisier's inventive scientific imagination, which ranged far beyond the demonstrable results of the investigations he had carried out, and a critical control that restrained him in most cases from giving free public run to that imagination. The combination enabled him to set his sights on distant goals, and usually protected him at the same time from undermining his present position.

III

From his letter to Black we can see that in the experiments on human respiration Lavoisier was mainly concerned to compare the respiratory rates under such conditions as abstinence and digestion, rest and exercise. In his memoir he suggested that he and Seguin were induced to orient the investigation in this way by incidental observations they had made during the preliminary experiments with guinea pigs. "We noticed," he wrote, "that respiration was accelerating during digestion, and that the animals were consuming more air; and we had equally begun to see that movement and agitation were augmenting these effects still more: but we were far from contented with such indecisive experiments."[35] They therefore tested these effects on the respiration of Seguin, who could deliberately control his state of nourishment and his movements. It is not clear how they arranged for Seguin to perform a measurable quantity of exercise. Lavoisier's memoir indicates that Seguin did work equivalent to lifting a fifteen-pound weight to a given height,[36] whereas Madame Lavoisier's drawing shows him working a foot treadle. Neither description is detailed enough to ascertain whether the treadle was linked to a mechanism that lifted a weight. However they may have contrived the technical details of these experiments, the outcome strikingly confirmed the expectations they had formed from their casual observations on the animals. "Movement and exercise," Lavoisier reported, "considerably augment all of these proportions." That is, in separate comparisons made during digestion and abstinence, the oxygen consumption was in both cases considerably higher when Seguin exercised than when he rested. For the case of abstinence, "M. Seguin having lifted a weight of fifteen pounds to a height of 613 feet during a quarter of an hour, his consumption of air during the same time was elevated to 800 cubic inches, that is to say, to 3,200 cubic inches per hour." Under the same conditions at rest, his consumption was only 1,210 cubic inches per hour. When he did the same amount-of work while digesting, he reached a consumption of 4,600 cubic inches per hour.[37]

Although "the temperature of the blood" remained constant when Seguin did this work, his pulse rate and his breathing "varied in a very remarkable manner." Lavoisier believed, in fact, that they had discovered two important laws: that the pulse rate increased in direct proportion to the total weight which a person lifted to a given height; and that the vital air consumed was directly proportional to the product of the pulse rate and the frequency of inspirations. These laws seemed sufficiently constant to him so that he asserted that by observing the acceleration of the circulation which resulted when a person exercised strenuously, one could calculate the "weight lifted to a given height which would be equivalent to the sum of the efforts he has made." One could compare in this way the "force" expended in activities which seemed to have no relation, such as reading or writing. "One could even evaluate," he declared, "what there is of a mechanical [measure] in the work of a philosopher who reflects, of a scholar who writes, of a musician who plays a piece of a symphony."[38] Lavoisier had once again captured a grand new vision.

If we accept literally Lavoisier's account of the course of his investigation, his momentous new insight connecting respiration with work emerged as an unanticipated development out of chance observations. Interested in measuring the consumption of oxygen under a variety of conditions, he and Seguin happened to notice that two of the conditions that seemed to influence the respiration of the animals serving as their subjects were digestion and unusually active movements. Exploring these effects under better-controlled conditions with Seguin as the subject, they found that both effects were significant. The effect of exercise was, in fact, far more marked than any other—far larger than the effect of external temperature, in contrast to what they would have expected from the basic theory that respiration replaces the heat lost to the surroundings. In this way Lavoisier came to appreciate that respiration must somehow be related to *travail* (work) as well as to animal heat. Because of his alertness to exploit the chance observation, therefore, he came to extend his theory of respiration in a direction not predictable from the existing theory.

We may immediately suspect, however, that there must be more below the surface; that some prior expectation had led Lavoisier to perceive the connection between the behavior of his guinea pigs and their breathing rates. As Karl Popper has vividly put it, to observe at all one "needs a chosen object, a definite task, an interest, a point of view, a problem."[39] There were any number of chance observations that Lavoisier might have made about the guinea pigs. Clearly, even if he was not actively looking for the particular connections he saw, they fell within a general "horizon of expectations." We may recall, in fact, that when he had first begun to think about respiration, back in 1775, it had already occurred to him that "it would be able to lead us to glimpse the cause of the movement of animals."[40] Even if he had totally forgotten about this old idea, the fact that he had once perceived the possibility of such a connection suggests that he was in some sense prepared in advance to notice it in these experiments carried out fifteen years later.

The fact that Lavoisier was able to convert the general notion of a connection between movement and respiration into a concrete test of the effect of a specific measure of muscular effort upon the respiratory rate suggests that he also had an appreciation for the special significance of the product of a weight and the height to which it is raised. Such a quantity had already been formalized in mechanics as an expression for a "force" equivalent to the *vis viva*, or force, of a body in motion. The product of the mass of a body and the height to which it would rise in consuming its *vis viva* was equal to the product of its mass and the square of its initial upward velocity. It happens that, in 1783, Lazare Carnot, a mathematician and engineer ten years younger than Lavoisier, had restated this relationship, calling MgH (where M = the total mass of a system, g = the force of gravity, and H = the height of rise or fall) the "moment of activity exerted by a force." According to Charles Gillispie, Carnot had converted this old expression in all but name to the conception later designated as "work." His purpose was to analyze the operation and the capacity of machines, considered as devices for transmitting motions.[41]

Lavoisier's use of the height to which Seguin lifted a weight appears to embody a similar general conception of the meaning of that quantity. At one point he equated the "weight lifted to a given height" with the "sum of the efforts"[42] Seguin had made, language resembling that of Carnot. It is just possible that Lavoisier might have been aware of the analysis Carnot submitted to the academy in an essay of 1783 on this subject. The difficulty with this interpretation is that Carnot's ideas made almost no impact until he returned to the subject long afterward. Moreover, it is not necessary to invoke so specific an influence, for Carnot was not so much discovering a new relation as giving formal expression to one that Gillispie has found was intuitively known to many people involved in technical activity involving machines during the late eighteenth century.[43] Lavoisier was probably aware of these relations through his general participation in that milieu. In order to apply them to his situation he needed mainly to perceive the human or animal body as a type of machine converting one form of motion to another. We can, in fact, surmise that the reason Lavoisier stressed the direct proportion he thought he had found between the "acceleration of the circulation" (the pulse rate), and the performance of work, while connecting the consumption of oxygen only indirectly with the work, was that circulation, and exercise in general, as forms of motion, fell in principle within the range of problems that Carnot and others had treated. There was no precedent available to extend such conversions of forces to include chemical processes. Although Lavoisier obviously knew the fundamental discovery was that the respiratory combustion itself increased in exercise, he had no conceptual means to express a direct causal connection between these two phenomena.

Almost as striking as Lavoisier's discovery itself was the long latent period between the time he first had the idea that respiration may be related to the cause of motion, and the time he first examined that possibility. For fifteen years he was completely silent about it. We cannot tell whether he finally remembered to take up what he had long ago had in mind, or whether the same idea occurred to him anew after he had lost sight of the original one. Whichever was the case, the explanation lies, I believe, in the fact that the whole recent history of respiration had imposed a pattern of thought that had no place for such a connection. The very comparison with combustion, which had stimulated so fruitfully the study of respiration, had restricted the viewpoint of those who pursued that analogy until it became an identity. The central defining property of combustions was that they released heat. Therefore, those like Priestley, Crawford, and Lavoisier, who studied respiration, fixed their attention on its corresponding property. Lavoisier had not only to define a category of "slow" combustion which did not produce immediately sensible heat, but to devise a means to measure the heat it did release, and he elevated the equivalence between the heats released in combustion and respiration to the status of his primary proof that respiration *is* a combustion.

In retrospect we can see that this preoccupation fostered a one-sided conception of the significance of respiration, that its *function* was to provide animal heat. The situation was an example of what Gaston Bachelard has tried to illuminate with his "notion of an *epistemological obstacle*." The very success of a given mode of thought or investigation makes it difficult to perceive or proceed in a different manner. In order to go beyond such boundaries, "the well-constructed mind must be reconstructed."[44] Lavoisier, the person who had done most of all to establish a theory of respiration based on its identity with combustion, was now the first to break the closed circle of identifications. How was he able to remove the "obstacle" that he himself had helped to raise? Part of the explanation may be in the fact that by 1790 his earlier endeavors to demonstrate the correspondence between respiration and combustion were for him solved problems. Although the addition of the formation of water to his theory had diminished the force of the conclusions he and Laplace had reached in the "Memoir on heat" from the comparison of the heat of combustion and respiration, Lavoisier showed no sign that he wished to reopen that question. Although respiration as the source of animal heat was still fundamental to his theory, that conception had now receded to the status of "acquired" background knowledge. He was now fixing his attention on previously unexplored effects upon respiration, and therefore freer to move beyond the bounds of the standard pattern of thought. Once he had entertained the connection between respiration and movement again, the new experimental results strongly reinforced it for him. The increase in Seguin's oxygen consumption when he sat in a colder medium, presumably requiring him to produce more heat to replace the greater losses, was noticeable but modest: a difference of fourteen degrees in temperature provoked a rise from 1,210 cubic inches of vital air per hour to 1,344 cubic inches. When Seguin lifted a weight for fifteen minutes, however, his consumption shot up to more than double his resting rate. After that dramatic result Lavoisier could hardly have avoided thinking of respiration as connected in some fundamental sense to *travail.*

These developments undoubtedly lowered the conceptual barriers Lavoisier had to cross to see respiration as more than the source of animal heat, but do not fully account for his ability to surmount the obstacle of an established pattern of thought. Nor could his metaphors have helped in this situation. The oil lamp and the candle do no mechanical work. He therefore had to transcend his metaphors as well as his literal interpretations of the past. Behind his achievement there is a residue of brilliant creative imagination that cannot be reduced to the influence of circumstances.

Lavoisier saw intuitively that respiration, which "is consuming at each instant a portion of the substance of the individual,"[45] is intimately connected with the "labor," the "activity," and the nourishment of the individual. He did not, and could not, formulate that relationship in the manner that it was formulated fifty years later, as a conversion of chemical energy to mechanical work; because it was during that interval that scientists gradually came to think in terms of processes in which one type of "force" is converted to another type, and to include "chemical force," as well as heat, among those conversions.[46] Such was Lavoisier's prescience, however, that when the chemists of that later era read his memoir, he appeared to them to have formulated the germinal statements of the principle that respiratory combustions are the source of "force" as well as heat. Jean-Baptiste Dumas, whose famous *Essay on the Chemical Statics of Organized Beings* of 1841 was inspired by Lavoisier's memoirs on respiration, probably read him that way.[47] In that sense Lavoisier's insight may have had a delayed impact somewhat like the work of Mendel.

IV

Combining the two new developments of his theory of respiration—that it increases with work, and must be balanced by nourishment—with the older view that respiration is the source of animal heat, Lavoisier was able to survey with breathtaking clarity how "compensations" among these interlocked processes permit humans to preserve an equilibrium under widely varying circumstances. In cold climates respiration accelerates, replacing the lost heat, while evaporative transpiration decreases. In hot surroundings these changes are reversed. When a person is inactive, he respires less, consumes less carbon and hydrogen, and requires less nourishment. When he labors and consumes more, he must digest more as well.[48] In one of the most quotable passages of his memoir on respiration he summed up these effects:

> The animal machine is therefore governed mainly by three types of regulators: respiration, which consumes hydrogen and carbon, and furnishes caloric; digestion, which replenishes, through the organs which secrete chyle, that which is lost in the lungs; transpiration, which augments or diminishes according as it is necessary to carry off more or less caloric.[49]

Lavoisier was characteristically eager to display the social relevance of his new theoretical synthesis. He noted with irony the fact that "the poor man who lives by the work of his hands, and is obliged to employ all of the force that nature has given him to earn his subsistence," must then consume more food than the idle wealthy person who can enjoy the abundance that is "physically necessary for the laboring man."[50] He did not dwell on this inequity, however, so much as on the implications of his view for health and disease. There is a limit to the compensations that the three regulatory mechanisms can maintain. If an individual consumes more hydrogen and carbon than his digestion can replace, he is subject not only to fatigue, but to "violent illnesses." If he eats too much, his respiration accelerates to remove the excess carbon and hydrogen in his blood, but if that is not enough to restore the equilibrium, he may fall victim to "putrid maladies and malignant fevers."[51] Thus Lavoisier was not immune to the penchant of his age for deducing broad medical consequences directly from a new physiological finding. By comparison with other medical systems of the time, however, his speculative excess was rather mild. His enthusiasm to demonstrate the social applicability of his science had from time to time broken through his generally critical spirit in the past. The need to appear serviceable to society in the new revolutionary era did not lessen such tendencies.

Almost as though to bring himself back down to earth after these visionary flights, Lavoisier then made an extraordinarily candid admission:

> I do not in any way conceal from myself an objection that one could make, and that I have made to myself, against the theory whose principal consequences I have just presented. There is no experiment that pronounces in a decisive manner whether the carbonic acid gas that is disengaged from the lungs during expiration is formed by the combination of the oxygen of the air with the car-

> bon of the blood; or whether instead that carbonic acid is already formed in the blood, and is in some way precipitated or disengaged by the oxygen gas of the air. The experiments which I have begun on digestion would seem to support the latter opinion; for an alimentary mass disengages a large quantity of carbonic acid gas just at the time that it is converted into chyle; and if it does not pass into the blood, one cannot see what its use is.
>
> There remain for me also uncertainties concerning the true quantity of water that is formed in respiration. Finally, I have not yet been able to determine whether or not in nature oxygen combines with the blood during respiration. I hope that the experiments I am planning will remove all these uncertainties. Perhaps I shall be obliged to make some modifications in the doctrine that I have presented in this manner. I shall not hestitate to modify my opinions, even to reverse my steps, if new experiments force me to abandon the first course that I have followed.[52]

Surely these are two of the most interesting, and most attractive, paragraphs Lavoisier ever wrote. He was at the time at the peak of his scientific success. The "assent of almost every physicist and chemist in Europe" was giving him ever greater confidence that the "truths" he had established in chemistry "have received the sanction of time."[53] He had not only won the allegiance of the ablest senior chemists in Paris, but gathered around him a coterie of younger men ready to follow him on the major issues of his science. He was, in short, in a position to support his scientific views not only with rational arguments and evidence, but with the great weight of his personal authority. At such a time, he was able to reassess a theory of respiration in which he had invested a decade and a half of thought and research, whose significance had become broader than ever through his most recent work, with sufficient detachment to call its entire structure into serious question. He did so because he had made a new observation that revealed to his open mind that he might have fundamentally misinterpreted his previous findings.

We should not underestimate the depth of Lavoisier's challenge to his own theory. The question he raised was not merely whether the carbonic acid of respiration is formed in the lungs or elsewhere, as Lagrange had contended. Lavoisier was entertaining the possibility that respiration was not even a combustion; that oxygen did not combine with carbon to form carbonic acid, but merely displaced carbonic acid that had entered the blood fully formed from the food. If that were so, there would be no more comparison to a burning lamp or candle, no more explanation for animal heat. There would be only a displacement of one gas by another, the significance of the exchange remaining quite unknown. Having acknowledged this crucial "objection," he went on to admit—what has been evident to us all along—that his calculation of the quantity of water formed during respiration was far from secure. Lavoisier retained, in the midst of the adulation he was now receiving, not only the capacity to doubt his long-held conclusions, but the courage to confess his doubts publicly to his peers in the Academy of Sciences.

This passage is also important for the information it includes that Lavoisier was undertaking a new kind of investigation, extending his interest in the "animal economy" experimentally, as well as theoretically, to the process of digestion. This was a marked departure from the range of research problems on which he had concentrated for the past seventeen years. We can readily see how the expansion of his conception of respiration brought the physiological problem of digestion for the first time into his domain of interests. To embark on a direct investigation of the chemical changes occurring within alimentary material during its passage through the digestive tract was nevertheless a bold venture into a new field for him; bolder even than his earlier excursion into the study of vegetation. This is the only reference to the specific nature of Lavoisier's experiments on digestion that I have been able to find. We can tell little, therefore, about the methods he used or the scope of his new investigation. At the very least it displayed the buoyant spirit of a man, heavily burdened with other duties, who still looked forward to new conquests in his cherished laboratory.

If Lavoisier possessed the critical insight to doubt his own theoretical positions, he was too optimistic to be long assailed by his doubts. Even before he read the above passage to the Academy he tacked onto it a reaffirmation of faith: "But I hope to reach a termination, and I believe that I am not far away from it; and that after having eliminated all the uncertainties, the true theory of respiration will no longer leave anything to be desired."[54]

On December 28 Joseph Black answered the letter in which Lavoisier had outlined the results of his respiration experiments. "The facts you have already ascertained relating to respiration," he wrote, "are especially interesting and make me hope for some important and capital discovery to be the result of your investigation. I shall esteem your early communication of them a very great favour."[55] When he received Black's remarks Lavoisier may have wondered why his distinguished colleague did not regard the results he had just communicated to him as important discoveries, but he would probably have agreed with Black that the best was yet to come.

V

One week after Lavoisier read his memoir on respiration he had it signed and certified by Tillet, the treasurer of the Academy: an unusual step to take *after* he had presented it publicly. Sometime after that, he rewrote the entire memoir in his own hand. In the original version he had inserted a note recognizing the crucial assistance of Seguin. In the revision he elevated Seguin to the status of co-author. After some hesitation about the order in which to list their names, he settled on "MM. Seguin and Lavoisier."[56] Throughout the text he changed phrases which had read "I have" done or thought, to "we have . . . " Had Lavoisier decided to be generous, or had Seguin complained that he had not received enough credit? Perhaps this change points to one of the earliest examples of the difficulties that have repeatedly arisen since then over how to allot recognition between the director of a laboratory who designs an investigation, provides the theoretical foundation, and writes the paper derived from it, and the assistant who performs a large share of the practical operations.[57] It is unfortunate that we cannot know more of the circumstances behind this telltale shift.

There was an additional motive for this change, based not on what had been done, but on grander plans for the future. Lavoisier also changed the title of the paper to "First memoir on the respiration of animals," and inserted following his review of the prior development of the subject, "Such was the state of our knowledge at the time that M. Seguin and I undertook a very extended investigation of the animal economy." He then modified this sentence to read ". . . at the time we formed the plan for a very extended investigation on almost all parts of the animal economy."[58] Evidently in the wake of his successful experiments on respiration Lavoisier was enlarging his horizons, and taking the person he had previously regarded as an assistant into full partnership. Retrospectively he portrayed his expanded goals as a plan he and Seguin together had deliberately set out in advance. Seguin's prior role was therefore also enhanced after the fact. In another added paragraph Lavoisier recognized Seguin's memoir on respiration of 1790: "M. Seguin adopted the various assertions [that Lavoisier had made since 1777 on the subject] and pulled them together in a memoir that he read to the Society of Medicine . . . "[59] By the time the published version of this statement appeared in 1793, Seguin's paper was treated as more than a review of the subject. "M. Seguin," it now read, "gave new development to this theory, and he confirmed it by new experiments in a memoir that he read to the Society of Medicine."[60] Both retrospectively and prospectively, Seguin's part in Lavoisier's venture was looming ever larger.

If these changes have a special sociological interest, others Lavoisier made in revising his memoir have a deeper intellectual significance. It is hardly surprising that he did not rest content with his statement of doubt about his whole enterprise in respiration. Working these paragraphs over, he at first merely softened the doubt. Retaining the basic admission that no experiment had established whether oxygen combines with carbon in the lungs or merely disengages preformed carbonic acid, he dropped the description of his experiments on digestion and the view that they supported the latter alternative. Instead he wrote only that "experiments that we intend to carry out on digestion will probably clarify this doubt." The second paragraph he left intact for the time being, except that he associated Seguin with the "uncertainties" that had previously been his alone.[61]

This minor modification did not long satisfy Lavoisier. He crossed out the section of the first paragraph posing the two alternatives he had outlined, as well as the entire second paragraph. To his opening sentence acknowledging objections that he did not conceal from himself, the beginning of the next sentence, "There is no experiment that pronounces in a decisive manner whether the carbonic acid gas that is disengaged [he deleted here "from the lungs"] during expiration is formed . . . ," he appended instead:

> immediately in the lungs, or during the course of the circulation by the combination of the oxygen of the air with the carbon of the blood. It would be possible that a portion of this carbonic acid was formed by digestion [he then wrote, but crossed out, "and by the decomposition of the aliments in the intestinal canal, that it circulates with the blood"], that it is introduced into the circulation with the chyle; finally that, having reached the lungs, it is disengaged from the blood in proportion as the oxygen combines with it [the blood] by means of a greater affinity.[62]

In making these successive changes, Lavoisier deftly transformed the "objections" he had earlier raised, from a deadly threat to his theory of respiration, to a benign readjustment. He still accepted as a real possibility that the carbonic acid he had found arising from the aliments undergoing digestion enters the blood and is exhaled; but he reduced the process to a secondary effect, accounting at most for a portion of the carbonic acid disengaged. He obviously did not base this conclusion on a quantitative comparison between the carbonic acid formed in digestion and that expired from the lungs. Rather it appears he simply decided that he could not let an objection deduced from a preliminary observation in a nascent physiological investigation of digestion upset a theory in which he had many strong reasons to maintain his belief. The episode might have amounted to a mere passing qualm that he overcame by his resolve not to be diverted from his path, except for the fact that in the course of disarming the objection he acquired a new perspective concerning an assumption he had held without visible question since he first began to think about respiration.

Having questioned whether the carbonic acid exhaled from the lungs is formed there, Lavoisier came to see that the alternative might be not that it is preformed in the blood all along, but that it is formed in the blood during the course of its circulation. There would then be a combustion after all, even if there was no experimental evidence that it takes place "immediately in the lungs." With that realization he gave up his simple presupposition that a respiratory combustion, like any other combustion, occurs where the combustible "immediately" encounters the oxygen, and accepted that the situation might be more complex than he had imagined.

After subduing the most dangerous of his "objections," Lavoisier must have felt less concern also over the other "uncertainties" he had raised. Recasting the second paragraph, he no longer mentioned the specific problem of how much water forms in respiration. He wrote only that the experiments he and Seguin were undertaking on digestion and on transpiration would probably lift whatever "uncertainties still remain with us on this subject." The open admission in the original paragraph that he might be forced to reverse his course now became more like an ideological assertion. If they were forced to "bring some changes to the doctrine" they were presenting, he now declared loftily, "these modifications of the initial ideas cost nothing to those who search for the truth for its own sake and with no other desire than to find it."[63]

Lavoisier's statements in the published form of the two paragraphs whose development we have followed have sometimes been interpreted as a manifestation of a continuing uncertainty over the location of the respiratory combustion. Much has been made of the controversy over the "site of respiration" in which his contemporaries and successors engaged, and Lavoisier himself has been portrayed as immersed in this question. Charles Culotta has most explicitly called it a "difficult problem for the French chemist." Lavoisier was, according to Culotta, "deeply concerned with his lung-site hypothesis."[64] The foregoing account suggests a far different interpretation. Lavoisier proposed no lung site "hypothesis." From 1774 until he raised the above "objections," he appears neither to have doubted, nor to have felt the need to support, the idea that the combustion occurs "immediately" in the lungs. He seems simply not to have imagined the situation in any other way. Now that his deeper questions about his theory led him to see that there had never been any experimental evidence for the assumption, he evinced no strong attachment to it. Whether he was influenced by Lagrange's argument or those of Girtanner and others we cannot say, for he did not mention them. At any rate, he went back to the general statement of his theory of respiration that he had retained in his rewritten draft, and struck out the phrase "which takes place in the lungs." That simple gesture symbolizes, I believe, how readily this willful yet flexible thinker could change his point of view when he found persuasive reasons to do so.

As he rewrote, and then modified further, the general statement of his theory of respiration Lavoisier made other small but important refinements. Eliminating the specific description of the combustion of a candle, he moved the paragraph "proving" his theory into juxtaposition with the two paragraphs comparing respiration to a lamp. He connected them by means of a new transition sentence, "The proofs of the identity between the effects of respiration and the combustion of oil can be deduced immediately from experiment."[65] Perhaps sensing that he was identifying respiration too literally with burning oil, he deleted the specification "of oil" from this sentence.[66] Subtle changes in the first two paragraphs also enhanced the metaphorical character of his comparison between an animal and a lamp. In their final form these finely crafted three paragraphs have stood as the cornerstone for the theory of respiration that has ever since Lavoisier guided investigation in that field:

> Starting from acquired knowledge, and confining ourselves to simple ideas which everyone can readily grasp, we would say to begin with, in general, that respiration is only a slow combustion of carbon and hydrogen, which is similar in every way to what takes place in a lamp or illuminated candle; and that from this point of view animals that respire are true combustible bodies which burn and consume themselves.
>
> In respiration, as in combustion, it is the air of the atmosphere which furnishes the oxygen and the caloric; but in respiration, it is the very substance of the animal, it is the blood, which furnishes the combustible; if animals do not regularly replenish through nourishment what they lose by respiration, the lamp will soon lack its oil; and the animal will perish, as a lamp is extinguished when it lacks nourishment.
>
> The proofs of this identity between the effects of respiration and of combustion can be deduced immediately from experiments. In fact, the air which has served for respiration no longer contains the same quantity of oxygen when it leaves the lungs; it includes not only carbonic acid gas, but, in addition, much more water than it contained before being inspired. Now, since vital air can be converted into carbonic acid gas only by an addition of carbon; and it can be converted into water only by the addition of hydrogen; and this double combination can take place only if the vital air loses a part of its specific caloric; it follows from this that the effect of respiration is to extract from the blood a portion of carbon and of hydrogen, and to deposit in its place a portion of its specific caloric, which, during the circulation, is distributed to all parts of the animal economy, and maintains that nearly constant temperature which one observes in all animals that respire.[67]

This succinct yet comprehensive statement highlights the qualities that made Lavoisier one of the most brilliant theorists in the history of biological thought. It focused unerringly on the general and essential features of the theory. It is as impressive for what it avoided as for what it included. Even though Seguin was nominally a joint author, neither these paragraphs nor the memoir as a whole bears any trace of the ideas with which Seguin had embellished Lavoisier's theory of respiration in his own previous writing. From the paragraph that Lavoisier had temporarily put in on the formation of "carbonated hydrogen" in digestion, we can see that he was tempted by Seguin's specification of the form in which the carbon and hydrogen burned in respiration exist in the blood—may in private have accepted it. But he had the wisdom to suppress that idea from his public presentation. Nor did Lavoisier follow Seguin's lead in attempting to integrate his theory with Crawford's theory of the distribution of animal heat. More secure in his own scientific judgment, the senior partner in this new joint venture had less need to fit his views into frameworks provided by others.

The omission of Seguin's version of Lavoisier's theory of respiration from the joint memoir highlights the fact that of all those who entered discussions of the topic, Lavoisier was the most successful at not getting mired in speculative debate over the internal locations or mechanisms through which the process takes place. Having now seen that there was no decisive experimental evidence to determine where in the body the combustions occur, he had made his theory more independent than ever of such conjectures. That does not mean that his theory of respiration was a purely chemical one. Lavoisier provided a profoundly physiological interpretation of the functional meaning of respiration; but it was an interpretation restricted to general principles that would be applicable no matter what the details of the internal mechanisms might turn out to be. That is one of the reasons that his theory endured long after the contributions to it made by his less critical followers had disappeared. As in so many situations before, Lavoisier demonstrated in this culminating statement of his theory of respiration that he dominated his scientific landscape as much by his appreciation for the limits of analysis as by his analytical mastery within those limits.

Lavoisier's theory of respiration was durable even though he was never able to ground it firmly in "proven facts." Laplace's advice to multiply the experiments purporting to demonstrate the identity between respiration and combustion still went unfulfilled. That demonstration had, in fact, lost even the force it once held, after Lavoisier revised his theory to include the formation of water. Far from regarding the quantity of heat produced by his guinea pig in the old experiments as equal to that produced by charcoal in forming the same amount of carbonic acid, he was now arguing that "animals disengage a greater quantity of caloric in a given time than that which should have resulted from the quantity of carbonic acid gas which their respiration produces in an equal time." The formation of water "explains that phenomenon perfectly,"[68] he claimed. To explain a discrepancy, however, is not to replace the proof which the presumed equality had been thought to provide before Lavoisier perceived the discrepancy as real. Moreover, the argument for the formation of water was itself still insecure. Even if the new calculation of the proportion of water to carbonic acid formed implies that it may have been based on a more substantial discrepancy between the oxygen consumed and that found in the carbonic acid formed than his original calculation had shown, he had yet to describe the experimental results from which he derived the new figures. Lavoisier's assertion that the expired air contains more water vapor than ordinary air was so general as to suggest that it did not rest on specific measurements. The carbon and hydrogen which the theory required the blood to furnish were still not identified in tangible form. Lavoisier was only being prudent, therefore, when he referred consistently to his *theory* of respiration.

What then distinguishes Lavoisier's "theory" of respiration from the "speculations" of his contemporaries other than our hindsight judgment that he was right and they were not? Their views were not devoid of experimental support, and his views were not fully supported by experiment. There is probably no ironclad methodological "demarcation principle" with which we can place his theory in a different category from the competing views. If we cannot define a difference in such terms, however, I think we can recognize a difference which does not rely on their respective degrees of contemporary influence or on their ultimate fates. The difference is not a matter of being more or less correct, or of being experimental rather than speculative. Doing our best to immerse ourselves in the context of the time, to free ourselves as far as we can from our presentist bias, we still discern the tighter control over the reasoning, the more purposeful ordering of investigations, the ability to focus on the essential and to discount the secondary, which appears to mark his contributions as superior to most of what others were saying and doing within the same domain. Lavoisier did not have a special access to the truth of the matter, denied to less talented contemporaries; but he did appear to have a firmer grip on the requirements for disciplined creative research.

By the time he rewrote his memoir on respiration, Lavoisier could report that he and Seguin were beginning experiments on transpiration, as well as on digestion.[69] Their research was now, in effect, covering all three of the "principal regulators" of the animal machine whose integrated actions Lavoisier had discussed theoretically. As suggested above, despite an assertion he added afterward to his memoir, he probably did not map out at the beginning a systematic plan to study the whole of the "animal economy." Rather, his point of view and his range of interests evolved as a natural outgrowth of the course of his research. He entered the field of digestion not as a separate research problem, but because the implications of his theory of respiration spread until they encompassed digestion as well, raising questions for him that he could answer only by extending his experiments in the same direction. Transpiration was also a problem that imposed itself on him because of the theoretical implications of respiration, and because of a striking result he encountered in his respiration experiments. In spite of the fact that the consumption of oxygen, the arterial pulse, and the frequency of breathing all increased dramatically in exercise, the "temperature of the blood remained nearly constantly the same, at least to within a few fractions of a degree."[70] An obvious corollary of his theory of respiration, however, was that when the oxygen consumption doubled, as it did when Seguin did his exercise, the heat production must double too. There must, therefore, be a powerful mechanism for ridding the body of this excess heat. Lavoisier had long been aware of the converse of this situation, that the rate of respiration does not increase or decrease in proportion to the change in the rate of heat loss due to warmer or colder surroundings. Already in his discussion of 1783 he had suggested that changes in the distribution of heat within the body, as well as evaporation, must be involved in maintaining the temperature under such circumstances. He had regarded such phenomena then as too complex to investigate at that time. The new situation in 1790 was different in that it focused attention on the one plausible means by which the surplus of heat produced could be disposed of at an *unchanged* external temperature; that was through the cooling effects of evaporation, a phenomenon explicable in terms of Joseph Black's potent concept of latent heat. Lavoisier had reason to believe, therefore, that an investigation of the elusive, even though frequently discussed, phenomenon of "invisible transpiration" from the surface of a human or animal might hold the key to solving this puzzle.

His entry into the investigations of digestion and transpiration followed a pattern common to many previous moves Lavoisier had made along the course of his experimental career. Seldom did he solve a problem without finding in that solution the starting point for another problem to investigate. That was one of the main reasons for his sustained scientific productivity. It meant that his research never "ran dry"; it kept moving, changing, growing, yet because each problem he took up was closely related to problems on which he had already worked, his research retained at the same time a cumulative continuity. He could almost always import into the new problem area methods and concepts adapted from the old, so that he seldom found himself in strange surroundings where he could not bring his accumulated experience to bear. The one obvious exception was when he took on the study of vegetation, and the relatively little progress he made there only reinforces our impression of the effectiveness of his more typical mode of progression. We know too little about the start of his research on digestion to tell to what extent he could apply his familiar techniques, to what extent he encountered unaccustomed physiological complexities, and how far he was able to advance. It is safe to assume, however, that he did not leap into the mainstream of physiological investigation. There is no evidence that he performed, or even contemplated performing, experiments on digestion of the type that Spallanzani, following the precedent of Réaumur, had recently carried out with such auspicious results. Lavoisier entered upon broader physiological investigations at just those points that touched upon his prior research pathway through the special problem of respiration.

* * *

I pointed out in the introduction to this book that Lavoisier's investigation of respiration was not an application of a chemistry of combustion previously worked out, that he developed his theory of respiration and his theory of combustion in intimate association with one another from the time he first became interested in processes which fix air. If historians have tended to accept the opposite view, that is probably in part because Lavoisier himself misled them. At the beginning of his memoir on respiration he contended that the "usage" and "effects" of respiration had been completely unknown until "very recently." He then provided an explanation for that ignorance. "The delay in our knowledge of such an important subject derives from the fact that there is a necessary connection in the sequence of our ideas, an indispensable order in the progress of the human spirit." It had been impossible to know anything about what happens in respiration before one had recognized: (1) that caloric is the constituent principle of gases; (2) that the air is composed of two gases; (3) that oxygen is the principle common to acids; (4) that carbonic acid is composed of seventy-two parts oxygen and twenty-eight parts carbon; (5) that caloric is disengaged during the combustion of carbon; (6) the composition of water. Lavoisier, of course, credited himself with having established all of these "truths."[71] According to his account, therefore, all of the central achievements of his "chemical revolution" had to be in place before he could even begin to study respiration successfully. When he went on to outline the steps in his investigation of respiration, he began with his first publication on the subject, of 1777, notwithstanding the fact that most of these six prerequisites had not been established then. Lavoisier was thus imposing on events an ideal order which did not even fit his own account of the actual historical steps. He was only doing, though perhaps in extreme form, what scientists almost invariably do when they recapitulate the prior investigations they invoke in support of a present conclusion. For the real historical pathway with its twists, turns, wasted motions, and impasses, they substitute a more logical sequence of the steps they *might* have followed had they known in advance where they would come out.

17

Dissonant Echoes

On January 29, 1791, a few weeks after Lavoisier had presented his memoir on respiration to the Academy of Sciences, his younger colleague Jean Hassenfratz read to that same body a memoir "on the combination of oxygen with the carbon and hydrogen of the blood, on the solution of oxygen in the blood, and on the manner in which caloric is disengaged." When Hassenfratz had last written on respiration, in 1789, it had been to defend Lavoisier's theory from the attack of Berlinghieri. He had assumed then that the combustion takes place in the lungs.[1] Two years later his objective was to "decide" between that view, as defined by Laplace, and the hypothesis of Lagrange that the oxygen combines with the carbon and hydrogen of the blood gradually, during the course of the circulation. Hassenfratz came down on the side of Lagrange.[2]

Lagrange had based his theory, at least to judge from the only existing summary of it in Hassenfratz's memoir, solely on the theoretical argument that the animal heat could not all be released in the lungs without making the lungs hotter than the rest of the body. Hassenfratz, on the other hand, believed that the resolution of the situation lay with experiments on the color changes of the blood. He cited those of Priestley, Hamilton, Crawford, Girtanner, and Fourcroy, adding some of his own to clinch his case. "I began," he wrote, "from two given facts that all physicians have affirmed many times, and which M. Fourcroy has reconfirmed in a rigorous manner at the Lycée." The first observation was that when venous blood is mixed with oxygen it becomes at first bright red, but gradually changes to a dark-wine color, even though the blood remains in continual contact with the oxygen, and is even shaken repeatedly with it. The second was that arterial blood in contact with any gas not containing oxygen becomes wine-colored. Hassenfratz interpreted these results to mean that "the red color of blood is the result of the solution of oxygen in the blood, and that the dark-wine color is the result of the abandonment of the blood by the oxygen in order to combine with the hydrogen and the carbon." His own experimental contribution to his argument was to react venous blood with oxygenated muriatic acid and with ordinary muriatic acid. Both acids decomposed the blood, but the oxygenated acid also turned it almost black, whereas the other acid did not change its color. The difference, Hassenfratz averred, was due to the fact that oxygenated muriatic acid contained oxygen in such a state that it "combines immediately with the hydrogen and carbon of the blood"; whereas in the second case oxygen is present only in a gaseous state, from which it cannot so easily enter those combinations. He supported his theory further by repeating an experiment of Girtanner. He mixed blood with oxygen gas until it was bright red, then sealed it hermetically into several tubes, some of which he left in darkness, the others in the light. The blood in all of the tubes gradually turned dark.[3]

Hassenfratz employed his explanation of the color changes he and others had produced in experiments on blood to elaborate on Lagrange's hypothesis. It is, he asserted, the oxygen which dissolves in the blood in the lungs which causes the blood to assume its bright arterial color. As the blood circulates, however, this oxygen gradually leaves the "total mass of the blood to combine with the hydrogen and carbon of the blood," so that by the time the blood returns through the veins to the lungs that combination has been completed, and the blood is entirely dark. In the lungs the carbonic acid and water are disengaged from the blood, while a new supply of oxygen is dissolved in it, restoring once again the arterial color. Since caloric is released by the combination of oxygen with carbon and hydrogen, most of the caloric produced is "disengaged during the grand progression" of the blood through the body. Hassenfratz allowed that some caloric is released in the lungs as well, by the condensation of the oxygen gas there, but claimed that "this heat is consumed in large part to vaporize the water which the expired air carries off with it." He went on to explain Crawford's measurements of the differential specific heats of arterial and venous blood. There were two concurring reasons. First, oxides have a greater specific heat than other substances, and the "arterial blood can be considered oxidized by comparison with venous blood." Second, arterial blood retains most of its caloric, because it is only during the course of the circulation that the caloric is released.[4]

The theory of respiration that Hassenfratz represented and supported in his memoir was viewed during the ensuing decades as an alternative to the theory associated with Lavoisier and Laplace,[5] and historians have therefore referred to them respectively as the "Lagrange-Hassenfratz" theory and the "Lavoisier-Laplace" theory.[6] There were, however, significant differences between the views of the persons whose names thus became linked, as well as in the type and quality of evidence each brought to bear on his position. There is no evidence that Lavoisier accepted the theory based on an analogy to latent heat which Laplace is reported to have contrived in order to evade Lagrange's objection. Rather, he came to realize, in 1790, that the question of where the combustion occurs was not yet answered. Because Seguin attempted in 1790 to connect

Lavoisier's theory of respiration with Crawford's theory of the distribution of heat, Mendelsohn has recently referred to a "Lavoisier-Crawford theory of animal heat,"[7] but Lavoisier himself never endorsed Seguin's synthesis. Hassenfratz linked Lavoisier and Crawford as believing that the combustion occurs in the lungs, at just about the time Lavoisier saw that his old assumption had no decisive support. Lagrange, a mathematician, based his theory, as far as we know, solely on the theoretically compelling argument that a combustion limited to the lungs was incompatible with the even distribution of heat. He did not involve himself with experiments, or considerations based on color changes in samples of withdrawn blood. Hassenfratz's argument was entirely based on such considerations. Thus, although their conclusions coincided, Lagrange and Hassenfratz were explaining different phenomena.

Hassenfratz believed that his approach was based on "direct experiments whose results were certain."[8] The fact that these experiments supported a view which appears in retrospect as a stage in the progression from which the modern theory of respiration emerged should not cause us to overrate the cogency of his observations or his reasoning. His interpretation of the color changes of blood was highly speculative; it involved two states of oxygen in the blood—solution and combinations with carbon and hydrogen—neither of which had been shown to exist. There were now available so many different observations on color changes of blood that one could justify almost any explanatory theory by selecting the observations which best fit one's particular mechanism. Like Girtanner, Seguin, and Crawford, Hassenfratz was seeking to describe the whole sequence of unobservable internal processes which intervene in respiration between the time that oxygen enters the lungs and that at which carbonic acid and water are expired from those organs. Like them, he was not up to the task. There are two particularly glaring examples of his loose reasoning. Where he had previously refuted Berlinghieri by asserting that water is not vaporized in the lungs, now that he no longer thought that the carbonic acid and water are formed there, he cheerfully adopted the opposite position on this point. When he tried to incorporate Crawford's measurements of the specific heats of arterial and venous blood into his theory, he proved nothing more than that he did not understand Crawford's concept of specific heat.

Linking Lavoisier all too readily with Crawford, Hassenfratz described both of them as having concluded, from the experiments of "Hamilton, Priestley, and several others," that "the color change which blood undergoes in the circulation derives from its combination with hydrogen gas."[9] Perhaps Hassenfratz had gained that impression by equating Seguin's views with those of Lavoisier. There is no indication, in anything we can be certain that he himself wrote, that Lavoisier ever adopted such a position. As far as we can tell he had, after briefly maintaining in 1777 the idea that oxygen absorbed into the blood may account for its red color, kept clear of arguments derived from the color changes which can be produced in blood outside the body. Similarly to Seguin, Hassenfratz was, within the conceptual envelope provided by Lavoisier's overall theory of respiration, following a mode of investigation originated by the phlogistonists. Hassenfratz too shows how much easier it was to adopt the general ideas of Lavoisier than to apply them with the disciplined imagination that enabled the master both to develop his theory in fruitful directions and to avoid trying to explain more than its experimental foundations could support.

II

During April or May of 1791, Lavoisier and Seguin presented a "second memoir on respiration" to the Academy. It is not evident which of the two read the paper at the meeting, but Seguin clearly wrote it.[10] Lavoisier had announced in his own memoir in November that Seguin would later describe the details of their experiments on animals.[11] The "second memoir" most likely represents Seguin's fulfillment of this charge. He did not, in fact, describe individual experimental results, but did give fuller accounts of the procedures they had followed in general. The memoir reveals that the two investigators did not rely exclusively on Seguin's eudiometric method, but resorted to a variety of means to determine the quantities of oxygen; that in the longer experiments they replenished the oxygen in the respiration chamber at intervals; that in the early experiments they did not absorb the carbonic acid until the end of the experiment, but during the course of the investigation they devised an ingenious technique for siphoning caustic alkali into dishes floating on the surface of the water, and for siphoning out saturated alkali, while the experiment continued.

Concerning the results, Seguin focused on various extremes they had observed, such as the largest and smallest quantities of oxygen consumed, and the maximum and minimum breathing rates of the animals. He outlined the questions they had posed, and the answers they had found, echoing in most respects the fuller discussions of the same points that Lavoisier had already presented.[12] At the end, however, Seguin branched out on his own with an interpretation of their finding that, "contrary to the opinions . . . of distinguished savants," the animals consumed equal quantities of vital air in a given time no matter how large the proportion of vital air was:

> One can reasonably conclude that the nature of blood is such that during its passage through the lungs it can lose only a portion of its carbonated hydrogen. From that one understands that any respirable air which will contain a sufficient quantity of vital air to burn this portion of the carbonated hydrogen must produce an effect analogous to any other respirable fluid composed almost entirely of vital air; the excess portion [of vital air] in this fluid beyond that quantity becoming absolutely inert.[13]

This was a clever idea. It made sense of a finding that had been very surprising in view of the general expectation that respiration, like other combustions, would become more rapid in pure vital air. It was not dissimilar to hypotheses that Lavoisier regularly offered in analogous circumstances. Unlike Lavoisier, who usually separated such speculative suggestions from what he believed his experiments had proven, however, Seguin went on to extol his explanation as "a new proof of the wisdom of nature and of the equilibrium which one encounters at each step in the state of health."[14] Moreover, the explanation reveals that Lavoisier's recent realization that there was no decisive experimental evidence for the combustion of carbon in the lungs did not induce in Seguin any doubt that the theoretical "carbonated hydrogen," which he had posited in his own earlier memoir on respiration as the form in which the respiratory hydrogen and carbon existed, is burned during the passage of the blood through the lungs.

By the time they presented Seguin's second memoir on respiration, Lavoisier and Seguin had embarked on the next phase of their general plan to study all of the parts of the animal economy. They now focused on transpiration, defined by Lavoisier as a process that "continuously removes water and that, combining it with caloric to reduce it to vapor, causes a cooling and prevents the animal machine from acquiring a temperature higher than that set by nature."[15] This cooling effect of transpiration had become important in the investigation of respiration, to explain why Seguin's temperature did not rise when he exercised, even though the large rise in his respiration must have produced more heat. In his discussion of the compensations by means of which animals and humans maintain an equilibrium under diverse conditions, Lavoisier viewed transpiration as one of the essential regulators. Now the two collaborators began seeking methods by which they could quantitatively measure the water removed by transpiration.

They must have seen from the start that there was no practical way to collect the water itself, so that the only route open to them was to determine it as a loss of weight. If they could establish the overall loss of weight of an individual during a given time, and deduct from that total the quantity due to respiration, the remainder would represent transpiration. Lavoisier was applying to this physiological problem the same principle of the balance that he had exploited so effectively to transform chemistry. In preparation for the effort they acquired a large, extremely sensitive balance, capable of weighing a 125-pound person with an error of no more than 18 grains. The balance was so delicate, in fact, that they believed they could detect the change in the weight of an individual during the time it took to carry out a weighing. In order to separate the losses attributable to transpiration through the skin from those due to respiration, the willing Seguin donned a taffeta suit impregnated with gum elastic so that neither air nor water could penetrate it. The suit completely covered his head, except for a tube cemented to his mouth so that he could breath through it without permitting anything except his respired air from escaping. He weighed himself before putting on the suit, and just after putting it on. He then sat quietly on the balance for three or four hours, weighed himself again, took off the suit, and weighed himself once more.[16] The difference between the first and last weights represented the loss of weight from respiration and transpiration together. The difference between the two weights with the suit on gave the loss due to "the effects of respiration."

The problem would have been solved, except for one "considerable difficulty." There was, in addition to cutaneous transpiration, a loss of weight due to pulmonary transpiration—the water evaporated from the lungs, as distinct from the water formed there from the combustion of hydrogen—which would be included in the effects of respiration, unless they could find a means to distinguish between the weights of these two quantities of water. The method by which they hoped to attain this end was to "measure with great precision," in a separate experiment, "the quantity of water and of carbonic acid exhaled, as well as the quantity of air before and after the experiment." Lavoisier designed an apparatus incorporating a long tube two-thirds filled with potassium acetate, a highly deliquescent salt. The expired water, absorbed in the tube, was measured by its increase in weight. The remaining dry air passed on into an apparatus, probably the usual caustic alkali bottle and a pneumatic chamber, allowing them to measure the overall change in volume and the quantity of carbonic acid produced. From these data they could calculate the quantity of water formed by the combustion of hydrogen, in the same manner that Lavoisier had originally demonstrated in 1785 that water is formed in respiration. By subtracting this calculated quantity from the weighed quantity of expired water, they could derive the quantity evaporated in pulmonary transpiration.[17] Lavoisier's analysis of the problem, and his solution, were in principle admirably lucid. As he himself commented, however, "The method that we employed, although simple in speculation, presented extreme difficulties in practice."[18] Whatever these difficulties were, it is unlikely that the two collaborators ever overcame them.

To the Academy on May 11, Lavoisier described verbally "the apparatus that had served for the experiments he has carried out jointly with M. Seguin. He also explained the results of these experiments."[19] We cannot tell how far along they were at this point, or whether the apparatus in question was Seguin's rubber suit or the long respiration tube. It is also uncertain just when he wrote and read to the Academy a "first memoir on the transpiration of animals." He is recorded as having continued, on June 10, the reading of a memoir on respiration which was, according to Daumas, actually this memoir on transpiration.[20]

In his memoir Lavoisier developed their overall approach and results, but described the experimental methods only in very general terms. As in their study of respiration, he apparently left the details for Seguin to report later. Along the way he acknowledged that in addition to practical difficulties encountered with the method for measuring the exhaled water and carbonic acid, there was a very serious theoretical difficulty. The calculation of water formed in respiration was dependent on the quantity of carbonic acid formed, because it was through the difference between the oxygen employed to form this carbonic acid, and the total oxygen consumed, that he calculated the water formed. The finding that he had reported in his memoir on respiration, that some carbonic acid may be released in digestion and enter the blood, now upset this calculation, however, because the preformed carbonic acid would be included in this measured quantity. Consequently, he wrote, the problem was "indeterminate," and there "could be many solutions, depending on whether one supposed that a greater or lesser quantity of carbonic acid and of water is disengaged already formed during the act of respiration." Unable to remove the obstacle that he had placed in his own path, Lavoisier simply hurdled it. Crossing out this negative view of the situation, he "supposed" that all of the carbonic acid disengaged was formed during the combustion, even though "this supposition is not demonstrated." Declining for now to discuss further "this very thorny problem that new experiments will clarify," he pushed on to a "provisional solution which appears to us the most probable."[21] Lavoisier carried out the calculations, and represented in the familiar balance sheet form the total loss of weight and the quantities of carbonic acid, water, carbon, and hydrogen contained in the respired gases and the pulmonary and cutaneous transpiration. We sense that in preparing this memoir Lavoisier was impatient to make public this representation of a result they had not yet reached. He indirectly acknowledged as much when he wrote that they were limiting themselves in this "first memoir" to presenting a general idea of the method "which has guided us," and that they would later publish full tables of their experimental results. "Those which we propose to publish," he admitted, "are not even completed yet."[22]

In the middle of his analysis of the experimental problem of separating the effects of transpiration and respiration, Lavoisier interjected, "It is first necessary to recall here several little-known circumstances which take place during respiration." He then gave a theoretical discussion of respiration that differed strikingly, in both tone and substance, from the treatment he had recently given in his memoir on respiration.

> It is necessary to know first of all, that a viscous humor, which is separated from the blood and filtered across the membranes of the lungs, exudes continuously into the bronchi, and if it becomes too abundant, forms the matter that is spit out. When analyzed, this matter is found to be composed mainly of water, of hydrogen, and of carbon.

> It is this humor which, being finely divided at the moment at which it leaves the extremely fine pores of the pulmonary membrane, is dissolved in the air introduced into the lungs by the act of respiration. From this dissolution results, as one knows, the carbonic acid and the water. It is accompanied by heat and a sort of combustion, and it is assisted by the temperature of the lungs, which is maintained continuously at 32 degrees . . . Réaumur.

In a third paragraph Lavoisier explained that the water would accumulate and suffocate the animal if it were not continuously evacuated. It is carried off because the cold air entering the lungs is warmed to the temperature of the blood, enabling it to dissolve more water.[23]

We are tempted to wonder whether the Lavoisier who wrote these passages, and read them to the Academy, can have been the same one who had discussed respiration with such critical caution in the brilliant memoir he had presented to the same assembly a few months earlier. There he had acknowledged the lack of experimental evidence that the combustion occurs in the lungs. Here he not only took it as an established fact that carbon and hydrogen are converted to carbonic acid and water in the lungs, but described the hidden circumstances under which that process takes place, and provided an explanation for it based on the physical and chemical properties of the substances involved. Moreover, though he had never espoused such a mechanism before, he now referred to it as something he was "recalling." He not only failed to give any reasons for having changed his mind in the short time since the previous memoir, but wrote as though he were oblivious to the view expressed there! If my interpretation of his previous writings is valid, Lavoisier had assumed up until 1790 that respiratory combustions occur in the lungs because he had not questioned his simple initial assumption. The situation was very different now, because he *had* questioned that view, had realized that there was no decisive support for it, and yet chose to ignore his own critique.

Following his table of the quantities of matter lost in transpiration and respiration Lavoisier predicted that they would "resolve the problem in a more rigorous manner . . . through new, more exact experiments. A more exact analysis than those we have made of the matter which exudes into the bronchi and experiments in digestion will probably remove all uncertainty in that respect."[24] Implicit in this claim is that he must have expected to be able to determine quantitatively the carbonic acid entering the blood from the digestive tract, and the carbon and hydrogen flowing into the lungs with the viscous humor. If he supposed he could do that in the near future, Lavoisier was indeed taking up the study of the "animal economy" with the heady optimism of one who knew little of the complexities involved.

As they continued their experiments, Lavoisier and Seguin expanded their ambitions. Inspired by the classic example of Sanctorius, who had lived much of his life on a balance, weighing everything he ate and excreted in order to establish the amount he lost by "insensible transpiration," they aspired to provide a modern equivalent, improved by their ability to discriminate the several forms of emanations. They hoped to ascertain the influence on the rate of transpiration of variations in all relevant conditions, such as the temperature and humidity, the diet, and the activity of the individual. Seguin's service as the subject for these experiments now grew to heroic proportions. He was weighed four times every day, and often had to remain in complete inactivity for hours on end, in order to establish the rate of his loss of weight with no exercise. He weighed all of his food, drink, and excretions day after day. The two collaborators having decided that cutaneous transpiration can itself be analyzed into two forms—insensible transpiration, or the evaporation of water, and sweating—Seguin sat in water baths for hours, or covered himself with oil, in order to distinguish the two forms by suppressing the action of the air on the surface of his body. Because there were supposed to be absorbent vessels in the skin as well as exhalant vessels, and he could not establish the absolute quantity of water evaporated from the skin unless he also knew whether any was absorbed, he sat in solutions of quinine and other fluids. If these were absorbed, he would be able to detect the fact by the medicinal action of such drugs on him. Not content with what he could accomplish by himself, he persuaded his brother and his friends to submit themselves to similar ordeals. Enlisting the aid of the hospitals, he subjected patients with venereal disease to sublimate baths in order to see if they could absorb this standard treatment for their affliction through their skins. For eleven long months Seguin devoted himself to this heavy task.[25]

In the meantime Lavoisier gradually dropped out of the investigation. During the year in which it went on, his extrascientific responsibilities again began to draw him relentlessly away from the laboratory. In January 1791, he became involved in efforts to reform the national finances, and by April he was a commissioner of the National Treasury. In March he was made a member of a commission to choose new units of measurement; from then on his most pressing research priority was the development of the metric system. By the end of the year he was treasurer both of the commission on weights and measures and the Academy of Sciences, and a member of a newly created Bureau de Consultation des Arts et Métiers. Meanwhile political attacks had begun both on the Academy and on himself, and Lavoisier was thrust into a leading role in the defense of the institution within which his scientific career had flourished.[26] There was no more relief from his multiplying burdens. In January 1792, he wrote that he "was overwhelmed by affairs and beginning to feel the weight of the immense loads imposed on him." He had promised to finish some memoirs to be included in an Italian translation of his *Elementary Treatise*, but he had to inform the translator that he no longer had time for it, or to carry out the experiments he had planned on digestion, the function of the chyle, and the blood.[27] Thus died his hope to extend his research into the problem of nutrition. By this time he must also have effectively withdrawn from the joint projects undertaken with Seguin. On February 21, 1792, Seguin read a "second memoir on transpiration" to the Academy, giving the details of the many experiments he had carried on during the preceding year.[28] Lavoisier took the occasion to announce that "the work begun in common with him had been continued by Seguin alone, and that the experiments in that memoir belonged entirely to him."[29] We cannot help wondering if, in addition to making certain that Seguin received full credit for his work, Lavoisier might also have wished to dissociate himself from Seguin's increasingly bizarre experimental exploits.

Lavoisier wrote his own "second memoir on the transpiration of animals" (though he included Seguin as joint author, just as Seguin included Lavoisier as joint author of *his* version). In general, schematic terms, he summarized the various means of suppressing contact between his skin and the air that Seguin had employed in attempting to dissociate the two forms of transpiration. The extra warmth that Seguin had felt under such circumstances prompted Lavoisier to a long digression on why people feel uncomfortable in humid air and in closed places, and on the role of clothing. He began the memoir by analyzing the apparently simple act of respiration into its "multitude" of component effects. These were "a decomposition of oxygen gas; a disengagement of caloric; a formation of water; and a filtration of viscous fluid, composed principally of hydrogen and carbon." Thus he now accorded this viscous fluid, which he had invoked simply to explain the hidden mechanism of respiration, the same status of certainty that he attributed to those measurable phenomena that he had demonstrated through laborious experimental effort. Moreover, he now extended the same mechanism to the skin. There too, a viscous fluid, composed of hydrogen and carbon, filtered through pores in the skin, and was removed from the surface by "a sort of respiration, of combustion, of formation of carbonic acid and water." Animals therefore respire not by their lungs alone, "but by means of the whole surface of their bodies." He gave no concrete experimental evidence for this bold new expansion of his theory of respiration. Perhaps it is just as well that he apparently did not carry out his intention to present this memoir to the Academy. It was found as a manuscript in his hand after his death, and published only in 1801, as an appendix to the third edition of his *Elementary Treatise*.[30]

From the foregoing account it is obvious that the investigation Lavoisier had begun so auspiciously in 1790 was by 1792 deteriorating precipitously. The experiments on digestion never got beyond a nascent stage. The beautifully designed experiments on respiration had given way to spectacular feats contrived to trap the elusive process of transpiration. The penetrating, cautious thinker of 1790, constructing the durable foundations for a theory of respiration independent of the unknown internal mechanisms, was by 1792 describing those very internal mechanisms, building ephemeral physiological systems on the slimmest of empirical foundations. Lavoisier was now engaging in those same hypothetical excesses, the avoidance of which had until recently distinguished his theory of respiration from the speculations of lesser figures around him. The master of the art of the soluble, who had always been able to distinguish so clearly between what his experiments could prove, what he could only suggest, and what must remain for future investigations to solve, was now embarked on a "vast new pathway," whose aim was no less than to examine the entire animal economy and—even beyond that—to arm himself to "attack the ancient colossus of . . . prejudice and of errors" constituting the structure of traditional medicine.[31] What had happened to alter so radically Lavoisier's scientific behavior?

We can probably not isolate a single explanatory factor, but there were several rapid, almost stimultaneous changes in his situation which may have acted synergistically upon Lavoisier's investigative style. One was the suddenness with which he entered a scientific field different from that to which he had been accustomed. He had, of course, not come lately to his interest in physiological processes, for he had been fixing his attention on respiration for nearly twenty years. Up until 1790, however, he had restricted his investigation to respiration as a form of combustion and a source of heat, aspects of the phenomenon that were amenable to treatment with the same repertoire of methods that he was developing for his chemical studies. Although he had discussed the broader physiological implications of the process, he had always done so in passing, tacitly recognizing that to explore them further would be to go beyond the scope of his own experimental pathway. The broader conception of respiration that he had assimilated by 1790, however, led him across a watershed. In order to pursue the problem further, he had to enter unfamiliar territory. If respiration was part of the overall material balance of the organism, as well as one of several regulators of its temperature, then to understand it involved understanding the whole of the "animal economy." To go on, therefore, confronted him with a fateful decision. The investigation of the animal economy was an old and extensively cultivated field—far older than chemistry—but a field in which he himself had no firsthand experience. Perhaps with an assurance bolstered by the astonishing magnitude of his success in chemistry, he seemed unawed by the difficulty of such a move. He brought to his new field the fresh insight that we often associate with crossing disciplinary boundaries. His analysis of the *problem* of transpiration, and his comprehension of the regulatory mechanisms maintaining equilibrium in animals, were, in fact, profound and penetrating. In some respects he could immediately see farther than those who had devoted their lives to physiology; but he moved without his habitual caution. He appears to have been unaware of the extent to which his inventive imagination had previously been tempered by the depth of his familiarity with the power and the limits of the methods in the field he had made his own.

A second obvious factor was that his burgeoning outside burdens prevented Lavoisier from engaging himself in his new enterprise with the intensity and the persistence that had marked his previous ventures. With time so limited, he was undoubtedly more tempted to take shortcuts when he could not quickly resolve the experimental problems he encountered. He was more willing to cross with his imagination the gaps that he would formerly have had the patience to fill in experimentally. Moreover, his increasing reliance on a less experienced associate not only to perform the experiments, but to report their details in separate memoirs, left Lavoisier more and more out of touch with the foundations for the inferences he wished to build on them. In his two memoirs on transpiration, Lavoisier described Seguin's results, and drew on them for his discussion, but his remoteness from them is clearly evident. We miss immediately those personal struggles to reconcile recalcitrant experimental data with the conclusions he wished them to support, that had so characterized his earlier investigations. By turning over to Seguin all of the details, he was unwittingly also handing over to his collaborator much of the scientific judgment that he had formerly exercised for himself. Lavoisier's experience has been repeated frequently in more recent times when directors of research have, for reasons less excusable than his, become too preoccupied with other matters to remain in close contact with the investigations carried out under their supervision.

Finally, the influence of Seguin's views themselves on Lavoisier's thinking is hard to miss. It should be evident that the origin of the elaborate respiratory mechanism Lavoisier postulated in his memoirs on transpiration was in Seguin's review of respiration of early 1790. There Seguin had described the hydrocarbonaceous fluid and had given the argument Lavoisier now used, that the finely divided state of this fluid enabled it to burn at the temperature of the blood. In his own memoir on transpiration Seguin continued to spread that oozing fluid liberally over his interpretations of his experimental results.[32] If Lavoisier seemed to be absorbing the more extravagant, less critical style of his youthful protégé, we may still wonder about what had happened to his independence of judgment. He had long threaded his way surefootedly through the thickets of speculative excesses current in his time. Why now would he succumb to temptations he had previously withstood? This question cannot be fully answered without more intimate access than we have to the personal relationship between the august leader of French chemistry and the eager young assistant he had promoted to collaborator. We can, however, guess that Seguin's energy and enthusiasm, the fact that he was willing to carry on devotedly the work that his mentor could no longer continue, gave Seguin special access to Lavoisier's sympathy and support.

It is not, of course, necessary to assume that Seguin originated the hypothetical mechanism that Lavoisier now adopted. I have done so because Seguin published such an idea at a time when Lavoisier had expressed no similar views. Nevertheless, it is possible that Lavoisier had already visualized the process privately in such a manner, but that he had at that time been careful not to discuss publicly conjectures he regarded as devoid of scientific proof. If so, Seguin could have picked up the idea in conversation while working in Lavoisier's laboratory. Lacking Lavoisier's reticence in such matters, Seguin might have put out as a scientific theory what Lavoisier at the time harbored only as a convenient way to imagine the unknown inner process. Under the changing circumstances just described, Lavoisier himself may eventually have lost sight of that distinction.

The degeneration of Lavoisier's research program was subtle. He did not suddenly abandon scientific investigation to indulge in speculative fancies. Despite his protestations in the preliminary discourse to his *Elementary Treatise,* he had never been able to proceed smoothly from the known to the unknown, restricting his inferences to the consequences flowing immediately from his experimental results. Always his vision had ranged in advance of what he could prove. Over and over he had had to press his data to conform to his expectations; to compensate for imperfect results by astute choices of assumptions. That was what he continued to do in 1791 and 1792; only the imaginative dimension was growing longer, while the experimental base was growing thinner. Under pressure of expanded ambitions and contracted time, he was growing a little more grandiose, and a little less careful.

Lavoisier himself was not necessarily satisfied with his memoirs on transpiration, or with the investigations on which they were built. We have seen in earlier situations that he had sometimes been carried along by enthusiasms that he later brought under control. Ideas that he put into early drafts sometimes disappeared, or were toned down in the final versions. At least once he had had the restraint not to publish a memoir that embodied a grand vision erected on shaky pilings—that on fermentation. There is one passage, in the second memoir on transpiration, in which he seemed to sense that he had got into deeper water than he expected:

> Although we may be still far from the goal that we propose to reach, we are pausing for a few moments in the vast course that we have undertaken to travel. In thus collecting our forces and our ideas, in reinforcing ourselves with the illumination of men of genius, of the medical savants who surround us, we are preparing ourselves to take up again with more courage the task which we have imposed upon ourselves.[33]

Perhaps this was just the rhetoric of an ambitious man seeking to impress on his audience the grandeur of his mission. Perhaps, however, it reveals also a vulnerable man, aware that he might have taken on more than he could manage.

In the end Lavoisier did not have the opportunity to decide whether or not to let his memoirs on transpiration enter the public record of his scientific activity. Long after Lavoisier's death, Seguin saw to it that the record of his own association with his mentor should be preserved and enhanced by the belated publication of those manuscripts documenting their joint endeavor.

The decline in the quality of Lavoisier's last investigation detracts little from his overall scientific stature; but it throws into sharper relief the magnitude of his previous achievement, and provides further perspective on the character of his long investigative odyssey. He has traditionally been portrayed as a person of such logic and rigor, such rigid discipline, such theoretical power and cool detachment, that his success was somehow inevitable. I also have maintained that the calibre of his investigation and of his reasoning consistently excelled that of his contemporaries in the same fields of inquiry. He was, however, never infallible. His mind was not a reasoning machine. He too was subject to enthusiasms alternating with doubts. He too could be boldly visionary at one moment, prudently cautious at another. He too could become so committed to a particular point of view that he could not see other sides of a problem or question. These were not shortcomings, but the forces behind his success. Michael Polanyi has argued eloquently that original discovery demands of the scientist "passionate pre-occupation with a problem," but also "submission to scientific standards for the appraisal and guidance of his efforts."[34] Had Lavoisier been as dispassionate as he is often depicted, it is doubtful that he could have engaged himself for so long as he did in the arduous struggle required to break with an established chemical system and to replace it piece by piece with a new one. For nearly twenty years he was able to check the ardor with which he pursued that aim by means of his critical detachment, his skepticism, and the discipline he imposed on his vision; but these were delicate balances. He had to maintain these balances alone, because he was so far ahead of everyone in his field that he had no one else against whom to measure his own standards. Finally, under extreme pressure, as his ambitions mounted and his many duties divided his energies, as his young collaborator impelled him onward, as the sobering effects of the direct encounter with experimental pitfalls receded from his weekly experience, the balance he had for so long sustained began to slip. The penetrating insight remained, but the vision began to mount toward heights where the critical check could not quite keep up.

III

Even as the outside pressures on him brought Lavoisier's personal scientific investigation to a standstill, the grand research plan he nurtured took on still larger dimensions. No longer limiting his purview to the animal economy, he set his sights on the great cycle of matter between the three kingdoms of nature. Plants obtain from the mineral kingdom the material which they organize into their substance. Animals nourish themselves on plants. Respiration and other processes such as fermentation or putrefation render back to the mineral kingdom the principles that plants and animals have successively borrowed from it.[35] Lavoisier now wished to understand all stages of this process; how the combustible bodies combine two by two, three by three, and four by four during vegetation and "animalization," as well as how they are again decomposed in respiration, fermentation, and other such processes.[36] Seeing that this goal was beyond his individual reach, he sought to organize collective investigative efforts. By the spring of 1792, probably at his urging, the Academy established a commission to undertake experiments on vegetation. The members, who included Lavoisier, Antoine-Laurent de Jussieu, Berthollet, Thouin, DesFontaines, and Fourcroy, assembled at the Jardin des Plantes and began to gather the apparatus necessary to begin the investigation. Hassenfratz and Seguin had already begun an independent collaborative investigation of the same problem. It would be surprising if Lavoisier were not also behind this joint undertaking by his two young supporters. On June 5 he wrote a draft proposal for an agreement by which Hassenfratz and Seguin would join forces with the commission.[37]

Having provided a means to get on with the problem of vegetation, Lavoisier called upon the European scientific community at large to forward his concern with the place of the animal economy in the cycle of nature. To stimulate investigations of animal nutrition the Academy, also most likely at his urging, offered a prize for a paper, to be submitted before January 1794, on an aspect of digestion. On July 28, 1792, he read at a meeting of the Academy a note he had composed defining the terms of the prize.[38] The note conveyed at the same time his vision of the overall material cycle of nature of which digestion composed one phase. Opening with a brief summary of the way in which plants derive their substance from the water, air, and earth, animals are nourished from plants, and the substances found in these processes are again decomposed, he asked:

> By what processes does nature carry out this marvelous circulation between the three kingdoms? How is she able to form the combustible, fermentable, and putrescent substances with materials that have none of these properties? These are, up until this time, impenetrable mysteries. One can nevertheless see vaguely that, since combustion and putrefaction are the means that nature employs to render to the mineral kingdom the materials that she had taken from there to form plants and animals, vegetation and animalization must be operations inverse to combustion and putrefaction.

After noting that the Academy had already established a commission to study vegetation, Lavoisier announced that the prize that the Academy had to offer should direct attention to "animalization, the nutrition of animals." Contestants were invited to investigate the chemical nature of the substances which serve as aliments to animals,

> the alterations which they undergo successively in the [digestive] canal which receives them, first by the mixture of saliva, second by the mixture of gastric juice, third by the mixture of bile. [The Academy] assumes [that the contestants will acquire] some analytical knowledge of the different fluids of these different humors. It assumes particularly [that they will attain] knowledge of the gas which is disengaged during the course of the digestion, the manner in which the digestion renders to the blood that which is continually removed from it by respiration.

He went on to say that the Academy was aware that no contestant would be able to solve the entire problem outlined in this paragraph, and it would consider awarding the prize to someone who could resolve a portion of it.[39] It should be evident that through the device of this prize Lavoisier was hoping to stimulate the scientists of Europe to take on those very problems that he had, less than two years earlier, thought he could resolve by himself. Time and circumstances had forced on him a more realistic assessment both of the magnitude of the task and of the limits of his own capacities.

Lavoisier's note stimulated a lively discussion in the Academy, and the text was heavily revised afterward.[40] The sections summarized above were only lightly altered, but a much more detailed description was added of the portion of the overall problem the Academy expected the contestants to solve. It proposed concentrating on the function of the liver and the bile. Where Lavoisier's draft had fixed on the chemical analysis of the fluids, the new instructions dwelt far more on the anatomical structure of the liver, and on the necessity to make comparative studies of the "diverse classes of animals."[41] Whereas he had viewed the problem almost entirely from the perspective of his own prior investigations and aspirations, the final note stressed the perspective of a zoologist and a comparative anatomist. Perhaps someone like Félix Vicq d'Azyr, the distinguished comparative anatomist of the Academy,[42] assisted in preparing the revisions. It might even be that the liveliness of the discussion derived from a feeling that Lavoisier was overstepping the bounds of his expertise in prescribing how a study of animal nutrition ought to be carried out. If so, this would have been the first of many debates between chemists and zoologists or physiologists over control of the mode of investigation of a process which lay on the common boundaries of their respective fields.

If he was no longer in a position to pursue personally his ambitious earlier plan to examine all the parts of the animal economy, Lavoisier must still have expected that he could play a leading part in defining the problems. In December 1792, he drew up a "plan for a treatise on chemistry." His outline included all of the topics in general chemistry that his previous *Elementary Treatise* contained. He intended, however, to treat in considerably more detail the chemistry of plant and animal matter. In addition he envisioned a special section on the animal economy and the economy of plants. The topics he listed for such a section were,

> The animal economy
> Respiration
> Transpiration
> Digestion
> The nature of the animal humors
> The economy of plants
> The nutrition of plants[43]

It is reasonable to infer that he had in mind to expound in detail the views he had outlined in his note for the Academy prize.

In the end, the onrush of political events thwarted even these literary plans. By the time Lavoisier sketched them out, the Academy itself was under siege, and he spent much of 1793 valiantly trying to fend off the threat of suppression which, in spite of his efforts, finally befell that institution of the ancien régime in August. By September he was under surveillance as a former tax farmer, and by November he was under arrest.[44] His hope to write a new treatise on chemistry synthesizing all of his investigations and the theoretical structure of his chemistry, as well as his views of the plant and animal economies, was reduced to an attempt to put together in a collected edition the scientific memoirs that he and his supporters had previously published. As he reviewed his old papers for this purpose, he made a few minor efforts to bring them up to date. In his memoir on the composition of carbonic acid, for example, he rewrote the concluding paragraph. He had, after using for eight years the proportions of seventy-two parts oxygen to twenty-eight carbon that he had established there, decided that that result, drawn from the aggregate of his experiments using different methods, was not right after all. Putting his trust in the single experiment he had made on highly purified *charbon de Bourdenne*, he adopted its result, seventy five parts oxygen to twenty-five carbon, for his new figure, though he feared that even that value "forced" the carbon somewhat. In some other places, such as the memoir of 1785 on alterations of the air, in which he had made the calculation showing that water is formed in respiration, he revised the calculation to conform to his new choice for the proportions of carbonic acid.[45] The change made no difference to the argument. From a position in which he could embark on a vast new investigative pathway, less than two years before, he had been reduced to a state in which he could do no more than add a few superficial touches to the corpus of his great achievements of the past. Even before it took Lavoisier's life, the revolution had all but smothered his mighty scientific spirit.

18

Reflections on the Creativity of One Scientist

After retracing Lavoisier's long investigative trail through the domains of plant and animal chemistry, what we have learned about the springs of his scientific creativity? First, we should acknowledge that no reconstruction based on written records can penetrate to the inmost recesses of thought. Those mysterious events during which one becomes aware that a novel idea, or a significant modification of an idea one already has, has "entered his head," are beyond recapturing, except in those rare cases in which the thinker has himself told of the experience. Even then he does not really know "where" the ideas have come from. Nor can we tell from the record the emotional reactions Lavoisier may have had at the high peaks of creativity in his scientific journey. Finally, we cannot bring the immediate visual scene into view before us. We cannot literally be present at "great moments of discovery."

Even if we accept these limitations, however, the exceptionally full documentation Lavoisier has left us has enabled us to approach very near to the germinal sources of the creative increments in his scientific investigations. We have been able to witness ideas put down on paper whose character, and the circumstances under which they are placed there, suggest that these are the earliest written traces of such thoughts, and that the unwritten development which separates them from some initial "flashes" of insight was probably short. We have been able to connect the origins of new ideas, or of their modifications, or of ways to represent them, to closely circumscribed circumstances, whether these be the conditions of a particular experiment or a stage in the construction of a memoir.

In no case have we been able to reconstruct exhaustively the steps in the formation of a concept, theory, or other idea from its earliest traces to the definitive form in which Lavoisier made it public. Were we able to do so, we would probably not find linear sequences of reasoning at all, for human thought does not proceed in the step-by-step fashion that its formalized reconstruction exhibits. It circles endlessly around on itself, views the same ideas over and over from slightly different perspectives, repeats itself many times, and occasionally in the midst of these iterative processes thrusts forward. Were we to have a complete record of the thought accompanying even a small innovation in Lavoisier's conceptual structure, it would probably be too intricate to describe on paper. Falling short of such an impossible description, we have been able to capture here and there samples of the emergence and growth of his scientific ideas at a level intimate enough to provide revealing glimpses of the nature of the process. Since these glimpses are embedded in specific situations, I have commented on them at those places in the narrative where they occurred, and shall not try to recapitulate them here. There are, however, a few characteristics that have appeared repeatedly enough to suggest some tentative generalizations.

Deep scientific discoveries are often regarded as being the result of conceptual "leaps." Since there must be logical gaps separating the previous structure of knowledge in a given area from the new, and since there are no strictly logical procedures for crossing such gaps, it is thought that scientists must get from one side to the other by means of some indivisible, if not unfathomable, perceptual shift. The famous stories of scientists who become aware all at once of the complete solutions to problems on which they had previously been blocked seem to verify this view. Such leaps undoubtedly happen. When we have available close records of scientific thought, as we do for Lavoisier, however, we can see that what appear at a distance as leaps often resolve at short range into smaller moves which narrow, if they do not entirely bridge over, the conceptual gaps involved.[1] The scientist may make not a single jump across the gap, but a prolonged passage through it. If there is no completely logical position between the two sides of the gap, the scientist may have to live for extended periods of time in a state of incoherence. Sometimes he may not notice the inconsistencies inherent in his mental framework, because the situation is complicated enough so that he cannot explore all of its finer structural connections at once. He may, however, be well aware of his state, but because he has committed himself to the passage, he must simply endure it until he can find his way to the far side. We have found Lavoisier more than once in such predicaments.

The individual moves which accumulate to form the "steps" in creative scientific thought may, in fact, be characteristically so minor that by themselves they are trivial. Although only a few such examples appeared visibly in the foregoing account of Lavoisier's investigations, they are probably representative of what would appear more pervasively if scientists kept even more minute records of their thought than Lavoisier did. It may be very common for scientists to "glide" along through many evanescent, barely sensible variations on ideas they are entertaining. Most of the variations cancel out, but occasionally they accumulate in a certain direction until the thinker recognizes a novelty significant enough to begin building deliberately upon it.

We have seen that, for Lavoisier, such small moves often grew into recognizably novel increments in his thought while he was composing drafts for a memoir. The process of writing a scientific paper seems to have been in his case a powerful stimulus to the formation of new insights. The reasons for that effect are self-evident. It is only when one organizes on paper a complicated argument, integrating it with the evidence one has to support it, that one must confront the ambiguities, the loopholes, the blurred edges of ideas that one cannot bring into sharp focus all at once in one's mental field. The nature of the records Lavoisier left behind undoubtedly introduces a bias in our picture. Because he preserved the successive drafts of his memoirs, we have an unusually full record of those ideas that developed as he wrote his formal papers. Had he discarded these drafts but kept a pocket notebook in which he jotted down ideas that occurred to him while he was away from his laboratory and his writing table, we might have obtained a quite different perspective. Nevertheless, the connection between scientific creativity and scientific writing deserves more attention than it receives in most discussions of the discovery process.

The extent to which Lavoisier developed his thought while writing his memoirs suggests a function for scientific papers that is not often emphasized. Scientific papers are characterized in many different ways: as reports of completed research, as announcements of discoveries, as vehicles for knowledge claims, as the end products of a process of "inscription,"[2] as the prime manifestation of the "context of justification," and as the necessary prerequisite for recognition as a practicing scientist. It has become commonplace to point out that as historical accounts of the discoveries they report, published scientific papers are misleading. For the actual pathway of thought and experiment they substitute the best combination of argument and evidence that the author can muster to justify the conclusions he has already reached. When, however, we have been able through laboratory records to approximate more closely the real historical course, we can perceive the relation between that course and its representation in the published paper in a more positive light. Although a scientific paper is everything that is implied in the above labels, it is, or at least for Lavoisier it was, far more. He was not merely contriving idealized or distorted versions of investigations, of which true versions already existed. He was transforming open-ended clusters of ideas and operations into organized, bounded investigative units. Not until he had chosen what to include and to exclude, clarified, linked together the parts, and rationalized what he had done did a coherent, completed investigation exist. Sometimes, as we have seen, he very nearly created an investigation on paper by bringing together experiments that had formerly been parts of other investigations. Producing his scientific papers was, in short, not a matter of reporting accurately or inaccurately on something he had previously done, but an integral part of the creative process.

If Lavoisier regularly changed and developed his views in the course of writing, he appears rarely to have done so in direct response to a specific experimental result. This difference may be in part an artifact. Perhaps he was simply less likely to put down deep reflections in his laboratory notebooks than to write them into the drafts for his memoirs. The pattern seems, however significantly related to his scientific style. In contrast to Priestley, who was forever being surprised by accidental observations that led him to change his mind about something, or to discover something new, Lavoisier most often found in the laboratory what he was looking for. That may be why some historians have thought that he made no novel discoveries. In fact, he made many unanticipated observations, but with the type of experiments he did, these were more likely to be setbacks than sources for discovery. Usually they were measurements which did not fit the interpretation he wished to draw from them. As we have seen, however, he seldom treated such an outcome as a refutation of his expected conclusion or as a starting point for the revision of a theory. Instead he made whatever reasonable assumptions he could to bring his result into line with his purpose. His responses contravene his own precept that "the sole means to preclude mistakes" consists of submitting reason "continuously to the test of experiment."[3] As in other ways, however, what Lavoisier practiced was more effective than what he advocated. J. R. Ravetz has developed the viewpoint that a new type of scientific method, its procedures and its apparatus, are bound to contain "pitfalls" to trap the unwary experimenter.[4] These pitfalls cannot be eliminated except through prolonged experience. Lavoisier was constrained to operate in the midst of innumerable pitfalls, because of the novelty of nearly every aspect of his investigative methods. Had he treated each anomalous result as a significant unexpected effect, he could not have accomplished anything truly significant. Generations of chemists and physiologists worked to refine the analytical methods Lavoisier had invented, before they could be made to yield highly precise and consistent results. In a more mature stage of development of the fields he pioneered, it might have been irresponsible to press the data as far as he did to support his premeditated conclusions. For him it was the only way to make sustained progress.

It is one thing to hold to one's conclusions in the face of results that for unexplained reasons do not entirely conform to them; but we have seen that Lavoisier also frequently used the results of experiments he knew to be flawed, and which he might have improved upon had he been more patient about eliminating all of the operational weak points that were within his technical capacity to remedy. Perhaps there were some individual cases in which he would have benefited by trying once or twice more than he did. In general, however, his willingness to settle for imperfect results was an aspect of his realism, and a factor in his success. By not allowing himself to bog down seeking a perfect analytical solution to any given problem, he was able to keep moving on, tackling the next problem opened up by the solution he accepted as good enough for the present. Lavoisier seems to have been quite aware of these considerations. There were so many sources of uncertainty that he could not hope to remove all of them. He asserted repeatedly in his papers that he did not regard the results he presented as "rigorous." Most openly in the "Memoir on heat," he said, "We cannot insist too much on that subject, that it is less the result of our experiments, than the method which we have used, that we are presenting."[5] If others were to adopt his methods, time would correct the inadequacies he could not expect to overcome all by himself in these first forays into new methodological terrain. His readiness to publish results based on experiments containing obvious flaws, in order to get on with his general program, made the most efficient use of his limited research time. Scientific creativity results sometimes from striving for perfection, but sometimes from making compromises appropriate to the circumstances.

The fact that Lavoisier often made do with imperfect experiments does not imply that he was a cursory experimentalist. In his attention to details in the construction of his apparatus and his procedures, in the repeated modifications he incorporated in his operations and equipment, he displayed a meticulous care, unsurpassed in his age.[6] He had, however, to apportion his time and resources according to the significance of a given result and the precision his purposes required. Fundamental quantities, such as the proportions of carbon and oxygen in carbonic acid, and of hydrogen and oxygen in water, he strove repeatedly to improve upon. He relied on these values for so many other calculations that he needed to have full confidence that they were the best he could attain. For other results that had fewer ulterior consequences for his interlocked structure of compositions and computations, he was more easily content with one or two experiments. When experimental pitfalls blocked his main investigative pathway, he devoted great energy and ingenuity to the effort to circumvent them. Although he never entirely solved the problem of analyzing sugar, or of carrying out a complete analysis of fermentation, his step-by-step responses to the difficulties he encountered showed him to be an able, inventive experimental tactician.

Correspondingly, the fact that Lavoisier did not submit his reasoning to the immediate test of experiment in the orthodox sense of his own "rule," or in the sense that Karl Popper's philosophy of falsification demands, does not signify that he ignored the sustained judgments of experimental results on his ideas. His system of thought was a sturdy growth that did not wilt easily in the face of a few empirical anomalies, but its growth was always conditioned and limited by the experimental environment in which he cultivated it. When Meusnier's arduous effort to reduce the data from a complicated gun barrel experiment led him to conclude that he could not come out with a plausible result unless he assumed that the charcoal in a background experiment contained inflammable air as well as *matière charbonneuse*, Lavoisier began to reconsider his interpretation of a whole range of analogous situations, reaching finally to a fundamental revision of his theory of respiration. The reasons for which he eventually abandoned his theory that fermentation decomposes water are complex, but one of the probable factors was that he was not able to develop decisive experimental support for the deduction that the quantity of water present should diminish during the operation.

We normally think of creativity as an individual affair; but an important source of Lavoisier's success was his capacity to engage in creative collaborations. He was one of the earliest of the great scientists of the past to exploit the fact that major scientific problems may require the joint efforts of scientists who can contribute expertise from different special areas of knowledge. Bucquet, Laplace, and Meusnier could supply for Lavoisier types of experience and insight that he could not duplicate from his own particular background. Moreover, he was obviously as skilled at collaborative research as at lone endeavors. He chose his collaborators well. They were men of independent stature and judgment, not likely to be dominated by him. He was able to attract them to become deeply involved in his problems. He drew on their knowledge to supplement his own. He worked with them closely enough so that, in spite of the different directions from which they came, it is impossible to disentangle all of their respective contributions to the joint phases of their investigations. His collaborators influenced the character and direction of his investigation during these periods, as well as his own approach to subsequent problems. Throughout, however, he maintained the general thrust and objectives of his own program, incorporating these strong partners into his enterprise without diluting his own definition of it.

In his last years the character of Lavoisier's collaborators changed. Seguin did not bring an independent base of experience, but was a younger follower who had learned what he knew of science from Lavoisier himself. He supplied enthusiasm, loyalty, willing hands, and ambition. To the extent that he may have influenced Lavoisier's own approach, the effects were less fortunate than those attributable to Lavoisier's earlier collaborators.

II

So far this chapter has reflected mainly on the intimate levels of Lavoisier's scientific creativity, and short-term characteristics of his experimental activity. Equally important are the long-range patterns of his sustained creative effort. Howard Gruber has particularly stressed the different time scales along which creative activity moves. He contrasts the extreme rapidity of thought, the relatively short time in which particular problems can be solved, and the slowness with which a new point of view develops.[7] We have followed Lavoisier for twenty years as he solved, or tried to solve, one problem after another within the bounds of a single, gradually evolving point of view. That point of view had already taken shape in Lavoisier's mind at the beginning of our story. Its formation is well described in Henry Guerlac's *Lavoisier—The Crucial Year.* The agenda that Lavoisier put down early in 1773, to study "the elastic fluid which is released from bodies," and "the operations by which one can succeed in fixing air," was the general expression of the point of view which guided all of his subsequent scientific work. Among the many problems that he took up within this framework, we have concentrated on those which involved, or were important to, the composition and processes of plants and animals. While Lavoisier was busy trying to solve one particular problem after another in order to deploy his general point of view in these areas, the point of view itself was in that process growing ever more comprehensive.

Gruber has also drawn attention to the idea that scientific thought develops in a process resembling *growth.* "Creative thinking," he writes, "is often thought of as an isolated act, but if instead it is treated as a growth process it may be easier to understand why progress is slow." Growth implies a continuity not readily dissipated by short-term impacts such as the results of individual experiments. "Like any other growing thing, a system of thought must change and yet retain its identity."[8] This point of view helps make sense of the progression of Lavoisier's views in the various areas of his investigations that we have followed. The very simple idea that respiration may separate a portion of the air and release matter of fire, for example, grew more concrete as Lavoisier's conception of air and of matter of fire itself grew clearer. It grew more specific as he compared it to the calcination of mercury, and more complete as he recognized the need to integrate two "effects" in the process, the formation of fixed air as well as the consumption of "pure air." The analogy to combustion, tacitly present from the beginning, but overshadowed for a time by Lavoisier's comparison between respiration and calcination, grew explicit as he generalized his conception of combustion itself. The idea that respiration is the source of animal heat, also included qualitatively from the beginning, grew clearer, and then grew tighter, as Lavoisier and Laplace demonstrated that respiration produces the same quantity of heat as the combustion of charbon. The theory grew more complicated with the addition of the formation of water, and finally it grew more comprehensive as he associated it with work as well as heat, and came to see that it involved the whole material balance of the animal economy. From the nascent sketches of an idea in 1774 and 1775, his conception of respiration grew into a mature theoretical structure. The analogy which stimulated its development shifted from a comparison to calcination, to a comparison to the combustion of charcoal, then to a comparison to the combustion of oil, yet throughout these changes we sense that Lavoisier was developing and modifying the same fundamental analogy. Despite the succession of changes recapitulated above, there is no doubt of the continuity, the lineal descent of Lavoisier's masterly statement in the "First memoir on animal respiration" of 1790 from his earliest notes on the subject. The stages in this growth were correlated with the experimental researches he was carrying on at the corresponding times, and conditioned by their outcomes. It is hard to imagine, however, any outcome of a given set of his experiments that might have induced Lavoisier to drop his basic point of view, to approach respiration from any other direction than its resemblance to combustion.

We have seen repeatedly that Lavoisier moved only gradually between conceptual positions that appear in retrospect to require simple choices between one alternative or another. For two years he harbored elements of the phlogiston theory at some times and under some circumstances, even as he was in the process of constructing another theory of combustion incompatible with it. During the same time he hovered somewhere between the conception of the air as a single, qualitatively changeable substance, and as a composite of two or more fixed species. It took him nearly as long to give up finally the idea that sugar contains preformed water, in favor of the view that only the elements of water are present; and nearly a decade to separate the elementary principle carbon from the *charbon* which was its most conspicuous source. I have characterized these long transitional states as periods in which a scientist must "live with incoherence." That such periods can be so prolonged, even though they must sometimes be uncomfortable, supports Gruber's position that changing one's point of view is a slow process of growth.

When we say that theories, points of view, or investigations *grow*, we should be aware that we have not thereby described these processes fully or literally. As Max Black, Robert Nesbit, Victor Turner, and others have pointed out, we are employing a metaphor, likening these processes to the growth of a living organism.[9] Intellectual growth, or the growth of an activity, shares some but not all of the features of organic growth. The shared meanings include the ideas of gradual change and a continuous identity. That identity, however, is far more problematic when applied to intellectual growth than in literal organic growth. In many cases we can be confident that the plant or animal which becomes larger and changes its form remains the "same" plant or animal, even if its appearance becomes altered beyond direct recognition. For ideas and investigations we have no enduring object on which to pin the continuing identity. We must rely on a judgment that underlying the changes some basic resemblances persist, and that circumstances suggest an ongoing stream of thinking or acting. The ongoing stream is, however, itself metaphorical. The thinking and acting are not literally continuous.

Sustained scientific creativity implies that an individual somehow manages to organize his life so as to direct himself for long periods of time toward coherent objectives; yet his activity need not be rigidly systematic. His overall goal encompasses more projects and problems than can be pursued at any one time, and there is no rule to determine the order in which they should be taken up. Gruber attempts to deal with this problem through the conception of a "network of enterprises." Once a person has taken up a project, according to this point of view, it tends to become a permanent concern, even though he may, for long stretches of time, not be doing anything about it.[10] Whether it is essential to the solution of a broader structure of problems or not, having identified himself with a subject, he tends to return to it. The organization of Lavoisier's scientific life seems to lend itself well to such a pattern. The study of respiration he identified as one of his enterprises in his general agenda in 1773, and he clearly retained it as such until the end of his life. Yet he did not have any notable ideas about it, as far as we can tell, until a year or so later; and he was actively engaged in experiments on respiration only for a few compact episodes—the spring and fall of 1776, the winters of 1782–83 and of 1783–84, and for much of 1790. These were not *isolated* episodes, because the continuity between them shows that Lavoisier identified himself permanently with the endeavor. He thought seriously about taking up the analysis of plant matter in 1774, but had no occasion to do so until 1779. After one foray, he did not systematically pursue the subject until after 1785. Then he kept at it as steadily as circumstances permitted, until the end of 1788. He carried out at least one experiment on fermentation in 1773, probably only one or two more between then and 1785. Then he pursued the subject intermittently, but without major breaks, until the summer of 1787. Thereafter he carried out one more recorded experiment on fermentation, in September 1788; but most of his research activities in the meantime were probably directed at obtaining other information he wanted to know in order to interpret the results of fermentation experiments. An extreme example of the proportion between latent period and active pursuit of an enterprise is Lavoisier's interest in vegetation. Having mentioned it in his agenda of 1773, he did not carry out any experiments on the subject until the summer of 1786. He planned to return to it the following year, but apparently never did. Yet this single incursion into the field itself was a manifestation of an interest permanent enough so that when he was no longer in a position to experiment, in 1792, he participated in, if he did not organize, the effort of the Academy of Sciences to undertake collective research on vegetation.

A striking feature of the organization of Lavoisier's research effort was the long-range continuity and coherence it exhibits in spite of frequent abrupt short-range shifts. He did not systematically complete any of the three major projects we have been following—respiration, plant and animal analysis, or fermentation—before turning to the next, but rotated from one to another in ways that defy completely logical explanation. If we had included in detail his investigations within general chemistry the patterns would appear still more convoluted. Moreover, we see that he repeatedly announced plans for continuing an investigation, but turned instead to one of the other strands in his network of enterprises. Research he claimed to be in progress was never finished. Memoirs whose publication he described as imminent never appeared. His apparent irresolution in following up his most immediate intentions contrasts with the remarkable consistency of the research trail he followed over the whole span of the years from 1772 to 1790. He was both vacillating and steady, an opportunist and a person who never lost sight of his ultimate scientific goals. Lavoisier was always planning ahead, yet forever having to alter his plans to fit local contingencies.

We cannot always specify what caused him to make the short-term shifts. Perhaps it was sometimes simply a matter of changing his mind about priorities when he had more projects in prospect than he could attend to at once. Sometimes he had to wait for the construction of the complicated equipment he utilized, and turned to something else in the meantime. In the case of the ice calorimeter, he had to schedule his research around rare weather conditions. His need to adapt his laboratory time to a busy schedule of other activities probably exaggerated this pattern of interruptions, making it, for example, much more difficult to pursue several possible lines of investigation at once; yet it is, I believe, a factor which we must always take into account when we seek to analyze the ordering of scientific research. Historians and philosophers commonly distinguish the actual course of an investigation from the rationalized reconstruction that the scientist presents after he has solved a given problem. We should distinguish similarly the ideal plans which an investigator holds in advance for his ongoing research from the modifications imposed upon him by contingent circumstances as he seeks to implement those plans. We emphasize that the reconstruction formulated afterward is normally more logical than the research itself. We should note that the advance plans too may be more logical than what can be carried out.[11]

His ability to combine short-range flexibility with long-range persistence of purpose was one of the characteristics that sustained Lavoisier's creative productivity. In a classic essay on creativity in science, Jacques Hadamard remarked that discovery can be stifled either by "attention too narrowly directed," or by its opposite—being "insufficiently faithful" to one's main idea. "In research, it may be detrimental to scatter our attention too much, while overstraining it too strongly in one particular direction may also be harmful to discovery."[12] Lavoisier avoided both extremes. He pursued a set of related general scientific problems which drew on a common and expanding pool of conceptual and methodological tools, but each having as well its own particular stages of development. When blocked for any reason on one project, he always had another to take up again, and progress in any one of these areas was likely to illuminate problems in one of the others. His accumulating experience with a repertoire of laboratory operations usable in different combinations in each of the areas enabled him to tackle progressively more difficult experimental problems. This manner of organizing his research over the years, his "faithfulness" to his main ideas over that time, was at least as important to his scientific accomplishment as was the brilliance or originality of any single piece of it. Lavoisier not only outshone but outdistanced his colleagues in the construction of a new chemistry of life.

This sustained effort is all the more impressive when we remind ourselves that Lavoisier's other responsibilities left him, on the average, with only one full day per week for experimental work. The rest of his scientific activity he had to squeeze into the hours of six to eight in the morning and seven to ten at night.[13] Nothing would have been easier than for this effort to be submerged in the press of administrative duties. Yet for most of that time he found the will and the energy to produce creative scientific investigations at a rate which would compare favorably with the productivity of many more recent scientists who have been able to do their research full-time.

If we accept the propositions that "the stream of thought is incredibly swift,"[14] and that a "thinking person goes over the same ground many times," varying his point of view as he does,[15] then the pace at which a scientist can carry on the slower operational side of his investigative endeavor should have significant effects on the nature of the interactions between thought and experiment. When a person can spend most of his active scientific life in the laboratory we would expect the most intimate interplay between individual results or problems encountered and solved in daily practice and the progression of fine conceptual changes which cumulatively bring about the growth of his theoretical framework. If, on the other hand, he can experiment less often, as Lavoisier was constrained to do, then we might expect more extended trains of subtle reformulations to go on in his mind in the larger intervals between experiments, resulting in more marked evolutions in viewpoint from one experiment to another. There are, unfortunately, no records of Lavoisier's thoughts intimate enough to discern development at a weekly level. We can, however, gain some insight into the nature of such effects by noting the similar effects on a larger scale resulting from Lavoisier's habit of dropping a particular problem for a long time and then returning to it. He took up plant analysis briefly in 1777, and did not come back to it until 1785. Intervening events had by then so modified his point of view that the analyses he carried out differed sharply from those he might have undertaken had he continued his initial approach in 1777. The theory of fermentation that he set out to demonstrate in 1785 had little in common with the theory of fermentation he had hoped to elucidate in 1773. The three major episodes in his experimental investigation of respiration also differed strikingly, in ways dependent largely on the lapses of time separating them. We cannot speculate on the patterns his investigation of respiration would have assumed had he been able to carry it out in one continuous project, or in what way his conclusions might have differed; but we can be certain that they *would* have differed.

The capacity to maintain over nearly twenty years a research program that appears in retrospect singularly coherent, despite the local pressures which threatened and diverted it along the way, can be explained partly in terms of personal drive, strength of will, steadiness of purpose, and the ability to organize one's life. It requires in addition the special and elusive quality of foresight—to be able to head persistently toward a destination one has never seen. Lavoisier displayed such ability on many levels. In 1773 he foresaw already that he could produce a revolution in chemistry. When he had made only a tentative analysis of the composition of one plant substance, sugar, he predicted that the extension of this approach to many plant and animal substances would open up a vast new pathway of investigation. When he had determined that two or three inflammable plant materials contained carbon and hydrogen, he was already confident that the same two constituents underlay the composition of all plant substances. He could visualize that the maintenance of a constant body temperature must involve control over the distribution of fluids in the body and over heat losses, when there was no direct evidence available concerning these processes. If we compare the agenda he set out for himself in 1773—to study the operations of vegetation, respiration, calcination, and combustion as processes which fix or release airs—with what he had done by 1790, we can see that this agenda did in fact guide his research through much of the seventeen years in between.

Foresight is the ability not only to perceive future opportunities, but to sense pitfalls lurking ahead in order to avoid them. When Lavoisier decided that a given analytical result was good enough to publish, even though he knew it to be far from "rigorous," he was making a judgment that a circumscribed additional effort was not likely to resolve the remaining difficulties, that a definitive solution must wait for a later stage of development. He thereby avoided wasting scarce time he could better apply to other problems. His avoidance of the kinds of sterile speculative webs others wove around his theory of respiration represented not only judgments that existing evidence was inadequate to support them, but predictions that with the methods available one could not build fruitful experiments around such views.

To see ahead is not to be able to specify the shape of the future in detail, only to detect enough of its vague outlines to know which direction to move in, to set one's priorities. Lavoisier's projections often proved wrong in detail afterward, but the general point of view embedded in them usually prevailed. The classificatory system into which he predicted plant substances would fit proved far too simple, but the viewpoint on which it was based, that the substances could be classified according to the proportions of the carbon, hydrogen, and oxygen composing them, survived. Lavoisier probably had no idea of how complicated the internal processes of respiration are, but the general theory of respiration he laid out was adaptable to the complexities he could not himself have envisioned. His sense of the length of time it would take to reach a goal he could foresee was far from infallible. Just before he had to withdraw from his last respiration experiments he seemed to feel that he would be able to resolve the remaining difficulties in what appears in retrospect an implausibly short time. The task which he set out for the Academy prize to be awarded after two years actually took scientists closer to fifty years to complete. Optimism, however, is probably at least as important for sustained scientific productivity as is foresight.

III

The main thrust of the preceding story has been to take us behind the public surface of Lavoisier's science, represented in his formal writings, in order to follow his private investigative trail. The public representations of that trail are, however, not merely distorted images of the true path, but a crucial phase in the creative process itself. I have already pointed out that Lavoisier finished creating an organized investigation only when he had finished composing the memoir which then served to justify it to his colleagues. In an earlier chapter, for a situation in which it was a special problem for him, I commented on the importance of the manner in which a scientist not only presents his own work, but situates it with respect to the prior state of the problem he hopes to advance. Lavoisier's skill at these aspects of his task was central to the success of his enterprise. He understood in a sophisticated way the function of scientific papers. He treated them not as transparent reports of his actual research pathway, but as logically reasoned arguments derived from it. Nevertheless, he did not present his arguments and conclusions as definitive. Polished though his memoirs were, after the successive stages of writing he put them through, they were still only progress reports: the best efforts he could make at the time, but imperfect, provisional statements, just as his experiments provided imperfect, provisional results. He never hesitated to return to analytical problems for which he had already published solutions, in order to improve on them. Nor did it embarrass him to revise theoretical positions without taking special notice of the differing earlier statements which he thereby supplanted. We may take these features of scientific literature for granted, but that is because Lavoisier's approach to science was so like that of our own age. We need only compare his publications with the refreshing but rambling tales of personal experimental adventures that Priestley published, or with the writings of someone like Girtanner who fancied he could achieve a universal synthesis of physiology in one or two articles, to see that in the realm of public presentation too, Lavoisier brought exceptional insight to his science.

Even though impressed by the skill with which Lavoisier presented his results in public, we may question his candor about the quality of the evidence on which his published results rested. Although the experiments he reported in detail always represented those he had actually carried out, he regularly created the impression that he had done many more, when the record suggests that he had done only a few. He acknowledged some of the sources of uncertainty in his experimental procedures, but seldom revealed the full extent of the adjustments to which he habitually resorted in order to "improve" the data, or to make them conform more closely to his expectations. One could even view his statements that his analyses were far from rigorous as contrivances to make him appear modest and cautious in his claims. If he was, in some respects, less than candid, he was tactically realistic. He was acutely aware of the need to win converts to his new chemical system.[16] A complete public display of all of his methodological difficulties might only lead those whom he hoped to attract to dismiss his approach as too unreliable to bet on for the future. He put the best light on these situations that he could, stretching the truth somewhat, but not so far as to deplete his credibility. The only criterion by which we can justify the wisdom of his judgment in such matters is that the subsequent development of the areas of general chemistry, plant and animal chemistry, and physiology, by those who did adopt his point of view, shows that he had not misled them about the value of his methods.

One feature of Lavoisier's public science cannot be construed as a strength. There is no way that his penchant for presenting quantitative results with long strings of numbers after the decimal point, or expressing weights in pounds, ounces, gros, grains, and sometimes even fractions of a grain, can be seen as realistic. We are probably more offended than his contemporaries, because we are so deeply conditioned to the restrictions on "significant figures." Contemporaries too, however, complained about the practice. When William Nicholson retranslated the annotated French edition of Kirwan's *Essay on Phlogiston* into English in 1789, he added in a preface a penetrating discussion of the liimits of accuracy of the quantities Lavoisier used in his calculations. He then commented,

> As a reference to weights in the experiments of Mr. Lavoisier is made to constitute a great part of the arguments . . . , I think it proper (highly as I esteem his talents) to take notice that his writings abound with specific gravities of elastic fluids, carried to five places of figures, which are so far from being given as estimate numbers, that they are used as elements in results, carried to six, seven, and even eight places of figures. If it be denied that these

> results are pretended to be true in the last figures, I must beg leave to observe that these long rows of figures, which in some instances extend to a thousand times the nicety of experiment, serve only to exhibit a parade which true science has no need of: and, more than this, that when the real degree of accuracy in experiments is thus hidden from our contemplation, we are somewhat disposed to doubt whether the *exactitude scrupuleuse* of the experiments be indeed such as to render the proofs *de l'ordre démonstratif.*[17]

I do not think that Lavoisier intended to deceive. His explanation that he simply reported the exact numbers that he obtained in his calculations can be confirmed by duplicating the calculations from his original data without rounding anything off. He seemed unaware that such a procedure was questionable. In his *Elementary Treatise* he included a chapter on weighing, in which he discussed very cogently the operational precautions necessary to attain the greatest possible precision; but he said nothing at all there about the degree of accuracy in the figures which was meaningful.[18] It is not easy to understand how a man who aimed to persuade, as Lavoisier did, and who was in many respects eminently persuasive, could persist in a practice which, as Nicholson's commentary shows, was apt to have just the opposite effect. It was a strange and prominent lapse in the sensitivity of a person otherwise well attuned to the psychological as well as the technical requirements for attaining his scientific goals.

IV

The pattern of sustained research from 1773 to 1790 which was so important to Lavoisier's scientific success required a determined will, foresight, and resourceful organization of his time. These attributes were as vital to his achievement as were the creative imagination and experimental skill he brought to his task. We can view such qualities as inherent to his individual scientific personality. They were manifested, however, within the very special environment of the Academy of Sciences. Lavoisier's serious approach to his enterprise can also be viewed, therefore, as a mark of what Charles Gillispie has recently described as the stage of near professionalism prevailing in the activities of the Academy during this era. The aura of competitive emulation within that body served to raise the scientific standards of the many aspirants to membership, and to sustain the diligence of those who entered the charmed circle.[19] The stable scientific role bestowed by membership in the Academy, and the mutual admiration for scientific achievements which members inspired in one another, must have reinforced Lavoisier's innate capacity for hard work, encouraging him to the persistent productivity necessary to retain or enhance his standing among his peers.

If the professional attitudes prevalent in the Academy probably urged Lavoisier onward toward his professional research style, the incompleteness of the professional status of academicians provided the impediments which limited the scope of his research. Although the academicians received pensions, these fell far short of their financial needs. They were required also to have outside posts or sources of income.[20] In Lavoisier's case such needs, together with the various duties incumbent upon an academician, account for the fact that he had just one full working day per week left over for research. Had he been able to experiment more often, the character of his experiments undoubtedly would have been different. He would then have had more time to refine each experimental operation and less need to rely on his skill at shoring up flawed results by maneuvers with the data. He might have been able to implement more of the various plans for continuing investigations which he dropped after publicly announcing them. His patterns of movement from one problem to another would have been quite different, and in some manner the nature and range of his conclusions would inevitably have been affected.

In his *Elementary Treatise* Lavoisier compared his method of reasoning in chemistry to the way in which mathematicians solve problems. He not only greatly admired the rigorous standard of the reasoning of mathematicians, but imitated it when he attempted to introduce algebraic equations to represent the balance between the materials and the products of a chemical operation. He was probably influenced to do so in part by his collaboration with two mathematicians. Both his admiration for mathematics and his associations with mathematicians were probably facilitated by the organization of the Academy. Because of its small size, a member came into contact with only a few colleagues from his own field, but mixed readily with leaders from other sciences. In this way he came to know not only Laplace, but Gaspard Monge, whom he also admired. The intellectual connection he sought to make between chemistry and mathematics thus reflected a type of social connection that the institutional structure of French science fostered.

Throughout this book I have focused on the intrinsic character of Lavoisier's scientific work rather than on the social context within which he pursued it. The above three examples, however, suggest ways in which studies like this one can promote a deeper examination of the interplay between science and its accompanying institutional conditions. Much has been claimed recently about the influences of the social context on the direction of scientific progress and on the nature of the content of science. Some even assert that scientific knowledge is solely the product of social processes. Too often, however, the connections adduced between the social milieu and the scientific activity are vague and global. Only by immersing ourselves fully in the fine structure of scientific investigation itself can we identify those aspects of it which may be sensitive to the attending institutional or other conditions; and only then can we locate the discrete impacts of the context upon the type of scientific knowledge produced. In the above cases, it is only when we have elucidated certain characteristics of Lavoisier's experimental practices which clearly impinged upon the nature of his conclusions, and have shown that these characteristics were dependent in part upon the time and resources that he had available for research, that we open an avenue for connecting the qualities of his science with the opportunities and obstacles that his institutional framework provided for him. Similarly, it is only when we can see the effects of the sustained pattern of movement of his research over the years on the contours of his scientific achievement that we can link the nature of that achievement to the ethos of the organization which may have helped him to sustain that pattern. It is only when we know how he tried to apply a mathematical model to his own work that we can assess the impact of an institutional environment which facilitated his contacts with mathematicians.

* * *

In this concluding chapter I have tried to draw out of the preceding narrative some of the general characteristics of Antoine Lavoisier's scientific work which may help to explain its creative success. Can what we learn from such a study of one scientist illuminate the nature of scientific creativity in general? Gruber warns us that "what we mean by creativity is the achievement of something unique, or at least very rare. There is no reason at all to think that any two creative people are alike in those key respects that lead us to label them as creative: what is most evident about each one is the uniqueness of his or her achievement."[21] It may be, however, that while the particular combinations of creative attributes that make up an individual are unique, and uniquely related to his or her scientific achievement, similar attributes recur in different combinations in different individuals. In treating three scientists—Claude Bernard, Hans Krebs, and Lavoisier—at the level of their daily laboratory work and thought, I have felt both the striking individual differences between them and the repetition of some basic common patterns. We need to explore many individual combinations if we are to move toward a general understanding of the elements of scientific creativity.

Notes
Index

Notes

In references to unnumbered pages in Lavoisier's manuscripts, I have placed page numbers in brackets. These numbers represent numbers I have used on the Xerox copies of these manuscripts with which I have worked. They are intended to serve as only an approximate guide to the location of the sources cited.

Introduction

1 Howard E. Gruber, *Darwin on Man: A Psychological Study of Scientific Creativity,* 2d ed. (Chicago: University of Chicago Press, 1981), pp. x–xii, 4; Gerald Holton, *The Scientific Imagination: Case Studies* (Cambridge: Cambridge University Press, 1976), p. viii. I have discussed this point of view in Frederic L. Holmes, "The Fine Structure of Scientific Creativity," *History of Science* 19 (1981):60–70.

2 Thomas Nickles, "Introductory Essay: Scientific Discovery and the Future of Philosophy of Science," in T. Nickles, ed., *Scientific Discovery, Logic, and Rationality,* Boston Studies in the Philosophy of Science, vol. 56 (Dordrecht: D. Reidel, 1978), pp. 1–60.

3 For example, S. F. Mason, *Main Currents of Scientific Thought: A History of the Sciences* (New York: Henry Schuman, 1953), pp. 249–250.

4 A. R. Hall, *The Scientific Revolution: 1500–1800* (Boston: Beacon Press, 1954), p. 332. See also Herbert Butterfield, *The Origins of Modern Science, 1300–1800,* 2d ed. rev. (Toronto: Clarke, Irwan, 1968), p. 206.

5 Henry Guerlac, *Lavoisier—The Crucial Year: The Background and Origin of His First Experiments on Combustion in 1772* (Ithaca: Cornell University Press, 1961), p. xvii.

6 J. R. Partington, *A History of Chemistry,* vol. 3 (London: Macmillan, 1962), p. 376.

7 Charles Coulston Gillispie, *The Edge of Objectivity: An Essay in the History of Scientific Ideas* (Princeton: Princeton University Press, 1960), p. 216.

8 Ibid., p. 215.

9 Ibid.; Henry Guerlac, "Lavoisier, Antoine-Laurent," in Charles C. Gillispie, ed., *Dictionary of Scientific Biography,* 16 vols. (New York: Charles Scribner's Sons,

1970–80), 8:66–91. Published also as Henry Guerlac, *Antoine-Laurent Lavoisier: Chemist and Revolutionary* (New York: Charles Scribner's Sons, 1975).

10 See note 5.

11 Leonard G. Wilson, "The Transformation of Ancient Concepts of Respiration in the Seventeenth Century," *Isis* 51(1959):161–172; Robert G. Frank, *Harvey and the Oxford Physiologists: A Study of Scientific Ideas and Social Interaction* (Berkeley: University of California Press, 1980); Diana Long Hall, *Why Do Animals Breathe?* (New York: Arno Press, 1981); Diana Long Hall, "'Bacon's Mansions': The Frustrations and Rewards of Respiratory Physiology in the Enlightenment," *Bulletin of the History of Medicine* 50(1976): 151–173; Everett Mendelsohn, *Heat and Life: The Development of the Theory of Animal Heat* (Cambridge, Mass.: Harvard University Press, 1964); G. J. Goodfield, *The Growth of Scientific Physiology* (London: Hutchinson, 1960), pp. 13–59.

12 Joseph S. Fruton, *Molecules and Life: Historical Essays on the Interplay of Chemistry and Biology* (New York: Wiley-Interscience, 1972), pp. 23–86.

13 Jon Eklund, *The Incompleat Chymist* (Washington, D.C.: Smithsonian Institution Press, 1975); Maurice Crosland, *Historical Studies in the Language of Chemistry* (Cambridge, Mass.: Harvard University Press, 1962).

Chapter 1. An Ambitious Agenda

1 Richard Lower, *De Corde,* in R. T. Gunther, ed., *Early Science in Oxford,* (London: Dawsons, 1968), 9:168.

2 An excellent concise description of these investigations and the prior state of the problem is in Leonard G. Wilson, "The Transformation of Ancient Concepts of Respiration in the Seventeenth Century." *Isis* 51(1959):161–172; Robert G. Frank, *Harvey and the Oxford Physiologists: A Study of Scientific Ideas and Social Interaction* (Berkeley: University of California Press, 1980), gives a compelling picture of the collaborative activities of the people involved in these investigations.

3 Henry Guerlac, *Lavoisier—The Crucial Year, The Background and Origin of His First Experiments on Combustion in 1772* (Ithaca: Cornell University Press, 1961), pp. 20–22.

4 The most complete account of the long period of investigation and frustration is Diana Long Hall, *Why Do Animals Breathe?* (New York: Arno Press, 1981).See also Diana Long Hall, "'Bacon's Mansions': The Frustrations and Rewards of Respiratory Physiology in the Enlightenment," *Bulletin of the History of Medicine* 50(1976): 151–173.

5 Stephen Hales, *Vegetable Staticks,* in Michael Hoskin, ed., *History of Science Library: Primary Sources* (New York: Science History Publications, 1969), pp. 133–147.

6 Henry Guerlac, "Joseph Black and Fixed Air: Part II," *Isis* 48(1957): 451–453. For further discussion of statements by "disciples" of Black, see Everett Mendelsohn, *Heat and Life: The Development of the Theory of Animal Heat* (Cambridge, Mass.: Harvard University Press, 1964), pp. 109–125.

7 Guerlac, "Joseph Black and Fixed Air," p. 455.

8 Joseph Priestley, "Observations et expériences sur différentes espèces d'air," *Observations sur la physique* 6(1773): 298, 301, 308, 311–312, 314–316.
9 Ibid., pp. 314, 316.
10 Ibid., pp. 313–314, 318–321.
11 Guerlac, *Lavoisier—The Crucial Year,* passim and pp. 70–71.
12 Antoine Lavoisier, *Opuscules physiques et chymiques* (Paris: Durand, Didot, Esprit, 1774), pp. 109–110. Although he did not publish this volume until 1774, it has been established that Lavoisier began presenting the material composing it at the Academy of Sciences in April 1773. See Maurice Daumas, *Lavoisier: Théoricien et expérimentateur* (Paris: Presses Universitaires, 1955), p. 30.
13 Lavoisier, *Opuscules,* pp. 124–131.
14 Lavoisier's plan of research has been reproduced in M. Berthelot, *La révolution chimique: Lavoisier* (Paris: Félix-Alcan, 1890), pp. 46–49, and Guerlac, *Lavoisier—The Crucial Year,* pp. 228–230.
15 See note 14.
16 See note 14. Lavoisier's vision of these processes as portions of a great chain of events may be viewed as an expression of a general trend in the eighteenth century to join the plant, animal, and mineral kingdoms, with the atmosphere, into a coherent picture of nature as a "circulation of matter." See Mikulas Teich, "Circulation, Transformation, Conservation of Matter and the Balancing of the Biological World in the Eighteenth Century," *Ambix* 29 (1982): 17–28.
17 Berthelot, *La révolution chimique,* pp. 233–238. (Summaries of Lavoisier's unpublished laboratory registers.)
18 Ibid., pp. 234–235, 240–242, 244–246.
19 Lavoisier, *Opuscules,* p. 131.
20 Lavoisier, Cahiers de laboratoire, Archives of the Académie des Sciences, Paris, R-1, f. 17. Berthelot, *La révolution chimique,* p. 235, quotes this passage, but reads "par les animaux" instead of "sur les animaux"—a crucial distortion of the meaning.
21 Berthelot, *La révolution chimique,* pp. 235–236.
22 Lavoisier, *Opuscules,* p. 110; Abbé Rozier, *Mémoire sur la meilleure manière de faire et de gouverner les vins* (Paris: Ruault, 1772), p. 151; Robert Kohler, "The Origin of Lavoisier's First Experiments in Combustion," *Isis* 63 (1972): 349–355; René Fric, "Contribution à l'étude des idées de Lavoisier sur la nature de l'air et sur la calcination des métaux," *Archives internationales d'histoire des sciences* 12 (1959): 161–162, 166–167. Fric's circumstantial dating is based on the fact that the *procès-verbaux* record that Lavoisier read a paper with a similar title at that meeting. If, however, the preserved draft was written later, Lavoisier's statements about fermentation might refer to the experiment described in the next paragraph, together with two concurrent experiments in which he noted that mixtures of wine and water, and of bran and water, eventually absorb air. Berthelot, *La révolution chimique,* p. 243.
23 Lavoisier, Cahiers, R-1, ff. 47v, 48. For discussion of the types of fermentation, see [Pierre-Joseph Macquer], *Dictionnaire de chymie,* 2 vols. (Paris: Lacombe, 1766), 1:494.
24 Lavoisier, *Opuscules,* pp. v–vi.
25 Lavoisier, *Opuscules,* pp. 237–248, 293–294, 320.

26 Ibid., pp. 302–307.
27 Ibid., pp. 309–310.
28 Lavoisier, Cahiers, R-1, f. 71. See also Lavoisier, *Opuscules*, pp. 350–351.
29 Daumas, *Lavoisier*, pp. 30–31.
30 Lavoisier, *Opuscules*, pp. iv–v.
31 Ibid., p. 319.
32 Henry Guerlac, *Antoine-Laurent Lavoisier: Chemist and Revolutionary* (New York: Charles Scribner's Sons, 1975), p. 82.
33 Lavoisier, Cahiers, R-2, ff. 20–22.
34 Lavoisier, *Opuscules*, pp. 312–314, 319–320.
35 Lavoisier, Cahiers, R-2, f. 23. (Photocopy in Archives of the Académie des Sciences. The original of Cahier R-2 is contained in the Bibliothèque Municipale de Perpignon, MS 61.) Above this passage is written "Expérience à revoir." It is possible, therefore, that the passage as a whole is not a record of an experiment actually performed, but a reminder to perform such an experiment—an alternative which would modify only slightly my comments on its significance.
36 See above, p. 7.
37 Lavoisier, *Opuscules*, pp. 304–305.
38 Ibid., pp. 305–307, 309–310, 350–351.
39 Joseph Priestley, *Experiments and Observations on Different Kinds of Air*, 2 vols. (London: J. Johnson, 1774–75), 1:70–71.
40 Ibid., 1:47.
41 Ibid., 1:194–195.
42 Ibid., 1:194. Mendelsohn has described lectures given by Andrew Duncan at Edinburgh in the winter of 1774 as "the earliest attempt to account for animal heat through the agency of phlogiston." Whether or not Priestley's discussion preceded that of Duncan, Mendelsohn's assertion would hold, because Priestley did not at this time associate respiration with animal heat. The similarity between these views, expressed nearly simultaneously, invites further exploration of the connections between Priestley's views and those of Duncan. Mendelsohn does not describe Priestley's investigations of respiration in detail. See Mendelsohn, *Heat and Life*, pp. 113–114.
43 Priestley, *Experiments and Observations*, 1:178.
44 Hales, *Vegetable Staticks*, p. 125.
45 Stephen Hales, *Statical Essays: Containing Haemastaticks* (London: Innys and Manby, 1733; facsimile reprint, New York: Hafner, 1964), table of contents and p. 292.
46 Priestley, *Experiments and Observations*, 1:108–115.
47 Berthelot, *La révolution chimique*, pp. 250–251.
48 See Lavoisier, Cahier, R-2, ff. 30–115.
49 Lavoisier, "Sur la calcination des métaux dans les vaisseaux fermés, et sur la cause de l'augmentation de poids qu'ils acquierent pendant cette opération," *Observations sur la physique* 2(1774):451. The revised version of this manuscript printed in Lavoisier's collected works replaces this conclusion with one reflecting a later stage in his thought. See *Oeuvres de Lavoisier*, 6 vols. (Paris: Imprimerie Impériale, 1862–93), 2:120.

50 Lavoisier, "Calcination des métaux," p. 449.
51 Lavoisier, Fiche 350, Archives of the Académie des Sciences.
52 Howard E. Gruber, *Darwin on Man: A Psychological Study of Scientific Creativity,* 2d ed. (Chicago: University of Chicago Press, 1981), p. 5.
53 Lavoisier, *Opuscules*, p. 280.
54 Henry Guerlac, "Chemistry as a Branch of Physics: Laplace's Collaboration with Lavoisier," *Historical Studies in the Physical Sciences* 7(1976):200–201.
55 Cyril Stanley Smith, personal conversation, 1963. See also Cyril Stanley Smith, *A History of Metallography* (Chicago: University of Chicago Press, 1960), p. xix.
56 Hales, *Vegetable Staticks*, pp. 85–107; Guerlac, *Lavoisier—The Crucial Year,* pp. 29–35.
57 Frederic L. Holmes, "Analysis by Fire and Solvent Extractions: The Metamorphosis of a Tradition," *Isis* 62(1970):129–148; Reinhard Löw, *Pflanzenchemie zwischen Lavoisier und Liebig* (Munich: Donau-Verlag, 1977), pp. 46–60.
58 Guerlac, *Antoine-Laurent Lavoisier,* pp. 52–53.
59 Holmes, "Analysis by Fire and Solvent Extractions," p. 144.
60 Lavoisier, Fiche 251, Archives of the Académie des Sciences, nos. 35–66.
61 Ibid., no. 57.
62 Lavoisier, Cahiers, R-2, f. 70.
63 Lavoisier, Cahiers, R-3, ff. 50–51. Berthelot, *La révolution chimique,* pp. 260–261, gives a condensed version of this passage, without indicating that he has left out significant portions of it. Berthelot also gives the impression that a discussion on "the nature of acids" is a continuation of these reflections, whereas in fact it begins on a separate page.
64 Lavoisier, *Opuscules*, pp. 274–276, 280.
65 Lavoisier, Cahiers, R-2, ff. 23, 30, 38–41.
66 Lavoisier, Fiche 170, Archives of the Académie des Sciences.
67 Ibid.
68 Lavoisier, "De l'élasticité et de la formation des fluides élastiques," Fiche 171, Archives of the Académie des Sciences, pp. 1–5.
69 Ibid., pp. 5–5v.
70 Ibid., p. 5v.
71 Ibid.
72 Ibid., p. 6.
73 Priestley, *Experiments and Observations*, 1:95.
74 Lavoisier, Fiche 171, p. 6.
75 Ibid., pp. 6–6v.
76 Ibid., p. 6v.
77 Ibid.
78 Lavoisier, "Sur la détonation du nitre," Fiche 169, Archives of the Académie des Sciences, p. 1.
79 Ibid., pp. 1–2.
80 Lavoisier, "Sur les acides en vapeurs appelés airs acides par M. Priestley," Fiche 168, Archives of the Académie des Sciences.
81 Ibid.

Chapter 2. Lavoisier in Midstream

1 The best-known recent comparison between scientific investigation and puzzle solving is in Thomas S. Kuhn, *The Structure of Scientific Revolutions*, 2d ed. (Chicago: University of Chicago Press, 1970), pp. 35–42. I am using the word *puzzle* in a more general sense than Kuhn does when characterizing "normal science."

2 Pierre Bayen, "Essai d'expériences chymiques, faites sur quelques précipités de mercure, dans la vue de découvrir leur nature," *Observations sur la physique* 3(1774):284.

3 Guerlac, *Lavoisier—The Crucial Year: The Background and Origin of his First Experiments on Combustion in 1772* (Ithaca: Cornell University Press, 1961), pp. 125–145.

4 Bayen, "Précipités de mercure," p. 284.

5 C. E. Perrin, "Prelude to Lavoisier's Theory of Calcination: Some Observations on *Mercurius Calcinatus per se*," *Ambix* 16(1969):140–151.

6 Bayen, "Précipités de mercure," pp. 129–145, 280–295. For a description of Meyer's *acidum pinque*, see J. R. Partington, *A History of Chemistry*, Vol. 3 (London: Macmillan, (1962), p. 145.

7 Bayen, "Précipités de mercure," pp. 288, 291.

8 Anon., "Discours sur le phlogistique," *Observations sur la physique* 3(1774):185–200.

9 Perrin, "Prelude to Lavoisier's Theory of Calcination," pp. 144–145.

10 C.-L. Cadet, "Observations et expériences de M. Cadet, sur le mercure précipité *per se*," *Observations sur la physique* 4(1775):55–60.

11 Brisson, Lavoisier, and Sage, "Rapport de messieurs les commissaires de l'Académie Royale des Sciences, concernant les expériences qui ont été faites sur le mercure précipité *per se* de M. Baumé, et sur celui qui a été préparé par M. Cadet," *Observations sur la physique* 4(1775):61–62.

12 Perrin, "Prelude to Lavoisier's Theory of Calcination," pp. 150–151. See also Henry Guerlac, *Antoine-Laurent Lavoisier: Chemist and Revolutionary* (New York: Charles Scribner's Sons, 1975), pp. 83–84. Similar claims have been made on behalf of Bayen. See Max Speter, *Lavoisier und seine Vorläufer* (Stuttgart: Ferdinand Enke, 1910), pp. 48–51. For a balanced evaluation of both claims, see Maurice Daumas, *Lavoisier: théoricien et expérimentateur* (Paris: Presses Universitaires, 1955), pp. 69–81.

13 Lavoisier, "Mémoire sur la nature du principe qui se combine avec les métaux pendant leur calcination, et qui en augmente le poids," *Observations sur la physique* 5(1775):429 n. 1, 430.

14 Ibid., p. 429 n. 1; Brisson, Lavoisier, and Sage, "Rapport," p. 62.

15 M. Berthelot, *La révolution chimique: Lavoisier* (Paris: Félix-Alcan, 1890), p. 264; Lavoisier, Fiche 1670, Archives of the Académie des Sciences.

16 Speter, *Lavoisier und seine Vorläufer,* p. 21.

17 Berthelot, *La révolution chimique*, pp. 264–265.

18 Ibid., p. 265.

19 Lavoisier, "La nature du principe," p. 429 n. 1.

20 Lavoisier, Cahiers, R-3, ff. 77–79.

21 Lavoisier, "La nature du principe," p. 432.
22 Lavoisier, Cahiers, R-3, f. 78.
23 Ibid.
24 Ibid., f. 79.
25 For a description of Magellan's general role in maintaining contacts between English and continental scientists, see Guerlac, *Lavoisier—The Crucial Year,* pp. 36–40.
26 J. Magellan, "Extrait d'une lettre sur de nouvelles expériences de M. Priestley, sur l'air fixe," *Observations sur la physique* 3(1774):145–147.
27 Lavoisier, "La nature du principe," pp. 429, 431–433.
28 James Bryant Conant, ed., *The Overthrow of the Phlogiston Theory: The Chemical Revolution of 1775–1789,* Harvard Case Histories in Experimental Science (Cambridge, Mass.: Harvard University Press, 1950), p. 22.
29 Gaston Bachelard, *La formation de l'esprit scientifique* (Paris: J. Vrin, 1975), pp. 13–22.
30 Lavoisier, "La nature du principe," p. 435.
31 See above, pp. 25–27.
32 See above, p. 26.
33 Lavoisier, "La nature du principe," p. 429.
34 Joseph Priestley, *Experiments and Observations on Different Kinds of Air,* 2 vols. (London: J. Johnson, 1774–75), 2:29–48; Joseph Priestley, "An Account of Further Discoveries on Air," *Philosophical Transactions of the Royal Society* 66(1775):387.
35 Priestley, "An Account," pp. 387–388.
36 Guerlac, *Antoine-Laurent Lavoisier,* p. 86.
37 Berthelot, *La révolution chimique,* pp. 267–269.
38 Lavoisier, Cahiers, R-4, f. 1.
39 Ibid., f. 2.
40 Ibid., ff. 4–8.
41 Ibid., ff. 7–8.
42 Ibid., ff. 1, 3. My interpretation that Lavoisier carried out these tests on the products of the earlier experiment only after producing and testing the nitrous air described above is tentative. It is based mainly on the fact that the quoted phrases are clearly added in the margins, and the fact that if he did not do them in this order, his nitrous air must have come from some unmentioned source.
43 Ibid., ff. 10–14; Berthelot, *La révolution chimique,* p. 271. I have not seen ff. 12 and 14, and have filled in my description of the outcome of the experiment from Lavoisier's later published account of the same, or a very similar, experiment. See Lavoisier, "Expériences sur la respiration des animaux," *Mémoires de l'Académie des Sciences,* (1777[1780]), pp. 186–187.
44 Guerlac, *Antoine-Laurent Lavoisier,* p. 91; Berthelot, *La révolution chimique,* p. 271.
45 Berthelot, *La révolution chimique,* p. 271.
46 Lavoisier, "Expériences sur la respiration des animaux," pp. 187–188. See Jon Eklund, *The Incompleat Chymist* (Washington, D.C.: Smithsonian Institution Press, 1975), pp. 2–3, for a discussion of the importance of analysis and synthesis in eighteenth-century chemistry.

47 Lavoisier, "Mémoire sur l'existence de l'air dans l'acide nitreux," *Recueil de mémoires et d'observations sur la formation et la fabrication du salpêtre* (Paris: Lacombe, 1776), pp. 601–617. For an incisive discussion of the development of Lavoisier's view of the role of "pure air" in acids, see Maurice Crosland, "Lavoisier's Theory of Acidity," *Isis* 64 (1973):306–325.

48 Lavoisier, "De l'air dans l'acide nitreux," p. 615.

49 Ibid., p. 610.

50 Speter, *Lavoisier und seine Vorläufer*, pp. 13, 32–33. For examples of Lavoisier's early reasoning within phlogiston chemistry, see Richard C. Jennings, "Lavoisier's Views on Phlogiston and the Matter of Fire before about 1770," *Ambix* 27(1981):206–209.

51 Lavoisier, "De l'air dans l'acide nitreux," pp. 616–617.

52 Ibid., p. 603.

53 Howard E. Gruber, *Darwin on Man: A Psychological Study of Scientific Creativity*, 2d ed. (Chicago: University of Chicago Press, 1981), p. 115.

54 René Fric, ed., *Oeuvres de Lavoisier: Correspondence*, 3 vols. (Paris: Editions Albin Michel, 1955–1964), 3:565.

55 Lavoisier, Cahiers, R-4, f. 16.

56 Lloyd G. Stevenson, *The Meaning of Poison* (Lawrence: University of Kansas Press, 1959), p. 9.

57 Priestley, *Experiments and Observations*, 1:194.

58 Ibid., 1:70–188.

59 For a similar comment, in the context of the thought of Aristotle and of Galileo, see Thomas S. Kuhn, "A Function for Thought Experiments," *The Essential Tension* (Chicago: University of Chicago Press, 1977), p. 258.

Chapter 3. The Emergence of a Theory of Respiration

1 Joseph Priestley, *Experiments and Observations on Different Kinds of Air*, 2 vols. (London: J. Johnson, 1774–75), 2:276–278.

2 Joseph Priestley, "Observations on Respiration, and the Use of the Blood," *Philosophical Transactions of the Royal Society*, (1776), p. 227.

3 See above, p. 3.

4 Priestley, "Observations on Respiration," pp. 237–248.

5 Lavoisier, Fiche 1696, Archives of the Académie des Sciences, contains the reprint, inscribed "M. Lavoisier, from the author," with a note from Magellan dated April 2, 1776.

6 Lavoisier, "Expériences sur la décomposition de l'air dans le poulmon, et sur un des principaux usages de la respiration dans l'économie animale," Fiche 1349, Archives of the Académie des Sciences, p. [6].

7 Ibid.

8 Ibid., pp. [6–7].

9 See above, p. 7.

10 See above, p. 29.

11 Lavoisier, "Expériences sur la décomposition . . . et sur un des principaux usages," p. [7].

12 Ibid., pp. [7–8].

13 On Trudaine de Montigny and his laboratory, see Suzanne Delorme, "Une famille de grands commis de l'état amis des sciences, au XVIIIe siècle les Trudaine," *Revue d'histoire des sciences* 3(1950):105–106. Charles Gillispie identified Etienne Mignot de Montigny for me. Personal communication, February 8, 1983. Lavoisier refers to him only as "M. de Montigny." For a biographical sketch of Montigny, see Charles Coulston Gillispie, *Science and Polity in France at the End of the Old Regime* (Princeton: Princeton University Press, 1980), p. 403.

14 Lavoisier, Cahiers, R-8, ff. 9–11.

15 Ibid., ff. 11–13.

16 Ibid., f. 13.

17 Ibid., ff. 13–15.

18 Ibid., f. 17.

19 See above, p. 12.

20 Lavoisier, Cahiers, R-8, f. 17.

21 Ibid., ff. 17–19.

22 Lavoisier, "Expériences sur la décomposition . . . et sur un des principaux usages," p.[10].

23 Lavoisier (untitled manuscript), Fiche 1349, p.[1].

24 Ibid., pp. [1–2].

25 Ibid.

26 Ibid.

27 Ibid., p.[3].

28 Ibid., pp. [3–4].

29 Lavoisier, "Expériences sur la décomposition de l'air dans le poulmon des animaux" (revision of "Expériences sur la décomposition . . . et sur un des principaux usages,"), Fiche 1349, pp. 1–2.

30 Lavoisier, "Expériences sur la décomposition . . . et sur un des principaux usages," pp.[2–8].

31 Ibid., p. [8].

32 See above, p. 19.

33 Lavoisier, "Exériences sur la décomposition . . . et sur un des principaux usages," p. [8].

34 Ibid., p. [7]. See also, Lavoisier, "Expériences sur la respiration des animaux et sur les changements qui arrivent à l'air en passant par leur poumon," *Mémoires de l'Académie des Sciences* (1777[1780]), p. 189.

35 Lavoisier, "Expériences sur la décomposition . . . et sur un des principaux usages," pp.[5–6].

36 Ibid., p.[5], note on left margin, and inserted loose sheet.

37 Ibid., p.[8].

38 Ibid., pp.[9–10].

39 Ibid., p.[10].

40 For an extended summary of the results of such practices, see [Pierre-Joseph Macquer], *Dictionnaire de chymie*, 2 vols. (Paris: Lacombe, 1766), 2:430–466. In this classification of neutral salts the composition and properties of unknown or little-known salts are regularly inferred from analogy to known ones.

41 Lavoisier, "Expériences sur la décomposition," (rev. version), pp. 1–9.
42 Ibid., pp. 9–10.
43 Lavoisier, "Expériences sur la décomposition . . . et sur un des principaux usages," p.[1].
44 Lavoisier, "Expériences sur la décomposition . . . dans le poulmon des animaux," p. 1.
45 Maurice Daumas, *Lavoisier: Théoricien et expérimentateur* (Paris: Presses Universitaires, 1955), p. 37.
46 Lavoisier, "Expériences sur la décomposition . . . dans le poulmon des animaux," p. 10.
47 Ibid., unpaginated portion.
48 Ibid.
49 Ibid.
50 Ibid.
51 Daumas, *Lavoisier,* p. 38; Henry Guerlac, *Antoine-Laurent Lavoisier: Chemist and Revolutionary* (New York: Charles Scribner's Sons, 1975), p. 141 n. 45.
52 Lavoisier, "Expériences sur la décomposition de l'air dans le poulmon, et sur un des principaux effets de la respiration dans l'économie animale," Fiche 1311, Archives of the Académie des Sciences.
53 Ibid., p. 1. It is not certain that the revisions were added between the two readings. I have assumed that timing as the most plausible, but they might have been made between the time of the second reading and publication.
54 Ibid., p. 10.
55 Lavoisier, "Mémoire sur la nature du principe qui se combine avec les métaux pendant leur calcination, et qui en augmente le poids," *Observations sur la physique* 5(1775):429–433.
56 Lavoisier, "Expériences sur la décomposition . . . et sur un des principaux effets," p. 10 verso.
57 Bruno Latour and Steve Woolgar, *Laboratory Life: The Social Construction of Scientific Facts* (Beverly Hills: Sage Publications, 1979), pp. 75–81.
58 Lavoisier, "Expériences sur la décomposition . . . et sur un des principaux effets," p. 11 verso.
59 Lavoisier, Cahiers, R-8, ff. 5–7.
60 Lavoisier, "Expériences sur la décomposition . . . et sur un des principaux effets," pp. 11 verso–12.

Chapter 4. Respiration and a General Theory of Combustion

1 Lavoisier, "Expériences sur la décomposition de l'air dans le poulmon et sur un des principaux usages de la respiration dans l'économie animale," Fiche 1349, Archives of the Académie des Sciences, p.[10].
2 Lavoisier, Cahiers, R-8, ff. 17–19.
3 Ibid., f. 19.
4 Stephen Hales, *Vegetable Staticks*, ed. Michael Hoskin, *History of Science Library: Primary Sources* (New York: Science History Publications, 1969), p. 147.
5 Lavoisier, Cahiers, R-8, ff. 21–25.

6 Lavoisier, "Expériences sur la respiration des animaux et sur les changements qui arrivent à l'air en passant par le poulmon," Fiche 1311, Archives of the Académie des Sciences, p. 12v.

7 Lavoisier, "Expériences et observations sur les fluides élastiques en général, et sur l'air de l'atmosphère en particulier," *Oeuvres*, 5:276; rpt. New York: Johnson Reprint Co., 1965. My interpretations depend upon the editorial note that states that the manuscript published for the first time in the *Oeuvres* is, "sous une forme peu différente," the same as the one he had read on May 10, 1777, and upon the assumption that this particular sentence was the same in the two manuscripts. The original manuscript, Lavoisier, Fiche 386, Archives of the Académie des Sciences, is missing.

8 Ibid., p. 271.

9 Lavoisier, "Fluides élastiques," pp. 273–275; J.-B. M. Bucquet, *Mémoire sur la manière dont les animaux sont affectés par différens fluides aériformes, méphitiques; et sur les moyens de remédier aux effets de ces fluides* (Paris: Imprimerie Royale, 1778), p. 51.

10 Lavoisier, "Fluides élastiques," pp. 276–281.

11 Ibid., pp. 278–279.

12 For a general discussion of the effects of conceptual changes on the meaning of experimental operations, see Thomas S. Kuhn, *The Structure of Scientific Revolutions*, 2d ed. (Chicago: University of Chicago Press, 1969), pp. 126–135.

13 Lavoisier, "Notes extraittes de M. Prisley," Fiche 172, Archives of the Académie des Sciences, p. 7.

14 Ibid.

15 Ibid., p. 7v.

16 Ibid.

17 Ibid., pp. 7v–8.

18 M. Berthelot, *La révolution chimique: Lavoisier* (Paris: Félix-Alcan, 1890), p. 267.

19 Ibid., pp. 244, 245.

20 Lavoisier, "Mémoire sur la calcination de l'étain dans les vaisseaux fermés," *Oeuvres*, 5:119.

21 Lavoisier, "Notice abrégée," Fiche 349ac, p. 1.

22 Henry Guerlac, "Chemistry as a Branch of Physics: Laplace's Collaboration with Lavoisier," *Historical Studies in the Physical Sciences* 7(1976):197–223; Lavoisier, "Notice abrégée," p. 3.

23 Lavoisier, "De la combinaison de la matière du feu avec les fluides évaporables, et de la formation des fluides élastiques aériformes," *Oeuvres*, 2:212–224.

24 [Wilhelm] Homberg, "Phosphore nouveau, ou suite des observations sur la matière fécale," *Mémoires de l'Académie des Sciences* (1711 [1714]), pp. 238–245.

25 [Pierre-Joseph Macquer], *Dictionnaire de chymie*, 2 vols. (Paris: Lacombe, 1766), 2:351.

26 [Lejay] de Suvigny, "Nouvelle théorie du pyrophore de M. Homberg," *Mémoires de Mathématique et de Physique, presentés à l'Académie Royale des Sciences par Divers Savans* 3(1760):180–208.

27 [Macquer], *Dictionnaire de chymie*, 1:244.

28 Ibid., 1:245.

29 Lavoisier, "Plans d'expériences à faire," Fiche 351, Archives of the Académie des Sciences, p. 1.

30 Lavoisier, "Notes extraittes," pp. 4, 4v.

31 Berthelot, *La révolution chimique*, p. 273.

32 Lavoisier, "Expériences sur la combinaison de l'alun avec les matières charbonneuses," *Mémoires de l'Académie des Sciences* (1777[1780]), pp. 363–372.

33 Lavoisier, "De la combustion des chandelles dans l'air atmosphérique et dans l'air pur," Fiche 1311(3), Archives of the Académie des Sciences, p.[2].

34 Lavoisier, "Etat des expériences faittes le 27 fevrier 1776," Fiche 353ac, Archives of the Académie des Sciences, pp. [1,4].

35 Lavoisier "Chandelles . . . dans l'air pur," pp. [20–21].

36 Ibid., pp. [14–15]. I have given only the original passages, leaving out small changes Lavoisier afterward made between the lines and in the margin.

37 For example, James Bryant Conant, *The Overthrow of the Phlogiston Theory* (Cambridge: Harvard University Press, 1956), regards the first direct "attack on the prevailing theory" as Lavoisier's "Reflections on phlogiston" of 1783; but Maurice Daumas, *Lavoisier: Théoricien et expérimentateur* (Paris: Presses Universitaires, 1955), p. 17, dates the first attacks in 1777: Max Speter, *Lavoisier und seine Vorläufer* (Stuttgart: Ferdinand Enke, 1910) p. 32, associated the attack with the published version of the memoir on candles: while Guerlac, "Chemistry as a Branch of Physics," p. 216, identifies it with the general memoir on combustion read on November 12, 1777.

38 Guerlac, "Chemistry as a Branch of Physics," pp. 202–203.

39 Michael Polanyi, *Personal Knowledge* (Chicago: University of Chicago Press, 1962), pp. 299–324.

40 Lavoisier, "Chandelles . . . dans l'air pur," pp. [17–20].

41 Denis I. Duveen and Herbert S. Klickstein, "A Letter from Guyton de Morveau to Macquart Relating to Lavoisier's Attack against the *Phlogiston* Theory," *Osiris* 12(1956): 345–347; see also Duveen and Klickstein, "A Case of Mistaken Identity: Macquer and Not Macquart," *Isis* 49(1958):73–74.

42 Lavoisier, "De la combustion des chandelles dans l'air atmosphérique, et dans l'air éminemment respirable," Fiche 1311(2), pp. 1–12.

43 Lavoisier, "Notice abrégée," pp. 5–6.

44 Lavoisier, "Combinaison de l'alun," p. 371.

45 Lavoisier, "Mémoire sur l'existence de l'air dans l'acide nitreux," *Oeuvres*, 2:130. For a summary of the background, see Henry Guerlac, *Antoine-Laurent Lavoisier: Chemist and Revolutionary* (New York: Charles Scribner's Sons, 1975), pp. 88–92.

46 Lavoisier, "Mémoire sur la combustion du phosphore de Kunckel, et sur la nature de l'acide qui résulte de cette combustion," *Oeuvres*, 2:139–144. Lavoisier read this memoir at the Academy on April 16, 1777. Lavoisier, "Mémoire sur la dissolution du mercure dans l'acide vitriolique et sur la résolution de cet acide en acide sulfureux aériforme et en air éminemment respirable," ibid., 2:194–198.

47 Anders Jahan Retzius, "Versuche mit Weinstein und dessen Säure," *Abhandlungen*

der Königlich-Schwedischen Akademie der Wissenschaften (Leipzig) 32(1770 [1774]): 210–226.

48 T. Bergman, "Herrn Bergmanns [*sic*] Abhandlung von der Zuckersäure," trans. C. E. Weigel, *Magazin vor Aerzte* 2(1777):868–887.

49 Some of the letters of Macquer to Bergman are included in *Torbern Bergman's Foreign Correspondence*, ed. G. Carlid and J. Nordström (Stockholm: Almquist and Wiksell, 1965), 1:229–255; but this volume does not contain letters from Bergman to his correspondents.

50 Lavoisier, Cahiers, R-4, ff. 126–127.

51 Ibid., ff. 128–131.

52 Ibid., ff. 132–133.

53 Lavoisier, "Notice abrégée," p. 7.

54 One might suppose that Lavoisier had carried out an additional experiment not recorded in the laboratory notebooks. That this is unlikely will become clear in Chapter 5.

55 Lavoisier, "Notice abrégée," pp. 7–9.

56 This statement would at first appear incorrect because the later-published memoir on acids carried the notation "Presented on September 5, 1777, read on November 23, 1779." See *Mémoires de l'Académie des Sciences* (1778[1781]), p. 535. As will be evident in Chapter 5, however, that memoir could not have been written before 1779. The note therefore refers only to the presentation of the abstract.

57 Lavoisier, "Sur la combustion," Fiche 1316, Archives of the Académie des Sciences.

58 Ibid., p. 2v.

59 Ibid., p. 3.

60 Ibid., pp. 3–4.

61 Ibid., pp. 4v–5.

62 Ibid., pp. 5–7.

63 Ibid., p. 7v.

64 Ibid., pp. 8–10.

65 Lavoisier, *Opuscules physiques et chymiques* (Paris: Durand, 1774), pp. 279–281.

66 Thomas S. Kuhn, *The Structure of Scientific Revolutions*, 2d ed. (Chicago: University of Chicago Press, 1970), pp. 92–110.

67 Ibid., pp. 89–90.

68 Ibid., pp. 111–118; See Norwood Russell Hanson, *Patterns of Discovery* (Cambridge: Cambridge University Press, 1975), pp. 4–19.

69 Lavoisier, "Sur la combustion," pp. 4–4v.

70 Ibid., p. 10.

71 Ibid., p. 10–10v.

72 See above, pp. 19, 29–30.

73 Everett Mendelsohn, *Heat and Life: The Development of the Theory of Animal Heat* (Cambridge, Mass.: Harvard University Press, 1964), p. 146, 165.

74 Lavoisier, "Sur la combustion," p. 10v.

75 Charles A. Culotta, "Respiration and the Lavoisier Tradition: Theory and Modification, 1777–1850," *Transactions of the American Philosophical Society* 62(1972):7.

76 Lavoisier, "Sur la combustion," p. 10v.
77 Ibid., p. 2v.
78 [Macquer], *Dictionnaire de chymie*, 1:273–276.
79 Lavoisier ["Sur la combustion"] (fair copy), Fiche 1316, Archives of the Académie of Sciences. p. [23].
80 Ibid., p. [11]; Guerlac, "Chemistry as a Branch of Physics," p. 216.
81 Duveen and Klickstein, "Letter," pp. 346–347.
82 Ibid., p. 347. See also Guerlac, "Chemistry as a Branch of Physics," p. 219.
83 Lavoisier ["sur la combustion"], pp. [4, 9–10, 23].
84 Ibid., p. [23].
85 Ibid., pp. [9, 10, 22–23].
86 Lavoisier, "Chandelles . . . dans l'air éminemment respirable," p. 8v; Daumas, *Lavoisier*, pp. 40–41.

Chapter 5. Collaboration and a Move toward Plant Chemistry

1 M. Berthelot, *La révolution chimique: Lavoisier* (Paris: Félix-Alcan, 1890), pp. 223, 280; Maurice Daumas, *Lavoisier: Théoricien et expérimentateur* (Paris: Presses Universitaires, 1955), pp. 98–99.
2 Henry Guerlac, *Antoine-Laurent Lavoisier: Chemist and Revolutionary* (New York: Charles Scribner's Sons, 1975), p. 124.
3 Lavoisier, "Introduction et plan d'un deuxième volume des Opuscules physiques et chemiques," *Oeuvres*, 5:267–269.
4 Fourcroy, "Eloge de M. Bucquet," *Journal de physique* 15(1780):257–260; J.-B. M. Bucquet, *Introduction à l'étude des corps naturels tirés du règne végétal* (Paris: Herissant, 1773).
5 Fourcroy, "Eloge," p. 259.
6 J.-B. M. Bucquet, *Mémoire sur la manière dont les animaux sont affectés par différens fluides aériformes, méphitiques; et sur les moyens de remédier aux effets de ces fluides* (Paris: Imprimerie Royale, 1778), pp. 1–34.
7 Lavoisier, "Rapport sur un mémoire relatif à l'acide méphitique," *Oeuvres*, 4:278.
8 Berthelot, *La révolution chimique*, p. 276.
9 Fourcroy, "Éloge," p. 263.
10 For further details see E. McDonald, "The Collaboration of Bucquet and Lavoisier," *Ambix* 13(1966):74–84. The "Notice abrégé de plusiers mémoires redigés en commun par MM. Bucquet et Lavoisier et sur lesquels ils prient l'assurance de leur donner date avant la séparation," Fiche 363, Archives of the Académie des Sciences, is missing from the Lavoisier archives.
11 Bucquet, *Animaux*, iii–xiii, 34–61.
12 Ibid., p. 55.
13 Ibid., pp. 61–86.
14 Ibid., pp. 87–93.
15 Ibid., pp. 61–62.
16 Ibid., p. viii.
17 Ibid., p. 89.
18 Lavoisier, Cahiers, R-4, f. 149.

19 Ibid., ff. 149–150.

20 Bucquet, *Animaux*, pp. 31–32.

21 Lavoisier, Cahiers, R-4, f. 151. The entry is actually dated January 27, 1777. Berthelot, *La révolution chimique*, p. 275, says "(c'est 1778)," a correction which seems obviously valid; Lavoisier, "Mémoire sur les altérations qui arrivent à l'air dans plusieurs circumstances où se trouvent les hommes réunis en société," *Mémoires de la Société de Médecine* 5(1782–83 [1787]):575–576.

22 Bucquet, *Animaux*, pp. 17–22; Lavoisier, "Expériences sur la respiration des animaux, et sur les changements qui arrivent à l'air en passant par leur poumon," *Mémoires de l'Académie des Sciences* (1777[1780]), p. 190; Lavoisier, "Mémoire sur la combustion des chandelles dans l'air atmosphérique et dans l'air éminemment respirable," *ibid.*, p. 195.

23 This date is taken from the *procès-verbaux* of the meeting. See Daumas, *Lavoisier*, pp. 41–42. The memoir itself says, "Relû 8 août 1778." I have assumed that "août" is a misprint for "avril." See Lavoisier, "Mémoire sur la nature du principe qui se combine avec les métaux pendant leur calcination, et qui en augmente le poids," *Mémoires de l'Académie des Sciences* (1775[1778]), p. 520.

24 Lavoisier, "La nature du principe," pp. 520–526. For a discussion of the original version, see above, pp. 48–52. A detailed comparison of the modified passages and their originals is given in English translation in James Bryant Conant, *The Overthrow of the Phlogiston Theory,* Harvard Case Histories in Experimental Science 2 (Cambridge, Mass.: Harvard University Press, 1956), pp. 22–28.

25 See, for example, Guerlac, *Antoine-Laurent Lavoisier,* pp. 86–87.

26 McDonald, "Collaboration," p. 83.

27 Lavoisier, "La nature du principe," p. 526.

28 Charles Coulston Gillispie, *Science and Polity in France at the End of the Old Regime* (Princeton: Princeton University Press, 1980), pp. 57–70; Henry Guerlac and Carl Perrin, "A Chronology of Lavoisier's Career," manuscript, n.d., p. 36.

29 Daumas, *Lavoisier,* p. 42.

30 Ibid., p. 99.

31 With the exception of a few analyses of airs and waters drawn from various places in or around Paris in the fall of 1778. See Berthelot, *La révolution chimique*, p. 281.

32 Lavoisier, Cahiers, R-4, f. 197. I have seen only the first page of the original laboratory record of this experiment, and have supplemented my account of it from the description Lavoisier gave in the first draft of his memoir "Sur la formation des acides en général et sur celle de l'acide du sucre en particulier," Fiche 1320, Archives of the Académie des Sciences, pp. 6–10.

33 Lavoisier, Cahiers, R-4, f. 197; Lavoisier, "La formation des acides" (first draft), pp. 6–10.

34 Lavoisier, Cahiers, R-6, ff. 68–71.

35 Lavoisier, "Sur la formation des acides en général et sur celle de l'acide du sucre en particulier," Fiche 1320, Archives of the Académie des Sciences, p. 1.

36 For an excellent exposition of this point of view, see Robert Siegfried, "Lavoisier's Table of Simple Substances: Its Origin and Interpretation," *Ambix* 29(1982):29–48.

37 See especially the final draft of Lavoisier's memoir on respiration, "Expériences sur la respiration des animaux et sur les changements qui arrivent à l'air en passant par

leur poulmon," Fiche 1311, Archives of the Académie des Sciences, pp. 8v–11, in which he changed six references to "dephlogisticated air," or "pure air," to "eminently respirable air."

38 Lavoisier, "Mémoire sur quelques fluides que l'on peut obtenir dans l'état aériforme, à un degré de chaleur peu supérieur à la température moyenne de la terre," *Oeuvres*, 2:263n.

39 Lavoisier "Acide du sucre," pp. 2–4.

40 Ibid., pp. 4–10.

41 Ibid., pp. 11–12.

42 Ibid., pp. 12–15.

43 The identity of these experiments can easily be established from the quantities of sugar, nitrous acid, and water used and the quantities of the products obtained.

44 See above, pp. 25–26.

45 Lavoisier, "Acide du sucre," pp.16–17.

46 Daumas, *Lavoisier*, p. 43; Lavoisier, *Oeuvres*, 2:194–198.

47 Lavoisier, "Considérations générales sur la nature des acides et sur les principes dont ils sont composés," Fiche 1320, Archives of the Académie des Sciences.

48 Ibid., p. [11].

49 Daumas, *Lavoisier*, pp. 43–44.

50 Lavoisier, "Considérations générales," pp.[7, 13].

51 Fourcroy, "Bucquet," p. 263.

52 Ibid., pp. 261–262.

53 Daumas, *Lavoisier*, p. 99.

54 Lavoisier, "Considérations générales sur la nature des acides et sur les principes dont il se sont composés," Fiche 1320, Archives of the Académie des Sciences, p. [3]. This manuscript is most easily distinguished from the manuscript cited in fn. 47, above, by the signature of Condorcet, his vertical line, and the notation "Lu le 17 novembre 1779, paraphé le 12 fevrier 1780." That indication leaves some confusion about the relation between the manuscripts. I have assumed that what Lavoisier read on November 17 was the preceding version. The published version, textually identical to the present one, confuses the situation further, by the notation "Présenté le 5 septembre 1777, lu le 23 nov. 1779." The second date might indicate that Lavoisier began reading on the seventeenth and finished reading at a subsequent meeting. The first date is, for obvious reasons impossible; only the abstract could have been presented then. Lavoisier (same title as preceding), *Mémoires de l'Académie des Sciences* (1778[1781]), p. 535.

Chapter 6. The Importance of Melting Ice

1 See Lavoisier to Cotte, December 27, 1781, Darmstäeder Collection of Lavoisier Documents, History of Science Collection, Cornell University.

2 On Dietrich, see C. E. Perrin, "A Lost Identity: Philippe Frederic, Baron de Dietrich (1748–1793)," *Isis* 73 (1982): 545–551.

3 Uno Boklund, "Scheele, Carl Wilhelm," in Charles C. Gillispie, ed. *Dictionary of Scientific Biography,* 16 vols. (New York: Charles Scribner's Sons, 1970–80), 12:147.

4 Lavoisier, "Réflexions sur la calcination et la combustion à l'occasion d'un ouvrage intitulé 'Traité chimique de l'air et du feu,'" *Oeuvres,* 2:391; Carl Wilhelm Scheele, *Chemische Abhandlung von der Luft und dem Feuer,* in *Sämmtliche physische und chemische Werke,* trans. Sigismund Hermbstädt, 2 vols., rpt. ed. (Wiesbaden: Martin Sändig, 1971), 1:13–200.

5 Scheele, *Von der Luft und dem Feuer,* pp. 200–204.

6 Ibid., pp. 204–210.

7 Ibid., p. 206.

8 Ibid., pp. 210–211.

9 Ibid., pp. 210–214.

10 Boklund, "Scheele," p. 147.

11 Joseph Priestley, "Sendschreiben an Hrn. R. Kirwan Esq. über Herrn Scheeles Abhandlung von der Luft und dem Feuer," in Scheele, *Werke,* 1:28–37.

12 Lavoisier, "Réflexions sur la calcination," p. 391; Maurice Daumas, *Lavoisier: Théoricien et expérimentateur* (Paris: Presses Universitaires, 1955), pp. 45–46; Henry Guerlac, "Chemistry as a Branch of Physics: Laplace's Collaboration with Lavoisier," *Historical Studies in the Physical Sciences* 7(1976):230 n. 83.

13 Lavoisier, "Réflexions sur la calcination," pp. 396–397.

14 Ibid., p. 402.

15 Ibid., pp. 397–398.

16 A.-L. Lavoisier and P.-S. de Laplace, "Mémoire sur la chaleur," *Mémoires de l'Académie des Sciences* (1780 [1783]), p. 404.

17 [Pierre-Joseph Macquer], *Dictionnaire de chymie,* 2 vols. (Paris: Lacombe, 1766), 1:247.

18 Lavoisier to Cotte, December 27, 1781, Darmstäeder Collection; Lavoisier, "Expériences faittes en 1781 et 1782 sur les dilatations de verre et des métaux depuis la terme de la congelation jusqu'à l'eau bouillante par MM. Laplace et Lavoisier," Fiche 1323, Archives of the Académie des Sciences.

19 Recent accounts of these developments can be found in Robert Fox, *The Caloric Theory of Gases, from Lavoisier to Regnault* (Oxford: Clarendon Press, 1971), pp. 20–34; Robert J. Morris, "Lavoisier and the Caloric Theory," *British Journal for the History of Science* 6(1972):9–12; A. L. Donovan, *Philosophical Chemistry in the Scottish Enlightenment* (Edinburgh: University Press, 1975), pp. 222–277; and Guerlac, "Chemistry as a Branch of Physics," pp. 223–234.

20 Fox, *The Caloric Theory of Gases,* p. 29; Morris, "Lavoisier and the Caloric Theory," pp. 9–12; Guerlac, "Chemistry as a Branch of Physics," pp. 230–234, 243. H. Magellan, "Sur la nouvelle théorie du feu élémentaire, et de la chaleur des corps," *Observations sur la physique* 17(1781):375–386; "Suite du mémoire sur le feu élémentaire et la chaleur," ibid., pp. 411–422; "Lettre de M. Magellan à l'auteur de ce journal," ibid., p. 370.

21 Magellan, "Suite du mémoire," pp. 411–412.

22 Ibid., p. 417.

23 Everett Mendelsohn, *Heat and Life: The Development of the Theory of Animal Heat* (Cambridge, Mass.: Harvard University Press, 1964), pp. 125–130.

24 Ibid., p. 146.

25 Guerlac, "Chemistry as a Branch of Physics," pp. 233–234, 240–241.
26 Ibid., p. 250.
27 Lavoisier and Laplace, "Chaleur," pp. 369–371.
28 Ibid., pp. 371–372; Guerlac, "Chemistry as a Branch of Physics," p. 241. For a detailed discussion of the ice calorimeter, its accuracy, its limitations, and later evaluations of the method, see T. H. Lodwig and W. A. Smeaton, "The Ice Calorimeter of Lavoisier and Laplace and Some of Its Critics," *Annals of Science* 31(1974): 1–18.
29 Berthelot, *La révolution chimique*, pp. 285–286; Lavoisier and Laplace, "Chaleur," pp. 363–365.
30 Lavoisier and Laplace, "Chaleur," pp. 363–364.
31 Ibid., pp. 367–368, 372–373.
32 Lavoisier, Cahiers, R-7, f. 55. This experiment is not directly recorded in the notebook, but referred to in the record of a subsequent similar experiment.
33 Laplace to Lavoisier, dated "ce dimanche matin," Archives de Chabrol. Sunday, February 2, 1783, would place the letter after the first experiment with a candle, and before the first respiration experiment. Roger Hahn allowed me to examine a copy of this letter which he received from Michelle Sadoun-Goupil. A later archivist has assigned the letter the date of "January 1784." I believe this date improbable, because it would have to have been written after the series of experiments carried out in the spring of 1783. There is no reference to previous experiments of the same nature, and the character of the letter suggests strongly that it was written at the beginning of this investigation.
34 Ibid.
35 Lavoisier, Cahiers, R-7, f. 53. In order to avoid an inversion of the order of dates in these pages of the notebook, Berthelot postulated that this and the following two experiments were performed in February 1784, rather than February 1783, the notebook having been unused for a few days less than a year. Berthelot, *La révolution chimique*, pp. 286–287. Berthelot was mistaken, however, for the experiments on respiration can be shown to have been the same ones described in the joint "Memoir on heat" in July 1783. Compare especially R-7, f. 54, with Lavoisier and Laplace, "Chaleur," p. 380.
36 Lavoisier, Cahiers, R-7, f. 54.
37 We cannot be certain that these were actually the first such experiments. Lavoisier and Laplace reported, however, just two experiments of this type in their memoir ("Chaleur," pp. 379–380). They appear to be the same experiments with minor corrections in the data. There is no need to assume, therefore, that they performed additional ones.
38 Mendelsohn, *Heat and Life*, p. 146.
39 Lavoisier, Cahiers, R-7, f. 55.
40 Ibid., f. 56.
41 Ibid., ff. 51–52; Berthelot, *La révolution chimique*, p. 286.
42 Lavoisier and Laplace, "Chaleur," p. 355.
43 Lavoisier, Cahiers, R-7, f. 57. The full title of the experiment is "Respiration des animaux quantité d'acide carbonique qu'il forme." It appears, however, as far as I

can judge from a xerox copy of this page, that the second half is one of the titles Lavoisier later added to many of the pages of his notebooks.

44 See Lavoisier and Laplace, "Chaleur," p. 397.

45 In the "Memoir on heat" Lavoisier used the figure of 0.47317 grains per cubic inch, based on measurements by de Luc.

46 Lavoisier, Cahiers, R-7, f. 57.

47 Thomas S. Kuhn, *The Structure of Scientific Revolutions*, 2d ed. (Chicago: University of Chicago Press, 1970), pp. 187–191.

48 Mendelsohn, *Heat and Life*, pp. 140–165, esp. pp. 146, 165; and p. 183.

49 Lavoisier, Cahiers, R-8, ff. 37–39.

50 Ibid., ff. 43–45.

51 Ibid., f. 47.

52 Ibid., ff. 49–50.

53 Ibid., f. 51.

54 Ibid., ff. 54–55.

55 See above, p. 26.

56 Daumas, *Lavoisier*, p. 48.

57 Lavoisier and Laplace, "Chaleur," pp. 378–379.

58 Ibid., pp. 379–380.

59 Guerlac, "Chemistry as a Branch of Physics," pp. 254–255.

60 Lavoisier and Laplace, "Chaleur," pp. 393–394.

61 Ibid., pp. 393, 397.

62 Ibid., pp. 394–396.

63 Ibid., p. 397.

64 Ibid.

65 Ibid., p. 398.

66 Ibid., pp. 398–400.

67 Ibid., pp. 400–401.

68 Ibid., pp. 401–402.

69 See above, p. 69.

70 Lavoisier and Laplace, "Chaleur," pp. 402–403. One reason that he was probably forced to rely more heavily upon the two closed experiments was that the second of the two open-chamber experiments they performed (excluding the earliest one, which was probably preliminary) they probably had to discard because of the moribund state of the animal at the end. See above, p. 180.

71 Ibid., p. 403.

72 Ibid., pp. 403–404.

73 Mendelsohn, *Heat and Life*, p. 156, notes that Adair Crawford "had shown already in 1781 that animals in colder air phlogisticate more air." Lavoisier and Laplace probably did not know of this result when they carried out these experiments.

74 Lavoisier and Laplace, "Chaleur," p. 405.

75 Douglas McKie, *Antoine Lavoisier: Scientist, Economist, Social Reformer* (New York: Collier Books, 1962), p. 102. In *The Growth of Scientific Physiology* (London: Hutchinson, 1960), pp. 42–45, G. J. Goodfield quotes verbatim McKie's ac-

count (from an earlier edition of the same book) of the experiment, and Lavoisier's own conclusion, with no comment on the issue.

76 Henry Guerlac, *Antoine-Laurent Lavoisier: Chemist and Revolutionary* (New York: Charles Scribner's Sons, 1975), p. 122.

77 Mendelsohn, *Heat and Life*, p. 149.

78 Charles A. Culotta, "Respiration and the Lavoisier Tradition: Theory and Modification, 1777–1850," *Transactions of the American Philosophical Society* 62(1972):5. Inspection of Culotta's statements in light of the foregoing account of Lavoisier and Laplace's investigation, or of their own memoir, readily reveals that Culotta himself was far more confused about the situation than Lavoisier ever was.

79 J. R. Partington, *A History of Chemistry*, Vol. 3 (London: Macmillan, 1962), p. 431.

80 Lavoisier and Laplace, "Chaleur," p. 398.

81 Ibid., pp. 398–400.

82 Ibid., p. 404.

83 Ibid., pp. 405, 407.

84 Ibid., p. 406.

85 Ibid.

86 William Harvey, "The First Anatomical Essay to Jean Riolan on the Circulation of the Blood," in *The Circulation of the Blood and Other Writings*, trans. Kenneth J. Franklin (London: Dent, Everyman's Library, 1963), p. 132.

87 Mendelsohn, *Heat and Life*, p. 151.

88 Lavoisier and Laplace, "Chaleur," pp. 406–407.

89 Ibid., pp. 407–408.

90 Ibid., p. 408.

91 See P. B. Medawar, *The Art of the Soluble* (Harmondsworth: Penguin Books, 1967), p. 11. See also Ernst Mayr, *The Growth of Biological Thought: Diversity, Evolution, and Inheritance* (Cambridge, Mass.: Belknap Press, 1982), pp. 832–834.

92 See Guerlac, *Antoine-Laurent Lavoisier*, p. 122: "The calorimeter provided a new instrument for the quantitative study of animal heat and the verification of Lavoisier's combustion theory of respiration." Mendelsohn, *Heat and Life*, pp. 149–150: "Respiration, Lavoisier and Laplace concluded, is a slow combustion." See also Joseph S. Fruton, *Molecules and Life: Historical Essays on the Interplay of Chemistry and Biology* (New York: Wiley-Interscience, 1972), p. 264.

Chapter 7. Water Divided.

1 Lavoisier and Laplace, "Memoire sur la chaleur," *Mémoires de l'Académie des Sciences* (1780[1783]), pp. 398, 404, 408.

2 Lavoisier, Cahiers, R-8, f. 35.

3 Ibid., f. 59, printed in *Lavoisier, Correspondence*, 2:739–740.

4 See F. L. Holmes, *Claude Bernard and Animal Chemistry* (Cambridge, Mass.: Harvard University Press, 1974), pp. 141–144.

5 Lavoisier, Cahiers, R-8, f. 63.

6 Maurice Daumas, *Lavoisier: Théoricien et expérimentateur* (Paris: Presses Universitaires de France, 1955), pp. 48–49; Henry Guerlac, "Chemistry as a Branch

of Physics; Laplace's Collaboration with Lavoisier," *Historical Studies in the Physical Sciences* 7(1976):241.

7 See, especially, J. R. Partington, *A History of Chemistry,* 4 vols. (London: Macmillan, 1962), 3:329–338, 436–453; Guerlac, "Chemistry as a Branch of Physics," pp. 261–266; and Carl Perrin, "Lavoisier, Monge and the Synthesis of Water," *British Journal for the History of Science* 6(1973):424–428.

8 Lavoisier, "Mémoire dans lequel on a pour objet de prouver que l'eau n'est point une substance simple, un élément proprement dit, mais qu'elle est susceptible de décomposition et de recomposition," *Oeuvres,* 2:341–343; Daumas, *Lavoisier,* p. 50; Lavoisier, "Extrait d'un mémoire lu à la séance publique de l'Académie Royale des Sciences du 12 novembre, sur la nature de l'eau, et sur les expérienes qui paroissent prouver que cette substance n'est point un élément proprement dit, mais qu'elle est susceptible de décomposition et de recomposition," *Observations sur la physique* 6(1783):452–455.

9 See above, p. 142.

10 Guerlac, "Chemistry as a Branch of Physics," p. 262.

11 Lavoisier, "Extrait," pp. 454–455.

12 See above, pp. 10–11.

13 Lavoisier, Cahiers, R-6, ff. 106–107.

14 Lavoisier, *Correspondance,* 2:757–758.

15 P.-S. de Laplace and A.-L. Lavoisier, "Mémoire contenant les expériences faites sur la chaleur pendant l'hiver de 1783 à 1784," in Lavoisier, *Oeuvres,* 2:724. For examples, see Lavoisier, Cahiers, R-8, ff. 173, 193.

16 For examples, Laplace and Lavoisier, "L'hiver de 1783 à 1784," pp. 725–726; Lavoisier, Cahiers, R-8, f. 193.

17 M. Berthelot, *La révolution chimique: Lavoisier* (Paris: Félix-Alcan, 1890), p. 294; Laplace and Lavoisier, "L'hiver de 1783 à 1784," pp. 725, 730–731.

18 Lavoisier, Cahiers, R-8, f. 173. Laplace and Lavoisier, "L'hiver de 1783 à 1784," pp. 725–726. Since Lavoisier wrote up these results for publication only in 1793, it is possible that he or Laplace formulated these comments on these other results much later; but it is more likely that the memoir only recalled inferences they had made at the time, because they did no further work on the problem during the intervening decade.

19 Lavoisier, Cahiers, R-8, ff. 179–181; Laplace and Lavoisier, "L'hiver de 1783 à 1784," p. 726.

20 Lavoisier, Cahiers, R-8, f. 193.

21 Laplace and Lavoisier, "L'hiver de 1783 à 1784," pp. 724–738; Berthelot, *La révolution chimique.* pp. 294–295.

22 Lavoisier, Cahiers, R-7, ff. 62–68.

23 Ibid., f. 66.

24 When Lavoisier wrote up the calorimetric measurements, nearly a decade later, for inclusion in his *Mémoires de chimie,* he reduced the heats of combustion to the value per pound of the combustible consumed, a less meaningful comparison than a common quantity of the air consumed or formed, and one not utilizing the complementary sets of combustion experiments. The heats released in the respiration of the guinea pigs he calculated for twenty-four hours, thus giving no basis of comparison

at all with the heats measured for the combustion of *charbon*. See Lavoisier and Laplace, "L'hiver de 1783 à 1784," p. 730.

25 Lavoisier, "Que l'eau n'est point une substance simple," pp. 344–345.

26 Lavoisier, *Opuscules physiques et chymiques* (Paris: Durand, Didot, Esprit, 1774), pp. 265–271.

27 Lavoisier, "Que l'eau n'est point une substance simple," p. 349.

28 Ibid., p. 346.

29 Lavoisier, Cahiers, R-7, ff. 69–71.

30 Lavoisier, "Que l'eau n'est point une substance simple," p. 350. For a full account of the history of the commission and Meusnier's contributions, see Charles Coulston Gillispie, *The Montgolfier Brothers and the Invention of Aviation, 1783–1784* (Princeton: Princeton University Press, 1983), pp. 25, 32–33, 67–68, 98–108.

31 Meusnier and Lavoisier, "Mémoire où l'on prouve, par la décomposition de l'eau, que ce fluide n'est point une substance simple, et qu'il y a plusieurs moyens d'obtenir en grand l'air inflammable qui y entre comme principe constituant," in Lavoisier, *Oeuvres*, 2:360–373.

32 Ibid., pp. 364, 369–370.

33 Lavoisier, Cahiers, R-7, f. 88–91. The same experiment is described more briefly in Meusnier and Lavoisier, "Décomposition de l'eau," pp. 370–371.

34 Meusnier and Lavoisier, "Décomposition de l'eau," p. 371.

35 Ibid., p. 366.

36 Lavoisier, Cahiers, R-7, ff. 91–92.

37 Ibid., f. 89.

38 Ibid., f. 92.

39 Ibid., ff. 88–97. The main calculations are contained on the right-hand pages, numbered consecutively, while a series of subsidiary calculations are entered on successive pages of the normally blank left side of the notebook. Berthelot, *La révolution chimique*, p. 289, attributes these calculations to Laplace. Daumas, *Lavoisier*, p. 53, and Guerlac, "Chemistry as a Branch of Physics," p. 270, follow Berthelot. Unless one can establish conclusively, however, that the handwriting is that of Laplace, it is far more natural to infer that the author was Meusnier, Lavoisier's chief collaborator in this series of experiments and the co-author of the memoir in which its results were first reported.

40 Lavoisier, Cahiers, R-7, f. 94 and left-hand facing page.

41 Ibid., facing f. 94.

42 Ibid.

43 Meusnier and Lavoisier, "Décomposition de l'eau," p. 367.

44 Lavoisier,Cahiers, R-7, facing ff. 94, 95.

45 Ibid., facing ff. 96, 97, f. 97.

46 Lavoisier, "Mémoire sur la formation de l'acide nommé air fixe ou acide crayeux, et que je désignerai désormais sous le nom d'acide du charbon," *Mémoires de l'Académie des Sciences* (1781[1784]), pp. 450–453.

47 Lavoisier, Cahiers, R-7, ff. 64–65.

48 Meusnier and Lavoisier, "Décomposition de l'eau," p. 371.

49 Lavoisier, "Acide du charbon," pp. 451–453.

50 See above, p. 203.

51 Walter Pagel, *Joan Baptista Van Helmont: Reformer of Science and Medicine* (Cambridge: Cambridge University Press, 1982), p. 53.
52 Lavoisier, "Sur la nature de l'eau et sur les expériences par lesquelles on a prétendu prouver la possibilité de son changement en terre," *Oeuvres*, 2:1–8.
53 Priestley, "Observations et expériences sur différentes espèces d'air," *Observations sur la physique* 6(1773):318–321.
54 Carl Wilhelm Scheele, *Sämmtliche physiche und chemische Werke*, trans. S. F. Hermbstädt, rpt. ed. (Wiesbaden: Martin Sändig, 1971), 1:203–204. For a summarized presentation of his extended investigations on vegetation, see Joseph Priestley, *Experiments and Observations on Different Kinds of Air* (Birmingham: Thomas Pearson, 1790; rpt., New York: Klaus Reprint Co., 1970), 3:247–347.
55 Jean Senebier, *Mémoires physico-chymiques sur l'influence de la lumière solaire pour modifer les êtres des trois règnes de la nature, et sur-tout ceux du règne végétal*, 3 vols. (Geneva: Barthelemi Chirol, 1782). The most comprehensive historical description of the work of Ingenhousz and of Senebier is Dorian Kottler, "Jean Senebier and the Emergence of Plant Physiology, 1775–1802: From Natural History to Chemical Science," Ph.D. diss., Johns Hopkins, 1973. The best published account is Leonard K. Nash, *Plants and the Atmosphere*, Harvard Case Histories in Experimental Science, ed. James B. Conant (Cambridge, Mass.: Harvard University Press, 1966).
56 Lavoisier, "Que l'eau n'est point une substnace simple," pp. 355–356.
57 Ibid., p. 341.
58 Lavoisier, "Mémoire sur la combustion des chandelles dans l'air atmospherique et dans l'air éminemment respirable," *Mémoires da l'Académie des Sciences*, (1777[1780]), p. 204.
59 Richard Kirwan astutely noticed this anomaly in Lavoisier's thought, in his defense of the phlogiston theory. Kirwan wrote: "Even charcoal he [Lavoisier] allowed at first to be an *unknown modification* of the inflammable principle, though at present he seems to think otherwise: if he allows it to contain the inflammable principle consolidated by unknown means, as ice is a modification of water, we shall hardly dispute it." R.Kirwan, *An Essay on Phlogiston and the Constitution of Acids: A New Edition* (London: J. Johnson, 1789), p. 6.
60 Lavoisier, "Que l'eau n'est point une substance simple," p. 341.
61 See above, p. 143.
62 Lavoisier, "Que l'eau n'est point une substance simple," pp. 357–359.

Chapter 8. Fixing the Composition of Fixed Air

1 Lavoisier, Cahiers, R-7, facing f. 95, f. 97 bis.
2 Lavoisier, "Mémoire dans lequel on a pour objet de prouver que l'eau n'est point une subtance simple, un élément proprement dit, mais qu'elle est susceptible de décomposition et de recomposition," *Oeuvres* 2:347.
3 Lavoisier, "Mémoire sur la formation de l'acide nommé air fixe ou acide crayeux, et que je désignerai désormais sous le nom d'acide du charbon," *Mémoires de l'Académie des Sciences* (1781[1784]), p. 449.
4 Lavoisier, Cahiers, R-7, f. 97.

5 Ibid., R-9, f. 28.
6 Ibid., f. 29, and facing page.
7 Ibid., R-8, ff. 219–221.
8 Ibid., R-9, f. 39.
9 Ibid., ff. 39–41.
10 Ibid., f. 42 and facing page.
11 Lavoisier, "Acide du charbon," pp. 450–452.
12 Ibid., pp. 452–453; Lavoisier, Cahiers, R-7, f. 65. The calculations in the memoir are identical to those in the notebook.
13 Lavoisier, "Acide du charbon," pp. 455–456; Cahiers, R-7, ff. 62–63 and facing page. Calculations identical.
14 Lavoisier, "Acide du charbon," p. 454. As I have argued above (p. 219), the use of the ratio 1:7.623 for the proportion of inflammable air confirms that Lavoisier recalculated the results of these experiments after Meusnier's analyses of April 10. It does not prove that he necessarily carried them out after completing the new series of experiments of May 10–June 5, as I have assumed. My interpretation would not be seriously altered if, in fact, Lavoisier had made the additional calculations on the earlier experiments before those on the later experiments.
15 Lavoisier, "Combination du principe oxygine avec la substance charbonneuse," Fiche 1329, Archives of the Académie des Sciences. This single page is inserted in the sheaf of folded pages comprising the first draft of the memoir by the second title, cited below. It is entirely crossed out. It is, of course, possible that this first effort continued on other pages that have been lost.
16 Lavoisier, "Mémoire sur la formation de l'acide nommé air fixe ou acide crayeux, et que je désignerai désormais sous le nom d'acide du charbon" (two drafts by the same title), Fiche 1329, Archives of the Académie des Sciences; Lavoisier, "Acide du charbon." I have assumed that the first of these drafts was a "first" draft, on the basis of its form. Lavoisier habitually wrote out first drafts with a very wide left-hand margin for corrections. There are also very many words and parts of words crossed out, sometimes rewritten without change, as one would expect of a first draft. In later drafts Lavoisier usually worked over successive fair copies.
17 From Lavoisier's statement ("Acide du charbon," p. 452) that "We have repeated and varied this experiment [on the combustion of charcoal] a great number of times," we might be led to conclude that there were other such experiments recorded neither in the notebooks nor in the memoir. This is, however, most likely another instance of the exaggerated impression Lavoisier habitually gave of the number of experiments he had performed. There are no experiments of this type in the memoir which cannot be found in the notebooks. If he had carried out others, in view of the fact that none of the ones he reported was totally satisfactory, he would certainly have published some of them—unless all of them happened to be even worse.
18 Ibid., pp. 458–463.
19 Compare ibid., pp. 465–466 with Lavoisier, "Que l'eau n'est point une substance simple," pp. 345–348.
20 Lavoisier, "Acide du charbon," p. 450.
21 Ibid., pp. 453–455.
22 Ibid., p. 458.

23 P. B. Medawar, *The Art of the Soluble* (Harmondsworth: Penguin Books, 1967), p. 169.

24 Lavoisier, "Acide du charbon," pp. 449, 454.

25 Ibid., pp. 459–462.

26 Lavoisier, "Acide du charbon" (first draft), n.p., final paragraph of main manuscript; "Acide du charbon," p. 467.

27 Daumas, *Lavoisier,* p. 54, notes the close concordance between Lavoisier's final result and the percent composition found by Dumas and Stas in 1840.

28 Henry Guerlac, *Antoine-Laurent Lavoisier: Chemist and Revolutionary* (New York: Charles Scribner's Sons, 1975), p. 124.

29 Lavoisier, "Acide du charbon" (first and second drafts); "Acide du charbon."

30 Lavoisier, "Acide du charbon," pp. 448–449.

31 One might think that for convenience we could now begin to refer to *charbon* and *substance charbonneuse* respectively by their eventual English equivalents, charcoal and carbon. That would, however, still create the impression of a more definitive clarification of nomenclature than had yet occurred. Besides the fact that Lavoisier revised these terms once more as part of the general reform of chemical nomenclature, English translation of his writings continued to blur the distinction.

Chapter 9. Water and Respiration

1 A detailed description of these events and the surviving documents recording them is given in Maurice Daumas and Denis Duveen, "Lavoisier's Relatively Unknown Large-Scale Decomposition and Synthesis of Water, February 27 and 28, 1785," *Chymia* 5(1959):113–129.

2 "Développement des dernières expériences sur la décomposition et la recomposition de l'eau," in Lavoisier, *Oeuvres*, 5:320–334. This article, probably edited but not necessarily written by Lavoisier, appeared originally in *Journal polytype des sciences et des arts*, February 26, 1786.

3 Lavoisier, *Traité élémentaire de chimie* (Paris: Cuchet, 1789), 1:100.

4 Denis I. Duveen and Herbert S. Klickstein, "Antoine-Laurent Lavoisier's Contributions to Medicine and Public Health," *Bulletin of the History of Medicine* 29 (1955):169–173.

5 W. A Smeaton, "Lavoisier's Membership of the Société Royale de Médicine," *Annals of Science* 12(1956):228–240.

6 Lavoisier, "Mémoire sur les altérations qui arrivent à l'air dans un grand nombre de circonstances," Fiche 1348, Archives of the Académie des Sciences. In the text I have translated the title as Lavoisier first wrote it. He then partially rewrote it as in the present citation.

7 Compare ibid., pp. [1–2] with Lavoisier, "Expériences et observations sur les fluides élastiques en général et sur l'air de l'atmosphère en particulier," *Oeuvres*, 5:271–272.

8 Lavoisier, "Altérations . . . dans un grand nombre de circonstances," pp. [5–11].

9 Ibid., pp. [12–15].

10 Ibid., pp. [15–18].

11 Ibid., p.[17].

12 Lavoisier, "Mémoire sur les altérations qui arrivent à l'air dans plusieurs circonstances où se trouvent les hommes réunies en société" (revised title), Fiche 1278, Archives of the Académie des Sciences, p. [1]; Lavoisier (same title), *Mémoires de la Société de Médicine* 5(1782–83 [1787]):569.

13 Lavoisier, "Altérations . . . dans un grand nombre de circonstances," pp. [7–8].

14 Ibid., p. [8].

15 See above, pp. 64–65.

16 Lavoisier, "Altérations . . . dans un grand nombre de circonstances," p. [4].

17 Ibid.

18 See above, pp. 180–182.

19 Lavoisier, "Mémoire sur la combinaison de l'acide nitreux avec les airs respirables," *Oeuvres,* 2:503–508.

20 Karl R. Popper, *The Logic of Scientific Discovery* (New York: Science Editons, 1961), p. 92.

21 See, for example, Thomas Nickles, "Introductory Essay," in Thomas Nickles, ed., *Scientific Discovery, Logic, and Rationality,* Boston Studies in the Philosophy of Science, Vol. 56 (Dordrecht: D. Reidel, 1980), pp. 8–18.

22 Lavoisier, "Altérations . . . dans plusieurs circonstances," pp.[6, 14]. These consecutive pages of the fair copy are separated by seven pages of a subsequent revision. I have eliminated from the translation several phrases which Lavoisier started to write but immediately crossed out.

23 Ibid., p. [14].

24 Everett Mendelsohn, *Heat and Life: The Development of the Theory of Animal Heat* (Cambridge, Mass.: Harvard University Press, 1964), p. 152; Charles A. Culotta, "Respiration and the Lavoisier Tradition: Theory and Modification, 1777–1850," *Transactions of the American Philosophical Society* 62(1972):5; Joseph S. Fruton, *Molecules and Life: Historical Essays on the Interplay of Chemistry and Biology* (New York: Wiley-Interscience, 1972), p. 264; Henry Guerlac, *Antoine-Laurent Lavoisier: Chemist and Revolutionary* (New York: Charles Scribner's Sons, 1975), p. 122.

25 See above, pp. 186–187.

26 See above, pp. 229 ff.

27 See, for example, Max Black, "More about Metaphor," in A. Ortony, ed., *Metaphor and Thought* (London: Cambridge University Press, 1980), pp. 19–43.

28 Lavoisier, Cahiers, R-8, f. 42.

29 Lavoisier,"Altérations . . . dans plusieurs circonstances," p. [4].

30 Lavoisier, Cahiers, R-8, f. 44.

31 Lavoisier, "Altérations . . . dans plusieurs circonstances," pp. [7–8].

32 Ibid., p. [9].

33 Ibid., p. [10].

34 Ibid.

35 Ibid.

36 Lavoisier, "Altérations," *Mémoires de la Société de Medicine,* 5:569–582.

37 Seguin and Lavoisier, "Premier mémoire sur la respiration des animaux," *Mémoires de l'Académie des Sciences* (1789 [1793]), p. 569.

38 Laplace and Lavoisier, "Mémoire contenant les expériences faites sur la chaleur pendant l'hiver de 1783 à 1784, in Lavoisier, *Oeuvres*, 2:724.

Chapter 10. The Composition of Inflammable Plant Substances

1 Lavoisier, "Mémoire sur la combinaison du principe oxygine avec l'esprit de vin, l'huile, et différents corps combustibles," *Oeuvres*, 2:588.

2 Lavoisier, "Observations diverses de chimie: Sur le changement de l'esprit de vin en eau" (first draft), Fiche 1343, Archives of the Académie des Sciences, p. [1].

3 For this judgment I have relied on the summaries of the laboratory records in M. Berthelot, *La révolution chimique: Lavoisier* (Paris: Félix-Alcan, 1890), pp. 225–310.

4 Lavoisier, "Observations diverses . . . sur le changement," p. [1].

5 C. J. Geoffroy, "Methode pour connoître et déterminer au juste la qualité des liqueurs spiritueuses qui portent le nom d'eau de vie et d'esprit de vin," *Mémoires de l'Académie des Sciences* (1718), pp. 37–50.

6 Lavoisier, "Observations diverses . . . sur le changement," p. [1].

7 Ibid.

8 Ibid., pp. [1–3].

9 Lavoisier, single sheet of paper headed "3 September 1784," Fiche 1343, Archives of the Académie des Sciences.

10 Lavoisier, "Observations diverses de chimie: Sur la combustion de l'esprit de vin et sa transmutation apparente en eau" (fair copy of "Observations diverses . . . sur le changement," with title revised afterward), Fiche 1343, p. [3], and loose sheet headed "September 3, 1784," Fiche 1343.

11 Maurice Daumas, *Lavoisier: Théoricien et expérimentateur* (Paris: Presses Universitaires, 1955), p. 55.

12 Lavoisier, "Observations diverses . . . sur la combustion," p. [3]. The title of the paper referred to the "apparent transmutation." See above, n. 10.

13 Ibid., p. [4]; Daumas, *Lavoisier*, p. 55.

14 Lavoisier, "Observations diverses . . . sur la combustion," p. [3].

15 Charles Coulston Gillispie, *The Edge of Objectivity: An Essay in the History of Scientific Ideas* (Princeton: Princeton University Press, 1960), p. 321.

16 Lavoisier, "Mémoire dans lequel on a pour objet de prouver que l'eau n'est point une substance simple, un élément proprement dit, mais qu'elle est susceptible de décomposition et de recomposition," *Oeuvres*, 2:357–358.

17 Lavoisier, "De la combinaison du principe oxygine avec l'esprit de vin, l'huille, et differens corps combustibles" (first draft), Fiche 1343, Archives of the Académie des Sciences, pp. [5–6]. Lavoisier made the same point, but with less emphasis and force, in the published version.

18 Ibid., pp. [6–10]; See also "Mémoire sur la combinaison du principe oxygine" (published version), pp. 589–590.

19 Lavoisier, "Mémoire sur la combinaison du principe oxygine," p. 589.

20 Ibid., p. 590.

21 Lavoisier, Cahiers, R-11, ff. 9–13.

22 Ibid., f. 9. On the following page (f. 10), there are calculations of the composition,

but from the fact that the new chemical nomenclature is used, it is evident that Lavoisier did not carry them out until several years later.

23 Lavoisier, "Mémoire sur la combinaison du principe oxygine," p. 594.

24 Lavoisier, Cahiers, R-11, ff. 11–13.

25 Lavoisier, "Mémoire sur la combinaison du principe oxygine," p. 595.

26 Lavoisier, Cahiers, R-11, ff. 14–16.

27 Ibid., f. 16.

28 Ibid., ff. 13, 12v.

29 Lavoisier, "De la combinaison du principe oxygine," p. [11].

30 Ibid., pp. [11–12].

31 Ibid., p. [5].

32 Ibid., pp. [11–12].

33 Ibid., p. [15].

34 I borrow the term "nascent" from Gerald Holton's description of his approach to understanding scientific activity in *The Scientific Imagination: Case Studies* (Cambridge: Cambridge University Press, 1978), p. vii.

35 Lavoisier, "De la combinaison du principe oxygine," pp. [13–15].

36 Gillispie, *The Edge of Objectivity*, pp. 231–232.

37 Lavoisier, "Sur la nature de l'eau et sur les expériences par lesquelles on a prétendu prouver la possibilité de son changement en terre," *Oeuvres*, 2:1–28. The standard historical account of these experiments is A. N. Meldrum, "Lavoisier's Work on the Nature of Water and the Supposed Transmutation of Water into Earth," *Archeion* 14 (1932): 246–247; Meldrum, "Lavoisier's Early Work in Science," *Isis* 19 (1933): 330–363; ibid. 20 (1934): 396–425. An important new interpretation of this work is J. B. Gough, "Lavoisier's Memoirs on the Nature of Water and Their Place in the Chemical Revolution," *Ambix* 30 (1983): 89–106.

38 An essential foundation for such a study is a collection of sixty-six small folded sheets, entitled. "Particular ideas and experiments to perform," dated between 1764 and 1767, on a variety of problems mostly in mineralogical chemistry. In one of them, note 46, dated June 7, 1767, Lavoisier described a dissolution of silver in nitrous acid which he had carried out, and for which he gave the weight of the silver, the weight of the nitrous acid calculated from its density, and the expected total weight of the solution, in his familiar balance sheet form. The collection of notes forms Fiche 251, Archives of the Académie des Sciences.

39 [Meusnier] (untitled), Fiche 1343, Archives of the Académie des Sciences. The inference that Meusnier is the author of the analysis is based on the similarity of the handwriting to that in entries in Lavoisier's laboratory notebooks that appear attributable to him; the fact that Meusnier collaborated with Lavoisier on the gun barrel experiments; and the mathematical nature of the analysis.

40 Lavoisier, "De la combinaison du principe oxygine," pp. [17, 20–21].

41 Ibid., pp. [22–23].

42 Lavoisier, "De la combinaison du principe oxygine" (fair copy), Fiche 1343, pp. [13–14].

43 Ibid., pp. [14–15]. See also "Mémoire sur la combinaison du principe oxygine," pp. 597–600. Compare with Lavoisier "Mémoire sur la formation de l'acide nommé air

fixe ou acide crayeux, et que je désignerai désormais sous le nom d'acide du charbon," *Mémoires de l'Académie des Sciences* (1781 [1784]), pp. 455–457.

44 Lavoisier, "De la combinaison du principe oxygine" (fair copy), pp. [14–15].

45 Ibid., pp. [14–16].

46 Ibid., pp. [8–13].

47 Ibid. pp. [23–24]. (Pages [17] onward of the "fair copy" are actually a further revision in Lavoisier's hand, and are identical to a section of the published version, *Oeuvres*, 2:590–593, 595–600.

48 Lavoisier, "De la combinaison du principe oxygine" (fair copy), p. [12]; "Mémoire sur la combinaison du principe oxygine," p. 595.

49 Lavoisier, "De la combinaison du principe oxygine" (fair copy rev.), pp. [26–33]; "Mémoire sur la combinaison du principe oxygine," pp. 597–600. One might expect that the changed constant would have caused Lavoisier trouble with the second experiment on wax, by increasing the "negative" deficit that he already attributed to experimental error. It did, in fact, increase this figure from 0.278 to 1.0 grains. He chose not to make that difference visible, but to hide it in the figures for fixed air, which do not quite come out to his standard proportions. This way of handling the situation may appear inconsistent with other responses described above, but since he knew in advance that there had to be an experimental error involved, he probably did not consider it worthwhile to discuss a problem which no longer entailed a theoretical question.

50 Daumas, *Lavoisier*, p. 57.

51 Lavoisier, "De la combinaison du principe oxygine," (first draft), p. [1].

52 Ibid. (fair copy), p. [1].

Chapter 11. Nature's Operations

1 [Pierre-Joseph Macquer], *Dictionnaire de chymie*, 2 vols. (Paris: Lacombe, 1766), 1:493–494; 2:526, 629–631.

2 Lavoisier, *Traité élémentaire de chimie* (Paris: Cuchet, 1789), 1:141–142.

3 [Macquer], *Dictionnaire de chymie*, 2:526.

4 See above p. 204.

5 [Anonymous], "Recueil de faites sur la fermentation et ses différentes effets," Lavoisier archives, Fiche 343, p. 2.

6 [Macquer], *Dictionnaire de chymie*, 1:493.

7 See Joseph S. Fruton, *Molecules and Life*, (New York: Wiley-Interscience, 1972), pp. 34–35.

8 Lavoisier, Cahiers, R-12, f. 25.

9 [Macquer], *Dictionnaire de chymie*, 2:532–535.

10 Ibid., 1:488.

11 Lavoisier, Cahiers, R-12, ff. 25–27. According to Berthelot what had actually taken place was a lactic fermentation, which caused the iron to dissolve. See M. Berthelot, *La révolution chimique: Lavoisier* (Paris: Félix-Alcan, 1890), p. 303.

12 Berthelot, *La révolution chimique*, p. 303.

13 Ibid., pp. 301–304.

14 Maurice Daumas, *Lavoisier: Théoricien et expérimentateur* (Paris: Presses Universitaires de France, 1955), p. 58.
15 Roger Hahn, *The Anatomy of a Scientific Institution: The Paris Academy of Sciences, 1666–1803* (Berkeley: University of California Press, 1971), pp. 99–101.
16 Berthelot, *La révolution chimique*, pp. 301, 303.
17 Ibid., p. 304; Daumas, *Lavoisier*, p. 58.
18 Joseph Priestley, *Experiments and Observations on Different Kinds of Air* (Birmingham: Thomas Pearson, 1790; rpt., New York: Kraus Reprint Co., 1970), 3:408, 416–419. This is a later, abridged account. Lavoisier did not make reference to a specific publication by Priestley.
19 Lavoisier, "Réflexions sur la décomposition de l'eau par les substances végétales et animales," *Mémoires de l'Académie des Sciences* (1786 [1788]), pp. 590–594.
20 Ibid., p. 594.
21 Stephen Hales, *Vegetable Staticks*, ed. Michael Hoskin, *History of Science Library: Primary Sources* (New York: Science History Publications, 1969), p. 97.
22 Ibid., pp. 97–98, 105, 120–121, 168–170, 178.
23 Lavoisier, "Reflexions sur la decomposition de l'eau," pp. 594–596. By the time this passage was published, in 1788, Lavoisier had adopted the new system of chemical nomenclature, and he changed the terms used in it to reflect that system. I have restored to this translation the older terms which he used when he originally wrote the paper.
24 Lavoisier, "Sur l'air qu'on tira des végétaux lorsqu'on les décompose par la distillation à feu nud," Fiche 390, Archives of the Académie des Sciences, pp. [11–12].
25 Ibid., p. [13].
26 Abbé Fontana, "Mémoire sur la nature de l'acide des animaux, des végétaux, et des substances gommeuses et résineuses," *Obsérvations sur la physique* 12 (1778): 26[64]–75; Fontana, "Supplément aux expériences sur les fourmis," ibid., pp. 169–189. Berthollet's general investigation of tartaric acid is described in Claude-Louis Berthollet, "Expériences sur l'acide tartareux," ibid. 7(1776):130–148, although the particular experiments in question do not appear to be included in this paper. Fontana summarized them in detail.
27 Lavoisier, "Considérations générales sur la nature des acides," Mémoires de l'Académie des Sciences (1777[1780]), p. 545.
28 Nicolas Deyeux, "Reflexions sur le mémoire de M. l'Abbé Fontana, où il s'agit de la nature de l'acide des fourmis," *Observations sur la physique* 12 (1778): 357–359.
29 This orientation is supported by the fact that he revised the title, on the left-hand margin, to read, "Reflexions sur les circonstances qui accompagnent la décomposition des végétaux soit dans la distillation soit dans la fermentation." Lavoisier, "Sur l'air," p. [1].
30 Ibid., p. [9].
31 Ibid., p. [14].
32 Ibid., pp. [18–21]. For the corresponding discussions in their final published form, see Lavoisier, "Reflexions sur la décomposition de l'eau," pp. 603–604.
33 Lavoisier, "Sur l'air," pp. [15–17].

34 See above, pp. 220–222.
35 Jean Senebier, *Mémoires physico-chimiques sur l'influence de la lumière solaire pour modifier les êtres des trois règnes de la nature, et sur-tout ceux du règne végétal*, 3 vols. (Geneva: Barthelemi Chirol, 1782), 3:330–344.
36 Lavoisier, Cahiers, R-12, ff. 113–119.
37 Ibid., ff. 121–123.
38 Ibid., ff. 125–129.
39 Ibid., ff. 131–133.
40 Senebier, *Mémoires physico-chimique sur l'influence de la lumière solaire*, Vol. 1.
41 Priestley, *Experiments and Observations*, 3:246–347.
42 See above, p. 156
43 Lavoisier, "Reflexions sur la decomposition de l'eau," p. 605.
44 Lavoisier, Cahiers, R-12, ff. 135–137.
45 Ibid., ff. 137–141.
46 Ibid., ff. 141–143.
47 Daumas, *Lavoisier*, p. 59; Lavoisier, "Reflexions sur la décomposition de l'eau par les substances végétales et animales," Fiche 1347, Archives of the Académie des Sciences. There is internal evidence that in writing this draft Lavoisier anticipated that he would give it at a public meeting. See p. [21].
48 Lavoisier, "Reflexions sur la décomposition de l'eau," Fiche 1347, p. [4].
49 Lavoisier, "Sur l'air," p. [14].
50 Lavoisier, "Reflexions sur la décomposition de l'eau," Fiche 1347, pp. [14–15].
51 Claude-Louis Berthollet, "Recherches sur la nature des substances animales et sur leur rapports avec les substances végétales," *Mémoires de l'Académie des Sciences* (1780 [1784]), pp. 120–125; Berthollet, "Précis d'observations sur l'analyse animale comparé à l'analyse végétale," *Observations sur la physique* 27(1786): 272–275; Berthollet, "Suite des recherches sur la nature des substances animales et sur leur rapport avec les substances végétales," ibid., pp. 389–395. On Berthollet's connections with Lavoisier, see Michelle Sadoun-Goupil, *Le chimiste Claude-Louis Berthollet (1748–1822)* (Paris: J. Vrin, 1977), pp. 16–17.
52 Lavoisier, "Reflexions sur la décomposition de l'eau," Fiche 1347, p. [15].
53 Ibid., pp. [19–21].
54 See above. pp. 65–66, 82–87.
55 Daumas, *Lavoisier*, pp. 59–60.

Chapter 12. Language, Organic Composition, and Fermentation

1 Maurice Daumas, *Lavoisier: Théoricien et expérimentateur* (Paris: Presses Universitaires, 1955), pp. 60–62; Guyton de Morveau, Antoine Lavoisier, Claude-Louis Berthollet, and Antoine de Fourcroy, *Méthode de nomenclature chimique* (Paris: Cuchet, 1787).
2 On this subject, see especially Maurice Crosland, *Historical Studies in the Language of Chemistry* (Cambridge, Mass.: Harvard University Press, 1962), and Robert Siegfried, "Lavoisier's Table of Simple Substances: Its Origin and Interpretation," *Ambix* 29 (1982) pp. 28–48.

3 Morveau, Lavoisier, et al., *Méthode*, pp. 31–32.
4 Ibid., pp. 35–36.
5 Ibid., p. 33.
6 Ibid., pp. 43–45.
7 Ibid., p. 17.
8 Ibid., pp. 30, 36.
9 Antoine Lavoisier, *Traité élémentaire de chimie*, 2 vols. (Paris: Cuchet, 1789), 1:192.
10 Lavoisier, Fiche 1452, Archives of the Académie des Sciences, p. [1]. This manuscript is attached to the fair copy of a memoir entitled "Sur la fermentation spiritueuse," with an archivist's notation that it is an "addition" to that memoir. From its contents, however, one can easily tell that it is an earlier draft of the addition Lavoisier made to his "Reflexions sur la décomposition de l'eau par les substances végétales et animales," *Mémoires de l'Académie des Sciences* (1786 [1788]), on pp. 597–599.
11 Lavoisier, Fiche 1452, pp. [2–4].
12 Ibid., pp. [4–5].
13 Ibid., p. [1]. I have numbered the pages of this manuscript without taking into account the missing page.
14 Ibid., p. [5].
15 Ibid., pp. [5–7].
16 Ibid.,, pp. [7–8].
17 Lavoisier, "Reflexions sur la decomposition de l'eau," pp. 597–598.
18 Lavoisier, *Traité élémentaire de chimie*, 2 vols. (Paris: Cuchet, 1789), 1:150–151.
19 Howard E. Gruber, "On the Relation between 'Aha Experiences' and the Construction of Ideas," *History of Science* 19(1981):44.
20 Lavoisier, "Reflexions sur la décomposition de l'eau," pp. 599–600.
21 Lavoisier, "Sur la fermentation spiritueuse" (fair copy), Fiche 1452, Archives of the Académie des Sciences, p. [5].
22 Lavoisier, Cahiers, R-11, f 51.
23 Lavoisier, Cahiers, R-11, ff. 54–55. See above, p. 233.
24 Ibid., ff. 56–59.
25 Ibid., R-12, ff. 143–144, 163.
26 Ibid., R-11, ff. 60–62.
27 Ibid., R-12, ff. 164–166.
28 Ibid., ff. 164–166, 178–181. For a general description of the method Lavoisier used to measure the specific gravities, see Lavoisier, *Traité élémentaire*, 2:337–339.
29 Lavoisier, Cahiers, R-12, ff. 182–183.
30 Lavoisier, "Reflexions sur la décomposition de l'eau," pp. 603–604.
31 Lavoisier, Cahiers, R-12, f. 169.
32 Ibid., ff. 171–175.
33 Ibid., f. 170.
34 Ibid., ff. 185–189. See J. R. Partington, *A History of Chemistry*, Vol. 3 (London: Macmillan, 1962), p. 232.

35 Lavoisier, Cahiers, R-12, ff. 190–191.
36 Ibid., f. 193.
37 See above, pp. 271–272.
38 Lavoisier, Cahiers, R-12, f. 197.
39 Edouard Grimaux, *Lavoisier, 1743–1794* (Paris: Félix-Alcan, 1888), pp. 167–186; M. Berthelot, *La révolution chimique: Lavoisier* (Paris: Félix-Alcan, 1890), p. 305.
40 Lavoisier, "Fermentation spiritueuse" (fair copy), p. [1].
41 The evidence for this date is circumstantial. The text of the manuscript makes it clear that Lavoisier intended it for a public meeting. It could not have been prepared before the conclusion of the fermentation experiment that ended on June 12, 1787. The memoir contains a composition for sugar which Fourcroy reported in the reply of the French chemists to Kirwan (see below, p. 357), which was ready for publication by January 1788. The minutes for the meeting of the Academy for November 14 record that "Lavoisier read a memoir," (Daumas, *Lavoisier,* p. 62), but give no indication of the subject. The only other plausible alternative is the public meeting normally held during the Easter season, for 1788. There is no record of Lavoisier's reading any memoir at this meeting, and no reason to consider it more likely than the November meeting.
42 Lavoisier, "Fermentation spiritueuse" (fair copy), p. [1].
43 Ibid., p. [9]; Lavoisier "27 avril 1787," in sheet of notes and calculations on fermentation, Fiche 345, Archives of the Académie des Sciences.
44 Lavoisier, "Résultat de la fermentation," Fiche 345, Archives of the Académie des Sciences. There are several similar sheets by the same title in the collection of notes.
45 Ibid.
46 Lavoisier, "Sur la fermentation spiritueuse" (first draft), Fiche 344, Archives of the Académie des Sciences, p. [10].
47 Lavoisier, "Résultat." See n. 44.
48 Lavoisier, "Fermentation spiritueuse" (first draft), p. [10].
49 Ibid., p. [2].
50 Lavoisier, *Traité élémentaire,* 1:vii–xi.
51 Lavoisier, "Fermentation spiritueuse" (first draft) pp. [2–4].
52 Ibid., pp. [4–8].
53 Ibid., p. [9].
54 Lavoisier, Fiche 345 (untitled page among notes and calculations).
55 Lavoisier, "Fermentation spiritueuse" (first draft), p. [12]; (fair copy), p. [14].
56 Lavoisier, "Fermentation spiritueuse" (fair copy), p. [12].
57 Ibid.
58 Lavoisier, "Fermentation spiritueuse" (first draft), p. [13].
59 Lavoisier, "Fermentation" (fair copy), pp. [13–14].
60 See, for example, Charles Coulston Gillispie, *The Edge of Objectivity: An Essay in the History of Scientific Ideas* (Princeton: Princeton University Press, 1960), pp. 209–216.
61 Lavoisier, "Fermentation spiritueuse" (fair copy), pp. [15–16].
62 Lavoisier, "Fermentation spiritueuse" (first draft), pp. [14–15].

63 Ibid., p. [12].
64 Lavoisier, "Fermentation spiritueuse" (fair copy), pp. [13–14].
65 Lavoisier, "Produit de la fermentation," Fiche 345, Archives of the Académie des Sciences.
66 Lavoisier, "Fermentation spiritueuse" (first draft), p. [8].
67 Lavoisier, "Fermentation spiritueuse" (fair copy), p. [12].
68 Daumas, *Lavoisier,* p. 62.

Chapter 13. The Trouble with Sugar

1 R. Kirwan, *An Essay on Phlogiston and the Constitution of Acids,* 2d ed. (London: J. Johnson, 1789), pp. 4–7. This edition contained, in addition to Kirwan's original chapters, English translations of the comments of the French chemists, with brief notes in reply by Kirwan.
2 See above, pp. 138–146.
3 Kirwan, *Essay on Phlogiston,* pp. 152–155.
4 Lavoisier, "Considérations générales sur la nature des acides," *Mémoires de l'Académie des Sciences* (1777 [1780]), p. 541.
5 Kirwan, *Essay on Phlogiston,* p. 155.
6 Lavoisier, "La nature des acides," pp. 538–545.
7 Kirwan, *Essay on Phlogiston,* p. 157
8 Maurice Daumas, *Lavoisier: Théoricien et expérimentateur* (Paris: Presses Universitaires, 1955), p. 62.
9 *Essai sur le phlogistique, et sur la constitution des acides, traduit de l'anglois de M. Kirwan, avec des notes de MM. de Morveau, Lavoisier, de la Place, Monge, Berthollet, et de Fourcroy* (Paris: Hôtel Serpente, 1788), p. 185.
10 Ibid., p. 186.
11 Kirwan, *Essay on Phlogiston,* p. 192.
12 *Essai sur le phlogistique,* pp. 186–187.
13 Ibid., p. 188.
14 Ibid.
15 Kirwan, *Essay on Phlogiston,* p. 157.
16 *Essai sur le phlogistique,* pp. 189–191.
17 Edouard Grimaux, *Lavoisier, 1743–1794* (Paris: Félix-Alcan, 1888), pp. 184–185.
18 Lavoisier, Cahiers, R-12, inserted at f. 223. Another loose sheet related to a different experiment, and dated April 29, 1788, is inserted at the same place. The nearest preceding date on the notebook pages themselves is also April 29 (f. 221).
19 See above, p. 348.
20 Lavoisier, Cahiers, R-12, f. 163.
21 See ibid., f. 182.
22 Lavoisier, "Matériaux de le fermentation" (notes attached to "Sur la fermentation spiritueuse," first draft), Fiche 345, Archives of the Académie des Sciences.
23 Ibid.

24 Lavoisier, "Produit de la fermentation," Fiche 345, Archives of the Académie des Sciences. Lavoisier made an error in subtraction. The difference should be 15 ounces, 1 gros, 42 grains.
25 Lavoisier, several untitled pages, Fiche 345, Archives of the Académie des Sciences.
26 M. Berthelot, *La révolution chimique: Lavoisier* (Paris: Félix-Alcan, 1890), pp. 306–308.
27 Lavoisier, Cahiers, R-12, f. 203.
28 Ibid., R-12, f. 203, R-13, f. 9; Berthelot, *La révolution chimique*, p. 308.
29 Lavoisier, Cahiers, R-13, ff. 11–12.
30 Ibid., R-12, f. 207.
31 Ibid., ff. 215–217.
32 Ibid., f. 219.
33 Ibid., ff. 219–223, and inserted loose sheet. Additional confirmation that Lavoisier relied on his carbonization analysis for the figure of 28 percent carbon in sugar is that he made an alternative calcuation of the composition "on the supposition that sugar contains 28.95 of carbon." (He meant to write 28.85, as the calculation on the back of the loose sheet shows.) This was the exact proportion resulting from that experiment.
34 Ibid., R-13, f. 13.
35 Ibid., ff. 20–21.
36 Ibid., R-12, f. 218.
37 See above, p. 272.
38 Lavoisier, Cahiers, R-11, facing f. 13. Lavoisier actually gave only the composition of the 93.5 grains of spirit of wine consumed in the experiment. He started to convert to the base of 100 parts spirit of wine, but left the amounts blank. The above is what he would have obtained by completing the computation. The right-hand column I obtained by repeating his procedure with the ratio 72:28. It agrees with his earlier published values, but is expressed in different units.
39 Ibid. For an interesting discussion of other examples of Lavoisier's effort to relate chemical balances to algebraic methods, see Charles Coulton Gillispie, *The Edge of Objectivity* (Princeton: Princeton University Press, 1960), pp. 242–246.
40 Lavoisier, "Calcul de 1er juillet 1788" (Pages attached to "Sur la fermentation spiritueuse," first draft, Fiche 345, Archives of the Académie des Sciences).
41 Lavoisier, Cahiers, R-12, f. 218.
42 Lavoisier, *Traité élémentaire de chimie*, 2 vols. (Paris: Cuchet, 1789), 1:67–68.
43 See above, p. 272.
44 Lavoisier, Cahiers, R-11, f. 10.
45 The composition for spirit of wine shown in the table in *Traité élémentaire*, 1:147, reduces to these proportions if one combines the weights for oxygen and for "hydrogen combined with oxygen," and converts the figures to grains and to a base of 100 grains of spirit of wine.
46 Lavoisier, Cahiers, R-12, f. 209.
47 See above, pp. 345–346.

48 The figures are:

Oxygen	29 pounds	10 ounces	6 gros	10.6 grains
Hydrogen combined with oxygen	5	3	6	18.8
Hydrogen combined with carbon	4	14	7	18.8
Carbon	17	13	6	9.8
Total	57	11	1	58.0

See Lavoisier, Cahiers, R-12, f. 209. Maurice Daumas, *Lavoisier: Théoricien et expérimentateur* (Paris: Presses Universitaires, 1955), p. 63, dates these calculations June 22, 1789, because a loose sheet, which he regards as part of the same "study", and which bears that date, is inserted at the same place. The loose sheet is, however, about an unrelated experiment. Daumas's date is ruled out by the fact that tables derived from these appeared in the *Traité élémentaire*.

49 Following the steps of Lavoisier's procedure shown at R-11, facing f.13, but setting m = fraction of oxygen in carbonic acid:

1. Using data from Lavoisier, *Traité élémentaire* 1:147, converted to a total of 93.50 grains spirit of wine, the quantity found in the original experiment:

$95.280m$ = oxygen contained in carbonic acid

x preformed water + z hydrogen + 110.317 oxygen = $95.280m$ + 108.537 water

$59.832 + 6.544 + 110.317 = 95.280m + 108.537$

$m = 0.715$

2. Using data from R-12, f. 209

$56.567 + 7.99 + 110.317 = 95.280m + 108.537$

$m = 0.696$

50 For a standard account, see Nicolas Lemery, *Cours de chymie*, 4th ed. (Paris, 1681), p. 762.

51 Lavoisier, Cahiers, R-13, f. 27.

52 Ibid., f. 28.

53 Ibid., ff. 29–33.

54 Ibid., f. 34; see Lemery, *Cours de chymie* pp. 588–592.

55 Lavoisier, *Traité élémentaire,* 1:205–206.

56 Lavoisier, Cahiers, R-13, ff. 31–44.

57 Lavoisier, *Traité élémentaire* 2:461–464.

58 The apparatus is preserved in the Musée des Techniques of the Conservatoire des Artes et Métiers, Paris.

59 See Daumas, *Lavoisier,* pp. 152–153.

60 Lavoisier, Cahiers, R-13, f. 66.

61 Ibid., f. 67, facing f. 67.

62 Lavoisier "Suite de l'expérience sur la corne du 6 août 88," Cahiers, R-13, n.p., following f. 67.

63 Lavoisier, Cahiers, R-13, ff. 46–58.
64 Frederic L. Holmes, "Analysis by Fire and Solvent Extractions: The Metamorphosis of a Tradition," *Isis* 62(1970):139.

Chapter 14. Plant and Animal Chemistry in the New Chemical System

1 Maurice Daumas, *Lavoisier: Théoricien et expérimentateur* (Paris: Presses Universitaires, 1955), pp. 63, 108–109.
2 Antoine Lavoisier, *Traité élémentaire de chimie*, 2 vols. (Paris: Cuchet, 1789), 1:132–138, 158.
3 Ibid., 1:116–120.
4 Ibid., 1:123–126. Evan Melhado has shown that the term "radical," which Lavoisier adopted from Guyton de Morveau, originated in Bergman's concept of a "radical acid." Melhado, *Jacob Berzelius: The Emergence of His Chemical System* (Madison: University of Wisconsin Press, 1981), pp. 68–69, 92–98.
5 Lavoisier, *Traité élémentaire*, 1:125, 128, 130–131.
6 Ibid., 1:127.
7 Ibid., 1:158.
8 Ibid., 1:127.
9 Lavoisier, "Calcul pour l'acide acéteux . . . pour l'air fixe," Fiche 345, Archives of the Académie des Sciences.
10 Lavoisier, *Traité élémentaire*, 1:146.
11 Lavoisier (untitled), Fiche 345, Archives of the Académie des Sciences.
12 Ibid.
13 Armand Seguin, "Extrait d'un ouvrage de M. Lavoisier," *Annales de chimie* 2 (1801 [2d ed.]): 239.
14 See below, p. 428.
15 Lavoisier, *Traité élémentaire*, 1:150–151. See above, p. 324.
16 Ibid., 1:149.
17 See above, pp. 360–362.
18 Lavoisier, *Traité élementaire*, 1:150.
19 Ibid., 1:140–141.
20 Henry Guerlac, *Antoine-Laurent Lavoisier: Chemist and Revolutionary* (New York: Charles Scribner's Sons, 1975), p. 119; Douglas McKie, *Antoine Lavoisier: Scientist, Economist, Social Reformer* (New York: Henry Schuman, 1952), pp. 203–204; J. R. Partington, *A History of Chemistry*, Vol. 3 (London: Macmillan, 1962), pp. 377–378.
21 Max Speter, *Lavoisier und seine Vorläufer* (Stuttgart: Ferdinand Enke, 1910), p. 46.
22 Ibid., p. 480.
23 Quoted in Guerlac, *Antoine-Laurent Lavoisier*, p. 119.
24 Ibid.
25 Partington, *A History of Chemistry*, 3:480.
26 Joseph S. Fruton, *Molecules and Life: Historical Essays on the Interplay of Chemistry and Biology* (New York: Wiley-Interscience, 1972), p. 40.

27 Lavoisier, *Traité élémentaire*, 1:143.

28 See above, pp. 372–373.

29 Lavoisier, *Traité élémentaire*, 1:151.

30 Ibid., 1:x–xi.

31 See above, pp. 342–346.

32 Lavoisier, *Traité élémentaire*, 1:142.

33 See above, pp. 357, 364–365.

34 Lavoisier, *Traité élémentaire*, 1:145.

35 Ibid., 1:148–149.

36 Emile Meyerson, *Identity and Reality*, trans. Kate Loewenberg (New York: Dover, 1962), pp. 169–175.

37 Lavoisier, *Traité élémentaire*, 1:141.

38 Ibid., 1:133–134.

39 Ibid., 1:147.

40 Ibid., 1:125.

41 Ibid., 1:127–128, 158.

42 Ibid., 1:120, 125, 138, 146, 152.

43 Daumas, *Lavoisier*, p. 152. The apparatus for combustion of oil and for fermentation are both on display in the Musée des Techniques of the Conservatoire des Arts et Métiers, in Paris. My description is based on personal observation there. See also Maurice Daumas, "Les appareils d'expérimentation de Lavoisier," *Chymie* 3 (1950):60–61.

44 Lavoisier, "Détails historiques sur la cause de l'augmentation de poids," *Oeuvres*, 2:104.

45 Frederic L. Holmes, "Analysis by Fire and Solvent Extractions: The Metamorphosis of a Tradition," *Isis* 62(1970):144–148.

46 Eliot F. Beach,"Beccari of Bologna: The Discoverer of Vegetable Protein," *Journal of the History of Medicine* 16(1961):361–363.

47 H. M. Rouelle, "Expériences," *Journal de médecine* 39(1773):251–265; "Observations sur les fécules ou parties vertes des plantes, et sur la matière glutineuse ou végéto-animale," ibid., 40(1773):59–66.

48 Jean-Baptiste Bucquet, *Introduction à l'étude des corps naturels tirés du règne végétal* (Paris: Herissant, 1773).

49 Claude-Louis Berthollet, "Observations sur la causticité des alkalis et de la chaux," *Mémoires de l'Académic des Sciences* (1782 [1785]), pp. 616–619; Antoine de Fourcroy, "Mémoire sur la nature de la fibre charnue ou musculaire et sur le siège de l'irritabilité," ibid. (1782–83 [1787]), pp. 502–505.

50 Louis-Claude Cadet, "Expériences sur la bile de l'homme et des animaux," *Mémoires de l'Académie des Sciences* (1767 [1770]), pp. 471–483.

51 Lavoisier, Cahiers, R-13, ff. 14, 19.

52 Charles van Bochaute, "Dissertation physiologico-chymique sur la bile," *Journal de physique* 13 (supplement) (1773):262.

53 For an important recent discussion of some of these developments, see Reinhard Löw, *Pflanzenchemie zwischen Lavoisier und Liebig* (Munich: Donau-Verlag, 1977).

Chapter 15. Responses to Lavoisier's Theory of Respiration

1 Antoine Lavoisier, *Traité élémentaire de chimie*, 2 vols. (Paris: Cuchet, 1789), 1:202; Lavoisier, Cahiers, R-12, f. 59.
2 Antoine Fourcroy, "Extrait d'un mémoire sur les propriétés médicinales de l'air vital," *Annales de chimie* 4 (1796):83–88.
3 Ibid., pp. 88–93. See above, p. 239.
4 Jean-Henri Hassenfratz, "Sur la combinaison d l'oxigène avec le carbone et l'hydrogène du sang, sur la dissolution de l'oxigène dans le sang, et sur la manière dont le calorique se dégage," *Annales de chimie* 9 (1791):266–267.
5 Most explicitly in Diana Long Hall, "The Iatrochemical Background of Lagrange's Theory of Animal Heat," *Journal of the History of Biology* 4 (1971): 245. Everett Mendelsohn, *Heat and Life: The Development of the Theory of Animal Heat* (Cambridge, Mass.: Harvard University Press, 1964), p. 171, treats Lagrange's view as a response to ideas expressed by Christoph Girtanner in 1790.
6 Hassenfratz, "Sur la combinaison de l'oxigène," p. 267.
7 Ibid.
8 For an extensive description of the ensuing debates, see Everett Mendelsohn, "The Controversy over the Site of Heat Production in the Body," *Proceedings of the American Philosophical Society* 105 (1961):412–420.
9 Adair Crawford, *Experiments and Observations on Animal Heat and the Inflammation of Combustible Bodies*, 2d ed. rev. (London: J. Johnson, 1788), pp. 280–284.
10 Ibid., pp. A3–A5, 96–305.
11 Ibid., pp. 308–319; Mendelsohn, *Heat and Life*, p. 154.
12 Crawford, *Animal Heat*, pp. 320–321, 326–327, 333–334.
13 Ibid., pp. 322–339.
14 Ibid., p. 339.
15 Ibid., pp. 340–348.
16 Ibid., pp. 351–352.
17 Ibid., p. 333.
18 Mendelsohn, *Heat and Life*, pp. 156–157; G. J. Goodfield, *The Growth of Scientific Physiology* (London: Hutchinson, 1960), pp. 52–53, 56–57; T. H. Lodwig and W. A. Smeaton, "The Ice Calorimeter of Lavoisier and Laplace and Some of Its Critics," *Annals of Science* 31 (1974):1–18.
19 Goodfield, *The Growth of Scientific Physiology* p. 53.
20 Crawford, *Animal Heat*, pp. 253–261; Laplace and Lavoisier, "Mémoire sur les expériences faites sur la chaleur pendant l'hiver de 1783 à 1784," in Lavoisier *Oeuvres*, 2:726–727.
21 H. M. Collins, "The Seven Sexes: A study in the Sociology of a Phenomenon, or the Replication of Experiments in Physics," *Sociology* 9 (1975):210–211. Collins argues that for marginal fields these practices can be explained as negotiations about the rules for making experiments.
22 Crawford, *Animal Heat*, p. 262.
23 See above, p. 221.
24 Crawford, *Animal Heat*, pp. 307, 361, 387–391.

25 See above, p. 63.
26 Crawford, *Animal Heat*, pp. 149–150.
27 Goodfield, *The Growth of Scientific Physiology*, p. 58.
28 Mendelsohn, *Heat and Life*, p. 164.
29 Crawford, *Animal Heat*, pp. 368–380.
30 See Karl Hufbauer, *The Formation of the German Chemical Community (1720–1795)* (Berkeley: University of California Press, 1982), pp. 96–106.
31 Léopold Vacca Berlinghieri, "Mémoire sur la chaleur," *Observations sur la physique* 35 (1789): 113–121.
32 "Observations de M. Hassenfratz, relatives à un mémoire de M. Berlinghieri," *Annales de chimie* 3 (1789):263–265.
33 Ibid., pp. 262–263.
34 Ibid., pp. 264–265.
35 Stuart Pierson, "Seguin, Armand," in Charles Gillispie, ed., *Dictionary of Scientific Biography*, 16 vols. (New York: Charles Scribner's Sons, 1970–80), 12:286–287; A. Fourcroy, "Recherches pour servir à l'histoire du gaz azote ou de la mofette, comme principe des matières animales," *Annales de chimie* 1 (1790):50; A. Seguin, "Extrait d'un ouvrage de M. Lavoisier," ibid. 2 (2d ed. 1801):247.
36 Armand Seguin, "Observations générales sur le calorique et ses differents effets, et réflexions sur la théorie de MM. Black, Crawford, Lavoisier, et de Laplace, sur la chaleur animale et sur celle qui se dégage pendant la combustion; avec un résumé de tout ce qui a été fait et écrit jusqu'à ce moment sur ce sujet," Première partie, *Annales de chimie* 3 (1789):148–242; Seguin, Seconde partie, ibid., 5 (2d ed., 1800):201–271.
37 A. Lavoisier, *Traité élémentaire de chimie*, 2 vols. (Paris: Cuchet, 1789) 1:6.
38 Seguin, "Première partie, pp. 183–229.
39 Seguin, Seconde partie, pp. 259–261.
40 Ibid., pp. 261–267.
41 Ibid., pp. 267–268.
42 Crawford, *Animal Heat*, pp. 344–345, 359, 362, 366–367.
43 See, for example, Lavoisier, "Mémoire dans lequel on a pour object de prouver que l'eau n'est point une substance simple, un élément proprement dit, mais qu'elle est susceptible de décomposition et de recomposition," *Oeuvres*, 2:335.
44 Seguin, Seconde partie, pp. 269–271.
45 A. Seguin, "Observations générales sur la respiration et sur la chaleur animale," *Observations sur la physique* 37 (1790):467–470. A handwritten manuscript of this memoir, identical to the published text, is preserved in the archives of the *Académie Nationale de Médecine*, Lavoisier-Seguin dossier, carton 174, no. 34. I wish to thank Caroline Hannaway for drawing my attention to this document.
46 Ibid., pp. 470–472.
47 See above. pp. 194–195.
48 See, for example, Charles Culotta, "Respiration and the Lavoisier Tradition: Theory and Modification, 1777–1850," *Transactions of the American Philosophical Society* 62 (1972):69. Everett Mendelsohn more cautiously draws distinctions between the views of Lavoisier and Seguin (*Heat and Life*, p. 161); but he considers that Seguin's paper "gave an indication of the direction [his collaborative works with

Lavoisier] would take in solving some of the problems raised by Crawford's and Lavoisier's theories" (ibid., p. 160).

49 Joseph Priestley, "Observations on Respiration," *Philosophical Transactions of the Royal Society* 80 (1790):106.

50 Ibid., pp. 107–108.

51 Ibid., pp. 108–109.

52 See above, pp. 255–256.

53 Joseph Priestley, *Experiments and Observations on Different Kinds of Air,* 3 vols., (Birmingham: Thomas Pearson, 1790; (facsimile ed., New York: Kraus Reprint Co., 1970), 3:543–550.

54 David M. Knight, "Girtanner, Christoph," *Dictionary of Scientific Biography,* 5:411; Christoph Girtanner, "Sur l'irritabilité, considérée comme principe de vie dans la nature organisée," Premier mémoire, *Observations sur la physique* 36 (1790):422–440; Girtanner, Second mémoire, ibid., 37, pt. II (1790): 147–148.

55 Girtanner, Premier mémoire, p. 437.

56 Girtanner, Second mémoire, pp. 139–147.

57 Ibid., pp. 140–141.

58 Ibid., p. 140.

59 Ibid., p. 149.

60 See Albrecht von Haller, *First Lines of Physiology* (Edinburgh: Charles Elliot, 1777; rpt., Sources of Science, No. 32, New York: Johnson Reprint Corp., 1966), pp. 9–20; von Haller, *Anfangsgründe der Physiologie,* trans. Johann Haller, 8 vols. (Berlin: C. F. Boss, 1759), 1:1–46; von Haller, *A Dissertation on the Sensible and Irritable Parts of Animals,* intro. Owsei Temkin (Baltimore: John Hopkins Press, 1936), pp. 42–46.

61 Girtanner, Second mémoire, p. 151.

Chapter 16. Lavoisier's Return to Respiration

1 Lavoisier, "Sur la respiration animale," Fiche 1349, Archives of the Académie des Sciences, p. [1].

2 Edouard Grimaux, *Lavoisier, 1743–1794* (Paris: Félix-Alcan, 1888), pp. 128, 201–202.

3 M. Berthelot, *La révolution chimique: Lavoisier* (Paris: Félix-Alcan, 1890) p. 307.

4 Henry Guerlac and Carl Perrin, "A Chronology of Lavoisier's Career, manuscript, n.d., pp. 69–71.

5 Lavoisier, "Respiration," p. [1].

6 See Figures 20 and 21.

7 See above, p. 441.

8 Lavoisier, "Respiration," p. [10].

9 See above, pp. 239–240, 244.

10 A. Seguin, "Mémoire sur l'eudiométrie," *Annales de chimie* 9 (1791):296.

11 Lavoisier, "Respiration," p. [11].

12 See above, p. 104.

13 Seguin, "L'eudiométrie," p. 297.

14 Ibid., pp. 298–303.
15 Lavoisier, "Respiration," pp. [11–12].
16 Ibid., p. [14].
17 The drawings are reproduced from Grimaux, *Lavoisier,* facing pp. 122 and 128. Among the implausible details are that, although the two drawings are supposed to depict comparable experiments in exercise and repose, the apparatus shown in one is entirely different from that in the other; that in the "repose" drawing the breathing tube is extravagently long, a feature which could only hinder the exchange of gases with the pneumatic chamber at the other end; that the flask inserted in the tube resembles the apparatus Lavoisier used for the synthesis of water; that the chamber breathed into in the "exercise" drawing makes no obvious sense; and that the foot treadle is not shown connected up with any mechanism on which Seguin could perform work.
18 Lavoisier, "Respiration," p. [18].
19 Aldo Mielo, ed., "Una lettera di A. Lavoisier a J. Black," *Archeion* 25 (1943):238–239.
20 Lavoisier, "Respiration," p. [10]. The passage in which Lavoisier made this statement was subsequently eliminated from the draft.
21 "Copie d'une lettre de M. Joseph Black à M. Lavoisier," *Annales de chimie* 8 (1791):225–229.
22 Lavoisier, "Respiration," p. [1]. The date of the reading is given on the fair copy of the memoir. (No first draft in Lavoisier's hand has survived.) According to the minutes of the Academy, the reading of the memoir was not completed on November 13, but continued on November 17 and December 7 and 11. See Maurice Daumas, *Lavoisier: Théoricien et expérimentateur* (Paris: Presses Universitaires, 1955) p. 64.
23 Lavoisier, "Respiration," p. [13].
24 Ibid., p. [14].
25 Ibid., pp. [12–13].
26 See above, p. 187.
27 See above, pp. 414–415.
28 Lavoisier, "Respiration," pp. [18–19]. In Seguin and Lavoisier, "Premier mémoire sur la respiration des animaux," *Mémoires de l'Académie des Sciences* (1789 [1793]), p. 577, he promised "in the forthcoming memoir" to give "with great accuracy the quantity of carbonic acid and of water which the quantity of [vital] air forms in the lungs." Such a memoir never appeared.
29 Lavoisier, "Respiration," p. [6].
30 W. H. S. Jones, *The Medical Writings of Anonymous Londinensis* (Cambridge: Cambridge University Press, 1947), p. 127.
31 M. D. Grmek, "Santorio, Santorio," in Charles C. Gillispie, ed., *Dictionary of Scientific Biography,* 16 vols. (New York: Charles Scribner's Sons, 1970–80), 12:101–104.
32 Lavoisier, "Respiration," pp. [8–10].
33 Ibid., p. [20].
34 See above, p. 386; Lavoisier, *Elementary Treatise,* 1:130.
35 Lavoisier, "Respiration," p. [14].

36 Ibid., p. [16].
37 Ibid. pp. [15–16].
38 Ibid., pp. [16–18].
39 Karl R. Popper, *Conjectures and Refutations: The Growth of Scientific Knowledge* (London: Routledge and Kegan Paul, 1963), pp. 46–47.
40 See above, p. 30.
41 Charles Coulston Gillispie, *Lazare Carnot Savant* (Princeton University Press, 1971), pp. 51–61.
42 Lavoisier, "Respiration," p. [16].
43 Charles Gillispie, letter to the author, September 21, 1982.
44 Gaston Bachelard, *La formation de l'esprit scientifique* (Paris: J. Vrin, 1975), pp. 13–16.
45 Seguin and Lavoisier, "Premier mémoire," p. 578.
46 Thomas K. Kuhn, "Energy Conservation as an Example of Simultaneous Discovery," in *The Essential Tension: Selected Studies in Scientific Tradition and Change* (Chicago: University of Chicago Press, 1977), pp. 73–82.
47 J. B. Dumas, *Essai de statique chimique des êtres organisés*, 2d ed. (Paris: Fortin, Masson, 1842), pp. 1–48; see esp. pp. 8, 43, 87. See also Dumas, "Essai de statique chimique des êtres organisés," *Annales de chimie et de physique*, 4 (1842):115–126.
48 Lavoisier, "Respiration," pp. [21–23].
49 Ibid., pp. [23–24].
50 Ibid., pp. [20–21].
51 Ibid., pp. [24–28].
52 Ibid., pp. [29–30].
53 Ibid., pp. [3–4].
54 Ibid., p. [30].
55 Joseph Black to Lavoisier, Edinburgh, Dec. 28, 1790, Lavoisier MS 1.34, Darmstäeder Collection, History of Science Collection, Cornell University (photocopy of original in Archives Nationales, Paris).
56 Seguin and Lavoisier, "Premier mémoire sur la respiration des animaux," Fiche 1349, Archives of the Académie des Sciences, p. 1.
57 See Robert K. Merton, "The Matthew Effect in Science," in *The Sociology of Science: Theoretical and Empirical Investigations* (Chicago: University of Chicago Press, 1973), pp. 439–459.
58 Seguin and Lavoisier, "Premier mémoire," Fiche 1349, p. 5.
59 Ibid.
60 Seguin and Lavoisier, "Premier mémoire," *Mémoires de l'Académie des Sciences* (1789), pp. 569–570.
61 Seguin and Lavoisier, "Premier mémoire," Fiche 1349, pp. 28–29.
62 Ibid.
63 Ibid., p. 29.
64 Charles A. Culotta, "Respiration and the Lavoisier Tradition: Theory and Modification, 1777–850," *Transactions of the American Philosophical Society* 62 (1972):4, 6.
65 Seguin and Lavoisier, "Premier mémoire," Fiche 1349, p. 6.

66 Seguin and Lavoisier, "Premier mémoire," *Mémoires de l'Académie des Sciences* (1789), p. 570.
67 Ibid., pp. 570–571.
68 Ibid., p. 569.
69 Ibid., pp. 580–583.
70 Ibid., p. 576.
71 Ibid., pp. 566–569.

Chapter 17. Dissonant Echoes

1 See above, p. 427.
2 J. Hassenfratz, "Sur la combinaison de l'oxigène avec le carbone et l'hydrogène du sang, sur la dissolution de l'oxigène dans le sang, et sur la manière dont le calorique se dégage," *Annales de chimie* 9 (1791):261–275.
3 Ibid., pp. 261–270.
4 Ibid., pp. 270–275.
5 Everett Mendelsohn, "The Controversy over the Site of Heat Production in the Body," *Proceedings of the American Philosophical Society* 105 (1961): 412–420.
6 Charles A. Culotta, "Respiration and the Lavoisier Tradition: Theory and Modification, 1777–1850," *Transactions of the American Philosophical Society* 62 (1972):8.
7 Everett Mendelsohn, *Heat and Life: The Development of the Theory of Animal Heat* (Cambridge, Mass.: Harvard University Press, 1964), p. 169.
8 Hassenfratz, "Sur la combinaison de l'oxigène," p. 268.
9 Ibid., p. 261.
10 The memoir itself, which was not published until 1814, gives as the date it was read "April 9, 1791." Lavoisier and Armand Seguin, "Second mémoire sur la respiration," *Annales de chimie* 91 (1814):318. Daumas maintains, however, on the basis of the minutes of the Academy meetings, that Lavoisier read this memoir on May 4, 1791. In addition to the general circumstances, the most direct evidence that Seguin was the author of this memoir is the reference in it to "my phosphoric eudiometer" ("Second mémoire," p. 322). See Maurice Daumas, *Lavoisier: Théoricien et expérimentateur* (Paris: Presses Universitaires, 1955), p. 64.
11 Lavoisier, "Sur la respiration animale," Fiche 1349, Archives of the Académie des Sciences, p. [10].
12 Lavoisier and Seguin, "Second mémoire," pp. 321–332.
13 Ibid., p. 333.
14 Ibid.
15 Seguin and Lavoisier, "Sur la transpiration des animaux," Fiche 1350, Archives of the Académie des Sciences, p. [1]. This draft is in Lavoisier's hand.
16 Lavoisier and A. Seguin, "Second mémoire sur la transpiration," *Annales de chimie* 90 (1814):6–9. The author of this memoir was Seguin. It is distinct from the memoir with similar title written by Lavoisier and published posthumously in the third edition of the *Traité de chimie*.
17 Seguin and Lavoisier "Sur la transpiration des animaux," pp. [7–12]: Seguin and

Lavoisier, "Premier mémoire sur la transpiration des animaux," in Lavoisier, *Oeuvres*, 2:707–709. The description of the apparatus for measuring the exhaled water and carbonic acid contained in Lavoisier's draft was deleted from the version that was later published.

18 Seguin and Lavoisier, "Premier mémoire sur la transpiration," p. 709.

19 Daumas, *Lavoisier*, p. 64.

20 Ibid., p. 65.

21 Seguin and Lavoisier, "Sur la transpiration des animaux," pp. [12–13].

22 Ibid., p. [16]. In the revised version that was later published these statements were modified, but were in substance similar. Seguin and Lavoisier, "Premier mémoire sur la transpiration," p. 710.

23 Seguin and Lavoisier, "Sur la transpiration des animaux," pp. [9–10].

24 Ibid., pp. [19–20].

25 Ibid., pp. [5–6]; Lavoisier and Seguin, "Second mémoire sur la transpiration," (by Seguin), pp. 6–28; A. Seguin, "Premier mémoire sur les vaisseaux exhalans," *Annales de chimie* 90 (1814):185–205.

26 Henry Guerlac and Carl Perrin, "A Chronology of Lavoisier's Career," manuscript, n.d., pp. 71–72; Roger Hahn, *The Anatomy of a Scientific Institution: The Paris Academy of Sciences, 1666–1803* (Berkeley: University of California Press, 1971), pp. 226–241.

27 Edouard Grimaux, *Lavoisier, 1743–1794* (Paris: Félix-Alcan, 1888), pp. 211–212.

28 Lavoisier and Seguin, "Second mémoire sur la transpiration," p. 5.

29 Daumas, *Lavoisier*, p. 65.

30 Seguin and Lavoisier, "Sur la transpiration des animaux: second mémoire," Fiche 1350, Archives of the Académie des Sciences; Lavoisier, "Second mémoire sur la transpiration des animaux," *Oeuvres*, 2:379–390.

31 Lavoisier, Ibid., p. 380; Seguin and Lavoisier, "Sur la transpiration des animaux," (draft), pp. [23–24].

32 Lavoisier and Seguin, "Second mémoire sur la transpiration," pp. 23–25.

33 Lavoisier, "Second mémoire sur la transpiration," *Oeuvres*, 2:380.

34 Michael Polanyi, *Personal Knowledge* (Chicago: University of Chicago Press, 1962), pp. 171, 300–301.

35 Lavoisier, Fiche 1648 (folded sheet), Archives of the Académie des Sciences, p. [1].

36 Lavoisier, "Combustibles hidrocarbonneux et hidro azoto carbonneux," Fiche 1260 (one of a series of loose sheets giving outlines of chapters for a projected treatise on chemistry).

37 Lavoisier, letter signed by "the academicians of the commission for experiments on vegetation," to M. Seguin and M. Hassenfratz, June 5, 1792, Fiche 384, Archives of the Académie des Sciences.

38 Daumas, *Lavoisier*, p. 65.

39 Lavoisier, Fiche 1648, entire.

40 Daumas, *Lavoisier*, p. 65.

41 "Prix proposé par l'Académie des Sciences, pour l'année 1794," *Mémoires de l'Académie des Sciences* (1789 [1792]), pp. 24–30.

42 P. Huard and M. J. Imbault-Huart, "Vicq d'Azyr, Félix," in C. C. Gillispie, ed.,

Dictionary of Scientific Biography, (New York: Charles Scribner's Sons, 1970–80), 14:14–17.

43 Lavoisier, "Table des chapitres d'un cours de chimie expérimentale rangée suivant l'ordre naturel des idées," Fiche 1260, Archives of the Académie des Sciences, last page.

44 Douglas McKie, *Antoine Lavoisier: Scientist, Economist, Social Reformer* (New York: Collier Books, 1962), pp. 247–274.

45 Lavoisier, *Mémoires de physique et de chimie* (n.p., n.d.), 1:209–210, 4:20–21.

Chapter 18. Reflections on the Creativity of One Scientist

1 For cogent comments on these questions in a different context, see Thomas Nickles, "Introductory Essay: Scientific Discovery and the Future of Philosophy of Science," in T. Nickles, ed., *Scientific Discovery, Logic, and Rationality* (Dordrecht: D. Reidel, 1978), p. 17.

2 See Bruno Latour and Steve Woolgar, *Laboratory Life: The Social Construction of Scientific Facts* (Beverly Hills: Sage Publications, 1979), pp. 45–53.

3 Lavoisier, *Traité élémentaire de chimie*, 2 vols. (Paris: Cuchet, 1789), 1:xi.

4 J. R. Ravetz, *Scientific Knowledge and Its Social Problems* (Harmondsworth: Penguin Books, 1973), pp.94–101.

5 Lavoisier and Laplace, "Mémoire sur la chaleur," Mémoires de l'Académie des Sciences (1780 [1783]), p. 398.

6 See Maurice Daumas, "Les appareils d'expérimentation de Lavoisier," *Chymia* 3 (1950):44–62.

7 Howard E. Gruber, *Darwin on Man: A Psychological Study of Scientific Creativity*, 2d ed. (Chicago: University of Chicago Press, 1981), pp. 5, 114.

8 Ibid., p. 120.

9 Victor Turner, *Dramas, Fields, and Metaphors: Symbolic Action in Human Society* (Ithaca: Cornell University Press, 1974), pp. 24–28.

10 Gruber, *Darwin on Man*, p. xxi; Howard E. Gruber, "On the Hypothesized Relation between Giftedness and Creativity," in D. Feldman, ed., *New Directions for Child Development* (San Francisco: Jossey-Bass, 1982), pp. 24–26.

11 I have raised this point also in the context of the investigations of Hans Krebs. Frederic L. Holmes, "Hans Krebs and the Discovery of the Ornithine Cycle," *Federation Proceedings* 39 (1980):224.

12 Jacques Hadamard, *An Essay on the Psychology of Invention in the Mathematical Field* (New York: Dover Publications, 1954), pp. 50, 53, 54.

13 Charles C. Gillispie, "Notice biographique de Lavoisier par Madame Lavoisier," *Revue d'histoire des sciences* 9 (1956):57.

14 Gruber, *Darwin on Man*, p. 114.

15 Howard E. Gruber, "On the Relation between 'Aha Experiences' and the Construction of Ideas," *History of Science* 19 (1981):51.

16 The allusion to Thomas Kuhn's conception of the conversion process in science is intentional. See Thomas S. Kuhn, *The Structure of Scientific Revolutions*, 2d ed. (Chicago: University of Chicago Press, 1970) pp. 150–159.

17 R. Kirwan, *An Essay on Phlogiston and the Constitution of Acids*, 2d ed. (London: J. Johnson, 1789), pp. x–xi.
18 Lavoisier, *Traité élémentaire de chimie*, 2 vols. (Paris: Cuchet, 1789), 2:327–336.
19 Charles Coulston Gillispie, *Science and Polity in France at the End of the Old Regime* (Princeton: Princeton University Press, 1980) pp. 83–84.
20 Ibid., p. 85; Roger Hahn, "Scientific Careers in Eighteenth-Century France," in Maurice Crosland, ed., *The Emergence of Science in Western Europe* (New York: Science History Publications, 1976), pp. 131–136.
21 Gruber, *Darwin on Man*, p. xx.

Index

Academy of Sciences: influence on Lavoisier's science, 500–502
Acid of chalk: synonym for fixed air, 136
Acid of *charbon*: synonym for fixed air, 235
Acid of sugar: discovery of, 110–11; formation from sugar, 110, 138–41; Lavoisier's experiments on, 111–13, 138–41; composition of, 353–58; renamed oxalic acid, 356
Acid of tartar (tartaric acid): isolation of, 110
Acidiform principle: 140–41; renamed oxygen principle, 146–47
Acids: may contain air, 10; formation of acid airs from, 37–39; Lavoisier's theory of, 57, 110–13, 117, 139–40, 144
Aeriform fluids, 101
Air: goodness of, 17, 95; from reduction of mercury, 44, 46–50
—common: restoration of by plants, 6, 220–21; composition of, 9, 11, 18, 19, 21, 23, 27, 57–58, 97, 134–135, 244–45; conversion to fixed air, 28–29; analysis and synthesis of, 56–57, 60–61, 66–67, 68, 74–75; salubrity of, 94–95, 134, 238–41
—species of: 52, 57, 154; effects of on animals, 9, 12, 15; densities of, 12, 97, 99, 243, 286; bases of, 102
Analogy: between respiration and combustion, 3, 6, 15–17, 91, 93, 123–24, 249–50; between respiration and calcination, 61, 74, 77–80, 84, 86; in scientific thought, 80, 220, 282–83, 350; in eighteenth century chemistry, 123, 169–70, 513
Analysis and synthesis: of air, 57, 60–61; of nitrous acid, 57
Animal economy, 19, 450, 461, 466, 473, 479, 483, 484–85
Animal heat:
—theories of: mechanical theories, 3; Joseph Black, 4; Lavoisier, 19–21, 29–30, 121, 123, 426, 429, 464; Lavoisier and Laplace, 189–90, 193, 195, 197–98, 258; Crawford, 158–60, 424, 426; Lagrange, 415–16, 469–71; Sequin, 432–33; Hassenfratz, 469–71; Andrew Duncan, 508*n*42
—distribution of in body: 159–60, 194–95, 433, 434
—experiments on: of Lavoisier and Laplace, 162–65, 183, 199, 205, 207; of Crawford, 417–18, 420–23
Animal matter: early idea of Lavoisier on, 24; discovery of mophette (nitrogen) in, 312; yeast as, 329; Lavoisier's distillation analyses of, 377–79, 380, 383, 408; composition of, 379; classes of, 408
Animalization, 483
Asphyxiation, 132–36
Atmosphere. *See* Air, common
Azote: definition of, xxiv, 318; constituent of animal matter, 325, 385–86, role in respiration, 446, 447–48. *See also* Mophette

Bachelard, Gaston: epistemological obstacle, 49, 456

Balance sheet method, xviii–xix, 281–82, 532*n*38
Balloon ascents, 211, 526*n*30
Bases of airs, 102
Baumé, Antoine, 43–44
Bayen, Pierre, 42–45, 510*n*12
Beccari, Iacopo Bartolomeo: separation of gluten and starch, 407
Bergman, Torbern: discovery of acid of sugar (oxalic acid), 110–11, 113, 139, 141, 145, 312; and asphyxiation, 134; concept of radical acid, 541*n*4
Berlinghieri, Léopold Vacca: criticism of Crawford, Lavoisier, 426–28, 469
Bernard, Claude: study of laboratory work of, 502
Berthelot, Marcelin: on Lavoisier and Bucquet, 131; on Lavoisier's nonscientific duties, 440; abstract of Lavoisier's laboratory notebooks, 509*n*63, 519*n*31, 522*n*35, 526*n*39; lactic acid fermentation in experiment of Lavoisier, 533*n*11
Berthollet, Claude-Louis: mentioned, 154, 355, 425, 431, 483; investigations of plant acids, 299–300, 320; discovery of mophette (nitrogen) in animal matter, 312, 408; and Lavoisier, 535*n*51
Bile: analysis by Cadet, 408; subject of prize proposed by Academy of Sciences, 484.
Black, Joseph: and fixed air (carbonic acid), xxiii, 4, 29, 318; and respiration, 4–5, 30, 449; tests for fixed air, 66; latent and specific heat, 158, 160, 467; and Lavoisier, 425, 444–47, 460.
Black, Max: on metaphors, 493
Blagden, Charles: mentioned, 201, 209
Blood: color change of, 3, 63–64, 78–79, 153, 430, 431, 432, 437, 469–70; role in respiration, 155–57, 199–201, 256; circulation as site of respiration, 415–16, 462–63, 470
Boerhaave, Hermann: water in spirit of wine, 265
Boyle, Robert: experiment on combustion and respiration in evacuated chamber, 3, 15; experiment on plants and water, 219; mentioned, 449
Brisson, Mathurin-Jacques: member of committee to examine reduction of mercury, 43
Brown, John: medical theory of excitability mentioned, 436
Bucquet, Jean-Baptiste: career, 130–31; collaboration with Lavoisier, 131–36, 239, 408, 415, 491; study of asphyxiation, 132–36, 138; death of, 145–46, 158

Cadet, Claude-Louis, de Gassicourt: member of committee to verify experiment of Lavoisier, 13; member of committee to examine reduction of mercury, 43–44; witness to experiment of Lavoisier, 45; analysis of bile, 408
Calcination: absorbs portion of air, 11, 18–19; of lead, 11, 18; weight gain in, 42; as slow combustion, 116; in Lavoisier's theory of combustion, 126. *See also* Mercury, Respiration
Caloric theory: views of Seguin, 428–29. *See also* Matter of fire
Calorimeter: invention of ice calorimeter, 160–61; experiment of Lavoisier and Laplace with, 161–67, 204–8, 258, 295; invention of water calorimeter of Crawford, 417–18, experiment of Crawford with, 418–22; comparison of accuracy of ice and water calorimeter, 422, 522*n*28
Candle:
—combustion of: 69, 91–93, 96, 105, 123–24, 180, 208, 221, 226, 419–21; cause of extinction of, 5; effects of various airs on, 12
—heat of combustion of, 162, 164, 165–66, 206, 418
Carbon, xxiii, 319. *See also Charbon*; *Matière charbonneuse*
Carbonated hydrogen (*hydrogène carboné*): theoretical substance oxidized in respiration, 431, 432–33, 437, 452, 464–65, 472–73, 475–76, 478, 480–81
Carbonic acid: definition of, xxiii, 318; combining proportions of, 367–68, 371, 373–74, 376, 398, 485; gas, water content of, 349, 389. *See also* Fixed air
Carnot, Lazare: analysis of relationship *MgH*, 455–56
Cavendish, Henry: and identification of inflammable air, 5; and synthesis of water, 202; and analysis of atmosphere, 245; and combination of nitrogen and oxygen, 294
Charbon: definition of, xxiii, 103–4; early views of Lavoisier on, 25–26, 36, 37–38;

combustion of, 26, 51, 116–18, 122–24, 180–86, 189, 190, 208, 209, 224–28, 327–28, 418, 435; heat of combustion of, 166, 191–92, 206; inflammable air (hydrogen) in, 210, 215–18; combustion of without air, 212–13, 295–96. *See also* Respiration and combustion
Charles brothers: balloon ascents of, 211
Chaulnes, Marie Joseph Louis d'Albert d'Ailly, Duc de: and density of fixed air, 94
Chemical element: Lavoisier's definition of, 319
Chemical equations: Lavoisier's use of, 280–83, 289, 341–45, 371–72, 394, 396
Chemical language, 303, 316–19, 387–88
Chemical nomenclature. *See* Nomenclature of eighteenth century chemistry
Cigna, Giovanni Francesco: mentioned, 71, 72
Circulation of matter: 482–83, 507
Classification of plant and animal matter, 386–88
Clouet, Jean-Baptiste: member of Gunpowder Commission, 138
Collaboration: Lavoisier and, 491
Collins, Harry: on replication of experiments, 423, 543*n*21
Combustion: of phosphorus, 1, 6, 9, 10, 11, 166, 186, 208; of sulfur, 1, 6, 9, 11; limited in closed space, 5, 34; of wax candles, 69, 91–93, 96, 105, 123–24, 180, 208, 221, 226, 412–21; of pyrophor, 102–5, 108–9; general theory of Lavoisier, 113–20, 126; as method of organic analysis, 264; of inflammable plant substances, 264–67, 270–76, 289–90, 340, 418; without air, 303; Kirwan and, 353; experiments of Crawford on, 418; of *charbon* (charcoal), *See Charbon*; and respiration, *See* Respiration
Composite bases in plant and animal matter, 386–87
Conant, James Bryant: on Lavoisier's conception of the air, 49, 52; on Lavoisier's attack on phlogiston, 516*n*37; gives translation of passages of Lavoisier on air, 519*n*24
Conceptual leaps in scientific discovery, 487
Conceptual obstacles, 49–50, 93–94, 95, 456–57
Conceptual passages, 120, 487
Condorcet, M.-J.-A.-N.C., Marquis de: signatures on Lavoisier's manuscripts, 82, 127, 143; suggests term "vital air," 141
Conservation of matter, 262, 267–69, 281–83, 284, 341–42, 394–96, 401–2
Control experiments, 311
Crawford, Adair: theory of animal heat, 158–60, 423–25; theory compared to Lavoisier's theory, 160, 195, 471; influence on Lavoisier and Laplace, 162, 164, 184; relation of respiration to outside temperature, 189, 523*n*73; measurements of heat of respiration and combustion, 411, 416–23; reactions to theory, 425–34, 544*n*48; mentioned, 449, 456, 465, 469
Crosland, Maurice: on chemical nomenclature, xxiii, 535*n*2; on Lavoisier's theory of acids, 512*n*47
Culotta, Charles: on Lavoisier and Laplace's calorimetric respiration experiments, 190, 524*n*78; on site of respiration, 463

Daumas, Maurice: on writing of Elementary Treatise, 385; on priority claims over reduction of mercury, 510*n*12; on Lavoisier's attack on phlogiston, 516*n*37; on decomposition of water, 529*n*1; on dates, 540*n*48, 548*n*10
Delorme, Suzanne: on Trudaine de Montigny, 513*n*13
Densities of airs, 12, 97, 99, 243, 286
Dephlogisticated air (pure air, vital air, oxygen gas): definition of, xxiii–xxiv; discovery of, 52–53; effects on animals, 52, 135–36; Lavoisier and, 53–56
DesFontaines, René Louiche: member of commission on vegetation, 483
Detonation of nitre: Lavoisier's notes on, 35–36; heat of, 166, 186
Deyeux, Nicolas: on composition of plant and animal acids, 300–301
Dietrich, Baron Phillippe-Frédéric: translation of Scheele's Chemical Treatise on Air and Fire, 151
Digestion: effects on rate of respiration, 445, 453–54; Lavoisier's views on role of, 452, 462, 475–76; Lavoisier's experiments on, 459–60, 461, 476, 478; prize offered by Academy of Sciences for investigation of, 484, 485
Donovan, Arthur L.: on Black's theory of latent and specific heat, 521*n*19

Duclos, Samuel Cottereau: Lavoisier's reading of, 24
DuHamel, Henri Louis, deMonceau: experiments on plants and water mentioned, 220
Dumas, Jean-Bapiste: influence of Lavoisier's theory of respiration on, 457
Duncan, Andrew: theory of animal heat, 508*n*42
Duveen, Denis: on decomposition and synthesis of water, 529*n*1

Eklund, Jon: on chemical nomenclature, xxiii; on analysis and synthesis, 511*n*46
Elastic fluids: fixed from, released into air, 11, 12–13; matter of fire in formation of, 31–32, 138. *See also* Air
Element, Chemical: Lavoisier's definition of, 319
Elementary fiber of animal body, 439
Eminently respirable air (vital air, oxygen gas), xxiv, 137, 141
"Epistemological obstacle," 49, 456
Equations. *See* Chemical equations
Erasistratus: experiment on insensible transpiration, 450
Ether: formation from spirit of wine, 327, 328; combustion of, 339–40
Eudiometric methods: adaptation of nitrous air test to, 170; Cavendish's use of, 245; of Seguin, 441–43
Evaporation: experiment of Lavoisier and Laplace, 101; cooling effect in lungs, 194–95, 426; cooling effect in transpiration, 458, 466–67
Exercise: effect on rate of respiration, 445–46, 453, 454
Expansion of metals and glass: experiment of Lavoisier and Laplace on, 158

Falsification: view of Karl Popper, 490
Fermentation: in Lavoisier's early research plan, 7–11, 18; Priestley and, 9–10; experiment of Abbé Rozier on, 10; definition of, 291–92
—acetous, 10, 294
—spirituous (vinous, alcoholic): as means to decompose water, 203, 222–23, 340, 347–48, 389–91; and germination, 304–5; Lavoisier's experiments on, 10–11, 204, 292–94, 309–10, 327, 328–33, 382–83; experimental apparatus, 309, 329, 349, 381–82, 404–5, 406 (Figure 17), 407 (Figure 18), 542*n*43; coalescence of Lavoisier's research on, 327; balance sheets for, 333, 342–45, 360–61, 372–73, 375–77, 388–90, 393–99, 402; Lavoisier's unpublished memoir on, 340–52; Lavoisier's theory of, 347–48, 389–93; as method for analysis of sugar, 357–58; equation of, 396–97, 402
—lactic, 533*n*11
Fire, Matter of. *See* Matter of fire
Fixed air (of Joseph Black): definition, xxiii; identification of, 4; formation in combustion, 4, 8, 31, 92; formation in fermentation, 4, 9–10; formation in respiration, 4, 6, 7, 8, 14, 29–30, 65–66, 69, 82, 93, 108, 121; effect on animals, 5, 8, 9, 12, 69, 94; absorption in limewater, 5; tests for, 11–12; from minium and chalk, 12–13, 18; relation to common air, 28–29, 31, 37, 50–51, 88, 96–100, 109, 116; as an acid, 37–39, 105, 116, 136; from reduction of mercury, 48–49; density of, 94, 252; composition of, 31–32, 98–99, 109, 116, 137; quantitative composition of, 149, 224–36, 285, 328, 435; base of, 184, 236. *See also* Carbonic acid
Fixed air (of Stephen Hales), xxiii, 23, 29, 297, 299
Flashes of insight, 19–20, 59, 122, 325, 486
Fontana, Abbé: and adaptation of nitrous air test, 170; mentioned, 201; and composition of plant acids, 299–300, 534*n*26
Foresight in scientific creativity, 497–98
Fortin, Nicolas: apparatus constructed for Lavoisier, 382, 404–5
Fourcroy, Antoine: on J.B. Bucquet, 132, 145; witness to synthesis of water, 201; and new nomenclature, 316, 318; discussion of sugar and oxalic acid, 355–58, 537*n*41; distinguished classes of animal matter, 408; associate of Lavoisier, 425; and Lavoisier's theory of respiration, 414–15, 448; and composition of air, 442; and color changes of blood, 469; member of committee on vegetation, 483
Fox, Robert: on specific and latent heat, 521*n*19
Frank, Robert: on early history of respiration, xxi, 506*n*2

Franklin, Benjamin: heard Lavoisier's paper on combustion, 127
Fric, René: on date of Lavoisier's memoir on calcination, 10
Fruton, Joseph: on history of fermentation, xxi–xxii; on Lavoisier's fermentation results, 397

Geoffroy, Claude-Joseph: experiment on spirit of wine, 265, 266 (Figure 8)
Germination: views of Lavoisier and Senebier on, 304–5; experiment of Lavoisier on, 305–9
Gillispie, Charles Coulston: on personality of Lavoisier, xx; on conservation of matter, 269; on balance sheet method, 281; on conceptions of work, 455; on professionalization in Academy of Sciences, 500; on E. Mignot de Montigny, 513*n*13; on ballooning and J.B. Meusnier, 526*n*30; on Lavoisier and algebra, 539*n*39
Girtanner, Christoph: system of physiology of, 436, 498–99; theory of respiration, 436–39, 450, 463; experiment on color changes of blood, 437, 469, 470; mentioned, 471
Goodfield, June: on history of respiration, xxi; on calorimetric measurements, 421, 523–24*n*75
Gough, J.B.: on Lavoisier's memoirs on water, 532*n*37
Growth processes in scientific thought, 492–93
Gruber, Howard: on case studies of scientific creativity, xvii; on flashes of insight, 20, 325; on inhibition of scientific change, 59; on time scales in scientific activity, 491; on growth processes, 492, 493; on networks of enterprise, 494; on uniqueness of creativity, 502
Guerlac, Henry: on weight gain in calcination, 42; on Magellan, 511*n*25; on specific and latent heat, 521*n*12
—on Lavoisier: origins of interest in fixation and release of airs, 6, 492; theory of matter of fire, 21, 101; influence of Hales on, 23; experiment with Laplace on evaporation, 101; attack on phlogiston, 106, 516*n*37; activities of, 129; and Laplace, investigation of respiration, 190, 524*n*92; fermentation results of, 397; theory of acids of, 516*n*45; identity of collaborator, 526*n*39
Guettard, Jean–Etienne: and Lavoisier's early mineralogical interests, 24
Gun barrel experiments of Lavoisier and Meusnier, 211–14, 232–33, 269, 282
Gunpowder Commission: Lavoisier's travels for, 137–38
Guyton de Morveau: investigation of weight gain in calcination, 42; and Lavoisier's attack on phlogiston, 107, 127; and new nomenclature, 316–19; and refutation of Kirwan, 355; and composition of air, 442; and term "radical," 541*n*4

Hadamard, Jacques: on creativity in science, 495
Hahn, Roger, 522*n*33
Hales, Stephen: definition of fixed air, xxiii, 29, 297; and respiration, 4, 14, 19–20; and Lavoisier, 14, 19–20, 23, 299, 311; and Priestley's nitrous air test, 16; and distillation of plant matter, 23, 26, 296–97; and combustion, 92; mentioned, 71, 72, 449
Hall, A. Rupert: on Lavoisier's experiments, xviii
Hall, Diana Long: on respiration in 18th century, xxi, 506*n*4; on Lagrange's theory of animal heat, 543*n*5
Haller, Albrecht von: and irritability, 436; concept of elemental fiber, 439
Hamilton, Dr. (friend of Crawford): experiment on color change of blood, 424, 430, 437, 469
Hanson, Norwood Russell: on Gestalt switches in scientific perception, 119
Harden, Arthur: on Lavoisier's fermentation results, 397
Harvey, William: on distribution of heat in blood, 195; views on blood and nourishment compared to later theories of respiration, 438
Hassenfratz, Jean-Henri: summary of Lagrange's theory of respiration, 415–16; disciple of the new chemistry, 425–26; refutation of criticism of Lavoisier's theory of heat, 426–28; theory of respiration, 469–72; investigation of vegetation, 483
Heat: absorbed and released in chemical reactions, 101–2, 161–62; of combustion, 162, 165–66, 186, 189, 192, 418, 525–26*n*24; heat released in respiration, 164–65, 189,

Heat: (*continued*)
418; theories of, 158, 184, 424–25, 426. *See also*, Animal heat; Caloric theory; Latent heat; Matter of fire; Specific heats
Henry, Prince of Prussia: visitor to Academy of Sciences, 267
Henry, Thomas: letter of Lavoisier to, 59
History of science: as history of ideas, xvi, 50; as history of investigation, xvi; as social history, xvi, 501–2; as case studies in scientific creativity, xvii, 502; and philosophy of science, xvii; criteria for evaluation of past science in, xvii–xviii
Holton, Gerald: on case studies of scientific creativity, xvii; on "nascent" moments in science, 532*n*34
Homberg, Wilhelm: discovery of pyrophor, 102
Hooke, Robert: experiment on lungs, 3
Horn: distillation of, 377–79, 380, 383
Hufbauer, Karl: on German phlogiston chemists, 544*n*30
Hydrogen: in new nomenclature, 318. *See also* Inflammable air
Hydrogène carboné. *See* Carbonated hydrogen
—Hydrocarbonaceous fluid. *See* Carbonated hydrogen

Incoherence in creative scientific thought, 29, 30–31, 35, 36–37, 39, 62, 119–20, 493, 512*n*59
Inflammable air: discovery of, 5; effect on animals, 5; constituent of plant substances, 25, 142–43, 203, 222; in synthesis of water, 201–2; production of, 202, 211–12; constituent of *charbon*, 210, 215–19; species of, modifications of, 221, 222, 527*n*59; burned in respiration, 246–57; renamed hydrogen gas, 318
Inflammable plant substances: composition of, 210, 222–23, 226, 263–90
Ingenhousz, Jan: experiment on action of plants on atmosphere, 220, 527*n*55
Insight, Flashes of. *See* Flashes of insight
Irritability: defined by Haller, 436: in system of physiology of Girtanner, 436–39
Irvine, William: theory of heat of, 158

Jennings, Richard G.: on Lavoisier and phlogiston, 512*n*50
Joseph II, Emperor of Austria-Hungary: visit to Academy of Sciences, 94, 238
Jussieu, Antoine-Laurent de: member of commission on vegetation, 483

Kirwan, Richard: defender of phlogiston theory, 353, 416; criticism of Lavoisier's analysis of acid of sugar, 353–55, 527*n*59; response to by Fourcroy, 355–58; mentioned, 499, 538*n*1
Kohler, Robert: on influence of fermentation on Lavoisier's thought, 10
Kottler, Dorian: on Ingenhousz and Senebier, 527*n*55
Krebs, Hans: on writing in scientific thought, 90; study of laboratory work of, 502, 550*n*11
Kuhn, Thomas S.: on Gestalt shifts in scientific revolutions, 119–20; on scientific problems perceived as like solved problems, 169; on puzzle-solving, 510*n*1; on incoherence in scientific thought, 512*n*59; on effects of conceptual change on experimental operations, 515*n*12; on scientific conversions, 515*n*12

Lagrange, Joseph Louis de: theory of respiration, 415–16, 425, 459, 463, 469–71
Lamétherie, Jean-Claude de, editor of *Observations sur la physique*: opposition to Lavoisier's chemical system, 425
Landriani, Chevalier: witness to experiment of Lavoisier, 362, 363
Language of chemistry: preliminary ideas of Lavoisier on, 303; reform of nomenclature, 316–19; nomenclature for plant oxides and acids, 387–88
Laplace, Pierre Simon: experiment with Lavoisier on evaporation, 101–2, 106, 138; experiment with Lavoisier on heat and respiration, 149, 162–201, 204–208; experiment with Lavoisier on expansion of metals and glass, 158; formulation of theory of heat, invention of calorimeter, 160–61; letters to Lavoisier on respiration, 162–63, 204–5; and synthesis of water, 201–2; and evolution of inflammable air from dilute acid, 202; theory of respiration, 416, 469, 470; as collaborator of Lavoisier, 491; mentioned, 230, 258, 355, 465, 492, 501, 526*n*39
Latent heat: discovery of by Black, 158; appli-

cation to calorimeter, by Lavoisier and Laplace, 160; application to theory of respiration by Laplace, 416; application to transpiration by Lavoisier, 467
Lavoisier, Antoine: scientific methods and style of, xviii–xix, 51–52, 62, 65–66, 80, 81–82, 84–85, 131–32, 195–96, 214, 232–35, 244–46, 250, 258–59, 286–88, 303–4, 311, 314–15, 323, 326, 344, 347, 350–51, 369–70, 399, 403, 407–9, 453, 458–60, 464–66, 467, 478–82, 486–502; character and personality of, xix–xx, 51, 59–60, 70–72, 106–8, 115, 127–28, 135, 137, 146, 156, 240–41, 347, 351, 400–401, 459, 481; research agenda of, 7–8; and mineralogical chemistry, 17–18, 532; and traditional chemistry, 24; rational reconstructions of experimental investigations, 48, 142–44, 230–32, 349–50, 468; and mathematics, 282–83, 289, 343–45, 371–72, 396, 399, 501–2, 539*n*39; plans to investigate physiological processes, 413, 461, 473, 478, 483–85
—theories of: fermentation, 10–11, 203, 347–48, 389–93; matter of fire (caloric), 18, 21, 28, 31–32, 34, 36, 37, 38, 97–98, 101–2, 126, 138, 155; respiration, 19–23, 29–31, 33, 78–89, 93–94, 121, 125, 193, 195, 241–44, 246–58, 449–66, 475–76, 478; acids, 57, 110, 113; combustion, 114–18, 126, 183–84, 303–4; vegetation, 220–22, 304, 313–14, 320; organic composition, 320–26, 385–88
—views on: absorption and release of airs, 8, 9, 18–19, 27; fixed air, 8, 11–12, 18, 27, 28–29, 31–32, 34, 36, 37–38, 45, 50–51, 96–100, 105, 109–10; composition of atmosphere, 11–13, 18–19, 23, 28, 31–32, 49–50, 51–52, 57–58, 61, 95–100, 106, 244–45; analysis of plant and animal matter, 23–27; phlogiston, 26–28, 32–33, 36, 38, 51, 58–59, 88–89, 96–98, 106, 114–16, 294; nature of *charbon*, 26–27, 36, 51, 58, 100, 109–10, 210, 218, 235–36; conservation of matter. *See* Conservation of matter
—Experiments on: combustion of phosphorus and sulfur, 1, 6; calcination and reduction of lead, 1, 6, 9, 13, 27, 210; fermentation, 10–11, 204, 292–94, 309–10, 327, 328–33, 382–83; respiration, 14, 60–61, 64–69, 162–65, 167–80, 183, 186–89, 193, 207, 413, 440–49, 472; reduction and calcination of mercury, 45–49, 53–57; nitrous acid, 57; combustion of candles and analysis of wax, 69, 91–93, 105, 162, 164, 165–66, 180, 208, 226, 284–86; evaporation, 101; combustion of pyrophor, 104–5, 108–9; formation and composition of acid of sugar, 111–13, 138–40; analysis of sugar, 142–43, 334–39, 342–43, 357, 362–65, 368–69, 379–80; combustion of *charbon*, 166, 180–83, 184–86, 208, 212–19, 224–27, 327–28; expansion of metals and glass, 158; blood in respiration, 200–1; measurements of specific heats, heats of combustion and heat released in respiration, 161–67, 204–8, 295; synthesis and decomposition of water, 201–2, 211–14, 237–38, 295–96; combustion and analysis of spirit of wine (alcohol), 264–69, 270–73, 275, 276–83, 371–72, 374–75; combustion and analysis of olive oil, 273–74, 283–84, 287; destructive distillation of plant substances, 297–99; germination, 305–9, analysis of various plant and animal matters, 370, 377–79, 380, 383–84; digestion, 459–60, 461–62, 466; transpiration, 466, 473–75, 476–77
—collaborative investigations: 491; with Trudaine de Montigny, 45, 67–70, 91; with Laplace, 101–2, 158, 160–98, 199–202, 204–8, 258–59; with Bucquet, 131–32, 134–36, 138, 145–46, 158, 239; with Meusnier, 211–19, 237–38, 267–69, 282; with Sequin, 411, 440–49, 453–54, 461–62, 466, 472–82
—influences of and interactions with other scientists: Black, 6, 8–9, 11–12, 14, 30, 444–47, 460; Priestley, 6–7, 9, 17, 30, 32–34, 37–39, 44, 48, 50, 53, 59–61, 64, 70–73, 81, 95, 96–98, 106–8, 128, 489; Hales, 6, 8, 14, 19–20, 23, 192, 244, 296–97, 299, 311; Rozier, 10; Macquer, 13, 107, 113, 116; Rouelle, 24; Stahl, 27, 36, 106, 108, 115–18, 128; Bergman, 111–13, 139, 141, 145; Scheele, 151–58, 192, 194, 196, 199–201, 301, 306; Crawford, 160–64, 194–95; Fontana, 299–300; Berthollet, 299–300, 312; Senebier, 304–5, 314

Lavoisier: (*continued*)
—scientific writing of: 73; character of in laboratory notebooks, xxii; importance of to development of his thought, 89–90, 247–48, 313–15, 352, 453, 461–64, 488
—extra-scientific activities mentioned: made director of Paris Arsenal, 56; pressing outside affairs (1777–1781), 129–30, 151; travels for Gunpowder Commission, 137–38; member commission on ballooning, 211; elected to Royal Society of Medicine, 238; Director of Academy (for 1785), 294; member of Provincial Assembly of Orléanais, 340, 358; increasing burdens of, from 1789 onward, 405–6, 440, 477–78, 485; effects of on research, 480, 496, 501
Lavoisier, Madame: translator of Kirwan's *Essay*, 355; drawings of respiration experiments, 441, 443, 444 (Figure 20), 445 (Figure 21), 453
Lead: calcination and reduction of, 6, 9, 13, 27, 209–10
Legendre, Adrien-Marie: present at synthesis of water, 201
Lodwig, T.H.: on accuracy of calorimeters, 421, 522*n*28
Löw, Reinhard: on plant analysis after Lavoisier, 542*n*53
Lower, Richard, 3
Lungs, as location for respiratory combustion: views of Lavoisier, 19, 22, 82, 87, 121, 125, 193, 194–95, 199, 255, 256, 449, 451, 452, 458–60, 462–63, 475–76; view of Lagrange, 415–16; view of Laplace, 416; view of Hassenfratz, 427, 469–70; view of Seguin, 430–31, 433–34; view of Girtanner, 437–39; later controversy, 548*n*5

McKie, Douglas: on Lavoisier and Laplace investigation of respiration, 190
Macquer, Pierre-Joseph: records results of experiment of Lavoisier, 13; present at experiment of Lavoisier on mercury calx, 45; definition of *charbon*, 103; and Lavoisier's attack on phlogiston, 107, 127; correspondent of Bergman, 111; produced acid from calx of arsenic, 113; defined calcination as slow combustion, 116, 126; use of term *gas*, 131; definition of fermentation, 291–92, 294; idea that vital air accelerates vital movements, 414; examples of use of analogy in chemistry of salts, 513*n*40
Magellan, Jean: letter about Priestley's nitrous air test, 48; summary of Crawford's theory of animal heat, 158–60
Manganese oxide: use as oxygenating agent for analysis of sugar, 380–81
Matière charbonneuse: meaning of, xxiii; use of by Suvigny, 103; use of by Lavoisier, 109–10, 143; as constituent of fixed air, 109; as constituent of plant matter, 143; as modification of inflammable principle, 221–22. *See also* Carbon; *Charbon*
Matter of fire: *See also*, Heat; Caloric theory
—early ideas of Lavoisier on: 18, 21; released in respiration, 19, 29; in relation between common and fixed air, 28, 31–32, 99; as constituent of all elastic fluids, 31–32; and phlogiston, 32–33, 38, 58, 96, 97, 118, 120; in fixed air, 34, 97; in *charbon*, 36; released from air in combustion, 36, 97, 118; malleability of concept, 37
—theory of 1777 of Lavoisier: 130, 138, 155; two forms of, 101; absorbed in evaporation, 101; absorbed or released in chemical operations, 101–2; combined with base to form an air (gas), 102, 116, 126, 127; disengaged in combustions, 115, 127; disengaged in respiration, 121–23, 124
Mayow, John: experiment on theory of respiration, 3; experiment repeated by others, 4, 5, 92
Medawar, Peter: on scientific papers, 231
Melhado, Evan: origin of term "radical," 541
Mendel, Gregor: mentioned, 457
Mendelsohn, Everett: on history of respiration, xxi; on respiration as analogous to combustion, 123; comparison of Crawford, Lavoisier theories of animal heat, 160; on Lavoisier and Laplace's "metabolic-heat studies," 165; on distribution of animal heat, 195; on "Lavoisier–Crawford theory of animal heat," 471; on Andrew Duncan and animal heat, 508*n*42; on Crawford, 523*n*73; on Lavoisier and Laplace's conclusions concerning respiration, 524*n*92; on site of heat production, 543*n*8; on views of Seguin and Lavoisier, 544*n*48
Mephitic acid: term coined by Lavoisier for fixed air, 105, 116
Mercury: reduction of calx of without charcoal, 42–46; experiments of Bayen with, 42–43;

committee to evaluate reduction of, 43–44; new air obtained from calx of by Priestley, 44, 52–53; experiments of Lavoisier with, 44–48, 53–57; analysis and synthesis of air, 56–57; calcination of compared to respiration, 74–75, 77–80, 84–85, 86–87, 93; oxide of, as oxygenating agent for analysis of plant matter, 362–64, 365–66, 370; effects of oxide of on irritability, 436

Metaphor: role of in Lavoisier's theory of respiration, 451–52, 457, 464

Meusnier, Jean-Baptiste: engineering of balloons, 211; experiments with Lavoisier on generation of inflammable air and analysis of water, 211–19, 233, 490, 526*n*39; analysis of Lavoisier's experiment on combustion of charcoal, 214–19, 224, 228, 229, 230; experiment with Lavoisier on synthesis and decomposition of water, 237; design of apparatus for combustion of spirit of wine, 267, 268 (Figure 9); experiment with Lavoisier on combustion of spirit of wine, 267–69; mathematical analysis for Lavoisier experiment on decomposition of water, 282, 532*n*39; as collaborator, 491

Meyer, Johann Friedrick: *acidum pinque*, 43, 510*n*6

Meyerson, Emile: on conservation of matter, 401

Mignot, Etienne de Montigny: 513*n*13; experiment with Lavoisier and Trudaine on respiration, 67–69, 70, 91

Milly, comte de: reduction of mercury calx, 43

Monge, Gaspard: synthesis of water, 202; and rebuttal of Kirwan, 355; Lavoisier's admiration for, 501

Montgolfier brothers balloon ascents, 211

Montigny, Etienne Mignot de: *See* Mignot, Etienne de Montigny

Montigny, Trudaine de: *See* Trudaine de Montigny

Mophette: meaning of, xxiv; Lavoisier's definition of, 57; as residue of calcination, 66; as residue of respiration, 67, 68, 77, 95; as constituent of animal matter, 312; renamed azote, 318. *See also* Azote

Morris, Robert V.: on specific and latent heats, 521*n*19

Nash, Leonard K.: on Ingenhousz and Senebier, 527*n*55

Nesbit, Robert: on metaphor of growth, 493

Nicholson, William: criticism of Lavoisier's presentation of results, 499–500

Nickles, Thomas: on conceptual gaps in scientific thought, 550*n*1

Nitrogen, xxiv. *See also* Mophette; Azote

Nitrous acid, xxiv; demonstration of composition, 57; revision of composition, 139

Nitrous air (nitric oxide), xxiv; views of Lavoisier on, 31–32, 38

Nitrous air test: invention and use of by Priestley, 16–17, 48, 435; use of by Lavoisier, 23, 46–48, 53–55; 59, 60–61, 68–69, 111–12; redefinition of by Lavoisier, 95–96; eudiometric adaptation of, 170; refinement of by Lavoisier, 244–45; imprecision of, 441

Nomenclature of eighteenth century chemistry, xxii–xxiv; new terms introduced by Lavoisier, 49, 105, 136, 137, 140–41, 146–47, 235–36; general reform of Lavoisier and associates, 316–19

Nutrition: relation to respiration, 450, 452, 464; prize offered by Academy of Sciences for study of, 483

Oil, Lavoisier's investigations of: early ideas on, 25; plans for experiments on, 25, 404, 405 (Figure 16); as product of plant analysis, 25, 312–13, 322–23; heat of combustion of, 206–7, 295; combustion and analysis of, 273–74, 283–84, 287–88; composition of, 283–84, 325, 386; distillation product of animal matter, 377–79

Oil lamp: burning of, compared to respiration, 449, 451–53, 463–64

Organic chemistry, roots of traceable to Lavoisier: invention of combustion method of analysis, 264, 289, 409; question of preexistence of water in organic substances, 278, 280; identification of elementary constituents of plant substances, 324; fermentation equation as prototype for organic reactions, 396, 402

Oxalic acid: composition of, 356–58. *See also* Acid of sugar

Oxides: of plant and animal matter in Lavoisier's classification system, 386–88; application to fermentation of sugar, 392–93

Oxygen: introduction of term, 146–47. *See also* Acidiform principle, Pure air, Emi-

Oxygen: (*continued*)
nently respirable air, Vital air
Oxygen gas, 317

Partington, J.R.: on Lavoisier and Laplace investigation of respiration, 190; on first chemical equation, 396; on Lavoisier's fermentation results, 397; on *acidum pinque*, 510*n*6
Perrin, Carleton: on calx of mercury, 42; on Dietrich, 520*n*2
Phlogiston: definition, xxiii; in Priestley's theory of respiration, 15–16, 63–64, 434–36; criticisms of theory by French chemists, 43; and definition of dephlogisticated air, 52–53; supporters of theory of, 107, 127, 425, 426; in Scheele's theory of respiration, 153–54; in Crawford's theory of animal heat, 158–59, 423–24; theory of Kirwan, 353, 527*n*59. *See also* Lavoisier, views on phlogiston
Phosphorus: combustion of, 1, 6; heat of combustion of, 166, 192
Physiological balance experiments, 450, 473–74, 476–77
Physiological regulation: Lavoisier's conception of, 457–58, 479
Physiological steady state: Lavoisier's grasp of, 195–96, 450, 457–58, 464
Pitfalls in experimentation, 489–90
Plant acids: discoveries of, 110–11, 301; extension of theory of acids to, 110–13, 138–40, 141, 145; composition of, 141, 299–301, 320, 355–57; in Lavoisier's classification, 387–88, 404
Plant and animal substances: Lavoisier's plans to investigate, 8–9, 23–27, 144, 145; solvent method of extraction of, 24, 130, 407–8; Rouelle and analysis of, 24, 407; Hales and distillation of, 296–97; classification of Lavoisier of, 386–88; contemporary progress in investigation of, 407–8. Lavoisier's investigations of specific substances, *See* Lavoisier, Experiments
—composition of: as *charbon* and inflammable air, 25; views of Lavoisier, 25, 301–2, 311–13, 319–26, 385–86, 402–3; views of Hales, 297; views of Berthollet, 299–300, 312; view of Fontana, 300; view of Deyeux, 300–301; view of Fourcroy, 355–56; elementary constituents identified, 312, 319–21, 323–24, 385–86; as *charbon* and water, 320; as compounds of three or four elements, 320–22, 385–86; double bases (radicals) in, 386–87, 402
Plant chemistry as focus of Lavoisier's later investigations, 261, 326
Plants: restoration of atmosphere by, 6, 220; action of sunlight on, 220; vegetation, 8, 219–21, 313–14, 483; germination, 304–9; economy of, 485
Polanyi, Michael: on personal commitment in science, 107; on passion and submission in science, 482
Popper, Karl: on consistency in theories, 246; on scientific observations, 454–55; on falsification, 490
Pott, Johann Heinrich: works of read by Lavoisier, 24
Priestley, Joseph: meaning of phlogiston and dephlogisticated air to, xxiii; discoveries of new species of airs, 5; use of mercury with pneumatic trough, 5; on respiration, 5–6, 15–16, 63–64, 411, 434–36, 508*n*42; discovery of restoration of air by plants, 6, 220, 308; discovery that agitation in water renders noxious air respirable, 9, 33; formation of fixed air in fermentation, 9–10; invention of nitrous air test, 16–19, 48; identification of respiration with combustion, 16–17, 126; explanation of limited combustion in closed space, 34; visit to Paris, 44; discovery of new air derived from mercury calx, 44, 52–53; conception of air, 53; meaning of vitiated air, 61; experiments on blood, 63–64; commentary on Scheele's views, 154; influence of theory of respiration on Crawford, 159–60, 423–24; reduction of minium in inflammable air, 209; experiments on charcoal, 295; opposition to new chemistry, 416, 425; experiments on respiration, 434–36; scientific style of, 489, 498. Relation to, influences on Lavoisier, *see* Lavoisier
Pringle, John: letter of Priestley to, 52
Professionalism in Lavoisier's research, 500–501
Pure air: Lavoisier's term for respirable, combustible portion of atmosphere, 57–58, 96. *See also* Eminently respirable air, Vital air, Oxygen
Pyrophor: discovery of by Homberg, 102; ex-

periments of Suvigny on, 103; experiments of Lavoisier on, 104–5, 108–9

Radicals: in composition of plant and animal substances, 387, 403, 541*n*4
Ravetz, J.R.: pitfalls in experimentation, 489
Réaumur, René-Antoine Ferchault de: experiments on digestion mentioned, 467
Replication of experiments, 423
Respiration: and combustion, 3, 15–16, 91, 93, 108, 120–26, 183, 189–94, 197, 208, 421, 451–53, 456, 464, 493; absorbs something from air, 3, 19, 21, 75; forms fixed air, 4, 5, 7, 8, 14, 29–30, 65–66, 69, 82, 93, 108, 121, 192–93, 434–35; causes loss of elasticity of air, 4–19; hypothetical internal mechanisms of, 4, 63, 78, 153–54, 430–31, 433, 437–38, 470, 472, 475–76; as source of animal heat, 4, 19–21, 29–30, 121–22, 159–60, 195; as corruption of air, 5; and phlogiston, 15–16, 63–64, 153–54, 159–60, 424, 434; as source of work, 29–30, 453–57; and calcination, 61, 74, 77–80, 93; compared to combustion of *charbon*, 121, 169–70, 193–94; forms water, 246–56, 418–20, 428, 430, 448–49, 465–66; cutaneous, 478. Location of in body, *See* Lungs
—effects of conditions on rate of: composition of atmosphere, 187–88, 414–15, 446, 448; temperature, 189, 444–45, 523*n*73; digestion, 445, 453–54; exercise, 445–46, 453–55, 457
—investigations and theories of, by: Boyle, Hooke, Lower, and Mayow, 3; Hales, 4; Black, 4–5; Priestley, 5–6, 15–17, 63–64, 411, 434–36, 508*n*42; Scheele, 152–53; Crawford, 416–23; Dr. Hamilton, 424; Girtanner, 436–39; Hassenfratz, 469–72. Lavoisier, *See* Lavoisier: Theories of, and Experiments on
—views on, of: Fourcroy, 414–15; Macquer, 414; Lagrange, 415–16; Laplace, 416; Berlinghieri, 426; Hassenfratz, 426–28; Seguin, 429–34, 472–73
—applications of theory of: to questions of salubrity of air, 94–95, 238–41; to medical theory, 415, 458; to social questions, 458
Retzius, Anders: and isolation of tartaric acid, 110
Rochefoucauld, duc de La: present for experiment of Lavoisier, 45
Rouelle, Guillaume-François: and analysis of plants by extraction, 24, 130, 407; teacher of Lavoisier, 24, 408; teacher of Bucquet, 130; classification of plant substances, 387
Rouelle, Hilaire Marin: discovery of vegetoanimal matter, 407–8
Roux, Augustin: predecessor of Bucquet, 130
Rozier, Abbè: and fermentation, 10

Sadoun-Goupil, Michelle: and letter of Laplace, 522*n*33; on Berthollet and Lavoisier, 535*n*51
Sage, Balthazar: and revival of asphyxiated bird, 94; and therapy for asphyxia, 133
Sanctorius (Santorio, Santorio): physiological balance experiments of, 450, 477
Scheele, Carl Wilhelm: isolation of plant acids by, 110, 145, 301, 408; on components of air, 151–52; on respiration, 152–54; experiments on blood in respiration, 152–53, 157, 169, 194, 196, 199–200; experiments on respiration of germinating seedlings, 152, 156, 306, 308; commentary by Lavoisier on treatise of, 154–57; refutation by Lavoisier of view of respiration of, 156, 192; discovery of pyromucic acid, 338
Scientific revolutions, 7, 119–20
Sequin, Armand: comment on Lavoisier's view of plant substances, 390–91; assistant to Lavoisier on respiration experiments, 411, 440–41, 443–47, 453–54, 472; follower of Lavoisier, 428; views on caloric 428–29; views on respiration, 429–34, 470–71, 544–45*n*48; theory of carbonated hydrogen substance consumed in respiration, 431, 432–33, 464–65, 472–73, 480–81; invention of eudiometric method by, 441–43, 548*n*10; made collaborator of Lavoisier, 460–61; experiments with Lavoisier on transpiration, 466, 473–78, 480; and posthumous publication of Lavoisier's memoirs, 482; investigation of vegetation, 483; as collaborator, 491
Senebier, Jean: experiments on vegetation, 220, 314, 527*n*55; theory of germination of, 304–5, 308, 314
Siegfried, Robert: on role of oxygen in Lavoisier's theoretical structure, 519*n*36; on new chemical nomenclature, 535*n*2

Smeaton, William: on accuracy of calorimeters, 421, 522*n*28
Smith, Cyril: on analogy of novel ideas and crystal formation, 22
Social context and scientific activity, xvi, 501–2
Spallanzani, Lazzaro: experiments on digestion, 201, 467
Specific heats: discovery of by Black, 158; method of Crawford for measuring, 158, 160; of arterial, venous blood, and respired airs, 158–59, 194–95, 416–17, 433; measurements by Lavoisier and Laplace of, 160, 161, 207
Speter, Max: on Lavoisier's early view of calcination, 45; on Lavoisier and phlogiston, 58, 516*n*37
Spirit of wine (alcohol): xxiv; formation of in fermentation, 10, 222–23, 331–32, 341, 346, 372, 392–94; composition of, 223, 277–78, 283, 325, 346 (Figure 13), 371–72, 374–75; combustion and analysis of, 264–73, 274–75, 276–81, 328, 340; water formed in combustion of, 265–69; water contained in, 278–79, 283, 325; conversion to ether, 327, 328
Stahl, Georg Ernst: phlogiston theory of, xxiii; Lavoisier's modifications of theory of, 27, 115, 118; mentioned as leader of phlogiston school, 28, 36, 43, 58; Lavoisier's attack on doctrine of, 106–8, 116, 119, 128
Sugar: as source of acid of sugar (oxalic acid): 110–12, 138–40, 353–56; composition of, 142, 320–24, 342–43, 346 (Figure 13), 357, 364–65, 368–69, 391–92, 394 (Figure 15), 398, 400; fermentation of, 292–94, 309–10, 327, 328–33, 344–46, 382–83, 392, 393–94
—analysis of: with nitrous acid (nitric acid), 142–43, 144–45; means available for, 334; with sulfuric acid, 335–37, 343, 364–65; by distillation, 337–39, 343; by fermentation, 343, 346 (Figure 13), 357; by oxygenation with metallic oxides, 362–64, 379–80
Suvigny, Lejay de: investigation of pyrophor, 103–4; use of term *matières charbonneuses*, 103–4, 109

Teich, Mikulas: on circulation of matter in nature, 507*n*16
Temperature: effect of on rate of respiration, 188–89, 196, 444–45, 523*n*73; uniformity of in animal body, 194, 432–33; constancy of in animals, 196, 466
Thouin, Andre: member of commission on vegetation, 483
Tillet, Mathieu: signed memoir of Lavoisier, 460
Transpiration: necessity of to maintain constant body temperature, 466–67; investigations of by Lavoisier and Seguin, 466, 473–79
Trudaine de Montigny, Jean-Chalres-Philibert: member of committee to verify Lavoisier's experiments, 13
—experiments with Lavoisier: on mercury calx, 45; on respiration and combustion, 67–69, 70, 91
Turner, Victor: on metaphor of growth, 493

Vallerius: experiments on plants and water, 220
Vandermonde, Alexandre-Theophile: present for synthesis of water, 201
Van Helmont, Joan Baptiste: use of term *gas*, 131; experiment on formation of plants from water, 219, 220
Vegetation: action of on air, 6, 152, 156, 220, 305–9, 313–14; in Lavoisier's research program, 8; Lavoisier's early interest in, 219; views of Lavoisier on, 203, 220–21, 304; decomposition of water by, 220–21; necessity of respirable air for, 304; commission to investigate, 483
———experiments on: by Priestley, 6, 220; by Scheele, 152, 156; by Ingenhousz, 220; by Senebier, 220; by Lavoisier, 305–9
Ventilation of public buildings, 95, 239–40
Vicq d'Azyr, Félix: possible role in formulating prize for study of nutrition, 484
Vital air (oxygen gas): definition of, xxiv; term suggested by Condorcet, 141. *See also* Eminently respirable air
Vitiated air: traditional meaning, 61; meaning altered in framework of Lavoisier, 76–77

Water: synthesis of, 149, 201–2, 237; combining proportions of, 215, 217, 237, 277, 287–88; transmutation of, 219–20, 532*n*37; as constituent of plant substances, 278–80, 285–86, 302, 320, 321, 324, 325, 345–46, 356

—decomposition of: with iron filings, 202–3, 211–12; with *charbon*, 212–13, 295–96; by vegetation, 220–21, 304, 308, 313–14; by fermentation, 222, 340–42, 347–48, 360–61, 389–91; not decomposed by fermentation, 390–92; by decomposition of plant matter, 297–98, 301–2, 311–12
—formation of: in combustion of charcoal, 215–19; in respiration, 246–47; in combustion of spirit of wine, 265–70
Wax: composition of, 284–86, 288–89. *See also*, Candles
Weights: system used by Lavoisier, xxiv
Wilson, Leonard G.: on respiration in seventeenth century, xxi, 506*n*2
Work: effects on rate of respiration, 445–46, 454; conception of in late eighteenth century mechanics, 455–56; Lavoisier's view of relation of respiration to, 457
Writing: and scientific creativity, 89–90, 352, 488

Yeast: as ferment, 292; use of by Lavoisier, 309; Lavoisier's examination of properties of, 327, 329; composition of, 394 (Figure 15)

DESIGNED BY CAMERON POULTER
COMPOSED BY GRAPHIC COMPOSITION, INC., ATHENS, GEORGIA
MANUFACTURED BY EDWARDS BROTHERS, INC., ANN ARBOR, MICHIGAN
TEXT AND DISPLAY LINES ARE SET IN BODONI

Library of Congress Cataloging in Publication Data
Holmes, Frederic Lawrence.
Lavoisier and the chemistry of life.
(Wisconsin publications in the history of science
and medicine; no. 4)
Includes index.
1. Respiration—Research—History. 2. Lavoisier,
Antoine Laurent, 1743–1794. 3. Creative ability in
science. 4. Biochemists—France—Biography. 5. Chemists
—France—Biography. I. Title. II. Series.
QP511.8.L38H65 1984 574.1'92'0924 [B] 84-40152
ISBN 0-299-09980-6